The Every-Day Life Of Abraham Lincoln

by

Francis Fisher Browne

Double 9
BOOKS

The Every-Day Life Of Abraham Lincoln
by Francis Fisher Browne

ISBN: 978-93-60465-23-0

Published by

DOUBLE 9 BOOKS

2/13-B, Ansari Road
Daryaganj, New Delhi – 110002
info@double9books.com
www.double9books.com
Tel. 011-40042856

ABOUT THE AUTHOR

FRANCIS FISHER BROWNE was an American editor, poet, and literary reviewer who was born December 1, 1843, and died May 11, 1913. The Chicago Literary Club, the Caxton Club (Chicago), and The Twilight Club of Pasadena (California) all made Browne an honorary member after all. He was one of their leaders. In the summer of 1893, he was in charge of the Committee on Congress at the World's Congress Auxiliary of the Columbian Exhibition, also known as the Chicago World's Fair. Browne was one of the most important intellectuals and writers in Chicago, Illinois, in the 20th century. Browne moved to Chicago from New England in 1867 and started the literary magazine The Dial. It was a revival of Margaret Fuller's transcendental periodical and a place for modernist literature to be published. Along the way, he became close with John Muir, John Burroughs, Walt Witman, and other well-known people. Born in South Halifax, Vermont, Browne was the son of William Goldsmith Browne and Eunice (Fisher) Browne. People know his father as a poet because of the song and hymn "A Hundred Years to Come." Browne learned how to print by working at The Chicopee Journal, his father's newspaper, while he was in high school in Chicopee, Massachusetts.

CONTENTS

PREFACE 8

CHAPTER I 11

CHAPTER II 34

CHAPTER III 47

CHAPTER IV 57

CHAPTER V 68

CHAPTER VI 76

CHAPTER VII 84

CHAPTER VIII 96

CHAPTER IX 111

CHAPTER X 124

CHAPTER XI 132

CHAPTER XII 153

CHAPTER XIII 167

CHAPTER XIV 182

CHAPTER XV 202

CHAPTER XVI 222

CHAPTER XVII 241

CHAPTER XVIII 256

CHAPTER XIX 266

CHAPTER XX 281

CHAPTER XXI 292

CHAPTER XXII 313

CHAPTER XXIII 323

CHAPTER XXIV 333

CHAPTER XXV 344

CHAPTER XXVI 357

CHAPTER XXVII 365

CHAPTER XXVIII 386

CHAPTER XXIX 399

INDEX 411

NOTES 494

"How beautiful to see
Once more a shepherd of mankind indeed.
Who loved his charge, but never loved to lead;
One whose meek flock the people joyed to be,
Not lured by any cheat of birth,
But by his clear-grained human worth,
And brave old wisdom of sincerity!
They knew that outward grace is dust;
They could not choose but trust
In that sure-footed mind's unfaltering skill,
And supple-tempered will
That bent like perfect steel to spring again and thrust.
His was no lonely mountain-peak of mind,
Thrusting to thin air o'er our cloudy bars,
A sea-mark now, now lost in vapors blind;
Broad prairie rather, genial, level-lined,
Fruitful and friendly for all human kind,
Yet also nigh to heaven and loved of loftiest stars.

"Great captains, with their guns and drums,
Disturb our judgment for the hour,
But at last silence comes;
These all are gone, and, standing like a tower,
Our children shall behold his fame,
The kindly-earnest, brave, foreseeing man,
Sagacious, patient, dreading praise, not blame,
New birth of our new soil, the first American."
    JAMES RUSSELL LOWELL.

PREFACE

PREFACE TO THE SECOND EDITION

The original edition of this book was published about twenty years after Lincoln's death at the close of the Civil War. At that time many of the men who had taken a prominent part in the affairs, military and civil, of that heroic period, many who had known Lincoln and had come in personal contact with him during the war or in his earlier years, were still living. It was a vivid conception of the value of the personal recollections of these men, gathered and recorded before it was too late, that led to the preparation of this book. It was intended to be, and in effect it was, largely an anecdotal Life of Lincoln built of material gathered from men still living who had known him personally. The task was begun none too soon. Of the hundreds who responded to the requests for contributions of their memories of Lincoln there were few whose lives extended very far into the second quarter-century after his death, and few indeed survive after the lapse of nearly fifty years, — though in several instances the author has been so fortunate as to get valuable material directly from persons still living (1913). Of the more than five hundred friends and contemporaries of Lincoln to whom credit for material is given in the original edition, scarcely a dozen are living at the date of this second edition. Therefore, the value of these reminiscences increases with time. They were gathered largely at first hand. They can never be replaced, nor can they ever be very much extended.

This book brings Lincoln the man, not Lincoln the tradition, very near to us. Browning asked, "And did you once see Shelley plain? And did he stop and speak to you?" The men whose narratives make up a large part of this book all saw Lincoln plain, and here tell us what he spoke to them, and how he looked and seemed while saying it. The great events of Lincoln's life, and impressions of his character, are given in the actual words of those who knew him—his friends, neighbors, and daily associates—rather than condensed and remolded into other form. While these utterances are in some cases rude and unstudied, they have often a power of delineation and a graphic force that more than compensate for any lack of literary quality.

In a work prepared on such a plan as this, some repetitions are unavoidable; nor are they undesirable. An event or incident narrated by different observers is thereby brought out with greater fulness of detail; and phases of Lincoln's many-sided character are revealed more clearly by the varied impressions of numerous witnesses whose accounts thus correct or verify each other. Some inconsistencies and contradictions are inevitable,— but these relate usually to minor matters, seldom or never to the great essentials of Lincoln's life and personality. The author's desire is to present material from which the reader may form an opinion of Lincoln, rather than to present opinions and judgments of his own.

Lincoln literature has increased amazingly in the past twenty-five years. Mention of the principal biographies in existence at the time of the original edition was included in the Preface. Since then there have appeared, among the more formal biographies, the comprehensive and authoritative work by Nicolay and Hay, the subsequent work by Miss Ida Tarbell, and that by Herndon and Weik, besides many more or less fragmentary publications. Some additions, but not many, have been made to the present edition from these sources. The recently-published Diary of Gideon Welles, one of the most valuable commentaries on the Civil War period now available, has provided some material of exceptional interest concerning Lincoln's relations with the members of his Cabinet.

In re-writing the present work, it has been compressed into about two-thirds of its former compass, to render it more popular both in form and in price, and to give it in some places a greater measure of coherency and continuity as an outline narrative of the Civil War. But its chief appeal to the interest of its readers will remain substantially what it was in the beginning, as set forth in its title, "The Every-day Life of Abraham Lincoln, by Those Who Knew Him."

F.F.B.

SANTA BARBARA, CAL., *April, 1913.*

PREFACE TO THE FIRST EDITION

This book aims to give a view, clearer and more complete than has been given before, of the personality of Abraham Lincoln. A life so full of incident and a character so many-sided as his can be understood only with the lapse of time. A sense of the exhaustless interest of that life and character, and the inadequacy of the ordinarily constructed biography to portray his many-sidedness, suggested the preparation of a work upon the novel plan here represented. Begun several years ago, the undertaking proved of such magnitude that its completion has been delayed beyond the anticipated time. The extensive correspondence, the exploration of available sources of information in the books, pamphlets, magazines, and newspapers of a quarter of a century, and in the scraps and papers of historical collections, became an almost interminable task. The examination and sifting of this mass of material, its verification amidst often conflicting testimony, and its final molding into shape, involved time and labor that can be estimated only by those who have had similar experience.

To the many who have kindly furnished original contributions, to others who have aided the work by valuable suggestions and information, to earlier biographies of Lincoln—those of Raymond, Holland, Barrett, Lamon, Carpenter, and (the best and latest of all) that of Hon. I.N. Arnold— hearty acknowledgment is made. Much that was offered could not be used. In the choice of material, from whatever source, the purpose has been to avoid mere opinions and eulogies of Lincoln and to give abundantly those actual experiences, incidents, anecdotes, and reminiscences which reveal the phases of his unique and striking personality.

It scarcely need be pointed out that this work does not attempt to give a connected history of the Civil War, but only to sketch briefly those episodes with which Lincoln is personally identified and of which some knowledge is essential to an understanding of his acts and character. Others are brought into prominence only as they are associated with the chief actor in the great drama. Many of them are disappearing,—fading into the smoky and lurid background. But that colossal central figure, playing one of the grandest roles ever set upon the stage of human life, becomes more impressive as the scenes recede.

F.F.B.

CHICAGO, *October, 1886.*

CHAPTER I

The year 1809—that year which gave William E. Gladstone to England— was in our country the birth-year of him who wears the most distinguished name that has yet been written on the pages of American history— ABRAHAM LINCOLN. In a rude cabin in a clearing, in the wilds of that section which was once the hunting-ground and later the battle-field of the Cherokees and other war-like tribes, and which the Indians themselves had named Kentucky because it was "dark and bloody ground," the great War President of the United States, after whose name History has written the word "Emancipator," first saw the light. Born and nurtured in penury, inured to hardship, coarse food, and scanty clothing,—the story of his youth is full of pathos. Small wonder that when asked in his later years to tell something of his early life, he replied by quoting a line from Gray's Elegy:

"The short and simple annals of the poor."

Lincoln's ancestry has been traced with tolerable certainty through five generations to Samuel Lincoln of Norfolk County, England. Not many years after the landing of the "Mayflower" at Plymouth—perhaps in the year 1638—Samuel Lincoln's son Mordecai had emigrated to Hingham, Massachusetts. Perhaps because he was a Quaker, a then persecuted sect, he did not remain long at Hingham, but came westward as far as Berks County, Pennsylvania. His son, John Lincoln, went southward from Pennsylvania and settled in Rockingham County, Virginia. Later, in 1782, while the last events of the American Revolution were in progress, Abraham Lincoln, son of John and grandfather of President Lincoln, moved into Kentucky and took up a tract of government land in Mercer County. In the Field Book of Daniel Boone, the Kentucky pioneer, (now in possession of the Wisconsin Historical Society), appears the following note of purchase:

"Abraham Lincoln enters five hundred acres of land on a Treasury warrant on the south side of Licking Creek or River, in Kentucky."

At this time Kentucky was included within the limits and jurisdiction of Virginia. In 1775 Daniel Boone had built a fort at Boonesborough, on the Kentucky river, and it was not far from this site that Abraham Lincoln,

President Lincoln's grandfather, located his claim and put up a rude log hut for the shelter of his family. The pioneers of Kentucky cleared small spaces and erected their humble dwellings. They had to contend not only with the wild forces of nature, and to defend themselves from the beasts of the forest,—more to be feared than either were the hostile Indians. The settlers were filled with terror of these stealthy foes. At home and abroad they kept their guns ready for instant use both night and day. Many a hard battle was fought between the Indian and the pioneer. Many an unguarded woodsman was shot down without warning while busy about his necessary work. Among these was Abraham Lincoln. The story of his death is related by Mr. I.N. Arnold. "Thomas Lincoln was with his father in the field when the savages suddenly fell upon them. Mordecai and Josiah, his elder brothers, were near by in the forest. Mordecai, startled by a shot, saw his father fall, and running to the cabin seized the loaded rifle, rushed to one of the loop-holes cut through the logs of the cabin, and saw the Indian who had fired. He had just caught the boy, Thomas, and was running toward the forest. Pointing the rifle through the logs and aiming at a medal on the breast of the Indian, Mordecai fired. The Indian fell, and springing to his feet the boy ran to the open arms of his mother at the cabin door. Meanwhile Josiah, who had run to the fort for aid, returned with a party of settlers. The bodies of Abraham Lincoln and the Indian who had been killed were brought in. From this time forth Mordecai Lincoln was the mortal enemy of the Indian, and it is said that he sacrificed many in revenge for the murder of his father."

In the presence of such dangers Thomas Lincoln spent his boyhood. He was born in 1778, and could not have been much more than four years old on that fatal day when in one swift moment his father lay dead beside him and vengeance had been exacted by his resolute boy brother. It was such experiences as these that made of the pioneers the sturdy men they were. They acquired habits of heroism. Their sinews became wiry; their nerves turned to steel. Their senses became sharpened. They grew alert, steady, prompt and deft in every emergency.

Of Mordecai Lincoln, the boy who had exhibited such coolness and daring on the day of his father's death, many stories are told after he reached manhood. "He was naturally a man of considerable genius," says one who knew him. "He was a man of great drollery. It would almost make you laugh to look at him. I never saw but one other man who excited in me the same disposition to laugh, and that was Artemus Ward. Abe Lincoln had a very high opinion of his uncle, and on one occasion remarked that Uncle Mord had run off with all the talents of the family."

Thomas Lincoln was twenty-eight years old before he sought a wife. His choice fell upon a young woman of twenty-three whose name was Nancy

Hanks. Like her husband, she was of English descent. Like his, her parents had followed in the path of emigration from Virginia to Kentucky. The couple were married by the Rev. Jesse Head, a Methodist minister located at Springfield, Washington County, Kentucky. They lived for a time in Elizabethtown, but after the birth of their first child, Sarah, they removed to Rock Spring farm, on Nolin Creek, in Hardin (afterward LaRue) County. In this desolate spot, a strange and unlikely place for the birth of one destined to play so memorable a part in the history of the world, on the twelfth day of February, 1809, Abraham Lincoln the President was born.

Of all the gross injustice ever done to the memory of woman, that which has been accorded to Nancy Hanks is the greatest. The story which cast a shadow upon her parentage, and on that of her illustrious son as well, should be sternly relegated to the oblivion whence it came. Mr. Henry Watterson, in his brilliant address on Lincoln, refers to him as "that strange, incomparable man, *of whose parentage we neither know nor care*." In some localities, particularly in Kentucky and South Carolina, the rumor is definite and persistent that the President was not the son of Thomas Lincoln, the illiterate and thriftless, but of one Colonel Hardin for whom Hardin County was named; that Nancy Hanks was herself the victim of unlegalized motherhood, the natural daughter of an aristocratic, wealthy, and well-educated Virginia planter, and that this accounted for many of her son's characteristics. The story has long since been disproved. Efforts to verify it brought forth the fact that it sprang into being in the early days of the Civil War and was evidently a fabrication born of the bitter spirit of the hour.

It was not from his father, however, that Lincoln inherited any of his remarkable traits. The dark coarse hair, the gray eyes, sallow complexion, and brawny strength, which were his, constituted his sole inheritance on the paternal side. But Nancy Hanks was gentle and refined, and would have adorned any station in life. She was beautiful in youth, with dark hair, regular features, and soft sparkling hazel eyes. She was unusually intelligent, and read all the books she could obtain. Says Mr. Arnold: "She was a woman of deep religious feeling, of the most exemplary character, and most tenderly and affectionately devoted to her family. Her home indicated a love of beauty exceptional in the wild settlement in which she lived, and judging from her early death it is probable that she was of a physique less hardy than that of those among whom she lived. Hers was a strong, self-reliant spirit, which commanded the love and respect of the rugged people among whom she dwelt."

The tender and reverent spirit of Abraham Lincoln, and the pensive melancholy of his disposition, he no doubt inherited from his mother. Amid the toil and struggle of her busy life she found time not only to teach him to read and write but to impress upon him ineffaceably that love of truth and justice, that perfect integrity and reverence for God, for which he was noted all his life. Lincoln always looked upon his mother with unspeakable affection, and never ceased to cherish the memory of her life and teaching.

A spirit of restlessness, a love of adventure, a longing for new scenes, and possibly the hope of improving his condition, led Thomas Lincoln to abandon the Rock Spring farm, in the fall of 1816, and begin life over again in the wilds of southern Indiana. The way thither lay through unbroken country and was beset with difficulties. Often the travellers were obliged to cut their road as they went. With the resolution of pioneers, however, they began the journey. At the end of several days they had gone but eighteen miles. Abraham Lincoln was then but seven years old, but was already accustomed to the use of axe and gun. He lent a willing hand, and bore his share in the labor and fatigue connected with the difficult journey. In after years he said that he had never passed through a more trying experience than when he went from Thompson's Ferry to Spencer County, Indiana. On arriving, a shanty for immediate use was hastily erected. Three sides were enclosed, the fourth remaining open. This served as a home for several months, when a more comfortable cabin was built. On the eighteenth of October, 1817, Thomas Lincoln entered a quarter-section of government land eighteen miles north of the Ohio river and about a mile and a half from the present village of Gentryville. About a year later they were followed by the family of Thomas and Betsy Sparrow, relatives of Mrs. Lincoln and old-time neighbors on the Rock Spring farm in Kentucky. Dennis Hanks, a member of the Sparrow household and cousin of Abraham Lincoln, came also. He has furnished some recollections of the President's boyhood which are well worth recording. "Uncle Dennis," as he was familiarly called, was himself a striking character, a man of original manners and racy conversation. A sketch of him as he appeared to an observer in his later days is thus given: "Uncle Dennis is a typical Kentuckian, born in Hardin County in 1799. His face is sun-bronzed and ploughed with the furrows of time, but he has a resolute mouth, a firm grip of the jaws, and a broad forehead above a pair of piercing eyes. The eyes seem out of place in the weary, faded face, but they glow and flash like two diamond sparks set in ridges of dull gold. The face is a serious one, but the play of light in the eyes, unquenchable by time, betrays a nature of sunshine and elate with life. A glance at the profile shows a face strikingly Lincoln-like,—prominent cheek bones, temple, nose, and chin; but best of all is that twinkling drollery in the eye that flashed in the White House during the dark days of the Civil War."

Uncle Dennis's recollections go back to the birth of Abraham Lincoln. To use his own words: "I rikkilect I run all the way, over two miles, to see

Nancy Hanks's boy baby. Her name was Nancy Hanks before she married Thomas Lincoln. 'Twas common for connections to gather in them days to see new babies. I held the wee one a minute. I was ten years old, and it tickled me to hold the pulpy, red little Lincoln. The family moved to Indiana," he went on, "when Abe was about nine. Mr. Lincoln moved first, and built a camp of brush in Spencer County. We came a year later, and he had then a cabin. So he gave us the shanty. Abe killed a turkey the day we got there, and couldn't get through tellin' about it. The name was pronounced Linkhorn by the folks then. We was all uneducated. After a spell we learnt better. I was the only boy in the place all them years, and Abe and me was always together."

Dennis Hanks claims to have taught his young cousin to read, write, and cipher. "He knew his letters pretty wellish, but no more. His mother had taught him. If ever there was a good woman on earth, she was one,—a true Christian of the Baptist church. But she died soon after we arrived, and Abe was left without a teacher. His father couldn't read a word. The boy had only about one quarter of schooling, hardly that. I then set in to help him. I didn't know much, but I did the best I could. Sometimes he would write with a piece of charcoal or the p'int of a burnt stick on the fence or floor. We got a little paper at the country town, and I made some ink out of blackberry briar-root and a little copperas in it. It was black, but the copperas ate the paper after a while. I made Abe's first pen out of a turkey-buzzard feather. We had no geese them days. After he learned to write his name he was scrawlin' it everywhere. Sometimes he would write it in the white sand down by the crick bank and leave it there till the waves would blot it out. He didn't take to books in the beginnin'. We had to hire him at first, but after he got a taste on't it was the old story—we had to pull the sow's ears to get her to the trough, and then pull her tail to get her away. He read a great deal, and had a wonderful memory—wonderful. Never forgot anything."

Lincoln's first reading book was Webster's Speller. "When I got him through that," said Uncle Dennis, "I had only a copy of the Indiana Statutes. Then Abe got hold of a book. I can't rikkilect the name. It told a yarn about a feller, a nigger or suthin', that sailed a flatboat up to a rock, and the rock was magnetized and drawed all the nails out, and he got a duckin' or drowned or suthin',—I forget now. [It was the "Arabian Nights."] Abe would lay on the floor with a chair under his head and laugh over them stories by the hour. I told him they was likely lies from beginnin' to end, but he learned to read right well in them. I borrowed for him the Life of Washington and the Speeches of Henry Clay. They had a powerful influence on him. He told me afterwards in the White House he wanted to live like Washington. His speeches show it, too. But the other book did the most amazin' work. Abe was a Democrat, like his father and all of us, when he began to read it. When he closed it he was a Whig, heart and soul, and he went on step by step till he became leader of the Republicans."

These reminiscences of Dennis Hanks give the clearest and undoubtedly the most accurate glimpse of Lincoln's youth. He says further, referring to the boy's unusual physical strength: "My, how he would chop! His axe would flash and bite into a sugar-tree or sycamore, and down it would come. If you heard him fellin' trees in a clearin' you would say there was three men at work, the way the trees fell. Abe was never sassy or quarrelsome. I've seen him walk into a crowd of sawin' rowdies and tell some droll yarn and bust them all up. It was the same after he got to be a lawyer. All eyes was on him whenever he riz. There was *suthin' peculiarsome* about him. I moved from Indiana to Illinois when Abe did. I bought a little improvement near him, six miles from Decatur. Here the famous rails were split that were carried round in the campaign. They were called *his* rails, but you never can tell. I split some of 'em. He was a master hand at maulin ' rails. I heard him say in a speech once, 'If I didn 't make these I made many just as good.' Then the crowd yelled."

One of his playmates has furnished much that is of interest in regard to the reputation which Lincoln left behind him in the neighborhood where he passed his boyhood and much of his youth. This witness says: "Whenever the court was in session he was a frequent attendant. John A. Breckenridge was the foremost lawyer in the community, and was famed as an advocate in criminal cases. Lincoln was sure to be present when he spoke. Doing the chores in the morning, he would walk to Booneville, the county seat of Warwick County, seventeen miles away, then home in time to do the chores at night, repeating this day after day. The lawyer soon came to know him. Years afterwards, when Lincoln was President, a venerable gentleman one day entered his office in the White House, and standing before him said: 'Mr. President, you don't know me.' Mr. Lincoln eyed him sharply for a moment, and then quickly replied with a smile, 'Yes I do. You are John A. Breckenridge. I used to walk thirty-four miles a day to hear you plead law in Booneville, and listening to your speeches at the bar first inspired me with the determination to be a lawyer.'"

Lincoln's love for his gentle mother, and his grief over her untimely death, is a touching story. Attacked by a fatal disease, the life of Nancy Hanks wasted slowly away. Day after day her son sat by her bed reading to her such portions of the Bible as she desired to hear. At intervals she talked to him, urging him to walk in the paths of honor, goodness, and truth. At last she found rest, and her son gave way to grief that could not be controlled.

In an opening in the timber, a short distance from the cabin, sympathizing friends and neighbors laid her body away and offered sincere prayers above her grave. The simple service did not seem to the son adequate tribute to the memory of the beloved mother whose loss he so sorely felt, but no minister could be procured at the time to preach a funeral sermon. In the spring, however, Abraham Lincoln, then a lad of ten, wrote to Elder Elkin, who had lived near them in Kentucky, begging that he would come and preach a sermon above his mother's grave, and adding that by granting this request he would confer a lasting favor upon his father, his sister, and himself. Although it involved a journey of more than a hundred miles on horseback, the good man cheerfully complied. Once more the neighbors and friends gathered about the grave of Nancy Hanks, and her son found comfort in their sympathy and their presence. The spot where Lincoln's mother lies is now enclosed within a high iron fence. At the head of the grave a white stone, simple, unaffected, and in keeping with the surroundings, has been placed. It bears the following inscription:

NANCY HANKS LINCOLN,
MOTHER OF PRESIDENT LINCOLN,
DIED OCTOBER 5, A.D. 1818.
AGED THIRTY-FIVE YEARS.
Erected by a friend of her martyred son.

Lincoln always held the memory of his mother in the deepest reverence and affection. Says Dr. J.G. Holland: "Long after her sensitive heart and weary hands had crumbled into dust, and had climbed to life again in forest flowers, he said to a friend, with tears in his eyes, 'All that I am or ever hope to be I owe to my sainted mother.'"

The vacant place of wife and mother was sadly felt in the Lincoln cabin, but before the year 1819 had closed it was filled by a woman who nobly performed the duties of her trying position. Thomas Lincoln had known Mrs. Sarah Johnston when both were young and living in Elizabethtown, Kentucky. They had married in the same year; and now, being alike bereaved, he persuaded her to unite their broken households into one.

By this union, a son and two daughters, John, Sarah, and Matilda, were added to the Lincoln family. All dwelt together in perfect harmony, the mother showing no difference in the treatment of her own children and the two now committed to her charge. She exhibited a special fondness for the little Abraham, whose precocious talents and enduring qualities she was quick to apprehend. Though he never forgot the "angel mother" sleeping on the forest-covered hill-top, the boy rewarded with a profound and lasting affection the devoted care of her who proved a faithful friend and helper during the rest of his childhood and youth. In her later life the step-mother spoke of him always with the tenderest feeling. On one occasion she said: "He never gave me a cross word or look, and never refused, in fact or appearance, to do anything I requested of him."

The child had enjoyed a little irregular schooling while living in Kentucky, getting what instruction was possible of one Zachariah Birney, a Catholic, who taught for a time close by his father's house. He also attended, as convenience permitted, a school kept by Caleb Hazel, nearly four miles away, walking the distance back and forth with his sister. Soon after coming under the care of his step-mother, the lad was afforded some similar opportunities for learning. His first master in Indiana was Azel Dorsey. The sort of education dispensed by him, and the circumstances under which it was given, are described by Mr. Ward H. Lamon, at one time Lincoln's law-partner at Springfield, Illinois. "Azel Dorsey presided in a small house near the Little Pigeon Creek meeting-house, a mile and a half from the Lincoln cabin. It was built of unhewn logs, and had holes for windows, in which greased paper served for glass. The roof was just high enough for a man to stand erect. Here the boy was taught reading, writing, and ciphering. They spelt in classes, and 'trapped' up and down. These juvenile contests were very exciting to the participants, and it is said by the survivors that Abe was even then the equal, if not the superior, of any scholar in his class. The next teacher was Andrew Crawford. Mrs. Gentry says he began teaching in the neighborhood in the winter of 1822-3. Crawford 'kept school' in the same little school-house which had been the scene of Dorsey's labors, and the windows were still adorned with the greased leaves of old copybooks that had come down from Dorsey's time. Abe was now in his fifteenth year, and began to exhibit symptoms of gallantry toward the other sex. He was growing at a tremendous rate, and two years later attained his full height of six feet and four inches. He wore low shoes, buckskin breeches, linsey-woolsey shirt, and a cap made of the skin of a 'possum or a coon. The breeches clung close to his thighs and legs, and failed by a large space to meet the tops of his shoes. He would always come to school thus, good-humoredly and laughing. He was always in good health, never sick, had an excellent constitution and took care of it."

Crawford taught "manners"—a feature of backwoods education to which Dorsey had not aspired. Crawford had doubtless introduced it as a refinement which would put to shame the humble efforts of his predecessor. One of the scholars was required to retire, and then to re-enter the room as a polite gentleman is supposed to enter a drawing-room. He was received at the door by another scholar and conducted from bench to bench until he had been introduced to all the young ladies and gentlemen in the room.

Lincoln went through the ordeal countless times. If he took a serious view of the performance it must have put him to exquisite torture, for he was conscious that he was not a perfect type of manly beauty. If, however, it struck him as at all funny, it must have filled him with unspeakable mirth to be thus gravely led about, angular and gawky, under the eyes of the precise Crawford, to be introduced to the boys and girls of his acquaintance.

While in Crawford's school the lad wrote his first compositions. The exercise was not required by the teacher, but, as Nat Grigsby has said, "he took it up on his own account." At first he wrote only short sentences against cruelty to animals, but at last came forward with a regular composition on the subject. He was annoyed and pained by the conduct of the boys who were in the habit of catching terrapins and putting coals of fire on their backs. "He would chide us," says Grigsby, "tell us it was wrong, and would write against it."

One who has had the privilege of looking over some of the boyish possessions of Lincoln says: "Among the most touching relics which I saw was an old copy-book in which, at the age of fourteen, Lincoln had taught himself to write and cipher. Scratched in his boyish hand on the first page were these lines:

Abraham Lincoln
his hand and pen.
he will be good but
god knows When"

The boy's thirst for learning was not to be satisfied with the meagre knowledge furnished in the miserable schools he was able to attend at long intervals. His step-mother says: "He read diligently. He read everything he could lay his hands on, and when he came across a passage that struck him he would write it down on boards, if he had no paper, and keep it until he had got paper. Then he would copy it, look at it, commit it to memory, and repeat it. He kept a scrap-book into which he copied everything which particularly pleased him." Mr. Arnold further states: "There were no libraries and but few books in the back settlements in which Lincoln lived. If by chance he heard of a book that he had not read he would walk miles to borrow it. Among other volumes borrowed from Crawford was Weems's Life of Washington. He read it with great earnestness. He took it to bed with him in the loft and read till his 'nubbin' of candle burned out. Then he placed the book between the logs of the cabin, that it might be near as soon as it was light enough in the morning to read. In the night a heavy rain came up and he awoke to find his book wet through and through. Drying it as well as he could, he went to Crawford and told him of the mishap. As he had no money to pay for the injured book, he offered to work out the value of it. Crawford fixed the price at three days' work, and the future President pulled corn for three days, thus becoming owner of the coveted volume." In addition to this, he was fortunate enough to get hold of Æsop's Fables, Pilgrim's Progress, and the lives of Benjamin Franklin and Henry Clay. He made these books his own by conning them over and over, copying the more impressive portions until they were firmly fixed in his memory. Commenting upon the value of this sort of mental training, Dr. Holland wisely remarks: "Those who have witnessed the dissipating effect of many books upon the minds of modern children do not find it hard to believe that Abraham Lincoln's poverty of books was the wealth of his life. The few he had did much to perfect the teaching which his mother had begun, and to form a character which for quaint simplicity, earnestness, truthfulness, and purity, has never been surpassed among the historic personages of the world."

It may well have been that Lincoln's lack of books and the means of learning threw him upon his own resources and led him into those modes of thought, of quaint and apt illustration and logical reasoning, so peculiar to him. At any rate, it is certain that books can no more make a character like Lincoln than they can make a poet like Shakespeare.

"By books may Learning sometimes befall,
But Wisdom never by books at all," —

a saying peculiarly true of a man such as Lincoln.

A testimonial to the influence of this early reading upon his childish mind was given by Lincoln himself many years afterwards. While on his way to Washington to assume the duties of the Presidency he passed through Trenton, New Jersey, and in a speech made in the Senate Chamber at that place he said: "May I be pardoned if, upon this occasion, I mention that away back in my childhood, in the earliest days of my being able to read, I got hold of a small book—such a one as few of the younger members have seen, Weems's Life of Washington. I remember all the accounts there given of the battle-fields and struggles for the liberties of the country; and none fixed themselves upon my imagination so deeply as the struggle here at Trenton. The crossing of the river, the contest with the Hessians, the great hardships endured at that time, all fixed themselves in my memory more than any single Revolutionary event; and you all know, for you have all been boys, how these early impressions last longer than any others. I recollect thinking then, boy even though I was, that there must have been something more than common that these men struggled for. I am exceedingly anxious that that thing which they struggled for, that something even more than

National Independence, that something that held out a great promise to all the people of the world for all time to come, I am exceedingly anxious that this Union, the Constitution, and the liberties of the people, shall be perpetuated in accordance with the original idea for which that struggle was made."

Another incident in regard to the ruined volume which Lincoln had borrowed from Crawford is related by Mr. Lamon. "For a long time," he says, "there was one person in the neighborhood for whom Lincoln felt a decided dislike, and that was Josiah Crawford, who had made him pull fodder for three days to pay for Weems's Washington. On that score he was hurt and mad, and declared he would have revenge. But being a poor boy, a fact of which Crawford had already taken shameful advantage when he extorted three days' labor, Abe was glad to get work anywhere, and frequently hired out to his old adversary. His first business in Crawford's employ was daubing the cabin, which was built of unhewn logs with the bark on. In the loft of this house, thus finished by his own hands, he slept for many weeks at a time. He spent his evenings as he did at home,—writing on wooden shovels or boards with 'a coal, or keel, from the branch.' This family was rich in the possession of several books, which Abe read through time and again, according to his usual custom. One of the books was the 'Kentucky Preceptor,' from which Mrs. Crawford insists that he 'learned his school orations, speeches, and pieces to write.' She tells us also that 'Abe was a sensitive lad, never coming where he was not wanted'; that he always lifted his hat, and bowed, when he made his appearance; and that 'he was tender and kind,' like his sister, who was at the same time her maid-of-all-work. His pay was twenty five cents a day; 'and when he missed time, he would not charge for it.' This latter remark of Mrs. Crawford reveals the fact that her husband was in the habit of docking Abe on his miserable wages whenever he happened to lose a few minutes from steady work. The time came, however, when Lincoln got his revenge for all this petty brutality. Crawford was as ugly as he was surly. His nose was a monstrosity—long and crooked, with a huge mis-shapen stub at the end, surmounted by a host of pimples, and the whole as blue as the usual state of Mr. Crawford's spirits. Upon this member Abe levelled his attacks, in rhyme, song, and chronicle; and though he could not reduce the nose he gave it a fame as wide as to the Wabash and the Ohio. It is not improbable that he learned the art of making the doggerel rhymes in which he celebrated Crawford's nose from the study of Crawford's own 'Kentucky Preceptor.'"

Lincoln's sister Sarah was warmly attached to him, but was taken from his companionship at an early age. It is said that her face somewhat resembled his, that in repose it had the gravity which they both inherited from their mother, but it was capable of being lighted almost into beauty by one of her brother's ridiculous stories or sallies of humor. She was a modest, plain, industrious girl, and was remembered kindly by all who knew her. She was married to Aaron Grigsby at eighteen, and died a year later. Like her brother, she occasionally worked at the houses of the neighbors. She lies buried, not with her mother, but in the yard of the old Pigeon Creek meeting-house.

A story which belongs to this period was told by Lincoln himself to Mr. Seward and a few friends one evening in the Executive Mansion at Washington. The President said: "Seward, you never heard, did you, how I earned my first dollar?" "No," rejoined Mr. Seward. "Well," continued Mr. Lincoln, "I belonged, you know, to what they call down South the 'scrubs.' We had succeeded in raising, chiefly by my labor, sufficient produce, as I thought, to justify me in taking it down the river to sell. After much persuasion, I got the consent of mother to go, and constructed a little flatboat, large enough to take a barrel or two of things that we had gathered, with myself and the bundle, down to the Southern market. A steamer was coming down the river. We have, you know, no wharves on the Western streams; and the custom was, if passengers were at any of the landings, for them to go out in a boat, the steamer stopping and taking them on board. I was contemplating my new flatboat, and wondering whether I could make it stronger or improve it in any way, when two men came down to the shore in carriages with trunks. Looking at the different boats, they singled out mine and asked, 'Who owns this?' I answered somewhat modestly, 'I do.' 'Will you take us and our trunks to the steamer?' asked one of them. 'Certainly,' said I. I was glad to have the chance of earning something. I supposed that each of them would give me two or three bits. The trunks were put on my flatboat, the passengers seated themselves on the trunks, and I sculled them out to the steamer. They got on board, and I lifted up their heavy trunks and put them on the deck. The steamer was about to put on steam again, when I called out to them that they had forgotten to pay me. Each man took from his pocket a silver half-dollar and threw it into the bottom of my boat. I could scarcely believe my eyes. Gentlemen, you may think it a little thing, and in these days it seems to me a trifle; but it was a great event in my life. I could scarcely credit that I, a poor boy, had earned a dollar in less than a day,—that by honest work I had earned a dollar. The world seemed wider and fairer to me. I was a more hopeful and confident being from that time."

Notwithstanding the limitations of every kind which hemmed in the life of young Lincoln, he had an instinctive feeling, born perhaps of his eager ambition, that he should one day attain an exalted position. The first betrayal of this premonition is thus related by Mr. Arnold:

"Lincoln attended court at Booneville, to witness a murder trial, at which one of the Breckenridges from Kentucky made a very eloquent speech for the defense. The boy was carried away with admiration, and was so enthusiastic that, although a perfect stranger, he could not resist expressing his admiration to Breckenridge. He wanted to be a lawyer. He went home, dreamed of courts, and got up mock trials, at which he would defend imaginary prisoners. Several of his companions at this period of his life, as well as those who knew him after he went to Illinois, declare that he was often heard to say, not in joke, but seriously, as if he were deeply impressed rather than elated with the idea: 'I shall some day be President of the United States.' It is stated by many of Lincoln's old friends that he often said while still an obscure man, 'Some day I shall be President.' He undoubtedly had for years some presentiment of this."

At seventeen Lincoln wrote a clear, neat, legible hand, was quick at figures and able to solve easily any arithmetical problem not going beyond the "Rule of Three." Mr. Arnold, noting these facts, says: "I have in my possession a few pages from his manuscript 'Book of Examples in Arithmetic' One of these is dated March 1, 1826, and headed 'Discount,' and then follows, in his careful handwriting: 'A definition of Discount,' 'Rules for its computation,' 'Proofs and Various Examples,' worked out in figures, etc.; then 'Interest on money' is treated in the same way, all in his own handwriting. I doubt whether it would be easy to find among scholars of our common or high schools, or any school of boys of the age of seventeen, a better written specimen of this sort of work, or a better knowledge of figures than is indicated by this book of Lincoln's, written at the age of seventeen."

In March, 1828, Lincoln went to work for old Mr. Gentry, the founder of Gentryville. "Early the next month the old gentleman furnished his son Allen with a boat and a cargo of bacon and other produce with which he was to go to New Orleans unless the stock should be sooner disposed of. Abe, having been found faithful and efficient, was employed to accompany the young man. He was paid eight dollars per month, and ate and slept on board." The entire business of the trip was placed in Abraham's hands. The fact tells its own story touching the young man's reputation for capacity and integrity. He had never made the trip, knew nothing of the journey, was unaccustomed to business transactions, had never been much upon the river, but his tact and ability and honesty were so far trusted that the trader was willing to risk the cargo in his care. The delight with which the youth swung loose from the shore upon his clumsy craft, with the prospect of a ride of eighteen hundred miles before him, and a vision of the great world of which he had read and thought so much, may be imagined. At this time he had become a very tall and powerful young man. He had reached the height of six feet and four inches, a length of trunk and limb remarkable even among the tall race of pioneers to which he belonged.

Just before the river expedition, Lincoln had walked with a young girl down to the river to show her his flatboat. She relates a circumstance of the evening which is full of significance. "We were sitting on the banks of the Ohio, or rather on the boat he had made. I said to Abe that the sun was going down. He said to me, 'That's not so; it don't really go down; it seems so. The earth turns from west to east and the revolution of the earth carries us under; we do the sinking, as you call it. The sun, as to us, is comparatively still; the sun's sinking is only an appearance.' I replied, 'Abe, what a fool you are!' I know now that I was the fool, not Lincoln. I am now thoroughly satisfied that he knew the general laws of astronomy and the movements of the heavenly bodies. He was better read then than the world knows or is likely to know exactly. No man could talk to me as he did that night unless he had known something of geography as well as astronomy. He often commented or talked to me about what he had read,—seemed to read it out of the book as he went along. He was the learned boy among us unlearned folks. He took great pains to explain; could do it so simply. He was diffident, too."

But another change was about to come into the life of Abraham Lincoln. In 1830 his father set forth once more on the trail of the emigrant. He had become dissatisfied with his location in southern Indiana, and hearing favorable reports of the prairie lands of Illinois hoped for better fortunes there. He parted with his farm and prepared for the journey to Macon County, Illinois. Abraham visited the neighbors and bade them goodbye; but on the morning selected for their departure, when it came time to start, he was missing. He was found weeping at his mother's grave, whither he had gone as soon as it was light. The thought of leaving her behind filled him with unspeakable anguish. The household goods were loaded, the oxen yoked, the family got into the covered wagon, and Lincoln took his place by the oxen to drive. One of the neighbors has said of this incident: "Well do I remember the day the Lincolns left for Illinois. Little did I think that I was looking at a boy who would one day be President of the United States!"

An interesting personal sketch of Thomas Lincoln is given by Mr. George B. Balch, who was for many years a resident of Lerna, Coles County, Illinois. Among other things he says: "Thomas Lincoln, father of the great President, was called Uncle Tommy by his friends and Old Tom Lincoln by other people. His property consisted of an old horse, a pair of oxen and a few sheep—seven or eight head. My father bought two of the sheep, they being the first we owned after settling in Illinois. Thomas Lincoln was a large, bulky man, six feet tall and weighing about two hundred pounds. He was large-boned, coarse-featured, had a large blunt nose, florid complexion, light sandy hair and whiskers. He was slow in speech and slow in gait. His whole appearance denoted a man of small intellect and less ambition. It is generally supposed that he was a farmer; and such he was, if one who tilled so little land by such primitive modes could be so called. He never planted more than a few acres, and instead of gathering and hauling his crop in a wagon he usually carried it in baskets or large trays. He was uneducated, illiterate, content with living from hand to mouth. His death occurred on the fifteenth day of January, 1851. He was buried in a neighboring country graveyard, about a mile north of Janesville, Coles County. There was nothing to mark the place of his burial until February, 1861, when Abraham Lincoln paid a last visit to his grave just before he left Springfield for Washington. On a piece of oak board he cut the letters T.L. and placed it at the head of the grave. It was carried away by some relic-hunter, and the place remained as before, with nothing to mark it, until the spring of 1876. Then the writer, fearing that the grave of Lincoln's father would become entirely unknown, succeeded in awakening public opinion on the subject. Soon afterward a marble shaft twelve feet high was erected, bearing on its western face this inscription:

> THOMAS LINCOLN
> FATHER OF
> THE MARTYRED PRESIDENT.
> BORN
> JAN. 6th, 1778
> DIED
> JAN. 15th, 1851.
> LINCOLN.

"And now," concluded Mr. Balch, "I have given all that can be known of Thomas Lincoln. I have written impartially and with a strict regard to facts which can be substantiated by many of the old settlers in this county. Thomas Lincoln was a harmless and honest man. Beyond this, one will search in vain for any ancestral clue to the greatness of Abraham Lincoln."

After reaching the new home in Illinois, young Lincoln worked with his father until things were in shape for comfortable living. He helped to build the log cabin, break up the new land and fence it in, splitting the rails with his own hands. It was these very rails over which so much sentiment was expended years afterward at an important epoch in Lincoln's political career. During the sitting of the State Convention at Decatur, a banner attached to two of these rails and bearing an appropriate inscription was brought into the assemblage and formally presented to that body amid a scene of unparalleled enthusiasm. After that they were in demand in every State of the Union in which free labor was honored. They were borne in processions by the people, and hailed by hundreds of thousands as a symbol of triumph and a glorious vindication of freedom and of the right and dignity of labor. These, however, were not the first rails made by Lincoln. He was a practiced hand at the business. As a memento of his pioneer accomplishment he preserved in later years a cane made from a rail which he had split on his father's farm.

The next important record of Lincoln's career connects him with Mr. Denton Offutt. The circumstances which brought him into this relation are thus narrated by Mr. J.H. Barrett: "While there was snow on the ground, at the close of the year 1830, or early in 1831, a man came to that part of Macon County where young Lincoln was living, in pursuit of hands to aid him in a flatboat voyage down the Mississippi. The fact was known that the youth had once made such a trip, and his services were sought for this occasion. As one who had his own subsistence to earn, with no capital but his hands, he accepted the proposition made him. Perhaps there was something of his inherited and acquired fondness for exciting adventure impelling him to this decision. With him were also employed his former fellow-laborer, John Hanks, and a son of his step-mother named John Johnston. In the spring of 1831 Lincoln set out to fulfil his engagement. The floods had so swollen the streams that the Sangamon country was a vast sea before him. His first entrance into that county was over these wide-spread waters in a canoe. The time had come to join his employer on his journey to New Orleans, but the latter had been disappointed by another person on whom he relied to furnish him a boat on the Illinois river. Accordingly all hands set to work, and themselves built a boat on that river, for their purposes. This done, they set out on their long trip, making a successful voyage to New Orleans and back."

Mr. Herndon says: "Mr. Lincoln came into Sangamon County down the North Fork of the Sangamon river, in a frail canoe, in the spring of 1831. I can see from where I write the identical place where he cut the timbers for his flatboat, which he built at a little village called Sangamon Town, seven miles northwest of Springfield. Here he had it loaded with corn, wheat, bacon, and other provisions destined for New Orleans, at which place he landed in the month of May, 1831. He returned home in June of that year, and finally settled in another little village called New Salem, on the high bluffs of the Sangamon river, then in Sangamon County and now in Menard County, and about twenty miles northwest of Springfield."

The practical and ingenious character of Lincoln's mind is shown in the act that several years after his river experience he invented and patented a device for overcoming some of the difficulties in the navigation of western rivers with which this trip had made him familiar. The following interesting account of this invention is given:

"Occupying an ordinary and commonplace position in one of the show-cases in the large hall of the Patent Office is one little model which in ages to come will be prized as one of the most curious and most sacred relics in that vast museum of unique and priceless things. This is a plain and simple model of a steamboat roughly fashioned in wood by the hand of Abraham Lincoln. It bears date 1849, when the inventor was known simply as a successful lawyer and rising politician of Central Illinois. Neither his practice nor his politics took up so much of his time as to prevent him from giving some attention to contrivances which he hoped might be of benefit to the world and of profit to himself. The design of this invention is suggestive of one phase of Abraham Lincoln's early life, when he went up and down the Mississippi as a flatboatman and became familiar with some of the dangers and inconveniences attending the navigation of the western rivers. It is an attempt to make it an easy matter to transport vessels over shoals and snags and 'sawyers.' The main idea is that of an apparatus resembling a noiseless bellows placed on each side of the hull of the craft just below the water line and worked by an odd but not complicated system of ropes, valves, and pulleys. When the keel of the vessel grates against the sand or obstruction these bellows are to be filled with air, and thus buoyed up the ship is expected to float lightly and gayly over the shoal which would otherwise have proved a serious interruption to her voyage. The model, which is about eighteen or twenty inches long and has the appearance of having been whittled with a knife out of a shingle and a cigar-box, is built without any elaboration or ornament or any extra apparatus beyond that necessary to show the operation of buoying the steamer over the obstructions. It is carved as one might imagine a retired railsplitter would whittle, strongly but not smoothly, and evidently made with a view solely to convey to the minds of the patent authorities, by the simplest possible means, an idea of the purpose and plan of the invention. The label on the steamer's deck informs us that the patent was obtained; but we do not learn that the navigation of the western rivers was revolutionized by this quaint conception. The modest little model has reposed here for many years, and the inventor has found it his task to guide the ship of state over shoals more perilous and obstructions more obstinate than any prophet dreamed of when Abraham Lincoln wrote his bold autograph across the prow of his miniature steamer."

At the conclusion of his trip to New Orleans, Lincoln's employer, Mr. Offutt, entered into mercantile trade at New Salem, a settlement on the

Sangamon river, in Menard County, two miles from Petersburg, the county seat. He opened a store of the class usually to be found in such small towns, and also set up a flouring-mill. In the late expedition down the Mississippi Mr. Offutt had learned Lincoln's valuable qualities, and was anxious to secure his help in his new enterprise. Says Mr. Barrett: "For want of other immediate employment, and in the same spirit which had heretofore actuated him, Abraham Lincoln entered upon the duties of a clerk, having an eye to both branches of his employer's business. This connection continued for nearly a year, all duties of his position being faithfully performed." It was to this year's humble but honorable service of young Lincoln that Mr. Douglas tauntingly alluded in one of his speeches during the canvass of 1858 as 'keeping a groggery.'

While engaged in the duties of Offutt's store Lincoln began the study of English grammar. There was not a text-book to be obtained in the neighborhood; but hearing that there was a copy of Kirkham's Grammar in the possession of a person seven or eight miles distant he walked to his house and succeeded in borrowing it. L.M. Green, a lawyer of Petersburg, in Menard County, says that every time he visited New Salem at this period Lincoln took him out upon a hill and asked him to explain some point in Kirkham that had given him trouble. After having mastered the book he remarked to a friend that if that was what they called a science he thought he could "subdue another." Mr. Green says that Lincoln's talk at this time showed that he was beginning to think of a great life and a great destiny. Lincoln said to him on one occasion that all his family seemed to have good sense but somehow none had ever become distinguished. He thought perhaps he might become so. He had talked, he said, with men who had the reputation of being great men, but he could not see that they differed much from others. During this year he was also much engaged with debating clubs, often walking six or seven miles to attend them. One of these clubs held its meetings at an old store-house in New Salem, and the first speech young Lincoln ever made was made there. He used to call the exercising "practicing polemics." As these clubs were composed principally of men of no education whatever, some of their "polemics" are remembered as the most laughable of farces. Lincoln's favorite newspaper at this time was the "Louisville Journal." He received it regularly by mail, and paid for it during a number of years when he had not money enough to dress decently. He liked its politics, and was particularly delighted with its wit and humor, of which he had the keenest appreciation.

At this era Lincoln was as famous for his skill in athletic sports as he was for his love of books. Mr. Offutt, who had a strong regard for him, according to Mr. Arnold, "often declared that his clerk, or salesman, knew more than any man in the United States, and that he could out-run, whip, or throw any man in the county. These boasts came to the ears of the 'Clary Grove Boys,' a set of rude, roystering, good-natured fellows, who lived in and around Clary's Grove, a settlement near New Salem. Their leader was Jack Armstrong, a great square-built fellow, strong as an ox, who was believed by his followers to be able to whip any man on the Sangamon river. The issue was thus made between Lincoln and Armstrong as to which was the better man, and although Lincoln tried to avoid such contests, nothing but an actual trial of strength would satisfy their partisans. They met and wrestled for some time without any decided advantage on either side. Finally Armstrong resorted to some foul play, which roused Lincoln's indignation. Putting forth his whole strength, he seized the great bully by the neck and holding him at arm's length shook him like a boy. The Clary Grove Boys were ready to pitch in on behalf of their champion; and as they were the greater part of the lookers-on, a general onslaught upon Lincoln seemed imminent. Lincoln backed up against Offutt's store and calmly awaited the attack; but his coolness and courage made such an impression upon Armstrong that he stepped forward, grasped Lincoln's hand and shook it heartily, saying: 'Boys, Abe Lincoln is the best fellow that ever broke into this settlement. He shall be one of us.' From that day forth Armstrong was Lincoln's friend and most willing servitor. His hand, his table, his purse, his vote, and that of the Clary Grove Boys as well, belonged to Lincoln. The latter's popularity among them was unbounded. They saw that he would play fair. He could stop a fight and quell a disturbance among these rude neighbors when all others failed."

Under whatever circumstances Lincoln was forced into a fight, the end could be confidently predicted. He was sure to thrash his opponent and gain the latter's friendship afterwards by a generous use of victory. Innumerable instances could be cited in proof of this statement. It is related that "One day while showing goods to two or three women in Offutt's store, a bully came in and began to talk in an offensive manner, using much profanity and evidently wishing to provoke a quarrel. Lincoln leaned over the counter and begged him, as ladies were present, not to indulge in such talk. The bully retorted that the opportunity had come for which he had long sought, and he would like to see the man who could hinder him from saying anything he might choose to say. Lincoln, still cool, told him that if he would wait until the ladies retired he would hear what he had to say and give him any satisfaction he desired. As soon as the women were gone the man became furious. Lincoln heard his boasts and his abuse for a time, and finding that he was not to be put off without a fight, said, 'Well, if you must be whipped, I suppose I may as well whip you as any other man.' This was just what the bully had been seeking, he said; so out of doors they went. Lincoln made short work of him. He threw him upon the ground, and held him there as if he had been a child, and gathering some 'smart-weed' which grew upon the spot he rubbed it into his face and eyes until the fellow bellowed with pain. Lincoln did all this without a particle of anger, and when the job was finished went immediately for water, washed his victim's face and did everything he could to alleviate his distress. The upshot of the matter was that the man became his life-long friend and was a better man from that day."

The chief repute of a sturdy frontiersman is built upon his deeds of prowess, and the fame of the great, rough, strong-limbed, kind-hearted Titan was spread over all the country around. Says Mr. Lamon: "On one occasion while he was clerking for Offutt a stranger came into the store and soon disclosed the fact that his name was Smoot. Abe was behind the counter at the moment, but hearing the name he sprang over and introduced himself. Abe had often heard of Smoot and Smoot had often heard of Abe. They had been as anxious to meet as ever two celebrities were, but hitherto they had never been able to manage it. 'Smoot,' said Lincoln, after a steady survey of his person, 'I am very much disappointed in you; I expected to see an old Probst of a fellow.' (Probst, it appears, was the most hideous specimen of humanity in all that country). 'Yes,' replied Smoot, 'and I am equally disappointed, for I expected to see a good-looking man when I saw you.' A few neat compliments like the foregoing laid the foundation of a lasting intimacy between the two men, and in his present distress Lincoln knew no one who would be more likely than Smoot to respond favorably to an application for money." After he was elected to the Legislature, says Mr. Smoot, "he came to my house one day in company with Hugh Armstrong. Says he, 'Smoot, did you vote for me?' I told him I did. 'Well,' says he, 'you must loan me money to buy suitable clothing, for I want to make a decent appearance in the Legislature.' I then loaned him two hundred dollars, which he returned to me according to promise."

Lincoln's old friend W.G. Greene relates that while he was a student at the Illinois College at Jacksonville he became acquainted with Richard Yates, then also a student. One summer while Yates was his guest during the vacation, Greene took him up to Salem and made him acquainted with Lincoln. They found the latter flat on his back on a cellar door reading a newspaper. Greene introduced the two, and thus began the acquaintance between the future War-Governor of Illinois and the future President.

Lincoln was from boyhood an adept at expedients for avoiding any unpleasant predicament, and one of his modes of getting rid of troublesome friends, as well as troublesome enemies, was by telling a story. He began these tactics early in life, and he grew to be wonderfully adept in them. If a man broached a subject which he did not wish to discuss, he told a story which changed the direction of the conversation. If he was called upon to answer a question, he answered it by telling a story. He had a story for everything; something had occurred at some place where he used to live that illustrated every possible phase of every possible subject with which he might have connection. He acquired the habit of story-telling naturally, as we learn from the following statement: "At home, with his step-mother and the children, he was the most agreeable fellow in the world. He was always ready to do everything for everybody. When he was not doing some special act of kindness, he told stories or 'cracked jokes.' He was as full of his yarns in Indiana as ever he was in Illinois. Dennis Hanks was a clever hand at the same business, and so was old Tom Lincoln." It was while Lincoln was salesman for Offutt that he acquired the *sobriquet* of "Honest Abe." Says Mr. Arnold: "Of many incidents illustrating his integrity, one or two may be mentioned. One evening he found his cash overran a little, and he discovered that in making change for his last customer, an old woman who had come in a little before sundown, he had made a mistake, not having given her quite enough. Although the amount was small, a few cents, he took the money, immediately walked to her house, and corrected the error. At another time, on his arrival at the store in the morning, he found on the scales a weight which he remembered having used just before closing, but which was not the one he had intended to use. He had sold a parcel of tea, and in the hurry had placed the wrong weight on the scales, so that the purchaser had a few ounces less of tea than had been paid for. He immediately sent the quantity required to make up the deficiency. These and many similar incidents are told regarding his scrupulous honesty in the most trifling matters. It was for such things as these that people gave him the name which clung to him as long as he lived."

It was in the summer of 1831 that Abraham Lincoln performed his first official act. Minter Graham, the school-teacher, tells the story. "On the day of the election, in the month of August, Abe was seen loitering about the polling place. It was but a few days after his arrival in New Salem. They were 'short of a clerk' at the polls; and, after casting about in vain for some one competent to fill the office, it occurred to one of the judges that perhaps the tall stranger possessed the needful qualifications. He thereupon accosted him, and asked if he could write. He replied, 'Yes, a little.' 'Will you act as clerk of the election to-day?' said the judge. 'I will try,' returned Abe, 'and do the best I can, if you so request.'" He did try accordingly, and, in the language of the schoolmaster, "performed the duties with great facility, firmness, honesty, and impartiality. I clerked with him," says Mr. Graham, "on the same day and at the same polls. The election books are now in the city of Springfield, where they can be seen and inspected any day."

That the foregoing anecdotes bearing on the early life of Abraham Lincoln are approximately correct is borne out by Lincoln himself. At the urgent request of Hon. Jesse W. Fell, of Bloomington, Illinois, Lincoln wrote a sketch of himself to be used during the campaign of 1860. In a note which accompanied the sketch he said: "Herewith is a little sketch, as you requested. There is not much to it, for the reason, I suppose, that there is not much of me. If anything be made out of it I wish it to be modest and not to go beyond the material." The letter is as follows:

I was born Feb. 12, 1809, in Hardin County, Kentucky. My parents were both born in Virginia, of undistinguishable families—second families, perhaps I should say. My mother, who died in my tenth year, was of a family of the name of Hanks, some of whom now reside in Adams, and others in Macon Counties, Illinois. My paternal grandfather, Abraham Lincoln, emigrated from Rockingham County, Virginia, to Kentucky, about 1781 or '2, where, a year or two later, he was killed by Indians, not in battle, but by stealth, when he was laboring to open a farm in the forest. His ancestors, who were Quakers, went to Virginia from Berks County, Pennsylvania. An effort to identify them with the New England family of the same name, ended in nothing more than a similarity of Christian names in both families, such as Enoch, Levi, Mordecai, Solomon, Abraham, and the like.

My father, at the death of his father, was but six years of age, and he grew up literally without education. He removed from Kentucky to what is now Spencer County, Indiana, in my eighth year. We reached our new home about the time the State came into the Union. It was a wild region, with many bears and other wild animals still in the woods. There I grew up. There were some schools, so called, but no qualification was ever required of a teacher beyond 'readin', writin' and cipherin'' to the Rule of Three. If a straggler, supposed to understand Latin, happened to sojourn in the neighborhood, he was looked upon as a wizard. There was absolutely nothing to excite ambition for education. Of course when I came of age I did not know much. Still, somehow, I could read, write, and cipher to the

Rule of Three, but that was all. I have not been to school since. The little advance I now have upon this store of education, I have picked up from time to time under the pressure of necessity.

I was raised to farm work, which I continued till I was twenty-two. At twenty-one I came to Illinois, and passed the first year in Macon County. Then I got to New Salem, at that time in Sangamon, now in Menard County, where I remained a year as a sort of clerk in a store. Then came the Black Hawk War, and I was elected a Captain of Volunteers—a success which gave me more pleasure than any I have had since. I went through the campaign, was elated, ran for the Legislature the same year (1832), and was beaten—the only time I have ever been beaten by the people. The next, and three succeeding biennial elections, I was elected to the Legislature. I was not a candidate afterwards. During this legislative period I had studied law, and removed to Springfield to practice it. In 1846 I was once elected to the Lower House of Congress, but was not a candidate for re-election. From 1849 to 1854, both inclusive, practiced law more assiduously than ever before. Always a Whig in politics, and generally on the Whig electoral tickets, making active canvasses. I was losing interest in politics, when the repeal of the Missouri Compromise aroused me again. What I have done since then is pretty well known.

If any personal description of me is thought desirable, it may be said, I am in height, six feet, four inches, nearly; lean in flesh, weighing, on an average, one hundred and eighty pounds; dark complexion, with coarse black hair, and gray eyes. No other marks or brands recollected.

Yours very truly,
A. LINCOLN.

CHAPTER II

The spring of 1832 brought a new turn in Lincoln's career. The year had been one of great advancement in many respects. He had made new and valuable acquaintances, read many books, mastered the grammar of his own tongue, won a multitude of friends. Those who could appreciate intelligence and character respected him, and those whose highest ideas of a man related to his physical prowess were devoted to him. Everyone trusted him. He was judge, arbitrator, referee, authority in all disputes, games, and matches whether of man-flesh or horse-flesh. He was the peacemaker in all quarrels. He was everybody's friend—the best-natured, most sensible, best-informed, most modest, unassuming, kindest, gentlest, roughest, strongest, best young fellow in all New Salem or the region about. But Mr. Offutt's trading enterprises ended disastrously in the year 1832. The store was closed, the mill was shut down, and Lincoln was out of business.

At the very moment, however, that he found himself adrift Illinois was filled with excitement over the Black Hawk War. The centre of alarm was in the Rock Valley, in the northern part of the State, which had been formerly the home of the Sac tribe of Indians. Discontented with their life on the reservation west of the Mississippi, to which they had been removed, the Sacs, with several other tribes, resolved to recover their old hunting-grounds. The warlike chief, Black Hawk, was at the head of the revolt, and his march toward the Rock river was signalized by a number of massacres. Governor Reynolds of Illinois issued a proclamation calling for volunteers to aid the regular troops in the emergency. Lincoln was one of the first to answer the call, the brave "Clary Grove Boys" also coming promptly to the rescue. "The volunteers gathered," writes Mr. Arnold, "at Rushville, in Schuyler County, at which place they were to be organized, and elected officers. Lincoln was a candidate for the place of captain, and in opposition to him was one William Kirkpatrick. The mode of election was novel. By agreement, each candidate walked off to some distance and took position by himself. The men were then to form, and those who voted for Kirkpatrick were to range on a line with their candidate. When the lines were formed, Lincoln's was three times as long as that of Kirkpatrick, and so Lincoln was declared elected. Speaking of this affair when President, he said that he was more gratified with this his first success than with any other election of his life. Neither Lincoln nor his company was in any engagement during the campaign, but there was plenty of hardships and fatigue, and some incidents occurred to illustrate his courage and power over men."

Many years afterward—in fact, while Lincoln was President—he referred to those early scenes in a way that illustrates his wonderful memory and his power of recalling the minutest incidents of his past life. Meeting an old Illinois friend, he naturally fell to talking of Illinois, and related several stories of his early life in that region. Particularly he remembered his share in the Black Hawk War. He referred to his part of the campaign lightly, and said that he saw but very little fighting. But he remembered coming on a camp of white scouts one morning just as the sun was rising. The Indians had surprised the camp and killed and scalped every man. "I remember just how those men looked," said Lincoln, "as we rode up the little hill where their camp was. The red light of the morning sun was streaming upon them as they lay, heads toward us, on the ground, and every man had a round red spot on the top of his head, about as big as a dollar, where the redskins had taken his scalp. It was frightful, but it was grotesque, and the red sunlight seemed to paint everything all over." Lincoln paused as if recalling the vivid picture, and added, somewhat irrelevantly, "I remember that one man had buckskin breeches on."

Lincoln also told a good story of his first experience in drilling raw troops during the Black Hawk War. He was crossing a field with a front of twenty men when he came to a gate through which it was necessary to pass. In describing the incident he said: "I could not, for the life of me, remember the proper word of command for getting my company *endwise*, so that it could pass through the gate. So, as we came near the gate, I shouted, 'Halt! this company is dismissed for two minutes, when it will fall in again on the other side of the gate.'" The manoeuvre was successfully executed.

During this campaign an incident occurred which well serves to show Lincoln's keen sense of justice, his great common sense, and his resoluteness when aroused. One day there came to the camp an old Indian, footsore and hungry. He was provided with a letter of safe-conduct from General Cass; but there was a feeling of great irritation against the Indians, and the men objected strongly to receiving him. They pronounced him a spy and his passport a forgery, and were rushing upon the defenseless Indian to kill him, when the tall figure of their captain, Lincoln, suddenly appeared between them and their victim. His men had never seen him so aroused, and they cowed before him. "Men," said he, "this must not be done! He must not be killed by us!" His voice and manner produced an effect on the mob. They paused, listened, fell back, and sullenly obeyed him, although there were still some murmurs of disappointed rage. At length one man, probably thinking he spoke for the crowd, cried out: "This is cowardly on your part, Lincoln!" Lincoln only gazed with contempt on the men who would have murdered one unarmed Indian but who quailed before his single hand. "If any man thinks I am a coward," said he, "let him test it." "Lincoln," was the reply, "you are larger and heavier than any of us." "That you can guard against," responded the captain. "Choose your weapons!" The insubordination ended, and the word "coward" was never associated with Lincoln's name again. He afterward said that at this time he felt that his life and character were both at stake, and would probably have been lost had he not at the supreme moment forgotten the officer and asserted the man. His men could hardly have been called soldiers. They were merely armed citizens, with a military organization in name only. Had he ordered them under arrest he would have created a serious mutiny; and to have them tried and punished would have been impossible.

It was while Lincoln was a militia captain that he made the acquaintance of a man who was destined to have an important influence on his life. This was Major John T. Stuart, afterwards his law-partner. Stuart was already a lawyer by profession. During the Black Hawk War he commanded one of the Sangamon County companies, and was soon afterward elected major of a spy battalion formed from some of these companies. He had the best of opportunities at this time to observe the merits of Captain Lincoln, and testifies that the latter was exceedingly popular among the soldiers on account of his excellent care of the men in his command, his never-failing good nature, and his ability to tell more stories and better ones than any man in the service. He was popular also among these hardy men on account of his great physical strength. For several years after the Black Hawk War Lincoln retained his military title and was usually addressed as "Captain Lincoln." But this in time was discontinued. Stuart's title of "Major," on the contrary, adhered to him through life. He was best known as "Major Stuart" down to the time of his death, which occurred early in the winter of 1886.

The time for which Captain Lincoln's company enlisted soon ran by, but the trouble with the Indians not being ended Governor Reynolds called for a second body of volunteers. Lincoln again responded, and was enrolled as a private in the independent company commanded by Elijah Iles of Springfield. A note of this occurrence, made in 1868 by Captain Iles, contains the following statement: "The term of Governor Reynolds's first call being about to expire, he made a second call, and the first levy was disbanded. I was elected a captain of one of the companies. We were mustered into service on the 29th of May, 1832, at the mouth of Fox river, now Ottawa, by Lieutenant Robert Anderson, Assistant Inspector General in the United States Army."

One day during the Black Hawk War there were in the camp on Rock river four men afterward famed in the history of the country. It was while Lincoln was a member of the company under command of Captain Iles. These men were Lieutenant Colonel Zachary Taylor, Lieutenant Jefferson Davis, Lieutenant Robert Anderson, and Private Abraham Lincoln. Lincoln and Anderson did not meet again until 1861, after the latter had evacuated Fort Sumter. Major Anderson then visited Washington and called at the White House to pay his respects to the President. After having expressed his thanks to Anderson for his conduct in South Carolina, Lincoln said, "Major, do you remember ever meeting me before?" "No, Mr. President, I do not remember having had the pleasure before," said Anderson. "Well," said Lincoln, "my memory is better than yours. You mustered me into the service of the United States in 1832 at Dixon's Ferry, during the Black Hawk War."

Lincoln displayed the same courage and fidelity in performing the duties of a soldier that had marked his conduct in all other relations of life. Father Dixon, the guide who was attached to Captain Iles's company of mounted rangers, remarks that in their marches when scouts were sent forward to examine thickets and ravines in which it was thought the enemy might be lurking it often became necessary for many of the men to dismount and attend to their riding gear. Whenever Lincoln was detailed for such service, however, his saddle was always in order.

During the contest between General Lewis Cass and General Zachary Taylor for the Presidency, in the year 1848, Lincoln made a speech in Congress in which he referred to his services in the Black Hawk War with characteristic humor:

"By the way, Mr. Speaker," he said, "did you know that I am a military hero? Yes, sir. In the days of the Black Hawk War I fought, bled, and came away. Speaking of General Cass's career reminds me of my own. I was not at Stillman's defeat, but I was about as near it as Cass was to Hull's surrender, and, like him, I saw the place very soon afterwards. It is quite certain that I did not break my sword, for I had none to break. But I bent my musket pretty badly on one occasion. If Cass broke his sword the idea is that he broke it in desperation. I bent my musket by accident. If General Cass went ahead of me in picking whortleberries, I guess I surpassed him in charges upon the wild onions. If he saw any live fighting Indians, it is more than I did, but I had a good many bloody struggles with the mosquitos, and although I never fainted from loss of blood I can truly say that I was often very hungry. Mr. Speaker, if I should ever conclude to doff whatever our Democratic friends may suppose there is in me of black-cockade Federalism, and thereupon they shall take me up as their candidate for the Presidency, I protest they shall not make fun of me as they have of General Cass by attempting to write me into a military hero."

Lincoln's popularity among his comrades in the field was so great that at the close of his military service, which had lasted three months, he was nominated as a candidate for the State Legislature. "His first appearance on the stump in the course of the canvass was at Pappsville, about eleven miles west of Springfield, upon the occasion of a public sale. The sale over, speech-making was about to begin, when Lincoln observed some strong symptoms of inattention in his audience which had taken that particular moment to engage in a a general fight. Lincoln saw that one of his friends was suffering more than he liked, and stepping into the crowd he shouldered them sternly away from his man until he met a fellow who refused to fall back. Him he seized by the nape of the neck and the seat of his breeches, and tossed him 'ten or twelve feet easily.' After this episode—as characteristic of him as of the times—he mounted the platform and delivered with awkward modesty the following speech: 'Gentlemen and Fellow-Citizens, I presume you all know who I am. I am humble Abraham Lincoln. I have been solicited by my friends to become a candidate for the Legislature. My politics are short and sweet, like the old woman's dance. I am in favor of a national bank. I am in favor of the internal-improvement system and a high protective tariff. These are my sentiments and political principles. If elected I shall be thankful. If not, it will be all the same.'"

Lincoln's friend, Mr. A.Y. Ellis, who was with him during a part of this campaign, says: "He wore a mixed-jeans coat, claw-hammer style, short in the sleeves and bobtail,—in fact, it was so short in the tail that he could not sit down on it,—flax and tow linen pantaloons, and a straw hat. I think he wore a vest, but I do not remember how it looked. He wore pot-metal boots. I went with him on one of his electioneering trips to Island Grove, and he made a speech which pleased his party friends very well, although some of the Jackson men tried to make sport of it. He told several good anecdotes in the speech, and applied them very well, I thought."

The election took place in August, and although Lincoln was defeated he received two hundred and seventy-seven out of the two hundred and eighty-four votes cast in his precincts. He was so little known outside of New Salem that the chances of election were hopelessly against him, yet the extraordinary evidence of favor shown by the vote of his fellow-townsmen was a flattering success in the midst of defeat. His failure to be elected, however, left him once more without occupation. He was without means, and felt the necessity of undertaking some business that would provide him an income, however small. It seems that at this time he considered seriously learning the blacksmith's trade, but while entertaining the idea an event occurred which opened the way in another direction. The particulars of this event are given by Mr. W.G. Greene. "A man named Reuben Radford," says

Mr. Greene, "was the keeper of a small store in the village of New Salem. A friend told him to look out for the 'Clary Grove boys' or they would smash him up. He said he was not afraid. He was a great big fellow. But his friend said, 'They don't come alone. If one can't whip you, two or three can, and they'll do it.' One day he left his store in charge of his brother, with injunctions that if the 'Clary Grove boys' came he must not let them have more than two drinks apiece. All the stores in those days kept liquor to sell and had a corner for drinking. The store was nicely fitted up, and had many things in glass jars nicely labelled. The 'Clary Grove boys' came, and took two drinks each. The clerk refused them any more as politely as he could. Then they went behind the counter and helped themselves. They got roaring drunk and went to work smashing everything in the store. The fragments on the floor were an inch deep. They left and went off on their horses whooping and yelling. Coming across some herds of cattle, they took the bells from their necks, fastened them to the tails of the leaders, and chased them over the country yelling like mad. Radford heard them, and, mounting his horse, rode in hot haste to the store. I had been sent that morning with grist to the mill, and had to pass the store. I saw Radford ride up, his horse a lather of foam. He dismounted, and looked in upon the wreck through the open door He was aghast at the sight, and said, 'I'll sell out this thing to the first man that comes along.' I rode up and said, 'I'll give you four hundred dollars for it.' 'Done!' said he. 'But,' I said, 'I have no money. I must have time.' 'How much?' 'Six months.' 'Agreed.' He drew up a note for four hundred dollars at six months, and I signed it. I began to think I was stuck. Then the boys came in, and among them was Lincoln. 'Cheer up, Billy,' he said. 'It's a good thing. We'll take an inventory.' 'No more inventories for me,' said I, not knowing what he meant. He explained that we should take an account of stock to see how much was left. We found that it amounted to about twelve hundred dollars. Lincoln and Berry consulted over it, and offered me two hundred and fifty dollars for my bargain. I accepted, stipulating that they should assume my notes. Berry was a wild fellow—a gambler. He had a fine horse, with a splendid saddle and bridle. He turned over the horse as part pay. Lincoln let Berry run the store, and it soon ran out. I had to pay the note. Lincoln said he would pay it some day and did, with interest." This ended Lincoln's brief career as a country merchant.

Many of the anecdotes in the foregoing pages touch upon Lincoln's ambition to fit himself for a public speaker. Even at this early day the settlers in New Salem were infected with the general desire to join in the march toward intellectual improvement. To aid in this object, they had established a club entitled the New Salem Literary Society. Before this association, the studious Lincoln was invited to speak. Mr. R.B. Rutledge, the brother of Anne Rutledge, says of the event: "About the year 1832 or 1833, Mr. Lincoln made his first effort at public speaking. A debating club, of which James Rutledge was president, was organized and held regular meetings. As Lincoln arose to speak, his tall form towered above the little assembly. Both hands were thrust down deep in the pockets of his pantaloons. A perceptible smile at once lit up the faces of the audience, for all anticipated the relation of some humorous story. But he opened up the discussion in splendid style, to the infinite astonishment of his friends. As he warmed with his subject, his hands would forsake his pockets and enforce his ideas by awkward gestures, but would very soon seek their easy resting-places. He pursued the question with reason and argument so pithy and forcible that all were amazed. The president, after the meeting, remarked to his wife that there was more in Abe's head than wit and fun; that he was already a fine speaker; that all he lacked was culture to enable him to reach the high destiny which he knew was in store for him."

On the 7th of May, 1833, Lincoln was appointed postmaster at New Salem by President Jackson. The duties of the position were light, there being only a weekly mail, and the remuneration was correspondingly small. "The office was too insignificant to be considered politically, and it was given to the young man because everybody liked him, and because he was the only man willing to take it who could make out the returns. He was exceedingly pleased with the appointment, because it gave him a chance to read every newspaper that was taken in the vicinity. He had never been able to get half the newspapers he wanted, and the office gave him the prospect of a constant feast. Not wishing to be tied to the office, as it yielded him no revenue that would reward him for the confinement, he made a post-office of his hat. Whenever he went out, the letters were placed in his hat. When an anxious looker for a letter met the postmaster he found also the post-office, and the public official, taking off his hat, looked over and delivered the mail wherever the public might find him. He kept the office until it was discontinued, or was removed to Petersburg."

A small balance due the government remained in the hands of Lincoln at the discontinuance of the office. Time passed on, and he had removed to Springfield and was practicing law, having his place of business in Dr. Henry's office. Meanwhile his struggle with poverty was unabated, and he had often been obliged to borrow money from his friends to purchase the barest necessities. It was at this juncture that the agent of the United States called for a settlement of his post-office accounts. The interview took place in the presence of Dr. Henry who thus describes it: "I did not believe he had the money on hand to meet the draft, and I was about to call him aside and loan him the money, when he asked the agent to be seated a moment. He went over to his trunk at his boarding-house and returned with an old blue sock with a quantity of silver and copper coin tied up in it. Untying the sock, he poured the contents on the table and proceeded to count the coin, which consisted of such silver and copper pieces as the country people were then in the habit of using in paying postage. On counting it up, there was found the exact amount of the draft to a cent, and in the identical coin which had been received. He never, under any circumstances, used trust funds."

When Lincoln was about twenty-three years of age, some time in 1832, he began studying law, using an old copy of Blackstone's Commentaries which he had bought at auction in Springfield. This work was soon mastered, and then the young man looked about him for more. His friend of the Black Hawk War, Major John T. Stuart, had a considerable law library for those days, and to him Lincoln applied in his extremity. The library was placed at his disposal, and thenceforth he was engrossed in the acquisition of its contents. But the books were in Springfield, where their owner resided; and New Salem was some fourteen miles distant. This proved no obstacle in the way of Lincoln, who made nothing of the walk back and forth in the pursuit of his purpose. Mr. Stuart's partner, Mr. H.C. Dummer, who took note of the youth in his frequent visits to the office, describes him as "an uncouth looking lad, who did not say much, but what he did say he said straight and sharp." "He used to read law," says Henry McHenry, "barefooted, seated in the shade of a tree just opposite Berry's grocery, and would grind around with the shade, occasionally varying his attitude by lying flat on his back and putting his feet up the tree," a situation which might have been unfavorable to mental application in the case of a man with shorter extremities. "The first time I ever saw Abe with a law-book in his hand," says Squire Godbey, "he was sitting astride Jake Bates's woodpile in New Salem. Says I, 'Abe, what are you studying?' 'Law,' says Abe. 'Good God Almighty!' responded I." It was too much for Godbey; he could not suppress the exclamation of surprise at seeing such a figure acquiring learning in such an odd situation. Mr. Arnold states that Lincoln made a practice of reading in his walks between Springfield and New Salem; and so intense was his application and so absorbed was he in his study that he would pass his best friends without observing them, and some people said that Lincoln was going crazy with hard study.

He soon began to make a practical application of his legal knowledge. He bought an old form-book and began to draw up contracts, deeds, leases, mortgages, and all sorts of legal instruments for his neighbors. He also began to exercise his forensic ability in trying small cases before justices of the peace and juries, and soon acquired a local reputation as a speaker, which gave him considerable practice. But he was able in this way to earn scarcely money enough for his maintenance. To add to his means, he took up the study of surveying, and soon became, like Washington, a skilful and accurate surveyor. John Calhoun, an intelligent and courteous gentleman, was at that time surveyor of the county of Sangamon. He became interested in Lincoln and appointed him his deputy. His work was so accurate and the settlers had such confidence in him that he was much sought after to survey, fix, and mark the boundaries of farms, and to plot and lay off the town of Petersburg. His accuracy must have been attained with some difficulty, for when he began to survey his chain was a grape-vine. He did not speculate in the land he surveyed. Had he done so the rapid advance in the value of real estate would have made it easy for him to make good investments. But he was not in the least like one of his own appointees when President, — a surveyor-general of a Western territory, who bought up much of the best land, and to whom the President said, "I am told, sir, you are *monarch of all you survey.*"

The nomination of Lincoln for the State Legislature on his return from the Black Hawk War was premature. The people of New Salem voted for him almost to a man, but his acquaintance had not then extended into the surrounding district far enough to insure his election. In the campaign of 1834 the choice of a candidate again fell upon him, and this time there was a prospect of success. Lincoln entered into the contest with earnestness, and used every legitimate means to secure a victory. Mr. Herndon relates the following incident of this campaign: "Lincoln came to my house, near Island Grove, during harvest. There were some thirty men in the field. He had his dinner, and then went out into the field where the men were at work. I introduced him, and the boys said they would not vote for a man unless he could 'make a hand.' 'Well, boys,' he said, 'if that is all that is needed I am sure of your votes.' He took hold of the cradle and led the way all around with perfect ease. The boys were satisfied. I don't think he lost a vote in that crowd. The next day there was speaking at Berlin. He went from my house with Dr. Barnett, who had asked me who this man Lincoln was. I told him he was a candidate for the Legislature. He laughed and said, 'Can't the party raise better material than that?' I said, 'Go to-morrow and hear him before you pass judgment.' When he came back I said, 'Doctor, what have you to say now?' 'Why, sir,' he said, 'he is a perfect *take-in*. He knows more than all the rest of them put together.'"

The result of the election was that Lincoln was chosen to represent the Sangamon district. When the Legislature convened at the opening session, he was in his place in the lower house; but he bore himself quietly in his new position. He had much to learn in his novel situation as one of the lawmakers of the State, and as a co-worker with an assembly comprising the most talented and prominent men gathered from all parts of Illinois. He was keenly watchful of the proceedings of the House, weighing every measure with scrutinizing sagacity, but except in the announcement of his vote his voice was seldom heard. At the previous session, Mr. G.S. Hubbard, afterwards a well-known citizen of Chicago, had exerted himself to procure the passage of an act for the construction of the Illinois and Michigan Canal. His effort was defeated; but he continued, as a lobbyist, to push the measure during several winters, until it was finally adopted. Lincoln lent him efficient aid in the accomplishment of his object. "Indeed," remarks Mr. Hubbard, "I very much doubt if the bill could have passed as easily as it did without his valuable help." "We were thrown much together," continues Mr. Hubbard, "our intimacy increasing. I never had a friend to whom I was more warmly attached. His character was almost faultless; possessing a warm and generous heart, genial, affable, honest, courteous to his opponents, persevering, industrious in research, never losing sight of the principal point under discussion, aptly illustrating by his stories which were always brought into good effect. He was free from political trickery or denunciation of the personal character of his opponents. In debate he was firm and collected. 'With malice toward none, with charity for all,' he won the confidence of the public, even his political opponents."

Of all the stories of Lincoln's boyhood and youth, the most profoundly touching is that of his love for Anne Rutledge. The existence of this romance was brief, but it is believed by many that it was the memory of it which threw over Lincoln that indescribable melancholy which seemed to shadow his whole life. The Rutledges from whom Anne was descended were an eminent family of the Carolinas. She was about nineteen years old when Lincoln knew her first. It was shortly after the Black Hawk War. She was a winsome girl, with fair hair and blue eyes, and Lincoln's heart was captivated by her sweet face and gentle manners. So attractive a girl was not, of course, without suitors, and Anne had been wooed by one James McNeill, a young man who had come to New Salem soon after the founding of the town. He had been more than ordinarily successful, and had bought a large farm a few miles north of the village. He was unmarried—at least he so represented himself—and paid devoted attention to Anne. They were engaged, although both had acquiesced in the wishes of Anne's parents that they should not be married until she was older.

About this time Lincoln appeared in New Salem and went to board at the Rutledge tavern. Here he saw Anne, and was much in her company. During the next year McNeill became restless and discontented. He said it was because he wanted to see his people. So he decided to go East on a visit. He sold out his interests in New Salem—an act not at all necessary if he were going only on a visit, and which in the light of after events had much significance—telling Anne that it was his hope to bring his father and mother back with him and establish them upon his farm. "This done," he said, "we will be married." He then set out on his journey.

It was late in the summer before Anne heard from him. He explained that he had been taken ill with chills and fever on the way, and had been long delayed in getting home. But the long wait had been a great strain upon Anne. Lincoln, meanwhile, had become the postmaster in New Salem, and it was to him that Anne came to inquire for letters. He watched her anxiety with sympathy, and in a way became her confidant. His tender heart, which never could resist suffering, was deeply touched at sight of her distress. Finally McNeill's letters ceased altogether; and then Anne confided to Lincoln something which McNeill had told her before he left, and which until now she had kept secret,—namely, that his name was not McNeill but McNamar. He had explained to her that he had made this change because his father had failed in business and that as his oldest son it was his duty to retrieve the family fortunes. So he had changed his name, and come West, hoping to return in a few years to his family a rich man. All this Anne had believed, and had not repeated until now.

All New Salem joined in declaring McNamar an impostor and his story a fabrication. "Who knew how many wives he had?" they said. With one accord Anne's friends denounced him; and although his story turned out afterward to be not altogether false, it is small wonder that Anne herself at last came to believe that either he was dead or had ceased to love her.

While matters were in this state, Lincoln ventured to show his love for Anne. It was a long time before she would listen; but, convinced at last that her former lover had deserted her, she promised, in the spring of 1835, to become his wife. But Lincoln had nothing on which to support a family,— in fact, could hardly support himself. Besides, Anne was anxious to go to school another year. So it was decided that she should spend the winter in an academy in Jacksonville, while Lincoln devoted himself to the study of the law. Then, when she should return from school, he would be a member of the bar and they could be married.

A happy spring and summer followed. All their friends took an interest in the lovers, and their prospects seemed bright. But Anne's health began to fail. She could not rid herself of her haunting memories. There was a possibility that she had wronged McNamar. What if he should love her still, and should return and find her wedded to another? Had she wronged both men? In her thoughts was perpetual conflict. The old love still persisted. Her conscience troubled her. She doubted, and was morbidly melancholy.

All this wore upon her; she fell ill. At last her condition became grave, then hopeless. Lincoln was sent for. Anne's last hour was passed alone with him. She died at sunset, August 25, 1835. An old neighbor who saw Lincoln just after his parting with the dying girl says: "There were signs of the most terrible distress in his face. His grief became frantic. He lost all self-control, even the consciousness of his own identity; and his closest friends in New Salem pronounced him insane, crazy, mad. They watched him with especial vigilance on dark and stormy days. At such times he raved piteously, often saying, 'I can never be reconciled to having the snow fall and the rain beat upon her grave.'" His old friend, Bowlin Greene, alone seemed possessed of the power to quiet him. He took him to his own home and kept him for several weeks, an object of undisguised solicitude. At last it seemed safe to permit him to return to his old haunts. Greene urged him to go back to the law; and he did so, but he was never the same man again. He was thin, haggard, and careworn. He was as one who had been at the brink of the grave. A long time afterward, when the grass had for nearly thirty years grown over the grave of Anne Rutledge, Lincoln was one day introduced to a man named Rutledge in the White House. He looked at him a moment, then grasped his hand and said with deep feeling: "I love the name of Rutledge to this day. Anne was a lovely girl. She was natural, well-educated. She would have made a good, loving wife. I did honestly and truly love her, and I think often, often of her now." Mr. Herndon has said that the love and the death of this young girl shattered Lincoln's purposes and tendencies. "He threw off his infinite sorrow only by leaping wildly into the political arena. He needed whip and spur to save him from despair."

The period of Abraham Lincoln's boyhood and youth had closed when he stood by the grave of Anne Rutledge. He had long been a man in stature. He was now a man in years; yet the rough path he had been forced to travel had made his progress toward maturity painfully slow. In spite of his low birth, of his dire poverty, of the rudeness and illiteracy of his associates, of the absence of refinement in his surroundings, of his scanty means of education, of his homely figure and awkward manners, of his coarse fare and shabby dress, he dared to believe there was an exalted career in store for him. He hewed out the foundations for it with indomitable spirit. It was to be grounded on manly virtues. It seems as though the boy felt the consecration of a high destiny from the very dawn of his intelligence, and it set him apart, secure amid the temptations and safe from the vices that corrupt many men. In the rough garb of the backwoodsman he preserved the instincts of a gentleman. He was the companion of bullies and boors. He shared their work and their sports, but he never stooped to their vulgarity. He very seldom drank with them, and they never heard him speak an oath. He could throw the stoutest in a wrestling match, and was ready, when brought to it, to whip any insolent braggart who made cruel use of his strength. He never flinched from hardship or danger, yet his heart was as soft and tender as a woman's. The great gentle giant had a feeling of sympathy for every living creature. He was not ashamed to rock a cradle, or to carry a pail of water or an armful of wood to spare a tired woman's arms. Though destitute of worldly goods, he was rich in friends. All the people of his acquaintance knew they could count on his doing the right thing always, so far as he was able. Hence they trusted and loved him; and the title of "Honest Abe," which he bore through life, was a seal of knighthood rarer and prouder than any king or queen could confer with the sword. Abraham Lincoln was one of nature's noblemen. He showed himself a hero in every circumstance of his boyhood and youth. The elements of greatness were visible even then. The boy who was true to duty, patient in privation, modest in merit, kind to every form of distress, determined to rise by wresting opportunities from the grudging hand of fate, was sure to make a man distinguished among his fellows,—a man noted among the great men of the world, as the boy had been among his neighbors in the wilds of Spencer County and New Salem.

The site of the town where Lincoln spent the last three years of the period covered in this portion of his biography is now a desolate waste. A gentleman who visited the spot during the summer of 1885 thus describes the mournful scene: "From the hill where I sit, under the shade of three trees whose branches make one, I look out over the Sangamon river and its banks covered apparently with primeval forests. Around are fields overgrown with weeds and stunted oaks. It was a town of ten or twelve years only. It began in 1824 and ended in 1836. Yet in that time it had a history which the world will not let die as long as it venerates the memory of the noble liberator and martyr President, Abraham Lincoln."

CHAPTER III

Abraham Lincoln's career as a lawyer covered a period of a quarter of a century, beginning about 1834 or '35, and ending with his election to the Presidency, in November, 1860. When he began his professional life he was an obscure and unpromising youth of twenty-five, with but little learning and fewer accomplishments, and without advantages of social influence or wealthy friends. Step by step, with patient industry and unflinching determination, he climbed the ladder of professional advancement until he stood among the foremost lawyers of the West. He had, indeed, won a national reputation; and when he laid aside his law books, a mature man of fifty, it was to enter upon the great honors and responsibilities of the Presidency of the American Republic.

Lincoln was devoted to his profession, and his success in it was earned by hard and constant application. But his natural taste for politics led him to take a full share in the activities of political life. He had already served a term in the Illinois Legislature (1834-35), and so well satisfied were his constituents that they renominated him for the succeeding term. In the canvass which followed he distinguished himself as a stump-speaker; showing, by his tact and ability, by the skill and ingenuity with which he met his opponents in debate, by his shrewdness in attack and readiness in retort, how much he had profited by the training of the previous years.

An incident illustrating his ready wit and his keen insight into human nature occurred early in this campaign, at Springfield, where a public discussion was held between the opposing candidates. An interesting version of this incident is given by Mr. Arnold: "There lived at this time in the most pretentious house in Springfield a prominent citizen named George Forquer. He had been long in public life, had been a leading Whig—the party to which Lincoln belonged—but had lately gone over to the Democrats, and had received from the Democratic administration an appointment to the lucrative post of Register of the Land Office at Springfield. Upon his handsome new house he had lately placed a lightning-rod, the first one ever put up in Sangamon County. As Lincoln was riding into town with his friends, they passed the fine house of Forquer, and observed the novelty of the lightning-rod, discussing the manner in which it protected the house from being struck by lightning. In this discussion there were seven Whig and seven Democratic candidates for the lower branch of the Legislature; and after several had spoken it fell to Lincoln to close the arguments. This he did with great ability. Forquer, though not a candidate, then asked to be heard for the Democrats in reply to Lincoln. He was a good speaker and well-known throughout the county. His special task that day was to attack and ridicule the young man from Salem. Turning to Lincoln, who stood within a few feet of him, he said: 'This young man must be taken down, and I am truly sorry that the task devolves upon me.' He then proceeded, in a very overbearing way, and with an assumption of great superiority, to attack Lincoln and his speech. Lincoln stood calm, but his flashing eye and pale cheek showed his indignation. As soon as Forquer had closed he took the stand and first answered his opponent's arguments fully and triumphantly. So impressive were his words and manner that a hearer believes that he can remember to this day, and repeat, some of the expressions. Among other things, he said: 'The gentleman commenced his speech by saying that this *young* man—alluding to me—must be taken down. I am not so young in years as I am in the tricks and trades of a politician; but, ' said he, pointing to Forquer, 'live long or die young, I would rather die now, than, like the gentleman, change my politics for a three thousand dollar office, and then feel obliged to erect a lightning-rod over my house to protect a guilty conscience from the vengeance of an offended God!'"

"It is difficult to-day," says Mr. Arnold, "to appreciate the effect on the old settlers, of this figure. This lightning-rod was the first which most of those present had ever seen. They had slept all their lives in their cabins in conscious security. Here was a man who seemed, to these simple-minded people, to be afraid to sleep in his own house without special and extraordinary protection from Almighty God. These old settlers thought nothing but the consciousness of guilt, the stings of a guilty conscience, could account for such timidity. Forquer and his lightning-rod were talked over in every settlement from Sangamon to the Illinois and the Wabash. Whenever he rose to speak thereafter, they said, 'There is the man who dare not sleep in his own house without a lightning-rod to keep off the vengeance of the Almighty.'"

Another amusing incident of the same campaign, and one which illustrates Lincoln's love of a practical joke, is given as follows: "Among the Democrats stumping the county at this time was one Dick Taylor, a most pompous person, who was always arrayed in the richest attire—ruffled shirts, seals, etc., besides a rich embroidered vest. Notwithstanding this array, he made great pretentions of being one of the 'hard-handed yeomanry,' and ridiculed with much sarcasm the 'rag barons' and 'manufacturing lords' of the Whig party. One day, when he was particularly aggravating in a speech of this kind, Lincoln decided on a little sport, and sidling up to Taylor suddenly threw open the latter's coat, showing to the astonished spectators a glittering mass of ruffled shirt, gold watch, and glittering jewels. The crowd shouted uproariously. Lincoln said: 'While he [Colonel Taylor] was making these charges against the Whigs over the country, riding in fine carriages, wearing ruffled shirts, kid gloves, massive gold watch-chains with large gold seals, and flourishing a heavy gold-headed cane, I was a poor boy, hired on a flatboat at eight dollars a month, and had only one pair of breeches to my name, and they were buckskin,—and if you know the nature of buckskin, when wet and dried by the sun it will shrink,—and mine kept shrinking until they left several inches of my legs bare between the tops of my socks and the lower part of my breeches. Whilst I was growing taller, they were becoming shorter and so much tighter that they left a blue streak around my legs that can be seen to this day. If you call this aristocracy, I plead guilty to the charge.'"

"The Saturday evening preceding the election," says Mr. Lamon, "the candidates were addressing the people in the Court House at Springfield. Dr. Early, one of the candidates on the Democratic side, made some charge which Mr. N.W. Edwards, one of the candidates on the Whig side, deemed untrue. Edwards climbed on a table, so as to be seen by Early and by everyone in the house, and at the top of his voice told Early that the charge was false. The excitement that followed was intense—so much so that fighting men thought a duel must settle the difficulty. Lincoln, by the programme, followed Early. He took up the subject in dispute and handled it fairly and with such ability that everyone was astonished and pleased. So that difficulty ended there. Then for the first time, aroused by the excitement of the occasion, he spoke in that tenor intonation of voice that ultimately settled down into that clear, shrill monotone style that afterwards characterized his public speaking, and enabled his audience, however large, to hear distinctly the lowest sound of his voice." Mr. Arnold says that Lincoln's reply to Dr. Early was "often spoken of as exhibiting wonderful ability, and a crushing power of sarcasm and ridicule. When he began he was embarrassed, spoke slowly and with some hesitation and difficulty. But becoming excited by his subject, he forgot himself entirely, and went on with argument and wit, anecdote and ridicule, until his opponent was completely crushed. Old settlers of Sangamon County who heard this reply speak of his personal transformation as wonderful. When Lincoln began, they say, he seemed awkward, homely, unprepossessing. As he went on, and became excited, his figure rose to its full height and became commanding and majestic. His plain face was illuminated and glowed with expression. His dreamy eye flashed with inspiration, and his whole person, his voice, his gestures, were full of the magnetism of powerful feeling, of conscious strength and true eloquence."

The inflexible honesty and fine sense of honor which lay at the foundation of Lincoln's character are nobly exhibited in the following letter to a former friend but now political opponent, Col. Robert Allen:

> DEAR COLONEL:—I am told that during my absence last week, you passed through this place, and stated publicly that you were in possession of a fact or facts which, if known to the public, would entirely destroy the prospects of N.W. Edwards and myself at the ensuing election, but that through favor to us you would forbear to divulge them. No one has needed favors more than I, and generally few have been less unwilling to accept them; but in this case favor to me would be injustice to the public, and therefore I must beg your pardon for declining it. That I once had the confidence of the people of Sangamon County is sufficiently evident; and if I have since done anything, either by design or misadventure, which if known would subject me to a forfeiture of that confidence, he who knows of that thing and conceals it is a traitor to his country's interest.
>
> I find myself wholly unable to form any conjecture of what fact or facts, real or supposed, you spoke. But my opinion of your veracity will not permit me for a moment to doubt that you at least believed what you said. I am flattered with the personal regard you manifested for me; but I do hope that on more mature reflection you will view the public interest as a paramount consideration, and therefore determine to let the worst come.
>
> I assure you that the candid statement of facts on your part, however low it may sink me, shall never break the ties of personal friendship between us.
>
> I wish an answer to this, and you are at liberty to publish both if you choose.
>
> Very respectfully,
> A. LINCOLN.
>
> COL. ROBERT ALLEN.

The campaign resulted in Lincoln's election to the Legislature of 1836. The nine delegates from Sangamon County happened to be men of remarkable stature, each one measuring six feet or more in height; and very naturally they were nicknamed the "Long Nine." Lincoln overtopped all the rest, and as a consequence was called "the Sangamon Chief." The State capital was then at Vandalia; and Lincoln's journey there from Springfield was made mainly on foot. As he was trudging along the muddy road, he fell in with Judge John Dean Caton, one of the early lawyers of Illinois, afterwards Chief Justice of the State, who became an intimate friend of Lincoln. Judge Caton gives an interesting account of their first meeting, which occurred at this time. "I first met Mr. Lincoln," says Judge Caton, "about the last of November, 1835, when on my way to Vandalia to join the Supreme Court, which met there the first Monday in December, at the same time as the meeting of the Legislature. There were a great many people and all sorts of vehicles on the road from Springfield to Vandalia. The roads were very bad, and most of the passengers got out and walked a considerable portion of the distance. It seemed almost like the movement of a little army. While walking thus along the side of the road I met Mr. Lincoln for the first time, and in the course of a two days' journey we became quite well acquainted. If he had been admitted to the bar at that time, he had not become known as a lawyer out of his own immediate circuit. He was going to Vandalia as a member of the Legislature. He was one of the 'Long Nine,' as it was called, from Sangamon County, who by their successful manoeuvring and united efforts succeeded in getting the seat of government moved from Vandalia to Springfield. During my stay of a few weeks in Vandalia I frequently met Mr. Lincoln. He was a very pleasant companion; but as we walked along the road on the occasion referred to, talking about indifferent subjects, nothing impressed me with any idea of his future greatness."

When Lincoln took his seat in the first session of the new Legislature at Vandalia, his mind was full of new projects. His real public service was now about to begin, and having spent his time in the previous Legislature mainly as an observer and listener he was determined during this session to identify himself conspicuously with the "liberal" progressive legislation, dreaming of a fame far different from that he actually obtained as an anti-slavery leader. As he remarked to his friend Speed, he hoped to obtain the great distinction of being called "the De Witt Clinton of Illinois."

It was at a special session of this Legislature that Lincoln first saw Stephen A. Douglas, his great political antagonist of the future, whom he describes as "the *least* man" he ever saw. Douglas had come into the State from Vermont only the previous year, and having studied law for several months considered himself eminently qualified to be State's attorney for the district in which he lived. General Linder says of the two men at this time: "I here had an opportunity, better than any I had previously possessed, of measuring the intellectual stature of Abraham Lincoln. He was then about twenty-seven years old—my own age. Douglas was four years our junior;

consequently he could not have been over twenty-three years old. Yet he was a very ready and expert debater, even at that early period of his life. He and Lincoln were very frequently pitted against each other, being of different politics. They both commanded marked attention and respect."

A notable measure effected by the "Long Nine" during this session of the Legislature was the removal of the State Capital from Vandalia to Springfield. It was accomplished by dint of shrewd and persistent management, in which Lincoln was a leading spirit. Mr. Robert L. Wilson, one of his colleagues, says: "When our bill to all appearance was dead beyond resuscitation, and our friends could see no hope, Lincoln never for a moment despaired. Collecting his colleagues in his room for consultation, his practical common-sense, his thorough knowledge of human nature, made him an overmatch for his compeers, and for any man I have ever known."

Lincoln's reputation as an orator was gradually extending beyond the circle of his friends and constituents. He was gaining notice as a ready and forcible speaker, with shrewd and sensible ideas which he expressed with striking originality and independence. He was invited to address the Young Men's Lyceum at Springfield, January 27, 1837, and read a carefully prepared paper on "The Perpetuation of Our Political Institutions," which was afterwards published in the Springfield "Weekly Journal." The address was crude and strained in style, but the feeling pervading it was fervent and honest, and its patriotic sentiment and sound reflection made it effective for the occasion. A few paragraphs culled from this paper, some of them containing remarkable prophetic passages, afford a clue to the stage of intellectual development which Lincoln had reached at the age of twenty-seven, and an interesting contrast with the terser style of his later years.

> In the great journal of things happening under the sun, we, the American people, find our account running under date of the nineteenth century of the Christian era. We find ourselves in the peaceful possession of the fairest portion of the earth, as regards extent of territory, fertility of soil, and salubrity of climate. We find ourselves under the government of a system of political institutions conducing more essentially to the ends of civil and religious liberty than any of which the history of former times tells us. We, when mounting the stage of existence, found ourselves the legal inheritors of these fundamental blessings. We toiled not in the acquisition or establishment of them; they are a legacy bequeathed us by a once hardy, brave and patriotic, but now lamented and departed race of ancestors. Theirs

was the task (and nobly they performed it) to possess themselves, and, through themselves, us, of this goodly land, and to uprear upon its hills and valleys a political edifice of liberty and equal rights; 'tis ours only to transmit these—the former unprofaned by the foot of an invader, the latter undecayed by the lapse of time and untorn by usurpation—to the latest generation that fate shall permit the world to know. This task, gratitude to our fathers, justice to ourselves, duty to posterity, all imperatively require us faithfully to perform.

How, then, shall we perform it? At what point shall we expect the approach of danger? Shall we expect some transatlantic military giant to step the ocean and crush us at a blow? Never! All the armies of Europe, Asia, and Africa combined, with all the treasure of the earth (our own excepted) in their military chest, with a Bonaparte for a commander, could not, by force, take a drink from the Ohio, or make a track on the Blue Ridge, in a trial of a thousand years! At what point, then, is the approach of danger to be expected? I answer, if it ever reach us, *it must spring up amongst ourselves*. It cannot come from abroad. If destruction be our lot, we must ourselves be its author and finisher. As a nation of free men, we must live through all time, or die by suicide. I hope I am not over-wary; but, if I am not, there is even now something of ill-omen amongst us. I mean the increasing disregard for law which pervades the country, the growing disposition to substitute the wild and furious passions in lieu of the sober judgment of the courts, and the worse than savage mobs for the executive ministers of justice. This disposition is awfully fearful in any community; and that it now exists in ours, though grating to our feelings to admit it, it would be a violation of truth and an insult to our intelligence to deny. Accounts of outrages committed by mobs form the every-day news of the times. They have pervaded the country from New England to Louisiana; they are neither peculiar to the eternal snows of the former, nor the burning sun of the latter. They are not the creature of climate; neither are they confined to the slaveholding or non-slaveholding States. Alike they spring up among the pleasure-hunting masters of Southern slaves and the order-loving citizens of the land of steady habits. Whatever their course may be, it is common to the whole country. Here, then, is one point at which danger may be expected. The question recurs, How shall we fortify against it? The answer is simple. Let every American, every lover of liberty, every well-wisher to his posterity, swear by the blood of the Revolution, never to violate in the least particular the laws of the country, and never to tolerate their violation by others. As the patriots of 'seventy-six' did to the support of the Declaration of Independence, so to the support of the Constitution and the Laws let every American pledge his life, his property, and his sacred honor; let every man remember that to violate the law is to trample on the blood of his father, and to tear the charter of his own and his children's liberty. Let reverence for the laws be breathed by every American mother to the lisping babe that prattles on her lap. Let it be taught in schools, in seminaries, and in colleges. Let it be written in primers, spelling-books, and in almanacs. Let it be preached from the pulpit, proclaimed in legislative halls, and enforced in courts of justice. And, in short, let it become the political religion of the nation.

During the years of Lincoln's service in the Illinois Legislature the Democratic party was strongly dominant throughout the State. The feeling on the subject of slavery was decidedly in sympathy with the South. A large percentage of the settlers in the southern and middle portions of Illinois were from States in which slave labor was maintained; and although the determination not to permit the institution to obtain a foothold in the new commonwealth was general, the people were opposed to any action which should affect its condition where it was already established. During the sessions of 1836-7 resolutions of an extreme pro-slavery character were carried through the Legislature by the Democratic party, aiming to prevent the Abolitionists from obtaining a foothold in the State. Lincoln could not conscientiously support the resolutions, nor hold his peace concerning them. He did not shrink from the issue, but at the hazard of losing his political popularity and the gratifying prospects that were opening before him he drew up a protest against the pro-slavery enactment and had it entered upon the Journal of the House. The state of public opinion in Illinois at that time may be judged by the fact that of the hundred Representatives in the House *only one* had the courage to sign the protest with him. Lincoln 's protest was as follows:

March 3, 1837.

The following protest, presented to the House, was read and ordered to be spread on the journals, to wit:

Resolutions upon the subject of domestic slavery having passed both branches of the General Assembly at its present session, the undersigned hereby protest against the passage of the same.

They believe that the institution of slavery is founded on both injustice and bad policy; but that the promulgation of abolition doctrines tends rather to increase than abate its evils.

They believe that the Congress of the United States has no power, under the Constitution, to interfere with the institution of slavery in the different States.

They believe that the Congress of the United States has the power, under the Constitution, to abolish slavery in the District of Columbia, but that the power ought not to be exercised, unless at the request of the people of the District.

The difference between these opinions and those contained in the said resolutions, is their reason for entering this protest.

(Signed)
DAN STONE,
A. LINCOLN,
Representatives from the County of Sangamon.

The great financial panic which swept over the country in 1837 rendered expedient an extra session of the Legislature, which was called together in July. General Lee D. Ewing had been elected to this session from Fayette County for the express purpose of repealing the law removing the capital from Vandalia to Springfield. "General Ewing was," says Mr. Linder, "a man of considerable notoriety, popularity, and talents. He had been a member of Congress from Illinois, and had filled various State offices in his time. He was a man of elegant manners, great personal courage, and would grace either the *salons* of fashion or the Senate chamber at Washington. The Legislature opened its special session (I was there as a spectator), and General Ewing sounded the tocsin of war. He said that 'the arrogance of Springfield, its presumption in claiming the seat of government, was not to be endured; that the law had been passed by chicanery and trickery; that the Springfield delegation had sold out to the internal improvement men, and had promised their support to every measure that would gain them a vote to the law removing the seat of government.' He said many other things, cutting and sarcastic. Lincoln was chosen by his colleagues to reply to Ewing; and I want to say here that this was the first time that I began to conceive a very high opinion of the talents and personal courage of Abraham Lincoln. He retorted upon Ewing with great severity, denouncing his insinuations imputing corruption to him and his colleagues, and paying back with usury all that Ewing had said, when everybody thought and believed that he was digging his own grave; for it was known that Ewing would not quietly pocket any insinuations that would degrade him personally. I recollect his reply to Lincoln well. After addressing the Speaker, he turned to the Sangamon delegation, who all sat in the same portion of the house, and said: 'Gentlemen, have you no other champion than this coarse and vulgar fellow to bring into the lists against me? Do you suppose that I will condescend to break a lance with your low and obscure colleague?' We were all very much alarmed for fear there would be a personal conflict between Ewing and Lincoln. It was confidently believed that a challenge must pass between them; but friends on both sides took the matter in hand, and it was settled without anything serious growing out of it."

When the legislative session ended, in February, 1837, Lincoln returned to a job of surveying which he had begun a year before at Petersburg, near his old home at Salem. He spent a month or two at Petersburg, completing the surveying and planning of the town. That his work was well and satisfactorily done is attested by many—among them by Mr. John Bennett, who lived in Petersburg at the time. "My earliest acquaintance with Lincoln," says Mr. Bennett, "began on his return from Vandalia, where he had spent the winter as a member of the Legislature from Sangamon County. Lincoln spent most of the month of March in Petersburg, finishing up the survey and planning of the town he had commenced the year before. I was a great deal in his company, and formed a high estimate of his worth and social qualities, which was strengthened by many years of subsequent social intercourse and business transactions, finding him always strictly honest. In fact, he was now generally spoken of in this region as 'Honest Abe.' After Menard County was formed out of a portion of Sangamon County, and the county seat established at Petersburg, Mr. Lincoln was a regular attendant at the courts. I was then keeping a hotel, and he was one of my regular customers. Here he met many of his old cronies of his early days at Salem, and they spent the most of the nights in telling stories or spinning long yarns, of which Mr. Lincoln was particularly fond."

CHAPTER IV

Lincoln's removal from New Salem to Springfield, where his more active life as a lawyer began, occurred in April, 1837, soon after the completion of his survey work at Petersburg. The event was closely connected with the removal of the State capital from Vandalia to Springfield, the law for which was passed at the legislative session of 1836-7. As has been stated, Lincoln was a member of that Legislature and was active in procuring the passage of the bill. The citizens of Springfield were very desirous of the removal of the capital to their town, and many of them were present at the session when the measure was up for discussion. They had thus become acquainted with Lincoln; they were favorably impressed as to his abilities and character, and pleased with his efforts in the matter in which they were so greatly interested. Through their influence and encouragement he chose Springfield as his future home.

Lincoln's first interview, after his arrival in Springfield, was with Mr. Joshua F. Speed, with whom he already had a slight acquaintance, and who details the circumstances of their meeting. "He had ridden into town," says Mr. Speed, "on a borrowed horse, with no earthly property save a pair of saddle-bags containing a few clothes. I was a merchant at Springfield, and kept a large country store, embracing dry goods, groceries, hardware, books, medicines, bed-clothes, mattresses,—in fact, everything that country people needed. Lincoln came into the store with his saddle-bags on his arm, and said he wanted to buy the fixings for a single bed. The mattresses, blankets, sheets, coverlid, and pillow, according to the figures made by me, would cost seventeen dollars. He said that was perhaps cheap enough, but small as the sum was he was unable to pay it. But if I would credit him till Christmas and his experiment as a lawyer was a success, he would pay then; adding, in the saddest tone, 'If I fail in this, I do not know that I can ever pay you.' As I looked up at him I thought then, and think now, that I never saw a sadder face. I said to him, 'You seem to be so much pained at contracting so small a debt, I think I can suggest a plan by which you can avoid the debt and at the same time attain your end. I have a large room with a double bed up-stairs which you are very welcome to share with me.' 'Where is your room?' said he. 'Up-stairs,' said I, pointing to a pair of winding stairs which led from the store to my room. He took his saddle-bags on his arm, went up-stairs, set them down on the floor, and came down with the most changed countenance. Beaming with pleasure, he exclaimed, 'Well, Speed, I'm moved!' Lincoln was then twenty-eight years old. He was a lawyer without a client, with no money, all his earthly wealth consisting of the clothes he wore and the contents of his saddle-bags."

Lincoln shared the same room with Mr. Speed during his early residence in Springfield, taking his meals with his companion at the house of Mr. William Butler, with whom he boarded for five years. His professional advancement at first was slow, and he had periods of great discouragement. An old settler of Illinois, named Page Eaton, says: "I knew Lincoln when he first came to Springfield. He was an awkward but hard-working young man. Everybody said he would never make a good lawyer because he was too honest. He came to my shop one day, after he had been here five or six months, and said he had a notion to quit studying law and learn carpentering. He thought there was more need of carpenters out here than lawyers." Soon after Lincoln's settlement in Springfield, he formed a law partnership with Major John T. Stuart, whom he had known for some years and who already had a good position at the bar. This partnership began, according to the statement of Major Stuart, on April 27, 1837. It continued just four years, when it was dissolved, and Lincoln and Judge Stephen T. Logan became partners. This latter partnership continued about two years, when, on September 20, 1843, the firm of Lincoln & Herndon was formed, and it continued to the time of Lincoln's death.

When Lincoln began to practice law, it was the custom in Illinois to "ride the circuit," a proceeding of which the older communities of the East know nothing. The State of Illinois, for instance, is divided into a number of districts, each composed of a number of counties, of which a single judge, appointed or elected as the case may be, for that purpose, makes the circuit, holding courts at each county seat. Railroads being scarce, the earlier circuit judges made their trips from county to county on horseback or in a gig; and the prominent lawyers living within the limits of the circuit made the tour of the circuit with the judge. It is said that when Lincoln first began to "ride the circuit" he was too poor to own a horse or vehicle, and was compelled to borrow from his friends. But in due time he became the proprietor of a horse, which he fed and groomed himself, and to which he was very much attached. On this animal he would set out from home, to be gone for weeks together, with no baggage but a pair of saddle-bags containing a change of linen, and an old cotton umbrella to shelter him from sun or rain. When he got a little more of this world's goods he set up a one-horse buggy, a very sorry and shabby-looking affair which he generally used when the weather promised to be bad. The other lawyers were always glad to see him, and landlords hailed his coming with pleasure; but he was one of those gentle, uncomplaining men whom they would put off with indifferent accommodations. It was a significant remark of a lawyer who was thoroughly acquainted with his habits and disposition that "Lincoln was never seated next the landlord at a crowded table, and never got a chicken-liver or the best cut from the roast." Lincoln once remarked to Mr. Gillespie that he never felt his own unworthiness so much as when in the presence of a hotel clerk or waiter. If rooms were scarce, and one, two, three, or four gentlemen were required to lodge together in order to accommodate some surly man who "stood upon his rights," Lincoln was sure to be one of the unfortunates. Yet he loved the life of the circuit, and never went home without reluctance.

In describing the many experiences of the lawyers who travelled the circuits at this period, Mr. Arnold says: "The State was settled with a hardy, fearless, honest, but very litigious population. The court-house was sometimes framed and boarded, but more frequently it was built of logs. The judge sat upon a raised platform behind a rough board, sometimes covered with green baize, for a table on which to write his notes. A small table stood on the floor in front for the clerk. In the center of the room was another larger table around which in rude chairs the lawyers were grouped, too often with their feet on top of it. Rough benches were placed there for the jury, the parties to the suit, witnesses and bystanders. The court-rooms were nearly always crowded for here were rehearsed and acted the dramas, the tragedies, and the comedies of real life. The court-house has always been a very attractive place to the people of the frontier. It supplied the place of theatres, lecture and concert rooms, and other places of interest and amusement in the older settlements and towns. The leading lawyers and judges were the star actors, and had each his partisans. Hence crowds attended the courts to see the judges, to hear the lawyers contend, with argument and law and wit, for success, victory, and fame. The merits and ability of the leading advocates, their success or discomfiture in examining or cross-examining a witness, the ability of this or that one to obtain a verdict, were canvassed at every cabin-raising, bee, or horse-race, and at every log-house and school in the county. Thus the lawyers were stimulated to the utmost exertion of their powers, not only by controversy and desire of success, but by the consciousness that their efforts were watched with eagerness by friends, clients, partisans, or rivals. From one to another of these rude court-houses the gentlemen of the bar passed, following the judge around his circuits from county to county, travelling generally on horseback, with saddle-bags, brushes, an extra shirt or two, and perhaps two or three law books. Sometimes two or three lawyers would unite and travel in a buggy, and the poorer and younger ones not seldom walked. But a horse was not an unusual fee, and in those days when horse thieves as clients were but too common, it was not long before a young man of ability found himself well mounted.

"There was very great freedom in social intercourse. Manners were rude, but genial, kind, and friendly. Each was always ready to assist his fellows, and selfishness was not tolerated. The relations between the bench and bar were familiar, free and easy. Flashes of wit and humor and repartee were constantly exchanged. Such was the life upon which Lincoln now entered; and there gathered with him around those pine tables of the frontier court-house a very remarkable combination of men, men who would have been leaders of the bar at Boston or New York, Philadelphia or Washington; men who would have made their mark in Westminster Hall, or upon any English circuit. At the capital were John T. Stuart, Stephen T. Logan, Edward D. Baker, Ninian W. Edwards, Josiah Lamborn, and many others. Among the leading lawyers from other parts of the State who practiced in the Supreme and Federal Courts at the capital were Stephen A. Douglas; Lyman Trumbull, for many years chairman of the judiciary committee of the United States Senate; O.H. Browning, Senator and member of the Cabinet at Washington; William H. Bissell, Member of Congress, and Governor of the State; David Davis, justice of the Supreme Court, Senator and Vice-President of the United States; Justin Butterfield of Chicago, and many others almost or quite equally distinguished. This 'circuit riding' involved all sorts of adventures. Hard fare at miserable country taverns, sleeping on the floor, and fording streams, were every-day occurrences. All such occurrences were met with good humor and often turned into sources of frolic and fun. In fording swollen streams, Lincoln was frequently sent forward as a scout or pioneer. His extremely long legs enabled him, by taking off his boots and stockings, and by rolling up or otherwise disposing of his trousers, to test the depth of the stream, find the most shallow water, and thus to pilot the party through the current without wetting his garments."

A gentleman who lived in one of the judicial circuits of Illinois in which Lincoln had an extensive though not very lucrative practice gives some graphic and interesting reminiscences. "The terms of the court were held quarterly and usually lasted about two weeks. They were always seasons of great importance and much gayety in the little town that had the honor of being the county seat. Distinguished members of the bar from surrounding and even from distant counties, ex-judges and ex-Members of Congress, attended and were personally and many of them popularly known to almost every adult, male and female, of the limited population. They came in by stages and on horseback. Among them the one whose arrival was looked forward to with the most pleasurable anticipations, and whose possible absence—although he almost never was absent—was feared with the liveliest emotions of anxiety, was 'Uncle Abe,' as he was lovingly called by us all. Sometimes he might happen to be a day or two late. Then, as the Bloomington stage came in at sundown, the bench and bar, jurors and citizens, would gather in crowds at the hotel where he always put up, to give him a welcome if, happily, he should arrive, and to experience the keenest feelings of disappointment if he should not. If he arrived, as he alighted and stretched out both his long arms to shake hands with those nearest to him and with those who approached, his homely face handsome in its broad and sunshiny smile, his voice touching in its kindly and cheerful accents, everyone in his presence felt lighter in heart and more joyous. He brought light with him. He loved his fellow-men with all the strength of his great nature, and those who came in contact with him could not help reciprocating the love."

Another old friend describes Lincoln as being at this time "very plain in his costume, as well as rather uncourtly in his address and general appearance. His clothing was of home Kentucky jean, and the first impression made by his tall, lank figure upon those who saw him was not specially prepossessing. He had not outgrown his hard backwoods experience, and showed no inclination to disguise or to cast behind him the honest and manly though unpolished characteristics of his earlier days. Never was a man further removed from all snobbish affectation. As little was there, also, of the demagogue art of assuming an uncouthness or rusticity of manner and outward habit with the mistaken notion of thus securing particular favor as 'one of the masses.' He chose to appear then, as in all his later life, precisely what he was. His deportment was unassuming, though without any awkwardness of reserve."

Mr. Crane, an old settler of Tazewell County, says he used to see Lincoln when passing through Washington, in that county, on his way to attend court at Metamora; and he remembers him as "dressed in a homespun coat that came below his knees and was out at both elbows."

Lincoln's tenderness of heart was displayed in his treatment of animals, toward which he was often performing unusual acts of kindness. On one occasion, as Mr. Speed relates, Lincoln and the other members of the Springfield bar had been attending court at Christiansburg, and Mr. Speed was riding with them toward Springfield. There was quite a party of these lawyers, riding two by two along a country lane. Lincoln and John J. Hardin brought up the rear of the cavalcade. "We had passed through a thicket of wild plum and crab-apple trees," says Mr. Speed, "and stopped to water our horses. Hardin came up alone. 'Where is Lincoln?' we inquired. 'Oh,' replied he, 'when I saw him last he had caught two young birds which the wind had blown out of their nests, and he was hunting the nest to put them back.' In a short time Lincoln came up, having found the nest and placed the young birds in it. The party laughed at him; but he said, 'I could not have slept if I had not restored those little birds to their mother.'"

Again, as Dr. Holland narrates, "Lincoln was one day riding by a deep slough or pit in which, to his exceeding pain, he saw a pig struggling, and with such faint efforts that it was evident that he could not extricate himself. Lincoln looked at the pig and the mud that enveloped him, and then looked ruefully at some new clothes in which he had but a short time before enveloped himself. Deciding against the claims of the pig he rode on; but he could not get rid of the vision of the poor brute, and at last, after riding two miles, he turned back, determined to rescue the animal at the expense of his new clothes. Arrived at the spot, he tied his horse, and coolly went to work to build of old rails a passage to the bottom of the hole. Descending on these rails, he seized the pig and dragged him out, but not without serious damage to the clothes he wore. Washing his hands in the nearest brook and wiping them on the grass, he mounted his gig and rode along. He then fell to examining the motive that sent him back to the release of the pig. At the first thought it seemed to be pure benevolence; but at length he came to the conclusion that it was selfishness, for he certainly went to the pig's relief in order (as he said to the friend to whom he related the incident) to 'take a pain out of his own mind.'"

Instances showing the integrity, candor, unselfishness, and humanity of Lincoln's conduct in his law practice could be multiplied indefinitely. The following are given by Dr. Holland: "The lawyers of Springfield, particularly those who had political aspirations, were afraid to undertake the defense of anyone who had been engaged in helping off fugitives slaves. It was a very unpopular business in those days and in that locality; and few felt that they could afford to engage in it. One who needed such aid went to Edward D. Baker, and was refused, distinctly and frankly on the ground that as a political man he could not afford it. The man applied to an ardent anti-slavery friend for advice. He spoke of Mr. Lincoln, and said, 'He's not afraid of an unpopular case. When I go for a lawyer to defend an arrested fugitive slave, other lawyers will refuse me. But if Mr. Lincoln is at home he will always take my case.'"

An old woman of seventy-five years, the widow of a revolutionary pensioner, came tottering into his law office one day, and told him that a certain pension agent had charged her the exorbitant fee of two hundred dollars for collecting her pension. Lincoln was satisfied by her representations that she had been swindled, and finding that she was not a resident of the town, and that she was poor, gave her money, and set about the work of procuring restitution. He immediately entered suit against the agent to recover a portion of his ill-gotten money. This suit was one of the most remarkable that Lincoln ever conducted. The day before the case came up he asked his partner, Mr. Herndon, to get him a "Life of Washington," and he spent the whole afternoon reading it. His speech to the jury was long remembered. The whole court-room was in tears as he closed with these words: "Gentlemen of the jury. Time rolls by. The heroes of '76 have passed away. They are encamped on the other shore. This soldier has gone to his rest, and now, crippled, blinded, and broken, his widow comes to you and to me, gentlemen of the jury, to right her wrongs. She was not always as you see her now. Once her step was elastic. Her face was fair. Her voice was as sweet as any that rang in the mountains of old Virginia. Now she is old. She is poor and defenceless. Out here on the prairies of Illinois, hundreds of miles from the scenes of her childhood, she appeals to you and to me who enjoy the privileges achieved for us by the patriots of the Revolution for our sympathetic aid and manly protection. I have but one question to ask you, gentlemen of the jury. Shall we befriend her?" During the speech the defendant sat huddled up in the court-room, writhing under the lash of Lincoln's tongue. The jury returned a verdict for every cent that Lincoln had asked. He became the old lady's surety for costs, paid her hotel bill and sent her home rejoicing. He made no charges for his own or his partner's services. A few days afterwards Mr. Herndon picked up a little scrap of paper in the office. He looked at it a moment, and burst into a roar of laughter. It was Lincoln's notes for the argument of this case. They were unique:—"No contract—Not professional services—Unreasonable charges—Money retained by Deft not given by Pl'ff.—Revolutionary War—Describe Valley Forge—Ice—Soldiers' bleeding feet—Pl'ff's husband—Soldiers leaving home for the army—*Skin Def't*—Close."

In his Autobiography, Joseph Jefferson tells how he visited Springfield with a theatrical company in the early days (1839) and planned to open a theatrical season in that godly town. But "a religious revival was in progress, and the fathers of the church not only launched forth against us in their sermons, but got the city to pass a new law enjoining a heavy license against our 'unholy' calling. I forget the amount, but it was large enough to be prohibitory." The company had begun the building of a new theatre; and naturally the situation was perplexing. In the midst of their trouble, says Mr. Jefferson, "a young lawyer called on the Managers. He had heard of the injustice, and offered, if they would place the matter in his hands, to have the license taken off,—declaring that he only wanted to see fair play, and he would accept no fee whether he failed or succeeded. The case was brought up before the council. The young lawyer began his harangue. He handled the subject with tact, skill, and humor, tracing the history of the drama from the time when Thespis acted in a cart, to the stage of to-day. He illustrated his speech with a number of anecdotes, and kept the council in a roar of laughter. His good humor prevailed, and the exorbitant tax was taken off. This young lawyer was very popular in Springfield, and was honored and beloved by all who knew him; and after the time of which I write he held rather an important position in the Government of the United States. He now lies buried in Springfield, under a monument commemorating his greatness and his virtues,—and his name was Abraham Lincoln."

Judge Gillespie tells a good story, to the effect that Lincoln and General U.P. Linder were once defending a man who was being tried on a criminal charge before Judge David Davis, who said at dinner-time that the case must be disposed of that night. Lincoln suggested that the best thing they could do would be to run Benedict, the prosecuting attorney, as far into the night as possible, in hopes that he might, in his rage, commit some indiscretion that would help their case. Lincoln began, but to save his life he could not speak one hour, and the laboring oar fell into Linder's hands. "But," said Lincoln, "he was equal to the occasion. He spoke most interestingly three mortal hours, about everything in the world. He discussed Benedict from head to foot, and put in about three-quarters of an hour on the subject of Benedict's whiskers." Lincoln said he never envied a man so much as he did Linder on that occasion. He thought he was inimitable in his capacity to talk interestingly about everything and nothing, by the hour.

But if Lincoln had not General Linder's art of "talking against time," his wit often suggested some readier method of gaining advantage in a case. On one occasion, a suit was on trial in the Circuit Court of Sangamon County, in which Lincoln was attorney for the plaintiff, and Mr. James C. Conkling, then a young man just entering practice, was attorney for the defendant. It was a jury trial, and Lincoln waived the opening argument to the jury, leaving Mr. Conkling to sum up his case for the defense. The latter spoke at considerable length, in a sophomoric style, laboring under the impression that unless he made an extraordinary exertion to influence the jury he would be quite eclipsed by Lincoln in his closing speech. But he was completely taken back by the unlooked-for light manner in which Lincoln treated the case in his closing. Lincoln proceeded to reply but, in doing so he talked on without making the slightest reference to the case on hearing or to the argument of Mr. Conkling. His summing-up to the jury was to the following effect: "Gentlemen of the jury: In early days there lived in this vicinity, over on the Sangamon river, an old Indian of the Kickapoo tribe by the name of Johnnie Kongapod. He had been taken in charge by some good missionaries, converted to Christianity, and educated to such extent that he could read and write. He took a great fancy to poetry and became somewhat of a poet himself. His desire was that after his death there should be placed at the head of his grave an epitaph, which he prepared himself, in rhyme, in the following words:

> "'Here lies poor Johnnie Kongapod;
>
> Have mercy on him, gracious God,
>
> As he would do if he were God
>
> And you were Johnnie Kongapod.'"

Of course all this had no reference to the case, nor did Lincoln intend it should have any. It was merely his way of ridiculing the eloquence of his opponent. The verdict of the jury was for the plaintiff, as Lincoln expected it would be; and this was the reason of his treating the case as he did.

A story somewhat similar to the above was told by the late Judge John Pearson shortly before his death. In the February term, 1850, of the Circuit Court of Vermilion County, Illinois, a case was being tried in which a young lady had brought suit for $10,000 against a recreant lover who had married another girl. The amount sued for was thought to be an enormous sum in those days, and the ablest talent to be found was brought into requisition by both sides. Richard Thompson and Daniel W. Voorhees were associated with O.L. Davis for the fair plaintiff. H.W. Beckwith, Ward Lamon, and Abraham Lincoln were for the defendant. The little town of Danville was crowded with people from far and near who had come to hear the big speeches. The evidence brought out in the trial was in every way against the defendant, and the sympathy of the public was, naturally enough, with the young lady plaintiff. Lincoln and his associate counsel plainly saw the hopelessness of their cause; and they wisely concluded to let their side of the case stand upon its merits, without even a plea of extenuating circumstances. Voorhees was young, ambitious, and anxious to display his oratory. He arranged with his colleagues at the beginning that he should make a speech, and he spent several hours in his room at the hotel in the preparation of an oratorical avalanche. It became generally known that Dan was going to out-do himself, and the expectation of the community was at its highest tension. The little old court-house was crowded. The ladies were out in full force. Voorhees came in a little late, glowing with the excitement of the occasion. It had been arranged that Davis was to open, Lincoln was to follow, and Voorhees should come next. Mr. Davis made a clear statement of the case, recited the character of the evidence, and closed with a plain logical argument. Then Lincoln arose, and stood in silence for a moment, looking at the jury. He deliberately re-arranged some of the books and papers on the table before him, as though "making a good ready," as he used to say, and began in a spirited but deliberate way: "Your Honor, the evidence in this case is all in, and doubtless all concerned comprehend its fullest import without the aid of further argument. Therefore we will rest our case here." This move, of course, cut off all future discussion. Voorhees, with his load of pyrotechnics was shut out. An ominous silence followed Lincoln's remark; then Voorhees arose, white with rage, and entered a protest against the tactics of the defense. All the others were disappointed, but amused, and the only consolation that Voorhees got out of this affair was a verdict for the full amount claimed by his client. But he never forgave Lincoln for thus "nipping" his great speech "in the bud."

Mr. Wickizer gives a story which illustrates the off-hand readiness of Lincoln's wit. "In the court at Bloomington Mr. Lincoln was engaged in a case of no great importance; but the attorney on the other side, Mr. S., a young lawyer of fine abilities, was always very sensitive about being beaten, and in this case he manifested unusual zeal and interest. The case lasted until late at night, when it was finally submitted to the jury. Mr. S. spent a sleepless night in anxiety, and early next morning learned, to his great chagrin, that he had lost the case. Mr. Lincoln met him at the court-house and asked him what had become of his case. With lugubrious countenance and melancholy tone, Mr. S. said, 'It's gone to hell!' 'Oh, well!' replied Lincoln, 'Never mind,—you can try it again there!'"

Lincoln was always ready to join in a laugh at his own expense, and used to tell the following story with intense enjoyment: "In the days when I used to be 'on the circuit' I was accosted in the cars by a stranger who said, 'Excuse me, sir, but I have an article in my possession which belongs to you.' 'How is that?' I asked, considerably astonished. The stranger took a jack-knife from his pocket. 'This knife,' said he, 'was placed in my hands some years ago with the injunction that I was to keep it until I found a man uglier than myself. I have carried it from that time to this. Allow me to say, sir, that I think you are fairly entitled to the property.'"

Mr. Gillespie says of Lincoln's passion for story-telling: "As a boon companion, Lincoln, although he never drank liquor or used tobacco in any form, was without a rival. No one would ever think of 'putting in' when he was talking. He could illustrate any subject, it seemed to me, with an appropriate and amusing anecdote. He did not tell stories merely for the sake of telling them, but rather by way of illustration of something that had happened or been said. There seemed to be no end to his fund of stories." Mr. Lamon states: "Lincoln frequently said that he lived by his humor and would have died without it. His manner of telling a story was irresistibly comical, the fun of it dancing in his eyes and playing over every feature. His face changed in an instant; the hard lines faded out of it, and the mirth seemed to diffuse itself all over him like a spontaneous tickle. You could see it coming long before he opened his mouth, and he began to enjoy the 'point' before his eager auditors could catch the faintest glimpse of it. Telling and hearing ridiculous stories was one of his ruling passions." A good illustration of this fondness for story-telling is given by Judge Sibley, of Quincy, Illinois, who knew Lincoln when practicing law at Springfield. One day a party of lawyers were sitting in the law library of the court-house at Springfield, awaiting the opening of court, and telling stories to fill the time. Judge Breese of the Supreme bench—one of the most distinguished of American jurists, and a man of great personal dignity—passed through the room where the lawyers were sitting, on his way to open court. Lincoln, seeing him, called out in his hearty way, "Hold on, Breese! Don't open court yet! Here's Bob Blackwell just going to tell a new story!" The judge passed on without replying, evidently regarding it as beneath the dignity of the Supreme Court to delay proceedings for the sake of a story.

CHAPTER V

In 1838 Lincoln was for a third time a candidate for the State Legislature. Mr. Wilson, one of his colleagues from Sangamon County, states that a question of the division of the county was one of the local issues. "Mr. Lincoln and myself," says Mr. Wilson, "among others residing in the portion of the county which sought to be organized into a new county, opposed the division; and it became necessary that I should make a special canvass through the northwest part of the county, then known as Sand Ridge. I made the canvass. Mr. Lincoln accompanied me, and being personally acquainted with everyone we called at nearly every house. At that time it was the universal custom to keep some whiskey in the house for private use and to treat friends. The subject was always mentioned as a matter of politeness, but with the usual remark to Mr. Lincoln, 'We know you never drink, but maybe your friend would like to take a little.' I never saw Mr. Lincoln drink. He often told me he never drank; had no desire for drink, nor for the companionship of drinking men."

The result of this canvass was that Lincoln was elected to the Legislature for the session of 1838-39. The next year he was elected for the session of 1840-41. This ended his legislative service, which comprised eight consecutive years, from 1834 to 1841. In these later sessions he was as active and prominent in the House as he had been in the earlier times when a member from New Salem.

Lincoln's faculty for getting the better of an adversary by an apt illustration or anecdote was seldom better shown than by an incident which occurred during his last term in the Legislature. Hon. James C. Conkling has given the following graphic description of the scene: "A gentleman who had formerly been Attorney-General of the State was also a member. Presuming upon his age, experience, and former official position, he thought it incumbent upon himself to oppose Lincoln, who was then one of the acknowledged leaders of his party. He at length attracted the attention of Lincoln, who replied to his remarks, telling one of his humorous anecdotes and making a personal application to his opponent which placed the latter in such a ridiculous attitude that it convulsed the whole House. All business was suspended. In vain the Speaker rapped with his gavel. Members of all parties, without distinction, were compelled to laugh. They not only laughed, they screamed and yelled; they thumped upon the floor with their canes; they clapped their hands and threw up their hats; they shouted and twisted themselves into all sorts of contortions, until their sides ached and the tears rolled down their cheeks. One paroxysm passed away, but was speedily succeeded by another, and again they laughed and screamed and yelled. Another lull occurred, and still another paroxysm, until they seemed to be perfectly exhausted. The ambition of Lincoln's opponent was abundantly gratified, and for the remainder of the session he lapsed into profound obscurity."

In June, 1842, ex-President Van Buren was journeying through Illinois with a company of friends. When near Springfield they were delayed by bad roads, and were compelled to spend the night at Rochester, some miles out. The accommodations at this place were very poor, and a few of the ex-President's Springfield friends proposed to go out to meet him and try to aid in entertaining him. Knowing Lincoln's ability as a talker and story-teller, they begged him to go with them and aid in making their guest at the country inn pass the evening as pleasantly as possible. Lincoln, with his usual good nature, went with them, and entertained the party for hours with graphic descriptions of Western life, anecdotes and witty stories. Judge Peck, who was of the party, and a warm friend of the ex-President, says that Lincoln was at his best. There was a constant succession of brilliant anecdotes and funny stories, accompanied by loud laughter in which Van Buren took his full share. "He also," says the Judge, "gave us incidents and anecdotes of Elisha Williams, and other leading members of the New York bar, going back to the days of Hamilton and Burr. Altogether there was a right merry time. Mr. Van Buren said the only drawback upon his enjoyment was that his sides were sore from laughing at Lincoln's stories for a week thereafter."

Lincoln's eight years of legislative service had given him considerable reputation in politics, and he had become the acknowledged leader of the Whig party in Illinois. In the exciting Presidential campaign of 1840, known as the "Log Cabin" campaign, he took a very active part. He had been nominated as Presidential Elector on the Harrison ticket, and stumped a large portion of the State. A peculiarly interesting reminiscence of Lincoln's appearance on one occasion during the "Log Cabin" campaign is furnished by Mr. G.W. Harris, who says: "In the fall of the year 1840 there came into the log school-house in a village in Southern Illinois where I, a lad, was a pupil, a tall, awkward, plain-looking young man dressed in a full suit of 'blue jean.' Approaching the master, he gave his name, and, apologizing for the intrusion, said, 'I am told you have a copy of Byron's works. I would like to borrow it for a few hours.' The book was produced and loaned to him. With his thanks and a 'Good-day' to the teacher, and a smile such as I have never seen on any other man's face and a look that took in all of us lads and lassies, the stranger passed out of the room. This was during a Presidential canvass. Isaac Walker, candidate for Democratic Elector, and Abraham Lincoln, candidate for Whig Elector, were by appointment to discuss political matters in the afternoon of that day. I asked for and got a half-holiday. I had given no thought to the matter until the appearance of Lincoln (for he it was) in the school-room. But, something in the man had aroused, not only in me but in others of the scholars, a strong desire to see him again and to hear him speak. Isaac Walker in his younger days had been a resident of the village. Lincoln was aware of this, and shrewdly suspected that Walker in his remarks would allude to the circumstance; so, having the opening speech, he determined to 'take the wind out of his sails.' He did so—how effectually, it is hardly necessary for me to say. He had borrowed Byron's works to read the opening lines of 'Lara':

"He, their unhoped, but unforgotten lord,
The long self-exiled chieftain, is restored.
There be bright faces in the busy hall,
Bowls on the board, and banners on the wall;

"He comes at last in sudden loneliness,
And whence they know not, why they need not guess;
They more might marvel, when the greeting's o'er,
Not that he came, but came not long before."

During this period Lincoln continued to enjoy the hospitality of Mr. Speed at Springfield. "After he made his home with me," says Mr. Speed, "on every winter's night at my store, by a big wood fire, no matter how inclement the weather, eight or ten choice spirits assembled, without distinction of party. It was a sort of social club without organization. They came there because they were sure to find Lincoln. His habit was to engage in conversation upon any and all subjects except politics. But one evening a political argument sprang up between Lincoln and Douglas, which for a time ran high. Douglas sprang to his feet and said: 'Gentlemen, this is no place to talk politics; we will discuss the questions publicly with you.'" A few days later the Whigs held a meeting and challenged the Democrats to a joint debate. The challenge was accepted. Douglas, Lamborn, Calhoun, and Jesse Thomas were deputed by the Democrats to meet Logan, Baker, Browning, and Lincoln on the part of the Whigs. The intellectual encounter between these noted champions is still described by those who witnessed it as "the great debate." It took place in the Second Presbyterian church at

Springfield, and lasted eight nights, each speaker occupying a night in turn. Mr. Speed speaks thus of Lincoln's effort: "Lincoln delivered his speech without manuscript or notes. He had a wonderful faculty in that way. He might be writing an important document, be interrupted in the midst of a sentence, turn his attention to other matters entirely foreign to the subject on which he was engaged, and then take up his pen and begin where he left off without reading the previous part of the sentence. He could grasp, exhaust, and quit any subject with more facility than any man I have ever seen or heard of." The subjoined paragraphs from the speech above referred to show the impassioned feeling which Lincoln poured forth that night. Those familiar with his admirable style in his later years would scarcely recognize him in these florid and rather over-weighted periods:

Many free countries have lost their liberty, and ours may lose hers; but if she shall, be it my proudest plume, not that I was the last to desert, but that I never deserted her. I know that the great volcano at Washington, aroused and directed by the evil spirit that reigns there, is belching forth the lava of political corruption in a current broad and deep, which is sweeping with frightful velocity over the whole length and breadth of the land, bidding fair to leave unscathed no green spot or living thing; while on its bosom are riding, like demons on the waves of hell, the imps of the Evil Spirit, and fiendishly torturing and taunting all those who dare resist its destroying course with the hopelessness of their effort; and knowing this, I cannot deny that all may be swept away. Broken by it, I too may be; bow to it, I never will. The probability that we may fall in the struggle ought not to deter us from the support of a cause which we deem to be just. It shall not deter me. If I ever feel the soul within me elevate and expand to those dimensions not wholly unworthy of its Almighty architect, it is when I contemplate the cause of my country deserted by all the world beside, and I, standing up boldly and alone, hurling defiance at her victorious oppressors. And here, without contemplating consequences, before high Heaven and in the face of the whole world, I swear eternal fidelity to the just cause, as I deem it, of the land of my life, my liberty, and my love. And who that thinks with me will not fearlessly adopt the oath I take? Let none falter who thinks he is right, and we may succeed. But if, after all, we shall fail, be it so. We shall have the proud consolation of saying to our conscience and to the departed shade of our country's freedom, that the cause approved by our judgments and adored by our hearts in disaster, in chains, in torture, and in death, we never failed in defending.

In this canvass Lincoln came again into collision with Douglas, the adversary whom he had met two years before and with whom he was to sustain an almost life-long political conflict. He also had occasion to show his courage and presence of mind in rescuing from a mob his distinguished friend, Col. E.D. Baker, afterwards a Senator of the United States. "Baker was speaking in a large room," says Mr. Arnold, "rented and used for the court sessions, and Lincoln's office was in an apartment over the court-room, communicating with it by a trap-door. Lincoln was in his office listening to Baker through the open trap-door, when Baker, becoming excited, abused the Democrats, many of whom were present. A cry was raised, 'Pull him off the stand!' The instant Lincoln heard the cry, knowing a general fight was imminent, his athletic form was seen descending from above through the opening of the trap-door, and, springing to the side of Baker, and waving his hand for silence, he said with dignity: 'Gentlemen, let us not disgrace the age and country in which we live. This is a land where freedom of speech is guaranteed. Baker has a right to speak. I am here to protect him, and no man shall take him from this stand if I can prevent it.' Quiet was restored, and Baker finished his speech without further interruption."

A similar occurrence, happening about the same period, is detailed by General Linder: "On a later occasion, when Colonel Baker and myself were both battling together in the Whig cause, at a convention held in Springfield, I made a speech at the State House, which I think now, looking back at it from this point, was the very best I ever made in my life. While I was addressing the vast assembly some ruffian in the galleries flung at me a gross personal insult accompanied with a threat. Lincoln and Colonel Baker, who were both present and were warm personal and political friends of mine, anticipating that I might be attacked when I left the State House, came upon the stand a little while before I concluded my speech and took their station on each side of me. When I was through, and after my audience had greeted me with three hearty cheers, each took one of my arms, and Lincoln said to me: 'Linder, Baker and I are apprehensive that you may be attacked by some of those ruffians who insulted you from the galleries, and we have come up to escort you to your hotel. We both think we can do a little fighting, so we want you to walk between us until we get you to your hotel. Your quarrel is our quarrel and that of the great Whig party of this nation. Your speech upon this occasion is the greatest that has been made by any of us, for which we wish to honor and defend you.' This I consider no ordinary compliment, coming from Lincoln, for he was no flatterer nor disposed to bestow praise where it was undeserved. Colonel Baker heartily concurred in all he said, and between those two glorious men I left the stand and we marched out of the State House through our friends, who trooped after us evidently anticipating what Lincoln and Baker had suggested to me, accompanying us to my hotel."

That Lincoln had an abundance of physical courage, and was well able to defend himself when necessity demanded, is clear from the incidents just given. Mr. Herndon, his intimate friend, adds his testimony on this point. As Lincoln was grand in his good nature, says Mr. Herndon, so he was grand in his rage. "Once I saw him incensed at a judge for giving an unfair decision. It was a terrible spectacle. At another time I saw two men come to blows in his presence. He picked them up separately and tossed them apart like a couple of kittens. He was the strongest man I ever knew, and has been known to lift a man of his own weight and throw him over a worm fence. Once in Springfield the Irish voters meditated taking possession of the polls. News came down the street that they would permit nobody to vote but those of their own party. Mr. Lincoln seized an axe-handle from a hardware store and went alone to open a way to the ballot-box. His appearance intimidated them, and we had neither threats nor collisions all that day."

An unsuspected side of Lincoln's character was shown, at this period of his life, in the affair with General Shields. With all his gentleness and his scrupulous regard for the rights of others, Lincoln was not one to submit to being bullied; while his physical courage had been proved in many a rough—and—tumble encounter, often against heavy odds, with the rude and boisterous spirits of his time. These encounters were usually with nature's weapons; but in the Shields affair—duel, it was sometimes called— he showed that he would not shrink from the use of more deadly weapons if forced to do so. In judging this phase of his character, account must be taken of his Kentucky birth and origin, and of the customs and standards of his time. James Shields (afterwards a distinguished Union General and U.S. Senator) was at this time (1842) living at Springfield, holding the office of State Auditor. He is described as "a gallant, hot-headed bachelor, from Tyrone County, Ireland." He was something of a beau in society, and was the subject of some satirical articles which, in a spirit of fun, Miss Mary Todd (afterwards Mrs. Lincoln) had written and published in a local journal. Shields was furious, and, demanding the name of the writer, Lincoln sent him word that he would assume full responsibility in the matter. A challenge to a duel followed, which Lincoln accepted and named broadswords as the weapons. General Linder states that Lincoln said to him that he did not want to kill Shields, and felt sure he could disarm him if they fought with broadswords, while he felt sure Shields would kill him if pistols were the weapons. It seems that Lincoln actually took lessons in broadsword exercise from a Major Duncan; and at the appointed time all parties proceeded to the chosen field, near Alton. But friends appeared on the scene while the preliminaries were being arranged, and succeeded in effecting a reconciliation. Major Lucas, of Springfield, who was on the field, stated that he "had no doubt Lincoln meant to fight. Lincoln was no coward, and he would unquestionably have held his own against his antagonist, for he was a powerful man and well skilled in the use of the broadsword. Lincoln said to me, after the affair was all over, 'I could have split him in two.'" But there can be little doubt that he was well pleased that the affair proved a bloodless one.

The mention of Miss Mary Todd, in the preceding paragraph, brings us to Lincoln's marriage with that lady, which occurred in 1842, he being then in his thirty—fourth year. Miss Todd was the daughter of the Hon. Robert T. Todd, of Lexington, Kentucky. She came to Springfield in 1839, to live with her sister, Mrs. Ninian W. Edwards. "She was young," says Mr. Lamon, "just twenty-one,—her family was of the best and her connections in Illinois among the most refined and distinguished people. Her mother having died when she was a little girl, she had been educated under the care of a French lady. She was gifted with rare talents, had a keen sense of the ridiculous, a ready insight into the weaknesses of individual character, and a most fiery and ungovernable temper. Her tongue and her pen were equally sharp. Highbred, proud, brilliant, witty, and with a will that bent every one else to her purpose, she took Lincoln captive. He was a rising politician, fresh from the people, and possessed of great power among them. Miss Todd was of aristocratic and distinguished family, able to lead through the awful portals of 'good society' whomsoever they chose to countenance. It was thought that a union between them could not fail of numerous benefits to both parties. Mr. Edwards thought so; Mrs. Edwards thought so; and it was not long before Mary Todd herself thought so. She was very ambitious, and even before she left Kentucky announced her belief that she was destined to be the wife of some future President. For a while she was courted by Douglas as well as by Lincoln. Being asked which of them she intended to have, she answered, 'The one that has the best chance of being President.' She decided in favor of Lincoln; and in the opinion of some of her husband's friends she aided to no small extent in the fulfilment of the prophecy which the bestowal of her hand implied." Mrs. Edwards, Miss Todd's sister, has related that "Lincoln was charmed with Mary's wit and fascinated with her quick sagacity, her will, her nature and culture. I have happened in the room," she says, "where they were sitting, often and often, and Mary led the conversation. Lincoln would listen, and gaze on her as if drawn by some superior power—irresistibly so. He listened, but seldom said a word."

Preparations were made for the marriage between Lincoln and Miss Todd. But they were interrupted by a painful occurrence—a sudden breaking out of a fit of melancholy, or temporary insanity, such as had afflicted Lincoln on a former occasion. This event has been made the subject of no little gossip, into which it is not now necessary or desirable to go, further than to mention that at about this time Lincoln seems to have formed a strong attachment for Miss Matilda Edwards, a sister of Ninian W. Edwards; and that the engagement with Miss Todd was for a time broken off. In consequence of these complications, Lincoln's health was seriously affected. He suffered from melancholy, which was so profound that "his friends were alarmed for his life." His intimate companion, Mr. Speed, endeavored to rescue him from the terrible depression, urging that he would die unless he rallied. Lincoln replied, "I am not afraid to die, and would be more than willing. But I have an irrepressible desire to live till I can be assured that the world is a little better for my having been in it."

Mr. Herndon gives as his opinion that Lincoln's insanity grew out of a most extraordinary complication of feelings—aversion to the marriage proposed, a counter—attachment to Miss Edwards, and a revival of his tenderness for the memory of Anne Rutledge. At all events, his derangement was nearly if not quite complete. "We had to remove razors from his room," says Mr. Speed, "take away all knives, and other dangerous things. It was terrible." Mr. Speed determined to do for him what Bowlin Greene had done on a similar occasion at New Salem. Having sold out his store on the first of January,

1841, he took Lincoln with him to his home in Kentucky and kept him there during most of the summer and fall, or until he seemed sufficiently restored to be given his liberty again, when he was brought back to Springfield. His health was soon regained, and on the 4th of November, 1842, the marriage between him and Miss Todd was celebrated according to the rites of the Episcopal Church. After the marriage Lincoln secured pleasant rooms for himself and wife at the Globe Tavern, at a cost of four dollars a week. In 1844 he purchased of the Rev. Nathan Dressar the plain dwelling which was his home for the ensuing seventeen years, and which he left in 1861 to enter the White House.

CHAPTER VI

In the spring of 1843 Lincoln was among the nominees proposed to represent the Sangamon district in Congress; but Col. Edward D. Baker carried the delegation, and was elected. In writing to his friend Speed, Lincoln treated the circumstance with his usual humor. "We had," he says, "a meeting of the Whigs of the county here last Monday to appoint delegates to a district convention. Baker beat me, and got the delegation instructed to go for him. The meeting, in spite of my attempt to decline it, appointed me one of the delegates; so that in getting Baker the nomination I shall be 'fixed' a good deal like a fellow who is made groomsman to the man who 'cut him out' and is marrying his own girl."

On the 20th of September, 1843, the partnership between Lincoln and Judge Logan was dissolved; and the same day a new association was formed with William H. Herndon, a relative of one of Lincoln's former friends of Clary Grove. It is said that in spite of their close friendship Mr. Herndon could not understand it when Lincoln one day plunged up the office stairs and said, "Herndon, should you like to be my partner?" "Don't laugh at me, Mr. Lincoln," was the response. Persistent repetition of the question could hardly gain a hearing; but at last Mr. Herndon said: "Mr. Lincoln, you know I am too young, and I have no standing and no money; but if you are in earnest, there is nothing in this world that would make me so happy." Nothing more was said till the papers were brought to Herndon to sign. The partnership of "Lincoln & Herndon" was a happy one, and continued until Lincoln became President, a period of nearly eighteen years.

The life of Henry Clay, which Lincoln read in his boyhood, had filled him with enthusiasm for the great Whig leader; and when the latter was nominated for the Presidency, in 1844, there was no more earnest adherent of his cause than the "Sangamon Chief," as Lincoln was now called. Lincoln canvassed Illinois and a part of Indiana during the campaign, meeting the chief Democratic speakers, and especially Douglas, in debate. Lincoln had not at this time heard the "silvery-tongued orator" of Kentucky; but two years later the opportunity was afforded and eagerly embraced. It is possible, as Dr. Holland remarks, that he "needed the influence of this visit to restore a healthy tone to his feelings, and to teach him that the person whom his imagination had transformed into a demigod was only a man, possessing the full measure of weaknesses common to men. In 1846 Lincoln learned that Clay was to deliver a speech at Lexington, Kentucky, in favor of gradual emancipation. This event seemed to give him an excuse for breaking away from his business and satisfying his desire to look his demigod in the face and hear the music of his eloquence. He accordingly went to Lexington, and arrived there in time to attend the meeting. On returning to his home from this visit he did not attempt to disguise his disappointment. Clay's speech was written and read; it lacked entirely the fire and eloquence which Lincoln had anticipated. At the close of the meeting Lincoln secured an introduction to the great orator and as Clay knew what a friend Lincoln had been to him, he invited his admirer and partisan to Ashland. No invitation could have delighted Lincoln more. But the result of his private intercourse with Clay was no more satisfactory than that which followed the speech. Those who have known both men will not wonder at this; for two men could hardly be more unlike in their motives and manners than the two thus brought together. One was a proud man; the other was a humble man. One was princely in his bearing; the other was lowly. One was distant and dignified; the other was as simple and approachable as a child. One received the deference of men as his due; the other received it with an uncomfortable sense of his unworthiness. A friend of Lincoln, who had a long conversation with him after his return from Ashland, found that his old enthusiasm was gone. Lincoln said that though Clay was polished in his manners, and very hospitable, he betrayed a consciousness of superiority that none could mistake."

For two years after the Presidential contest between Clay and Polk, Lincoln devoted himself assiduously to his law practice. But in 1846 he was again active in politics, this time striving for a seat in the National Congress. His chief opponent among the Whig candidates was his old friend John J. Hardin, who soon withdrew from the contest, leaving Mr. Lincoln alone in the field. The candidate on the Democratic ticket was Peter Cartwright, the famous Methodist preacher. It was supposed from his great popularity as a pulpit orator that Mr. Cartwright would run far ahead of his ticket. Instead of this, Lincoln received a majority of 1,511 in his district, which in 1844 had given Clay a majority of only 914 and in 1848 had allowed the Whig candidate for Congress to be defeated by 106 votes.

Lincoln took his seat in the Thirtieth Congress in December, 1847, the only Whig member from Illinois. Among the notable members of this Congress were ex-president John Quincy Adams; Andrew Johnson, elected Vice-President with Lincoln on his second election; A.H. Stephens, afterwards Vice-President of the Confederacy; Toombs, Rhett, Cobb, and others who afterwards became leaders of the Rebellion. In the Senate were Daniel Webster, Simon Cameron, Lewis Cass, Mason, Hunter, John C. Calhoun, and Jefferson Davis.

Lincoln entered Congress as the Illinois leader of the Whig party. He was reputed to be an able and effective speaker. In speaking of the impression he made upon his associates, the Hon. Robert C. Winthrop says: "I recall vividly the impressions I then formed both of his ability and amiability. We were old Whigs together, and agreed entirely upon all questions of public interest. I could not always concur in the policy of the party which made him President, but I never lost my personal regard for him. For shrewdness, sagacity, and keen practical sense, he has had no superior in our day or generation."

Alexander H. Stephens, writing seventeen years after Lincoln's death, recalled their service together in Congress. "I knew Mr. Lincoln well and intimately," said Mr. Stephens. "We both were ardent supporters of General Taylor for President in 1848. Lincoln, Toombs, Preston, myself, and others, formed the first Congressional Taylor Club, known as 'The Young Indians,' and organized the Taylor movement which resulted in his nomination. Mr. Lincoln was careless as to his manners and awkward in his speech, but possessed a strong, clear, vigorous mind. He always attracted and riveted the attention of the House when he spoke. His manner of speech as well as of thought was original. He had no model. He was a man of strong convictions, and what Carlyle would have called an *earnest* man. He abounded in anecdote. He illustrated everything he was talking about by an anecdote, always exceedingly apt and pointed; and socially he always kept his company in a roar of laughter."

Alluding to his first speech in Congress—on some post-office question of no special interest—Lincoln wrote to his friend Herndon that his principal object was to "get the hang of the House"; adding that he "found speaking here and elsewhere about the same thing. I was about as badly scared as when I spoke in court, but no more so."

Lincoln's mental power, as well as his self-confidence, developed rapidly under the responsibilities of his new position. During his term of service in the House he was zealous in the performance of his duties, alert to seize every opportunity to strike a blow for his party and acquit himself to the satisfaction of his constituents. In January, 1848, he made a telling speech in support of the "Spot Resolutions," in which his antagonism to the course of the Administration in regard to the war on Mexico was uncompromisingly announced. These resolutions were offered for the purpose of getting from President Polk a statement of facts regarding the beginning of the war. In this speech Lincoln warned the President not to try to "escape scrutiny by fixing the public gaze upon the exceeding brightness of military glory— that attractive rainbow that rises in showers of blood, that serpent's eye that charms but to destroy." In writing, a few days after the delivery of this speech, to Mr. Herndon, Lincoln said: "I will stake my life that if you had been in my place you would have voted just as I did. Would you have voted what you felt and knew to be a lie? I know you would not. Would you have gone out of the House—skulked the vote? I expect not. If you had skulked one vote you would have had to skulk many more before the end of the session. Richardson's resolutions, introduced before I made any move or gave any vote upon the subject, make a direct question of the justice of the war; so no man can be silent if he would. You are compelled to speak; and your only alternative is to tell the *truth* or tell a *lie*. I cannot doubt which you would do."

Lincoln's position on the Mexican War has been generally approved by the moral sense of the country; but it gave his political enemies an opportunity, which they were not slow to improve, for trying to make political capital out of it and using it to create a prejudice against him. Douglas in particular never missed an opportunity of referring to it. In the great joint debate in 1858 he spoke of Lincoln's having "distinguished himself in Congress by his opposition to the Mexican War, taking the side of the common enemy against his own country." No better refutation of these oft-repeated charges could be made than that given by Lincoln himself on this occasion. "The Judge charges me," he said, "with having, while in Congress, opposed our soldiers who were fighting in the Mexican War. I will tell you what he can prove by referring to the record. You remember I was an old Whig; and whenever the Democratic party tried to get me to vote that *the war had been righteously begun* by the President, I would not do it. But whenever they asked for any money or land-warrants, or anything to pay the soldiers, I gave *the same vote that Judge Douglas did. Such* is the truth, and the Judge has a right to make all he can out of it."

The most ambitious utterance of Lincoln during this term in Congress was that of July 27, 1848, when he took for his subject the very comprehensive one of "The Presidency and General Politics." It was a piece of sound and forcible argumentation, relieved by strong and effective imagery and quiet humor. A considerable portion of it was occupied with an exposure of the weaknesses of General Cass, the Presidential candidate opposed to General Taylor. Lincoln ridiculed Cass with all the wit at his command. An extract from this speech has already been quoted in this work, in the account of Lincoln in the Black Hawk War. Another passage, equally telling, relates to the vacillating action of General Cass on the Wilmot Proviso. After citing a number of facts in reference to the case, Lincoln says: "These extracts show that in 1846 General Cass was for the Proviso *at once*; that in March, 1847, he was still for it, *but not just then*; and that in December, 1847, he was *against it* altogether. This is a true index to the whole man. When the question was raised, in 1846, he was in a blustering hurry to take ground for it. He sought to be in advance, and to avoid the uninteresting position of a mere follower. But soon he began to see glimpses of the great Democratic ox-gad waving in his face, and to hear indistinctly a voice saying, 'Back! Back, sir! Back a little!' He shakes his head and bats his eyes and blunders back to his position of March, 1847. But still the gad waves, and the voice grows more distinct and sharper still, 'Back, sir! Back, I say! Further back!' And back he goes to the position of December, 1847, at which the gad is still and the voice soothingly says, 'So! Stand still at that!'"

Again, after extended comment on the extra charges of General Cass upon the Treasury for military services, he continued in a still more sarcastic vein: "But I have introduced General Cass's accounts here chiefly to show the wonderful physical capacities of the man. They show that he not only did the labor of several men *at the same time*, but that he often did it *at several places* many hundred miles apart *at the same time*. And at eating, too, his capacities are shown to be quite as wonderful. From October, 1821, to May, 1822, he ate ten rations a day in Michigan, ten rations a day here in Washington, and near five dollars' worth a day besides, partly on the road between the two places. And then there is an important discovery in his example—the art of being paid for what one eats, instead of having to pay for it. Hereafter if any nice young man shall owe a bill which he cannot pay in any other way he can just board it out. Mr. Speaker, we have all heard of the animal standing in doubt between two stacks of hay and starving to death. The like of that would never happen to General Cass. Place the stacks a thousand miles apart, he would stand stock-still midway between them and eat them *both at once*; and the green grass along the line would be apt to suffer some, too, at the same time. By all means make him President, gentlemen. He will feed you bounteously—if—if—there is any left after he shall have helped himself."

Lincoln's most important act in the Congress of 1848-9 was the introduction of a bill for the gradual abolition of slavery in the District of Columbia. But the state of feeling on the subject of emancipation was so feverish at the time that the bill could not even be got before the House.

The Whig National Convention met at Philadelphia the first of June, to nominate a candidate for the Presidency. Lincoln attended the Convention as a delegate from Illinois. During the campaign of 1848 he labored earnestly for the election of General Taylor. This campaign made him known more generally throughout the country, as he spoke in New York and New England as well as in Illinois and the West.

While in Washington, Lincoln kept up a free correspondence with his friend and law-partner Herndon, which affords many interesting glimpses of his thoughts and views. In one of these letters, endeavoring to incite Herndon to political ambition, he wrote: "Nothing could afford me more satisfaction than to learn that you and others of my young friends at home were doing battle in the contest, endearing themselves to the people and taking a stand far above any I have ever been able to reach in their admiration. I cannot conceive that other old men feel differently. Of course, I cannot demonstrate what I say; but I was young once, and I am sure I was never ungenerously thrust back. The way for a young man to rise is to improve himself in every way he can, never suspecting that anybody wishes to hinder him. Allow me to assure you that suspicion and jealousy never did help any man in any situation. There may sometimes be ungenerous attempts to keep a young man down; and they will succeed, too, if he allows his mind to be diverted from its true channel, to brood over the attempted injury. Cast about and see if this feeling has not injured every person you have ever known to fall into it. Now, in what I have said I am sure you will suspect nothing but sincere friendship. I would save you from a fatal error. You have been a laborious, studious young man. You are far better informed on almost all subjects than I have ever been. You cannot fail in any laudable object unless you allow your mind to be improperly directed. I have some the advantage of you in the world's experience, merely by being older; and it is this that induces me to offer you this advice."

It will be observed that, in this letter Lincoln speaks of himself as an "old man." This had been a habit with him for years; and yet at this date he was under thirty-nine. He was already beginning to be known as "Old Abe." Hon. E.B. Washburne states that he remembers hearing him thus called, in Chicago, in July, 1847. "One afternoon," says Mr. Washburne, "several of us sat on the sidewalk under the balcony in front of the Sherman House, and among the number was the accomplished scholar and unrivalled orator, Lisle Smith, who suddenly interrupted the conversation by exclaiming, 'There is Lincoln on the other side of the street! *Just look at old Abe!*' And from that time we all called him 'Old Abe.' No one who saw him can forget his personal appearance at that time. Tall, angular, and awkward, he had on a short-waisted, thin, swallow-tail coat, a short vest of the same material, thin pantaloons scarcely coming down to his ankles, a straw hat, and a pair of brogans, with woollen socks."

During the summer following the expiration of Lincoln's term in Congress (March 4, 1849) he made a strong effort to secure the position of Commissioner of the General Land Office, but without success. The place was given to Justin Butterfield of Chicago. It was a severe disappointment to Lincoln. Major Wilcox, who at the period referred to lived in McDonough County, Illinois, and in early days was a Whig politician, visited Washington to aid Lincoln in seeking this appointment, and has furnished a graphic account of the circumstances and of Lincoln's appearance at the national capital in the novel capacity of an office-seeker. Major Wilcox says that in June, 1849, he went to Washington and had an interview with the newly-inaugurated President, General Taylor, regarding Lincoln's appointment to the desired office. The interview was but partially satisfactory, the President remarking that he was favorable to Lincoln, but that Mr. Butterfield was very strongly urged for the place and the chances of appointment were in his favor. Lincoln had arranged to be in Washington at a time specified, after Major Wilcox should have had opportunity to look the ground over. Major Wilcox says that he went to the railroad depot to meet Lincoln at the train. It was in the afternoon, towards night. The day had been quite warm, and the road was dry and dusty. He found Lincoln just emerging from the depot. He had on a thin suit of summer clothes, his coat being a linen duster, much soiled. His whole appearance was decidedly shabby. He carried in his hand an old-fashioned carpet-sack, which added to the oddity of his appearance. Major Wilcox says if it had been anybody else he would have been rather shy of being seen in his company, because of the awkward and unseemly appearance he presented. Lincoln immediately began to talk about his chances for the appointment; whereupon Major Wilcox related to him everything that had transpired, and what President Taylor had said to him. They proceeded at once to Major Wilcox's room, where they sat down to look over the situation. Lincoln took from his pocket a paper he had prepared in the case, which comprised eleven reasons why he should be appointed Commissioner of the General Land Office. Amongst other things Lincoln presented the fact that he had been a member of Congress from Illinois two years; that his location was in the West, where the government lands were; that he was a native of the West, and had been reared under Western influences. He gave reasons why the appointment should be given to Illinois, and particularly to the southern part of the State. Major Wilcox says that he was forcibly struck by the clear, convincing, and methodical statement of Lincoln as contained in these eleven reasons why he should have the appointment. But it was given to Mr. Butterfield.

After Lincoln became President, a Member of Congress asked him for an appointment in the army in behalf of a son of the same Justin Butterfield. When the application was presented, the President paused, and after a moment's silence, said: "Mr. Justin Butterfield once obtained an appointment I very much wanted, in which my friends believed I could have been useful, and to which they thought I was fairly entitled. I hardly ever felt so bad at any failure in my life. But I am glad of an opportunity of doing a service to his son." And he made an order for his commission. In lieu of the desired office, General Taylor offered Lincoln the post of Governor, and afterwards of Secretary, of Oregon Territory; but these offers he declined. In after years a friend remarked to him, alluding to the event: "How fortunate that you declined! If you had gone to Oregon you might have come back as Senator, but you would never have been President." "Yes, you are probably right," said Lincoln; and then, with a musing, dreamy look, he added: "I have all my life been a fatalist. What is to be, will be; or, rather, I have found all my life, as Hamlet says,—

'There's a divinity that shapes our ends,

Rough-hew them how we will.'"

CHAPTER VII

Retiring, somewhat reluctantly, from Washington life, which he seems to have liked very much, Lincoln returned to Springfield in 1849 and resumed the practice of the law. He declined an advantageous offer of a law-partnership at Chicago, made him by Judge Goodrich, giving as a reason that if he went to Chicago he would have to sit down and study hard, and this would kill him; that he would rather go around the circuit in the country than to sit down and die in a big city. So he settled down once more in the rather uneventful and fairly prosperous life of a country lawyer.

A gentleman who knew Lincoln intimately in Springfield, in his maturity, has given the following capital description of him. "He stands six feet four inches high in his stockings. His frame is not muscular, but gaunt and wiry; his arms are long, but not disproportionately so for a person of his height; his lower limbs are not disproportioned to his body. In walking, his gait, though firm, is never brisk. He steps slowly and deliberately, almost always with his head inclined forward and his hands clasped behind his back. In matters of dress he is by no means precise. Always clean, he is never fashionable; he is careless, but not slovenly. In manner he is remarkably cordial and at the same time simple. His politeness is always sincere but never elaborate and oppressive. A warm shake of the hand and a warmer smile of recognition are his methods of greeting his friends. At rest, his features, though those of a man of mark, are not such as belong to a handsome man; but when his fine dark gray eyes are lighted up by any emotion, and his features begin their play, he would be chosen from among a crowd as one who had in him not only the kindly sentiments which women love but the heavier metal of which full-grown men and Presidents are made. His hair is black, and, though thin, is wiry. His head sits well on his shoulders, but beyond that it defies description. It nearer resembles that of Clay than that of Webster; but it is unlike either. It is very large, and phrenologically well proportioned, betokening power in all its developments. A slightly Roman nose, a wide-cut mouth, and a dark complexion, with the appearance of having been weather-beaten, complete the description."

Of Lincoln's life at this period, another writer says: "He lived simply, comfortably, and respectably, with neither expensive tastes nor habits. His wants were few and simple. He occupied a small unostentatious house in Springfield, and was in the habit of entertaining, in a very simple way, his friends and his brethren of the bar during the terms of the court and the sessions of the Legislature. Mrs. Lincoln often entertained small numbers of friends at dinner and somewhat larger numbers at evening parties. In his modest and simple home everything was orderly and refined, and there was always, on the part of both Mr. and Mrs. Lincoln, a cordial and hearty Western welcome which put every guest at ease. Yet it was the wit and humor, anecdote, and unrivalled conversation of the host which formed the chief attraction and made a dinner at Lincoln's cottage an event to be remembered. Lincoln's income from his profession was now from $2,000 to $3,000 per annum. His property consisted of his house and lot in Springfield, a lot in the town of Lincoln which had been given to him, and 160 acres of wild land in Iowa which he had received for his services in the Black Hawk War. He owned a few law and miscellaneous books. All his property may have been of the value of $10,000 or $12,000."

Lincoln was at this time the father of two sons: Robert Todd, born on the 1st day of August, 1843; and Edward Baker, born on the 10th of March, 1846. In a letter to his friend Speed, dated October 22 of the latter year, Lincoln writes: "We have another boy, born the 10th of March. He is very much such a child as Bob was at his age, rather of a *longer* order. Bob is 'short and low, ' and I expect he always will be. He talks very plainly, almost as plainly as anybody. He is quite smart enough. I sometimes fear he is one of the little *rare-ripe* sort that are smarter at about five than ever after. He has a great deal of that sort of mischief that is the offspring of much animal spirits. Since I began this letter a messenger came to tell me Bob was lost; but by the time I reached the house his mother had found him and had him whipped. By now, very likely, he is run away again."

December 21, 1850, a third son, William Wallace, was born to him; and on April 4, 1853, a fourth and last child, named Thomas.

"A young man bred in Springfield," says Dr. Holland, "speaks of a vision of Lincoln, as he appeared in those days, that has clung to his memory very vividly. The young man's way to school led by the lawyer's door. On almost any fair summer morning he would find Lincoln on the sidewalk in front of his house, drawing a child backward and forward in a little gig. Without hat or coat, wearing a pair of rough shoes, his hands behind him holding to the tongue of the gig, and his tall form bent forward to accommodate himself to the service, he paced up and down the walk forgetful of everything around him and intent only on some subject that absorbed his mind. The young man says he remembers wondering in his boyish way how so rough and plain a man should happen to live in so respectable a house. The habit of mental absorption, or 'absent-mindedness' as it is called, was common with him always, but particularly during the formative periods of his life. The New Salem people, it will be remembered, thought him crazy because he passed his best friends in the street without seeing them. At the table, in his own family, he often sat down without knowing or realizing where he was, and ate his food mechanically. When he 'came to himself' it was a trick with him to break the silence by the quotation of some verse of poetry from a favorite author. It relieved the awkwardness of the situation, served as a 'blind' to the thoughts which had possessed him, and started conversation in a channel that led as far as possible from the subject that he had set aside."

Mr. Lamon has written with great freedom of the sorrow that brooded over Lincoln's home. Some knowledge of the blight which this cast upon his life is necessary for a right interpretation of the gloomy moods that constantly oppressed him and left their indelible impress on his face and character. Mr. Lamon states unreservedly that Lincoln's marriage was an unhappy one. The circumstances preceding his union with Miss Todd have been related. Mr. Lamon says: "He was conscientious and honorable and just. There was but one way of repairing the injury he had done Miss Todd, and he adopted it. They were married; but they understood each other, and suffered the inevitable consequences. Such troubles seldom fail to find a tongue; and it is not strange that in this case neighbors and friends, and ultimately the whole country, came to know the state of things in that house. Lincoln scarcely attempted to conceal it. He talked of it with little or no reserve to his wife's relatives, as well as to his own friends. Yet the gentleness and patience with which he bore this affliction from day to day and from year to year was enough to move the shade of Socrates. It touched his acquaintances deeply, and they gave it the widest publicity." Mrs. Colonel Chapman, daughter of Dennis Hanks and a relative of Lincoln, made him a long visit previous to her marriage. "You ask me," says she, "how Mr. Lincoln acted at home. I can say, and that truly, he was all that a husband, father, and neighbor should be, kind and affectionate to his wife and child ('Bob' being the only one they had when I was with them), and very pleasant to all around him. Never did I hear him utter an unkind word."

It seems impossible to arrive at all the causes of Lincoln's melancholy disposition. He was, according to his most intimate friends, totally unlike other people,—was, in fact, "a mystery." But whatever the history or the cause,—whether physical reasons, the absence of domestic concord, a series of painful recollections of his mother, of early sorrows and hardships, of Anne Rutledge and fruitless hopes, or all these combined,—Lincoln was a terribly sad and gloomy man. "I do not think that he knew what happiness was for twenty years," says Mr. Herndon. "'Terrible' is the word which all his friends used to describe him in the black mood. 'It was terrible! It was terrible!' said one to another." Judge Davis believes that Lincoln's hilarity was mainly simulated, and that "his stories and jokes were intended to whistle off sadness." "The groundwork of his social nature was sad," says Judge Scott. "But for the fact that he studiously cultivated the humorous, it would have been very sad indeed. His mirth always seemed to me to be put on; like a plant produced in a hot-bed, it had an unnatural and luxuriant growth." Mr. Herndon, Lincoln's law-partner and most intimate friend, describes him at this period as a "thin, tall, wiry, sinewy, grizzly, raw-boned man, looking 'woe-struck.' His countenance was haggard and careworn, exhibiting all the marks of deep and protracted suffering. Every feature of the man—the hollow eyes, with the dark rings beneath; the long, sallow, cadaverous face intersected by those peculiar deep lines; his whole air; his walk; his long silent reveries, broken at long intervals by sudden and startling exclamations, as if to confound an observer who might suspect the nature of his thoughts,—showed he was a man of sorrows, not sorrows of to-day or yesterday, but long-treasured and deep, bearing with him a continual sense of weariness and pain. He was a plain, homely, sad, weary-looking man, to whom one's heart warmed involuntarily because he seemed at once miserable and kind."

Mr. Page Eaton, an old resident of Springfield, says: "Lincoln always did his own marketing, even after he was elected President and before he went to Washington. I used to see him at the butcher's or baker's every morning, with his basket on his arm. He was kind and sociable, and would always speak to everyone. He was so kind, so childlike, that I don't believe there was one in the city who didn't love him as a father or brother." "On a winter's morning," says Mr. Lamon, "he could be seen wending his way to the market, with a basket on his arm and at his side a little boy whose small feet rattled and pattered over the ice-bound pavement, attempting to make up by the number of his short steps for the long strides of his father. The little fellow jerked at the bony hand which held his, and prattled and questioned, begged and grew petulant, in a vain effort to make his father talk to him. But the latter was probably unconscious of the other's existence, and stalked on, absorbed in his own reflections. He wore on such occasions an old gray shawl, rolled into a coil and wrapped like a rope around his neck. The rest of his clothes were in keeping. 'He did not walk cunningly—Indian-like—but cautiously and firmly.' His tread was even and strong. He was a little pigeon-toed; and this, with another peculiarity, made his walk very singular. He set his whole foot flat on the ground, and in turn lifted it all at once—not resting momentarily upon the toe as the foot rose nor upon the heel as it fell. He never wore his shoes out at the heel and the toe, as most men do, more than at the middle. Yet his gait was not altogether awkward, and there was manifest physical power in his step. As he moved along thus, silent and abstracted, his thoughts dimly reflected in his sharp face, men turned to look after him as an object of sympathy as well as curiosity. His melancholy, in the words of Mr. Herndon, '*dripped from him* as he walked.' If, however, he met a friend in the street, and was roused by a hearty 'Good-morning, Lincoln!' he would grasp the friend's hand with one or both of his own, and with his usual expression of 'Howdy! howdy!' would detain him to hear a story; something reminded him of it; it happened in Indiana, and it must be told, for it was wonderfully pertinent. It was not at home that he most enjoyed seeing company. He preferred to meet his friends abroad,—on a street-corner, in an office, at the court-house, or sitting on nail-kegs in a country store." Mrs. Lincoln experienced great difficulty in securing the punctual attendance of her husband at the family meals. Dr. Bateman has repeatedly seen two of the boys pulling with all their might at his coat-tails, and a third pushing in front, while *paterfamilias* stood upon the street cordially shaking the hand of an old acquaintance.

After his breakfast-hour, says Mr. Lamon, he would appear at his office and go about the labors of the day with all his might, displaying prodigious industry and capacity for continuous application, although he never was a fast worker. Sometimes it happened that he came without his breakfast; and then he would have in his hands a piece of cheese or bologna sausage, and a few crackers, bought by the way. At such times he did not speak to his partner, or his friends if any happened to be present; the tears perhaps struggling into his eyes, while his pride was struggling to keep them back. Mr. Herndon knew the whole story at a glance. There was no speech between them, but neither wished the visitors at the office to witness the scene. So Lincoln retired to the back office while Mr. Herndon locked the front one and walked away with the key in his pocket. In an hour or more the latter would return and perhaps find Lincoln calm and collected. Otherwise he went out again and waited until he was so. Then the office was opened and everything went on as usual.

"His mind was filled with gloomy forebodings and strong apprehensions of impending evil, mingled with extravagant visions of personal grandeur and power. He never doubted for a moment that he was formed for some 'great or miserable end.' He talked about it frequently and sometimes calmly. Mr. Herndon remembers many of these conversations in their office at Springfield and in their rides around the circuit. Lincoln said the impression had grown in him all his life; but Mr. Herndon thinks it was about 1840 that it took the character of a 'religious conviction.' He had then suffered much, and considering his opportunities he had achieved great things. He was already a leader among men, and a most brilliant career had been promised him by the prophetic enthusiasm of many friends. Thus encouraged and stimulated, and feeling himself growing gradually stronger and stronger in the estimation of 'the plain people' whose voice was more potent than all the Warwicks, his ambition painted the rainbow of glory in the sky, while his morbid melancholy supplied the clouds that were to overcast and obliterate it with the wrath and ruin of the tempest. To him it was fate, and there was no escape or defense. The presentiment never deserted him. It was as clear, as perfect, as certain as any image conveyed by the senses. He had now entertained it so long that it was as much a part of his nature as the consciousness of identity. All doubts had faded away, and he submitted humbly to a power which he could neither comprehend nor resist. He was to fall,—fall from a lofty place and in the performance of a great work."

On one occasion Lincoln visited Chicago as counsel in a case in the U.S. District Court. The Hon. N.B. Judd, an intimate friend, was also engaged upon the case, and took Mr. Lincoln home with him as a guest. The following account of this visit is given by Mrs. Judd in Oldroyd's Memorial Album: "Mr. Judd had invited Mr. Lincoln to spend the evening at our pleasant home on the shore of Lake Michigan. After tea, and until quite late, we sat on the broad piazza, looking out upon as lovely a scene as that which has made the Bay of Naples so celebrated. A number of vessels were availing themselves of a fine breeze to leave the harbor, and the lake was studded with many a white sail. I remember that a flock of sea-gulls were flying along the beach, dipping their beaks and white-lined wings in the foam that capped the short waves as they fell upon the shore. Whilst we sat there the great white moon appeared on the rim of the eastern horizon and slowly crept above the water, throwing a perfect flood of silver light upon the dancing waves. The stars shone with the soft light of a midsummer night, and the breaking of the low waves upon the shore added the charm of pleasant sound to the beauty of the night. Mr. Lincoln, whose home was far inland from the great lakes, seemed greatly impressed with the wondrous beauty of the scene, and carried by its impressiveness away from all thought of jars and turmoil of earth. In that mild, pleasant voice, attuned to harmony with his surroundings, as was his wont when his soul was stirred by aught that was lovely or beautiful, Mr. Lincoln began to speak of the mystery which for ages enshrouded and shut out those distant worlds above us from our own; of the poetry and beauty which was seen and felt by seers of old when they contemplated Orion and Arcturus as they wheeled, seemingly around the earth, in their nightly course; of the discoveries since the invention of the telescope, which had thrown a flood of light and knowledge on what before was incomprehensible and mysterious; of the wonderful computations of scientists who had measured the miles of seemingly endless space which separated the planets in our solar system from our central sun, and our sun from other suns. He speculated on the possibilities of knowledge which an increased power of the lens would give in the years to come. When the night air became too chilling to remain longer on the piazza we went into the parlor. Seated on the sofa, his long limbs stretching across the carpet and his arms folded behind him, Mr. Lincoln went on to speak of other discoveries, of the inventions which had been made during the long cycles of time lying between the present and those early days when the sons of Adam began to make use of material things about them and invent instruments of various kinds in brass and gold and silver. He gave us a short but succinct account of all the inventions referred to in the Old Testament, from the time when Adam walked in the garden of Eden until the Bible record ended, 600 B.C. I said, 'Mr. Lincoln, I did not know you were such a Bible student.' He replied: 'I must be honest, Mrs. Judd, and tell you just how I come to know so much about these early inventions.' He then went on to say that in discussing with some friend the relative age of the discovery and use of the precious metals he went to the Bible to satisfy himself and became so interested in his researches that he made memoranda of the different discoveries and inventions. Soon after, he was invited to lecture before some literary society, I think in Bloomington. The interest he had felt in the study convinced him that the subject would interest others, and he therefore prepared and delivered his lecture on The Age of Different Inventions. 'Of course,' he added, 'I could not after that forget the order or time of such discoveries and inventions.'"

In all the years that had passed since Lincoln left his father's humble house, he had preserved an affectionate interest in the welfare of its various members. He paid them visits whenever he could find opportunity, and never failed to extend his aid and sympathy whenever needed. He had risen to success in his profession, was widely known throughout his section, and though still a poor man he had good prospects and considerable influence. Yet he ever retained a considerate regard and remembrance for the poor and obscure relatives he had left plodding in the humble ways of life. He never assumed the slightest superiority to them. Whenever, upon his circuit, he found time, he always visited them. Countless times he was known to leave his companions at the village hotel after a hard day's work in the court-room and spend the evening with these old friends and companions of his humbler days. On one occasion, when urged not to go, he replied, "Why, Aunt's heart would be broken if I should leave town without calling upon her," —yet he was obliged to walk several miles to make the call. As his fortunes improved he often sent money and presents to his father and step-mother, bought land for them, and tried in every way to make them comfortable and happy. The father was gratified at these marks of affection, and felt great pride in the rising prosperity of his son. Mr. Herndon says that "for years Lincoln supported or helped to support his aged father and mother. It is to his honor that he dearly loved his step-mother, and it is equally true that she idolized her step-son. He purchased a piece of property in Coles County as a home for his father and mother, and had it deeded in trust for their use and benefit."

In 1851 Lincoln's father died, at the age of seventy-three. The following letter, written a few days before this event, reveals the affectionate solicitude of the son:

Springfield, Jan. 12,1851.

DEAR BROTHER:—On the day before yesterday I received a letter from Harriet, written at Greenup. She says she has just returned from your house, and that father is very low and will hardly recover. She also says that you have written me two letters, and that, although you do not expect me to come now, you wonder that I do not write. I received both your letters; and although I have not answered them, it is not because I have forgotten them, or not been interested about them, but because it appeared to me I could write nothing which could do any good. You already know I desire that neither father nor mother shall be in want of any comfort, either in health or sickness, while they live; and I feel sure you have not failed to use my name, if necessary, to procure a doctor or anything else for father in his present sickness. My business is such that I could hardly leave home now, if it were not, as it is, that my wife is sick a-bed. I sincerely hope father may yet recover his health; but, at all events, tell him to remember to call upon and confide in our great and good and merciful Maker, who will not turn away from him in any extremity. He notes the fall of a sparrow, and numbers the hairs of our heads; and He will not forget the dying man who puts his trust in Him. Say to him, that if we could meet now it is doubtful whether it would not be more painful than pleasant; but that if it be his lot to go now he will soon have a joyous meeting with loved ones gone before, and where the rest of us, through the help of God, hope ere long to join them.

Write me again when you receive this.

Affectionately,
A. LINCOLN.

The step-brother, John Johnston, to whom the foregoing letter is addressed, was the cause of considerable anxiety to Lincoln. It was with him that their parents resided, and frequent were his appeals to Lincoln to extricate him from some pecuniary strait into which he had fallen through his confirmed thriftlessness and improvidence. "John Johnston," Mr. Herndon says, "was an indolent and shiftless man, one who was 'born tired.' Yet he was clever, generous and hospitable." The following document affords a hint of Lincoln's kindly patience as well as of his capacity for sound practical advice when it was much needed:

> DEAR JOHNSTON:—Your request for eighty dollars I do not think it best to comply with now. At the various times when I have helped you a little you have said to me, 'We can get along very well now'; but in a very short time I find you in the same difficulty again. Now, this can only happen by some defect in your conduct. What that defect is, I think I know. You are not lazy, and still you are an idler. I doubt whether, since I saw you, you have done a good whole day's work in any one day. You do not very much dislike to work, and still you do not work much, merely because it does not seem to you that you could get much for it. This habit of uselessly wasting time is the whole difficulty; and it is vastly important to you, and still more so to your children, that you should break the habit. It is more important to them, because they have longer to live, and can keep out of an idle habit before they are in it easier than they can get out after they are in. You are now in need of some money; and what I propose is that you shall go to work, 'tooth and nail,' for somebody who will give you money for it. Let father and your boys take charge of things at home, prepare for a crop, and make the crop, and you go to work for the best money-wages, or in discharge of any debt you owe, that you can get; and, to secure you a fair reward for your labor, I now promise you, that, for every dollar you will, between this and the first of next May, get for your own labor, either in money or as your own indebtedness, I will then give you one other dollar. By this, if you hire yourself at ten dollars a month, from

me you will get ten more, making twenty dollars a month for your work. In this I do not mean you shall go off to St. Louis, or the lead-mines, or the gold-mines in California; but I mean for you to go at it, for the best wages you can get, close to home, in Coles County. Now, if you will do this you will soon be out of debt, and, what is better, you will have a habit that will keep you from getting in debt again. But if I should now clear you out of debt, next year you would be in just as deep as ever. You say you would almost give your place in heaven for $70 or $80. Then you value your place in heaven very cheap; for I am sure you can, with the offer I make, get the seventy or eighty dollars for four or five months' work. You say, if I will furnish you the money, you will deed me the land, and if you don't pay the money back, you will deliver possession. Nonsense! If you can't now live with the land, how will you then live without it? You have always been kind to me, and I do not mean to be unkind to you. On the contrary, if you will but follow my advice, you will find it worth more than eighty times eighty dollars to you.

Affectionately your brother,
A. LINCOLN.

In other letters he wrote even more sharply to his thriftless step-brother.

Shelbyville, Nov. 4, 1851

DEAR BROTHER:—When I came into Charleston, day before yesterday, I learned that you are anxious to sell the land where you live, and move to Missouri. I have been thinking of this ever since, and cannot but think such a notion is utterly foolish. What can you do in Missouri better than here? Is the land any richer? Can you there, any more than here, raise corn and wheat and oats without work? Will any body there, any more than here, do your work for you? If you intend to go to work, there is no better place than right where you are; if you do not intend to go to work, you can not get along anywhere. Squirming and crawling about from place to place can do no good. You have raised no crop this year; and what you really want is to sell the land, get the money and spend it. Part with the land you have, and, my life upon it, you will never after own a spot big enough to bury you in. Half of what you will get for the land you will spend in moving to Missouri, and the other half you will eat and drink and wear out, and no foot of land will be bought. Now, I feel it is my duty to have no hand in such a piece of foolery. I feel that it is so even on your own account, and particularly on mother's account. The eastern forty acres I intend to keep for mother while she lives; if you will not cultivate it, it will rent for enough to support her; at least, it will rent for something. Her dower in the other two forties she can let you have, and no thanks to me. Now, do not misunderstand this letter. I do not write it in any unkindness. I write it in order, if possible, to get you to face the truth, which truth is, you are destitute because you have idled away all your time. Your thousand pretences for not getting along better are all nonsense. They deceive nobody but yourself. *Go to work* is the only cure for your case.

Sincerely yours,
A. LINCOLN.

In still another letter he reveals his tender solicitude for his step-mother, as well as his care for his step-brother's unfortunate children.

Shelbyville, Nov. 9, 1851

DEAR BROTHER:—When I wrote you before, I had not received your letter. I still think as I did; but if the land can be sold so that I get $300 to put at interest for mother, I will not object, if she does not. But before I will make a deed, the money must be had, or secured beyond all doubt, at ten per cent. As to Abram, I do not want him on my own account; but I understand he wants to live with me, so that he can go to school, and get a fair start in the world, which I very much wish him to have. When I reach home, if I can make it convenient I will take him, provided there is no mistake between us as to the object and terms of my taking him.

In haste, as ever,
A. LINCOLN.

In speaking of Lincoln's regard for his step-mother, it is interesting also to learn her opinion of him. A gentleman visiting the old lady after her son's death says: "She is eighty-four years old, and quite feeble. She is a plain, unsophisticated old lady, with a frank, open countenance, a warm heart full of kindness toward others, and in many respects very much like the President. Abraham was evidently her idol; she speaks of him still as her 'good boy,' and with much feeling said, 'He was always a good boy, and willing to do just what I wanted. He and his step-brother never quarrelled but once, and that, you know, is a great deal for step-brothers. I didn't want him elected President. I knowed they would kill him.'" She died in April, 1869, and was buried by the side of her husband, Thomas Lincoln.

CHAPTER VIII

The ten years following the close of Lincoln's Congressional service, in 1849, were given to the uninterrupted practice of the law, to which he devoted himself laboriously and successfully, though not with great pecuniary gains. His legal fees were regarded by his brethren at the bar as "ridiculously small." His practice had extended to the Supreme Court of his State and to the United States District and Circuit Courts, and he was occasionally retained for cases in other States. With greater love of money and less sympathy for his fellows, he might have acquired a fortune in his profession.

Lincoln never speculated. Apparently he had no great desire to acquire wealth. He had many opportunities in the days of the State's early growth to make good and safe investments, but he never took advantage of them. Many of his fellow lawyers were becoming wealthy, but Lincoln still rode the circuit wearing the familiar gray shawl about his shoulders, carrying a carpet-bag filled with papers and a change of underclothing, and a faded, green cotton umbrella with "A. Lincoln" in large white muslin letters on the inside. The knob was gone from the handle of the umbrella and a piece of twine kept it from falling open. A young lawyer who saw him for the first time thus—one who grew to love him and who afterwards gave his life for the Union—in relating the circumstance a long time afterward, exclaimed: "He was the *ungodliest* figure I ever saw."

An interesting and vivid description of Lincoln's personal appearance and manner in the trial of a case is furnished by one who was a witness of the scenes which he so admirably describes. The writer says: "While living in Danville, Illinois, in 1854, I saw Abraham Lincoln for the first time. The occasion of his visit was as prosecutor of a slander suit brought by Dr. Fithian against a wealthy farmer whose wife died under the doctor's hands. The defense was represented by Edward A. Hannegan, of Indiana, ex-United States Senator and afterward Minister to Berlin, an able and eloquent man; and O.B. Ficklin, who, after Douglas and Lincoln, was considered the best lawyer in Illinois. Lincoln had all he could do to maintain himself against his two formidable adversaries, but he was equal to the occasion. The trial lasted three or four days, the examination of witnesses consuming most of the time. In this part of the work Lincoln displayed remarkable tact. He did not badger the witnesses, or attempt to confuse them. His questions were plain and practical, and elicited answers that had a direct bearing upon the case. He did nothing for effect, and made no attempt to dazzle the jury or captivate the audience. When he arose to speak he was confronted by an audience that was too numerous for all to find seats in the court-room. He was attired in a fine broadcloth suit, silk hat, and polished boots. His neck was encircled by an old-fashioned silk choker. He perspired freely, and used a red silk handkerchief to remove the perspiration. His clothes fitted him, and he was as genteel-looking as any man in the audience. The slouchy appearance which he is said to have presented on other occasions was conspicuously absent here. As he stood before the vast audience, towering above every person around him, he was the centre of attraction. I can never forget how he looked, as he cast his eyes over the crowd before beginning his argument. His face was long and sallow; high cheek bones; large, deep-set eyes, of a grayish-brown color, shaded by heavy eyebrows; high but not broad forehead; large, well-formed head, covered with an abundance of coarse black hair, worn rather long, through which he frequently passed his fingers; arms and legs of unusual length; head inclined slightly forward, which made him appear stoop-shouldered. His features betrayed neither excitement nor anxiety. They were calm and fixed. In short, his appearance was that of a man who felt the responsibility of his position and was determined to acquit himself to the best of his ability. I do not remember the points of his speech; but his manner was so peculiar, so different from that of other orators whom I have heard, that I can never forget it. He spoke for almost two hours, entirely without notes and with an eloquence that I have never heard surpassed. He was all life, all motion; every muscle and fibre of his body seemed brought into requisition. His voice was clear, distinct, and well modulated. Every word was clean-cut and exactly suited to its place. At times he would stoop over until his hands almost swept the floor. Then he would straighten himself up, fold his arms across his breast, and take a few steps forward or back. This movement completed, he would fling his arms above his head, or thrust them beneath his coat-tails, elevating or depressing his voice to suit the attitude assumed and the sentiment expressed. Arms and legs were continually in motion. It seemed impossible for him to stand still. In the midst of the most impassioned or pathetic portions of his speech, he would extend his long arms toward the judge or jury, and shake his bony fingers with an effect that is indescribable. He held his audience to the last; and when he sat down there was a murmur of applause which the judge with difficulty prevented from swelling to a roar. The argument must have been as able as the manner of the speaker was attractive, for the verdict was in favor of his client.

"When he had retired to his hotel after the trial, and while conversing with a number of gentlemen who had called to pay their respects to him, Lincoln was informed that an old colored woman, who had known him years before in Kentucky, wished to see him. She was too feeble to come to him, and desired him to go to her. Ascertaining where she lived, Lincoln started at once, accompanied by a boy who acted as pilot. He found the woman in a wretched hovel in the outskirts of the town, sick and destitute. He remembered her very well, as she had belonged to the owner of the farm upon which Lincoln was born. He gave her money to supply her immediate wants, promised her that he would see she did not suffer for the necessaries of life, and when he returned to town hunted up a physician and engaged him to give the old woman all the medical attention that her case demanded."

Mr. G.W. Harris, whose first meeting with Lincoln in a log school-house has been previously described in these pages, subsequently became a clerk in Lincoln's law-office at Springfield, and furnishes some excellent reminiscences of that interesting period. "A crack-brained attorney who lived in Springfield, supported mainly by the other lawyers of the place, became indebted, in the sum of two dollars and fifty cents, to a wealthy citizen of the county, a recent comer. The creditor, failing after repeated efforts to collect the amount due him, came to Mr. Lincoln and asked him to bring suit. Lincoln explained the man's condition and circumstances, and advised his client to let the matter rest; but the creditor's temper was up, and he insisted on having suit brought. Again Lincoln urged him to let the matter drop, adding, 'You can make nothing out of him, and it will cost you a good deal more than the debt to bring suit.' The creditor was still determined to have his way, and threatened to seek some other attorney who would be more willing to take charge of the matter than Lincoln appeared to be. Lincoln then said, 'Well, if you are determined that suit shall be brought, I will bring it; but my charge will be ten dollars.' The money was paid him, and peremptory orders were given that the suit be brought that day. After the client's departure, Lincoln went out of the office, returning in about an hour with an amused look on his face. I asked what pleased him, and he replied, 'I brought suit against — —, and then hunted him up, told him what I had done, handed him half of the ten dollars, and we went over to the squire's office. He confessed judgment and paid the bill.' Lincoln added that he didn't see any other way to make things satisfactory for his client as well as the rest of the parties.

"Mr. Lincoln had a heart that was more a woman's than a man's— filled to overflowing with sympathy for those in trouble, and ever ready to relieve them by any means in his power. He was ever thoughtful of others' comforts, even to the forgetting of himself. In those early days his face wore a sad look when at rest—a look that made you feel that you would like to take from him a part of his burden. One who knew him then and had known his career since would be inclined to think that he already felt premonitions of the heavy burdens that his broad shoulders were to bear, and the sorrows that his kind heart would have to endure.

"Mr. Lincoln was fond of playing chess and checkers, and usually acted cautiously upon the defensive until the game had reached a stage where aggressive movements were clearly justified. He was also somewhat fond of ten-pins, and occasionally indulged in a game. Whatever may have been his tastes in his younger days, at this period of his life he took no interest in fishing-rod or gun. He was indifferent to dress, careless almost to a fault of his personal appearance. The same indifference extended to money. So long as his wants were supplied—and they were few and simple—he seemed to have no further use for money, except in the giving or the lending of it, with no expectation or desire for its return, to those whom he thought needed it more than he. Debt he abhorred, and under no circumstances would he incur it. He was abstemious in every respect. I have heard him say that he did not know the taste of liquor. At the table he preferred plain food, and a very little satisfied him.

"Under no circumstances would he, as an attorney, take a case he knew to be wrong. Every possible means was used to get at the truth before he would undertake a case. More cases, by his advice, were settled without trial than he carried into the courts; and that, too, without charge. When on one occasion I suggested that he ought to make a charge in such cases, he laughingly answered, 'They wouldn't want to pay me; they don't think I have earned a fee unless I take the case into court and make a speech or two.' When trivial cases were brought to him, such as would most probably be carried no farther than a magistrate's office, and he could not induce a settlement without trial, he would generally refer them to some young attorney, for whom he would speak a good word at the same time. He was ever kind and courteous to these young beginners when he was the opposing counsel. He had a happy knack of setting them at their ease and encouraging them. In consequence he was the favorite of all who came in contact with him. When his heart was in a case he was a powerful advocate. I have heard more than one attorney say that it was little use to expect a favorable verdict in any case where Lincoln was opposing counsel, as his simple statements of the facts had more weight with the jury than those of the witnesses.

"As a student (if such a term could be applied to Mr. Lincoln) one who did not know him might have called him indolent. He would pick up a book and run rapidly over the pages, pausing here and there. At the end of an hour—never, as I remember, more than two or three hours—he would close the book, stretch himself out on the office lounge, and with hands under his head and eyes shut he would digest the mental food he had just taken.

"In the spring of 1846, war between the United States and Mexico broke out. Mr. Lincoln was opposed to the war. He looked upon it as unnecessary and unjust. Volunteers were called for. John J. Hardin, who lost his life in that war, and Edward D. Baker, who was killed at Ball's Bluff during our Civil War—both Whigs—were engaged in raising regiments. Meetings were held and speeches made. At one of them, after Baker and others had spoken, Lincoln, who was in the audience, was called for, and the call was repeated until at last he ascended the platform. He thanked the audience for the compliment paid him in the wish they had expressed to hear him talk, and said he would gladly make them a speech if he had anything to say. But he was not going into the war; and as he was not going himself, he did not feel like telling others to go. He would simply leave it to each individual to do as he thought his duty called for. After a few more remarks, and a story 'with a nib to it,' he bowed himself off the platform.

"About a year after this, Mr. Lincoln was seeking to be nominated as a candidate for Congress. Finding the writing of letters (at his dictation) to influential men in the different counties and even precincts of the district somewhat burdensome, I suggested printing circulars. He objected, on the ground that a printed letter would not have the same effect that a written one would; the latter had the appearance of personality, it was more flattering to the receiver, and would more certainly gain his assistance, or at least his good-will. In discussing the probabilities of his nomination, I remarked that there was so much unfairness, if not downright trickery, used that it appeared to me almost useless to seek a nomination without resort to similar means. His reply was: 'I want to be nominated; I would like to go to Congress; but if I cannot do so by fair means, I prefer to stay at home.' He was nominated, and in the following fall was elected by a majority over three times as large as the district had ever before given.

"Mr. Lincoln, like many others in their callow days, scribbled verses; and so far as I was capable of judging, their quality was above the average. It was accidentally that I learned this. In arranging the books and papers in the office, I found two or three quires of letter-paper stitched together in book form, nearly filled with poetical effusions in Mr. Lincoln's handwriting, and evidently original. I looked through them somewhat hurriedly, and when Lincoln came in I showed him the manuscript, asking him if it was his. His response was, 'Where did you find it?' and rolling it up, he put it in his coat-tail pocket; and I saw it no more. Afterwards, in speaking of the matter to Mr. Lincoln's partner, he said, 'I believe he has at times scribbled some verses; but he is, I think, somewhat unwilling to have it known.'"

Lincoln's love of poetry is further shown by the following incident, related by a gentleman who visited the old law-office of Lincoln & Herndon, at Springfield. He says: "I took up carelessly, as I stood thinking, a handsome octavo volume lying on the office table. It opened so persistently at one place, as I handled it, that I looked to see what it was, and found that somebody had thoroughly thumbed the pages of 'Don Juan.' I knew Mr. Herndon was not a man to dwell on it, and it darted through my mind that perhaps it had been a favorite with Lincoln. 'Did Mr. Lincoln ever read this book?' I said, hurriedly. 'That book!' said Herndon, looking up from his writing and taking it out of my hand. 'Oh, yes; he read it often. It is the office copy.'" Lincoln was so fond of the book that he kept it ready to his hand.

Mr. John T. Stuart, Lincoln's first law-partner, says of him that his accounts were correctly kept, but in a manner peculiar to himself. Soon after their law-partnership was formed, Mr. Stuart was elected to Congress, thereafter spending much of his time in Washington. Lincoln conducted the business of the firm in his absence. When Mr. Stuart reached home, at the close of the first session of Congress, Lincoln proceeded to give him an account of the earnings of the office during his absence. The charges for fees and entry of receipts of money were not in an account book, but stowed away in a drawer in Lincoln's desk, among the papers in each case. He proceeded to lay the papers before Mr. Stuart, taking up each case by itself. The account would run in this way:

Fees charged in this case...............$

Amount collected.......................$

Stuart's half..........................$

The half that belonged to Mr. Stuart would invariably accompany the papers in the case. Lincoln had the reputation of being very moderate in his charges. He was never grasping, and seemed incapable of believing that his services could be worth much to anyone.

One of the most famous cases in which Lincoln engaged was that of William D. Armstrong, son of Jack and Hannah Armstrong of New Salem, the child whom Lincoln had rocked in the cradle while Mrs. Armstrong attended to other household duties. Jack Armstrong, it will be remembered, was an early friend of Lincoln's, whom he had beaten in a wrestling-match on his first arrival in New Salem. He and his wife had from that time treated the youth with the utmost kindness, giving him a home when he was out of work, and showing him every kindness it was in their power to offer.

Lincoln never forgot his debt of gratitude to them; and when Hannah, now a widow, wrote to him of the peril her boy was in, and besought him to help them in their extremity, he replied promptly that he would do what he could. The circumstances were these: "In the summer of 1857, at a camp-meeting in Mason County, one Metzgar was most brutally murdered. The affray took place about half a mile from the place of worship, near some wagons loaded with liquor and provisions. Two men, James H. Norris and William D. Armstrong, were indicted for the crime. Norris was tried in Mason County, convicted of manslaughter, and sentenced to the penitentiary for a term of eight years. The popular feeling being very high against Armstrong in Mason County, he took a change of venue to Cass County, and was there tried (at Beardstown) in the spring of 1858. Hitherto Armstrong had had the services of two able counsellors; but now their efforts were supplemented by those of a most determined and zealous volunteer. The case was so clear against the accused that defense seemed almost useless. The strongest evidence was that of a man who swore that at eleven o'clock at night he saw Armstrong strike the deceased on the head; that the moon was shining brightly, and was nearly full; and that its position in the sky was just about that of the sun at ten o'clock in the morning, and by it he saw Armstrong give the mortal blow." This was fatal, unless the effect could be broken by contradiction or impeachment. Lincoln quietly looked up an almanac, and found that at the time this witness declared the moon to have been shining with full light there was no moon at all. Lincoln made the closing argument. "At first," says Mr. Walker, one of the counsel associated with him, "he spoke very slowly and carefully, reviewing the testimony and pointing out its contradictions, discrepancies and impossibilities. When he had thus prepared the way, he called for an almanac, and showed that at the hour at which the principal witness swore he had seen, by the light of the full moon, the mortal blow given, *there was no moon*. The last fifteen minutes of his speech were as eloquent as I ever heard; and such were the power and earnestness with which he spoke to that jury, that all sat as if entranced, and, when he was through, found relief in a gush of tears." Said one of the prosecutors: "He took the jury by storm. There were tears in Mr. Lincoln's eyes while he spoke, but they were genuine. His sympathies were fully enlisted in favor of the young man, and his terrible sincerity could not help but arouse the same passion in the jury. I have said a hundred times that it was Lincoln's speech that saved that man from the gallows." "Armstrong was not cleared by any want of testimony against him, but by the irresistible appeal of Mr. Lincoln in his favor," says Mr. Shaw, one of the associates in the prosecution. His mother, who sat near during Lincoln's appeal, says: "He told the stories about our first acquaintance, and what I did for him and how I did it. Lincoln said to me, 'Hannah, your son will be cleared before sundown.' He and the other lawyers addressed the jury, and closed the case. I went down to Thompson's pasture. Stator came to me and told me that my son was cleared and a free man. I went up to the court-house; the jury shook hands with me, so did the court, so did Lincoln. We were all affected, and tears were in Lincoln's eyes. He then remarked to me, 'Hannah, what did I tell you? I pray to God that William may be a good boy hereafter; that this lesson may prove in the end a good lesson to him and to all.' After the trial was over, Lincoln came down to where I was in Beardstown. I asked him what he charged me; told him I was poor. He said, 'Why, Hannah, I shan't charge you a cent—never. Anything I can do for you I will do willingly and without charges.' He wrote to me about some land which some men were trying to get from me, and said, 'Hannah, they can't get your land. Let them try it in the Circuit Court, and then you appeal it. Bring it to the Supreme Court, and Herndon and I will attend to it for nothing.'"

Lincoln regarded himself not only as the legal adviser of unfortunate people, but as their friend and protector; and he would never press them for pay for his services. A client named Cogdal was unfortunate in business, and gave Lincoln a note in payment of legal fees. Soon afterwards he met with an accident by which he lost a hand. Meeting Lincoln some time after, on the steps of the State House, the kind lawyer asked him how he was getting along. "Badly enough," replied Mr. Cogdal. "I am both broken up in business and crippled." Then he added, "I have been thinking about that note of yours." Lincoln, who had probably known all about Mr. Cogdal's troubles, and had prepared himself for the meeting, took out his pocket-book, and saying, with a laugh, "Well you needn't think any more about it," handed him the note. Mr. Cogdal protesting, Lincoln said, "Even if you had the money, I would not take it," and hurried away.

Mr. G.L. Austin thus describes an incident of Lincoln's career at the bar: "Mr. Lincoln was once associated with Mr. Leonard Swett in defending a man accused of murder. He listened to the testimony which witness after witness gave against his client, until his honest heart could stand it no longer; then, turning to his associate, he said: 'Swett, the man is guilty; you defend him; I can't.' Swett did defend him, and the man was acquitted. When proffered his share of the large fee, Lincoln most emphatically declined it, on the ground that 'all of it belonged to Mr. Swett, whose ardor and eloquence saved a guilty man from justice.'"

At a term of court in Logan County, a man named Hoblit had brought suit against a man named Farmer. The suit had been appealed from a justice of the peace, and Lincoln knew nothing of it until he was retained by Hoblit to try the case in the Circuit Court. G.A. Gridley, then of Bloomington, appeared for the defendant. Judge Treat, afterwards on the United States bench, was the presiding judge at the trial. Lincoln's client went upon the witness stand and testified to the account he had against the defendant, gave the amount due after allowing all credits and set-offs, and swore positively that it had not been paid. The attorney for the defendant simply produced a receipt in full, signed by Hoblit prior to the beginning of the case. Hoblit had to admit the signing of the receipt, but told Lincoln he "supposed the cuss had lost it." Lincoln at once arose and left the court-room. The Judge told the parties to proceed with the case; and Lincoln not appearing, Judge Treat directed a bailiff to go to the hotel and call him. The bailiff ran across the street to the hotel, and found Lincoln sitting in the office with his feet on the stove, apparently in a deep study, when he interrupted him with: "Mr. Lincoln, the Judge wants you." "Oh, does he?" replied Lincoln. "Well, you go back and tell the Judge I cannot come. Tell him I have to *wash my hands*." The bailiff returned with the message, and Lincoln's client suffered a non-suit. It was Lincoln's way of saying he wanted nothing more to do with such a case.

Lincoln would never advise clients into unwise or unjust lawsuits. He would always sacrifice his own interests, and refuse a retainer, rather than be a party to a case which did not command the approval of his sense of justice. He was once waited upon by a lady who held a real-estate claim which she desired to have him prosecute, putting into his hands, with the necessary papers, a check for two hundred and fifty dollars as a retaining fee. Lincoln said he would look the case over, and asked her to call again the next day. Upon presenting herself, he told her that he had gone through the papers very carefully, and was obliged to tell her frankly that there was "not a peg" to hang her claim upon, and he could not conscientiously advise her to bring an action. The lady was satisfied, and, thanking him, rose to go. "Wait," said Lincoln, fumbling in his vest pocket; "here is the check you left with me." "But, Mr. Lincoln," returned the lady, "I think you have earned that." "No, no," he responded, handing it back to her; "that would not be right. I can't take pay for doing my duty." To a would-be client who had carefully stated his case, to which Lincoln had listened with the closest attention, he said: "Yes, there is no reasonable doubt that I can gain your case for you. I can set a whole neighborhood at loggerheads; I can distress a widowed mother and her six fatherless children, and thereby get for you six hundred dollars, which rightfully belongs, it appears to me, as much to the woman and her children as it does to you. You must remember that some things that are *legally* right are not *morally* right. I shall not take your case, but will give you a little advice, for which I will charge you nothing. You seem to be a sprightly, energetic man. I would advise you to try your hand at *making six hundred dollars some other way*."

Senator McDonald states that he saw a jury trial in Illinois, at which Lincoln defended an old man charged with assault and battery. No blood had been spilled, but there was malice in the prosecution, and the chief witness was eager to make the most of it. On cross-examination, Lincoln "gave him rope" and drew him out; asked him how long the fight lasted and how much ground it covered. The witness thought the fight must have lasted half an hour and covered an acre of ground. Lincoln called his attention to the fact that nobody was hurt, and then with an inimitable air asked him if he didn't think it was "a mighty small crop for an acre of ground." The jury rejected the prosecution's claim.

Many of the stories told of Lincoln at the bar are extremely ridiculous, and represent him in anything but a dignified light. But they are a part of the character of the man, and should be given wherever there is reason to suppose they are genuine. Besides, they are usually full of a humor that is irresistible. Such an incident is given by the Hon. Lawrence Weldon, Lincoln's old friend and legal associate in Illinois. "I can see him now," says Judge Weldon, "through the decaying memories of thirty years, standing in the corner of the old court-room, and as I approached him with a paper I did not understand, he said: 'Wait until I fix this plug for my *gallus*, and I will pitch into that like a dog at a root.' While speaking, he was busily engaged in trying to connect his suspender with his trousers by making a 'plug' perform the function of a button. Lincoln liked old-fashioned words, and never failed to use them if they could be sustained as proper. He was probably accustomed to say 'gallows,' and he never adopted the modern word 'suspender.'"

On a certain occasion Lincoln appeared at the trial of a case in which his friend Judge Logan was his opponent. It was a suit between two farmers who had had a disagreement over a horse-trade. On the day of the trial, Mr. Logan, having bought a new shirt, open in the back, with a huge standing collar, dressed himself in extreme haste, and put on the shirt with the *bosom at the back*, a linen coat concealing the blunder. He dazed the jury with his knowledge of "horse points"; and as the day was sultry, took off his coat and "summed" up in his shirt-sleeves. Lincoln, sitting behind him, took in the situation, and when his turn came he remarked to the jury: "Gentlemen, Mr. Logan has been trying for over an hour to make you believe he knows more about a horse than these honest old farmers who are witnesses. He has quoted largely from his 'horse doctor,' and now, gentlemen, I submit to you," (here he lifted Logan out of his chair, and turned him with his back to the jury and the crowd, at the same time flapping up the enormous standing collar) "what dependence can you place in his horse knowledge, when he *has not sense enough to put on his shirt?*" Roars of laughter greeted this exposition, and the verdict was given to Lincoln.

The preceding incident leads to another, in which Lincoln himself figures as a horse-trader. The scene is a very humorous one; and, as usual in an encounter of wit, Lincoln came out ahead. He and a certain Judge once got to bantering each other about trading horses; and it was agreed that the next morning at nine o'clock they should make a trade, the horses to be unseen up to that hour,—and no backing out, under a forfeit of twenty-five dollars. At the hour appointed the Judge came up, leading the sorriest looking specimen of a nag ever seen in those parts. In a few minutes Lincoln was seen approaching with a *wooden saw-horse* upon his shoulders. Great were the shouts and the laughter of the crowd; and these increased, when Lincoln, surveying the Judge's animal, set down his saw-horse, and exclaimed: "Well, Judge, this is the first time I ever *got the worst of it* in a horse-trade!"

There has been much discussion as to Lincoln's rank and ability as a lawyer. Opinion among his contemporaries seems to have been somewhat divided. Mr. Herndon felt warranted in saying that he was at the same time a very great and a very insignificant lawyer. His mind was logical and direct. Generalities and platitudes had no charm for him. He had the ability to seize the strong points of a case and present them with clearness and compactness. His power of comparison was great. He rarely failed in a legal discussion to use this mode of reasoning. Yet he knew practically nothing of the rules of evidence, of pleading, of practice, as laid down in the text-books, and seemed to care little about them. Sometimes he lost cases of the plainest justice which the most inexperienced lawyer could have won. He looked upon two things as essential to his success in a case. One was time; he was slow in reasoning and slow in speech. The other was confidence that the cause he represented was just. "If either of these were lacking," said Mr. Herndon, "Lincoln was the weakest man at the bar. When it fell to him to address the jury he often relied absolutely on the inspiration of the moment,—but he seldom failed to carry his point."

Among the great number of opinions of Lincoln's rank as a lawyer, expressed by his professional brethren, a few may properly be given in closing this chapter, which is devoted chiefly to Mr. Lincoln's professional career. First we may quote the brief but emphatic words of the distinguished jurist, Judge Sidney Breese, Chief Justice of Illinois, who said: "For my single self, I have for a quarter of a century regarded Mr. Lincoln as the finest lawyer I ever knew, and of a professional bearing so high-toned and honorable, as justly, and without derogating from the claims of others, entitling him to be presented to the profession as a model well worthy of the closest imitation."

Another distinguished Chief Justice, Hon. John Dean Caton; says: "In 1840 or 1841, I met Mr. Lincoln, and was for the first time associated with him in a professional way. We attended the Circuit Court at Pontiac, Judge Treat presiding, where we were both engaged in the defense of a man by the name of Lavinia. That was the first and only time I was associated with him at the bar. He practiced in a circuit that was beyond the one in which I practiced, and consequently we were not brought together much in the practice of the law. He stood well at the bar from the beginning. I was a younger man, but an older lawyer. He was not admitted to the bar till after I was. I was not closely connected with him. Indeed, I did not meet him often, professionally, until I went on the bench in 1842; and he was then in full practice before the Supreme Court, and continued to practice there regularly at every term until he was elected President. Mr. Lincoln understood the relations of things, and hence his deductions were rarely wrong from any given state of facts. So he applied the principles of law to the transactions of men with great clearness and precision. He was a close reasoner. He reasoned by analogy, and enforced his views by apt illustration. His mode of speaking was generally of a plain and unimpassioned character, and yet he was the author of some of the most beautiful and eloquent passages in our language, which, if collected, would form a valuable contribution to American literature. The most punctilious honor ever marked his professional and private life."

The Hon. Thomas Drummond, for many years Judge of the United States District Court at Chicago, said: "It is not necessary to claim for Mr. Lincoln attributes or qualities which he did not possess. He had enough to entitle him to the love and respect and esteem of all who knew him. He was not skilled in the learning of the schools, and his knowledge of the law was acquired almost entirely by his own unaided study and by the practice of his profession. Nature gave him great clearness and acuteness of intellect and a vast fund of common-sense; and as a consequence of these he had much sagacity in judging of the motives and springs of human conduct. With a voice by no means pleasing, and, indeed, when excited, in its shrill tones sometimes almost disagreeable; without any of the personal graces of the orator; without much in the outward man indicating superiority of intellect; without great quickness of perception,—still, his mind was so vigorous, his comprehension so exact and clear, and his judgments so sure, that he easily mastered the intricacies of his profession, and became one of the ablest reasoners and most impressive speakers at our bar. With a probity of character known to all, with an intuitive insight into the human heart, with a clearness of statement which was itself an argument, with an uncommon power and facility of illustration, often, it is true, of a plain and homely kind, and with that sincerity and earnestness of manner to carry conviction, he was perhaps one of the most successful jury lawyers we have ever had in the State. He always tried a case fairly and honestly. He never intentionally misrepresented the testimony of a witness or the arguments of an opponent. He met both squarely, and, if he could not explain the one or answer the other, substantially admitted it. He never misstated the law according to his own intelligent view of it. Such was the transparent candor and integrity of his nature that he could not well or strongly argue a side or a cause that he thought wrong. Of course, he felt it his duty to say what could be said, and to leave the decision to others; but there could be seen in such cases the inward struggle in his own mind. In trying a cause he might occasionally dwell too long or give too much importance to an inconsiderable point; but this was the exception, and generally he went straight to the citadel of a cause or a question, and struck home there, knowing if that were won the outwork would necessarily fall. He could hardly be called very learned in his profession, and yet he rarely tried a cause without fully understanding the law applicable to it. I have no hesitation in saying he was one of the ablest lawyers I have ever known. If he was forcible before the jury he was equally so with the court. He detected with unerring sagacity the marked points of his opponents' arguments, and pressed his own views with overwhelming force. His efforts were quite unequal, and it may have been that he would not on some occasions strike one as at all remarkable; but let him be thoroughly aroused, let him feel that he was right and that some great principle was involved in his case, and he would come out with an earnestness of conviction, a power of argument, and a wealth of illustration, that I have never seen surpassed.... Simple in his habits, without pretensions of any kind, and distrustful of himself, he was willing to yield precedence and place to others, when he ought to have claimed them for himself. He rarely, if ever, sought office except at the urgent solicitations of his friends. In substantiation of this, I may be permitted to relate an incident which now occurs to me. Prior to his nomination for the Presidency, and, indeed, when his name was first mentioned in connection with that high office, I broached the subject upon the occasion of meeting him here. His response was, 'I hope they will select some abler man than myself.'"

Mr. C.S. Parks, a lawyer associated with Lincoln for some years, furnishes the following testimony concerning his more prominent qualities: "I have often said that for a man who was for a quarter of a century both a lawyer and a politician he was the most *honest* man I ever knew. He was not only morally honest, but intellectually so. He could not reason falsely; if he attempted it, he failed. In politics he would never try to mislead. At the bar, when he thought he was wrong, he was the weakest lawyer I ever saw."

Hon. David Davis, afterwards Associate Justice U.S. Supreme Court and U.S. Senator, presided over the Eighth Judicial Circuit of Illinois during the remaining years of Lincoln's practice at the bar. He was united to Lincoln in close bonds of friendship, and year after year travelled with him over the circuit, put up with him at the same hotels, and often occupied the same room with him. "This simple life," says Judge Davis, "Mr. Lincoln loved, preferring it to the practice of the law in the city. In all the elements that constitute the great lawyer, he had few equals. He seized the strong points of a cause, and presented them with clearness and great compactness. He read law-books but little, except when the cause in hand made it necessary; yet he was unusually self-reliant, depending on his own resources, and rarely consulting his brother lawyers either on the management of his case or the legal questions involved. He was the fairest and most accommodating of practitioners, granting all favors which he could do consistently with his duty to his client, and rarely availing himself of an unwary oversight of his adversary. He hated wrong and oppression everywhere, and many a man, whose fraudulent conduct was undergoing review in a court of justice, has withered under his terrific indignation and rebuke."

Mr. Speed says: "As a lawyer, after his first year he was acknowledged to be among the best in the State. His analytical powers were marvellous. He always resolved every question into its primary elements, and gave up every point on his own side that did not seem to be invulnerable. One would think, to hear him present his case in the court, he was giving his case away. He would concede point after point to his adversary. But he always reserved a point upon which he claimed a decision in his favor, and his concessions magnified the strength of his claim. He rarely failed in gaining his cases in court."

The special characteristics of Lincoln's practice at the bar are thus ably summed up: "He did not make a specialty of criminal cases, but was engaged frequently in them. He could not be called a great lawyer, measured by the extent of his acquirement of legal knowledge; he was not an encyclopædia of cases; but in the clear perception of legal principles, with natural capacity to apply them, he had great ability. He was not a case lawyer, but a lawyer who dealt in the deep philosophy of the law. He always knew the cases which might be quoted as absolute authority, but beyond that he contented himself in the application and discussion of general principles. In the trial of a case he moved cautiously. He never examined or cross-examined a witness to the detriment of his side. If the witness told the truth, he was safe from his attacks; but woe betide the unlucky and dishonest individual who suppressed the truth or colored it against Mr. Lincoln's side. His speeches to the jury were very effective specimens of forensic oratory. He talked the vocabulary of the people, and the jury understood every point he made and every thought he uttered. I never saw him when I thought he was trying to make an effort for the sake of mere display; but his imagination was simple and pure in the richest gems of true eloquence. He constructed short sentences of small words, and never wearied the minds of the jury by mazes of elaboration."

CHAPTER IX

At the death of Henry Clay, in June, 1852, Lincoln was invited to deliver a eulogy on Clay's life and character before the citizens of Springfield. He complied with the request on the 16th of July. The same season he made a speech before the Scott Club of Springfield, in reply to the addresses with which Douglas had opened his extended campaign of that summer, at Richmond, Virginia. Except on these two occasions, Lincoln took but little part in politics until the passage of the Nebraska Bill by Congress in 1854. The enactment of this measure impelled him to take a firmer stand upon the question of slavery than he had yet assumed. He had been opposed to the institution on grounds of sentiment since his boyhood; now he determined to fight it from principle. Mr. Herndon states that Lincoln really became an anti-slavery man in 1831, during his visit to New Orleans, where he was deeply affected by the horrors of the traffic in human beings. On one occasion he saw a slave, a beautiful mulatto girl, sold at auction. She was felt over, pinched, and trotted around to show bidders she was sound. Lincoln walked away from the scene with a feeling of deep abhorrence. He said to John Hanks, *"If I ever get a chance to hit that institution, John, I'll hit it hard!"* Again, in the summer of 1841, he was painfully impressed by a scene witnessed during his journey home from Kentucky, described in a letter written at the time to the sister of his friend Speed, in which he says: "A fine example was presented on board the boat for contemplating the effect of conditions upon human happiness. A man had purchased twelve negroes in different parts of Kentucky, and was taking them to a farm in the South. They were chained six and six together; a small iron clevis was around the left wrist of each, and this was fastened to the main chain by a shorter one, at a convenient distance from the others, so that the negroes were strung together like so many fish upon a trot-line. In this condition they were being separated forever from the scenes of their childhood, their friends, their fathers and mothers, brothers and sisters, and many of them from their wives and children, and going into perpetual slavery."

Judge Gillespie records a conversation which he had with Lincoln in 1850 on the slavery question, remarking by way of introduction that the subject of slavery was the only one on which he (Lincoln) was apt to become excited. "I recollect meeting him once at Shelbyville," says Judge Gillespie, "when he remarked that something must be done or slavery would overrun the whole country. He said there were about six hundred thousand non-slaveholding whites in Kentucky to about thirty-three thousand slaveholders; that in the convention then recently held it was expected that the delegates would represent these classes about in proportion to their respective numbers; but when the convention assembled, there was not a single representative of the non-slaveholding class; everyone was in the interest of the slaveholders; 'and,' said he, 'the thing is spreading like wildfire over the country. In a few years we will be ready to accept the institution in Illinois, and the whole country will adopt it.' I asked him to what he attributed the change that was going on in public opinion. He said he had recently put that question to a Kentuckian, who answered by saying, 'You might have any amount of land, money in your pocket, or bank-stock, and while travelling around nobody would be any wiser; but if you had a darkey trudging at your heels, everybody would see him and know that you owned a slave. It is the most ostentatious way of displaying property in the world; if a young man goes courting, the only inquiry is as to how many negroes he owns.' The love for slave property was swallowing up every other mercenary possession. Its ownership not only betokened the possession of wealth, but indicated the gentleman of leisure who scorned labor. These things Mr. Lincoln regarded as highly pernicious to the thoughtless and giddy young men who were too much inclined to look upon work as vulgar and ungentlemanly. He was much excited, and said with great earnestness that this spirit ought to be met, and if possible checked; that slavery was a great and crying injustice, an enormous national crime, and we could not expect to escape punishment for it. I asked him how he would proceed in his efforts to check the spread of slavery. He confessed he did not see his way clearly; but I think he made up his mind that from that time he would oppose slavery actively. I know that Lincoln always contended that no man had any right, other than what mere brute force gave him, to hold a slave. He used to say it was singular that the courts would hold that a man never lost his right to property that had been stolen from him, but that he instantly *lost his right to himself* if he was stolen. Lincoln always contended that the cheapest way of getting rid of slavery was for the nation to buy the slaves and set them free."

While in Congress, Lincoln had declared himself plainly as opposed to slavery; and in public speeches not less than private conversations he had not hesitated to express his convictions on the subject. In 1850 he said to Major Stuart: "The time will soon come when we must all be Democrats or Abolitionists. When that time comes, *my mind is made up*. The slavery question cannot be compromised." The hour had now struck in which Lincoln was to espouse with his whole heart and soul that cause for which finally he was to lay down his life. In the language of Mr. Arnold, "He had bided his time. He had waited until the harvest was ripe. With unerring sagacity he realized that the triumph of freedom was at hand. He entered upon the conflict with the deepest conviction that the perpetuity of the Republic required the extinction of slavery. So, adopting as his motto, 'A house divided against itself cannot stand,' he girded himself for the contest. The years from 1854 to 1860 were on his part years of constant, active, and unwearied effort. His position in the State of Illinois was central and commanding. He was now to become the recognized leader of the anti-slavery party in the Northwest, and in all the Valley of the Mississippi. Lincoln was a practical statesman, never attempting the impossible, but seeking to do the best thing practicable under existing circumstances. He knew that prohibition in the territories would result in no more slave states and no slave territory. And now, when the repeal of the Missouri Compromise shattered all parties into fragments, he came forward to build up the Free Soil party and threw into the conflict all his strength and vigor. The conviction of his duty was deep and sincere. Hence he pleaded the cause of liberty with an energy, ability, and power which rapidly gained for him a national reputation. Conscious of the greatness of his cause, inspired by a genuine love of liberty, animated and made strong by the moral sublimity of the conflict, he solemnly announced his determination to speak for freedom and against slavery until—in his own words—wherever the Federal Government has power, 'the sun shall shine, the rain shall fall, and the wind shall blow upon no man who goes forth to unrequited toil.'"

The absorbing political topic in 1855 was the contest in Kansas, which proved the battle-ground for the struggle over the introduction of slavery into the territories north of the line established by the "Missouri Compromise." Lincoln's views on the subject are defined in a notable letter to his friend Joshua Speed, a resident of Kentucky. The following passages show, in Lincoln's own words, where he stood on the slavery question at this memorable epoch:

SPRINGFIELD, AUGUST 24, 1855.

Dear Speed:—You know what a poor correspondent I am. Ever since I received your very agreeable letter of the twenty-second of May, I have been intending to write you in answer to it. You suggest that in political action now, you and I would differ. You know I dislike slavery, and you fully admit the abstract wrong of it. So far, there is no cause of difference. But you say that sooner than yield your legal right to the slave, especially at the bidding of those who are not themselves interested, you would see the Union dissolved. I am not aware that any one is bidding you yield that right—very certainly I am not. I leave the matter entirely to yourself. I also acknowledge your rights and my obligations under the Constitution, in regard to your slaves. I confess I hate to see the poor creatures hunted down, and caught, and carried back to their stripes and unrequited toil; but I bite my lip and keep quiet. In 1841 you and I had together a tedious low-water trip on a steamboat from Louisville to St. Louis. You may remember, as I well do, that from Louisville to the mouth of the Ohio, there were on board ten or a dozen slaves, shackled together with irons. That sight was a continual torment to me; and I see something like it every time I touch the Ohio, or any other slave border. It is not fair for you to assume that I have no interest in a thing which has, and continually exercises, the power of making me miserable. You ought rather to appreciate how much the great body of the people of the North do crucify their feelings in order to maintain their loyalty to the Constitution and the Union.

I do oppose the extension of slavery, because my judgment and feelings so prompt me; and I am under no obligations to the contrary. If for this you and I must differ, differ we must. You say, if you were President you would send an army and hang the leaders of the Missouri outrages upon the Kansas elections; still, if Kansas fairly votes herself a slave State, she must be admitted, or the Union must be dissolved. But how if she votes herself a slave State unfairly—that is, by the very means for which you would hang men? Must she still be admitted, or the Union dissolved? That will be the phase of the question when it first becomes a practical one. In your assumption that there may be a fair decision of the slavery question in Kansas, I plainly see you and I would differ about the Nebraska law. I look upon that enactment not as a law but a violence from the beginning. It was conceived in violence, passed in violence, is maintained in violence, and is being executed in violence. I say it was conceived in violence, because the destruction of the Missouri Compromise under the Constitution was nothing less than violence. It was passed in violence, because it could not have passed at all but for the votes of many members in violent disregard of the known will of their constituents. It is maintained in violence, because the elections since clearly demand its repeal; and the demand is openly disregarded. That Kansas will form a slave constitution, and with it will ask to be admitted into the Union, I take to be already a settled question, and so settled by the very means you so pointedly condemn. By every principle of law ever held by any court, North or South, every negro taken to Kansas is free; yet in utter disregard of this—in the spirit of violence merely—that beautiful Legislature gravely passes a law to hang any man who shall venture to inform a negro of his legal rights. This is the substance and real object of the law. If, like Haman, they should hang upon the gallows of their own building, I shall not be among the mourners for their fate. In my humble sphere I shall advocate the restoration of the Missouri Compromise so long as Kansas remains a Territory; and, when, by all these foul means, it seeks to come into the Union as a slave State, I shall oppose it.... You inquire where I now stand. That is a disputed point. I think I am a Whig; but others say there are no Whigs, and that I am an Abolitionist. When I was in Washington I voted for the Wilmot Proviso as good as forty times, and I never heard of any attempt to unwhig me for that. I now do no more than oppose the extension of slavery. I am not a Know-Nothing—that is certain. How could I be? How can anyone who abhors the oppression of the negroes be in favor of degrading classes of white people? Our progress in degeneracy appears to me to be pretty rapid. As a nation we began by declaring that 'all men are created equal.' We now practically read it 'all men are created equal, except negroes.' When the Know-Nothings get control, it will read, 'all men are created equals, except negroes and foreigners and Catholics.' When it comes to that, I should prefer emigrating to some other country where they make no pretense of loving liberty—to Russia for instance, where despotism can be taken pure, and without the base alloy of hypocrisy.

Your friend forever,
A. LINCOLN.

Lincoln was soon accorded an opportunity to cross swords again with his former political antagonist, Douglas, who had lately come from his place in the Senate Chamber at Washington, where he had carried the obnoxious Nebraska Bill against the utmost efforts of Chase, Seward, Sumner, and others, to defeat it. As Mr. Arnold narrates the incident,—"When, late in September, 1854, Douglas returned to Illinois he was received with a storm of indignation which would have crushed a man of less power and will. A bold and courageous leader, conscious of his personal power over his party, he bravely met the storm and sought to allay it. In October, 1854, the State Fair being then in session at Springfield, with a great crowd of people in attendance from all parts of the State, Douglas went there and made an elaborate and able speech in defense of the repeal of the Missouri Compromise. Lincoln was called upon by the opponents of this repeal to reply, and he did so with a power which he never surpassed and had never before equalled. All other issues which had divided the people were as chaff, and were scattered to the winds by the intense agitation which arose on the question of extending slavery, not merely into free territory, but into territory which had been declared free by solemn compact. Lincoln's speech occupied more than three hours in delivery, and during all that time he held the vast crowd in the deepest attention."

Mr. Herndon said of this event: "This anti-Nebraska speech of Mr. Lincoln was the profoundest that he made in his whole life. He felt burning upon his soul the truths which he uttered, and all present felt that he was true to his own soul. His feelings once or twice came near stifling utterance. He quivered with emotion. He attacked the Nebraska Bill with such warmth and energy that all felt that a man of strength was its enemy, and that he intended to blast it, if he could, by strong and manly efforts. He was most successful, and the house approved his triumph by loud and continued huzzas, while women waved their white handkerchiefs in token of heartfelt assent. Douglas felt the sting, and he frequently interrupted Mr. Lincoln; his friends felt that he was crushed by the powerful argument of his opponent. The Nebraska Bill was shivered, and, like a tree of the forest, was torn and rent asunder by hot bolts of truth. At the conclusion of this speech, every man, woman, and child felt that it was unanswerable." In speaking of the same occasion, Mr. Lamon says: "Many fine speeches were made upon the one absorbing topic; but it is no shame to any one of these orators that their really impressive speeches were but slightly appreciated or long remembered beside Mr. Lincoln's splendid and enduring performance,— enduring in the memory of his auditors, although preserved upon no written or printed page."

A few days after this encounter, Douglas spoke in Peoria, and was followed by Lincoln with the same crushing arguments that had served him at the State Fair, and with the same triumphant effect. His Peoria speech was written out by him and published after its delivery. A few specimens will show its style and argumentative power.

> Argue as you will, and as long as you will, this is the naked front and aspect of the measure; and in this aspect it could not but produce agitation. Slavery is founded in the selfishness of man's nature; opposition to it, in his love of justice. These principles are an eternal antagonism; and when brought into collision so fiercely as slavery extension brings them, shocks, throes, and convulsions must ceaselessly follow. Repeal the Missouri Compromise; repeal all compromises; repeal the Declaration of Independence; repeal all past history,—you still cannot repeal human nature. It still will be the abundance of man's heart, that slavery extension is wrong; and out of the abundance of his heart, his mouth will continue to speak.... When Mr. Pettit, in connection with his support of the Nebraska Bill, called the Declaration of Independence 'a self-evident lie,' he only did what consistency and candor require all other Nebraska men to do. Of the forty-odd Nebraska Senators who sat present and heard him, no one rebuked him.... If this had been said among Marion's men, Southerners though they were, what would have become of the man who said it? If this had been said to the men who captured Andre, the man who said it would probably have been hung sooner than Andre was. If it had been said in old Independence Hall seventy-eight years ago, the very doorkeeper would have throttled the man, and thrust him into the street.... Thus we see the plain, unmistakable spirit of that early age towards slavery was hostility to the principle, and toleration only by necessity. But now it is to be transformed into a 'sacred right.' Nebraska brings it forth, places it on the high road to extension and perpetuity, and with a pat on its back says to it: 'Go, and God speed you.' Henceforth it is to be the chief jewel of the nation, the very figurehead of the ship of state. Little by little, but steadily as man's march to the grave, we have been giving the old for the new faith. Nearly eighty years ago we began by declaring that all men are created equal; but now from that beginning we have run down to

that other declaration, 'that for *some* men to enslave others is a sacred right of self-government.' ... In our greedy chase to make profit of the negro, let us beware lest we cancel and tear to pieces even the white man's charter of freedom.... If all earthly power were given me, I should not know what to do as to the existing institution. My first impulse would be to free all the slaves, and send them to Liberia—to their own native land. But, if they were all landed there in a day, they would all perish in the next ten days; and there are not surplus shipping and surplus money enough to carry them there in many times ten days. What then? Free them all, and keep them among us as underlings? Is it quite certain that this betters their condition? I think I would not hold one in slavery at any rate; yet the point is not clear enough for me to denounce people upon. What next? Free them, and make them politically and socially our equals? My own feelings will not admit of this; and, if mine would, we well know that those of the great mass of white people will not. A universal feeling, whether well or ill founded, cannot be safely disregarded. We cannot then make them equals. It does seem to me that systems of gradual emancipation might be adopted; but, for their tardiness in this, I will not undertake to judge our brethren of the South.

Our Republican robe is soiled—trailed in the dust. Let us repurify it. Let us turn and wash it white, in the spirit, if not the blood, of the Revolution. Let us turn slavery from its claims of 'moral right,' back upon its existing legal rights and its arguments of 'necessity.' Let us return it to the position our fathers gave it, and there let it rest in peace. Let us re-adopt the Declaration of Independence, and with it the practices and policy which harmonize with it. Let North and South—let all Americans—let all lovers of liberty everywhere—join in the great and good work. If we do this, we shall not only have saved the Union, but we shall have so saved it as to make and to keep it forever worthy of the saving. We shall have so saved it that the succeeding millions of free and happy people, the world over, shall rise up and call us blessed to the latest generations.

It was in one of these speeches that Lincoln's power of repartee was admirably illustrated by a most laughable retort made by him to Douglas. Mr. Ralph E. Hoyt, who was present, says: "In the course of his speech, Mr.

Douglas had said, 'The Whigs are all dead.' For some time before speaking, Lincoln sat on the platform with only his homely face visible to the audience above the high desk before him. On being introduced, he arose from his chair and proceeded to straighten himself up. For a few seconds I wondered when and where his head would cease its ascent; but at last it did stop, and 'Honest Old Abe' stood before us. He commenced, 'Fellow-citizens: My friend, Mr. Douglas, made the startling announcement to-day that the Whigs are all dead. If this be so, fellow-citizens, you will now experience the novelty of hearing a speech from a dead man; and I suppose you might properly say, in the language of the old hymn:

"Hark! from the tombs a doleful sound!"'

This set the audience fairly wild with delight, and at once brought them into full confidence with the speaker."

Hating slavery though he did, Lincoln was steadily opposed to all forms of unlawful or violent opposition to it. At about the time of which we are speaking a party of Abolitionists in Illinois had become so excited over the Kansas struggle that they were determined to go to the aid of the Free-State men in that territory. As soon as Lincoln learned of this project, he opposed it strongly. When they spoke to him of "Liberty, Justice, and God's higher law," he replied in this temperate and judicious strain:

Friends, you are in the minority—in a sad minority; and you can't hope to succeed, reasoning from all human experience. You would rebel against the Government, and redden your hands in the blood of your countrymen. If you have the majority, as some of you say you have, you can succeed with the ballot, throwing away the bullet. You can peaceably, then, redeem the Government and preserve the liberties of mankind, through your votes and voice and moral influence. *Let there be peace.* In a democracy, where the majority rule by the ballot through the forms of law, these physical rebellions and bloody resistances are radically wrong, unconstitutional, and are treason. Better bear the ills you have than fly to those you know not of. Our own Declaration of Independence says that governments long established should not be resisted for trivial causes. Revolutionize through the ballot-box, and restore the Government once more to the affection and hearts of men, by making it express, as it was intended to do, the highest spirit of justice and liberty. Your attempt, if there be such, to resist the laws of Kansas by force, will be criminal and wicked; and all your feeble attempts will be follies, and end in bringing sorrow on your heads, and ruin the cause you would freely die to preserve.

No doubt was felt of Lincoln's sympathies; indeed, he is known to have contributed money to the Free-State cause. But it is noticeable that in this exciting episode he showed the same coolness, wisdom, moderation, love of law and order that so strongly characterized his conduct in the stormier period of the Civil War, and without which it is doubtful if he would have been able to save the nation.

Some interesting recollections of the events of this stirring period, and of Lincoln's part in them, are given by Mr. Paul Selby, for a long time editor of the "State Journal" at Springfield, and one of Lincoln's old-time friends and political associates. "While Abraham Lincoln had the reputation of being inspired by an almost unbounded ambition," says Mr. Selby, "it was of that generous quality which characterized his other attributes, and often led him voluntarily to restrain its gratification in deference to the conflicting aspirations of his friends. All remember his magnanimity towards Col. Edward D. Baker, when the latter was elected to Congress from the Springfield District in 1844, and the frankness with which he informed Baker of his own desire to be a candidate in 1846—when for the only time in his life, he was elected to that body. In 1852, Richard Yates of Jacksonville, then recognized as one of the rising young orators and statesmen of the West, was elected to Congress for the second time from the Springfield District. It was during the term following this election that the Kansas-Nebraska issue was precipitated upon the country by Senator Douglas, in the introduction of his bill for the repeal of the Missouri Compromise. Yates, in obedience to his impulses, which were always on the side of freedom, took strong ground against the measure—notwithstanding the fact that a majority of his constituents, though originally Whigs, were strongly conservative, as was generally the case with people who were largely of Kentucky and Tennessee origin. In 1854 the Whig party, which had been divided on the Kansas-Nebraska question, began to manifest symptoms of disintegration; while the Republican party, though not yet known by that name, began to take form. At this time I was publishing a paper at Jacksonville, Yates's home; and although from the date of my connection with it, in 1852, it had not been a political paper, the introduction of a new issue soon led me to take decided ground on the side of free territory. Lincoln at once sprang into prominence as one of the boldest, most vigorous and eloquent opponents of Mr. Douglas's measure, which was construed as a scheme to secure the admission of slavery into all the new territories of the United States. At that time Lincoln's election to a seat in Congress would probably have been very grateful to his ambition, as well as acceptable in a pecuniary point of view; and his prominence and ability had already attracted the eyes of the whole State toward him in a special degree. Having occasion to visit

Springfield one day while the subject of the selection of a candidate was under consideration among the opponents of the Kansas-Nebraska Bill, I encountered Mr. Lincoln on the street. As we walked along, the subject of the choice of a candidate for Congress to succeed Yates came up, when I stated that many of the old-line Whigs and anti-Nebraska men in the western part of the district were looking to him as an available leader. While he seemed gratified by the compliment, he said: 'No; Yates has been a true and faithful Representative, and should be returned.' Yates was renominated; and although he ran ahead of his ticket, yet so far had the disorganization of the Whig party then progressed, and so strong a foothold had the pro-slavery sentiment obtained in the district, that he was defeated by Major Thomas L. Harris, of Petersburg, whom he had defeated when he first entered the field as a candidate four years before. While it is scarcely probable that Lincoln, if he had been a candidate, could have changed the result, yet the prize was one which he would then have considered worth contending for; and if the nomination could have been tendered him without doing injustice to his friend, he would undoubtedly have accepted it gladly and thrown all the earnestness and ability which he possessed into the contest. This instance only illustrates a feature of his character which has so often been recognized and commented upon—his generosity toward those among his political friends who might be regarded as occupying the position of rivals."

In 1854, during Lincoln's absence from Springfield, he was nominated as a candidate for the State Legislature. It was in one of Lincoln's periods of profound depression, and it was with the greatest difficulty that he could be persuaded to accept the nomination. "I went to see him," says one of his close political friends, Mr. William Jayne, "in order to get his consent to run. This was at his house. He was then the saddest man I ever saw—the gloomiest. He walked up and down the floor, almost crying; and to all my persuasions to let his name stand in the paper, he said, 'No, I can't. You don't know all. I say you don't begin to know one-half; and that's enough.'" His name, however, was allowed to stand, and he was elected by about 600 majority. But Lincoln was then extremely desirous of succeeding General James Shields, whose term in the United States Senate was to expire the following March. The Senate Chamber had long been the goal of his ambition. He summed up his feelings in a letter to Hon. N.B. Judd, some years after, saying, "I would rather have a full term in the United States Senate than the Presidency." He therefore resigned his seat in the Legislature—the fact that a majority in both houses was opposed to the Nebraska Bill allowing him to do so without injury to his party—and became a candidate for the Senate. But the act was futile. When the Legislature met, in February, 1855, to make choice of a Senator, a clique of anti-Nebraska Democrats held out so firmly against the nomination of Lincoln that there was danger of the Whigs leaving their candidate altogether. In this dilemma Lincoln was consulted. Mr. Lamon thus describes the incident: "Lincoln said, unhesitatingly, 'You ought to drop me and go for Trumbull; that is the only way you can defeat Matteson.' Judge Logan came up about that time, and insisted on running Lincoln still; but the latter said, 'If you do, you will lose both Trumbull and myself; and I think the cause in this case is to be preferred to men.' We adopted his suggestion, and took up Trumbull and elected him, although it grieved us to the heart to give up Lincoln." Mr. Parks, a member of the Legislature at this time, and one of Lincoln's intimate friends, said: "Mr. Lincoln was very much disappointed, for I think it was the height of his ambition to get into the United States Senate. Yet he manifested no bitterness toward Mr. Judd or the other anti-Nebraska Democrats by whom politically he was beaten, but evidently thought their motives were right. He told me several times afterwards that the election of Trumbull was the best thing that could have happened."

Hon. Elijah M. Haines, ex-Speaker of the Illinois Legislature, a resident of the State for over half a century, and one of Lincoln's early friends, was a member of the Legislature during the Senatorial struggle just referred to. His familiarity with all its incidents lends value to his distinct and vivid recollections. "Abraham Lincoln had been elected a member of the House on the Fusion ticket, with Judge Stephen T. Logan, for the district composed of Sangamon County," writes Mr. Haines. "But it being settled that the Fusion party—which was an anti-Douglas combination, including Whigs, Free-Soilers, Know-Nothings, etc.—would have a majority of the two houses on ballot, Mr. Lincoln was induced to become a candidate for United States Senator, for the support of that party. He therefore did not qualify as a member. Although Mr. Lincoln never acquired the reputation of being an office-seeker, yet it happened frequently that his name would be mentioned in connection with some important position. He became quite early in life one of the prominent leaders of the Whig party of the State, and for a long time, in connection with a few devoted associates, led the forlorn hope of that party. During a period of about twenty years there was seldom more than one Whig member in the Illinois delegation of Congressmen. The Sangamon district, in which Mr. Lincoln lived, was always sure to elect a Whig member when the party was united; but it contained quite a number of aspiring Whig orators, and there was a kind of understanding between them that no one who attained the position of Representative in Congress should hold it longer than one term; that he would then give way for the next favorite. Mr. Lincoln had held the position once, and its return to him was far in the future. The Fusion triumph in the

Legislature was considered by the Whig element as a success, in which they acknowledged great obligation to Mr. Lincoln. That element in the Fusion party therefore urged his claims as the successor of General Shields. His old associate and tried friend in the Whig cause, Judge Logan, became the champion of his interests in the House of Representatives. I was present and saw something of Mr. Lincoln during the early part of the session, before the vote for Senator was taken. He was around among the members much of the time. His manner was agreeable and unassuming; he was not forward in pressing his case upon the attention of members, yet before the interview would come to a close some allusion to the Senatorship would generally occur, when he would respond in some such way as this: 'Gentlemen, that is rather a delicate subject for me to talk upon; but I must confess that I would be glad of your support for the office, if you shall conclude that I am the proper person for it.' When he had finished, he would generally take occasion to withdraw before any discussion on the subject arose. When the election of Senator occurred, in February, Lincoln received 45 votes—the highest number of any of the candidates, and within six votes of enough to secure his election. This was on the first ballot, after which Lincoln's votes declined. After the ninth ballot, Mr. Lincoln stepped forward—or, as Mr. Richmond expresses it, *leaned* forward from his position in the lobby—and requested the committee to withdraw his name. On the tenth ballot Judge Trumbull received fifty-one votes and was declared elected." Thus were Lincoln's political ambitions again frustrated. But their realization was only delayed for the far grander triumph that was so soon to come, although no man then foresaw its coming.

CHAPTER X

The year 1856 saw the dissolution of the old Whig party. It had become too narrow and restricted to answer the needs of the hour. A new platform was demanded, one that would admit the great principles and issues growing out of the slavery agitation. A convention of the Whig leaders throughout the country met at Pittsburgh, Pennsylvania, on the 22d of February of that year, to consider the necessity of a new organization. A little later, Mr. Herndon, in the office of Lincoln, prepared a call for a convention at Bloomington, Illinois, "summoning together all those who wished to see the government conducted on the principles of Washington and Jefferson." This call was signed by the most prominent Abolitionists of Illinois, with the name of A. LINCOLN at the head. The morning after its publication, Major Stuart entered Mr. Herndon's office in a state of extreme excitement, and, as the latter relates, demanded: "'Sir, did Mr. Lincoln sign that Abolition call which is published this morning?' I answered, 'Mr. Lincoln did not sign that call.' 'Did Lincoln authorize you to sign it?' 'No, he never authorized me to sign it.' 'Then do you know that you have ruined Mr. Lincoln?' 'I did not know that I had ruined Mr. Lincoln; did not intend to do so; thought he was a made man by it; that the time had come when conservatism was a crime and a blunder.' 'You, then, take the responsibility of your acts, do you?' 'I do, most emphatically.' However, I instantly sat down and wrote to Mr. Lincoln, who was then in Pekin or Tremont—possibly at court. He received my letter, and instantly replied, either by letter or telegraph—most likely by letter—that he adopted *in toto* what I had done, and promised to meet the radicals—Lovejoy and such like men—among us." Mr. Herndon adds: "Never did a man change as Lincoln did from that hour. No sooner had he planted himself right on the slavery question than his whole soul seemed burning. *He blossomed right out.* Then, too, other spiritual things grew more real to him."

Mr. Herndon had been an Abolitionist from birth. It was an inheritance with him; but Lincoln's conversion was a gradual process, stimulated and confirmed by the influence of his companion. "From 1854 to 1860," says Mr. Herndon, "I kept putting into Lincoln's hands the speeches and sermons of Theodore Parker, Wendell Phillips, and Henry Ward Beecher. I took 'The Anti-Slavery Standard' for years before 1856, 'The Chicago Tribune,' and

'The New York Tribune'; kept them in my office, kept them purposely on my table, and would read to Lincoln the good, sharp, solid things, well put. Lincoln was a natural anti-slavery man, as I think, and yet he needed watching,—needed hope, faith, energy; and I think I *warmed him*."

It is stated that "when Herndon was very young—probably before Mr. Lincoln made his first protest in the Legislature of the State in behalf of liberty—Lincoln once said to him: 'I cannot see what makes your convictions so decided as regards the future of slavery. What tells you the thing must be rooted out?' 'I feel it in my bones,' was Herndon's emphatic answer. 'This continent is not broad enough to endure the contest between freedom and slavery!' It was almost in these very words that Lincoln afterwards opened the great contest with Douglas. From this time forward he submitted all public questions to what he called 'the test of Bill Herndon's *bone philosophy*'; and their arguments were close and protracted."

Lincoln's attitude on slavery aroused formidable opposition among his friends, and even in his own family. Mrs. Lincoln was decidedly pro-slavery in her views. Once while riding with a friend she said: "If my husband dies, his spirit will never find me residing outside the limits of a slave State." But opposition, whether from without or within, could never swerve him from a course to which conscience and reason clearly impelled him. Long before Mr. Herndon published the call for the Bloomington convention, he had said to a deputation of men from Chicago, in answer to the inquiry whether Lincoln could be trusted for freedom: "Can you trust yourselves? If you can, you can trust Lincoln forever."

The convention met at Bloomington, May 29, 1856. One of its chief incidents was a speech by Lincoln. This speech was one of the great efforts of his life, and had a powerful influence on the convention. "Never," says one of the delegates, "was an audience more completely electrified by human eloquence. Again and again his hearers sprang to their feet, and by long continued cheers expressed how deeply the speaker had aroused them." "It was there," says Mr. Herndon in one of his lectures, "that Lincoln was baptized and joined our church. He made a speech to us. I have heard or read all of Mr. Lincoln's great speeches; and I give it as my opinion that the Bloomington speech was the grand effort of his life. Heretofore, and up to this moment, he had simply argued the slavery question on grounds of policy,—on what are called the *statesman's* grounds,—never reaching the question of the radical and eternal right. Now he was newly baptized and freshly born; he had the fervor of a new convert; the smothered flame broke out; enthusiasm unusual to him blazed up; his eyes were aglow with inspiration; he felt a new and more vital justice; his heart was alive to the right; his sympathies burst forth; and he stood before the throne of the eternal Right, in presence of his God, and then and there unburdened his penitential and fired soul. This speech was fresh, new, genuine, odd, original; filled with fervor not unmixed with a divine enthusiasm; his head breathing out through his tender heart its truths, its sense of right, and its feeling of the good and for the good. This speech was full of fire and energy and force; it was logic; it was pathos; it was enthusiasm; it was justice, equity, truth, right, and good, set ablaze by the divine fires of a soul maddened by wrong; it was hard, heavy, knotty, gnarly, edged, and heated. I attempted for about fifteen minutes, as was usual with me then, to take notes; but at the end of that time I threw pen and paper to the dogs, and lived only in the inspiration of the hour. If Mr. Lincoln was six feet four inches high usually, *at Bloomington he was seven feet*, and inspired at that. From that day to the day of his death, he stood firm on the right. He felt his great cross, had his great idea, nursed it, kept it, taught it to others, and in his fidelity bore witness of it to his death, and finally sealed it with his precious blood."

The committee on resolutions at the convention found themselves, after hours of discussion, unable to agree; and at last they sent for Lincoln. He suggested that all could unite on the principles of the Declaration of Independence and hostility to the extension of slavery. "Let us," said he, "in building our new party make our cornerstone the Declaration of Independence; let us build on this rock, and the gates of hell shall not prevail against us." The problem was mastered, and the convention adopted the following:

> *Resolved*, That we hold, in accordance with the opinions and practices of all the great statesmen of all parties for the first sixty years of the administration of the government, that under the Constitution Congress possesses full power to prohibit slavery in the territories; and that while we will maintain all constitutional rights of the South, we also hold that justice, humanity, the principles of freedom, as expressed in our Declaration of Independence and our National Constitution, and the purity and perpetuity of our government, require that that power should be exerted to prevent the extension of slavery into territories heretofore free.

The Bloomington convention concluded its work by choosing delegates to the National Republican convention to be held at Philadelphia the following month, for the nomination of candidates for the Presidency and Vice-presidency of the United States. And thus was organized the Republican party in Illinois, which revolutionized the politics of the State and elected Lincoln to the Presidency.

The people of Bloomington seem to have had but little sympathy with this convention. A few days later, Herndon and Lincoln tried to hold a ratification meeting; but only three persons were present—Lincoln, Herndon, and John Pain. "When Lincoln came into the court-room where the meeting was to be held," says Herndon, "there was an expression of sadness and amusement on his face. He walked to the stand, mounted it in a kind of mockery—mirth and sadness all combined—and said, 'Gentlemen, this meeting is larger than I thought it would be. I knew that Herndon and myself would come, but I did not know that anyone else would be here; and yet another has come—you, John Pain. These are sad times, and seem out of joint. All seems dead; but the age is not yet dead; it liveth as sure as our Maker liveth. Under all this seeming want of life and motion, the world does move nevertheless. Be hopeful. And now let us adjourn and appeal to the people.'"

The National convention of the Republican party met at Philadelphia in June, 1856, and adopted a declaration of principles substantially based upon those of the Bloomington convention. John C. Fremont was nominated as candidate for President. Among the names presented for Vice-president was that of Abraham Lincoln, who received 110 votes. William L. Dayton received 259 votes and was unanimously declared the nominee. Fremont and Dayton thus became the standard-bearers of the new national party. When the news reached Lincoln, in Illinois, that he had received 110 votes as nominee for the Vice-presidency, he could not at first believe that he was the man voted for, and said, "No, it could not be; it must have been the great Lincoln of Massachusetts!" He was then in one of his melancholy moods, full of depression and despondency.

In the stirring presidential campaign of 1856, Lincoln was particularly active, and rendered most efficient service to the Republican party. He spoke constantly, discussing the great question of "slavery in the territories" in a manner at once original and masterly. A graphic picture of one of these campaign gatherings is furnished by Hon. William Bross, afterwards Lieutenant-Governor of Illinois. "I first met Mr. Lincoln, to know him," says Governor Bross, "at Vandalia, the old capital of the State, in October, 1856. There was to be a political meeting in front of the old State House, in the center of the square, at 2 o'clock. Soon after that hour the sonorous voice of Dr. Curdy rang through the town: 'O, yes! O, yes! All ye who want to hear public speaking, draw near!' The crowd at once began to gather from all sides of the square. The Doctor then introduced the first speaker, and he proceeded to make the best presentation he could of the principles of the newly-formed Republican party, and the reasons why Fremont, 'the gallant pathfinder of the West,' should be elected President. About the time the first speaker closed his remarks, Hon. Ebenezer Peck and Abraham Lincoln arrived and took the stand; and both made able and effective speeches. After that, Lincoln and I frequently met during the canvass, and often afterwards I spoke with him from the same platform. The probable result of an election was often canvassed, and a noticeable fact was that in most cases he would mark the probable result below rather than above the actual majority."

Some lively reminiscences of Lincoln's appearance and efforts in this campaign are given by Mr. Noah Brooks, the well-known journalist and author, who at that time lived in Northern Illinois and attended many of the great Republican mass-meetings. "At one of these great assemblies in Ogle County," says Mr. Brooks, "to which the country people came on horseback, in farm wagons, or afoot, from far and near, there were several speakers of local celebrity. Dr. Egan of Chicago, famous for his racy stories, was one; and Joe Knox of Bureau County, a stump speaker of renown, was another attraction. Several other orators were 'on the bills' for this long-advertised 'Fremont and Dayton rally,' among them being a Springfield lawyer who had won some reputation as a close reasoner, and a capital speaker on the stump. This was Abraham Lincoln, popularly known as 'Honest Abe Lincoln.' In those days he was not so famous in our part of the State as the two speakers whom I have named. Possibly he was not so popular among the masses of the people; but his ready wit, his unfailing good humor, and the candor which gave him his character for honesty, won for him the admiration and respect of all who heard him. I remember once meeting a choleric old Democrat striding away from an open-air meeting where Lincoln was speaking, striking the earth with his cane as he stumped along, and exclaiming, 'He's a dangerous man, sir! A d——d dangerous man! He makes you *believe* what he says, in spite of yourself!' It was Lincoln 's manner. He admitted away his whole case apparently—and yet, as his political opponents complained, he usually carried conviction with him. As he reasoned with his audience, he bent his long form over the railing of the platform, stooping lower and lower as he pursued his argument, until, having reached his point, he clinched it, usually with a question, and then suddenly sprang upright, reminding one of the springing open of a jack-knife blade. At the Ogle County meeting to which I refer, Lincoln led off, the raciest speakers being reserved for the latter part of the political entertainment. I am bound to say that Lincoln did not awaken the boisterous applause which some of those who followed him did, but his speech made a more lasting impression. It was talked about for weeks afterward in the neighborhood, and it probably changed many votes; for that was the time when Free-soil votes were being made in Northern Illinois."

Mr. Brooks had made Lincoln's acquaintance early in the day referred to; and after Lincoln had spoken, and while some of the other orators were entertaining the audience, the two drew a little off from the crowd and fell into a discussion over the political situation and prospects. "We crawled under the pendulous branches of a tree," says Mr. Brooks, "and Lincoln, lying flat on the ground, with his chin in his hands, talked on, rather gloomily as to the present but absolutely confident as to the future. I was dismayed to find that he did not believe it possible that Fremont could be elected. As if half pitying my youthful ignorance, but admiring my enthusiasm, he said, 'Don't be discouraged if we don't carry the day this year. We can't do it, that's certain. We can't carry Pennsylvania; those old Whigs down there are too strong for us. But we shall sooner or later elect our President. I feel confident of that.' 'Do you think we shall elect a Free-soil President in 1860?' I asked. 'Well, I don't know. Everything depends on the course of the Democracy. There's a big anti-slavery element in the Democratic party, and if we could get hold of that we might possibly elect our man in 1860. But it's doubtful, very doubtful. Perhaps we shall be able to fetch it by 1864; perhaps not. As I said before, the Free-soil party is bound to win in the long run. It may not be in my day; but it will be in yours, I do really believe.'" The defeat of Fremont soon verified Lincoln's prediction on that score.

A peculiarly interesting episode of Lincoln's life belongs to this period, though unrelated to political events. This was the meeting, in a professional way, with Edwin M. Stanton, at that time a prominent lawyer of Pittsburgh, afterwards the great War Secretary of President Lincoln's cabinet. The circumstances were briefly these: Among Lincoln's law cases was one connected with the patent of the McCormick Reaper; and in the summer of 1857 he visited Cincinnati to argue the case before Judge McLean of the United States Circuit Court. It was a case of great importance, involving the foundation patent of the machine which was destined to revolutionize the harvesting of grain. Reverdy Johnson was on one side of the case, and E.M. Stanton and George Harding on the other. It became necessary, in addition, to have a lawyer who was a resident of Illinois; and inquiry was made of Hon. E.B. Washburne, then in Congress, as to whether he knew a suitable man. The latter replied that "there was a man named Lincoln at Springfield, who had considerable reputation in the State." Lincoln was retained in the case, and came on to Cincinnati with a brief. Stanton and Harding saw in their associate counsel "a tall, dark, uncouth man, who did not strike them as of any account, and, indeed, they gave him hardly any chance." An interesting account of this visit, and of various incidents connected with it, has been prepared by the Hon. W.M. Dickson of Cincinnati. "Mr. Lincoln came to the city," says Mr. Dickson, "a few days before the argument took place, and remained during his stay at the house of a friend. The case was one of large importance pecuniarily, and in the law questions involved. Reverdy Johnson represented the plaintiff. Mr. Lincoln had prepared himself with the greatest care; his ambition was to speak in the case, and to measure swords with the renowned lawyer from Baltimore. It was understood between his client and himself, before his coming, that Mr. Harding of Philadelphia was to be associated with him in the case, and was to make the 'mechanical argument.' Mr. Lincoln was a little surprised and annoyed after reaching Cincinnati, to learn that his client had also associated with him Mr. Edwin M. Stanton, of Pittsburgh, and a lawyer of our own bar; the reason assigned being that the importance of the case required a man of the experience and power of Mr. Stanton to meet Mr. Johnson. The reasons given did not remove the slight conveyed in the employment, without consultation with Lincoln, of this additional counsel. He keenly felt it, but acquiesced. The trial of the case came on; the counsel for defense met each morning for consultation. On one of these occasions one of the counsel moved that only two of them should speak in the case. This motion was also acquiesced in. It had always been understood that Mr. Harding was to speak to explain the mechanism of the reapers. So this motion excluded either Mr. Lincoln or Mr. Stanton. By the custom of the bar, as between counsel of equal standing and in the absence of any action of the client, the original counsel speaks. By this rule Mr. Lincoln had precedence. Mr. Stanton suggested to Mr. Lincoln to make the speech. Mr. Lincoln answered, 'No; you speak,' Mr. Stanton replied, 'I will,' and taking up his hat, said he would go and make preparation. Mr. Lincoln acquiesced in this, but was deeply grieved and mortified; he took but little more interest in the case, though remaining until the conclusion of the trial. He seemed to be greatly depressed, and gave evidence of that tendency to melancholy which so marked his character. His parting on leaving the city cannot be forgotten. Cordially shaking the hand of his hostess, he said: 'You have made my stay here most agreeable, and I am a thousand times obliged to you; but as for repeating my visit, I must say to you I never expect to be in Cincinnati again. I have nothing against the city, but things have so happened here as to make it undesirable for me ever to return.' Thus untowardly met for the first time, Lincoln and Stanton. Little did either then suspect that they were to meet again on a larger theatre, to become the chief actors in a great historical epoch."

If Lincoln was "surprised and annoyed" at the treatment he received from Stanton, the latter was no less surprised, and a good deal more disgusted, on seeing Lincoln and learning of his connection with the case. He made no secret of his contempt for the "long, lank creature from Illinois," as he afterwards described him, "wearing a dirty linen duster for a coat, on the back of which the perspiration had splotched wide stains that resembled a dirty map of the continent." He blurted out his wrath and indignation to his associate counsel, declaring that if "that giraffe" was permitted to appear in the case he would throw up his brief and leave it. Lincoln keenly felt the affront, but his great nature forgave it so entirely that, recognizing the singular abilities of Stanton beneath his brusque exterior, he afterwards, for the public good, appointed him to a seat in his cabinet.

Lincoln, says Mr. Dickson, "remained in Cincinnati about a week, moving freely about. Yet not twenty men in the city knew him personally, or knew he was here; not a hundred would have known who he was had his name been given to them. He came with the fond hope of making fame in a forensic contest with Reverdy Johnson. He was pushed aside, humiliated and mortified. He attached to the innocent city the displeasure that filled his bosom, and shook its dust from his feet."

In his Autobiography, Moncure D. Conway records a glimpse of Lincoln during his Cincinnati visit that seems worth transcribing. "One warm evening in 1859, passing through the market-place in Cincinnati, I found there a crowd listening to a political speech in the open air. The speaker stood on the balcony of a small brick house, some lamps assisting the moonlight. Something about the speaker, and some words that reached me, led me to press nearer. I asked the speaker's name, and learned that it was Abraham Lincoln. Browning's description of the German professor, 'Three parts sublime to one grotesque,' was applicable to this man. The face had a battered and bronzed look, without being hard. His nose was prominent, and buttressed a strong and high forehead. His eyes were high-vaulted, and had an expression of sadness; his mouth and chin were too close together, the cheeks hollow. On the whole, Lincoln's appearance was not attractive until one heard his voice, which possessed variety of expression, earnestness, and shrewdness in every tone. The charm of his manner was that he had no manner; he was simple, — direct, humorous. He pleasantly repeated a mannerism of his opponent, — 'This is what Douglas calls his *gur-reat per-rinciple.*' But the next words I remember were these: '*Slavery is wrong.*'"

CHAPTER XI

The year 1858 is memorable alike in the career of Lincoln and in the political history of the country. It was distinguished by the joint discussions between the two great political leaders of Illinois, which rank among the ablest forensic debates that have taken place since the foundation of the republic. The occasion was one to call out the greatest powers of the two remarkable men who there contested for political supremacy. It was not alone that Lincoln and Douglas were opposing candidates for a high office—that of Senator of the United States: they were the champions and spokesmen of their parties at a critical period when great issues were to be discussed and great movements outlined and directed. It was naturally expected that the winner in the contest would become the political leader of his State. Little was it imagined that the loser would become the leader and savior of the Nation.

On the 21st of April the Democratic convention of Illinois met at Springfield and announced Stephen A. Douglas, then United States Senator, as its choice for another term. June 16 the Republican convention met at the same place and declared unanimously that "Abraham Lincoln is our first and only choice for United States Senator to fill the vacancy about to be created by the expiration of Mr. Douglas's term of office." For a number of days previous to the meeting of the Republican convention Lincoln had been engaged in preparing a speech for the occasion. It was composed after his usual method—the separate thoughts jotted down as they came to him, on scraps of paper at hand at the moment, and these notes were arranged in order and elaborated into a finished essay, copied on large sheets of paper in a plain and legible handwriting. This was the speech which afterwards came to be so celebrated as the "house-divided-against-itself" speech. Lincoln was gravely conscious of its unusual importance, and gave great care and deliberation to its composition. The evening of June 16—the day of his nomination by the convention—Lincoln went to his office, accompanied by his friend Herndon, and having locked the door proceeded to read his speech. Slowly and distinctly he read the first paragraph, and then turned to Herndon with, "What do you think of that?" Mr. Herndon was startled at its boldness. "I think," said he, "it is all true. But is it entirely politic to read or speak it as it is written?" "That makes no difference," said Lincoln. "That expression is a truth of all human experience,—'a house divided against itself cannot stand.' The proposition is indisputably true, and has been true for more than six thousand years; I want to use some universally known figure, expressed in simple language, that may strike home to the minds of men in order to rouse them to the peril of the times." Mr. Herndon was convinced by Lincoln's language, and advised him to deliver the speech just as it was written. Lincoln was satisfied, but thought it would be prudent to consult a few other friends in the matter, and about a dozen were called in. "After seating them at the round table," says John Armstrong, one of the number, "he read that clause or section of his speech which reads, 'a house divided against itself cannot stand,' etc. He read it slowly and cautiously, so as to let each man fully understand it. After he had finished the reading, he asked the opinions of his friends as to the wisdom or policy of it. Every man among them condemned the speech in substance and spirit, especially that section quoted above, as unwise and impolitic if not untrue. They unanimously declared that the whole speech was too far in advance of the times. Herndon sat still while they were giving their respective opinions of its unwisdom and impolicy; then he sprang to his feet and said, 'Lincoln, deliver it *just as it reads*. If it is in advance of the times, let us lift the people to its level. The speech is true, wise, and politic, and will succeed now or in the future. Nay, it will aid you, if it will not make you President of the United States.' Mr. Lincoln sat still a moment, then rose from his chair, walked backwards and forwards in the hall, stopped, and said: 'Friends, I have thought about this matter a great deal, have weighed the questions from all corners, and am thoroughly convinced the time has come when this speech should be uttered; and if it be that I must go down because of it, then let me go down linked to truth—die in the advocacy of what is right and just. This nation cannot live on injustice; "a house divided against itself cannot stand," I say again and again.' This was spoken with emotion—the effects of his love of truth, and sorrow from the disagreement of his friends."

On the next evening the speech was delivered to an immense audience in the hall of the House of Representatives at Springfield. "The hall and lobbies and galleries were even more densely crowded and packed than at any time during the day," says the official report; and as Lincoln "approached the speaker's stand, he was greeted with shouts and hurrahs, and prolonged cheers." The prophetic sentences which dropped first from the lips of the speaker were freighted with a solemn import which even he could scarcely have divined in full. The seers of old were not more inspired than he who now, out of the irresistible conviction of his heart, said to his surprised and unbelieving listeners:

If we could first know where we are and whither we are tending, we could then better judge what to do and how to do it. We are now far on in the fifth year since a policy was initiated with the avowed object and confident promise of putting an end to slavery agitation. Under the operation of that policy, that agitation has not only not ceased, but has constantly augmented. In my opinion it will not cease until a crisis shall have been reached and passed. 'A house divided against itself cannot stand.' I believe this Government cannot endure, permanently, half slave and half free. I do not expect the Union to be dissolved—I do not expect the house to fall—but I do expect it will cease to be divided. It will become all one thing or all the other. Either the opponents of slavery will arrest the further spread of it, and place it where the public mind shall rest in the belief that it is in course of ultimate extinction, or its advocates will push it forward till it shall become alike lawful in all the States—old as well as new—North as well as South.

Mr. Jeriah Bonham, an old citizen of Illinois, relates that he was present as a delegate at the Springfield convention and heard the famous speech of Lincoln. According to Mr. Bonham, "The speech was prepared with unusual care, every paragraph and sentence carefully weighed. The firm bedrock of principles, the issues of the campaign on which he proposed to stand and fight his battles, were all well considered, and his arguments were incontrovertible. In that memorable speech culminated all the grand thoughts he had ever uttered, embodying divinity, statesmanship, law, and morals, and even fraught with prophecy. As he advanced in this argument he towered to his full height, forgetting himself entirely as he grew warm in his work. Men and women who heard that speech well remember the wonderful transformation wrought in Lincoln's appearance. The plain, homely man towered up majestically; his face lit as with angelic light; the long, bent, angular figure, like the strong oak of the forest, stood erect, and his eyes flashed with the fire of inspiration."

The party that had nominated Lincoln for the Senate was not prepared to endorse his restriction of the coming struggle to the single issue of the slavery question. His friends dreaded the result of his uncompromising frankness, while politicians quite generally condemned it. Even so stanch a friend as Leonard Swett, whose devotion to Lincoln never wavered throughout his whole career, shared these apprehensions. Says Mr. Swett: "The first ten lines of that speech defeated him. The sentiment of the 'house divided against itself' seemed wholly inappropriate. It was a speech made at the commencement of a campaign, and apparently made for the campaign. Viewing it in this light alone, nothing could have been more unfortunate or inappropriate. It was saying the wrong thing first; yet he felt that it was an abstract truth, and that standing by the speech would ultimately find him in the right place. I was inclined at the time to believe these words were hastily and inconsiderately uttered; but subsequent facts have convinced me they were deliberate and had been well matured."

A few days after the delivery of this speech, a gentleman named Dr. Long called on Lincoln and gave him a foretaste of the remarks he was to hear during the next few months. "Well, Lincoln," said he, "that foolish speech of yours will kill you—will defeat you in this contest, and probably for all offices for all time to come. I am sorry, sorry, very sorry. I wish it was wiped out of existence. Don't you wish so too?" Laying down the pen with which he had been writing, and slowly raising his head and adjusting his spectacles, Lincoln replied: "Well, Doctor, if I had to draw a pen across and erase my whole life from existence, and I had one poor gift or choice left as to what I should save from the wreck, *I should choose that speech*, and leave it to the world unerased."

The Senatorial campaign was now well begun. Douglas opened it by a speech at Chicago on the 9th of July. Lincoln was present, and on the next evening spoke in reply from the same place—the balcony of the Tremont House. A week later Douglas spoke at Bloomington, with Lincoln again in the audience. The notion of a joint discussion seems to have originated with Lincoln, who on the 24th of July addressed a note to Douglas as follows:

> HON. S.A. DOUGLAS—My Dear Sir:— Will it be agreeable to you to make an arrangement for you and myself to divide time, and address the same audiences during the present canvass? Mr. Judd, who will hand you this, is authorized to receive your answer, and, if agreeable to you, to enter into the terms of such arrangement. Your obedient servant, A. LINCOLN.

The result of this proposal was an agreement that there should be a joint discussion between the two candidates in each of the seven Congressional districts in which they had not both already been heard. Places were named and dates fixed extending to the middle of October. It was agreed that the opening speech on each occasion should occupy one hour; the reply, one hour and a half; the close, half an hour; and that Mr. Douglas should have the first and last voice in four of the seven meetings.

The champions who were thus to enter the lists in a decisive trial of forensic strength and skill are forcibly contrasted by Mr. Speed, who says:

"They were the respective leaders of their parties in the State. They were as opposite in character as they were unlike in their persons. Lincoln was long and ungainly; Douglas was short and compact. Douglas, in all elections, was the moving spirit and manager. He was content with nothing short of a blind submission to himself. He could not tolerate opposition to his will within his party organization. He held the reins and controlled the movements of the Democratic chariot. With a large State majority, with many able and ambitious men in it, he stepped to the front in his youth and held his place till his death. Lincoln, on the other hand, shrank from any controversy with his friends. His party being in a minority in the State, he was forced to the front because his friends thought he was the only man with whom they could win. In a canvass his friends had to do all the management. He knew nothing of how to reach the people except by addressing their reason. If the situation had been reversed—Lincoln representing the majority and Douglas the minority—I think it most likely Lincoln would never have had the place. He had no heart for a fight with friends."

The Hon. James G. Blaine has given a masterly description and analysis of the comparative powers of the two illustrious debaters. Douglas, says Mr. Blaine, "was everywhere known as a debater of singular skill. His mind was fertile in resources. He was a master of logic. No man perceived more quickly than he the strength or the weakness of an argument, and no one excelled him in the use of sophistry and fallacy. Where he could not elucidate a point to his own advantage, he would fatally becloud it for his opponent. In that peculiar style of debate which in intensity resembles a physical combat, he had no equal. He spoke with extraordinary readiness. There was no halting in his phrase. He used good English, terse, vigorous, pointed. He disregarded the adornments of rhetoric—rarely used a simile. He was utterly destitute of humor, and had slight appreciation of wit. He never cited historical precedents except from the domain of American politics. Inside that field his knowledge was comprehensive, minute, critical; beyond it his learning was limited. He was not a reader. His recreations were not in literature. In the whole range of his voluminous speaking, it would be difficult to find either a line of poetry or a classical allusion. But he was by nature an orator, and by long practice a debater. He could lead a crowd almost irresistibly to his own conclusions. He could, if he wished, incite a mob to desperate deeds. He was, in short, an able, audacious, almost unconquerable opponent in public discussion. It would have been impossible to find any man of the same type able to meet him before the people of Illinois. Whoever attempted it would probably have been destroyed in the first encounter. But the man who was chosen to meet him, who challenged him to the combat, was radically different in every phase of character. Scarcely could two men be more unlike in mental and moral constitution than Abraham Lincoln and Stephen A. Douglas. Lincoln was calm and philosophic. He loved the truth for the truth's sake. He would not argue from a false premise, or be deceived himself or deceive others by a false conclusion. He had pondered deeply on the issues which aroused him to action. He had given anxious thought to the problems of free government, and to the destiny of the Republic. He had marked out a path of duty for himself, and he walked it fearlessly. His mental processes were slower but more profound than those of Douglas. He did not seek to say merely the thing which was best for that day's debate, but the thing which would stand the test of time and square itself with eternal justice. He wished nothing to appear white unless it was white. His logic was severe and faultless. He did not resort to fallacy, and could detect it in his opponent and expose it with merciless directness. He had an abounding sense of humor, and always employed it in illustration of his argument—but never for the mere sake of provoking merriment. In this respect he had the wonderful aptness of Franklin. He often taught a great truth with the felicitous brevity of an Aesop fable. His words did not flow in an impetuous torrent, as did those of Douglas; but they were always well chosen, deliberate and conclusive."

Mr. Arnold, in the course of an extended comparison, says: "At the time of these discussions, both Lincoln and Douglas were in the full maturity of their powers. Douglas was forty-five and Lincoln forty-nine years of age. Physically and mentally, they were as unlike as possible. Douglas was short, not much more than five feet high, with a large head, massive brain, broad shoulders, a wide, deep chest, and features strongly marked. He impressed every one, at first sight, as a strong, sturdy, resolute, fearless man. Lincoln's herculean stature has already been described. A stranger who listened to him for five minutes would say: 'This is a kind, genial, sincere, genuine man; a man you can trust, plain, straightforward, honest, and true.' If this stranger were to hear him make a speech, he would be impressed with his clear good sense, by his wit and humor, by his general intelligence, and by the simple, homely, but pure and accurate language he used. In his long residence at Washington, Douglas had acquired the bearing and manners of a gentleman and a man of the world. But he was always a fascinating and attractive man, and always and everywhere personally popular. He had been for years carefully and thoroughly trained on the stump, in Congress, and in the Senate, to meet in debate the ablest speakers in the State and Nation. For years he had been accustomed to meet on the floor of the Capitol the leaders of the old Whig and Free-soil parties. Among them were Webster and Seward, Fessenden and Crittenden, Chase, Trumbull, Hale and others of nearly equal eminence; and his enthusiastic friends insisted that never, either in single conflict or when receiving the assault of the senatorial leaders of a whole party, had he been discomfited. His style was bold, vigorous, and aggressive; at times even defiant. He was ready, fluent, fertile in resources, familiar with national and party history, severe in denunciation, and he handled with skill nearly all the weapons of debate. His iron will and restless energy, together with great personal magnetism, made him the idol of his friends and party. His long, brilliant, and almost universally successful career, gave him perfect confidence in himself, and at times he was arrogant and overbearing.... Lincoln also was a thoroughly trained speaker. He had met successfully, year after year, at the bar and on the stump, the ablest men of Illinois and the Northwest, including Lamborn, Stephen T. Logan, John Calhoun, and many others. He had contended, in generous emulation, with Hardin, Baker, Logan, and Browning; and had very often met Douglas, a conflict with whom he always courted rather than shunned. His speeches, as we read them to-day, show a more familiar knowledge of the slavery question than those of any other statesman of our country. This is especially true of the Peoria speech and the Cooper Institute speech. Lincoln was powerful in argument, always seizing the strong points, and demonstrating his propositions with a clearness and logic approaching the certainty of mathematics. He had, in wit and humor, a great advantage over Douglas. Then he had the better temper; he was always good humored, while Douglas, when hard pressed, was sometimes irritable. Douglas perhaps carried away the more popular applause; Lincoln made the deeper and more lasting impression. Douglas did not disdain an immediate *ad captandum* triumph; while Lincoln aimed at permanent conviction. Sometimes, when Lincoln's friends urged him to raise a storm of applause, which he could always do by his happy illustrations and amusing stories, he refused, saying, 'The occasion is too serious; the issues are too grave. I do not seek applause, or to amuse the people, but to *convince* them.' It was observed in the canvass that while Douglas was greeted with the loudest cheers, when Lincoln closed the people seemed serious and thoughtful, and could be heard all through the crowd, gravely and anxiously discussing the subjects on which he had been speaking."

Soon after the arrangements for the debate had been made, Senator Douglas visited Alton, Illinois. A delegation of prominent Democrats there paid their respects to him, and during the conversation one of them congratulated Douglas on the easy task he would have in defeating Lincoln; at the same time expressing surprise at the champion whom he had selected. Douglas replied: "Gentlemen, you do not know Mr. Lincoln. I have known him long and well, and I know that I shall have anything but an easy task. I assure you I *would rather meet any other man in the country than*

Abraham Lincoln." This was Douglas's mature opinion of the man of whom, years before, he had said, in his characteristic way: "Of all the d——d Whig rascals about Springfield, Abe Lincoln is the ablest and honestest." On another occasion, Douglas said: "I have known Lincoln for nearly twenty-five years. There were many points of sympathy between us when we first got acquainted. We were both comparatively boys, and both struggling with poverty in a strange land. I was a school-teacher in the town of Winchester, and he a flourishing grocery-keeper in the town of Salem. He was more successful in his occupation than I was in mine, and hence more fortunate in the world's goods. Lincoln is one of those peculiar men who perform with admirable skill everything they undertake. I made as good a school-teacher as I could, and when a cabinet-maker I made as good bedsteads and tables as I could—although my old boss says that I succeeded better with *bureaus* and *secretaries* than with anything else. But I believe that Lincoln was always more successful in business than I, for his business enabled him to get into the Legislature. I met him there, however, and had a sympathy with him because of the up-hill struggle we both had had in life. He was then just as good at telling an anecdote as now. He could beat any of the boys in wrestling or running a foot-race, in pitching quoits or pitching a copper; and the dignity and impartiality with which he presided at a horse-race or fist-fight excited the admiration and won the praise of everybody that was present. I sympathized with him because he was struggling with difficulties, and so was I. Mr. Lincoln served with me in the Legislature of 1836; then we both retired, and he subsided, or became submerged, and was lost sight of as a public man for some years. In 1846, when Wilmot introduced his celebrated proviso, and the Abolition tornado swept over the country, Lincoln again turned up as a Member of Congress from the Sangamon district. I was then in the Senate of the United States, and was glad to welcome my old friend."

Lincoln, in a speech delivered two years before the joint debate, had spoken thus of Senator Douglas: "Twenty-two years ago, Judge Douglas and I first became acquainted; we were both young then—he a trifle younger than I. Even then, we were both ambitious—I perhaps quite as much as he. With me, the race of ambition has been a failure—a flat failure; with him, it has been one of splendid success. His name fills the nation, and is not unknown even in foreign lands. I affect no contempt for the high eminence he has reached; so reached that the oppressed of my species might have shared with me in the elevation, I would rather stand on that eminence than wear the richest crown that ever pressed a monarch's brow."

A few days before the first discussion was to take place, Lincoln, who had become conscious that some of his party friends distrusted his ability to meet successfully a man who, as the Democrats declared and believed, had never had his equal on the stump, met an old friend from Vermilion County, and, shaking hands, inquired the news. His friend replied, "All looks well; our friends are wide awake, but they are looking forward with some anxiety to these approaching joint discussions with Douglas." A shade passed over Lincoln's face, a sad expression came and instantly passed, and then a blaze of light flashed from his eyes, and with his lips compressed and in a manner peculiar to him, half serious and half jocular, he said: "My friend, sit down a minute, and I will tell you a story. You and I, as we have travelled the circuit together attending court, have often seen two men about to fight. One of them, the big or the little giant, as the case may be, is noisy and boastful; he jumps high in the air, strikes his feet together, smites his fists, brags about what he is going to do, and tries hard to 'skeer' the other man. The other man says not a word; his arms are at his side, his fists are clenched, his teeth set, his head settled firmly on his shoulders; he saves his breath and strength for the struggle. *This man will whip*, as sure as the fight comes off. Good-bye, and remember what I say."

The spirit and purpose with which Lincoln went into the contest are shown also in the following words: "I shall not ask any favors at all. Judge Douglas asks me if I wish to push this matter to the point of personal difficulty. I tell him, *No!* He did not make a mistake, in one of his early speeches, when he called me an 'amiable' man, though perhaps he did when he called me an 'intelligent' man. I again tell him, *No!* I very much prefer, when this canvass shall be over, however it may result, that we at least part without any bitter recollections of personal difficulties."

The speeches in these joint discussions were entirely extemporaneous in form, yet they were reported and printed in all the prominent papers in the West, and found eager readers throughout the country. The voice and manner, which add so much to the effect of a speaker, could not be reproduced on the printed page; nor could full justice be done, in a hasty transcript, to the force and fitness of the language employed. Still, the impressions of those who heard them at the time, as well as later and cooler analyses of them, have agreed in pronouncing these debates among the most able and interesting on record. The scenes connected with the different meetings were intensely exciting. Vast throngs were invariably in attendance, while a whole nation was watching the result. "At Freeport," says an observer, "Mr. Douglas appeared in an elegant barouche drawn by four white horses, and was received with great applause. But when Mr. Lincoln came up, in a 'prairie schooner,'—an old-fashioned canvas-covered pioneer wagon,—the enthusiasm of the vast throng was unbounded."

At Charleston Lincoln opened and closed the day's debate. It was the fourth discussion, and there was no more doubt of his ability to sustain the conflict. According to Mr. Arnold, "Douglas's reply to Lincoln was mainly a defense. Lincoln's close was intensely interesting and dramatic. His logic and arguments were crushing, and Douglas's evasions were exposed with a power and clearness that left him utterly discomfited. Republicans saw it. Democrats realized it, and a sort of panic seized them, and ran through the crowd of upturned faces. Douglas realized his defeat, and, as Lincoln's blows fell fast and heavy, he lost his temper. He could not keep his seat; he rose and walked rapidly up and down the platform, behind Lincoln, holding his watch in his hand, and obviously impatient for the call of 'time.' A spectator says: 'He was greatly agitated, his long grizzled hair waving in the wind, like the shaggy locks of an enraged lion.' It was while Douglas was thus exhibiting to the crowd his eager desire to stop Lincoln, that the latter, holding the audience entranced by his eloquence, was striking his heaviest blows. The instant the secondhand of his watch reached the point at which Lincoln's time was up, Douglas, holding up the watch, called out: 'Sit down, Lincoln, sit down! Your time is up!' Turning to Douglas, Lincoln said calmly: 'I will. I *will* quit. I believe my time *is* up. ' 'Yes, ' said a voice from the platform, 'Douglas has had enough; it is time you let up on him. '"

The institution of slavery was, of course, the topic around which circled all the arguments in these joint discussions. It was the great topic of the hour—the important point of division between the Republican and Democratic parties. Lincoln's exposition of the subject was profound and masterly. At the meeting in Quincy the issue was defined and the argument driven home with unsparing logic and directness. In closing the debate, he said:

> I wish to return to Judge Douglas my profound thanks for his public annunciation here to-day, to be put on record, that his system of policy in regard to the institution of slavery contemplates that it shall last *forever*. We are getting a little nearer the true issue of this controversy, and I am profoundly grateful for this one sentence. Judge Douglas asks you, 'Why cannot the institution of slavery, or, rather, why cannot the nation, part slave and part free, continue as our fathers made it forever?' In the first place, I insist that our fathers *did not* make this nation half slave and half free, or part slave and part free. I insist that they found the institution of slavery existing here. They did not make it so, but they left it so, because they knew of no way to get rid of it at that time. When Judge Douglas undertakes to say that,

as a matter of choice, the fathers of the Government made this nation part slave and part free, he assumes what is historically a *falsehood*. More than that; when the fathers of the Government cut off the source of slavery by the abolition of the slave-trade, and adopted a system of restricting it from the new Territories where it had not existed, I maintain that they placed it where they understood, and all sensible men understood, it was in the course of ultimate extinction; and when Judge Douglas asks me why it cannot continue as our fathers made it, I ask him why he and his friends could not let it remain as our friends made it? It is precisely all I ask of him in relation to the institution of slavery, that it shall be placed upon the basis that our fathers placed it upon. Mr. Brooks, of South Carolina, once said, and truly said, that when this Government was established, no one expected the institution of slavery to last until this day; and that the men who formed this Government were wiser and better than the men of these days; but the men of these days had experience which the fathers had not, and that experience had taught them the invention of the cotton-gin, and this had made the perpetuation of the institution of slavery a necessity in this country. Judge Douglas could not let it stand upon the basis on which our fathers placed it, but removed it, and put it upon the cotton-gin basis. It is a question, therefore, for him and his friends to answer — why they could not let it remain where the fathers of the Government originally placed it.

In these debates Lincoln often seemed like one transfigured — carried away by his own eloquence and the force of his conviction. He said to a friend during the canvass: "Sometimes, in the excitement of speaking, I seem to see the end of slavery. I feel that the time is soon coming when the sun shall shine, the rain shall fall, on no man who shall go forth to unrequited toil.... How this will come, when it will come, by whom it will come, I cannot tell; — but that time will surely come." Again, at the first encounter at Alton, he uttered these pregnant sentences:

On this subject of treating slavery as a wrong, and limiting its spread, let me say a word. Has anything ever threatened the existence of this Union save and except this very institution of slavery? What is it that we hold most dear among us? Our own liberty and prosperity. What has ever threatened our liberty and prosperity, save and except this institution of slavery? If this is true, how do you propose to improve the condition of things by enlarging slavery?—by spreading it out and making it bigger? You may have a wen or cancer upon your person, and not be able to cut it out lest you bleed, to death; but surely it is no way to cure it to ingraft it and spread it over your whole body—that is no proper way of treating what you regard a wrong. This peaceful way of dealing with it as a wrong—restricting the spread of it, and not allowing it to go into new countries where it has not already existed—that is the peaceful way, the old-fashioned way, the way in which the fathers themselves set us the example. Is slavery wrong? That is the real issue. That is the issue that will continue in this country when these poor tongues of Judge Douglas and myself shall be silent. It is the eternal struggle between these two principles—right and wrong—throughout the world. They are two principles that have stood face to face from the beginning of time; and will ever continue to struggle. The one is the common right of humanity, and the other the divine right of kings. It is the same principle, in whatever shape it develops itself. It is the same spirit that says: 'You work, and toil, and earn bread, and I'll eat it.' No matter in what shape it comes, whether from the mouth of a king who seeks to bestride the people of his own nation and live by the fruit of their labor, or from one race of men as an apology for enslaving another race, it is the same tyrannical principle.

On still another occasion he used these unmistakable words:

My declarations upon this subject of negro slavery may be misrepresented, but cannot be misunderstood. I have said that I do not understand the Declaration to mean that all men were created equal in all respects. They are not our equal in color. But I suppose that it does mean to declare that all men are created equal in some respects; they are equal in their right to 'life, liberty, and the pursuit of happiness.' Certainly the negro is not our equal in color, perhaps not in many other respects; still, *in the right to put into his mouth the bread that his own hands have earned, he is the equal of every other man, white or black.*

The Every-Day Life Of Abraham Lincoln | 143

It is not in the scope of this narrative to print extended quotations from the speeches made in this memorable contest, but rather to give such reminiscences and anecdotes, and description by eye-witnesses, as will best serve to bring the scenes and actors vividly to mind. Fortunately, many such records are still in existence, and from them some most entertaining personal accounts have been obtained. Among these is an impressive pen-picture of Lincoln on the stump, as admirably sketched by the Rev. Dr. George C. Noyes, of Chicago. "Mr. Lincoln in repose," says Dr. Noyes, "was a very different man in personal appearance from Mr. Lincoln on the platform or on the stump, when his whole nature was roused by his masterful interest in the subject of his discourse. In the former case he was, as has often been described, a man of awkward and ungainly appearance and exceedingly homely countenance. In the latter case, he was a man of magnificent presence and remarkably impressive manner. The writer retains to this day a very vivid impression of his appearance in both these characters, and both on the same day. It was in Jacksonville, in the summer of 1858, and during the great contest with Douglas, when the prize contended for was a seat in the United States Senate. The day was warm; the streets were dusty, and filled with great crowds of people. When Lincoln arrived on the train from Springfield, he was met by an immense procession of people on horseback, in carriages, in wagons and vehicles of every description, and on foot, who escorted him through the principal streets to his hotel. The enthusiasm of the multitude was great; but Lincoln's extremely homely face wore an expression of sadness. He rode in a carriage near the head of the procession, looking dust-begrimed and worn and weary; and though he frequently lifted his hat in recognition of the cheers of the crowds lining the streets, I saw no smile on his face, and he seemed to take no pleasure in the demonstrations of enthusiasm which his presence called forth. His clothes were very ill-fitting, and his long arms and hands protruded far through his coat sleeves, giving him a peculiarly uncouth appearance. Though I had often seen him before, and had heard him in court—always with delight in his clearness and cogency of statement, his illuminating humor, and his conspicuous fairness and candor—yet I had never before seen him when he appeared so homely; and I thought him about the ugliest man I had ever seen. There was nothing in his looks or manner that was prepossessing. Such he appeared as he rode in the procession on the forenoon of that warm summer day. His appearance was not different in the afternoon of that day, when, in the public square, he first stood before the great multitude who had assembled there to hear him. His powers were aroused gradually as he went on with his speech. There was much play of humor. 'Judge Douglas has,' he said, 'one great advantage of me in this contest. When he stands before his admiring friends, who gather in great numbers to hear him, they can easily see, with half an eye, all kinds of *fat offices* sprouting out of his fat and jocund face, and, indeed, from every part of his plump and well-rounded body. His appearance is therefore irresistibly attractive. His friends expect him to be President, and they expect their reward. But when I stand before the people, not the sharpest vision is able to detect in my lean and lank person, or in my sunken and hollow cheeks, *the faintest sign or promise* of an office. I am not a candidate for the Presidency, and hence there is no beauty in me that men should desire me. ' The crowd was convulsed with laughter at this sally. As the speech went on, the speaker, though often impressing his points with apposite and laughter-provoking stories, grew more and more earnest. He showed that the government was founded in the interest of freedom, not slavery. He traced the steady aggressions of the slave power step by step, until he came to declare and to dwell upon the fact of the irrepressible conflict between the two. Then, as he went on to show, with wonderful eloquence of speech and of manner, that the country must and would ultimately become, not all slave, but all free, he was transfigured before his audience. His homely countenance fairly glowed with the splendor of his prophetic speech; and his body, no longer awkward and ungainly, but mastered and swayed by his thought, became an obedient and graceful instrument of eloquent expression. The whole man seemed to speak. He seemed like some grand Hebrew prophet, whose face was glorified by the bright visions of a better day which he saw and declared. His eloquence was not merely that of clear and luminous statement, felicitous illustration, or excited yet restrained feeling; it was the eloquence also of *thought*. With something of the imaginative, he united rare dialectic power. He felt the truth before he expounded it, but when once it was felt by him, then his logical power came into remarkably effective play. Step by step he led his hearers onward, till at last he placed them on the summit whence they could see all the landscape of his subject in harmonious and connected order. Of these two contrasted pictures of Lincoln, it is only the last which shows him as he was in his real and essential greatness. And not this fully; for it was in his character that he was greatest. He was not merely a thinker, but a thinker for man, directing his thought to the ends of justice, freedom, and humanity. If he desired and sought high position, it was only that he might thus better serve the cause of freedom to which he was devoted. From the time when he withdrew, in a spirit of magnanimity that was never appreciated, in favor of a rival candidate for the United States Senate, it was evident that the *cause* was more to him than any personal advantage or advancement."

Another graphic description of Lincoln's appearance and manner on the stump is given by Mr. Jeriah Bonham, whose account of the famous "house-divided-against-itself" speech has already found a place in this narrative. "When Mr. Lincoln took the stand," says Mr. Bonham, "he did not, on rising, show his full height, but stood in a stooping posture, his long-tailed coat hanging loosely around his body, and descending over an ill-fitting pair of pantaloons that covered his not very symmetrical legs. He began his speech in a rather diffident manner, seeming for awhile at a loss for words; his voice was irregular, even a little tremulous, as he began his argument. As he proceeded he seemed to gain more confidence, his form straightened up, his face brightened, his language became free and animated. Soon he had drawn the attention of the crowd by two or three well-told stories that illustrated his argument; and then he became eloquent, carrying his audience at will, as tumultuous applause greeted every telling point he made."

Mrs. John A. Logan, in her "Recollections of a Soldier's Wife," says: "I always like to think of Mr. Lincoln as he was when I saw him with the eyes of an opponent. His awkwardness has not been exaggerated, but it gave no effect of self-consciousness. There was something about his ungainliness and his homely face which would have made anyone who simply passed him in the street remember him. His very awkwardness was an asset in public life, in that it attracted attention to him. Douglas, on the other hand, won by the magnetism of his personality. Lincoln did not *seem* to have any magnetism, though of course he actually did have the rarest and most precious kind. Give Mr. Lincoln five minutes and Mr. Douglas five minutes before an audience which knew neither, and Mr. Douglas would make the greater impression. But give them each an hour, and the contrary would be true."

In the party that attended Lincoln in the Senatorial campaign was the Hon. Andrew Shuman, afterwards Lieutenant-Governor of Illinois and one of the veteran journalists of Chicago. Mr. Shuman was detailed to report the joint debates for his paper; and he accompanied Lincoln through nearly all of the campaign, travelling with him by night—sometimes occupying the same room, and when in crowded quarters the same bed. He thus saw much of Lincoln, and had the best of opportunities for studying his character; not only hearing all his public speeches, but having long conversations with him in private, and listening to the stories, anecdotes, and gay or grave discourse by which the journeys and the frequent "waits" were enlivened. The group consisted of several gentlemen, including Norman B. Judd of Chicago, afterwards a member of Congress; Robert R. Hitt, who was Lincoln's shorthand reporter, afterwards member of Congress from Illinois; Mr. Villard, later the President of the Northern Pacific Railroad, then a newspaper correspondent; Mr. Shuman; and, at various times, other politicians and journalists. Of this party Lincoln was always the leading spirit in conversation. He would tell stories himself, and draw out stories from others; and his laugh, though not the loudest, was always the heartiest. Then he would pass to soberer themes, and discuss them with a tinge of that melancholy which, however he might be surrounded, never seemed far distant from him. At night, stopping at the country tavern or at some friend's house, the evenings would be spent in discussion and story-telling, or perhaps in a humorous review of the events of the day; and after retiring, Lincoln would entertain his companion, often far into the night, discoursing on many varied subjects,—politics, literature, views of human life and character, or the prominent men and measures then before the country.

One day, according to Governor Shuman, Lincoln had been announced to speak in a town in the extreme southern part of Illinois, in the very heart of "Egypt," where there was a strong pro-slavery sentiment; and it was feared there might be trouble, as Lincoln's anti-slavery tendencies were well known. To make matters worse, a party of Kentuckians and Missourians had come over to attend the meeting, and it was noised about that they would not allow Lincoln to speak. He heard of it, and both he and his friends were somewhat apprehensive of trouble. The place of the meeting was a grove in the edge of the town, the speakers occupying an improvised stand. The gathering was a large one, and it had every appearance of a Southern crowd. It was customary in those times for the men in that section of the country to carry pistols and ugly-looking knives strapped to their persons, on public occasions. It was a semi-barbarous community, and their hatred of the Abolitionists, as they called all anti-slavery men, was as intense as was their love of bad whiskey. Lincoln privately told his friends, who in that locality were very few in number, that "if only they will give me a fair chance to say a few opening words, I'll fix them all right." Before mounting the speaker's stand he was introduced to many of the crowd, and shook their hands in the usual Western way. Getting a small company of the rough-looking fellows around him, he opened on them. "Fellow-citizens of Southern Illinois— fellow-citizens of the State of Kentucky—fellow-citizens of Missouri," he said, in a tone more of conversation than of oratory, looking them straight in the eye, "I am told that there are some of you here present who would like to make trouble for me. I don't understand why they should. I am a plain, common man, like the rest of you; and why should not I have as good a right to speak my sentiments as the rest of you? Why, good friends, I am one of you; I am not an interloper here! I was born in Kentucky, raised in Illinois, just like the most of you, and worked my way right along by hard scratching. I know the people of Kentucky, and I know the people of Southern Illinois, and I think I know the Missourians. I am one of them, and therefore ought to know them, and they ought to know me better, and if they did know me better they would know that I am not disposed to make them trouble; then why should they, or any one of them, want to make trouble for me? Don't do any such foolish thing, fellow-citizens. Let us be friends, and treat each other like friends. I am one of the humblest and most peaceable men in the world—would wrong no man, would interfere with no man's rights; and all I ask is that, having something to say, you will give me a decent hearing. And, being Illinoisans, Kentuckians, and Missourians—brave and gallant people—I feel sure that you will do that. And now let us reason together, like the honest fellows we are." Having uttered these words, his face the very picture of good-nature and his voice full of sympathetic earnestness, he mounted the speaker's stand and proceeded to make one of the most impressive speeches against the further extension of slavery that he ever made in his life. He was listened to attentively; was applauded when he indulged in flashes of humor, and once or twice his eloquent passages were lustily cheered. His little opening remarks had calmed the threatening storm, had conquered his enemies, and he had smooth sailing. From that day to the time of his death, Abraham Lincoln held a warm place in the respect of very many of those rough and rude "Egyptians," and he had no warmer supporters for the Presidency, or while he was President, than they were.

Mr. Leonard Volk, the sculptor who afterwards made an excellent bust of Lincoln, says: "My first meeting with Abraham Lincoln was in 1858, when the celebrated Senatorial contest opened between him and Stephen A. Douglas. I was invited by the latter to accompany him and his party by a special train to Springfield, to which train was attached a platform-car having on board a cannon, which made considerable noise on the journey. At Bloomington we all stopped over night, as Douglas had a speech to make there in the evening. The party went to the Landon House—the only hotel, I believe, in the place at that time. While we were sitting in the hotel office after supper, Mr. Lincoln entered, carrying an old carpet-bag in his hand, and wearing a weather-beaten silk hat—too large, apparently, for his head—a long, loosely-fitting frock-coat of black alpaca, and vest and trousers of the same material. He walked up to the counter, and, saluting the clerk pleasantly, passed the bag over to him, and inquired if he was too late for supper. The clerk replied that supper was over, but perhaps enough could be 'scraped up' for him. 'All right,' said Mr. Lincoln; 'I don't want much.' Meanwhile, he said, he would wash the dust off. He was certainly very dusty; it was the month of June, and quite warm. While he was so engaged, several old friends, who had learned of his arrival, rushed in to see him, some of them shouting, 'How are you, Old Abe?' Mr. Lincoln grasped them by the hand in his cordial manner, with the broadest and pleasantest smile on his rugged face. This was the first good view I had of the 'coming man.' The next day we all stopped at the town of Lincoln, where short speeches were made by the contestants, and dinner was served at the hotel; after which, as Mr. Lincoln came out on the plank-walk in front, I was formally presented to him. He saluted me with his natural cordiality, grasping my hand in both his large hands with a vice-like grip, and looking down into my face with his beaming, dark, full eyes, said: 'How do you do? I am glad to meet you. I have read of you in the papers. You are making a statue of Judge Douglas for Governor Matteson's new house.' 'Yes, sir,' I answered; 'and sometime when you are in Chicago, and can spare the time, I would like to have you sit to me for a bust.' 'Yes, I will, Mr. Volk; I shall be glad to, the first opportunity I have.' All were soon on board the long train, crowded with people, going to hear the speeches at Springfield. The train stopped on the track, near Edward's Grove, in the northern outskirts of the town, where staging was erected and a vast crowd waited under the shade of the trees. On leaving the train, most of the passengers climbed over the fences and crossed the stubble-field, taking a short-cut to the grove,—among them Mr. Lincoln, who stalked forward alone, taking immense strides, the before-mentioned carpet-bag and an umbrella in his hands, and his coat skirts flying in the breeze. I managed to keep pretty close in the rear of the tall, gaunt figure, with the head craned forward, apparently much over the balance, like the Leaning Tower of Pisa, that was moving something like a hurricane across that rough stubble-field."

The contest between Lincoln and Douglas seemed to be, as expressed by Dr. Newton Bateman, "one between sharpness and greatness." Lincoln seemed to Dr. Bateman, "a man strongly possessed by a belief to which he was earnestly striving to win the people over; while the aim of Mr. Douglas seemed rather to be simply to defeat Mr. Lincoln." Yet, although Lincoln was usually earnest and considerate of his opponent, he could, when occasion required, bring his powers of humor and sarcasm into play in a very effective manner. A few pointed illustrations may be given. In his speech at Galesburg, Douglas sneeringly informed the citizens that "Honest Abe" had been a liquor-seller. Lincoln met this with the candid admission that once in early life he had, under the pressure of poverty, accepted and for a few months held a position in a store where it was necessary for him to retail liquor. "But the difference between Judge Douglas and myself is just this," he added, "that while I was *behind* the bar, he was *in front* of it."

At the close of the joint discussion at Alton, Douglas led off with a speech an hour long, in which he showed no little irritability. The campaign was evidently wearing on him. Lincoln, on the contrary, was in capital spirits. "He sat taking in the speech of Douglas with seeming immobility," says Mr. Jeriah Bonham, who was present, "and when it was ended, he rose to reply. As in the opening of all his speeches, he spoke slowly, did not rise to his full height, leaning forward in a stooping posture at first, his person showing all the angularities of limb and face. For the first five or ten minutes he was both awkward and diffident, as in almost monotonous tones he began to untangle the meshes of Douglas's sophistry. Proceeding, he gained confidence gradually; his voice rang out strong and clear; his tall form towered to its full height; his face grew radiant with impassioned feeling, as he poured forth an outburst of crushing argument and inspiring eloquence. The people became wild with enthusiasm, but his voice rang loud above their cheers. Frequently in his speech he would turn toward Douglas, and say with emphasis, 'You *know* these things are so, Mr. Douglas! ' or 'You know these things are *not* so, Mr. Douglas! ' At one time he bent his long body over his adversary, pouring in his arguments so sharply, that Douglas, chafing under the attack, rose to explain; but Lincoln would not allow it. 'Sit down, Mr. Douglas!' said he peremptorily. 'I did not interrupt you, and you shall not interrupt me. You will have opportunity to reply to me—if you can—in your closing speech.'"

A good story is told of the occasion on which Lincoln and Douglas spoke in Chicago. A well-known citizen who on account of his age was known familiarly as "Father Brewster"—a man of standing, and a member of the Board of Education—was one of the listeners on the platform. Lincoln admired the old gentleman very much, and the admiration was mutual. They sat together while Douglas made the opening speech. He spoke for more than an hour, and never more brilliantly. When Lincoln's turn came he could see that Father Brewster was exceedingly anxious as to the outcome. Lincoln arose, let out all the joints in his long body, slowly removed his overcoat and laid it across Mr. Brewster's knees. "Father Brewster," he said, "will you hold my overcoat *while I stone Stephen?*" Everybody shouted and cheered, and even Douglas joined in the laugh at his own expense.

Beneath the humors and excitements of the campaign, the prevailing tone of Lincoln's thought was deeply serious and reflective. Toward the close, when indications pointed to his defeat for the Senate, he seemed somewhat depressed, and occasionally his old habitual melancholy would steal over him and impart to his words a touching pathos. On such an occasion, in one of the smaller cities of Illinois, Douglas, having the first speech, made an unusually brilliant effort. He carried the crowd with him; and when Lincoln rose to reply, it was evident that he felt his disadvantage—felt, too, that do what he would final defeat was probable. He made a good speech, but not one of his best. Concluding his argument, he stopped and stood silent for a moment, looking around upon the throng of half-indifferent, half-friendly faces before him, with those deep-sunken weary eyes that always seemed full of unshed tears. Folding his hands, as if they too were tired of the hopeless fight, he said, in his peculiar monotone: "My friends, it makes little difference, very little difference, whether Judge Douglas or myself is elected to the United States Senate; but the great issue which we have submitted to you to-day is far above and beyond any personal interests or the political fortunes of any man. And, my friends, that issue will live and breathe and burn when the poor, feeble, stammering tongues of Judge Douglas and myself are silent in the grave." The crowd swayed as if smitten by a mighty wind. The simple words, and the manner in which they were spoken, touched every heart to the core.

Lincoln spoke in all about fifty times during the campaign. At its close, says Mr. Arnold, "both Douglas and Lincoln visited Chicago. Douglas was so hoarse that he could hardly articulate, and it was painful to hear him attempt to speak. Lincoln's voice was clear and vigorous, and he really seemed in better tone than usual. His dark complexion was bronzed by the prairie sun and winds; his eye was clear, his step firm, and he looked like a trained athlete, ready to enter, rather than one who had closed, a conflict."

Of the speeches in this campaign, Mr. Henry J. Raymond, the distinguished journalist, pronounced the following well-considered opinion: "While Douglas fully sustained his previous reputation, and justified the estimate his friends had placed upon his abilities, he labored under the comparative disadvantage of being much better known to the country at large than was his antagonist. During his long public career, people had become partially accustomed to his manner of presenting arguments and enforcing them. The novelty and freshness of Lincoln's addresses, on the other hand, the homeliness and force of his illustrations, their wonderful pertinence, his exhaustless humor, his confidence in his own resources, engendered by his firm belief in the justice of the cause he so ably advocated, never once rising, however, to the point of arrogance or superciliousness, fastened upon him the eyes of the people everywhere, friends and opponents alike. It was not strange that more than once, during the course of the unparalleled excitement which marked this canvass, Douglas should have been thrown off his guard by the singular self-possession displayed by his antagonist, and by the imperturbable firmness with which he maintained and defended a position once taken. The unassuming confidence which marked Lincoln's conduct was early imparted to his supporters, and each succeeding encounter added largely to the number of his friends, until they began to indulge the hope that a triumph might be secured in spite of the adverse circumstances under which the struggle was commenced."

Samuel Bowles, editor of the Springfield (Mass.) "Republican," said that Lincoln "handled Douglas as he would an eel—by main strength. Sometimes, perhaps, he handled him so strongly that he *slipped through his fingers*."

"In this canvass," says Mr. Lamon, "Mr. Lincoln earned a reputation as a popular debater second to that of no man in America—certainly not second to that of his famous antagonist. He kept his temper; he was not prone to personalities; he was fair, frank, and manly; and, if the contest had shown nothing else, it would have shown at least that 'Old Abe' could behave like a gentleman under very trying circumstances. His marked success in these discussions was probably no surprise to the people of the Springfield district, who knew him as well as they did Mr. Douglas, or even better. But in the greater part of the State, and throughout the Union, the series of brilliant victories successively won by an obscure man over an orator of such wide experience and renown was received with exclamations of astonishment alike by listeners and readers."

Caleb Cushing, the distinguished Massachusetts lawyer, was one of those acute minds whose attention was attracted to Lincoln by his debates with Douglas. Mr. Cushing said that these debates showed Lincoln to be the superior of Douglas "in every vital element of power"; and added that "the world does not yet know how much of a man Lincoln really is." It was soon to know him much more clearly. In less than two years after the great debate this lately obscure Illinois lawyer was elected President of the United States.

CHAPTER XII

On the 2d of November, 1858, the State election was held in Illinois. The chief significance of this election was due to the fact that the Legislature then chosen would decide whether Douglas or Lincoln should be sent to the Senate at Washington. The result showed that Lincoln had, by his hard efforts, won a victory for his cause and for his party, but not for himself. The Republican State ticket was elected by a majority of about 4,000 votes; but in the Legislature a number of members held over from the election of two years before, and the Republican gains, though considerable, were not quite sufficient to overcome this adverse element. When the Legislature met, Douglas was re-elected to the Senate by a small majority. It is said that Lincoln was deeply grieved by his defeat. When some one inquired of him how he felt over the result, he answered that he felt "like the boy that stubbed his toe,—'it hurt too bad to laugh, and he was too big to cry!'"

A few days after his return to Springfield, there was pressed on the attention of the defeated candidate a matter which must have been peculiarly unwelcome at the time, but which was accepted with habitual fortitude. What this matter was is revealed in the following letter:

SPRINGFIELD, NOV. 16, 1858.

HON. N.B. JUDD—*My Dear Sir*:—Yours of the 15th is just received. I wrote you the same day. As to the pecuniary matter, I am willing to pay according to my ability, but I am the poorest hand living to get others to pay. I have been on expense so long, without earning anything, that I am absolutely without money now for even household expenses. Still, if you can put in two hundred and fifty dollars for me towards discharging the debt of the committee, I will allow it when you and I settle the private matter between us. This, with what I have already paid with an outstanding note of mine, will exceed my subscription of five hundred dollars. This, too, is exclusive of my ordinary expenses during the campaign, all of which, being added to my loss of time and business, bears pretty heavily upon one no better off than I am. But as I had the post of honor, it is not for me to be over-nice.

You are feeling badly. *And this, too, shall pass away;* never fear.

Yours as ever,
A. LINCOLN.

Hon. E.M. Haines, who was a member of the Legislature of 1858-9, and a supporter of Lincoln for the Senate, states that Lincoln seemed greatly depressed by his defeat, and that his friends were also somewhat disheartened regarding his future prospects, and neglected him to some extent. "Some time after the Senatorial election," says Mr. Haines, "Governor Bissell gave a reception at his house, which I attended with my wife. After we had paid our respects to the Governor and Mrs. Bissell, we passed on to an adjoining room, where there was quite a throng of people engaged in conversation. Mr. Lincoln was standing near the centre of the room, entirely alone, with his usual sad countenance, and apparently unnoticed by anyone. I said to my wife, 'Here is Mr. Lincoln; he looks as if he had lost all his friends; come and have an introduction to him, and cheer him up.' Mr. Lincoln received us very cordially, and we entered into a general conversation, apparently unnoticed, and attracting no attention from others as they passed and repassed around us. Dancing was going on in the adjacent rooms, and Mr. Lincoln invited my wife to join him in the dancing, which she did, and he apparently took much pleasure in the recreation. My wife afterwards related to me much that Mr. Lincoln said in their conversation during the evening. His despondency became much dispelled after they became engaged in conversation; indeed, she said that he seemed to be putting forth an effort to get out of the gloomy condition which had come upon him from the result of his Senatorial canvass. He had occasion during their conversation to refer to his age, remarking incidentally that he was almost fifty years old; whereupon, as if suddenly reflecting that his age was a good part of a man's life, and as if unwilling to relinquish his hold upon the future, he suddenly braced himself up, and said, 'But, Mrs. Haines, I feel that I am good for another fifty years yet.'"

During the winter following the Senatorial debate Lincoln was occupied with his private affairs. The love of public speaking had become so strong with him that he prepared a lecture and delivered it to the public at several places during the winter. It was somewhat humorous in character, but was not much of a success, and he soon declined further invitations to deliver it. To one correspondent he wrote, in March, 1859: "Your note, inviting me to deliver a lecture in Galesburg, is received. I regret to say that I cannot do so now. I must stick to the courts for awhile. I read a sort of a lecture to three different audiences during the last month and this; but I did so under circumstances which made it a waste of time, of no value whatever."

The following autumn (1859) Senator Douglas visited Ohio and made speeches for the Democratic party there. From the Republican ranks there arose a cry for Lincoln, whose superiority to Douglas in the great debate of the preceding year was still fresh in the public mind. He promptly answered it, and spoke in that State with marked effect. At Cincinnati he addressed himself especially to Kentuckians, and said, in a strain which is now seen to be prophetic:

I should not wonder if there were some Kentuckians in this audience; we are close to Kentucky; but whether that be so or not, we are on elevated ground, and by speaking distinctly I should not wonder if some of the Kentuckians would hear me on the other side of the river. For that purpose I propose to address a portion of what I have to say to the Kentuckians. I say, then, in the first place, to the Kentuckians, that I am what they call, as I understand it, a 'Black Republican.' I think slavery is wrong, morally and politically. I desire that it should be no further spread in these United States, and I should not object if it should gradually terminate in the whole Union. While I say this for myself, I say to you Kentuckians, that I understand you differ radically with me upon this proposition; that you believe slavery is a good thing; that slavery is right; that it ought to be extended and perpetuated in this Union. Now, there being this broad difference between us, I do not pretend, in addressing myself to you Kentuckians, to attempt proselyting you; that would be a vain effort. I will tell you, so far as I am authorized to speak for the opposition, what we mean to do with you. We mean to treat you, as nearly as we possibly can, as Washington, Jefferson, and Madison treated you. We mean to leave you alone, and in no way to interfere with your institution; to abide by all and every compromise of the Constitution, and, in a word, coming back to the original proposition, to treat you, so far as degenerated men (if we have degenerated) may, according to the examples of those noble fathers—Washington, Jefferson and Madison. We mean to remember that you are as good as we; that there is no difference between us, other than the difference of circumstances. We mean to recognize and bear in mind always, that you have as good hearts in your bosoms as other people, or as we claim to have, and treat you accordingly. We mean to marry your girls, when we have a chance—the white ones, I mean—and I have the honor to inform you that I once did have a chance in that way. I have told you what we mean to do. I want to know now what *you* mean to do. I often hear it intimated that you mean to divide the Union whenever a Republican, or anything like it, is elected President of the United States. [A voice—'That is so.'] 'That is so,' one of them says; I wonder if he is a Kentuckian? [A voice—'He is a Douglas man.'] Well, then, I want to know what you are going to do with your half of it? Are you going to split the Ohio down through, and push your half off a piece? Or are you going to keep it right alongside of us outrageous fellows? Or are you going to build up a wall some way between your country and ours, by which that movable property of yours can't come over here any more, to the danger of your losing it? Do you think you can better yourselves on that subject by leaving us here under no obligation whatever to return those specimens of your movable property that come hither? You have divided the Union because we would not do right with you, as you think, upon that subject; when we cease to be under obligations to do anything for you, how much better off do you think you will be? Will you make war upon us and kill us all? Why, gentlemen, I think you are as gallant and as brave men as live; that you can fight as bravely in a good cause, man for man, as any other people living; that you have shown yourselves capable of this upon various occasions; but man for man, you are not better than we are, and there are not so many of you as there are of us. You will never make much of a hand at whipping us. If we were fewer in numbers than you, I think that you could whip us; if we were equal, it would likely be a drawn battle; but being inferior in numbers, you will make nothing by attempting to master us.

The Hon. W.M. Dickson, whose interesting account of Lincoln's first visit to Cincinnati and the disappointments attending it has already been given in this narrative, says of this second visit as contrasted with the obscurity of the first: "Lincoln returned to the city with a fame wide as the continent, with the laurels of the Douglas contest on his brow, and the Presidency almost in his grasp. He returned, greeted with the thunder of cannon, the strains of martial music, and the joyous plaudits of thousands of citizens thronging the streets. He addressed a vast concourse on Fifth Street Market;

was entertained in princely style at the Burnet House; and there received with courtesy the foremost citizens, come to greet this Western rising star."

In December of the same year Lincoln visited Kansas and addressed the people of that troubled State upon the political questions then before the country. At Leavenworth, Atchison, Elwood, and other places, he was met by large gatherings of eager listeners who were charmed and convinced by his fresh and reassuring utterances. His journeys were complete ovations, and he returned to Illinois leaving a host of new friends behind him. As several of Lincoln's biographers make no reference to his Kansas visit, and the entire matter seems more or less obscured, the following letter, lately written by Mr. Harry W. Stewart, of Carlsbad, New Mexico, is of much interest: "I have recently seen a reference to Lincoln's visit to Kansas as if the fact were not clearly established. In this connection I may offer a personal recollection of my father, James G. Stewart, who was a physician practicing in the little town of Elwood, Kansas, from 1856 to 1860. He said that both Lincoln and Seward came out and spoke in St. Joseph, Mo., just across the river from Elwood. On each occasion a large following of 'free state' men went over to St. Jo to hear the speech and incidentally to support the speaker in case of violence, which had been freely predicted. According to this reminiscence, Lincoln crossed the Missouri into Kansas, my father having the honor of taking him in a buggy to a small town fourteen miles distant from Elwood in Doniphan County. They drove out to Troy, where Mr. Lincoln made a speech. From here I think he went on to Lawrence and other places before returning to St. Joseph, but have no account of his movements beyond Troy. I think it was in the year 1858 and must have been in the summer time, for the party took Mr. Lincoln over the Missouri on a ferry. It did not make trips oftener than about once in two hours. When Lincoln came to the bank on the Missouri side the boat had just gone. There was no waiting-room or benches to sit on and some of the party were inclined to think they were in hard luck. When Lincoln found out how it was, he said: 'It's all right. We'll sit right down on the sand and wait for the boat.' Then they all sat down on the ground and listened to genuine Lincoln stories till the time was up. My father often spoke with delight of this incident. I have looked in vain in Lincoln histories for a more definite account of this Kansas trip. Of the actual fact there can be no doubt."

Lincoln's fame, as we have seen, had now extended to the East, where he seems to have been looked upon as a rising man and an interesting figure in national politics. Invitations to visit the East now began to reach him. In the following February (1860) he went to Brooklyn, for the purpose of delivering a lecture in Mr. Beecher's church. The invitation had given him much pleasure, and he prepared himself thoroughly; indeed, it is said that no effort of his life cost him so much labor as this. In the Plymouth congregation of Brooklyn there was an association of young men which was successful in getting an annual course of six lectures of the highest order. This association discerned in Lincoln a man worthy of a place in its course, and invited him to give such a lecture. Meanwhile, some prominent Republican politicians of New York had heard of him as a possible candidate for the Presidency, and desired him to make a speech in that city in order to determine whether he would be the man to present to the Republican National convention in case Mr. Seward could not be nominated. Lincoln informed these gentlemen of his Brooklyn engagement, but said he would speak in New York if the Brooklyn club gave its consent. That club agreed to this arrangement; and thus it was decided that Lincoln's speech should be delivered in New York City, instead of Brooklyn, as had been first intended. Mr. R.C. McCormick, who was a member of the committee in charge of the arrangements, says: "When Mr. Lincoln came to New York City, there was some confusion in the arrangements. He had at first been invited to appear in Brooklyn, but upon deliberation his friends thought it best that he should be heard in New York. Reaching the Astor House on Saturday, February 25, he was surprised to find by announcement in the public prints that he was to speak at the Cooper Institute. He said he must review his address if it was to be delivered in New York. What he had prepared for Mr. Beecher's church-folks might not be altogether appropriate to a miscellaneous political audience. Saturday was spent in a review of the speech, and on Sunday morning he went to Plymouth church, where apparently he greatly enjoyed the service. On Monday morning I waited upon him with several members of the Young Men's Republican Union, into whose hands the preparations for the meeting at the Cooper Institute had fallen. We found him in a suit of black, much wrinkled from its careless packing in a small valise. He received us cordially, apologizing for the awkward and uncomfortable appearance he made in his new suit, and expressing himself surprised at being in New York. His form and manner were indeed very odd, and we thought him the most unprepossessing public man we had ever met. I spoke to him of the manuscript of his forthcoming address, and suggested to him that it should be given to the press at his earliest convenience, in order that it might be published in full on the morning following its delivery. He appeared in much doubt as to whether any of the papers would care to print it; and it was only when I accompanied a reporter to his room and made a request for it, that he began to think his words might be of interest to the metropolitan public. He seemed wholly ignorant of the custom of supplying slips to the different journals from the office first putting the addresses in type, and was charmingly innocent of the machinery so generally used, even by some of our most popular orators, to give success and *éclat* to their public efforts.

The address was written upon blue foolscap paper, all in his own hand, and with few interlineations. I was bold enough to read portions of it, and had no doubt that its delivery would create a marked sensation throughout the country. Lincoln referred frequently to Douglas, but always in a generous and kindly manner. It was difficult to regard them as antagonists. Many stories of the famous Illinois debates were told us, and in a very short time his frank and sparkling conversation won our hearts and made his plain face pleasant to us all. During the day it was suggested that he should be taken up Broadway and shown the city, of which he knew but little — stating, I think, that he had been here but once before. At one place he met an Illinois acquaintance of former years, to whom he said, in his dry, good-natured way: 'Well, B., how have you fared since you left Illinois?' To which B. replied, 'I have made a hundred thousand dollars, and lost all. How is it with you, Mr. Lincoln?' 'Oh, very well,' said Lincoln. 'I have the cottage at Springfield, and about eight thousand dollars in money. If they make me Vice-president with Seward, as some say they will, I hope I shall be able to increase it to twenty thousand; and that is as much as any man ought to want.' We visited a photographic establishment upon the corner of Broadway and Bleeker streets, where he sat for his picture, the first taken in New York. At the gallery he met and was introduced to Hon. George Bancroft, and had a brief conversation with that gentleman, who welcomed him to New York. The contrast in the appearance of the men was most striking; the one courtly and precise in his every word and gesture, with the air of a trans-Atlantic statesman; the other bluff and awkward, his very utterance an apology for his ignorance of metropolitan manners and customs. 'I am on my way to Massachusetts,' he said to Mr. Bancroft, 'where I have a son at school, who, if report be true, already knows much more than his father.'"

On the evening of February 27 a large and brilliant audience gathered at Cooper Institute, to hear the famous Western orator. The scene was one never to be forgotten by those who witnessed it. Upon the platform sat many of the prominent men of the Republican party, and in the body of the hall were many ladies. The meeting was presided over by the distinguished citizen and poet William Cullen Bryant, of whom Mr. Lincoln afterward said, "It was worth a journey to the East merely to see such a man." The orator of the evening was introduced by Mr. Bryant with some very complimentary allusions, especially to his controversy with Douglas. "When Mr. Lincoln came on the platform and was introduced by Mr. Bryant," says one who was present, "he seemed a giant in contrast with him. His first sentence was delivered in a peculiarly high-keyed voice, and disappointed us. In a short time the sharp points of his address began to come, and he had not been speaking for half an hour before his audience seemed wild with enthusiasm." Another account says: "His manner was, to a New York audience, a very strange one, but it was captivating. He held the vast meeting spell-bound, and as one by one his oddly expressed but trenchant and convincing arguments confirmed the soundness of his political conclusions, the house broke out in wild and prolonged enthusiasm. I think I never saw an audience more thoroughly carried away by an orator." This speech was full of trenchant passages, which called forth tumultuous applause. The following is a specimen:

> I defy anyone to show that any living man in the whole world ever did, prior to the beginning of the present century (and I might almost say prior to the beginning of the last half of the present century), declare that, in his understanding, any proper division of local from Federal authority, or any part of the Constitution, forbade the Federal Government to control slavery in the Federal territories. To those who now so declare, I give not only our fathers who framed the government under which we live, but with them all other living men within the century in which it was framed, among whom to search, and they shall not be able to find the evidence of a single man agreeing with them.

Referring to the South, and the growing political discontent in that quarter, he said:

> Let all who believe that our fathers understood this question just as well as, and even better than, we do now, speak as they spoke and act as they acted upon it. This is all Republicans ask—all Republicans desire—in relation to slavery. As those fathers marked it, so let it be again marked, as an evil not to be extended, but to be tolerated and protected only because, and so far as, its actual presence among us makes that toleration and protection a necessity. Let all the guarantees those fathers gave it be not grudgingly but fully and fairly maintained.

His counsel to the young Republican party was timely and full of wisdom.

> A few words now to Republicans: It is exceedingly desirable that all parts of this great Confederacy shall be at peace, and in harmony one with another. Let us Republicans do our part to have it so. Even though much provoked, let us do nothing through passion and ill-temper. Even though

the Southern people will not so much as listen to us, let us calmly consider their demands, and yield to them, if in our deliberate view of our duty we possibly can.

The address closed with the following impressive words:

Wrong as we think slavery is, we can yet afford to let it alone where it is, because that much is due to the necessity arising from its actual presence in the nation; but can we, while our votes will prevent it, allow it to spread into the National Territories, and to overrun us here in these free States? If our sense of duty forbids this, then let us stand by our duty, fearlessly and effectively. Let us be diverted by none of those sophistical contrivances wherewith we are so industriously plied and belabored—contrivances such as groping for some middle ground between the right and the wrong, vain as the search for a man who should be neither a living man nor a dead man,—such as a policy of 'don't care' on a question about which all true men do care,—such as Union appeals, beseeching true Union men to yield to Disunionists, reversing the divine rule, and calling not the sinners but the righteous to repentance,—such as invocations of Washington, imploring men to unsay what Washington said and undo what Washington did. Neither let us be slandered from our duty by false accusations against us, nor frightened from it by menaces of destruction to the Government nor of dungeons to ourselves. Let us have faith that right makes might; and in that faith, let us to the end dare to do our duty as we understand it.

The Cooper Institute speech made a profound impression upon the public. All who saw and heard Lincoln on that occasion felt the influence of his strange but powerful personality; and acute minds recognized in the unsophisticated Western lawyer a new force in American politics. This speech made Lincoln known throughout the country, and undoubtedly did more than anything else to secure him the nomination for the Presidency. Aside from its extensive publication in the newspapers, various editions of it appeared in pamphlet form, one of the best of which was issued by Messrs. C.C. Nott and Cephas Brainard, who appended to their edition an estimate of the speech that is well worth reprinting here: "No one who has not actually attempted to verify its details can understand the patient research and historical labor which it embodies. The history of our earlier politics is scattered through numerous journals, statutes, pamphlets, and letters; and these are defective in completeness and accuracy of statement, and in indexes and tables of contents. Neither can any one who has not travelled over this precise ground appreciate the accuracy of every trivial detail, or the self-denying impartiality with which Mr. Lincoln has turned from the testimony of 'the fathers' on the general question of slavery to present the single question which he discusses. From the first line to the last, from his premises to his conclusion, he travels with a swift, unerring directness which no logician ever excelled,—an argument complete and full, without the affectation of learning, and without the stiffness which usually accompanies dates and details. A single easy, simple sentence of plain Anglo-Saxon words contains a chapter of history that, in some instances, has taken days of labor to verify, and must have cost the author months of investigation to acquire; and though the public should justly estimate the labor bestowed on the facts which are stated, they cannot estimate the greater labor involved on those which are omitted—how many pages have been read—how many works examined—what numerous statutes, resolutions, speeches, letters, and biographies have been looked through. Commencing with this address as a political pamphlet, the reader will leave it as an historical work—brief, complete, profound, impartial, truthful,—which will survive the time and the occasion that called it forth, and be esteemed hereafter no less for its intrinsic worth than for its unpretending modesty."

Lincoln's oldest son, Robert, was at this time a student in Harvard University, and, chiefly to visit him, Lincoln made a brief trip to New England. While there he spoke at Concord and Manchester in New Hampshire; at Woonsocket in Rhode Island; and at Hartford, New Haven, Norwich, Meriden, and Bridgeport in Connecticut. These speeches were heard with delight by large audiences, and received hearty praise from the press. At Manchester, "The Mirror," a neutral paper, published the following remarks on Lincoln's style of oratory: "He spoke an hour and a half, with great fairness, great apparent candor, and with wonderful interest. He did not abuse the South, the administration, or the Democrats, nor indulge in any personalities, with the exception of a few hits at 'Douglas's notions.' He is far from prepossessing in personal appearance, and his voice is disagreeable; and yet he wins attention and good-will from the start. He indulges in no flowers of rhetoric, no eloquent passages. He is not a wit, a humorist, or a clown; yet so fine a vein of pleasantry and good-nature pervades what he says, gliding over a deep current of poetical arguments, that he keeps his hearers in a smiling mood, ready to swallow all he says. His sense of the ludicrous is very keen; and an exhibition of that is the clincher of all his arguments—not the ludicrous acts of persons, but ludicrous ideas. For the first half-hour his opponents would agree with every word he uttered; and from that point he began to lead them off little by little, until it seemed as if he had got them all into his fold."

The Rev. John. P. Gulliver, of Norwich, Connecticut, has given a most interesting reminiscence of Lincoln's speech in that city while on his tour through New England. On the morning following the speech he met Lincoln on a railroad train, and entered into conversation with him. In speaking of his speech, Mr. Gulliver remarked to Lincoln that he thought it the most remarkable one he ever heard. "Are you sincere in what you say?" inquired Lincoln. "I mean every word of it," replied the minister; "indeed, I learned more of the art of public speaking last evening than I could from a whole course of lectures on rhetoric." Then Lincoln informed him of a "most extraordinary circumstance" that had occurred at New Haven a few days previous. A professor of rhetoric in Yale College, he had been told, came to hear him, took notes of his speech, and gave a lecture on it to his class the following day, and, not satisfied with that, followed him to Meriden the next evening and heard him again for the same purpose. All this seemed to Lincoln to be "very extraordinary." He had been sufficiently astonished by his success in the West, but he had no expectation of any marked success in the East, particularly among literary and learned men. "Now," said Lincoln, "I should like very much to know what it is in my speech which you thought so remarkable, and which interested my friend the professor so much." Mr. Gulliver's answer was: "The clearness of your statements, the unanswerable style of your reasoning, and especially your illustrations, which were romance and pathos and fun and logic all welded together." After Mr. Gulliver had fully satisfied his curiosity by a further exposition of the politician's peculiar power, Lincoln said: "I am much obliged to you for this. I have been wishing for a long time to find someone who would make this analysis for me. It throws light on a subject which has been dark to me. I can understand very readily how such a power as you have ascribed to me will account for the effect which seems to be produced by my speeches. I hope you have not been too flattering in your estimate. Certainly I have had a most wonderful success for a man of my limited education." Mr. Gulliver then inquired into the processes by which he had acquired his education, and was rewarded with many interesting details. When they were about to part, the minister said: "Mr. Lincoln, may I say one thing to you before we separate?" "Certainly; anything you please," was the response. "You have just spoken," said Mr. Gulliver, "of the tendency of political life in Washington to debase the moral convictions of our representatives there, by the admixture of considerations of mere political expediency. You have become, by the controversy with Mr. Douglas, one of our leaders in this great struggle with slavery, which is undoubtedly the struggle of the nation and the age. What I would like to say is this, and I say it with a full heart: Be true to your principles, and we will be true to you, and God will be true to us all." Mr. Lincoln, touched by the earnestness of his interlocutor, took his hand in both his own, and, with his face full of sympathetic light, exclaimed: "I say *amen* to that! *amen to that!*"

After the New England tour, Lincoln returned to his home in Springfield. As often happens, those least appreciative of his success were his own neighbors; and certain reflections gained vogue concerning his motives in visiting the East. It was charged that he had been mercenary; that his political speeches had been paid for. Something of this sort having been brought to Lincoln's notice, he disposed of the matter in the following manly and characteristic letter:

C.F. McNEILL, ESQ.—*Dear Sir:*—Reaching home yesterday, I found yours of the 23d March, enclosing a slip from the 'Middleport Press.' It is not true that I ever charged anything for a political speech in my life; but this much is true: Last October I was requested by letter to deliver some sort of speech in Mr. Beecher's church in Brooklyn, $200 being offered in the first letter. I wrote that I could do it in February, provided they would take a political speech if I could find time to get up no other. They agreed; and subsequently I informed them the speech would have to be a political one. When I reached New York, I learned for the first time that the place was changed to Cooper Institute. I made the speech, and left for New England, where I have a son at school, neither asking for pay nor having any offered me. Three days after, a check for $200 was sent me, and I took it, and did not know it was wrong. My understanding now is—though I knew nothing of it at the time—that they did charge for admittance at the Cooper Institute, and that they took in more than twice $200. I have made this explanation to you as a friend; but I wish no explanation made to our enemies. What they want is a squabble and a fuss; and that they can have if we explain; and they cannot have it if we don't. When I returned through New York from New England, I was told by the gentleman who sent me the check that a drunken vagabond in the club, having learned something about the $200, made the exhibition out of which the 'Herald' manufactured the article quoted by the 'Press' of your town. My judgment is, and therefore my request is, that you give no denial, and no explanations.

Thanking you for your kind interest in the matter, I remain,

Yours truly, A. LINCOLN.

It appears that on the Sunday which Lincoln spent in New York City he visited a Sunday School in the notorious region called Five Points, and there made a short address to the scholars. After his return to Springfield, one of his neighbors, hearing of this, thought it would be a good subject for bantering Lincoln about, and accordingly visited him for that purpose. This neighbor was generally known as "Jim," just as Lincoln was called "Abe." The following account of his visit, furnished by Mr. Edward Eggleston, shows that he did not derive as much fun from the "bantering" as he had expected: "He started for 'Old Abe's' office; but bursting open the door impulsively, found a stranger in conversation with Mr. Lincoln. He turned to retrace his steps, when Lincoln called out, 'Jim! What do you want?' 'Nothing.' 'Yes, you do; come back.' After some entreaty 'Jim' approached Mr. Lincoln, and remarked, with a twinkle in his eye, 'Well, Abe, I see you have been making a speech to Sunday School children. What's the matter?' 'Sit down, Jim, and I'll tell you all about it.' And with that Lincoln put his feet on the stove, and began: 'When Sunday morning came, I didn't know exactly what to do. Mr. Washburne asked me where I was going. I told him I had nowhere to go; and he proposed to take me down to the Five Points Sunday School, to show me something worth seeing. I was very much interested by what I saw. Presently, Mr. Pease came up and spoke to Mr. Washburne, who introduced me. Mr. Pease wanted us to speak. Washburne spoke, and then I was urged to speak. I told them I did not know anything about talking to Sunday Schools, but Mr. Pease said many of the children were friendless and homeless, and that a few words would do them good. Washburne said I must talk. And so I rose to speak; but I tell you, Jim, I didn't know what to say. I remembered that Mr. Pease said they were homeless and friendless, and I thought of the time when I had been pinched by terrible poverty. And so I told them that I had been poor; that I remembered when my toes stuck out through my broken shoes in winter; when my arms were out at the elbows; when I shivered with the cold. And I told them there was only one rule; that was, always do the very best you can. I told them that I had always tried to do the very best I could; and that, if they would follow that rule, they would get along somehow. That was about what I said. And when I got through, Mr. Pease said it was just the thing they needed. And when the school was dismissed, all the teachers came up and shook hands with me, and thanked me; although I did not know that I had been saying anything of any account. But the next morning I saw my remarks noticed in the papers.' Just here Mr. Lincoln put his hand in his pocket, and remarked that he had never heard anything that touched him as had the songs which those children sang. With that he drew forth a little book, saying that they had given him one of the books from which they sang. He began to read a piece with all the earnestness of his great, earnest soul. In the middle of the second verse his friend 'Jim' felt a choking in his throat and a tickling in his nose. At the beginning of the third verse he saw that the stranger was weeping, and his own tears fell fast. Turning toward Lincoln, who was reading straight on, he saw the great blinding tears in his eyes, so that he could not possibly see the pages. He was repeating that little song from memory. How often he had read it, or how long its sweet and simple accents continued to reverberate through his soul, no one can know."

CHAPTER XIII

In the latter part of the year 1859, after Lincoln had gained considerable national prominence through events already briefly narrated, some of his friends began to consider the expediency of bringing him forward as a candidate for the Presidency in 1860. The young Republican party had thus far been in the minority, and the necessity was generally felt of nominating a man who would not render himself objectionable by advocating extreme or unpopular measures. The subject was mentioned to Lincoln, but he seems not to have taken it very seriously. He said that there were distinguished men in the party who were more worthy of the nomination, and whose public services entitled them to it. Toward spring in 1860 Lincoln consented to a conference on the subject with some of his more intimate friends. The meeting took place in a committee-room in the State House. Mr. Bushnell, Mr. Hatch (then Secretary of State), Mr. Judd (Chairman of the Republican State Central Committee), Mr. Peck, and Mr. Grimshaw were present. They were unanimous in opinion as to the expediency and propriety of making Lincoln a candidate. But he was still reluctant; he doubted that he could get the nomination even if he wished it, and asked until the next morning to consider the matter. The next day he authorized his friends to work for him, if they so desired, as a candidate for the Presidency, at the National Republican convention to be held in May at Chicago.

It is evident that while Lincoln had no serious expectation of receiving the nomination, yet having consented to become a candidate he was by no means indifferent on the subject. The following confidential letter to his friend N.B. Judd shows his feelings at this time.

SPRINGFIELD, ILL., FEBRUARY 9, 1860.

HON. N.B. JUDD—*Dear Sir:*—I am not in a position where it would hurt much for me not to be nominated on the national ticket; but I am where it would hurt some for me not to get the Illinois delegates. What I expected when I wrote the letter to Messrs. Dole and others is now happening. Your discomfited assailants are more bitter against me, and they will, for revenge upon me, lay to the Bates egg in the South and the Seward egg in the North, and go far towards squeezing me out in the middle with nothing. Can you not help me a little in this matter in your end of the vineyard? (I mean this to be private.)

Yours as ever, A. LINCOLN.

It would seem that the original intention of Lincoln's friends had been to bring him out as a candidate for the Vice-Presidency. Hon. E.M. Haines states that as early as the spring of 1859, before the adjournment of the Legislature of which he was a member, some of the Republican members discussed the feasibility of urging Lincoln's name for the Vice-Presidency. Lincoln appears not to have taken very strongly to the suggestion. "I recollect," says Mr. Haines, "that one day Mr. Lincoln came to my desk in the House of Representatives, to make some inquiry regarding another member; and during the conversation, referring to his growing reputation, I remarked to him that I did not know that we would be able to make him President, but perhaps we could do the next best thing, and make him Vice-President. He brightened up somewhat, and answered by a story which I do not clearly recall, but the application of which was that he scarcely considered himself a big enough man for President, while the Vice-Presidency was scarcely big enough office for one who had aspired to a seat in the Senate of the United States."

On the 9th and 10th of May, 1860, the Republicans of Illinois met in convention at Decatur. Lincoln was present, although he is said to have been there as a mere spectator. It was, Mr. Lamon tells us, "A very large and spirited body, comprising the most brilliant as well as the shrewdest men in the party. It was evident that something of more than usual importance was expected to transpire. A few moments after the convention organized, 'Old Abe' was seen squatting, or sitting on his heels, just within the door of the convention building. Governor Oglesby rose and said, amid increasing silence, 'I am informed that a distinguished citizen of Illinois, and one whom Illinois will ever delight to honor, is present; and I wish to move that this body invite him to a seat on the stand.' Here the Governor paused, as if to work curiosity up to the highest point; then he shouted the magic name, '*Abraham Lincoln!*' A roar of applause shook every board and joist of the building. The motion was seconded and passed. A rush was made for the hero, who still sat on his heels. He was seized and jerked to his feet. An effort was made to 'jam him through the crowd' to his place of honor on the stage; but the crowd was too dense. Then he was 'boosted'—lifted up bodily—and lay for a few seconds sprawling and kicking upon the heads and shoulders of the great throng. In this manner he was gradually pushed toward the stand, and finally reached it, doubtless to his great relief, 'in the arms of some half-dozen gentlemen,' who set him down in full view of his clamorous admirers. 'The cheering was like the roar of the sea. Hats were thrown up by the Chicago delegation, as if hats were no longer useful.' Mr. Lincoln rose, bowed, smiled, blushed, and thanked the assembly as well as he could in the midst of such a tumult. A gentleman who saw it all says, 'I then thought him one of the most diffident and worst-plagued men I ever saw.' At another stage of the proceedings, Governor Oglesby rose again with another provoking and mysterious speech. 'There was,' he said, 'an old Democrat outside who had something he wished to present to the convention.' 'Receive it!' 'Receive it!' cried some. 'What is it?' 'What is it?' yelled some of the lower Egyptians, who seemed to have an idea that the 'old Democrat' might want to blow them up with an infernal machine. The door opened; and a fine, robust old fellow, with an open countenance and bronzed cheeks, marched into the midst of the assemblage, bearing on his shoulder 'two small triangular heart rails,' surmounted by a banner with this inscription: '*Two rails from a lot made by Abraham Lincoln and John Hanks, in the Sangamon Bottom, in the year 1830.*' The sturdy rail-bearer was old John Hanks himself, enjoying the great field-day of his life. He was met with wild and tumultuous cheers, prolonged through several minutes; and it was observed that the Chicago and Central-Illinois men sent up the loudest and longest cheering. The scene was tempestuous and bewildering. But it ended at last; and now the whole body, those in the secret and those out of it, clamored for a speech from Mr. Lincoln, who in the meantime 'blushed,' but seemed to shake with inward laughter. In response to the repeated calls he rose and said: 'Gentlemen, I suppose you want to know something about those things' (pointing to old John and the rails). 'Well, the truth is, John Hanks and I did make rails in the Sangamon Bottom. I don't know whether we made those rails or not; the fact is, I don't think they are a credit to the makers' (laughing as he spoke). 'But I do know this: I made rails then, and I think I could make better ones than these now.' By this time the innocent Egyptians began to open their eyes; they saw plainly enough the admirable Presidential scheme unfolded to their view. The result of it all was a resolution declaring that 'Abraham Lincoln is the first choice of the Republican party of Illinois for the Presidency, and instructing the delegates to the Chicago convention to use all honorable means to secure his nomination, and to cast the vote of the State as a unit for him.'"

On the 16th of May, 1860, the National Republican convention met at Chicago. An immense building called "The Wigwam," erected for the occasion, was filled with an excited throng numbering fully twelve thousand. After the usual preliminaries the convention settled down to the serious work of nominating a candidate for the Presidency. From the outset the contest was clearly between Abraham Lincoln of Illinois and William

H. Seward of New York. On the first ballot, Seward's vote of 173-1/2 was followed by Lincoln with 102—the latter having more than double the vote of his next competitor, Simon Cameron of Pennsylvania (51 votes), who was followed by Salmon P. Chase of Ohio (49 votes) and Edward Bates of Missouri (48 votes). A contrast between these two remarkable men, Seward and Lincoln, now political antagonists but soon to be intimately associated at the head of the Government—one as President and the other as his prime minister—is most interesting and instructive. Seward was a trained statesman and experienced politician of ripe culture and great sagacity, the acknowledged leader of the Republican party, New York's ex-Governor and now its most distinguished Senator. His position and career were therefore far more conspicuous than those of Lincoln. His supporters in the convention were well-organized, bold, confident, and expected that he would be nominated by acclamation. Lincoln, on the other hand, was still essentially a country lawyer, who had come into prominence mainly as the competitor of Senator Douglas in Illinois in 1858. With all his native strength of mind and force of character, he was, compared with the polished Seward, a rude backwoodsman, unskilled in handling the reins of government, unfamiliar with the wiles of statecraft, and unused to the company of diplomats and social leaders. His political reputation, and his support in the convention, were chiefly Western. Yet his Cooper Institute speech, delivered three months before the convention met, had done much for him in the East; and the homely title of "Honest Old Abe" had extended throughout the free States. Unlike Seward, he had no political enemies, and was the second choice of most of the delegates whose first choice was some other candidate.

In political management and strategy the Western men at the convention soon showed that they were at best a match for those from the East. Soon after the opening of the convention, Lincoln's friends saw that there was an organized body of men in the crowd who cheered vociferously whenever Seward's name was mentioned. "At a meeting of the Illinois delegation at the Tremont House," says Mr. Arnold, "on the evening of the first day, at which Judd, Davis, Cook and others were present, it was decided that on the second day Illinois and the West should be heard. There was then living in Chicago a man whose voice could drown the roar of Lake Michigan in its wildest fury; nay, it was said that his shout could be heard on a calm day across that lake. Cook of Ottawa knew another man living on the Illinois river, a Dr. Ames, who had never found his equal in his ability to shout and hurrah. He was, however, a Democrat. Cook telegraphed to him to come to Chicago by the first train. These two men with stentorian voices met some of the Illinois delegation at the Tremont House, and were instructed to organize each a body of men to cheer and shout, which they speedily did, out of the crowds which were in attendance from the Northwest. They were placed on opposite sides of the Wigwam, and instructed that when they saw Cook take out his white handkerchief they were to cheer and not to cease until he returned it to his pocket. Cook was conspicuous on the platform, and at the first utterance of the name of Lincoln, simultaneously with the wave of Cook's handkerchief, there went up such a cheer, such a shout as had never before been heard, and which startled the friends of Seward as the cry of 'Marmion' on Flodden Field 'startled the Scottish foe.' The New Yorkers tried to follow when the name of Seward was spoken, but, beaten at their own game, their voices were drowned by the cheers for Lincoln. This was kept up until Lincoln was nominated, amidst a storm of applause probably never before equalled at a political convention."

The result on the first ballot, with Seward leading Lincoln by 71-1/2 votes, has already been given. On the second ballot Seward gained 11 votes, giving him 184-1/2; while Lincoln made the astonishing gain of 78 votes, giving him a total of 181 and reducing Seward's lead of 71-1/2 votes to 3-1/2 votes. There was no longer doubt of the result. The third ballot came, and Lincoln, passing Seward who had fallen off 3-1/2 votes from the previous ballot, ran rapidly up to 231-1/2 votes—233 being the number required to nominate. Lincoln now lacked but a vote and a half to make him the nominee. At this juncture, the chairman of the Ohio delegation rose and changed four votes from Chase to Lincoln, giving him the nomination. The Wigwam was shaken to its foundation by the roaring cheers. The multitude in the streets answered the multitude within, and in a moment more all the volunteer artillery of Chicago joined in the grand acclamation. After a time the business of the convention proceeded, amid great excitement. All the votes that had heretofore been cast against Lincoln were cast for him before this ballot concluded. The convention completed its work by the nomination of Hannibal Hamlin of Maine for Vice-President.

Mr. F.B. Carpenter, who was present at Lincoln's nomination, furnishes a graphic sketch of this dramatic episode. "The scene surpassed description. Men had been stationed upon the roof of the Wigwam to communicate the result of the different ballots to the thousands outside, far outnumbering the packed crowd inside. To these men one of the secretaries shouted: 'Fire the salute! Lincoln is nominated!' Then, as the cheering inside died away, the roar began on the outside, and swelled up from the excited masses like the noise of many waters. This the insiders heard, and to it they replied. Thus deep called to deep with such a frenzy of sympathetic enthusiasm that even the thundering salute of cannon was unheard by many on the platform. When the excitement had partly subsided, Mr. Evarts of New York arose, and in appropriate words expressed his grief that Seward had not been nominated. He then moved that the nomination of Abraham Lincoln be made unanimous. Governor John A. Andrew of Massachusetts and Hon. Carl Schurz of Wisconsin seconded the motion, and it was carried. Then the enthusiasm of the multitude burst out anew. A large banner, prepared by the Pennsylvania delegation, was conspicuously displayed, bearing the inscription, 'Pennsylvania good for twenty thousand majority for the people's candidate, Abe Lincoln.' Delegates tore up the sticks and boards bearing the names of their several States, and waved them aloft over their heads. A brawny man jumped upon the platform, and pulling his coat-sleeves up to his elbows, shouted: 'I can't stop! Three times three more cheers for our next President, Abe Lincoln!' A full-length portrait of the candidate was produced upon the platform. Mr. Greeley telegraphed to the N.Y. Tribune: 'There was never another such scene in America.' Chicago went wild. One hundred guns were fired from the top of the Tremont House. At night the city was in a blaze of glory. Bonfires, processions, torchlights, fire-works, illuminations and salutes, 'filled the air with noise and the eye with beauty.' 'Honest Old Abe' was the utterance of every man in the streets. The Illinois delegation before it separated 'resolved' that the millennium had come."

Governor Andrew, who was destined to have highly important and intimate relations with Lincoln during the Civil War, records his first impressions of him in a few vivid sentences. "Beyond the experiences of the journey from Boston to Chicago," says Andrew's biographer, "beyond even the strain and excitement of those hours in caucus and convention, was the impression made on him by Lincoln as he saw him for the first time." Andrew was one of the committee of delegates who went to Springfield to notify Lincoln of his nomination at Chicago. He and the other delegates, he says, "saw in a flash that here was a man who was master of himself. For the first time they understood that he whom they had supposed to be little more than a loquacious and clever State politician, had force, insight, conscience; that their misgivings were vain.... My eyes were never visited with the vision of a human face in which more transparent honesty and more benignant kindness were combined with more of the intellect and firmness which belong to masculine humanity. I would trust my case with the honesty and intellect and heart and brain of Abraham Lincoln as a lawyer; and I would trust my country's cause in the care of Abraham Lincoln as its chief magistrate, while the wind blows and the water runs."

Dr. J.G. Holland gives a vivid picture of Lincoln's reception of the exciting news. "In the little city of Springfield," says Dr. Holland, "in the heart of Illinois, two hundred miles from where these exciting events were in progress, sat Abraham Lincoln, in constant telegraphic communication with his friends in Chicago. He was apprised of the results of every ballot, and with some of his friends sat in the 'Journal' office receiving and commenting upon the dispatches. It was one of the decisive moments of his life—a moment on which hung his fate as a public man, his place in history. He fully appreciated the momentous results of the convention to himself and the nation, and foresaw the nature of the great struggle which his nomination and election would inaugurate. At last, in the midst of intense excitement, a messenger from the telegraph office entered with the decisive dispatch in his hand. Without handing it to anyone, he took his way solemnly to the side of Mr. Lincoln, and said: 'The convention has made a nomination, and Mr. Seward is—the second man on the list.' Then he jumped upon the editorial table and shouted, 'Gentlemen, I propose three cheers for Abraham Lincoln, the next President of the United States!' and the call was boisterously responded to. He then handed the dispatch to Mr. Lincoln, who read it in silence, and then aloud. After exchanging greetings and receiving congratulations from those around him, he strove to get out of the crowd, and as he moved off he remarked to those near him: 'Well, there is a little woman who will be interested in this news, and I will go home and tell her,' and he hurried on, with the crowd following and cheering."

As soon as the news spread about Springfield a salute of a hundred guns was fired, and during the afternoon Lincoln's friends and neighbors thronged his house to tender their congratulations and express their joy. "In the evening," says one narrator, "the State House was thrown open and a most enthusiastic meeting held by the Republicans. At the close they marched in a body to the Lincoln mansion and called for the nominee. Mr. Lincoln appeared, and after a brief, modest, and hearty speech, invited as many as could get into the house to enter; the crowd responding that after the fourth of March they would give him a larger house. The people did not retire until a late hour, and then moved off reluctantly, leaving the excited household to their rest."

Among the more significant and intimate of the personal reminiscences of Lincoln are those by Mr. Leonard W. Volk, the distinguished sculptor already mentioned in these pages. Mr. Volk arrived in Springfield on the day of Lincoln's nomination, and had some unusually interesting conversation with him. He had already, only a month before, made the life-mask of Lincoln that became so well and favorably known. It is one of the last representations showing him without a beard. The circumstances and incidents attending the taking of this life-mask, as narrated by Mr. Volk, are well worth reproducing here. "One morning in April, 1860," says Mr. Volk, "I noticed in the paper that Abraham Lincoln was in Chicago,—retained

as one of the counsel in a 'Sand-bar' trial in which the Michigan Central Railroad was either plaintiff or defendant. I at once decided to remind him of his promise to sit to me, made two years before. I found him in the United States District Court room, his feet on the edge of the table, and his long dark hair standing out at every imaginable angle. He was surrounded by a group of lawyers, such as James F. Joy, Isaac N. Arnold, Thomas Hoyne, and others. Mr. Arnold obtained his attention in my behalf, when he instantly arose and met me outside the rail, recognizing me at once with his usual grip of both hands. He remembered his promise, and said, in answer to my question, that he expected to be detained by the case for a week. He added: 'I shall be glad to give you the sittings. When shall I come, and how long will you need me each time?' Just after breakfast every morning would, he said, suit him the best, and he could remain till court opened at ten o'clock. I answered that I would be ready for him the next morning (Thursday). 'Very well, Mr. Volk, I will be there, and I'll go to a barber and have my hair cut before I come.' I requested him not to let the barber cut it too short, and said I would rather he would leave it as it was; but to this he would not consent....
He was on hand promptly at the time appointed; indeed, he never failed to be on time. My studio was in the fifth story. There were no elevators in those days, and I soon learned to distinguish his step on the stairs, and am sure he frequently came up two, if not three, steps at a stride. When he sat down the first time in that hard, wooden, low-armed chair which I still possess, and which has been occupied by Douglas, Seward, and Generals Grant and Dix, he said, 'Mr. Volk, I have never sat before to sculptor or painter—only for daguerreotypes and photographs. What shall I do?' I told him I would only take the measurements of his head and shoulders that time, and that the next morning I would make a cast of his face, which would save him a number of sittings. He stood up against the wall, and I made a mark above his head, and then measured up to it from the floor and said: 'You are just twelve inches taller than Judge Douglas; that is, just six feet four inches.'

"Before commencing the cast next morning, and knowing Mr. Lincoln's fondness for a story, I told him one in order to remove what I thought an apprehensive expression—as though he feared the operation might be dangerous. He sat naturally in the chair when I made the cast, and saw every move I made in a mirror opposite, as I put the plaster on without interference with his eyesight or his free breathing through the nostrils. It was about an hour before the mould was ready to be removed, and being all in one piece, with both ears perfectly taken, it clung pretty hard, as the cheek-bones were higher than the jaws at the lobe of the ear. He bent his head low, and worked the cast off without breaking or injury; it hurt a little, as a few hairs of the tender temples pulled out with the plaster and made his eyes water.

"He entered my studio on Sunday morning, remarking that a friend at the hotel (Tremont House) had invited him to go to church, 'but,' said Mr. Lincoln, 'I thought I'd rather come and sit for the bust. The fact is,' he continued, 'I don't like to hear cut-and-dried sermons. No—when I hear a man preach, I like to see him act as *if he were fighting bees!*' And he extended his long arms, at the same time suiting the action to the words. He gave me on this day a long sitting of more than four hours, and when it was concluded we went to our family apartment to look at a collection of photographs which I had made in 1855-6-7 in Rome and Florence. While sitting in the rocking-chair, he took my little son on his lap and spoke kindly to him, asking his name, age, etc. I held the photographs up and explained them to him; but I noticed a growing weariness, and his eyelids closed occasionally as if he were sleepy, or were thinking of something besides Grecian and Roman statuary and architecture. Finally he said, 'These things must be very interesting to you, Mr. Volk; but the truth is, I don't know much of history, and all I do know of it I have learned from law books.'

"The sittings were continued daily till the Thursday following; and during their continuance he would talk almost unceasingly, telling some of the funniest and most laughable of stories, but he talked little of politics or religion during these sittings. He said, 'I am bored nearly every time I sit down to a public dining-table by some one pitching into me on politics.' Many people, presumably political aspirants with an eye to future prospects, besieged my door for interviews, but I made it a rule to keep it locked, and I think Mr. Lincoln appreciated the precaution. On our last sitting I noticed that Mr. Lincoln was in something of a hurry. I had finished the head, but desired to represent his breast and brawny shoulders as nature presented them; so he stripped off his coat, waistcoat, shirt, cravat, and collar, threw them on a chair, pulled his undershirt down a short distance, tying the sleeves behind him, and stood up without a murmur for an hour or so. I then said I had done, and was a thousand times obliged to him for his promptness and patience, and offered to assist him to re-dress, but he said, 'No, I can do it better alone.' I kept at my work without looking toward him, wishing to catch the form as accurately as possible while it was fresh in my memory. He left hurriedly, saying he had an engagement, and with a cordial 'Good-bye! I will see you again soon,' passed out. A few minutes after, I recognized his steps rapidly returning. The door opened and in he came, exclaiming, 'Hello, Mr. Volk! I got down on the sidewalk, and found I had forgotten to put on my undershirt, and thought it wouldn't do to go through the streets this way.' Sure enough, there were the sleeves of that garment dangling below the skirts of his broadcloth frock-coat! I went at once to his assistance, and helped to undress and re-dress him all right, and out he went with a hearty laugh at the absurdity of the thing."

Returning to the visit with Lincoln at Springfield on the day of his nomination, Mr. Volk says. "The afternoon was lovely—bright and sunny, neither too warm nor too cool; the grass, trees, and the hosts of blooming roses, so profuse in Springfield, appeared to be vying with the ringing bells and waving flags. I went straight to Mr. Lincoln's unpretentious little two-story house. He saw me from his door or window coming down the street, and as I entered the gate he was on the platform in front of the door, and quite alone. His face looked radiant. I exclaimed: 'I am the first man from Chicago, I believe, who has the honor of congratulating you on your nomination for President.' Then those two great hands took both of mine with a grasp never to be forgotten. And while shaking them, I said: 'Now that you will doubtless be the next President of the United States, I want to make a statue of you, and shall do my best to do you justice.' Said he, 'I don't doubt it, for I have come to the conclusion that you are an honest man,' and with that greeting I thought my hands were in a fair way of being crushed. I was invited into the parlor, and soon Mrs. Lincoln entered, holding a rose-bouquet in her hand, which she presented to me after the introduction; and in return I gave her a cabinet-size bust of her husband, which I had modelled from the large one, and happened to have with me. Before leaving the house it was arranged that Mr. Lincoln would give Saturday forenoon to obtaining full-length photographs to serve me for the proposed statue. On Saturday evening, the committee appointed by the convention to notify Mr. Lincoln formally of his nomination, headed by Mr. Ashmun of Massachusetts, reached Springfield by special train, bearing a large number of people, two or three hundred of whom carried rails on their shoulders, marching in military style from the train to the old State House Hall of Representatives, where they stacked them like muskets. The evening was beautiful and clear, and the entire population was astir. The bells pealed, flags waved, and cannon thundered forth the triumphant nomination of Springfield's distinguished citizen. The bonfires blazed brightly, and especially in front of that prim-looking white house on Eighth street. The committee and the vast crowd following it passed in at the front door, and made their exit through the kitchen door in the rear, Mr. Lincoln giving them all a hearty shake of the hand as they passed him in the parlor. By appointment, I was to cast Mr. Lincoln's hands on the Sunday following this memorable Saturday, at nine A.M. I found him ready, but he looked more grave and serious than he had appeared on the previous days. I wished him to hold something in his right hand, and he looked for a piece of pasteboard, but could find none. I told him a round stick would do as well as anything. Thereupon he went to the wood-shed, and I heard the saw go, and he soon returned to the dining-room (where I did the work), whittling off the end of a piece of broom-handle. I remarked to him that he need not whittle off the edges. 'Oh, well,' said he, 'I thought I would like to have it nice.' When I had successfully cast the mould of the right hand, I began the left, pausing a few moments to hear Mr. Lincoln tell me about a scar on the thumb. 'You have heard that they call me a rail-splitter, and you saw them carrying rails in the procession Saturday evening; well, it is true that I did split rails, and one day, while I was sharpening a wedge on a log, the axe glanced and nearly took my thumb off, and there is the scar, you see.' The right hand appeared swollen as compared with the left, on account of excessive hand-shaking the evening before; this difference is distinctly shown in the cast. That Sunday evening I returned to Chicago with the moulds of his hands, three photographic negatives of him, the identical black alpaca campaign suit of 1858, and a pair of Lynn newly-made pegged boots. The clothes were all burned up in the great Chicago fire. The casts of the face and hands I saved by taking them with me to Rome, and they have crossed the sea four times. The last time I saw Mr. Lincoln was in January, 1861, at his house in Springfield. His little parlor was full of friends and politicians. He introduced me to them all, and remarked to me aside that since he had sat to me for his bust, eight or nine months before, he had lost forty pounds in weight. This was easily perceptible, for the lines of his jaws were very sharply defined through the short beard which he was allowing to grow. Then he turned to the company and explained in a general way that I had made a bust of him before his nomination, and that he was then giving daily sittings to another sculptor; that he had sat to him for a week or more, but could not see the likeness, though he might yet bring it out. 'But,' continued Mr. Lincoln, 'in two or three days after Mr. Volk began my bust, there was the animal himself!' And this was about the last, if not the last, remark I ever heard him utter, except the good-bye and his good wishes for my success."

Saturday, May 19, the committee of the Chicago convention arrived at Springfield to notify Mr. Lincoln of his nomination. The Hon. George Ashmun, as chairman of the committee, delivered the formal address, to which Lincoln listened with dignity, but with an air of profound sadness, as though the trials in store for him had already "cast their shadows before." In response to the address, Lincoln said:

MR. CHAIRMAN AND GENTLEMEN OF THE COMMITTEE:—I tender to you and through you to the Republican National convention, and all the people represented in it, my profoundest thanks for the high honor done me, which you now formally announce. Deeply and even painfully sensible of the great responsibility which is inseparable from this high honor—a responsibility which I could almost wish had fallen upon some one of the far more eminent men and experienced statesmen whose distinguished names were before the convention—I shall, by your leave, consider more fully the resolutions of the convention, denominated the platform, and, without unnecessary and unreasonable delay, respond to you, Mr. Chairman, in writing, not doubting that the platform will be found satisfactory, and the nomination gratefully accepted. And now I will not longer defer the pleasure of taking you, and each of you, by the hand.

A letter was then handed Lincoln containing the official notice, accompanied by the resolutions of the convention. To this letter he replied, a few days later, as follows:

SPRINGFIELD, ILLINOIS, MAY 23, 1860.

SIR—I accept the nomination tendered to me by the convention over which you presided, of which I am formally apprised in a letter of yourself and others acting as a Committee of the Convention for that purpose. The declaration of principles and sentiments which accompanies your letter meets my approval, and it shall be my care not to violate it, or disregard it in any part. Imploring the assistance of Divine Providence, and with due regard to the views and feelings of all who were represented in the convention, to the rights of all the States and Territories and people of the nation, to the inviolability of the Constitution, and the perpetual union, harmony and prosperity of all, I am most happy to co-operate for the practical success of the principles declared by the convention.

In June Mr. Douglas was nominated for the Presidency by the Democratic convention, which met at Baltimore on the 18th. Mr. Douglas made a personal canvass, speaking in most of the states, North and South, and exerting all the powers of which he was master to win success. The campaign, as Mr. Arnold states, "has had no parallel. The enthusiasm of the people was like a great conflagration, like a prairie fire before a wild tornado. A little more than twenty years had passed since Owen Lovejoy, brother of Elijah Lovejoy, on the bank of the Mississippi, kneeling on the turf not then green over the grave of the brother who had been killed for his fidelity to freedom, had sworn eternal war against slavery. From that time on, he and his associate Abolitionists had gone forth preaching their crusade against oppression, with hearts of fire and tongues of lightning; and now the consummation was to be realized of a President elected on the distinct ground of opposition to the extension of slavery. For years the hatred of that institution had been growing and gathering force. Whittier, Bryant, Lowell, Longfellow, and others, had written the lyrics of liberty; the graphic pen of Mrs. Stowe, in 'Uncle Tom's Cabin,' had painted the cruelties of the overseer and the slaveholder; but the acts of slaveholders themselves did more to promote the growth of anti-slavery than all other causes. The persecutions of Abolitionists in the South; the harshness and cruelty attending the execution of the fugitive laws; the brutality of Brooks in knocking down, on the floor of the Senate, Charles Sumner, for words spoken in debate: these and many other outrages had fired the hearts of the people of the free States against this barbarous institution. Beecher, Phillips, Channing, Sumner, and Seward, with their eloquence; Chase with his logic; Lincoln, with his appeals to the principles of the Declaration of Independence, and to the opinions of the founders of the republic, his clear statements, his apt illustrations, and, above all, his wise moderation,—all had swelled the voice of the people, which found expression through the ballot-box, and which declared that slavery should go no further."

Among the various reminiscences of the memorable Presidential campaign of 1860, some of peculiar interest are furnished by Dr. Newton Bateman, President of Knox College, Illinois. Dr. Bateman had known Lincoln since 1842; and from the year 1858, when Dr. Bateman was elected State Superintendent of Public Instruction in Illinois, to the close of Lincoln's residence in Springfield in 1861, they saw each other daily. The testimony of so intimate an acquaintance, and one so well qualified to judge the character and abilities of men, is of unusual value; and it is worth noting that Dr. Bateman remarks that, while he was always an admirer of Lincoln, yet the greatness of the man grew upon him as the years pass by. In his professional and public work, says Dr. Bateman, Lincoln not only proved himself equal to every emergency and to every successive task, but made, from the outset, the impression upon the mind of those who knew him of being in possession of great reserve force. Perhaps the secret of this lies in part in the fact that he was accustomed to ponder deeply upon the ultimate principles of government and society, and strove to base his discussions upon the firm ground of ethical truth. Says Dr. Bateman, "He was the saddest man I ever knew." It was a necessity of his nature to be much alone; and he said that all his serious work—by which he meant the process of getting down to the bed-rock of first principles—must be done in solitude. Upon one occasion he called Dr. Bateman to him, and spent more than two hours in earnest conversation upon the most serious themes. At the close, Dr. Bateman said: "I did not know, Mr. Lincoln, that it was your habit to think so deeply upon this class of subjects." "Didn't you?" said Mr. Lincoln. "I can almost say that I think of *nothing else*."

One day there entered Lincoln's room a tall Southerner, a Colonel Somebody from Mississippi, whose eye's hard glitter spoke supercilious distrust and whose stiff bearing betokened suppressed hostility. It was beautiful, says Dr. Bateman, to see the cold flash of the Southerner's dark eye yield to a warmer glow, and the haughty constraint melt into frank good-nature, under the influence of Lincoln's words of simple earnestness and unaffected cordiality. They got so far in half an hour that Lincoln could say, in his hearty way: "Colonel, how tall are you?" "Well, taller than you, Mr. Lincoln," replied the Mississippian. "You are mistaken there," retorted Lincoln. "Dr. Bateman, will you measure us?" "You will have to permit me to stand on a chair for that," responded the Doctor. So a big book was adjusted above the head of each, and pencil marks made at the respective points of contact with the white wall. Lincoln's altitude, as thus indicated, was a quarter inch above that of the Colonel. "I knew it," said Lincoln. "They raise tall men down in Mississippi, but you go home and tell your folks that *Old Abe tops you a little.*" The Colonel went away much mollified and impressed. "My God!" said he to Dr. Bateman, as he went out. "There's going to be war; but could my people know what I have learned within the last hour, there need be no war."

During the Presidential campaign, the vote of the city of Springfield was canvassed house by house. There were at that time twenty-three clergymen residing in the city (not all pastors). All but three of these signified their intention to vote *against* Lincoln. This fact seemed to grieve him somewhat. Soon after, in conversing upon the subject with Dr. Bateman, he said, as if thinking aloud: "These gentlemen know that Judge Douglas does not care a cent whether slavery in the territories is voted up or voted down, for he has repeatedly told them so. They know that I *do* care." Then, drawing from a breast pocket a well-thumbed copy of the New Testament, he added, after a pause, tapping upon the book with his bony finger: "I do not so understand this book."

The poet Bryant was conspicuous among the prominent Eastern men who favored Lincoln's nomination for the Presidency in 1860. He had introduced Lincoln to the people of New York at the Cooper Institute meeting of the previous winter, and was a firm believer in the Western politician. After the convention Mr. Bryant wrote Lincoln a most friendly and timely letter, full of good feeling and of wise advice. Especially did he warn Lincoln to be cautious in committing himself to any specific policy, or making pledges or engagements of any kind. Mr. Bryant's letter contained much political wisdom, and was written in that scholarly style for which he was distinguished. But it could not surpass the simple dignity and grace of Lincoln's reply:

SPRINGFIELD, ILL., JUNE 28, 1860.

Please accept my thanks for the honor done me by your kind letter of the 16th. I appreciate the danger against which you would guard me; nor am I wanting in the *purpose* to avoid it. I thank you for the additional strength your words give me to maintain that purpose.

Your friend and servant, A. LINCOLN.

Mr. A.J. Grover relates that about this time he met Lincoln, and had a memorable conversation with him on the Fugitive Slave Law. Lincoln detested this law, but argued that until it was declared unconstitutional it must be obeyed. This was a short time after the rescue of a fugitive slave at Ottawa, Illinois, by John Hossack, James Stout, Major Campbell, and others, after Judge John D. Caton, acting as United States Commissioner, had given his decision remanding him to the custody of his alleged owner; and the rescuers were either in prison or out on bail, awaiting their trials. Says Mr. Grover: "When Mr. Lincoln had finished his argument I said, 'Constitutional or not, I will never obey the Fugitive Slave Law. I would have done as Hossack and Stout and Campbell did at Ottawa. I will never catch and return slaves in obedience to any law or constitution. I do not believe a man's liberty can be taken from him constitutionally without a trial by jury. I believe the law to be not only unconstitutional, but most inhuman.' 'Oh,' said Mr. Lincoln, and I shall never forget his earnestness as he emphasized it by striking his hand on his knee, 'it is ungodly! it is ungodly! no doubt it is ungodly! but it is the law of the land, and we must obey it as we find it.' I said: 'Mr. Lincoln, how often have you sworn to support the Constitution? We propose to elect you President. How would you look taking an oath to support what you declare is an ungodly Constitution, and asking God to help you?' He felt the force of the question, and, inclining his head forward and running his fingers through his hair several times, seemed lost in reflection; then he placed his hand upon my knee and said, very earnestly: 'Grover, it's no use to be always *looking up these hard spots*!'" In the terrible years then almost upon him, Lincoln found many such "hard spots" without taking the trouble to look them up.

CHAPTER XIV

The Presidential campaign of 1860, with its excitements and struggles, its "Wide-awake" clubs and boisterous enthusiasm throughout the North, and its bitter and threatening character throughout the South, was at last ended; and on the 6th of November Abraham Lincoln was elected President of the United States.[A] His cause had been aided not a little by an unexpected division in the Democratic party. Douglas had been nominated for the Presidency by this party in its convention at Baltimore on the 18th of June; but he was bitterly opposed by the extreme slavery element of the Democracy, and this faction held a convention of its own at Baltimore ten days later and nominated for President John C. Breckenridge of Kentucky. There was still another party, though a very minor one, in the field—the "Constitutional Union Party," based chiefly on a desire to avoid the issue of slavery in national politics—which on the 9th of May had nominated John Bell of Tennessee as its candidate for the Presidency, with Edward Everett of Massachusetts for the Vice-Presidency. There were thus four tickets in the field—the Republican, including if not representing the anti-slavery element in the North; the Democratic, which was pro-slavery in its tendencies but had so far failed to satisfy the Southern wing—now grown alarmed and restless at the growth and tendencies of the Republican party—that this element nominated as a third ticket an out-and-out pro-slavery candidate; and (fourth) a "Constitutional Union" ticket, representing a well-meant but fatuous desire to keep slavery out of national politics altogether.

This eventful contest was therefore determined largely on sectional lines, with slavery as the great underlying issue. Lincoln's gratification at his election was not untempered with disappointments. While he had a substantial majority of the electoral vote (180 to 123), the popular vote was toward a million (930,170), more against him than for him. Fifteen States gave him no electoral vote, and in nine States' he received not a single popular vote. The slave States—"the Solid South"—were squarely against him. Lincoln saw the significance of this, and it filled him with regret and apprehension. But he faced the future without dismay, and with a calm resolve to do his duty. With all his hatred of slavery, loyalty to the Constitution had always been paramount in his mind; and those who knew him best never doubted that it would continue so.

Lincoln took no active part in the campaign, preferring to remain quietly at his home in Springfield. Scarcely was the election decided than he was beset with visitors from all parts of the country, who came to gratify curiosity or solicit personal favors of the incoming President. The throng became at last so great, and interfered so much with the comfort of Lincoln's home, that the Executive Chamber in the State House was set apart as his reception room. Here he met all who chose to come—"the millionaire and the menial, the priest and the politician, men, women, and children, old friends and new friends, those who called for love and those who sought for office. From morning until night this was his occupation; and he performed it with conscientious care and the most unwearying patience." The situation at the Lincoln home at this time, and the spirit prevailing there, is well depicted by one of these callers, Mr. R.C. McCormick, whose interesting account of his meeting with Lincoln in New York City has already been quoted in these pages. "In January, 1861," says Mr. McCormick, "at the instance of various friends in New York who wished a position in the Cabinet for a prominent Kentuckian, I went to Springfield armed with documents for his consideration. I remained there a week or more, and was at the Lincoln cottage daily. Of the numerous formal and informal interviews that I witnessed, I remember all with the sincerest pleasure. I never found the man upon whom rested the great responsibilities of the nation impatient or ill-humored. The plainest and most tedious visitors were made welcome and happy in his presence; the poor commanded as much of his time as the rich. His recognition of old friends and companions in frontier life, whom many elevated as he had been would have found it convenient to forget, was especially hearty. His correspondence was already immense, and the town was alive with cabinet-makers and office-seekers; but he met all with a calm temper." Mr. Don Piatt relates that he had met Lincoln during the Presidential campaign, and had been invited to visit Springfield. He did so, and was asked to supper at the Lincoln house. "It was a plain, comfortable structure," says Mr. Piatt, "and the supper was mainly of cake, pies, and chickens, the last evidently killed in the morning, to be eaten that evening. After the supper we sat far into the night, talking over the situation. Mr. Lincoln was the homeliest man I ever saw. His body seemed to me a huge skeleton in clothes. Tall as he was, his hands and feet looked out of proportion, so long and clumsy were they. Every movement was awkward in the extreme. He sat with one leg thrown over the other, and the pendent foot swung almost to the floor. And all the while two little boys, his sons, clambered over those legs, patted his cheeks, pulled his nose, and poked their fingers in his eyes, without reprimand. He had a face that defied artistic skill to soften or idealize. It was capable of few expressions, but those were extremely striking. When in repose, his face was dull, heavy, and repellent. It brightened like a lit lantern when animated. His dull eyes would fairly sparkle with fun, or express as kindly a look as I ever saw, when moved by some matter of human interest."

Hon. George W. Julian, of Indiana, was another visitor to the Lincoln home in January. He says: "I had a curiosity to see the famous 'rail-splitter,' as he was then familiarly called, and as a member-elect of the Thirty-seventh Congress I desired to form some acquaintance with the man who was to play so conspicuous a part in the impending national crisis. On meeting him I found him far better looking than the campaign pictures had represented him. His face, when lighted up in conversation, was not unhandsome, and the kindly and winning tones of his voice pleaded for him like the smile that played about his rugged features. He was full of anecdote and humor, and readily found his way to the hearts of those who enjoyed a welcome to his fireside. His face, however, was sometimes marked by that touching expression of sadness which became so noticeable in the years following. On the subject of slavery I was gratified to find him less reserved and more emphatic than I had expected. I was much pleased with our first Republican Executive, and I returned home more fully inspired than ever with the purpose to sustain him to the utmost in facing the duties of his great office."

The wide range of these callers and their diverse errands are illustrated by examples furnished by Mr. Lamon. Two tall, ungainly fellows,— "Suckers," as they were called,—entered Lincoln's room one day while he was engaged in conversation with a friend. They lingered bashfully near the door, and Lincoln, noticing their embarrassment, rose and said good-naturedly, "How do you do, my good fellows? What can I do for you? Will you sit down?" The spokesman of the pair, the shorter of the two, declined to sit, and explained the object of the call. He had had a talk about the relative height of Lincoln and his companion, and had asserted his belief that they were of exactly the same height. He had come in to verify his judgment. Lincoln smiled, then got his cane, and placing the end of it upon the wall said, "Here, young man, come under here!" The young man came under the cane, as Lincoln held it, and when it was perfectly adjusted to his height Lincoln said, "Now come out and hold up the cane." This he did, while Lincoln stepped under. Rubbing his head back and forth to see that it worked easily under the measurement, he stepped out, and declared that the young man had guessed with remarkable accuracy—that he and the tall fellow were exactly of the same height. Then he shook hands with them and sent them on their way. The next caller was a very different person—an old and modestly dressed woman who tried to explain that she knew Lincoln. As he did not at first recognize her, she tried to recall to his memory certain incidents connected with his rides upon the circuit—especially his dining at her house upon the road at different times. Then he remembered her and her home. Having fixed her own place in his recollection, she tried to recall to him a certain scanty dinner of bread and milk that he once ate at her house. He could not remember it—on the contrary, he only remembered that he had always fared well at her house. "Well," said she, "one day you came along after we had got through dinner, and we had eaten up everything, and I could give you nothing but a bowl of bread and milk; you ate it, and when you got up you said it was *good enough for the President of the United States*." The good woman, remembering the remark, had come in from the country, making a journey of eight or ten miles, to relate to Lincoln this incident, which in her mind had doubtless taken the form of prophecy. Lincoln placed her at her ease, chatted with her of old times, and dismissed her in the most happy and complacent frame of mind.

Among the judicious friends of Lincoln who gave him timely counsel at this important epoch of his life was Judge John D. Caton, who, though a Democrat, was a far-sighted man who saw plainly the tendency of political affairs and was anxious for the preservation of the Union. "I met Lincoln in Springfield," writes Judge Caton, "and we had a conference in the law-library. I told him it was plain that he had a war on his hands; that there was a determination on the part of the South to secede from the Union, and that there would be throughout the North an equal determination to maintain the Union. I advised him to avoid bringing on the war by precipitate action, but let the Southerners begin it; to forbear as long as forbearance could be tolerated, in order to unite the North the more effectually to support his hands in the struggle that was certain to come; that by such a course the great body of the people of the North, of all parties, would come to his support. Mr. Lincoln listened intently, and replied that he foresaw that the struggle was inevitable, but that it would be his desire and effort to unite the people in support of the Government and for the maintenance of the Union; that he was aware that no single party could sustain him successfully, and that he must rely upon the great masses of the people of all parties, and he would try to pursue such a course as would secure their support. The interview continued perhaps an hour."

Judge David Davis, a most intimate and confidential friend of Lincoln, states that the latter was firmly determined to appoint "Democrats and Republicans alike to office." Mr. Lamon corroborates the statement, pointedly remarking: "He felt that his strength lay in conciliation at the outset; that was his ruling conviction during all those months of preparation for the great task before him. It showed itself not only in the appointments which he sought to make but in those which he did make. Harboring no jealousies, entertaining no fears concerning his personal interests in the future, he called around him the most powerful of his late rivals—Seward, Chase, Bates—and unhesitatingly gave into their hands powers which most Presidents would have shrunk from committing to their equals, and much more to their superiors, in the conduct of public affairs." In a noted instance where the most powerful influence was brought to bear upon Lincoln to induce him to make what he regarded as an unworthy appointment, he exclaimed: "All that I am in the world—the Presidency and all else—I owe to the opinion of me which the people express when they call me 'Honest Old Abe.' Now, what would they think of their *honest* Abe if he should make such an appointment as the one proposed?"

Hon. Leonard Swett, who knew Lincoln from 1848 to the time of his death, and had "traveled the circuit" with him in Illinois, relates that soon after the election he and Judge Davis advised Lincoln to consult Thurlow Weed regarding the formation of the Cabinet and on political affairs generally. "Mr. Lincoln asked me," says Mr. Swett, "to write Mr. Weed and invite him to a conference at Lincoln's house in Springfield. I did so, and the result was that Judge Davis, Thurlow Weed, and myself spent a whole day with him in discussing the men and measures of his administration. At that meeting, which took place in less than a month after Lincoln's election, or early in December, 1860, Lincoln became convinced that war was imminent between the North and the South. Mr. Weed was a very astute man, and had a wonderful knowledge of what was going on. He told Lincoln of preparations being made in the Southern States that could mean nothing less than war. It was a serious time with all of us, of course, but Lincoln took it with the imperturbability that always distinguished him."

The account given by Thurlow Weed, the veteran New York editor and journalist, of his visit to Lincoln on this occasion is of peculiar interest. Mr. Weed remained in Springfield two or three days in close consultation with the President-elect, the formation of the new Cabinet being the subject principally discussed. After expressing gratification at his election, and an apprehension of the dangers which threatened the incoming administration, says Mr. Weed, in his autobiography, "Mr. Lincoln remarked, smiling, that he supposed I had had some experience in cabinet-making; that he had job on hand, and as he had never learned that trade he was disposed to avail himself of the suggestions of friends. The question thus opened became the subject of conversation, at intervals, during that and the following day. I say at intervals, because many hours were consumed in talking of the public men connected with former administrations, interspersed, illustrated, and seasoned pleasantly with Mr. Lincoln's stories, anecdotes, etc. And here I feel called upon to vindicate Mr. Lincoln, as far as my opportunities and observation go, from the frequent imputation of telling indelicate and ribald stories. I saw much of him during his whole Presidential term, with familiar friends and alone, when he talked without restraint; but I *never heard him use a profane or indecent word, or tell a story that might not be repeated in the presence of ladies."*

"Mr. Lincoln observed," continues Mr. Weed, "that the making of a Cabinet, now that he had it to do, was by no means as easy as he had supposed; that he had, even before the result of the election was known, assuming the probability of success, fixed upon the two leading members of his Cabinet, but that in looking about for suitable men to fill the other departments he had been much embarrassed, partly from his want of acquaintance with the prominent men of the day, and partly because he believed that while the population of the country had immensely increased *really great men were scarcer than they used to be....* As the conversation progressed, Lincoln remarked that he intended to invite Governor Seward to take the State Department and Governor Chase the Treasury Department, remarking that aside from their long experience in public affairs and their eminent fitness they were prominently before the people and the convention as competitors for the Presidency, each having higher claims than his own for the place which he was to occupy. On naming Hon. Gideon Welles as the man he thought of as the representative of New England in the Cabinet, I remarked that I thought he could find several New England gentlemen whose selection for a place in his Cabinet would be more acceptable to the people of New England. 'But,' said Mr. Lincoln, 'we must remember that the Republican party is constituted of two elements, and that we must have men of Democratic as well as of Whig antecedents in the Cabinet.' ... In the course of our conversations Mr. Lincoln remarked that it was particularly pleasant to him to reflect that he was coming into office unembarrassed by promises. He owed, he supposed, his exemption from importunities to the circumstance that his name as a candidate was but a short time before the people, and that only a few sanguine friends anticipated the possibility of his nomination. 'I have not,' said he, 'promised an office to any man, nor have I, but in a single instance, mentally committed myself to an appointment.'"

"In this way two days passed very pleasantly," says Mr. Weed, "the conversation being alternately earnest and playful. I wish it were possible to give, in Mr. Lincoln's amusing but quaint manner, the many stories, anecdotes, and witticisms with which he interlarded and enlivened what with almost any of his predecessors in the high office of President would have been a grave, dry consultation. The great merit of Mr. Lincoln's stories, like Captain Bunsby's opinion, 'lays in the application on it.' They always and exactly suited the occasion and the object, and none to which I ever listened seemed far-fetched or pointless. I will attempt to repeat one of them.

If I have an especial fondness for any particular luxury, it manifests itself in a remarkable way when properly made December sausages are placed before me. While at breakfast, Judge Davis, noticing that, after having been bountifully served with sausage, like Oliver Twist I wanted some more, said, 'You seem fond of our Illinois sausages.' To which I responded affirmatively, adding that I thought the article might be relied on where pork was cheaper than dogs. 'That,' said Mr. Lincoln, 'reminds me of what occurred down at Joliet, where a popular grocer supplied all the villagers with sausages. One Saturday evening, when his grocery was filled with customers for whom he and his boys were busily engaged in weighing sausages, a neighbor with whom he had had a violent quarrel that day, came into the grocery and made his way up to the counter holding by the tail two enormous dead cats which he deliberately threw on to the counter, saying, 'This makes seven to-day. I'll call around Monday and get my money for them.'"

During the months intervening between his election and his departure for Washington, Lincoln maintained a keen though quiet watchfulness of the threatening aspect of affairs at the national capital and throughout the South. He was careful not to commit himself by needless utterances as to his future policy; but in all his demeanor, as a friend said, he displayed the firmness and determination, without the temper, of Jackson. In December following his election he wrote the following letters to his intimate friend, Hon. E.B. Washburne, then a member of Congress from Illinois:

SPRINGFIELD, ILL., Dec. 13, 1860.

HON. E.B. WASHBURNE—*My Dear Sir*: Your long letter received. Prevent, as far as possible, any of our friends from demoralizing themselves and our cause by entertaining propositions for compromise of any sort on the slavery extension. There is no possible compromise upon it but which puts us under again, and leaves us all our work to do over again. Whether it be a Missouri line, or Eli Thayer's Popular Sovereignty, it is all the same. Let either be done, and immediately filibustering and extending slavery recommences. On that point hold firm, as with a chain of steel.

Yours as ever, A. LINCOLN.

SPRINGFIELD, ILL., Dec. 21, 1860.

HON. E.B. WASHBURNE—*My Dear Sir*: Last night I received your letter giving an account of your interview with General Scott, and for which I thank you. Please present my respects to the General, and tell him confidentially that I shall be obliged to him to be as well prepared as he can to either *hold* or retake the forts, as the case may require, at and after the inauguration.

Yours as ever, A. LINCOLN.

The Southern States, led on by South Carolina, which formally severed its connection with the Union November 17, 1860 (only eleven days after Lincoln's election), were preparing to dissolve their alliance with the Free States. Mississippi passed the ordinance of secession January 9, 1861; Florida followed on the 10th; Alabama on the 11th; Georgia on the 19th; Louisiana on the 25th; and Texas on the 1st day of February. The plans of the seceders went on, unmolested by the Buchanan administration. Southerners in the Cabinet and in Congress conspired to deplete the resources of the Government, leaving it helpless to contest the assumptions of the revolted States. The treasury was deliberately bankrupted; the ships of the navy were banished to distant ports; the Northern arsenals were rifled to furnish arms for the seceded States; the United States forts and armaments on the Southern coast were delivered into the hands of the enemy, with the exception of Fort Sumter, which was gallantly held by Major Robert Anderson. While this system of bold and unscrupulous treachery was carried on by men in the highest places of trust, the chief executive of the nation remained a passive spectator. The South was in open rebellion, and the North was powerless to interfere. The weeks prior to the inauguration of the new administration dragged slowly along, each day adding fresh cause for anxiety and alarm.

Amidst these portentous scenes Lincoln, watching them from a distance, maintained his calm and vigilant attitude. No one knew better than he the significance of these ominous events that were taking place at the nation's capital and in the disaffected States; but there was nothing he could do about them. His time for action had not yet come. He said little, but enough to show unmistakably what he thought of the situation and what course he had resolved upon to meet it. As early as December 17, 1860—a little more than a month after his election—in writing to Thurlow Weed, he said: "*My opinion is that no State can in any way get out of the Union without the consent of the other States; and that it is the duty of the President to run the machine as it is.*" He had been made the pilot of the ship of State, and his duty and purpose were to save the vessel.[B] Upon this mighty task were concentrated all the powers of his intellect and will; and through all the desperate voyage that followed he never wavered or faltered in his course, from the time of his supreme resolve, made in the quiet of his country home, to the hour when

> "From fearful trip the victor ship came in with object won"—

but with her more than heroic but now victorious Captain "fallen cold and dead" upon her deck.

As the winter wore away, and the time for Lincoln's inauguration as President drew near, he began making preparation for leaving the familiar scenes where his life had thus far been spent. Early in February he made a parting visit to his relatives in Coles County, to whom in this hour of grave trial and anxiety his heart turned with fresh yearning. He spent a night at Charleston, where his cousin Dennis Hanks, and Mrs. Colonel Chapman, a daughter of Dennis, resided. We are told that "the people crowded by hundreds to see him; and he was serenaded by 'both the string and brass bands of the town, but declined making a speech." The following morning he passed on to Farmington, to the home of his beloved step-mother, who was living with her daughter, Mrs. Moore. Mr. Lamon relates that "the meeting between him and the old lady was of a most affectionate and tender character. She fondled him as her own 'Abe,' and he her as his own mother." Then Lincoln and Colonel Chapman drove to the house of John Hall, who lived on the old 'Lincoln farm' where Abe split the celebrated rails and fenced in the little clearing in 1830. Thence they went to the spot where Lincoln's father was buried. The grave was unmarked and utterly neglected. Lincoln said he wanted to 'have it enclosed, and a suitable tombstone erected,'" and gave the necessary instructions for this purpose. "We then returned," says Colonel Chapman, "to Farmington, where we found a large crowd of citizens—nearly all old acquaintances—waiting to see him. His reception was very enthusiastic, and seemed to gratify him very much. After taking dinner at his stepsister's (Mrs. Moore's), he returned to Charleston. Our conversation during the trip was mostly concerning family affairs. On the way down to Farmington Mr. Lincoln spoke to me of his step-mother in the most affectionate manner; said she had been his best friend, and that no son could love a mother more than he loved her. He also told me of the condition of his father's family at the time he married his step-mother, and of the change she made in the family, and of the encouragement he had received from her.... He spoke of his father, and related some amusing incidents of the bull-dog's biting the old man on his return from New Orleans; of the old man's escape, when a boy, from an Indian who was shot by his uncle Mordecai, etc. He spoke of his uncle Mordecai as being a man of very great natural gifts. At Charleston we found the house crowded by people wishing to see him. The crowd finally became so great that it was decided to hold a public reception at the Town Hall that evening at seven o'clock; until then Lincoln wished to be left with relatives and friends. At the Town Hall large numbers of people from the town and surrounding country, irrespective of party, called to see him. His reception by his old acquaintances was very gratifying to him."

A characteristic anecdote showing Lincoln's friendship and love of old associations is told among those relating to his last days at Springfield. When he was about to leave for Washington he went to the dingy little law office, sat down on the couch, and said to his law-partner, Herndon, "Billy, you and I have been together nearly twenty years, and have never 'passed a word.' Will you let my name stay on the old sign till I come back from Washington?" The tears started to Mr. Herndon's eyes. He put out his hand. "Mr. Lincoln," said he, "I will never have any other partner while you live"; and to the day of the assassination all the doings of the firm were in the name of "Lincoln & Herndon."

Governor Bross, of Illinois, relates that he was with Lincoln at Springfield on the day before he left for Washington. "We were walking slowly to his home from some place where we had met, and the condition and prospects of the country, and his vast responsibility in assuming the position of President, were the subjects of his thoughts. These were discussed with a breadth and anxiety full of that pathos peculiar to Mr. Lincoln in his thoughtful moods. He seemed to have a thorough prescience of the dangers through which his administration was to pass. No President, he said, had ever had before him such vast and far-reaching responsibilities. He regarded war—long, bitter, and dreadful—as almost sure to come. He distinctly and reverently placed his hopes for the result in the strength and guidance of Him on whom Washington relied in the darkest hours of the Revolution. He would take the place to which Providence and his countrymen had called him, and do the best he could for the integrity and the welfare of the Republic. For himself, he scarcely expected ever to see Illinois again."

On the morning of the 11th of February, 1861, Lincoln left his home in Springfield for the scene where he was to spend the most anxious, toilsome, and painful years of his life. An elaborate programme had been prepared for his journey to Washington, which was to conduct him through the principal cities of Indiana, Ohio, New York, New Jersey, Pennsylvania, and Maryland, and consume much of the time intervening before the 4th of March. Special trains, preceded by pilot-engines, were prepared for his accommodation. He was accompanied at his departure by his wife and three sons, and a party of friends, including Governor Yates, ex-Governor Moore, Dr. W.M. Wallace (his brother-in-law), N.B. Judd, O.H. Browning, Ward H. Lamon, David Davis, Col. E.E. Ellsworth, and John M. Hay and J.G. Nicolay, the two latter to be his private secretaries. Mr. Lamon thus graphically describes the incidents of his leave-taking: "It was a gloomy day; heavy clouds floated overhead, and a cold rain was falling. Long before eight o'clock a great mass of people had collected at the railway station. At precisely five minutes before eight, Mr. Lincoln, preceded by Mr. Wood, emerged from a private room in the depot building, and passed slowly to the car, the people falling back respectfully on either side, and as many as possible shaking his hands. Having reached the train, he ascended the rear platform, and, facing about to the throng which had closed around him, drew himself up to his full height, removed his hat, and stood for several seconds in profound silence. His eye roved sadly over that sea of upturned faces, as if seeking to read in them the sympathy and friendship which he never needed more than then. There was an unusual quiver in his lip, and a still more unusual tear on his shriveled cheek. His solemn manner, his long silence, were as full of melancholy eloquence as any words he could have uttered. What did he think of? Of the mighty changes which had lifted him from the lowest to the highest estate on earth? Of the weary road which had brought him to this lofty summit? Of his poor mother lying beneath the tangled underbrush in a distant forest? Of that other grave in the quiet Concord cemetery? Whatever the character of his thoughts, it is evident that they were retrospective and sad. To those who were anxiously waiting to catch his words it seemed long until he had mastered his feelings sufficiently to speak. At length he began, in a husky voice, and slowly and impressively delivered his farewell to his neighbors. Imitating his example, many in the crowd stood with heads uncovered in the fast-falling rain." Abraham Lincoln spoke none but true and sincere words, and none more true and heartfelt ever fell from his lips than these, so laden with pathos, with humility, with a craving for the sympathy of his friends and the people, and for help above and beyond all earthly power and love.

My Friends:—No one not in my position can realize the sadness I feel at this parting. To this people I owe all that I am. Here I have lived more than a quarter of a century. Here my children were born, and here one of them lies buried. I know not how soon I shall see you again. I go to assume a task more difficult than that which has devolved upon any other man since the days of Washington. He never would have succeeded except for the aid of Divine Providence, upon which he at all times relied. I feel that I cannot succeed without the same Divine blessing which sustained him; and on the same Almighty Being I place my reliance for support. And I hope you, my friends, will all pray that I may receive that Divine assistance, without which I cannot succeed, but with which success is certain. Again I bid you an affectionate farewell.

The route chosen for the journey to Washington, as has been stated, was a circuitous one. It seems to have been Lincoln's desire to meet personally the people of the great Northern States upon whose devotion and loyalty he prophetically felt he must depend for the salvation of the Republic. Everywhere he met the warmest and most generous greetings from the throngs assembled at the railway stations in the various cities through which he passed. At Indianapolis, where the first important halt was made, cannon announced the arrival of the party, and a royal welcome was accorded the distinguished traveler. In this, as in the other cities at which he stopped, Lincoln made a brief address to the people. His remarks were well considered and temperate; his manner was serious, his expressions thoughtful and full of feeling. He entreated the people to be calm and patient; to stand by the principles of liberty inwrought into the fabric of the Constitution; to have faith in the strength and reality of the Government, and faith in his purpose to discharge his duties honestly and impartially. He referred continually to his trust in the Almighty Ruler of the Universe to guide the nation safely out of its present peril and perplexity. "I judge," he said at Columbus, "that all we want is time and patience, and a reliance in that God who has never forsaken His people." Again, he said: "Let the people on both sides keep their self-possession, and just as other clouds have cleared away in due time, so will this; and this great nation shall continue to prosper as heretofore." Alluding more definitely to his purposes for the future, he declared: "I shall do all that may be in my power to promote a peaceful settlement of all our difficulties. The man does not live who is more devoted to peace than I am—none who would do more to preserve it. *But it may be necessary to put the foot down firmly.*"

At the conclusion of Lincoln's speech at Columbus, a tremendous crowd surged forward to shake his hand. Says Dr. Holland: "Every man in the crowd was anxious to wrench the hand of Abraham Lincoln. He finally gave both hands to the work, with great good nature. To quote one of the reports of the occasion: 'People plunged at his arms with frantic enthusiasm, and all the infinite variety of shakes, from the wild and irrepressible pump-handle movement to the dead grip, was executed upon the devoted *dexter* and *sinister* of the President. Some glanced at his face as they grasped his hand; others invoked the blessings of heaven upon him; others affectionately gave him their last gasping assurance of devotion; others, bewildered and furious, with hats crushed over their eyes, seized his hands in a convulsive grasp, and passed on as if they had not the remotest idea who, what, or where they were.' The President at last escaped, and took refuge in the Governor's residence, although he held a levee at the State House in the evening, where in a more quiet way he met many prominent citizens."

At Cincinnati, where Lincoln had had so distasteful an experience a few years before, a magnificent ovation greeted him. The scene is described by one who witnessed it—Hon. William Henry Smith, at that time a resident of Cincinnati. "It was on the 13th of February that Mr. Lincoln reached the Queen City. The day was mild for mid-winter, but the sky was overcast with clouds, emblematic of the gloom that filled the hearts of the unnumbered thousands who thronged the streets and covered the house-tops. Lincoln rode in an open carriage, standing erect with uncovered head, and steadying himself by holding on to a board fastened to the front part of the vehicle. A more uncomfortable ride than this, over the bouldered streets of Cincinnati, cannot well be imagined. Perhaps a journey over the broken roads of Eastern Russia, in a tarantass, would secure to the traveler as great a degree of discomfort. Mr. Lincoln bore it with characteristic patience. His face was very sad, but he seemed to take a deep interest in everything. It was not without due consideration that the President-elect touched on the border of a slave State on his way to the capital. In his speech in reply to the Mayor of Cincinnati, recognizing the fact that among his auditors were thousands of Kentuckians, he addressed them directly, calling them 'Friends,' 'Brethren.' He reminded them that when speaking in Fifth Street Market square in 1859 he had promised that when the Republicans came into power they would treat the Southern or slave-holding people as Washington, Jefferson, and Madison treated them; that they would interfere with their institutions in no way, but abide by all and every compromise of the Constitution, and 'recognize and bear in mind always that you have as good hearts in your bosoms as other people, or as we claim to have, and treat you accordingly.' Then, to emphasize this, he said—in a passage omitted by Mr. Raymond and all other biographers of Lincoln—

> And now, fellow-citizens of Ohio, have you who agree in political sentiment with him who now addresses you ever entertained other sentiments towards our brethren of Kentucky than those I have expressed to you? [*Loud and repeated cries of 'No!' 'No!'*] If not, then why shall we not, as heretofore, be recognized and acknowledged as brethren again, living in peace and harmony, one with another? [*Cries of 'We will!'*] I take your response as the most reliable evidence that it may be so, along with other evidence, trusting to the good sense of the American people, on all sides of all rivers in America, under the Providence of God, who has never deserted us, that we shall again be brethren, forgetting all parties—ignoring all parties.

"This statesmanlike expression of conservative opinion," continues Mr. Smith, "alarmed some of the Republicans, who feared that the new President might sell out his party; and steps were taken, later in the day, to remind him of certain principles deemed fundamental by those who had been attracted to the party of Freedom. The sequel will show how this was done, and how successfully Mr. Lincoln met the unexpected attack. In the evening I called, with other citizens, at Mr. Lincoln's rooms at the Burnet House to pay my respects. Mr. Lincoln had put off the melancholy mood that appeared to control him during the day, and was entertaining those present with genial, even lively, conversation. The pleasant entertainment was interrupted by the announcement that a delegation of German workingmen were about to serenade Mr. Lincoln. Proceeding to the balcony, there were seen the faces of nearly two thousand of the substantial German citizens who had voted for Mr. Lincoln because they believed him to be a stout champion of free labor and free homesteads. The remarks of their spokesman, Frederick Oberkleine, set forth in clear terrrrms what they expected. He said:

> We, the German free workingmen of Cincinnati, avail ourselves of this opportunity to assure you, our chosen Chief Magistrate, of our sincere and heartfelt regard. You earned our votes as the champion of Free Labor and Free Homesteads. Our vanquished opponents have, in recent times, made frequent use of the terms "Workingmen" and "Workingmen's Meetings," in order to create an impression that the mass of workingmen were *in favor of compromises between the interests of free labor and slave labor, by which the victory just won would be turned into a defeat.* This is a despicable device of dishonest men. *We spurn such compromises. We firmly adhere to the principles which directed our votes in your favor. We trust that you, the self-reliant because self-made man, will uphold the Constitution and the laws against secret treachery and avowed treason.* If to this end you should be in need of men, the German free workingmen, with others, will rise as one man at your call, ready to risk their lives in the effort to maintain the victory already won by freedom over slavery.

"This was bringing the rugged issue boldly to the front, and challenging the President-elect to meet the issue or risk the loss of the support of an important section of his own party. Oberkleine spoke with great effect, but the remarks were hardly his own. Some abler man had put into his mouth these significant words. Mr. Lincoln replied, very deliberately, but without hesitation, as follows:

MR. CHAIRMAN:—I thank you, and those you represent, for the compliment paid me by the tender of this address. In so far as there is an allusion to our present national difficulty, and the suggestion of the views of the gentlemen who present this address, I beg you will excuse me from entering particularly upon it. I deem it due to myself and the whole country, in the present extraordinary condition of the country and of public opinion, that I should wait and see the last development of public opinion before I give my views or express myself at the time of the inauguration. I hope at that time to be false to nothing you have been taught to expect of me. [*Cheers.*]

I agree with you, Mr. Chairman, and with the address of your constituents, in the declaration that workingmen are the basis of all governments. That remark is due to them more than to any other class, for the reason that there are more of them than of any other class. And as your address is presented to me not only on behalf of workingmen, but especially of Germans, I may say a word as to classes. I hold that the value of life is to improve one's condition. Whatever is calculated to advance the condition of the honest, struggling laboring man, so far as my judgment will enable me to judge of a correct thing, I am for that thing.

An allusion has been made to the Homestead Law. I think it worthy of consideration, and that the wild lands of the country should be distributed so that every man should have the means and opportunity of benefiting his condition. [*Cheers.*] I have said that I do not desire to enter into details, nor will I.

In regard to Germans and foreigners, I esteem foreigners no better than other people—nor any worse. [*Laughter and cheers.*] They are all of the great family of men, and if there is one shackle upon any of them it would be far better to lift the load from them than to pile additional loads upon them. [*Cheers.*] And inasmuch as the continent of America is comparatively a new country, and the other countries of the world are old countries, there is more room here, comparatively speaking, than there is elsewhere; and if they can better their condition by leaving their old homes, there is nothing in my heart to forbid them coming, and I bid them all God speed. [*Cheers.*] Again, gentlemen, thanking you for your address, I bid you good night.

"If anyone," says Mr. Smith, "had expected to trap Mr. Lincoln into imprudent utterances, or the indulgence of the rhetoric of a demagogue, this admirable reply showed how completely they were disappointed. The preservation of this speech is due to my accidental presence. The visitation of the Germans was not on the programme, and none of the representatives of the press charged with the duty of reporting the events of the day were present. Observing this, I took short-hand notes on the envelope of an old letter loaned me for the occasion, and afterwards wrote them out. The words of Mr. Lincoln, exactly as spoken, are given above."

At Cleveland the party remained over for a day, and Lincoln was greeted with the usual friendly enthusiasm. An immense crowd met him at the depot, and he was escorted to the Weddell House, where a reception was given him in the evening. Hon. A.G. Riddle, then a resident of Cleveland, and a newly elected member of the Congress which was to share with Lincoln the burdens and responsibilities of the Civil War, was present on that occasion, and furnishes the following interesting personal recollections of it: "I saw Abraham Lincoln for the first time, at the Weddell House that evening. He stood on the landing-place at the top of a broad stairway, and the crowd approached him from below. This gave him an exaggerated advantage of his six feet four inches of length. The shapelessness of the lathy form, the shock of coarse black hair surmounting the large head, the retreating forehead—these were not apparent where we stood. My heart sprang up to him—the coming man. Of the thousand times I afterward saw him, the first view remains the most distinct impression; and never again to me was he more imposing. As we approached, someone whispered of me to him; he took my hand in both his for an instant, and we wheeled into the already crowded rooms. His manner was strongly Western; his speech and pronunciation Southwestern. Wholly without self-consciousness with men, he was constrained and ill at ease when surrounded, as he several times was, by fashionably dressed ladies. One incident of the evening I particularly recall. Ab McElrath was in the crowd—a handsome giant, an Apollo in youth, of about Mr. Lincoln's height. What brought it about, I do not know; but I saw them standing back to back, in a contest of altitude—Mr. Lincoln and Ab McElrath—the President-elect, the chosen, the nation's leader in the thick-coming darkness, and the tavern-keeper and fox-hunter. The crowd applauded.

"Mr. Lincoln presented me to the gentlemen of his party—Mr. Browning, Mr. Judd, and Mr. Lamon, I remember, as I later became very well acquainted with them; also the rough-looking Colonel Sumner of the army. Mr. Lincoln invited me to accompany him for at least a day on his eastward journey. I joined him the next morning at the station. The vivacity of the night before had utterly vanished, and the rudely sculptured cliffy face struck me as one of the saddest I had ever seen. The eyes especially had a depth of melancholy which I had never seen in human eyes before. Some things he wished to know from me, especially regarding Mr. Chase, whom, among others, he had called to Springfield. He asked me no direct questions, but I very soon found myself speaking freely to him, and was able to explain some not well-known features of Ohio politics—and much to his satisfaction, as he let me see. There was then some talk of Mr. Seward, and more of Senator Cameron. All three had been his rivals at Chicago, and were, as I then thought, in his mind as possible Cabinet ministers; although no word was said by him of such an idea in reference to either. Presently he conducted me to Mrs. Lincoln, whom I had not before seen. Presenting me, he returned to the gentlemen of the party, and I saw little more of him except once when he returned to us, before I left the train. Mrs. Lincoln impressed me very favorably, as a woman of spirit, intelligence, and decided opinions, which she put very clearly. Our conversation was mainly of her husband. I remarked that all the likenesses I had ever seen of him did him injustice. This evidently pleased her. I suggested that a full beard from the under lip down (his face was shaven) would relieve and help him very much. This interested her, and we discussed it and the character of his face quite fully. The impression I then formed of this most unfortunate lady was only deepened by the pleasant acquaintance she permitted, down to the time of the national calamity, which unsettled her mind as I always thought."

Of the New York City visit, an excellent account is given by the distinguished preacher and writer, Dr. S. Irenæus Prime. "The country was at that moment," says Dr. Prime, "in the first throes of the great rebellion. Millions of hearts were beating anxiously in view of the advent to power of this untried man. Had he been called of God to the throne of power at such a time as this, to be the leader and deliverer of the people? As the carriage in which he sat passed slowly by me on the Fifth avenue, he was looking weary, sad, feeble, and faint. My disappointment was excessive; so great, indeed, as to be almost overwhelming. He did not look to me to be the man for the hour. The next day I was with him and others in the Governor's room in the City Hall, when the Mayor of the city made an official address. Mr. Lincoln's reply was so modest, firm, patriotic, and pertinent, that my fears of the day before began to subside, and I saw in this new man a promise of great things to come. It was not boldness or dash, or high-sounding pledges; nor did he while in office, with the mighty armies of a roused nation at his command, ever assume to be more than he promised in that little upper chamber in New York, on his journey to the seat of Government, to take the helm of the ship of state then tossing in the storm."

Before the end of the journey, strong fears prevailed in the minds of Lincoln's friends that an attempt would be made to assassinate him before he should reach Washington. Every precaution was taken to thwart such endeavor; although Lincoln himself was disturbed by no thought of danger. He had done, he contemplated doing, no wrong, no injustice to any citizen of the United States; why then should there be a desire to strike him down? Thus he reasoned; and he was free from any dread of personal peril. But the officials of the railroads over which he was to pass, and his friends in Washington, felt that there was cause for apprehension. It was believed by them that a plot existed for making away with Lincoln while passing through Baltimore, a city in the heart of a slave State, and rife with the spirit of rebellion. Detectives had been employed to discover the facts in the matter, and their reports served to confirm the most alarming conjectures. A messenger was despatched from Washington to intercept the Presidential party and warn Lincoln of the impending danger. Dr. Holland states that "the detective and Mr. Lincoln reached Philadelphia nearly at the same time, and there the former submitted to a few of the President's friends the information he had secured. An interview between Mr. Lincoln and the detective was immediately arranged, and took place in the apartments of the former at the Continental Hotel. Mr. Lincoln, having heard the officer's statement in detail, then informed him that he had promised to raise the American flag on Independence Hall the following morning— the anniversary of Washington's birthday—and that he had accepted an invitation to a reception by the Pennsylvania Legislature in the afternoon of the same day. 'Both of these engagements I will keep,' said Mr. Lincoln, 'if it costs me my life.' For the rest, he authorized the detective to make such arrangements as he thought proper for his safe conduct to Washington."

In the meantime, according to Dr. Holland, General Scott and Senator Seward, both of whom were in Washington, learned from independent sources that Lincoln's life was in danger, and concurred in sending Mr. Frederick W. Seward to Philadelphia to urge upon him the necessity of proceeding immediately to Washington in a quiet way. The messenger arrived late on Thursday night, after Lincoln had retired, and requested an audience. Lincoln's fears had already been aroused, and he was cautious, of course, in the matter of receiving a stranger. But satisfied that the messenger was indeed the son of Mr. Seward, he received him. Nothing needed to be done except to inform him of the plan entered into with the detective, by which the President was to arrive in Washington early on Saturday morning, in advance of his family and party.

On the morning of the 22d, Lincoln, as he had promised, attended the flag-raising at Independence Hall in Philadelphia, the historic building in which had been adopted the Declaration of Independence. The occasion was a memorable one, and Lincoln's address eloquent and impressive. "All the political sentiments I entertain," said he, "have been drawn from the sentiments which were given to the world from this hall." He spoke calmly but firmly of his resolve to stand by the principles of the immortal Declaration and of the Constitution of his country; and, as though conscious of the dangers of his position, he added solemnly: "I have said nothing but what I am willing to live by, *and, if it be the pleasure of Almighty God, to die by.*"

From Philadelphia Lincoln went immediately to Harrisburg, and attended the reception given him by the Pennsylvania Legislature, in the afternoon of the same day. Then, leaving his hotel in the evening, attended only by Mr. Lamon and the detective (Mr. Allan Pinkerton), he was driven to the depot, where he took the regular train for Washington. The train passed through Baltimore in the night, and early the next morning (February 23) reached the capital. Mr. Washburne, who had been notified to be at the depot on the arrival of the train, says: "I planted myself behind one of the great pillars in the old Washington and Baltimore depot, where I could see and not be observed. Presently, the train came rumbling in on time. When it came to a stop I watched with fear and trembling to see the passengers descend. I saw every car emptied, and there was no Mr. Lincoln. I was well-nigh in despair, and when about to leave I saw three persons slowly emerge from the last sleeping-car. I could not mistake the long, lank form of Mr. Lincoln, and my heart bounded with joy and gratitude. He had on a soft low-crowned hat, a muffler around his neck, and a short overcoat. Anyone who knew him at that time could not have failed to recognize him at once; but I must confess he looked more like a well-to-do farmer from one of the back towns of Jo Daviess County, coming to Washington to see the city, take out his land warrant and get the patent for his farm, than the President of the United States. The only persons that accompanied Mr. Lincoln were Pinkerton, the well-known detective, and Ward H. Lamon. When they were fairly on the platform, and a short distance from the car, I stepped forward and accosted the President: 'How are you, Lincoln?' At this unexpected and rather familiar salutation the gentlemen were apparently somewhat startled; but Mr. Lincoln, who had recognized me, relieved them at once by remarking in his peculiar voice: 'This is only Washburne!' Then we all exchanged congratulations, and walked out to the front of the depot, where I had a carriage in waiting. Entering the carriage (all four of us), we drove rapidly to Willard's Hotel, entering on Fourteenth Street, before it was fairly daylight."

General Stone, who was in command at Washington at that time, states that both General Scott and himself "considered it almost a certainty that

Mr. Lincoln could not pass through Baltimore alive on the day fixed," and adds: "I recommended that Mr. Lincoln should be officially warned; and suggested that it would be best that he should take the train that evening from Philadelphia, and so reach Washington early the next day. General Scott directed me to see Mr. Seward, to whom he wrote a few lines, which he handed me. I did not succeed in finding Mr. Seward until past noon. I handed him the General's note. He listened attentively to what I said, and asked me to write down my information and suggestions. Then, taking the paper I had written, he hastily left. The note I wrote was what Mr. Frederick Seward carried to Mr. Lincoln in Philadelphia. Mr. Lincoln has stated that it was *this note* which induced him to change his journey as he did. *The stories of disguises are all nonsense.* Mr. Lincoln merely took the sleeping-car in the night train."

There is little doubt that the fears of Lincoln's friends regarding his passage through Baltimore were well grounded; and that but for the timely warnings and precautions the assassination of April, 1865, might have taken place in February of 1861.

CHAPTER XV

The week following Lincoln's arrival in Washington, and preceding his inauguration, was for him one of incessant activity. From almost the first moment he was engrossed either in preparations for his inauguration and the official responsibilities which would immediately follow that event, or in receiving the distinguished callers who hastened to meet him and in discussing with them the grave aspects of political affairs. Without rest or opportunity to survey the field that lay before him, or any preparations save such as the resources of his own strong character might afford him, he was plunged instantly into the great political maelstrom in which he was to remain for four long years, and whose wild vortex might well have bewildered an eye less sure, a will less resolute, and a brain less cool than his. As Emerson put it, "The new pilot was hurried to the helm in a tornado."

"Mr. Lincoln's headquarters," says Congressman Riddle of Ohio, "were at Willard's Hotel; and the few days before the inauguration were given up to a continuous reception in the broad corridor of the second floor, near the stairway. I remember a notable morning when the majestic General Scott, in full dress, sword, plumes, and bullion, came to pay his respects to the incoming President. The scene was impressive. By the unknown law that ruled his spirits, Mr. Lincoln was at his best, complete master of himself and of all who came within the magic of his presence. Never was he happier, speaking most of the time, flashing with anecdote and story. That time now seems as remote as things of a hundred years ago. The war antiquated all that went before it. The Washington, the men, the spirit of that now ancient time, have faded past all power to recall and reproduce them. The real Washington was as essentially Southern as Richmond or Baltimore. 'Lincoln and his vandals,' fresh from the North and West, were thronging the wide, squat, unattractive city, from which the bolder and braver rebel element had not yet departed."

Dr. George B. Loring, of Massachusetts, who was one of the first to meet Lincoln after his arrival in Washington, says: "I saw him on his arrival, and when he made his first appearance in a public place. I was standing in the upper hall of Willard's Hotel, conversing with a friend and listening to the confused talk of the crowded drawing-room adjoining. As we stood there, a tall and awkward form appeared above the stairs, especially conspicuous, as it came into view, for a new and stylish hat. It was evidently President Lincoln, whom neither of us had seen before. As soon as his presence was known, the hall was thronged from the drawing-rooms. He seemed somewhat startled by the crowd, did not remove his hat, wended his way somewhat rapidly and with mere passing recognition, and took shelter in his room. When the crowd had dispersed, my friend and myself—although we had opposed his election—called upon him to pay our respects. He received us with great cordiality, spoke freely of the difficulties by which he was surrounded, and referred with evident satisfaction to the support he had received in Massachusetts. 'I like your man Banks,' said he, 'and have tried to find a place for him in my Cabinet; but I am afraid I shall not quite fetch it.' He bore the marks of anxiety in his countenance, which, in its expression of patience, determination, resolve, and deep innate modesty, was extremely touching."

Before leaving Springfield Lincoln had prepared his inaugural message with great care, and placed it in a "gripsack" for transportation to Washington. An odd incident, by which the message came near being lost on the journey, was afterwards related by Lincoln to a friend. When the party reached Harrisburg Lincoln asked his son Robert where the message was, and was taken aback by his son's confession that in the excitement caused by the enthusiastic reception he believed he had let a waiter have the gripsack. Lincoln, in narrating the incident, said: "My heart went up into my mouth, and I started downstairs, where I was told that if a waiter had taken the gripsack I should probably find it in the baggage-room. Going there, I saw a large pile of gripsacks and other baggage, and thought that I discovered mine. My key fitted it, but on opening there was nothing inside but a few paper collars and a flask of whisky. A few moments afterward I came across my own gripsack, with the document in it all right."

The fourth of March soon came, and with it the impressive ceremonies of Lincoln's inauguration as President. A good description of the scene is given by Dr. J.G. Holland. "The morning broke beautifully clear, and it found General Scott and the Washington police in readiness. In the hearts of the surging crowds there was anxiety; but outside all looked as usual on such occasions, with the exception of an extraordinary display of soldiers. The public buildings, the schools, and most of the places of business, were closed during the day, and the stars and stripes were floating from every flag-staff. There was a great desire to hear Lincoln's inaugural; and at an early hour Pennsylvania Avenue was full of people wending their way to the east front of the Capitol where it was to be delivered. As the Presidential party reached the platform erected for the ceremonies, Senator

Baker of Oregon, one of Lincoln's old friends and political rivals in Illinois, introduced him to the assembly. There was not a very hearty welcome given to the President as he stepped forward to read his inaugural. The reading was listened to with profound attention, those passages which contained any allusion to the Union being vociferously cheered. None listened more carefully than Mr. Buchanan and Judge Taney, the latter of whom, with noticeable agitation, administered the oath of office to Mr. Lincoln when his address was ended."

Another eye-witness has described the dramatic scene, and the principal actors in it, in the following graphic paragraphs: "Near noon I found myself a member of the motley crowd gathered around the side entrance to Willard's Hotel. Soon an open barouche drove up, and the only occupant stepped out. A large, heavy, awkward-moving man, far advanced in years, short and thin gray hair, full face plentifully seamed and wrinkled, head curiously inclined to the left shoulder, a low-crowned, broad-brimmed silk hat, an immense white cravat like a poultice thrusting the old-fashioned standing collar up to the ears, dressed in black throughout, with swallow-tail coat not of the newest style. It was President Buchanan, calling to take his successor to the Capitol. In a few minutes he reappeared, with Mr. Lincoln on his arm; the two took seats side by side, and the carriage rolled away, followed by a rather disorderly and certainly not very imposing procession. I had ample time to walk to the Capitol, and no difficulty in securing a place where everything could be seen and heard to the best advantage. The attendance at the inauguration was, they told me, unusually small; many being kept away by anticipated disturbance, as it had been rumored—not without good grounds—that General Scott himself was fearful of an outbreak, and had made all possible military preparations to meet the emergency. A square platform had been built out from the steps to the eastern portico, with benches for distinguished spectators on three sides. Senator Douglas, the only one I recognized, sat at the extreme end of the seat on the right of the narrow passage leading from the steps. There was no delay, and the gaunt form of the President-elect was soon visible, slowly making his way to the front. To me, at least, he was completely metamorphosed—partly by his own fault, and partly through the efforts of injudicious friends and ambitious tailors. He was raising (to gratify a very young lady, it is said) a crop of whiskers, of the blacking-brush variety, coarse, stiff, and ungraceful; and in so doing spoiled, or at least seriously impaired, a face which, though never handsome, had in its original state a peculiar power and pathos. On the present occasion the whiskers were reinforced by brand-new clothes from top to toe; black dress coat instead of the usual frock; black cloth or satin vest, black pantaloons, and a glossy hat evidently just out of the box.

To cap the climax of novelty, he carried a huge ebony cane, with a gold head the size of an egg. In these, to him, strange habiliments, he looked so miserably uncomfortable that I could not help pitying him. Reaching the platform, his discomfort was visibly increased by not knowing what to do with hat and cane; and so he stood there, the target for ten thousand eyes, holding his cane in one hand and his hat in the other, the picture of helpless embarrassment. After some hesitation, he pushed the cane into a corner of the railing, but could not find a place for the hat, except on the floor, where I could see he did not like to risk it. Douglas, who fully took in the situation, came to the rescue of his old friend and rival, and held the precious hat until the owner needed it again; a service which, if predicted two years before, would probably have astonished him. The oath of office was administered by Chief Justice Taney, whose black robes, attenuated figure, and cadaverous countenance reminded me of a galvanized corpse. Then the President came forward and read his inaugural address in a clear and distinct voice. It was attentively listened to by all; but the closest listener was Douglas, who leaned forward as if to catch every word, nodding his head emphatically at those passages which most pleased him. I must not forget to mention the presence of a Mephistopheles in the person of Senator Wigfall of Texas, who stood with folded arms leaning against the doorway of the Capitol, looking down upon the crowd and the ceremony with a contemptuous air which sufficiently indicated his opinion of the whole performance. To him, the Southern Confederacy was already an accomplished fact."

"Under the shadow of the great Eastern portico of the Capitol," says General John A. Logan, "with the retiring President and Cabinet, the Supreme Court Justices, the Foreign Diplomatic Corps, and hundreds of Senators, Representatives, and other distinguished persons filling the great platform on either side and behind them, Abraham Lincoln stood bareheaded before full thirty thousand people, upon whose uplifted faces the unveiled glory of the mild Spring sun now shone—stood reverently before that far greater and mightier Presence termed by himself, 'My rightful masters, the American people'—and pleaded in a manly, earnest, and affectionate strain with 'such as were dissatisfied' to listen to the 'better angels' of their nature. 'Temperate, reasonable, kindly persuasive'—it seems strange that Lincoln's inaugural address did not disarm at least the personal resentment of the South toward him, and sufficiently strengthen Union-loving people there against the red-hot Secessionists, to put the 'brakes' down on rebellion."

The address was devoted almost exclusively to the great absorbing topic of the hour—the attempt of the Southern States to withdraw from the Union and erect an independent republic. The calm, firm, moderate, judicious spirit which pervaded Lincoln's address is apparent in the following quotations, which contain its most significant and memorable passages:

Fellow-Citizens of the United States:—In compliance with a custom as old as the Government itself, I appear before you to address you briefly, and to take in your presence the oath prescribed by the Constitution of the United States to be taken by the President "before he enters on the execution of his office." ... Apprehension seems to exist among the people of the Southern States, that by the accession of a Republican Administration their property and their peace and personal security are to be endangered. There has never been any reasonable cause for such apprehension. Indeed, the most ample evidence to the contrary has all the while existed and been open to their inspection. It is found in nearly all the published speeches of him who now addresses you. I do but quote from one of those speeches when I declare that "I have no purpose, directly or indirectly, to interfere with the institution of slavery in the States where it exists. I believe I have no lawful right to do so, and I have no inclination to do so." Those who nominated and elected me did so with full knowledge that I had made this and many similar declarations, and have never recanted them.... I now reiterate these sentiments; and, in doing so, I only press upon the public attention the most conclusive evidence of which the case is susceptible, that the property, peace, and security of no section are to be in anywise endangered by the now incoming Administration. I add, too, that all the protection which, consistently with the Constitution and the laws, can be given, will be cheerfully given to all the States, when lawfully demanded, for whatever cause—as cheerfully to one section as to another.... I hold that, in contemplation of universal law, and of the Constitution, *the Union of these States is perpetual.* Perpetuity is implied, if not expressed, in the fundamental law of all National Governments. It is safe to assert that no Government proper ever had a provision in its organic law for its own termination. Continue to execute all the express provisions of our National Constitution, and the Union will endure forever.... I therefore consider that, in view of the Constitution and the laws, the Union is unbroken, and to the extent of my ability I shall take care, as the Constitution itself expressly enjoins upon me, that the laws of the Union be faithfully executed in all the States. Doing this I deem to be only a simple duty on my part; and I shall perform it, so far as practicable, unless my rightful masters, the American people, shall withhold the requisite means, or, in some authoritative manner, direct the contrary. I trust this will not be regarded as a menace, but only as the declared purpose of the Union that it will constitutionally defend and maintain itself. In doing this, there need be no bloodshed or violence; and there shall be none, unless it be forced upon the national authority. The power confided to me will be used to hold, occupy, and possess the property and places belonging to the Government, and to collect the duties and imposts; but beyond what may be but necessary for these objects, there will be no invasion, no using of force against or among the people anywhere.... Physically speaking, we cannot separate. We cannot remove our respective sections from each other, nor build an impassable wall between them. A husband and wife may be divorced, and go out of the presence and beyond the reach of each other; but the different parts of our country cannot do this. They cannot but remain face to face; and intercourse, either amicable or hostile, must continue between them. It is impossible, then, to make that intercourse more advantageous or more satisfactory after separation than before. Can aliens make treaties easier than friends can make law? Can treaties be more faithfully enforced between aliens than laws can among friends? Suppose you go to war, you cannot fight always; and when, after much loss on both sides and no gain on either, you cease fighting, the identical old questions, as to terms of intercourse, are again upon you.... This country, with its institutions, belongs to the people who inhabit it. Whenever they shall grow weary of the existing Government, they can exercise their constitutional right of amending it, or their revolutionary right to dismember or overthrow it. I cannot be ignorant of the fact that many worthy and patriotic citizens are desirous of having the National Constitution amended. While I make no recommendation of amendments, I fully recognize the rightful authority of the people over the whole subject, to be exercised in either of the modes prescribed in the instrument itself; and I should, under existing circumstances, favor rather than oppose a fair opportunity being afforded the people to act upon it.... The Chief Magistrate derives all his authority from the people, and they have conferred none upon him to fix terms for the separation of the States. The people themselves can do this also, if they choose; but the Executive, as such, has nothing to do with it. His duty is to administer the present Government as it came to his hands, and to transmit it, unimpaired by him, to his successor.... By the frame of the Government under which we live, the same people have wisely given their public servants but little power for mischief; and have, with equal wisdom, provided for the return of that little to their own hands at very short intervals. While the people retain their virtue and vigilance, no administration, by any extreme of wickedness or folly, can very seriously injure the Government in the short space of four years.

My countrymen, one and all, think calmly and well upon this whole subject. Nothing valuable can be lost by taking time. If there be an object to hurry any of you in hot haste to a step which you would never take deliberately, that object will be frustrated by taking time; but no good can be frustrated by it. Such of you as are now dissatisfied still have the old Constitution unimpaired, and, on the sensitive point, the laws of your own framing under it; while the new administration will have no immediate power, if it would, to change either. If it were admitted that you who are dissatisfied hold the right side in the dispute, there still is no single good reason for precipitate action. Intelligence, patriotism, Christianity, and a firm reliance on Him who has never yet forsaken this favored land, are still competent to adjust, in the best way, all our present difficulty.

In your hands, my dissatisfied fellow-countrymen, and not in mine, is the momentous issue of civil war. The Government will not assail you. You can have no conflict without being yourselves the aggressors. You have no oath registered in heaven to destroy the Government; while I shall have the most solemn one to "preserve, protect, and defend" it.

I am loth to close. We are not enemies, but friends. We must not be enemies. Though passion may have strained, it must not break, our bonds of affection. The mystic chords of memory, stretching from every battlefield and patriot grave to every living heart and hearthstone all over this broad land, will yet swell the chorus of the Union, when again touched, as surely they will be, by the better angels of our nature.

At the close of the address, which was delivered with the utmost earnestness and solemnity, Lincoln, "with reverent look and impressive emphasis, repeated the oath to preserve, protect, and defend the Constitution of his country. Douglas, who knew the conspirators and their plots, with patriotic magnanimity then grasped the hand of the President, gracefully extended his congratulations, and the assurance that in the dark future he would stand by him, and give to him his utmost aid in upholding the Constitution and enforcing the laws of his country."

"At the inauguration," says Congressman Riddle, "I stood within a yard of Mr. Lincoln when he pronounced his famous address. How full of life and power it then was, with the unction of his utterance! Surely, we thought, the South, which rejected the concessions of Congress, would accept him. How dry and quaint, yet ingenious, much of that inaugural appears to me now, when the life and soul seem to have gone out of it! A sad thing—a spectre of the day—will forever haunt my memory: Poor old President Buchanan, short, stout, pale, white-haired, yet bearing himself resolutely throughout, linked by the arm to the new President, into whom from himself was passing the qualifying unction of the Constitution, jostled hither and thither, as already out of men's sight, yet bravely maintaining the shadow of dignity and place. How glad he must have been to take leave of his successor at the White House when all was ended!"

The formalities of the inauguration concluded, Lincoln passed back through the Senate Chamber, and, again escorted by Mr. Buchanan, was conducted to the White House, where the cares and anxieties of his position immediately descended upon him. "Strange indeed," says General Logan, "must have been the thoughts that crowded through the brain and oppressed the heart of Abraham Lincoln that night—his first at the White House. The City of Washington swarmed with rebels and rebel sympathizers, and all the departments of Government were honeycombed with treason and shadowed with treachery and espionage. Every step proposed or contemplated by the Government would be known to the so-called Government of the Confederate States almost as soon as thought of. All means to thwart and delay the carrying out of the Government's purposes that the excuses of routine and red tape admitted of would be used by the traitors within the camp to aid the traitors without. No one knew all this better than Mr. Lincoln. With no army, no navy, not even a revenue cutter left—with forts and arsenals, ammunition and arms, in possession of the South, with no money in the National Treasury, and the National credit blasted—the position must, even to his hopeful nature, have seemed desperate. Yet even in this awful hour, he was sustained by confidence in the good effects of his conciliatory message to the South, and by his trust in the patriotism of the people and the Providence of God."

Mr. Welles, the incoming Secretary of the Navy, in writing of the period immediately following the inauguration, says: "A strange state of things existed at that time in Washington. The atmosphere was thick with treason. Party spirit and old party differences prevailed amidst the accumulating dangers. Secession was considered by most persons as a political party question, not as rebellion. Democrats to a large extent sympathized with the Rebels more than with the Administration. The Republicans, on the other hand, were scarcely less partisan and unreasonable ... clamorous for the removal of all Democrats, indiscriminately, from office."

The President's first official act was the announcement of his Cabinet, which was composed of the following persons: William H. Seward, Secretary of State; Simon Cameron, Secretary of War; Salmon P. Chase, Secretary of the Treasury; Gideon Welles, Secretary of the Navy; Caleb B. Smith, Secretary of the Interior; Montgomery Blair, Postmaster General; and Edward Bates, Attorney General. Lincoln had selected these counselors with grave deliberation. In reply to the remonstrances urged, on political grounds, against the appointment of one or two of them, he had said: "The times are too grave and perilous for ambitious schemes and personal rivalries. I need the aid of all of these men. They enjoy the confidence of their several States and sections, and they will strengthen the administration." On another occasion he remarked: "It will require the utmost skill, influence, and sagacity of all of us, to save the country; let us forget ourselves, and join hands like brothers to save the Republic. If we succeed, there will be glory enough for all."

Speculations have been almost endless as to how the Cabinet came to be made up as it was. But the truth is, according to Secretary Welles, that it was practically made up in Springfield almost as soon as Lincoln found himself elected. In Lincoln's own words, as given by Mr. Welles: "On the day of the Presidential election the operator of the telegraph in Springfield placed his instrument at my disposal. I was there without leaving, after the returns began to come in, until we had enough to satisfy us how the election had gone. This was about two in the morning of Wednesday. I went home, but not to get much sleep; for I then felt, as I never had before, the responsibility that was upon me. I began at once to feel that I needed support,—others to share with me the burden. This was on Wednesday morning, and before the sun went down I had made up my Cabinet. It was almost the same that I finally appointed."

The only two members of the Cabinet who served from the beginning to the end of Lincoln's administration were Welles and Seward. Stanton was not appointed until January 13, 1862, succeeding Simon Cameron. Chase left the Treasury Department to become Chief Justice, and was succeeded in the Treasury Department by ex-Governor Fessenden of Vermont, who in his turn was succeeded by Hugh McCulloch. The Attorney General's chair was filled successively by Bates and Speed. Caleb B. Smith was the first Secretary of the Interior, succeeded (January 1, 1863) by John P. Usher. The first Postmaster General was Montgomery Blair, who was followed (September 4, 1864) by ex-Governor Dennison of Ohio. The appointment that gave the greatest surprise of any in the Cabinet was that of Stanton as Secretary of War. Stanton had been in Buchanan's cabinet as Attorney General. He had been outspoken, almost brutal, in his scornful hostility to Lincoln, and the appointment by him was as great a surprise to Stanton as his acceptance of it was to everyone. When asked, somewhat incredulously, what he would do as War Secretary Stanton replied, "*I will make Abe Lincoln President of the United States.*" Of the character of this remarkable man, Mr. Alonzo Rothschild, in his interesting study of the relations between Lincoln and Stanton ("Lincoln, Master of Men," p. 229), says: "Intense earnestness marked Stanton's every act. So sharply were all his faculties focused upon the purpose of the hour that he is to be classed among the one-idea men of history. Whatever came between him and his goal encountered an iron will.... Quick to penetrate through the husks of fraud into the very nubbin of things, he was even more swiftly moved by relentless wrath to insist upon exposure and punishment. The brief career [as Attorney General] in Buchanan's cabinet had been long enough to demonstrate his almost savage hostility toward official dishonesty, as well as his moral courage to grapple with treason in high places. Above all, he evinced a loyalty to the Union that rose above the party creed of a lifetime—that might demand of him any sacrifice however great."

The first weeks of President Lincoln's residence in the Executive Mansion were occupied with the arduous work of selecting loyal and capable men for responsible positions in the Government service. The departments at Washington were filled with disloyal men, who used the means and influence pertaining to their places to aid the rebellious States. It was of vital importance that these faithless officials should be removed at the earliest moment, and their positions filled with men of tried integrity. Lincoln desired to appoint for this purpose stanch, competent, and trustworthy citizens, regardless of party distinctions. But the labor involved in this duty was enormous and exhausting. There was a multitude of vacant places, there were difficult questions to be considered in a majority of cases, and there was a host of applicants and their friends to be satisfied. Mr. Charles A. Dana relates a circumstance which hints at the troubles encountered by Lincoln in this province of his Presidential duties. "The first time I saw Mr. Lincoln," says Mr. Dana, "was shortly after his inauguration. He had appointed Mr.

Seward to be his Secretary of State; and some of the Republican leaders of New York, who had been instrumental in preventing Mr. Seward's nomination to the Presidency and in securing that of Mr. Lincoln, had begun to fear that they would be left out in the cold in the distribution of the offices. Accordingly several of them determined to go to Washington, and I was asked to go with them. We all went up to the White House together, except Mr. Stanton, who stayed away because he was himself an applicant for office. Mr. Lincoln received us in the large room upstairs in the east wing of the White House, where the President had his working office, and stood up while General Wadsworth, who was our principal spokesman, stated what was desired. After the interview was begun, a big Indianian, who was a messenger in attendance in the White House, came into the room and said to the President, 'She wants you.' 'Yes, yes,' said Mr. Lincoln, without stirring. Soon afterward the messenger returned again, exclaiming, 'I say she wants you.' The President was evidently annoyed, but instead of going out after the messenger he remarked to us: 'One side shall not gobble up everything. Make out a list of the places and men you want, and I will endeavor to apply the rule of give and take.' General Wadsworth answered: 'Our party will not be able to remain in Washington, but we will leave such a list with Mr. Carroll, and whatever he agrees to will be agreeable to us.' Mr. Lincoln continued, 'Let Mr. Carroll come in to-morrow, and we will see what can be done.'"

Lincoln was regarded with violent animosity by all who were in sympathy with the peculiar prejudices of the slave States. The inhabitants of the District of Columbia looked upon him with especial dislike. He was to them an odious embodiment of the abhorred principles of Abolitionism. As an illustration of this bitter feeling, Mr. Arnold narrates the following anecdote: "A distinguished South Carolina lady—one of the Howards—the widow of a Northern scholar, called upon him out of curiosity. She was very proud and aristocratic, and was curious to see a man who had been represented to her as a monster, a mixture of the ape and the tiger. She was shown into the room where were Mr. Lincoln and Senators Seward, Hale, Chase, and other prominent members of Congress. As Mr. Seward, whom she knew, presented her to the President, she hissed in his ear: 'I am a South Carolinian.' Instantly reading her character, he turned and addressed her with the greatest courtesy, and dignified and gentlemanly politeness. After listening a few moments, astonished to find him so different from what he had been described to her, she said: 'Why, Mr. Lincoln, you look, act, and speak like a kind, good-hearted, generous man.' 'And did you expect to meet a savage?' said he. 'Certainly I did, or even something worse,' replied she. 'I am glad I have met you,' she continued, 'and now the best way to preserve peace is for you to go to Charleston and show the people what you are, and tell them you have no intention of injuring them.' Returning home, she found a party of Secessionists, and on entering the room she exclaimed, 'I have seen him! I have seen him!' 'Who?' they inquired. 'That terrible monster, Lincoln, and I found him a gentleman, and I am going to his first levee after his inauguration.' At his first reception, this tall daughter of South Carolina, dressing herself in black velvet, with two long white plumes in her hair, repaired to the White House. She was nearly six feet high, with black eyes and black hair, and in her velvet and white feathers she was a striking and majestic figure. As she approached the President he recognized her immediately. 'Here I am again,' said she, 'that South Carolinian.' 'I am glad to see you,' replied he, 'and to assure you that the first object of my heart is to preserve peace, and I wish that not only you but every son and daughter of South Carolina were here, that I might tell them so.' Mr. Cameron, Secretary of War, came up, and after some remarks he said, 'South Carolina [which had already seceded] is the prodigal son.' 'Ah, Mr. Secretary,' said she, 'if South Carolina is the prodigal son, Uncle Sam, our father, ought to divide the inheritance, and let her go; but they say you are going to make war upon us; is it so?' 'Oh, come back,' said Lincoln, 'tell South Carolina to come back now, and we will kill the fatted calf.'"

The impression which Lincoln made on those who met him at the outset of his career as President, and their varied comments and descriptions, are matters of peculiar interest. At first, many people did not understand him— hardly knew what to make of a personality so unlike any they had ever seen in high places before. But he soon began to show those qualities of calm self-reliance, quickness to grasp the essential factors of a situation and readiness to meet it, courage, patience, firmness, breadth of view and kindliness, practical tact and wisdom, which were a surprise to all who knew him, and are now seen to be but a rapid and logical unfolding, under the stimulus of his enormous responsibilities, of his great natural powers. The test had come, the crisis was upon him; and he met them marvelously well.

General W.T. Sherman contributes an interesting reminiscence at this point. "One day," says General Sherman, "my brother, Senator Sherman, took me with him to see Mr. Lincoln. We found the room full of people. Mr. Lincoln sat at the end of a table, talking with three or four gentlemen, who soon left. John walked up, shook hands, and took a chair near him, holding in his hand some papers referring to minor appointments in the State of Ohio, which formed the subject of conversation. Mr. Lincoln took the papers, said he would refer them to the proper heads of departments, and would be glad to make the appointments asked for, if not already promised. John then turned to me, and said, 'Mr. President, this is my brother, Colonel

Sherman, who is just up from Louisiana; he may give you some information you want.' 'Ah!' said Mr. Lincoln, 'how are they getting along down there?' I said, 'They think they are getting along swimmingly—they are preparing for war.' 'Oh, well!' said he, '*I guess we'll manage to keep house.*' I was silenced, said no more to him, and we soon left. I was sadly disappointed, and remember that I broke out on John, cursing the politicians generally, saying, 'You have got things in a — — of a fix, and you may get them out as best you can,' adding that the country was sleeping on a volcano that might burst forth at any minute, but that I was going to St. Louis to take care of my family, and would have no more to do with it. John begged me to be more patient, but I said I would not; that I had no time to wait, that I was off for St. Louis; and off I went."

The apartment which Lincoln used as an office in which to transact daily business and to receive informal visits was on the second floor of the White House. Its simple equipments are thus described by Mr. Arnold: "It was about twenty-five by forty feet in size. In the centre, on the west, was a large white marble fireplace, with big old-fashioned brass andirons, and a large and high brass fender. A wood fire was burning in cool weather. The large windows opened on the beautiful lawn to the south, with a view of the unfinished Washington Monument, the Smithsonian Institution, the Potomac, Alexandria, and on down the river toward Mt. Vernon. Across the Potomac were Arlington Heights and Arlington House, late the residence of Robert E. Lee. On the hills around, during nearly all Lincoln's administration, were the white tents of soldiers, field fortifications and camps, and in every direction could be seen the brilliant colors of the national flag. The furniture of this room consisted of a large oak table covered with cloth, extending north and south; and it was around this table that the Cabinet sat when it held its meetings. Near the end of the table, and between the windows, was another table, on the west side of which the President sat in a large armchair, and at this table he wrote. A tall desk with pigeon-holes for papers stood against the south wall. The only books usually found in this room were the Bible, the United States Statutes, and a copy of Shakespeare. There were a few chairs and two plain hair-covered sofas. There were two or three map frames, from which hung military maps on which the position and movements of the armies were traced. On the mantel was an old and discolored engraving of General Jackson and a later photograph of John Bright. Doors opened into this room from the room of the Secretary, and from the outside hall running east and west across the House. A bell cord within reach of his hand extended to the Secretary's office. A messenger who stood at the door opening from the hall took in the cards and names of visitors. Here, in this plain room, Lincoln spent most of his time while President.

Here he received everyone, from the Chief Justice and Lieutenant-General to the private soldier and humblest citizen. Custom had fixed certain rules of precedence, and the order in which officials should be received. Members of the Cabinet and the high officers of the army and navy were generally promptly admitted. Senators and members of Congress were received in the order of their arrival. Sometimes there would be a crowd of them waiting their turn. While thus waiting, the loud ringing laugh of Mr. Lincoln would be heard by the waiting and impatient crowd. Here, day after day, often from early morning to late at night, Lincoln sat, listened, talked, and decided. He was patient, just, considerate, and hopeful. The people came to him as to a father. He saw everyone, and many wasted his precious time. Governors, Senators, Congressmen, officers, clergymen, bankers, merchants — all classes approached him with familiarity. This incessant labor, the study of the great problems he had to decide, the worry of constant importunity, the quarrels of officers of the army, the care, anxiety, and responsibility of his position, wore upon his vigorous frame."

Mr. Ben. Perley Poore states that "the White House, while Mr. Lincoln occupied it, was a fertile field for news, which he was always ready to give those correspondents in whom he had confidence; but the surveillance of the press — first by Secretary Seward, and then by Secretary Stanton — was as annoying as it was inefficient.... Often when Mr. Lincoln was engaged, correspondents would send in their cards, bearing requests for some desired item of news or for the verification of some rumor. He would either come out and give the coveted information, or he would write it on the back of the card and send it to the owner. He wrote a legible hand, slowly and laboriously perfecting his sentences before he placed them on paper. The long epistles that he wrote to his generals he copied himself, not wishing anyone else to see them, and these copies were kept in pigeon-holes for reference.... Mr. Lincoln used to wear at the White House in the morning, and after dinner, a long-skirted faded dressing-gown, belted around his waist, and slippers. His favorite attitude when listening — and he was a good listener — was to lean forward, and clasp his left knee with both hands, as if fondling it, and his face would then wear a sad and wearied look. But when the time came for him to give an opinion on what he had heard, or to tell a story which something 'reminded him of,' his face would lighten up with its homely, rugged smile, and he would run his fingers through his bristly black hair, which would stand out in every direction like that of an electric experiment doll."

John G. Nicolay, afterward Lincoln's private secretary, says: "The people beheld in the new President a man six feet four inches in height, a stature which of itself would be hailed in any assemblage as one of the outward signs of leadership; joined to this was a spare but muscular frame, and large strongly-marked features corresponding to his unusual stature. Quiet in demeanor but erect in bearing, his face even in repose was not unattractive; and when lit up by his open, genial smile, or illuminated in the utterance of a strong or stirring thought, his countenance was positively handsome. His voice, pitched in rather a high key, but of great clearness and penetration, made his public remarks audible to a wide circle of listeners."

Henry Champion Deming says of Lincoln's appearance at this time: "Conceive a tall and giant figure, more than six feet in height, not only unencumbered with superfluous flesh, but reduced to the minimum working standard of cord and sinew and muscle, strong and indurated by exposure and toil, with legs and arms long and attenuated, but not disproportionately to the long and attenuated trunk; in posture and carriage not ungraceful, but with the grace of unstudied and careless ease rather than of cultivated airs and high-bred pretensions. His dress is uniformly of black throughout, and would attract but little attention in a well-dressed circle, if it hung less loosely upon him, and if the ample white shirt collar were not turned over his cravat in Western style. The face that surmounts this figure is half Roman and half Indian, bronzed by climate, furrowed by life struggles, seamed with humor; the head is massive and covered with dark, thick, and unmanageable hair; the brow is wide and well developed, the nose large and fleshy, the lips full, cheeks thin and drawn down in strong, corded lines, which, but for the wiry whiskers, would disclose the machinery which moves the broad jaw. The eyes are dark gray, sunk in deep sockets, but bright, soft and beautiful in expression, sometimes lost and half abstracted, as if their glance was reversed and turned inward, or as if the soul which lighted them was far away. The teeth are white and regular, and it is only when a smile, radiant, captivating, and winning as was ever given to mortal, transfigures the plain countenance, that you begin to realize that it is not impossible for artists to admire and women to love it."

Mr. John Bigelow, who was appointed consul to Paris in 1861, and was afterwards minister to France, describes in his "Retrospections of an Active Life" his first visit to Lincoln and the impressions gained by him at that early period in Lincoln's official career. "The day following my arrival in Washington Preston King, Senator from New York, invited me to go with him to be presented to President Lincoln, an invitation which of course I embraced with alacrity; for as yet I had not met him, and knew him only by his famous senatorial campaign against Douglas in Illinois and the masterly address which he delivered at the Cooper Institute shortly before his nomination in New York.... The new President received us in his private room at an early hour of the morning; another gentleman was with him at the time, a member of the Senate, I believe. We were with him from a half to three-quarters of an hour. The conversation, in which I took little or no part, turned upon the operations in the field. I observed no sign of weakness in anything the President said; neither did I hear anything that particularly impressed me, which, under the circumstances, was not surprising. What did impress me, however, was what I can only describe as a certain lack of sovereignty. He seemed to me, nor was it in the least strange that he did, like a man utterly unconscious of the space which the President of the United States occupied that day in the history of the human race, and of the vast power for the exercise of which he had become personally responsible. This impression was strengthened by Mr. Lincoln's modest habit of disclaiming knowledge of affairs and familiarity with duties, and frequent avowals of ignorance, which, even where it exists, it is as well for a captain as far as possible to conceal from the public. The authority of an executive officer largely consists in what his constituents think it is. Up to that time Mr. Lincoln had had few opportunities of showing the nation the qualities which won all hearts and made him one of the most conspicuous and enduring historic characters of the century."

Some uncommonly vivid "first impressions" of Lincoln are given in the Journals of Ralph Waldo Emerson, who early in February of 1862 made a visit to Washington for the purpose of delivering a lecture before the Smithsonian Institution—a lecture which Lincoln is said to have attended. A day or two afterwards Emerson was taken by Senator Sumner of Massachusetts to call at the White House. "The President impressed me," says Emerson, "more favorably than I had hoped. A frank, sincere, well-meaning man, with a lawyer's habit of mind, good clear statement of his facts; correct enough, not vulgar, as described, but with a sort of boyish cheerfulness, or that kind of sincerity and jolly good meaning that our class-meetings on Commencement Days show, in telling our old stories over. When he has made his remark he looks up at you with great satisfaction, and shows all his white teeth, and laughs.... When I was introduced to him he said, 'Oh, Mr. Emerson, I once heard you say in a lecture that a Kentuckian seems to say by his air and manners, "Here am I; if you don't like me, the worse for you."'" (The point of this of course is that Lincoln was himself a Kentuckian.) A day or two later Emerson again called on the President, this time in the company of Secretary Seward. It being Sunday evening, Seward asked the President if he had been to church, to which the latter answered that he had not— that he had been reading, for the first time, Senator Sumner's speech in the Senate on the Trent affair. This was followed by some general conversation on the Trent affair, in which the President expressed his gratification at the friendly attitude taken in the matter by France and Spain.

Private Secretary Hay thus writes of Lincoln's character and disposition: "All agree that the most marked characteristic of Mr. Lincoln's manners was his simplicity and artlessness; this immediately impressed itself upon the observation of those who met him for the first time, and each successive interview deepened the impression. People seemed delighted to find in the ruler of the nation freedom from pomposity and affectation, mingled with a certain simple dignity which never forsook him. Though oppressed with the weight of responsibility resting upon him as President of the United States, he shrank from assuming any of the honors, or even the titles, of the position. After years of intimate acquaintance with Mr. Lincoln, the writer cannot now recall a single instance in which he spoke of himself as President, or used that title for himself except when acting in an official capacity. He always spoke of his position and office vaguely, as, 'this place,' 'here,' or other modest phrase. Once, speaking of the room in the Capitol used by the Presidents of the United States during the close of a session of Congress, he said, 'That room, you know, that they call'—dropping his voice and hesitating—'the President's room.' To an intimate friend who addressed him always by his own proper title, he said, 'Now call me Lincoln, and I'll promise not to tell of the breach of etiquette—if *you*, won't—and I shall have a resting-spell from "Mister President."' With all his simplicity and unacquaintance with courtly manners, his native dignity never forsook him in the presence of critical polished strangers; but mixed with his angularities and *bonhomie* was something which spoke the fine fiber of the man; and while his sovereign disregard of courtly conventionalities was somewhat ludicrous, his native sweetness and straightforwardness of manner served to disarm criticism and impress the visitor that he was before a man pure, self-poised, collected, and strong in unconscious strength. Of him, an accomplished foreigner, whose knowledge of the courts was more perfect than that of the English language, said, 'He seems to me one grand *gentilhomme* in disguise. '" Mr. Hay adds that Lincoln 's simplicity of manner "was marked in his total lack of consideration of what was due his exalted station. He had an almost morbid dread of what he called 'a scene'—that is, a demonstration of applause, such as always greeted his appearance in public. The first sign of a cheer sobered him; he appeared sad and oppressed, suspended conversation, and looked out into vacancy; and when it was over, resumed the conversation just where it was interrupted, with an obvious feeling of relief.... Speaking of an early acquaintance who was an applicant for an office which he thought him hardly qualified to fill, the President said, 'Well, now, I never thought M—— had any more than average ability, when we were young men together; really I did not.' [A pause.] 'But, then, I suppose he thought just the same about me; he had reason to, and—here I am!'"

General Carl Schurz says: "In the White House, as in his simple home in Springfield, Mr. Lincoln was the same plain, unaffected, unpretentious citizen. He won the admiration and affection of even the most punctilious of the foreign diplomats by the tenderness of his nature and the touching simplicity of his demeanor.... He was, in mind and heart, the very highest type of development of a plain man. He was a born leader of men, and the qualities that made him a leader were of the plain, common-sense type.... Lincoln had one great advantage over all the chief statesmen of his day. He had a thorough knowledge of the plain people. He knew their habits, their modes of thought, their unfailing sense of justice and right. He relied upon the popular feeling, in great measure, for his guidance."

Mrs. Harriet Beecher Stowe said of the qualities which Lincoln exhibited in the White House: "Lincoln is a strong man, but his strength is of a peculiar kind; it is not aggressive so much as passive; and among passive things, it is like the strength not so much of a stone buttress as of a wire cable. It is strength swaying to every influence, yielding on this side and on that, to popular needs, yet tenaciously and inflexibly bound to carry its great end.... Slow and careful in coming to resolutions, willing to talk with every person who has anything to show on any side of a disputed subject, long in weighing and pondering, attached to constitutional limits and time-honored landmarks, Lincoln certainly was the *safest* leader a nation could have at a time when the *habeas corpus* must be suspended and all the constitutional and minor rights of citizens be thrown into the hands of their military leader. A reckless, bold, theorizing, dashing man of genius might have wrecked our Constitution and ended us in a splendid military despotism."

The fear lest the virulent enemies of the administration should attempt to assassinate Lincoln was so wide-spread that military measures were enforced to protect him from secret assault. General Charles P. Stone, to whom the duty was entrusted of establishing the necessary precautions, has furnished a brief report on the subject. "From the first," says General Stone, "I took, under the orders of the General-in-chief, especial care in guarding the Executive Mansion—without, however, doing it so ostentatiously as to attract public attention. It was not considered advisable that it should appear that the President of the United States was, for his personal safety, obliged to surround himself by armed guards. Mr. Lincoln was not consulted in the matter. But Captain Todd, formerly an officer of the regular army, who was, I believe, the brother-in-law of Mr. Lincoln, was then residing in the Presidential Mansion, and with him I was daily and nightly in communication, in order that in case of danger one person in the President's household should know where to find the main body of the guard, to the officer commanding which Captain Todd was each night introduced. Double sentries were placed in the shrubbery all around the mansion, and the main body of the guard was posted in a vacant basement-room, from which a staircase led to the upper floors. A person entering by the main gate and walking up to the front door of the Executive Mansion during the night could see no sign of a guard; but from the moment anyone entered the grounds by any entrance, he was under the view of at least two riflemen standing silent in the shrubbery, and any suspicious movement on his part would have caused his immediate arrest; while inside, the call of Captain Todd would have been promptly answered by armed men. The precautions were taken before Fort Sumter was fired on, as well as afterward. One night near midnight," continues General Stone, "I entered the grounds for the purpose of inspecting the guard, and was surprised to see a bright light in the East room. As I entered the basement I heard a loud noise, as of many voices talking loudly, mingled with the ringing of arms, coming from the great reception room. On questioning the commander of the guard, I learned that many gentlemen had entered the house at a late hour, but they had come in boldly; no objection had been made from within, but on the contrary Captain Todd had told him all was right. I ascended the interior staircase and entered the East room, where I found more than fifty men, among whom were Hon. Cassius M. Clay and General Lane. All were armed with muskets, which they were generally examining, and it was the ringing of many rammers in the musket barrels which had caused the noise I had heard. Mr. Clay informed me that he and a large number of political friends, *deeming it very improper that the President's person should in such times be unguarded*, had formed a voluntary guard which would remain there every night and see to it that Mr. Lincoln was well protected. I applauded the good spirit exhibited, but did not, however, cease the posting of the outside guards, nor the nightly inspections myself as before, until the time came when others than myself became responsible for the safety of the President."

It is stated that Lincoln "had an almost morbid dislike to an escort, or guard, and daily exposed himself to the deadly aim of an assassin." To the remonstrances of friends, who feared his constant exposure to danger, he had but one answer: "If they kill me, the next man will be just as bad for them; and in a country like this, where our habits are simple, and must be, assassination is always possible, and will come if they are determined upon it." A cavalry guard was once placed at the gates of the White House for a while, and Lincoln said that he "worried until he got rid of it." He once remarked to Colonel Halpine: "It would never do for a President to have guards with drawn sabers at his door, as if he fancied he were, or were trying to be, or were assuming to be, an emperor." While the President's family were at their summer-house, near Washington, he rode into town of a morning, or out at night, attended by a mounted escort; but if he returned to town for a while after dark, he rode in unguarded, and often alone, in his open carriage. On more than one occasion, the same writer tells us, he "has gone through the streets of Washington at a late hour of the night with the President, without escort, or even the company of a servant, walking all the way, going and returning. Considering the many open and secret threats to take his life, it is not surprising that Lincoln had many thoughts about his coming to a sudden and violent end. He once said that he felt the force of the expression, 'To take one's life in his hand'; but that he would not like to face death suddenly. He said that he thought himself a great coward physically, and was sure that he would make a poor soldier, for unless there was something inspiring in the excitement of a battle he was sure that he would drop his gun and run at the first symptom of danger. That was said sportively, and he added, 'Moral cowardice is something which I think I never had.'"

CHAPTER XVI

The Confederate attack upon Fort Sumter—a United States fort situated at the mouth of Charleston Harbor, South Carolina—April 12, 1861, was the signal that civil war had actually begun. Lincoln had thus far maintained a conciliatory policy toward the States in rebellion, hoping to the last that good sense and reason prevailing over rash and violent impulses would induce them to resume their allegiance to the Government. Their resort to arms and capture of forts and property of the United States decided the course of the administration; and on the 15th of April—forty-two days after his accession to the Presidency—Lincoln issued a proclamation asking for the immediate enlistment of 75,000 volunteers,[C] and summoning Congress to convene in an extra session on the 4th of July. The call was sent forth in the following form:

PROCLAMATION.

By the President of the United States.

WHEREAS, the laws of the United States have been for some time past and now are opposed and the execution thereof obstructed in the States of South Carolina, Georgia, Alabama, Florida, Mississippi, Louisiana and Texas, by combinations too powerful to be suppressed by the ordinary course of judicial proceedings, or by the powers vested in the marshals by law; now, therefore, I, ABRAHAM LINCOLN, President of the United States, in virtue of the power in me vested by the Constitution and the laws, have thought fit to call forth, and hereby do call forth, the militia of the several States of the Union, to the aggregate number of seventy-five thousand, in order to suppress said combinations and to cause the laws to be duly executed.

The details of this object will be immediately communicated to the State authorities through the War Department. I appeal to all loyal citizens to favor, facilitate, and aid this effort to maintain the honor, the integrity and existence of our National Union, and the perpetuity of popular government, and to redress wrongs already long enough endured. I deem it proper to say that the first service assigned to the forces hereby called forth will probably be to repossess the forts, places, and property which have been seized from the Union; and in every event the utmost care will be observed, consistently with the objects aforesaid, to avoid any devastation, any destruction of, or interference with, property, or any disturbance of peaceful citizens of any part of the country; and I hereby command the persons composing the combinations aforesaid to disperse and retire peaceably to their respective abodes, within twenty days from this date.

Deeming that the present condition of public affairs presents an extraordinary occasion, I do hereby, in virtue of the power in me vested by the Constitution, convene both Houses of Congress. The Senators and Representatives are, therefore, summoned to assemble at their respective chambers, at twelve o'clock, noon, on Thursday, the fourth day of July next, then and there to consider and determine such measures as, in their wisdom, the public safety and interest may seem to demand.

In witness whereof I have hereunto set my hand and caused the seal of the United States to be affixed.

Done at the City of Washington, this fifteenth day of April, in the year of our Lord one thousand eight hundred and sixty-one, and of the independence of the United States the eighty-fifth.

By the President, ABRAHAM LINCOLN.
WILLIAM H. SEWARD, Secretary of State.

The issue of this proclamation created the wildest enthusiasm throughout the North. Scarcely a voice was raised against it, as it was seen to be a measure of absolute necessity and of self-defense on the part of the Government. "Every Northern State," says Mr. Henry I. Raymond, "responded promptly to the President's demand, and from private persons, as well as by the Legislatures, men, arms, and money were offered in unstinted profusion, and with the most zealous alacrity, in support of the Government. Massachusetts was first in the field, and on the first day after the issue of the proclamation her Sixth regiment, completely equipped, started from Boston for the national capital. Two more regiments were also made ready, and took their departure within forty-eight hours."

The Sixth Massachusetts regiment was attacked on its way to Washington, on the 19th of April, by a mob in Baltimore, carrying a Confederate flag, and several of its members were killed or severely wounded. "This," continues Mr. Raymond, "inflamed to a still higher point the excitement which already pervaded the country. The whole Northern section of the Union felt outraged that troops should be assailed and murdered on their way to protect the capital of the nation. In Maryland, where the secession party was strong, there was also great excitement, and the Governor of the State and the Mayor of Baltimore united in urging, for prudential reasons, that no more troops should be brought through that city." In answer to the remonstrances of Governor Hicks and a committee from Maryland, who presented their petition in person, Lincoln, intent on avoiding every cause of offense, and with a forbearance that now seems incredible, replied: "Troops must be brought here; but I make no point of bringing them through Baltimore. Without any military knowledge myself, of course I must leave details to General Scott. He hastily said this morning, in the presence of these gentlemen, 'March them around Baltimore, and not through it.' I sincerely hope the General, on fuller reflection, will consider this practical and proper, and that you will not object to it. By this, a collision of the people of Baltimore with the troops will be avoided, unless they go out of their way to seek it. I hope you will exert your influence to prevent this. Now and ever, I shall do all in my power for peace, consistently with the maintenance of the Government."

One of the most encouraging incidents of this opening chapter of the war was the announcement that Stephen A. Douglas, the great leader of the Democracy and the life-long political opponent of Lincoln, had declared his purpose to stand by the Government. The effect of this action, at this crisis, was most salutary; it ranged the Northern Democrats with the defenders of the Union, and gave Lincoln a united North as the act of no other individual could have done. From that time until his death Douglas never faltered in his loyalty, and stood by the Government with a zeal and patriotism which were above all lower considerations of person or of party. On Sunday, the 14th of April, when Washington was thrilling with excitement over the fall of Fort Sumter, Douglas called on the President and after a brief conversation authorized a statement to be telegraphed throughout the country that he was "fully prepared to sustain the President in the exercise of all his Constitutional functions, to preserve the Union, maintain the Government, and defend the Federal capital. A firm policy and prompt action were necessary. The capital was in danger, and must be defended at all hazards, and at any expense of men and money." Faithful to his pledge, Douglas immediately set out upon a tour through the Northwest, to strengthen, by his words and presence, the spirit of loyalty among the people. He made a series of eloquent speeches on his journey to Chicago, where he arrived worn and spent with the fatigue and excitement of his undertaking. It was the last and noblest service of his life. Illness ensued, and after a few weeks of suffering he passed away, June 3, at the age of forty-eight. His death was an irreparable loss, mourned by the President and the nation.

The President's call for troops was succeeded on the 19th of April by a proclamation declaring a blockade of Southern ports. The text of this document is historically important, as definitely formulating the attitude and policy of the Government.

> *Whereas,* An insurrection against the Government of the United States has broken out in the States of South Carolina, Georgia, Alabama, Florida, Mississippi, Louisiana, and Texas, and the laws of the United States for the collection of the revenue cannot be efficiently executed therein, conformably to that provision of the Constitution which requires duties to be uniform throughout the United States:
>
> *And whereas,* A combination of persons, engaged in such insurrection, have threatened to grant pretended letters of marque to authorize the bearers thereof to commit assaults on the lives, vessels, and property of good citizens of the country lawfully engaged in commerce on the high seas, and in waters of the United States:
>
> *And whereas,* An Executive Proclamation has already been issued, requiring the persons engaged in these disorderly proceedings to desist therefrom, calling out a militia force for the purpose of repressing the same, and convening Congress in extraordinary session to deliberate and determine thereon:
>
> Now, therefore, I, ABRAHAM LINCOLN, President of the United States, with a view to the same purposes before mentioned, and to the protection of the public peace, and the lives and property of quiet and orderly citizens pursuing their lawful occupations, until Congress shall have assembled and deliberated on the said unlawful proceedings, or until the same shall have ceased, have further deemed it advisable to set on foot a blockade of

the ports within the States aforesaid, in pursuance of the laws of the United States, and of the laws of nations in such cases provided. For this purpose a competent force will be posted so as to prevent entrance and exit of vessels from the ports aforesaid. If, therefore, with a view to violate such blockade, a vessel shall approach or shall attempt to leave any of the said ports, she shall be duly warned by the commander of one of the blockading vessels, who shall indorse on her register the fact and date of such warning; and if the same vessel shall again attempt to enter or leave the blockaded port, she will be captured and sent to the nearest convenient port, for such proceedings against her and her cargo, as prize, as may be deemed advisable.

And I hereby proclaim and declare, that if any person, under the pretended authority of said States, or under any other pretense, shall molest a vessel of the United States, or the persons or cargo on board of her, such person will be held amenable to the laws of the United States for the prevention and punishment of piracy.

By the President, ABRAHAM LINCOLN.
WILLIAM H. SEWARD, Secretary of State.
WASHINGTON, April 19, 1861.

On the 27th of April the President issued a proclamation by which the blockade of Southern ports was extended to the ports of North Carolina and Virginia. And on the 16th of May, by another proclamation, the President directed the commander of the United States forces in Florida to "permit no person to exercise any office or authority upon the islands of Key West, Tortugas, and Santa Rosa, which may be inconsistent with the laws and Constitution of the United States; authorizing him, at the same time, if he shall find it necessary, to suspend the writ of *habeas corpus*, and to remove from the vicinity of the United States fortresses all dangerous and suspected persons."

The Virginia Convention which passed the ordinance of secession (April 17) having appointed a committee to wait upon the President and "respectfully ask him to communicate to this Convention the policy which the Federal Executive intends to pursue in regard to the Confederate States," Lincoln in reply thus clearly outlined the policy and purposes of the Government:

In answer I have to say, that having at the beginning of my official term expressed my intended policy as plainly as I was able, it is with deep regret and mortification I now learn there is great and injurious uncertainty in the public mind as to what that policy is and what course I intend to pursue. Not having as yet seen occasion to change, it is now my purpose to pursue the course marked out in the Inaugural Address. I commend a careful consideration of the whole document as the best expression I can give to my purposes. As I then and therein said, I now repeat: "The power confided in me will be used to hold, occupy, and possess property and places belonging to the Government, and to collect the duties and imposts; but beyond what is necessary for these objects there will be no invasion, no using of force against or among the people anywhere." By the words "property and places belonging to the Government," I chiefly allude to the military posts and property which were in possession of the Government when it came into my hands. But if, as now appears to be true, in pursuit of a purpose to drive the United States authority from these places, an unprovoked assault has been made upon Fort Sumter, I shall hold myself at liberty to repossess, if I can, like places which had been seized before the Government was devolved upon me; and in any event I shall, to the best of my ability, repel force by force. In case it proves true that Fort Sumter has been assaulted, as is reported, I shall, perhaps, cause the United States mails to be withdrawn from all the States which claim to have seceded, believing that the commencement of actual war against the Government justifies and possibly demands it. I scarcely need to say that I consider the military posts and property situated within the States which claim to have seceded, as yet belonging to the Government of the United States as much as they did before the supposed secession. Whatever else I may do for the purpose, I shall not attempt to collect the duties and imposts by any armed invasion of any part of the country; not meaning by this, however, that I may not land a force deemed necessary to relieve a fort upon the border of the country. From the fact that I have quoted a part of the Inaugural Address, it must not be inferred that I repudiate any other part, the whole of which I reaffirm, except so far as what I now say of the mails may be regarded as a modification.

ABRAHAM LINCOLN.

In the early period of Lincoln's administration he was hopeful that many serious phases of the threatened trouble might be averted, and that the better judgment of the citizens of the South might prevail. "For more than a month after his inauguration," says Secretary Welles, "President Lincoln indulged the hope, I may say felt a strong confidence, that Virginia would not secede but would adhere to the Union.... That there should be no cause of offense, no step that would precipitate or justify secession, he enjoined forbearance from all unnecessary exercise of political party authority." But he was very decided and determined as to what his duty was and what his action would be if the secessionists and disunionists pressed their case. He said: "The disunionists did not want me to take the oath of office. I have taken it, and I intend to administer the office for the benefit of the people, in accordance with the Constitution and the law." He was especially anxious that Kentucky should not be plunged into a rebellious war, as he saw that this State would be of the utmost importance to the Union cause. Soon after the bombardment of Fort Sumter a conference was held between the President and a number of prominent Kentuckians then in Washington, at which Lincoln expressed himself in the most earnest words. Kentucky, he declared, "must not be precipitated into secession. She is the key to the situation. With her faithful to the Union, the discord in the other States will come to an end. She is now in the hands of those who do not represent the people. The sentiment of her State officials must be counteracted. We must arouse the young men of the State to action for the Union. We must know what men in Kentucky have the confidence of the people, and who can be relied on for good judgment, that they may be brought to the support of the Government at once." He paid a high tribute to the patriotism of the Southern men who had stood up against secession. "But," said he, "they are, as a rule, beyond the meridian of life, and their counsel and example do not operate quickly, if at all, on the excitable nature of young men who become inflamed by the preparations for war, and who in such a war as this will be, if it goes on, are apt to go in on the side that gives the first opportunity. The young men must not be permitted to drift away from us. I know that the men who voted against me in Kentucky will not permit this Government to be swept away by any such issue as that framed by the disunionists."

As Mr. Markland, a prominent Kentuckian, relates, in his reminiscences of the period: "Immediately a campaign for the Union was begun in Kentucky. The State could not be dragooned into open secession, therefore the neutrality policy was adopted. That policy was more rigidly observed by Mr. Lincoln than it was by his opponents, but he was not misled by it. Judge Joseph Holt made eloquent appeals for the Union through the columns of the press and from the forum, as did the Speeds, the Goodloes, and many others of prominence. Rousseau, Jacobs, Poundbaker, and others, stood guard in the Legislature, and by their eloquence stayed the tide of disunion there. The labors of Judge Holt, the Speeds, the Goodloes, Cassius M. Clay, and their followers, had brought forth fruit for the Union. The patriotic men in the Legislature had done their work well. The men in the camps on the north side of the Ohio river moved over into Kentucky, and the invasion of Confederates which was to sweep Kentucky into secession was at an end. Kentucky was saved to the Union by the wise counsel and pacific policy of Abraham Lincoln."

A special session of Congress convened on the 4th of July, in obedience to the summons of the President in his proclamation of April 15. The following day the message of the Executive rehearsed to the joint Houses the circumstances which had rendered their assembling necessary. It portrayed in clear and succinct words the situation of affairs, the aggressive acts of the States aiming to disrupt the Federal Union, and the measures adopted by the administration to frustrate their attempts. The assailants of the Government, said the President, "have forced upon the country the distinct issue, 'immediate dissolution or blood.' And this issue embraces more than the fate of these United States. It presents to the whole family of man the question whether a constitutional Republic or Democracy—a Government of the people by the same people—can or cannot maintain its territorial integrity against its own domestic foes. It presents the question whether discontented individuals, too few in numbers to control administration according to organic law in any case, can always, upon the pretenses made in this case, or on any other pretenses, or arbitrarily, without any pretense, break up their Government, and thus practically put an end to free government upon the earth. It forces us to ask, 'Is there, in all Republics, this inherent and fatal weakness? Must a Government, of necessity, be too strong for the liberties of its own people, or too weak to maintain its own existence?'" The message requested of Congress "the legal means for making this contest a short and decisive one; that you place at the control of the Government, for the work, at least four hundred thousand men and $400,000,000. That number of men is about one-tenth of those of proper ages within the regions where, apparently, all are willing to engage; and the sum is less than a twenty-third part of the money value owned by the men who seem ready to devote the whole. A debt of $600,000,000 now is a less sum per head than was the debt of our Revolution when we came out of that struggle; and the money value in the country now bears even a greater proportion to what it was then than does the population. Surely each man has as strong a motive now to preserve our liberties as each had then to establish them." The message dwelt upon the encouraging facts "that the free institutions we enjoy have developed the powers and improved the condition of our whole people beyond any example in the world. Of this we now have a striking and an impressive illustration. So large an army as the Government has now on foot was never before known without a soldier in it but had taken his place there of his own free choice. But more than this; there are many single regiments whose members, one and another, possess full practical knowledge of all the arts, sciences, professions, and whatever else, whether useful or elegant, is known in the world; and there is scarcely one from which there could not be selected a President, a Cabinet, a Congress, and perhaps a Court, abundantly competent to administer the Government itself." Finally, and eloquently, the message demonstrated the significance of the war in its effect upon the liberties and prayers of all mankind. This message again illustrates Lincoln's singular power of stating clearly and convincingly the nature and exigencies of the struggle for the Preservation of the Union. Said he:

> This is essentially a people's contest. On the side of the Union it is a struggle for maintaining in the world that form and substance of government whose leading object is to elevate the condition of men; to lift artificial weights from all shoulders; to clear the paths of laudable pursuits for all; to afford all an unfettered start and a fair chance in the race of life. Yielding to partial and temporary departures, from necessity, this is the leading object of the Government for whose existence we contend. I am most happy to believe that the plain people understand and appreciate this. It is worthy of note that while, in this the Government's hour of trial, large numbers of those in the army and navy who have been favored with the offices have resigned and proved false to the hand which had pampered them, not one common soldier or common sailor is known to have deserted his flag. Great honor is due to those officers who remained true, despite the example of their treacherous associates; but the greatest honor, and most important fact of all, is the unanimous firmness of the common soldiers and common sailors. To the last man, so far as known, they have successfully resisted the traitorous efforts of those whose commands but an hour before they obeyed as absolute law. This is the patriotic instinct of plain people. They understand, without an argument, that destroying the Government which was

made by Washington means no good to them. Our popular Government has often been called an experiment. Two points in it our people have already settled—the successful establishing and the successful administering of it. One still remains—its successful maintenance against a formidable internal attempt to overthrow it. It is now for them to demonstrate to the world that those who can fairly carry an election can also suppress a rebellion; that ballots are the rightful and peaceful successors of bullets; and that when ballots have fairly and constitutionally decided, there can be no successful appeal back to bullets; that there can be no successful appeal, except to ballots themselves, at succeeding elections. Such will be a great lesson of peace: teaching men that what they cannot take by an election, neither can they take by a war; teaching all the folly of being the beginners of a war.

Through the early summer of 1861 Washington was alive with preparations for a military movement against the enemy in Virginia. Troops from the North were constantly arriving, and as rapidly as possible were assigned to different organizations and drilled in the art of war. "Few comparatively know or can appreciate the actual condition of things and the state of feeling of the members of the Administration in those days," says Secretary Welles. "Nearly sixty years of peace had unfitted us for any war; but the most terrible of all wars, a civil war, was upon us, and it had to be met. Congress had adjourned without making any provision for the storm, though aware it was at hand and soon to burst upon the country. A new Administration, its members scarcely acquainted with each other, and differing essentially in the past, was compelled to act, promptly and decisively." The burden upon the President began to grow tremendous; but he did not shrink or falter.

> Upon his back a more than Atlas-load,
>
> The burden of the Commonwealth, was laid;
>
> He stooped, and rose up to it, though the road
>
> Shot suddenly downwards, not a whit dismayed.

He labored incessantly in urging forward the preparations for the great struggle which, however he might regret it, he now saw was inevitable. He was in daily conference with the officers of the army and of the War Department, and was present at innumerable reviews and parades of the soldiers. The 4th of July was memorable for a grand review of all the New

York troops in and about the city. It was a brilliant and impressive scene. Says a spectator, Hon. A.G. Riddle: "As they swept past—twenty-five thousand boys in blue—their muskets flashing, bands playing, and banners waving, I stood near a distinguished group surrounding the President, and noted his countenance as he turned to the massive moving column. All about him were excited, confident, exultant. He stood silent, pale, profoundly sad, as though his prophetic soul saw what was to follow. He seemed to be gazing beyond the splendid pageant before him, upon things hidden from other eyes. Was there presaged to him a vision of that grander review of our victorious armies at the close of the war, which he was not to see?"

A few days later, all the troops in Washington crossed the Long Bridge and marched, gallant and exultant, straight toward the enemy in Virginia. The advance of our army resulted, on the 21st of July, in the shameful disaster at Bull Run. The North was filled with surprise and dismay, and even the stoutest hearts were burdened with anxiety for the future. Lincoln at first shared somewhat in the general depression, but his elastic spirits quickly rallied from the shock. Three or four days after the battle, some gentlemen who had been on the field called upon him. He inquired very minutely regarding all the circumstances of the affair, and after listening with the utmost attention, said, with a touch of humor: "So it's your notion that we *whipped the rebels*, and then *ran away from them!*" Not long after this, the President made a personal visit to the army in Virginia. General Sherman, at that time connected with the Army of the Potomac, says: "I was near the river-bank, looking at a block-house which had been built for the defense of the aqueduct, when I saw a carriage coming by the road that crossed the Potomac river at Georgetown by a ferry. I thought I recognized in the carriage the person of President Lincoln. I hurried across a bend, so as to stand by the roadside as the carriage passed. I was in uniform, with a sword on, and was recognized by Mr. Lincoln and Mr. Seward, who rode side by side in an open hack. I inquired if they were going to my camp, and Mr. Lincoln said: 'Yes; we heard that you had got over the big scare, and we thought we would come over and see the boys.' The roads had been much changed and were rough. I asked if I might give directions to his coachman; he promptly invited me to jump in, and to tell the coachman which way to drive. Intending to begin on the right and follow round to the left, I turned the driver into a side-road which led up a very steep hill, and, seeing a soldier, called to him and sent him up hurriedly to announce to the Colonel whose camp we were approaching that the President was coming. As we slowly ascended the hill, I discovered that Mr. Lincoln was full of feeling, and wanted to encourage our men. I asked if he intended to speak to them, and he said he would like to. I asked him then to please discourage all cheering, noise, or any sort of confusion; that we had had enough of it before Bull Run to ruin any set of men, and that what we needed were cool, thoughtful, hard-fighting soldiers—no more hurrahing, no more humbug. He took my remarks in the most perfect good-nature. Before we had reached the first camp, I heard the drum beating the 'assembly,' saw the men running for their tents, and in a few minutes the regiment was in line, arms presented, and then brought to an 'order' and 'parade rest.' Mr. Lincoln stood up in the carriage, and made one of the neatest, best, and most feeling addresses I ever listened to, referring to our late disaster at Bull Run, the high duties that still devolved on us, and the brighter days yet to come. At one or two points the soldiers began to cheer, but he promptly checked them, saying: 'Don't cheer, boys. I confess I rather like it myself, but Colonel Sherman here says that it is not military; and I guess we had better defer to his opinion.' In winding up, he explained that, as President, he was commander-in-chief; that he was resolved that the soldiers should have everything that the law allowed; and he called on one and all to appeal to him personally in case they were wronged. The effect of this speech was excellent. We passed along in the same manner to all the camps of my brigade; and Mr. Lincoln complimented me highly for the order, cleanliness, and discipline that he observed. Indeed, he and Mr. Seward both assured me that it was the first bright moment that they had experienced since the battle."

"In the crowd at Fort Corcoran," continues General Sherman, "I saw an officer with whom I had had a little difficulty that morning. His face was pale and his lips were compressed. I foresaw a scene, but sat on the front seat of the carriage as quiet as a lamb. This officer forced his way through the crowd to the carriage, and said: 'Mr. President, I have a cause of grievance. This morning I went to speak to Colonel Sherman, and he threatened to shoot me.' Mr. Lincoln, who was still standing, said, 'Threatened to *shoot you?*' 'Yes, sir, he threatened to shoot me.' Mr. Lincoln looked at him, then at me; and stooping his tall, spare form toward the officer, said to him in a loud stage-whisper, easily heard for some yards around: 'Well, if I were you, and he threatened to shoot, *I would not trust him,* for *I believe he would do it.*' The officer turned about and disappeared, and the men laughed at him. Soon the carriage drove on, and as we descended the hill I explained the facts to the President, who answered, 'Of course I didn't know anything about it, but I thought you knew your own business best.' I thanked him for his confidence, and assured him that what he had done would go far to enable me to maintain good discipline; and it did."

The days following the Bull Run disaster were full of depression and discouragement, but Lincoln bore up bravely. He began to feel the terrible realities of his position, and saw himself brought face to face with the most awful responsibilities that ever rested upon human shoulders. A disrupted Union, the downfall of the great American Republic, so long predicted by envious critics of our institutions, seemed about to be accomplished. At the best, the Union could be saved only by the shedding of seas of priceless blood and the expenditure of untold treasures. And *he* must act, control, choose, and direct the measures of the Government and the movements of its vast armies. And what if all should fail? What if the resources of the Government should prove inadequate, and its enemies too powerful to be subdued by force? No wonder he was appalled and well-nigh overwhelmed by the dark prospect before him.

Rev. Robert Collyer tells of seeing Lincoln in the summer of 1861, on the steps of the White House, "answering very simply and kindly to the marks of respect some soldiers had come to pay him, who stood in deep ranks on the grass, that had been top-dressed with compost enough to cover the whole District of Columbia, as the chairman of the committee that had to pass the account told me. And once, curiously, I saw *only his feet*. It was soon after the battle of Bull Run, when some say that *we* ran, and some say that *they* ran. And all was quiet on the Potomac; but the nation was stamping and champing the bit. And passing the White House one day, I saw three pairs of feet on the sill of an open window; and pausing for a moment, a good-natured fellow said, '*That's the Cabinet a sittin'*, and *them big feet's old Abe's*.' So, lecturing in Boston not long after, I said, like a fool as I was, 'That's about all they are good for in Washington, to point their feet out o' window and talk, but go nowhere and do nothing.' When, indeed, the good President's heart was even then breaking with anxiety and trouble."

"One day," says Mr. A.G. Riddle, "I called at the White House to present a distinguished stranger, who had important matters to bring to Mr. Lincoln's notice. It was evening—cold, rainy, and cheerless. The Executive Mansion was gloomy and silent. At Mr. Lincoln's door we were told by the attendant to enter. We found the room quite dark, and seemingly vacant. I advanced a step or two, to determine if anyone were present, and was arrested by a strange apparition, at first not distinguishable: the long, seemingly lifeless, limbs of a man, as if thrown upon a chair and left to sprawl in unseemly disorder. A step further, and the fallen head disclosed the features of the President. I turned back; a word from my companion reached the drooping figure, and a sepulchral voice bade us advance. We came upon a man, in some respects the most remarkable of any time, in the hour of his prostration and weakness—in the depths of that depression to which his inherited melancholy at times reduced him, now perhaps coming to overwhelm him as he thought of the calamities of his country."

An old and intimate friend from Springfield, who visited Lincoln at this period, found the door of his office in the White House locked; but going through a private room and a side entrance, he found the President lying on a sofa, evidently greatly disturbed and much excited, manifestly displeased with the outlook. Jumping up from his reclining position, he advanced, saying: "You know better than any man living that from my boyhood up my ambition was to be President. I am President of one part of this divided country at least; but look at me! I wish I had never been born! I've a white elephant on my hands, one hard to manage. With a fire in my front and rear, having to contend with the jealousies of the military commanders, and not receiving that cordial co-operation and support from Congress that could reasonably be expected, with an active and formidable enemy in the field threatening the very life-blood of the Government, my position is anything but a bed of roses."

But in the darkest hours of the nation's peril, Lincoln never wavered in his purpose. Anxious and careworn, his heart bleeding with grief for the losses of our brave soldiers, and harassed by the grave duties constantly demanding his attention, he had but one purpose,—to go on unfalteringly and unhesitatingly in his course until the supremacy of the Government was restored in every portion of its territory. He wrote in a private letter: "I expect to maintain this contest until successful, or till I die, or am conquered, or my term expires, or Congress or the country forsake me."

Besides his invincible will and courage, Lincoln had one important resource in his dark hours, an ever-ready relief for his overcharged emotions. Byron said that he sometimes laughed in order that he might not weep. Lincoln's life long solace was his love of story-telling. Hon. Hugh McCulloch, afterward Secretary of the Treasury, relates that about a week after the battle of Bull Run he called at the White House, in company with a few friends, and was amazed when, referring to something which had been said by one of the company about the battle that was so disastrous to the Union forces, the President remarked, in his usual quiet manner, "That reminds me of a story," which he told in a manner so humorous as almost to lead his listeners to believe that he was free from care and apprehension. Mr. McCulloch could not then understand how the President could feel like telling a story, when Washington was in danger of being captured and the whole North was dismayed. He learned his mistake afterwards, however, and perceived that his estimate of Lincoln before his election was well grounded, and that he possessed even higher qualities than he had been given credit for; that he was "a man of sound judgment, great singleness and tenacity of purpose, and extraordinary sagacity; that story-telling was to him a safety-valve, and that he indulged in it, not only for the pleasure it afforded him, but for a temporary relief from oppressing cares." It is related that on the morning after the battle at Fredericksburg, Hon. I.N. Arnold, then a member of Congress from Illinois, called on the President, and to his amazement found him engaged in reading "Artemus Ward." Making no reference to that which occupied the universal thought, he asked Mr. Arnold to sit down while he read to him Artemus' description of his visit to the Shakers. Shocked at this proposition, Mr. Arnold said: "Mr. President, is it possible that with the whole land bowed in sorrow and covered with a pall in the presence of yesterday's fearful reverse, you can indulge in such levity?" Throwing down the book, with the tears streaming down his cheeks and his huge frame quivering with emotion, Lincoln answered: "Mr. Arnold, if I could not get momentary respite from the crushing burden I am constantly carrying, my heart would break!"

Ralph Waldo Emerson said: "His broad good humor, running easily into jocular talk, in which he delighted, and in which he excelled, was a rich gift to this wise man. It enabled him to keep his secret, to meet every kind of man, and every rank in society; to take off the edge of the severest decisions, to mask his own purpose and sound his companion, and to catch, with true instinct, the temper of every company he addressed. And, more than all, it is to a man of severe labor, in anxious and exhausting crises, the natural restorative, good as sleep, and is the protection of the overdriven brain against rancor and insanity."

Even amidst the stern realities of war, Lincoln was keenly appreciative of anything that disclosed the comic or grotesque side of men or happenings, — largely, doubtless, for the relief afforded him. At the beginning of Lee's invasion of Pennsylvania, in June, 1863, when the Union forces under Colonel Milroy were driven out of Harper's Ferry by the Confederates, great consternation and alarm were caused by reports that the Army of the Potomac had been routed and was retreating before Lee, who was pressing forward toward Harrisburg, the capital of Pennsylvania. Mr. Welles records in his Diary (June 17, 1863) that he was at the War Department with the President and Secretary Stanton, when "a messenger came in from General Schenck, declaring that the stragglers and baggage-trains of Milroy had run away in affright, and squads of them on different parallel roads had alarmed each other, and each fled in terror with all speed to Harrisburg. This alone was asserted to be the basis of the great panic which had alarmed Pennsylvania and the country. The President," continues Mr. Welles, "was in excellent humor. He said this flight would be a capital joke for Orpheus C. Kerr[D] to get hold of. He could give scope to his imagination over the terror of broken squads of panic-stricken teamsters, frightened at each other and alarming all Pennsylvania. General Meigs, who was present, inquired with great simplicity who this person (Orpheus C. Kerr) was. 'Why,' said the President, 'have you not read those papers? They are in two volumes; anyone who has not read them is a heathen.' He said he had enjoyed them greatly—except when they attempted to play their wit on him, which did not strike him as very successful, but rather disgusted him. 'Now, the hits that are given to you, Mr. Welles, or to Chase,' he said, 'I can enjoy; but I daresay they may have disgusted you while I was laughing at them. So *vice versa* as regards myself.'"

Hon. Lawrence Weldon relates that on one occasion he called upon the President to inquire as to the probable outcome of a conflict between the civil and military authorities for the possession of a quantity of cotton in a certain insurrectionary district. As soon as the inquiry had been made, Lincoln's face began lighting up, and he said: "What has become of our old friend Bob Lewis, of DeWitt County? Do you remember a story that Bob used to tell us about his going to Missouri to look up some Mormon lands that belonged to his father? You know that when Robert became of age he found among the papers of his father a number of warrants and patents for lands in Northeast Missouri, and he concluded the best thing he could do was to go to Missouri and investigate the condition of things. It being before the days of railroads, he started on horseback, with a pair of old-fashioned saddlebags. When he arrived where he supposed his land was situated, he stopped, hitched his horse, and went into a cabin standing close by the roadside. He found the proprietor, a lean, lank, leathery looking man, engaged in the pioneer business of making bullets preparatory to a hunt. On entering, Mr. Lewis observed a rifle suspended in a couple of buck-horns above the fire. He said to the man, 'I am looking up some lands that I think belong to my father,' and inquired of the man in what section he lived. Without having ascertained the section, Mr. Lewis proceeded to exhibit his title papers in evidence, and, having established a good title, as he thought, said to the man, 'Now, that is my title. What is yours?' The pioneer, who had by this time become somewhat interested in the proceedings, pointed his long finger toward the rifle. Said he, 'Young man, do you see that gun?' Mr. Lewis frankly admitted that he did. 'Well,' said he, 'that is my title, and if you don't get out of here pretty d——d quick you will feel the force of it.' Mr. Lewis very hurriedly put his title papers in his saddlebags, mounted his pony and galloped down the road, and, as Bob says, the old pioneer snapped his gun twice at him before he could turn the corner. Lewis said that he had never been back to disturb that man's title since. 'Now,' said Mr. Lincoln, 'the military authorities have the same title against the civil authorities that closed out Bob's Mormon title in Missouri.'" Judge Weldon says that after this anecdote he understood what would be the policy of the Government in the matter referred to as well as though a proclamation had been issued.

The tedium of meetings of the Cabinet was often relieved, and troublesome matters before it were illuminated, by some apt and pithy story. Secretary Welles tells of such an occasion when "Seward was embarrassed about the Dominican [sic] question. To move either way threatened difficulty. On one side was Spain, on the other side the negro. The President remarked that the dilemma reminded him of the interview between two negroes, one of whom was a preacher endeavoring to admonish and enlighten the other. 'There are,' said Josh the preacher, 'two roads for you, Joe. Be careful which you take. One ob dem leads straight to hell, de odder go right to damnation.' Joe opened his eyes under the impressive eloquence and visions of an awful future, and exclaimed, 'Josh, take which road you please; I go troo de wood.' 'I am not disposed to take any new trouble,' said the President, 'just at this time, and shall neither go for Spain nor the negro in this matter, but shall take to the woods.'"

It is related that Charles Sumner, who was a very tall man, and proud of his height, once worried the President about some perplexing matter, when Lincoln sought to change the subject by abruptly challenging his visitor to measure backs. "Sumner," said Mr. Lincoln, "declined to stand up with me, back to back, to see which was the tallest man, and made a fine speech about this being the time for uniting our fronts against the enemy, and not our backs. But I guess he was afraid to measure, though he is a good piece of a man. I have never had much to do with Bishops where I live, but, do you know, Sumner is *my idea of a Bishop*."

A good story of President Lincoln and General Scott is reported by Major-General Keyes, who at the beginning of the war was on the staff of General Scott, then commander-in-chief of the armies of the United States. "I was sent," says General Keyes, "by my chief to the President with a message that referred to a military subject, and that led to a discussion. Finding that Mr. Lincoln's observations were beginning to tangle my arguments, I said, 'That is the opinion of General Scott, and you know, Mr. President, he is a very able military man.' 'Well,' said the President, 'if he is as *able* a military man as he is *unable* as a politician, I give up. ' This was said with an expression of the eye, which he turned on me, that was peculiar to him, and which signified a great deal. The astounding force of Mr. Lincoln's observation was not at all diminished by the fact that I had long suspected that my chief lacked something which is necessary to make a successful politician."

Among the numerous delegations which thronged Washington in the early part of the war was one from New York, which urged very strenuously the sending of a fleet to the southern cities—Charleston, Mobile, and Savannah—with the object of drawing off the rebel army from Washington. Lincoln said the object reminded him of the case of a girl in New Salem, who was greatly troubled with a "singing" in her head. Various remedies were suggested by the neighbors, but nothing seemed to afford any relief. At last a man came along—"a common-sense sort of man," said he, inclining his head towards his callers pleasantly,—"who was asked to prescribe for the difficulty. After due inquiry and examination, he said the cure was very simple. 'What is it?' was the question. 'Make a plaster of *psalm-tunes*, and apply to her feet, and draw the singing *down*,' was the rejoinder." Still better was his reply to another delegation of New York millionaires who waited upon him in 1862, after the appearance of the rebel ram "Merrimac," and represented to him that they were very uneasy about the unprotected situation of their city, which was exposed to attack and bombardment by rebel rams; and they requested him to detail a gun-boat to defend the city. The gentlemen were fifty in number, very dignified and respectable in appearance, and stated that they represented in their own right $100,000,000. Lincoln did not wish to offend these gentlemen, and yet he intended to give them a little lesson. He listened with great attention, and seemed to be much impressed by their presence and their statements. Then he replied, very deliberately: "Gentlemen, I am by the Constitution commander-in-chief of the army and navy of the United States; and, as a matter of law, can order anything done that is practicable to be done. But, as a matter of fact, I am not in command of the gun-boats or ships of war; as a matter of fact, I do not know exactly where they are, but presume they are actively engaged. It is impossible for me, in the present condition of things, to furnish you a gun-boat. The credit of the Government is at a very low ebb; greenbacks are not worth more than forty or fifty cents on the dollar; and in this condition of things, if I was worth half as much as you, gentlemen, are represented to be, and as badly scared as you seem to be, I *would build a gun-boat and give it to the Government.*" A gentleman who accompanied the delegation says he never saw one hundred millions sink to such insignificant proportions, as the committee recrossed the threshold of the White House, sadder but wiser men.

"Mr. Lincoln had his joke and his 'little story' over the disruption of the Democracy. He once knew, he said, a sound churchman, of the name of Brown, who was the member of a very sober and pious committee, having in charge the erection of a bridge over a dangerous and rapid river. Several architects had failed, and at last Brown said he had a friend named Jones who had built several bridges, and could undoubtedly build that one. So Mr. Jones was called in. 'Can you build this bridge?' inquired the committee. 'Yes,' replied Jones, 'or any other. I could build a bridge to h—l, if necessary.' The committee were shocked, and Brown felt called upon to defend his friend. 'I know Jones so well,' said he, 'and he is so honest a man, and so good an architect, that if he states soberly and positively that he can build a bridge to ... to ... the infernal regions, why, I believe it; but I feel bound to say that I have my doubts about the abutment on the other side.' 'So,' said Mr. Lincoln, 'when politicians told me that the Northern and Southern wings of the Democracy could be harmonized, why, I believed them, of course; but I always had my *doubts about the abutment on the other side.'*"

A delegation once called on Lincoln to ask the appointment of a gentleman as commissioner to the Sandwich Islands. They presented their case as earnestly as possible, and, besides his fitness for the place, they urged that he was in bad health and a residence in that balmy climate would be of great benefit to him. The President closed the interview with the good-humored remark: "Gentlemen, I am sorry to say that there are eight other applicants for that place, and they are *all sicker than your man.*"

CHAPTER XVII

In November of 1861 occurred one of the most important and perilous episodes of the war; one whose full significance was not understood, except by a few cool heads, until long afterwards. Two influential Southern politicians, Mason and Slidell, had been sent by the Confederate Government as Commissioners to Great Britain and France, to try to secure the recognition of the Confederacy; and while on board the British steamer "Trent" they were taken prisoners by the U.S. steamer "San Jacinto," and were brought to Washington. Great Britain loudly protested against what she regarded as an unwarrantable seizure of passengers under the British flag, and for a time excitement ran high and war with England seemed almost inevitable. Fortunately for our country, the controversy was amicably settled by the surrender of the prisoners, without any sacrifice of the dignity of the Government of the United States. As stated by "Hosea Biglow," —

> We gave the critters back, John,
>
> Cos Abraham thought 't was right;
>
> It wa'nt your bullyin' clack, John,
>
> Provokin' us to fight.

The statesmanship displayed by our Government throughout this difficult affair was of the highest order. Credit for it has been given to Mr. Seward, the Secretary of State, by whom the correspondence and negotiations were conducted. Few men could have managed these details better; yet the course that was so happily determined on was undoubtedly due to the good sense and shrewd wisdom of the President. He not only dictated the policy to be followed by Mr. Seward in his despatches to the American Minister in London, but the more important documents were revised and materially altered by Lincoln's own hand. His management of the Trent affair alone, it has been said, would suffice to establish his reputation as the ablest diplomatist of the war. Coming, as it did, at a time when Lincoln was overwhelmed with the burden of home affairs, it showed the surprising resources of his character. The readiness and ability with which he met this perilous emergency, in a field in which he had had absolutely no experience or preparation, was equaled only by his cool courage and self-reliance in following a course radically opposed to the prevailing public sentiment, to the views of Congress, and to the advice of his own Cabinet. The Secretary of the Navy had hastened to approve officially the act of Captain Wilkes, commander of the "San Jacinto," and Secretary Stanton "cheered and applauded" it. Even Mr. Seward, cautious and conservative diplomat as he was, at-first "opposed any concession or surrender of the prisoners." But Lincoln said significantly, "*One war at a time.*" Events have long since afforded the most ample vindication of his course in this important matter. He avoided a foreign war, while at the same time, by committing Great Britain to the doctrine of "peace between neutrals," gained a substantial diplomatic victory over that government.

An excellent account of the circumstances of the Trent affair is given by Benson J. Lossing, the author and historian, who was in Washington when the events occurred. "The act of Captain Wilkes," says Mr. Lossing, "was universally applauded by all loyal Americans, and the land was filled with rejoicings because two of the most mischievous men among the enemies of the Government were in custody. For the moment, men did not stop to consider the law or the expediency involved in the act. Public honors were tendered to Captain Wilkes, and resolutions of thanks were passed by public bodies. The Secretary of the Navy wrote him a congratulatory letter on the 'great public services' he had rendered in 'capturing the rebel emissaries, Mason and Slidell,' and assured him that his conduct had 'the emphatic approval of the department.' The House of Representatives tendered him their thanks for the service he had done. But there was one thoughtful man in the nation, in whom was vested the tremendous executive power of the Republic at that time, and whose vision was constantly endeavoring to explore the mysteries of the near future, who held calmer and wiser thoughts than most men at that critical moment, because his feelings were kept in subjection to his judgment by a sense of heavy responsibility. That man was Abraham Lincoln. The writer was in the office of the Secretary of War when the telegraphic despatch announcing the capture of Mason and Slidell was brought in and read. He can never forget the scene that ensued. Led by Secretary Stanton, who was followed by Governor Andrew of Massachusetts and others who were present, cheer after cheer was heartily given by the company. A little later, the writer was favored with a brief interview with the President, when the clear judgment of that far-seeing and sagacious statesman uttered through his lips the words which formed the suggestion of, and the keynote to, the judicious action of the Secretary of State afterwards. 'I fear the traitors will prove to be white elephants,' said Mr. Lincoln. 'We must stick to American principles concerning the rights of neutrals,' he continued. 'We fought Great Britain for insisting, by theory and practise, on the right to do just what Captain Wilkes has just done. If Great Britain shall now protest against the act, and demand their release, we must give them up, apologize for the act as a violation of our own doctrines, and thus *forever bind her over to keep the peace in relation to neutrals*, and so acknowledge that she has been wrong for sixty years.' Great Britain did protest and make the demand, and at the same time made preparations for war against the United States. On the same day that Lord John Russell sent the protest and demand to Lord Lyons, the British Minister at Washington, Secretary Seward forwarded a despatch to Minister Adams in London, informing him that this Government disclaimed the act of Captain Wilkes, and giving assurance that it was ready to make a satisfactory arrangement of all difficulties arising out of the unauthorized act. These despatches passed each other in mid-ocean. The Government, in opposition to popular sentiment, decided at once to restore Mason and Slidell to the protection of the British flag. It was soon afterwards done, war between the two nations was averted, and, in the language of President Lincoln, the British Government was 'forever bound to keep the peace in relation to neutrals.' The wise statesmanship exhibited at that critical time was originated by Abraham Lincoln."

Lincoln once confessed that the Trent affair, occurring as it did at a very critical period of the war, had given him great uneasiness. When asked whether it was not a great trial to surrender the two captured Commissioners, he said: "Yes, that was a pretty bitter pill to swallow, but I contented myself with believing that England's triumph in the matter would be short-lived, and that after ending our war successfully we could if we wished call England to account for the embarrassments she had inflicted upon us. I felt a good deal like the sick man in Illinois who was told he probably hadn't many days longer to live, and that he ought to make peace with any enemies he might have. He said the man he hated worst of all was a fellow named Brown, in the next village, and he guessed he had better begin on him. So Brown was sent for, and when he came the sick man began to say, in a voice as meek as Moses', that he wanted to die at peace with all his fellow-creatures, and hoped he and Brown could now shake hands and bury all their enmity. The scene was becoming altogether too pathetic for Brown, who had to get out his handkerchief and wipe the gathering tears from his eyes. It wasn't long before he melted and gave his hand to his neighbor, and they had a regular love-feast. After a parting that would have softened the heart of a grindstone, Brown had about reached the room door, when the sick man rose up on his elbow and said, 'But, see here, Brown, if I *should* happen to get well, mind *that old grudge stands!*' So I thought if this nation should happen to get well, we might want that old grudge against England to stand."

Other controversies with England arose during the progress of the war—over the fitting out of Confederate cruisers at English ports to prey upon the commerce of the United States, over captured mails, etc.—in which all of Lincoln's sagacity and patience were needed to avert an open rupture with the British government. That the strain was severe and the danger great is made clear by an entry in Mr. Welles's Diary, in which he says: "We are in no condition for a foreign war. Torn by dissensions, an exhausting civil war on our hands, we have a gloomy prospect, but a righteous cause that will ultimately succeed. God alone knows through what trials, darkness, and suffering we are to pass." Again, in dealing with the French invasion of Mexico, Lincoln—as Mr. John Bigelow (then minister to France) puts it—"wisely limited himself to a firm repetition of the views and principles held by the United States in relation to foreign invasion," and thereby gained a diplomatic victory. How well "the old grudge against England" stood is shown by the substantial damages obtained from her, some years after the war, on the claims against the Alabama and other privateers, the foundations of which had been wisely laid by President Lincoln.

In the autumn of 1861 was originated the plan of a new naval vessel, which became the "Monitor"—the forerunner of the modern iron-clad, and the formidable little craft that beat back the "Merrimac" ram at Hampton Roads, March 9, 1862, saved the Federal Navy, and revolutionized naval architecture. The interesting story of the project, and of Lincoln's relation to it, is thus told: "The invention belongs to Captain John Ericsson, a man of marvelous ability and most fertile brain; but the creation of the 'Monitor' belongs to two distinguished iron-masters of the State of New York, viz.: the Hon. John F. Winslow and his partner in business, the Hon. John A. Griswold. These two gentlemen were in Washington in the autumn of 1861, for the adjustment of some claims against the Government for iron plating furnished by them for the war-ship 'Galena.' There, through Mr. C.S. Bushnell, the agent of Captain Ericsson, they learned that the plans and specifications for a naval machine, or a floating iron battery, presented by Captain Ericsson, found no favor with the special board appointed by Congress in 1861 to examine and report upon the subject of iron-clad ships of war. Ericsson and his agent, Mr. Bushnell, were thoroughly disheartened and demoralized at this failure to interest the Government in their plans. The papers were placed in the hands of Messrs. Winslow and Griswold, with the earnest request that they would examine them, and, if they thought well of them, use their influence with the Government for their favorable consideration. Mr. Winslow carefully read the papers and became satisfied that Ericsson's plan was both feasible and desirable. After conference with his friend and partner, Mr. Griswold, it was determined to take the whole matter to President Lincoln. Accordingly, an interview was arranged with Mr. Lincoln, to whom the plans of Captain Ericsson were presented, with all the unction and enthusiasm of an honest and mastering conviction, by Mr. Winslow and Mr. Griswold, who had now become thoroughly interested in the undertaking. The President listened with attention and growing interest. When they were done, Mr. Lincoln said, 'Gentlemen, why do you bring this matter to me? Why not take it to the Department having these things in charge?' 'It has been taken already to the Department, and there met with a repulse, and we come now to you with it, Mr. President, to secure your influence. We are here not simply as business men, but as lovers of our country, and we believe most thoroughly that here is something upon which we can enter that will be of vast benefit to the Republic,' was the answer. Mr. Lincoln was roused by the terrible earnestness of Mr. Winslow and his friend Griswold, and said, in his inimitable manner, 'Well, I don't know much about ships, though I once contrived a canal-boat—the model of which is down in the Patent Office—the great merit of which was that it could run where there was no water. But I think there is something in this plan of Ericsson's. I'll tell you what I will do. I will meet you to-morrow at ten o'clock, at the office of Commodore Smith, and we will talk it all over.' The next morning the meeting took place according to the appointment. Mr. Lincoln was present. The Secretary of the Navy, with many of the influential men of the Navy Department, also were there. The office where they met was rude in its belongings. Mr. Lincoln sat upon a rough box. Mr. Winslow, without any knowledge of naval affairs other than that which general reading would give, entered upon his task with considerable trepidation, but his whole heart was in it, and his showing was so earnest, practical, and patriotic, that a profound impression was made. 'Well,' said Mr. Lincoln, after Mr. Winslow had finished, 'well, Commodore Smith, what do you think of it?' The Commodore made some general and non-committal reply, whereupon the President, rising from the box, added, 'Well, I think there is something in it. Good morning, gentlemen,' and went out. From this interview grew a Government contract with Messrs. Winslow and Griswold for the construction of the 'Monitor,' the vessel to be placed in the hands of the Government within a hundred days at a cost of $275,000. The work was pushed with all diligence till the 30th of January, 1862, when the ship was launched at Greenpoint, one hundred and one days from the execution of the contract, thus making the work probably the most expeditious of any recorded in the annals of mechanical engineering."

At the assembling of Congress in December, 1861, Lincoln presented his first Annual Message. Among its most noteworthy passages was that which touched upon the relations between labor and capital—a subject so prominent in our later day. It was alluded to in its connection with the evident tendency of the Southern Confederacy to discriminate in its legislation in favor of the moneyed class and against the laboring people. On this point the President said:

> In my present position, I could scarcely be justified were I to omit raising a warning voice against this approach of returning despotism. It is not needed nor fitting here, that a general argument should be made in favor of popular institutions; but there is one point, with its connections, not so hackneyed as most others, to which I ask a brief attention. It is the effort to place *capital* on an equal footing with, if not above, *labor*, in the structure of government. It is assumed that labor is available only in connection with capital; that nobody labors unless somebody else, owning capital, somehow, by the use of it, induces him to labor. This assumed, it is next considered whether it is best that capital shall *hire* laborers, and thus induce them to work by their own consent, or *buy* them, and drive them to it without their consent. Having proceeded so far, it is naturally concluded that all laborers are either hired laborers or what we call slaves. And further, it is assumed that whoever is once a hired laborer is fixed in that condition for life. Now, there is no such relation between capital and labor as assumed; nor is there any such thing as a free man being fixed for life in the condition of a hired laborer. Both these assumptions are false, and all inferences from them are groundless. Labor is prior to and independent of capital. Capital is only the fruit of labor, and could never have existed if labor had not first existed. Labor is the superior of capital, and deserves much the higher consideration. Capital has its rights, which are as worthy of protection as any other rights. Nor is it denied that there is, and probably always will be, a relation between labor and capital, producing mutual benefits. The error is in assuming that the whole labor of community exists within that relation. A few men own capital, and those few avoid labor themselves, and, with their capital, hire or buy another few to labor for them. A large majority belong to neither class—neither work for others, nor have others working for them. In most of the Southern States, a majority of the whole people of all colors are neither slaves nor masters; while in the North, a large majority are neither

hirers nor hired. Men, with their families—wives, sons, and daughters—work for themselves, on their farms, in their houses, and in their shops, taking the whole product to themselves, and asking no favors of capital on the one hand, nor of hired laborers or slaves on the other. It is not forgotten that a considerable number of persons mingle their own labor with capital—that is, they labor with their own hands, and also buy or hire others to labor for them; but this is only a mixed, not a distinct class. No principle stated is disturbed by the existence of this mixed class. Again, as has already been said, there is not, of necessity, any such thing as the free hired laborer being fixed to that condition for life. Many independent men everywhere in these States, a few years back in their lives, were hired laborers. The prudent, penniless beginner in the world labors for wages awhile, saves a surplus with which to buy tools or land for himself; then labors on his own account another while, and at length hires another new beginner to help him. This is the just and generous and prosperous system, which opens the way to all, gives hope to all, and consequent energy and progress and improvement of condition to all. No men living are more worthy to be trusted than those who toil up from poverty—none less inclined to take, or touch, aught which they have not honestly earned. Let them beware of surrendering a political power which they already possess, and which, if surrendered, will surely be used to close the door of advancement against such as they, and to fix new disabilities and burdens upon them till all of liberty shall be lost.

The struggle *of* to-day is not altogether *for* to-day—it is for a vast future also. With a reliance on Providence, all the more firm and earnest, let us proceed in the great task which events have devolved upon us.

The reception given at the White House on New Year's day, 1862, was a brilliant and memorable affair. It was attended by distinguished army officers, prominent men from civil life, and the leading ladies of Washington society. "Army uniforms preponderated over black dress coats, and the young Germans of Blenker's division were gorgeously arrayed in tunics embroidered with gold on the collars and cuffs, sword-belts of gold lace, high boots, and jingling spurs." It was such a scene as that before the battle of Waterloo, when the

... capital had gathered then
Her beauty and her chivalry, and bright
The lamps shone o'er fair women and brave men;
A thousand hearts beat happily; and when
Music arose, with its voluptuous swell,
Soft eyes looked love to eyes that spake again,
And all went merry as a marriage bell.

How many of these brave men were destined never to see another New Year's day; and how many of those soft eyes would soon be dimmed with tears! Something of this feeling must have come over the sad soul of Lincoln. An eye-witness says that he "looked careworn and thoughtful, if not anxious; yet he had a pleasant word for all."

Early in 1862 an event occurred which added to the sorrow that seemed to enshroud the life of Lincoln, and afforded a glimpse into the depths of his tender and sorrowful nature. It was the death of his son Willie, a bright and promising boy, to whom his father was devotedly attached. "This," says Dr. J.G. Holland, "was a new burden; and the visitation which, in his firm faith in Providence, he regarded as providential, was also inexplicable. Why should he, with so many burdens upon him, and with such necessity for solace in his home and his affections, be brought into so tender a trial? It was to him a trial of faith, indeed. A Christian lady of Massachusetts, who was officiating as nurse in one of the hospitals, came in to attend the sick children. She reports that Mr. Lincoln watched with her about the bedside of the sick ones, and that he often walked the room, saying sadly: 'This is the hardest trial of my life. Why is it? Why is it?' In the course of conversations with her, he questioned her concerning her situation. She told him she was a widow, and that her husband and two children were in heaven; and added that she saw the hand of God in it all, and that she had never loved Him so much before as she had since her affliction. 'How is that brought about?' inquired Mr. Lincoln. 'Simply by trusting in God, and feeling that He does all things well,' she replied. 'Did you submit fully under the first loss?' he asked. 'No,' she answered, 'not wholly; but as blow came upon blow, and all were taken, I could and did submit, and was very happy.' He responded, 'I am glad to hear you say that. Your experience will help me to bear my afflictions.' On being assured that many Christians were praying for him on the morning of the funeral, he wiped away the tears that sprang in his eyes, and said, 'I am glad to hear that. I want them to pray for me. I need their prayers.' As he was going out to the burial, the good lady expressed her sympathy with him. He thanked her gently, and said, 'I will try to go to God with my sorrows.' A few days afterward she asked him if he could trust

God. He replied, 'I think I can. I will try. I wish I had that childlike faith you speak of, and I trust He will give it to me.' And then he spoke of his mother, whom so many years before he had committed to the dust among the wilds of Indiana. In this hour of his great trial, the memory of her who had held him upon her bosom and soothed his childish griefs came back to him with tenderest recollections. 'I remember her prayers,' said he, 'and they have always followed me. They have clung to me all my life.'"

An interesting passage in the secret history of the war at this period is narrated by one of the chief actors, Mr. A.M. Ross, a distinguished ornithologist of Canada, whose contribution embodies also so many interesting details of Lincoln's daily life that it seems worth giving rather fully. A few months after the inauguration of President Lincoln, Mr. Ross received a letter from the Hon. Charles Sumner, requesting him to come to Washington at his earliest convenience. "The day after my arrival in Washington," says Mr. Ross, "I was introduced to the President. Mr. Lincoln received me very cordially, and invited me to dine with him. After dinner he led me to a window, distant from the rest of the party, and said: 'Mr. Sumner sent for you at my request; we need a confidential person in Canada to look after our interests, and keep us posted as to the schemes of the Confederates in Canada. You have been strongly recommended to me for the position. Your mission shall be as confidential as you please; no one here but your friend Mr. Sumner and myself shall have any knowledge of your position. Think it over tonight, and if you can accept the mission come up and see me at nine o'clock tomorrow morning.' When I took my leave of him, he said, 'I hope you will decide to serve us.' The position thus offered was one not suited to my tastes, but, as Mr. Lincoln appeared very desirous that I should accept it, I concluded to lay aside my prejudices and accept the responsibilities of the mission. I was also persuaded to this conclusion by the wishes of my friend, Mr. Sumner.

"At nine o'clock next morning, I waited upon the President, and announced my decision. He grasped my hand in a hearty manner, and said: 'Thank you, thank you; I am glad of it. You must help us to circumvent the machinations of the rebel agents in Canada. There is no doubt they will use your country as a communicating link with Europe, and also with their friends in New York. It is quite possible, also, that they may make Canada a base from which to harass and annoy our people along the frontier.'

"After a lengthy conversation relative to private matters connected with my mission, I rose to leave, when he said, 'I will walk down to Willard's with you; the hotel is on my way to the Capitol, where I have an engagement at noon.' Before we reached the hotel a man came up to the President and thrust a letter into his hand, at the same time applying for some office in Wisconsin. I saw that the President was offended at the rudeness, for he passed the letter back without looking at it, saying, 'No, sir! I am not going to open shop here.' This was said in a most emphatic manner, but accompanied by a comical gesture which caused the rejected applicant to smile. As we continued our walk, the President spoke of the annoyances incident to his position, saying: 'These office-seekers are a curse to the country; no sooner was my election certain, than I became the prey of hundreds of hungry, persistent applicants for office, whose highest ambition is to feed at the Government crib.' When he bade me good-bye, he said, 'Let me hear from you once a week at least.' As he turned to leave me, a young army officer stopped him and made some request, to which the President replied with a good deal of humor, 'No, I can't do that; I must not interfere; they would scratch my eyes out if I did. You must go to the proper department.'

"Some time later," says Mr. Ross, "I again visited Washington. On my arrival there (about midnight) I went direct to the Executive Mansion, and sent my card to the President, who had retired. In a few minutes the porter returned and requested me to accompany him to the President's office, where Mr. Lincoln would shortly join me. The room into which I was ushered was the same in which I had spent several hours with the President on the occasion of my first interview with him. Scattered about the floor and lying open on the table were several military maps and documents, indicating recent use. In a few minutes the President came in and welcomed me in a most friendly manner; I expressed my regret at disturbing him at such an hour. He replied in a good-humored manner, saying, 'No, no! You did right; you may waken me up whenever you please. I have slept with one eye open ever since I came to Washington; I never close both, except when an office-seeker is looking for me.' I then laid before the President the 'rebel mail.' He carefully examined the address of each letter, making occasional remarks. At length he found one addressed to Franklin Pierce, ex-President of the United States, then residing in New Hampshire; and another to ex-Attorney-General Cushing, a resident of Massachusetts. He appeared much surprised, and remarked with a sigh, but without the slightest tone of asperity, 'I will have these letters enclosed in official envelopes, and sent to these parties.' When he had finished examining the addresses, he tied up all those addressed to private individuals, saying, 'I won't bother with them; but these look like official letters; I guess I'll go through them now.' He then opened them, and read their contents, slowly and carefully. While he was thus occupied, I had an excellent opportunity of studying this extraordinary man. A marked change had taken place in his countenance since my first interview with him. He looked much older, and bore traces of having passed through months of painful anxiety and trouble. There was a sad and serious look in his eyes that spoke louder than words of the disappointments, trials, and discouragements he had encountered since the war began. The wrinkles about the eyes and forehead were deeper; the lips were firmer, but indicative of kindness and forbearance. The great struggle had brought out the hidden riches of his noble nature, and developed virtues and capacities which surprised his oldest and most intimate friends. He was simple, but astute; he possessed the rare faculty of seeing things just as they are. He was a just, charitable, and honest man.

"When Mr. Lincoln finished reading the letters, I rose to go, saying that I would go to Willard's, and have a rest. 'No, no,' said the President, 'it is now three o'clock; you shall stay with me while you are in town; I'll find you a bed'; and leading the way, he took me into a bedroom, saying, 'Take a good sleep; you shall not be disturbed.' Bidding me 'good night,' he left the room to go back and pore over the rebel letters until daylight, as he afterwards told me. I did not awaken from my sleep until eleven o'clock in the forenoon, soon after which Mr. Lincoln came into my room, and laughingly said, 'When you are ready, I'll pilot you down to breakfast,' which he did. Seating himself at the table near me, he expressed his fears that trouble was brewing on the New Brunswick border; he said he had gathered further information on that point from the correspondence, which convinced him that such was the case. He was here interrupted by a servant, who handed him a card, upon reading which he arose, saying, 'The Secretary of War has received important tidings; I must leave you for the present; come to my room after breakfast and we'll talk over this New Brunswick affair."

"On entering his room again, I found him busily engaged in writing, at the same time repeating in a low voice the words of a poem which I remembered reading many years before. When he stopped writing I asked him who was the author of that poem. He replied, 'I do not know. I have written the verses down from memory, at the request of a lady who is much pleased with them.' He passed the sheet, on which he had written the verses, to me, saying, 'Have you ever read them?' I replied that I had, many years previously, and that I should be pleased to have a copy of them in his handwriting, when he had time and an inclination for such work. He said, 'Well, you may keep that copy, if you wish.'"

Hon. William D. Kelly, a Member of Congress from Pennsylvania, relates that during the time of McClellan's Peninsular campaign he called at the White House one morning, and while waiting to see the President, Senator Wilson of Massachusetts entered the chamber, having with him four distinguished-looking Englishmen. The President, says Mr. Kelly, "had evidently had an early appointment, and had not completed his toilet. He was in slippers, and his pantaloons, when he crossed one knee over the other, disclosed the fact that he wore heavy blue woollen stockings. It was an agreeable surprise to learn that the chief of the visiting party was Professor Goldwin Smith of Canada, one of the firmest of our British friends. As the President rose to greet them, he was the very impersonation of easy dignity, notwithstanding the negligence of his costume. With a tact that never deserted him, he opened the conversation with an inquiry as to the health of his friend John Bright, whom he said he regarded as a friend of our country and of freedom everywhere. The visitors having been seated, the magnitude of recent battles was referred to by Professor Smith as preliminary to the question whether the enormous losses which were so frequently occurring would not so reduce the industrial resources of the North as to affect seriously the prosperity of individual citizens and consequently the revenue of the country. He justified the question by proceeding to recite the number of killed, wounded, and missing, reported after some of the great battles recently fought. There were two of Mr. Lincoln's official friends who lived in dread of his little stories. Neither of them was gifted with humor, and both could understand his propositions, which were always distinct and clean cut, without such familiar illustrations as those in which he so often indulged; and they were chagrined whenever they were compelled to hear him resort to his stories in the presence of distinguished strangers. They were Senator Wilson of Massachusetts and Mr. Stanton, Secretary of War; and, as Professor Smith closed his arithmetical statement, the time came for the Massachusetts Senator to bite his lips, for the President, crossing his legs in such a manner as to show that his blue stockings were long as well as thick, said that, in settling such matters as that, we must resort to 'darkey arithmetic.' 'To darkey arithmetic!' exclaimed the dignified representative of the learning and higher thought of Great Britain and her American Dominion. 'I did not know, Mr. President, that you have two systems of arithmetic' 'Oh, yes,' said the President; 'I will illustrate that point by a little story. Two young contrabands, as we have learned to call them, were seated together, when one said to the other, "Jim, do you know 'rithmetic?" Jim answered, "No; what is 'rithmetic?" "Well," said the other, "it's when you add up things. When you have one and one, and you put dem togedder, dey makes two. And when you subtracts things, when if you have two things and you takes one away, only one remains." "Is dat 'rithmetic?" "Yah." "Well, 'tain't true, den. It's no good!" Here a dispute arose, when Jim said, "Now, you 'spose three pigeons sit on that fence, and somebody shoot one of dem; do t'other two stay dar? I guess not! dey flies away quickern odder feller falls." And, Professor, trifling as the story seems, it illustrates the arithmetic you must use in estimating the actual losses resulting from our great battles. The statements you have referred to give the killed, wounded, and missing at the first roll-call after the battle, which always exhibits a greatly exaggerated total, especially in the column of missing.'"

Mr. Goldwin Smith, the gentleman referred to in the foregoing anecdote, has summarized his impressions of Lincoln in the following paragraph: "Such a person as Abraham Lincoln is quite unknown to our official circles or to those of Continental nations. Indeed, I think his place in history will be unique. He has not been trained to diplomacy or administrative affairs, and is in all respects one of the people. But how wonderfully he is endowed and equipped for the performance of the duties of the chief executive officer of the United States at this time! The precision and minuteness of his information on all questions to which we referred was a succession of surprises to me."

Still terser, but hardly less expressive, is Emerson's characterization of Lincoln as one who had been "permitted to do more for America than any other American man."

A striking passage by Mr. Norman Hapgood should have place among these tributes. "Lincoln had no artificial aids. He merely proved the weapon of finest temper in the fire in which he was tested. In the struggle for survival in a national upheaval, he not only proved the living power of integrity and elasticity, but he easily combined with his feats of strength and shrewdness some of the highest flights of taste. As we look back across the changes of his life,—see him passing over the high places and the low, and across the long stretches of the prairie; spending years in the Socratic arguments of the tavern, and anon holding the rudder of state in grim silence; choosing jests which have the freshness of earth, and principles of eternal right, judging potentates and laborers in the clear light of nature, and at ease with both; alone by virtue of a large and melancholy soul, at home with every man by virtue of love and faith,—this figure takes its place high in our minds and hearts, not solely through the natural right of strength and success, but also because his strength is ours, and the success won by him rested on the fundamental purity and health of the popular will of which he was the leader and the servant. Abraham Lincoln was in a deep and lasting sense the first American."

Mr. John Bigelow, already quoted in these pages, summarized Lincoln's character and achievements in a passage of singular eloquence and force. "Lincoln's greatness must be sought for in the constituents of his moral nature. He was so modest by nature that he was perfectly content to walk behind any man who wished to walk before him. I do not know that history has made a record of the attainment of any corresponding eminence by any other man who so habitually, so constitutionally, did to others as he would have them do to him. Without any pretensions to religious excellence, from the time he first was brought under the observation of the nation he seemed, like Milton, to have walked 'as ever in his great Taskmaster's eye.' St. Paul hardly endured more indignities and buffetings without complaint. He was not a learned man. He was not even one who would deserve to be called in our day an educated man—knew little rather than much of what the world is proud of. He had never been out of the United States, or seen much of the portion of them lying east of the Alleghany Mountains. But the spiritual side of his nature was so highly organized that it rendered superfluous much of the experience which to most men is indispensable—the choicest prerogative of genius. It lifted him unconsciously above the world, above most of the men who surrounded him, and gave him a wisdom in emergencies which is bestowed only on those who love their fellow-man as themselves.... In the ordinary sense of the word, Mr. Lincoln was not a statesman. Had he come to power when Van Buren did, or when Cleveland did, he would probably have left Washington at the close of his term as obscure as either of them. The issues presented to the people of the United States at the Presidential election of 1860 were to a larger extent moral questions, humanly speaking, than were those presented at any other Presidential election. They were: first, the right of the majority to rule; second, the right of eight millions, more or less, of our fellow-beings to their freedom; and, third, the institutions and traditions which Washington planted and Jefferson watered, with the sacrifices necessary for their preservation. These questions subordinated all other political issues, and appealed more directly and forcibly to the moral sentiments of this nation than any issues they had ever before been called to settle either at the ballot-box or by force of arms. A President was needed at Washington to represent these moral forces. Such a President was providentially found in Lincoln ... a President who walked by faith and not by sight; who did not rely upon his own compass, but followed a cloud by day and a fire by night, which he had learned to trust implicitly."

A very graphic summing-up of Lincoln in person and character is that of Mr. John G. Nicolay, one of his private secretaries, who knew him intimately and understood him well. "President Lincoln was of unusual stature, six feet four inches, and of spare but muscular build," says Mr. Nicolay. "He had been in youth remarkably strong and skilful in the athletic games of the frontier, where, however, his popularity and recognized impartiality oftener made him an umpire than a champion. He had regular and prepossessing features, dark complexion, broad, high forehead, prominent cheek bones, gray, deep-set eyes, and bushy, black hair, turning to gray at the time of his death. Abstemious in his habits, he possessed great physical endurance. He was almost as tender-hearted as a woman. 'I have not willingly planted a thorn in any man's bosom,' he was able to say. His patience was inexhaustible. He had naturally a most cheerful and sunny temper, was highly social and sympathetic, loved pleasant conversation, wit, anecdote, and laughter. Beneath this, however, ran an undercurrent of sadness; he was occasionally subject to hours of deep silence and introspection that approached a condition of trance. In manner he was simple, direct, void of the least affectation, and entirely free from awkwardness, oddity, or eccentricity. His mental qualities were a quick analytic perception, strong logical powers, a tenacious memory, a liberal estimate and tolerance of the opinions of others, ready intuition of human nature; and perhaps his most valuable faculty was rare ability to divest himself of all feeling or passion in weighing motives of persons or problems of state. His speech and diction were plain, terse, forcible. Relating anecdotes with appreciating humor and fascinating dramatic skill, he used them freely and effectively in conversation and argument. He loved manliness, truth, and justice. He despised all trickery and selfish greed. In arguments at the bar he was so fair to his opponent that he frequently appeared to concede away his client's case. He was ever ready to take blame on himself and bestow praise on others. 'I claim not to have controlled events,' he said, 'but confess plainly that events have controlled me.' The Declaration of Independence was his political chart and inspiration. He acknowledged a universal equality of human rights. 'Certainly the negro is not our equal in color,' he said, 'perhaps not in many other respects; still, in the right to put into his mouth the bread that his own hands have earned, he is the equal of every other man, white or black.' He had unchanging faith in self-government. 'The people,' he said, 'are the rightful masters of both congresses and courts, not to overthrow the Constitution, but to overthrow the men who pervert the Constitution.' Yielding and accommodating in non-essentials, he was inflexibly firm in a principle or position deliberately taken. 'Let us have faith that right makes might,' he said, 'and in that faith let us to the end dare to do our duty as we understand it.' ..."

CHAPTER XVIII

President Lincoln's Cabinet, while containing men of marked ability and fitness for their positions, was in some respects about as ill-assorted and heterogeneous a body of men as were ever called to serve together as ministers and advisers of a great government. Its selection was a surprise to the country. Mr. John Bigelow said it "had the appearance of being selected from a grab-bag." "Not one of the members," continues Mr. Bigelow, "was a personal or much of a political friend of Mr. Lincoln; not one of them had ever had any experience or training in any executive office, except Welles of Connecticut, if he could be claimed as an exception because of having served three years in a bureau of the Navy in Washington. Of military administration, still less of actual war, no member knew anything by experience. The heads of the two most important departments, the Secretaries of State and the Treasury, were both disappointed candidates for the chair occupied by Mr. Lincoln. It was nothing less than Providential that the President was so happily constituted as neither to share nor to provoke any of the jealousies or envies of either of them, and by his absolute freedom from every selfish impulse gradually compelled them all to look up to him as the one person in whose singleness of eye they could all and always confide. Not immediately, but in the course of two or three years, they got into the habit of turning to him like quarrelling children to their mother to settle all the questions that temporarily divided them."

These Cabinet ministers were a devoted and patriotic body of men, but their misconceptions of their respective rights and duties were at first grotesque. Mr. Seward, a man of far greater administrative experience than Lincoln, assumed that he, rather than the President, was to be the master mind of the new administration. "Premier" he at first called himself. Mr. Stanton, the Secretary of War, thought the Navy should be a sort of adjunct to the War Department—an error of which Secretary Welles of the Navy Department speedily relieved him. These two men were altogether too unlike to get on well together. The cold and somewhat stately Welles was repelled by Stanton's impulsiveness and violence, while Stanton was exasperated by Welles's calmness and lack of excitability. "Lincoln's ministers had no idea that he towered above them," says Mr. John T. Morse, Jr., "and no one of them was at all overawed by him in those days. Presiding over them at the

Cabinet, casually meeting them, chatting with them or lounging as was his habit in Stanton's room, Lincoln seemed only officially superior to them. One of them had expected to be President, and another meant to be; a third dared to be insolent and unruly; it seemed to be only by a chance of politics that these men stood to him as junior partners to a senior, or like a board of directors to the president of a corporation."

The unfriendly feeling existing between members of the Cabinet comes out in many entries in Welles's Diary. "Pressing, assuming, violent, impatient, intriguing, harsh, and arbitrary," are examples of the terms in which Stanton is spoken of by Welles His contempt for the Committee on the Conduct of the War is expressed in no less stinging words. The members of this committee "are most of them narrow and prejudiced partisans, mischievous busybodies, and a discredit to Congress. Mean and contemptible partisanship colors all their acts." It is amusing to note that while Secretary Welles was thus outspoken in his criticisms of others, he himself did not escape calumny. One critic (Thurlow Weed, who, it may be remembered, had objected to Welles's appointment to a Cabinet position when Lincoln suggested it to him in their consultation at Springfield before the inauguration) declared that "It is worse than a fault, it is a crime, to keep that old imbecile at the head of the Navy Department." And another critic expressed the uncomplimentary opinion that "If Lincoln would send old Welles back to Hartford, it would be better for the Navy and for the country."

The accounts of the earliest Cabinet meetings, as given by Secretary Welles, who was nearly always present, are full of interest. "Cabinet meetings, which at that exciting period should have been daily, were infrequent, irregular, and without system," says Mr. Welles. "The Secretary of State notified his associates when the President desired a meeting of the heads of Departments. It seemed unadvisable to the Premier—as he liked to be called and considered—that the members should meet often, and they did not. Consequently there was very little concerted action. At the earlier meetings there was little or no formality; the Cabinet meetings were a sort of privy council or gathering of equals, much like a Senatorial caucus, where there was no recognized leader and the Secretary of State put himself in advance of the President. No seats were assigned or regularly taken. The Secretary of State was invariably present some little time before the Cabinet assembled, and from his former position as the chief executive of the largest State in the Union as well as from his recent place as a Senator, and from his admitted experience and familiarity with affairs, assumed, and was allowed, as was proper, to take the lead in consultations and also to give tone and direction to the manner and mode of proceedings. The President, if he did not actually wish, readily acquiesced in, this. Mr. Lincoln, having never had experience in administering the Government, State or National, deferred to the suggestions and course of those who had. Mr. Seward was not slow in taking upon himself to prescribe action and to do most of the talking, without much regard to the modest chief, but often to the disgust of his associates, particularly Mr. Bates, who was himself always courteous and respectful, and to the annoyance of Mr. Chase, who had had, like Mr. Seward, experience as a chief magistrate. Discussions were desultory and without order or system; but in the summing-up and conclusions the President, who was a patient listener and learner, concentrated results, and often determined questions adverse to the Secretary of State, regarding him and his opinions, as he did those of his other advisers, for what they were worth and generally no more."

It was perhaps natural, in a country so long free from wars as ours had been, that the Civil War should be regarded as a sort of political affair to be directed from Washington rather than by commanders in the field. For the first year or so the feeling was quite general that military affairs should be directed by Congress, acting through its Committee on the Conduct of the War, and by the Secretary of War, who complained bitterly that he was not allowed to assume control of military movements and that his plans were thwarted by McClellan (whom he especially hated). The President himself did not escape this condemnation. The feeling at this time is expressed in a sentence in Stanton's complaint, reflected through Chase, that "the President takes counsel of none but army officers in army matters." Chase declared to Welles, according to the latter, that the Treasury as well as other departments "ought to be informed of the particulars of every movement." The generals engaged in planning the campaigns and fighting the battles of the war, and their commander-in-chief the President, could hardly fail to find their task an uphill one when ideas so naïve and fatuous as these prevailed. It is no wonder that General Grant recorded in his Memoirs the opinion that the great difficulty with the Army of the Potomac during the first year of the war was its proximity to Washington; that the conditions made success practically impossible; and that neither he, nor General Sherman, nor any officer known to him, could have succeeded in General McClellan's place, under the conditions that then existed. Gradually, and by slow and often painful experience, a clearer conception of the meaning and methods of war prevailed. In this, as in so many things, Lincoln's insight was first and surest. By patience, tact, shrewdness, firmness, and diplomatic skill, he held the Cabinet together and stimulated its members to their best efforts for the common cause.

But the personal frictions and dissensions in the Cabinet, and the more or less meddlesome attitude of leaders in the Senate and the House, at times sorely tried the strength and patience of the harassed President, compelling him to act the part of peacemaker, and sometimes of judge and arbiter as well. At one time Secretary Stanton threatened to resign; and Chase declared that in that case he should go with him. Stanton and Welles were in frequent antagonism, Welles stating in his Diary that Stanton assumed, or tried to assume, that the Navy should be subject to the direction of the War Department. Seward was "meddlesome" toward other departments; "runs to the President two or three times a day; wants to be Premier," etc., says Welles. "Between Seward and Chase there was perpetual rivalry and mutual but courtly distrust; they entered the Cabinet as rivals, and in cold courtesy so continued." The most serious of these Cabinet embroglios occurred late in December of 1862, while Lincoln was well-nigh overwhelmed by Burnside's dreadful repulse at Fredericksburg. The gist of the affair, as given by Mr. Welles, is that the opposition to Seward in the Senate grew to such a point that a committee was appointed to wait on the President and request Seward's removal from the office of Secretary of State. The President, Mr. Welles tells us, was "shocked and grieved" at this demonstration. He asked all the members of his Cabinet to meet the Senate committee with him. All the members of the Cabinet were present except Seward, who had already sent the President his resignation. The meeting was attended also by Senators Collamer, Fessenden, Harris, Trumbull, Grimes, Howard, Sumner, and Pomeroy. The President, says Mr. Welles, opened the subject for which the meeting was called, taking a conciliatory tone toward the Senators, and requesting from each in turn an expression of opinion as to the wisdom of dropping Seward from the Cabinet. Most of them were strongly of the opinion that Seward ought to go. The President presented his own views, which were, in effect, that it would be a mistake to let Seward leave the Cabinet at that particular time. "He managed his own case," says Mr. Welles, "speaking freely, and showing great tact, shrewdness, and ability." The meeting continued until nearly midnight, and the matter was left still in the President's hands. The next morning Mr. Welles called early at the White House and found Lincoln practically decided not to accept Seward's resignation, saying that it would never do to take the course prescribed by the Senators; that "the Government would cave in; it could not stand—would not hold water; the bottom would be out," etc. He requested Welles to go at once to Seward and ask him not to press his resignation. Lincoln's intuitional mind seemed at once to connect Secretary Chase with the attack on Seward. Before Welles left the room, the President rang a bell and directed that a message be sent to Chase requesting him to come at once to the White House. When Welles returned from his interview with Seward, who readily promised to withdraw his resignation at the President's request, he found both Chase and Seward waiting for the President. The latter soon came in, and his first words were to ask Welles if he "had seen the man," to which Welles answered that he had, and that he assented to what had been asked of him. The dramatic scene that followed is thus described by Mr. Welles in his Diary: "The President turned to Chase and said, 'I sent for you, for this matter is giving me great trouble.' Chase said he had been painfully affected by the meeting last evening, which was a total surprise to him; and, after some not very explicit remarks as to how he was affected, informed the President he had prepared his resignation of the office of Secretary of the Treasury. 'Where is it?' said the President quickly, his eye lighting up in a moment. 'I brought it with me,' said Chase, taking the paper from his pocket; 'I wrote it this morning.' 'Let me have it,' said the President, reaching his long arm and fingers toward Chase, who held on, seemingly reluctant to part with the letter, which was sealed, and which he apparently hesitated to surrender. Something further he wished to say; but the President was eager and did not perceive it, and took and hastily opened the letter. 'This,' said he, looking toward me with a triumphant air, 'cuts the Gordian Knot. I can now dispose of this subject without difficulty, I see my way clear.' Chase sat by Stanton, fronting the fire; the President beside the fire, his face toward them, Stanton nearest him. I was on the sofa, near the east window. 'Mr. President,' said Stanton, with solemnity, 'I informed you day before yesterday that I was ready to tender you my resignation. I wish you, sir, to consider my resignation at this time in your possession.' 'You may go to your department,' said the President; 'I don't want yours. This,' holding out Chase's letter, 'is all I want; this relieves me; my way is clear; the trouble is ended. I will detain neither of you longer.' We all rose to leave," concludes Mr. Welles. "Chase and myself came downstairs together. He was moody and taciturn. Someone stopped him on the lower stairs, and I passed on."

A few days later, the President requested both Seward and Chase to withdraw their resignations and resume their duties. This was done, and the trouble was ended for the time. Both Secretaries had got their lessons, and profited by them. By the exercise of tact and patience, with firmness and decision when required, the President had let it be known that he was the head and chief of the Administration.

Next to the President, it was not Secretary Seward, the "Premier" as he wished to be regarded, but the War Secretary, Stanton, who was the master-mind of the Cabinet. He was the incarnation of energy, the embodiment of patriotic zeal. With all his faults of temper and disposition, he was a man of singular fitness for the responsible position he occupied, and his services to the Government can hardly be overestimated. He had been a Democrat, a member of Buchanan's Cabinet, and was, says Dr. Holland, "the first one in that Cabinet to protest against the downright treason into which it was drifting. He was a man of indomitable energy, devoted loyalty, and thorough honesty. Contractors could not manipulate him, traitors could not deceive him. Impulsive, perhaps, but true; wilful, it is possible, but placable; impatient, but persistent and efficient,—he became at once one of the most marked and important of the members of the Cabinet." Lincoln and Stanton together were emphatically "a strong team."

Stanton was not a member of Lincoln's first Cabinet, but came into it at the beginning of 1862, in place of Simon Cameron, who had just been appointed Minister to Russia. A very interesting account of Cameron's personal relations with Lincoln, the causes that led to his retirement from the Cabinet, and the appointment of Stanton in his place, is given by Cameron himself. He had been the choice of the Pennsylvania delegation for President, at the Chicago Convention in 1860, and it was largely due to him that Lincoln received the nomination. "After the election," said Mr. Cameron, "I made a trip to the West at Mr. Lincoln's request. He had, by letter, tendered me the position of either Secretary of War or Secretary of the Treasury; but when I went to see him he said that he had concluded to make Mr. Seward Secretary of State, and he wanted to give a place to Mr. Chase. 'Salmon P. Chase,' said he, 'is a very ambitious man.' 'Very well,' said I, 'then the War Department is the place for him. We are going to have an armed conflict over your election, and the place for an ambitious man is in the War Department. There he will have lots of room to make a reputation.' These thoughts of mine, that we were to have war, disturbed Mr. Lincoln very much, and he seemed to think I was entirely too certain about it. Finally, when he came to make up his Cabinet, doubtless remembering what I had said about the War Department, he appointed me Secretary of War."

"There has been," continues Mr. Cameron, "a great deal of misstatement as to Mr. Stanton's appointment as my successor. Stanton had been my attorney from the time I went into the War Department until he took my place as Secretary. I had hardly made a move in which the legality of any question could arise. I had taken his advice. I believed in the vigorous prosecution of the war from the start, while Mr. Seward believed in dallying and compromising, and Mr. Chase was constantly agitated about the expenditure of money; therefore it was that I was careful to have the advice of an able lawyer. When the question of changing me from the War Department to the Russian mission came up, Mr. Lincoln said to me, 'Whom shall I appoint in your place?' My prompt response was, 'Edwin M. Stanton.' 'But,' said he, 'I had thought of giving it to Holt.' 'Mr. Lincoln,' said I, 'if I am to retire in the present situation of affairs, it seems but proper that a friend of mine, or at least a man not unfriendly to me, should be appointed in my place. If you give Mr. Stanton the position, you will not only accomplish this object but will please the State of Pennsylvania and also get an excellent officer.' 'Very well,' said Mr. Lincoln, 'you go and see him, and if he will accept the place he shall have it.' I left the White House and started to find Stanton, passing through the Treasury Department on my way. As I passed Mr. Chase's office, I stepped in and told him what had occurred between the President and myself. He said, 'Let's send for Stanton; bring him here and talk it over.' 'Very well,' said I, and a messenger was at once sent. Stanton came immediately, and I told him of the conference between the President and myself. He agreed to accept. We walked to the White House, and the matter was settled.

"One of the troubles in the Cabinet which brought about this change was that I had recommended in my annual report, in the fall of 1861, that the negroes should be enlisted as soldiers after they left their masters. This advanced step was regarded by most of the Cabinet with alarm. Mr. Lincoln thought it would frighten the border States out of the Union, and Mr. Seward and Mr. Chase thought it would never do at all."

Just before the retirement of Mr. Cameron, a number of influential Senators waited upon the President and represented to him that inasmuch as the Cabinet had not been chosen with reference to the war and had more or less lost the confidence of the country, and since the President had decided to select a new war minister, they thought the occasion was opportune to change the whole seven Cabinet ministers. They therefore earnestly advised him to make a clean sweep, select seven new men, and so restore the waning confidence of the country. The President listened with patient courtesy, and when the Senators had concluded, he said, with a characteristic gleam of humor in his eye: "Gentlemen, your request for a change of the whole Cabinet because I have made one change, reminds me of a story I once heard in Illinois of a farmer who was much troubled by skunks. They annoyed his household at night, and his wife insisted that he should take measures to get rid of them. One moonlight night he loaded his old shot-gun and stationed himself in the yard to watch for the intruders, his wife remaining in the house anxiously awaiting the result. After some time she heard the shotgun go off, and in a few minutes the farmer entered the house. 'What luck had you?' said she. 'I hid myself behind the woodpile,' said the old man, 'with the shot-gun pointed toward the hen-roost, and before long there appeared, not one skunk, but *seven*. I took aim, blazed away, and killed one—and he raised such a fearful smell I concluded it was best to let the other six alone.'" The Senators retired, and nothing more was heard from them about Cabinet reconstruction.

Of the character and abilities of Secretary Stanton, and the relations between him and the President, General Grant has admirably said: "I had the fullest support of the President and Secretary of War. No General could want better backing; for the President was a man of great wisdom and moderation, the Secretary a man of enormous character and will. Very often where Lincoln would want to say *Yes*, his Secretary would make him say *No*; and more frequently, when the Secretary was driving on in a violent course, the President would check him. United, Lincoln and Stanton made about as perfect a combination as I believe could, by any possibility, govern a great nation in time of war.... The two men were the very opposite of each other in almost every particular, except that each possessed great ability. Mr. Lincoln gained influence over men by making them feel that it was a pleasure to serve them. He preferred yielding his own wish to gratify others, rather than to insist upon having his own way. It distressed him to disappoint others. In matters of public duty, however, he had what he wished, but in the least offensive way. Mr. Stanton never questioned his own authority to command, unless resisted. He cared nothing for the feeling of others." In a further comparison of the two men, General Grant said: "Lincoln was not timid, and he was willing to trust his generals in making and executing plans. The Secretary [Stanton] was very timid, and it was impossible for him to avoid interfering with the armies covering the capital when it was sought to defend it by an offensive movement against the army guarding the Confederate capital. He could see our weakness, but he could not see that the enemy was in danger. The enemy would not have been in danger if Mr. Stanton had been in the field."

With all his force of character, and his overbearing disposition, Stanton did not undertake to rule the President—though this has sometimes been asserted. He would frequently overawe and browbeat others, but he was never imperious in dealing with Lincoln. Mr. Watson, for some time Assistant Secretary of War, and Mr. Whiting, Solicitor of the War Department, with many others in a position to know, have borne positive testimony to this fact. Hon. George W. Julian, a member of the House Committee on the Conduct of the War, says: "On the 24th of March, 1862, Secretary Stanton sent for the Committee for the purpose of having a confidential conference as to military affairs. Stanton was thoroughly discouraged. He told us the President had gone back to his first love, General McClellan, and that it was needless for him or for us to labor with him." This language clearly shows that Lincoln, not Stanton, was the dominant mind.

Wherever it was possible, Lincoln gave Stanton his own way, and did not oppose him. But there were occasions when, in a phrase used by Lincoln long before, it was "necessary to *put the foot down firmly*." Such an occasion is described by General J.B. Fry, Provost Marshal of the United States during the war. An enlistment agent had applied to the President to have certain credits of troops made to his county, and the President promised him it should be done. The agent then went to Secretary Stanton, who flatly refused to allow the credits as described. The agent returned to the President, who reiterated the order, but again without effect. Lincoln then went in person to Stanton's office. General Fry was called in by Stanton to state the facts in the case. After he concluded, Stanton remarked that Lincoln must see, in view of such facts, that his order could not be executed. What followed is thus related by General Fry: "Lincoln sat upon a sofa, with his legs crossed, and did not say a word until the Secretary's last remark. Then he said, in a somewhat positive tone, 'Mr. Secretary, I reckon you'll have to execute the order.' Stanton replied, with asperity, 'Mr. President, I cannot do it. The order is an improper one, and I cannot execute it.' Lincoln fixed his eye upon Stanton, and in a firm voice and with an accent that clearly showed his determination, he said, 'Mr. Secretary, *it will have to be done.*' Stanton then realized that he was overmatched. He had made a square issue with the President, and had been defeated. Upon an intimation from him, I withdrew, and did not witness his surrender. A few minutes after I reached my office I received instructions from the Secretary to carry out the President's order."

Vice-President Wheeler relates a characteristic incident illustrating the relations between Lincoln and Stanton. The President had promised Mr. Wheeler an appointment for an old friend as army paymaster, stating that the Secretary of War would instruct the gentleman to report for duty. Hearing nothing further from the matter, Mr. Wheeler at length called upon the Secretary and reminded him of the appointment. Mr. Stanton denied all knowledge of the matter, but stated, in his brusque manner, that the name would be sent in, with hundreds of others, to the Senate for its consideration. Mr. Wheeler argued that his friend had been appointed by the Commander-in-chief of the Army, and that it was unjust to ask him to wait for the tardy action of the Senate upon the nomination, and that he was entitled to be mustered in at once. But all in vain; the only reply that could be got from the iron Secretary was, "You have my answer; no argument." Mr. Wheeler went to the chief clerk of the department, and asked for the President's letter directing the appointment. Receiving it, he proceeded to the White House, although it was after executive hours. "I can see Mr. Lincoln now," says Mr. Wheeler, "as he looked when I entered the room. He wore a long calico dressing-gown, reaching to his heels; his feet were encased in a pair of old-fashioned leathern slippers, such as we used to find in the old-time country hotels, and which had evidently seen much service in Springfield. Above these appeared the home-made blue woollen stockings which he wore at all seasons of the year. He was sitting in a splint rocking-chair, with his legs elevated and stretched across his office table. He greeted me warmly. Apologizing for my intrusion at that unofficial hour, I told him I had called simply to ascertain which was the paramount power in the Government, he or the Secretary of War. Letting down his legs and straightening himself up in his chair, he answered, 'Well, it is generally supposed *I am*. What's the matter?' I then briefly recalled the facts attending Sabin's appointment, when, without comment, he said, 'Give me my letter.' Then, taking his pen, he indorsed upon it:

> Let the within named J.A. Sabin be mustered AT ONCE. It is due to him and to Mr. W., under the circumstances.
>
> A. LINCOLN."

Armed with this peremptory order, Mr. Wheeler called on Stanton the next morning. The Secretary was furious. He charged Mr. Wheeler with interfering with his prerogatives. Mr. Wheeler remarked that he would call the next morning for the order to muster in. He called accordingly, and, handing him the order, in a rage, Stanton said, "I hope I shall never hear of this matter again."

It is related by Hon. George W. Julian, already quoted, that on a certain occasion a committee of Western men, headed by Mr. Lovejoy, procured from the President an important order looking to the exchange and transfer of Eastern and Western soldiers, with a view to more effective work. "Repairing to the office of the Secretary, Mr. Lovejoy explained the scheme, as he had before done to the President, but was met with a flat refusal. 'But we have the President's order, sir,' said Lovejoy. 'Did Lincoln give you an order of that kind?' said Stanton. 'He did, sir.' 'Then he is a d— —d fool,' said the irate Secretary. 'Do you mean to say the President is a d— —d fool?' asked Lovejoy, in amazement. 'Yes, sir, if he gave you such an order as that.' The bewildered Illinoisan betook himself at once to the President, and related the result of his conference. 'Did Stanton say I was a d— —d fool?' asked Lincoln, at the close of the recital. 'He did, sir, and repeated it.' After a moment's pause, and looking up, the President said, 'If Stanton said I was a d— —d fool, then *I must be one*, for he is nearly always right, and generally says what he means. *I will step over and see him*.'" The two men met, and the matter was easily adjusted. It was this rare combination of good-humor and firmness with an understanding of the other's trials and appreciation of his good qualities, that reduced the friction of official life and enabled Lincoln and Stanton to work together, in the main harmoniously and efficiently, in their great task of prosecuting the war and maintaining the integrity of the Union.

CHAPTER XIX

Early in 1862 Lincoln began giving more of his personal attention to military affairs. He was dissatisfied with the slow movements and small achievements of our armies, and sought to infuse new zeal and energy into the Union commanders. He also began a careful study of the great military problems pressing for solution; and he seemed resolved to assume the full responsibilities of his position, not only as the civil head of the Government but as the commander-in-chief of the armies and navies of the United States. In this he was influenced by no desire for personal control of the commanders in the field or interference with their plans; he always preferred to leave them the fullest liberty of action. But he felt that the situation demanded a single head, ready and able to take full responsibility for the most important steps; and, true to himself and his habits of a lifetime, he neither sought responsibility nor flinched from it.

The leading officers of the Union army were mostly young and inexperienced men, and none of them had as yet demonstrated the capacity of a great commander. At best it was a process of experiment, to see what generals and what strategic movements were most likely to succeed. In order to be able to judge correctly of measures and men, Lincoln undertook to familiarize himself with the practical details of military affairs and operations. Here was developed a new and unsuspected phase of his character. The plain country lawyer, unversed in the art of war, was suddenly transformed into the great civil ruler and military chieftain. "He was already," says Mr. A.G. Riddle, "one of the wariest, coolest, and most skilful managers of men. *A born strategist*, he was now rapidly mastering the great outline ideas of the art of war." "The elements of selfishness and ferocity which are not unusual with first-class military chiefs," said General Keyes, a prominent officer of the Union army, "were wholly foreign to Lincoln's nature. Nevertheless, *there was not one of his most trusted warlike counselors in the beginning of the war who equaled him in military sagacity.*" His reliance, in the new duties and perils that confronted him, was upon his simple common-sense, his native power of judgment and discernment. "Military science," says a distinguished officer, "is common-sense applied to the affairs of war." While Lincoln made no claim to technical knowledge in this sphere, and preferred to leave details to his subordinates, he yet developed an insight into military problems and an understanding of practical operations in the field which enabled him not only to approve or disapprove judiciously, but to direct and plan. A striking confirmation of this is given by Mr. J.M. Winchell, who thus relates what happened in a personal interview with the President:

"I was accompanied by one of Mr. Lincoln's personal friends; and when we entered the well-known reception-room, a very tall, lanky man came quickly forward to meet us. His manner seemed to me the perfection of courtesy. I was struck with the simplicity, kindness, and dignity of his deportment, so different from the clownish manners with which it was then customary to invest him. His face was a pleasant surprise, formed as my expectations had been from the poor photographs then in vogue, and the general belief in his ugliness. I remember thinking how much better-looking he was than I had anticipated, and wondering that anyone should consider him ugly. His expression was grave and care-worn, but still enlivened with a cheerfulness that gave me instant hope. After a brief interchange of commonplaces, he entered on a description of the situation, giving the numbers of the contending armies, their movements, and the general strategical purposes which should govern them both. Taking from the wall a large map of the United States, and laying it on the table, he pointed out with his long finger the geographical features of the vicinity, clearly describing the various movements so far as known, reasoning rigidly from step to step, and creating a chain of probabilities too strong for serious dispute. His apparent knowledge of military science, and his familiarity with the special features of the present campaign, were surprising in a man who had been all his life a civilian, engrossed with politics and the practise of the law, and whose attention must necessarily be so much occupied with the perplexing detail of duties incident to his position. It was clear that he made the various campaigns of the war a subject of profound and intelligent study, forming opinions thereon as positive and clear as those he held in regard to civil affairs."

Toward the end of January, 1862, Lincoln sought to overcome the inertia that seemed settling upon the Union forces by issuing the "President's General Order, No. I," directing that, on the 22d day of February following, "a general movement of the land and naval forces of the United States" be made against the insurgent forces, and giving warning that "the heads of departments, and especially the Secretaries of War and of the Navy, with all their subordinates, and the General-in-Chief, with all other commanders and subordinates of land and naval forces, will severally be held to their strict and full responsibilities for prompt execution of this order." This order, while it doubtless served to infuse activity into commanders and officials, did not result in any substantial successes to our arms. The President, worn by his ceaseless activities and anxieties, seems to have been momentarily disheartened at the situation. Admiral Dahlgren, who was in command of the Washington navy-yard in 1862, narrates that one day, at this period, "the President drove down to see the hundred-and-fifty-pounder cannon fired. For the first time I heard the President speak of the bare possibility of our being two nations—as if alluding to a previous suggestion. He could not see how the two could exist so near each other. He was evidently much worried at our lack of military success, and remarked that *'no one seemed ready.'*"

It is difficult to portray the worry and perplexity that beset Lincoln's life, and the incessant demands upon his attention, in his efforts to familiarize himself, as he felt compelled to do, with the practical operations of the war. Admiral Dahlgren, who saw him almost daily, relates that one morning the President sent for him, and said, "Well, Captain, here's a letter about some new powder." He read the letter and showed the sample of powder,—adding that he had burned some of it and it did not seem a good article; there was too much residuum. "Now I'll show you," said he. So he got a small sheet of paper and placed some of the powder on it, then went to the fire, and with the tongs picked up a coal, which he blew, with his spectacles still on his nose; then he clapped the coal to the powder, and after the explosion, remarked: "There is too much left there." There is something almost grotesque, but touching and pathetic as well, in this picture of the President of the United States, with all his enormous cares and responsibilities, engaged in so petty a matter as testing a sample of powder. And yet so great was his anxiety for the success of the armies and navies under his control that he wished to become personally satisfied as to every detail. He did not wish our armies or our war-vessels to lose battles on account of bad powder. "At another time," Admiral Dahlgren has related, "the President sent for me regarding some new invention. After the agent of the inventor left, the President began on army matters. 'Now,' said he, 'I am to have a sweat of five or six days'" (alluding to an impending battle, for the result of which he was very anxious). Again: "The President sent for me. Some man in trouble about arms; President holding a breech-loader in his hand. He asked me about the iron-clads, and Charleston." And again: "Went to the Department and found the President there. He looks thin, and is very nervous. Said they were doing nothing at Charleston, only asking for one iron-clad after another. The canal at Vicksburg was of no account, and he wondered how any sensible man could favor it. He feared the favorable state of public expectation would pass away before anything was done. Then he leveled a couple of jokes at the doings at Vicksburg and Charleston." No wonder the sympathetic Dahlgren, witnessing the sufferings of the tortured President, should exclaim: "*Poor gentleman! How thin and wasted he is!*"

The gloomy outlook in the Spring of 1862 was relieved by the substantial victories of General Burnside in North Carolina and of General Grant in Tennessee. The President was cheered and elated by these successes. It is related that General Burnside, visiting Washington at this time, called on the President, and that "the meeting was a grand spectacle. The two stalwart men rushed into each other's arms, and warmly clasped each other for some minutes. When General Burnside was about to leave, the President inquired, 'Is there anything, my dear General, that I can do for you?' 'Yes! yes!' was the quick reply, 'and I am glad you asked me that question. My three brigadiers, you know; everything depended on them, and they did their duty grandly!—Oh, Mr. President, we owe so much to them! I should so much like, when I go back, to take them their promotions.' 'It shall be done!' was Lincoln's hearty response, and on the instant the promotions were ordered, and General Burnside had the pleasure of taking back with him to Foster, Reno, and Parke their commissions as Major-Generals."

Our brightening prospects impelled the President to issue, on the 10th of April, the following proclamation, breathing his deeply religious spirit:

It has pleased Almighty God to vouchsafe signal victories to the land and naval forces engaged in suppressing an internal rebellion, and at the same time to avert from our country the dangers of foreign intervention and invasion. It is therefore recommended to the people of the United States that at their next weekly assemblages in their accustomed places of public worship which shall occur after the notice of this Proclamation shall have been received, they especially acknowledge and render thanks to our Heavenly Father for these inestimable blessings; that they then and there implore spiritual consolation in behalf of all those who have been brought into affliction by the casualties and calamities of sedition and civil war; and that they reverently invoke the Divine guidance for our national counsels, to the end that they may speedily result in the restoration of peace, harmony, and unity throughout our borders, and hasten the establishment of fraternal relations among all the countries of the earth.

ABRAHAM LINCOLN.

Early in May the President determined on a personal visit to Fortress Monroe, in order to learn what he could from his own observation of affairs in that region. The trip was a welcome respite from the cares and burdens of official life, and he gave himself up, as far as he could, to its enjoyment. The Secretary of War (Stanton) and the Secretary of the Treasury (Chase) accompanied the President. A most interesting account of the expedition is given by General Viele, who was a member of the party and thus had an opportunity to observe Lincoln closely. "When on the afternoon of May 4," says General Viele, "I was requested by the Secretary of War to meet him within an hour at the navy-yard, with the somewhat mysterious caution to speak to no one of my movements, I had no conception whatever of the purpose or intention of the meeting. It was quite dark when I arrived there simultaneously with the Secretary, who led the way to the wharf on the Potomac, to which a steamer was moored that proved to be a revenue cutter, the 'Miami.' We went on board and proceeded at once to the cabin, where to my surprise I found the President and Mr. Chase, who had preceded us. The vessel immediately got under way and steamed down the Potomac.... After supper the table was cleared, and the remainder of the evening was spent in a general review of the situation, which lasted long into the night. The positions of the different armies in the field, the last reports from their several commanders, the probabilities and possibilities as they appeared to each member of the group, together with many other topics, relevant and irrelevant, were discussed, interspersed with the usual number of anecdotes from the never-failing supply with which the President's mind was stored. It was a most interesting study to see these men relieved for the moment from the surroundings of their onerous official duties. The President, of course, was the centre of the group—kind, genial, thoughtful, tender-hearted, magnanimous Abraham Lincoln! It was difficult to know him without knowing him intimately, for he was as guileless and single-hearted as a child; and no man ever knew him intimately who did not recognize and admire his great abilities, both natural and acquired, his large-heartedness and sincerity of purpose.... He would sit for hours during the trip, repeating passages of Shakespeare's plays, page after page of Browning, and whole cantos of Byron. His inexhaustible stock of anecdotes gave to superficial minds the impression that he was not a thoughtful and reflecting man; whereas the fact was directly the reverse. These anecdotes formed no more a part of Mr. Lincoln's mind than a smile forms a part of the face. They came unbidden, and, like a forced smile, were often employed to conceal a depth of anxiety in his own heart, and to dissipate the care that weighed upon the minds of his associates. Both Mr. Chase and Mr. Stanton were under great depression of spirits when we started, and Mr. Chase remarked with a good deal of seriousness that he had forgotten to write a very important letter before leaving. It was too late to remedy the omission, and Mr. Lincoln at once drove the thought of it from his mind by telling him that a man was sometimes lucky in forgetting to write a letter, for he seldom knew what it contained until it appeared again some day to confront him with an indiscreet word or expression; and then he told a humorous story of a sad catastrophe that happened in a family, which was ascribed to something that came in a letter—a catastrophe so far beyond the region of possibility that it set us all laughing, and Mr. Chase lost his anxious look. That reminded Mr. Stanton of the dilemma he had been placed in, just before leaving, by the receipt of a telegram from General Mitchell, who was in Northern Alabama. The telegram was indistinct, and could not be clearly understood; there was no time for further explanation, and yet an immediate answer was required; so the Secretary took the chances and answered back, 'All right; go ahead.' 'Now, Mr. President,' said he, 'if I have made a mistake, I must countermand my instructions.' 'I suppose you meant,' said Mr. Lincoln, 'that it was all right if it was good for him, and all wrong if it was not. That reminds me,' said he, 'of a story about a horse that was sold at the cross-roads near where I once lived. The horse was supposed to be fast, and quite a number of people were present at the time appointed for the sale. A small boy was employed to ride the horse backward and forward to exhibit his points. One of the would-be buyers followed the boy down the road and asked him confidentially if the horse had a splint. 'Well, mister,' said the boy, 'if it's good for him he's got it, but if it isn't good for him he hasn't.' 'And that's the position,' said the President, 'you seem to have left General Mitchell in. Well, Stanton, I guess he'll come out right; but at any rate you can't help him now.' ... Mr. Lincoln always had a pleasant word to say the last thing at night and the first thing in the morning. He was always the first one to awake, although not the first to rise. The day-time was spent principally upon the quarter-deck, and the President entertained us with numerous anecdotes and incidents of his life, of the most interesting character. Few were aware of the physical strength possessed by Mr. Lincoln. In muscular power he was one in a thousand. One morning, while we were sitting on deck, he saw an axe in a socket on the bulwarks, and taking it up, he held it at arm's length at the extremity of the helve with his thumb and forefinger, continuing to hold it there for a number of minutes. The most powerful sailors on board tried in vain to imitate him. Mr. Lincoln said he could do this when he was eighteen years of age, and had never seen a day since that time when he could not.[E]

"It was late in the evening," continues General Viele, "when we arrived at Fortress Monroe.... Answering the hail of the guard-boats, we made a landing, and the Secretary of War immediately despatched a messenger for General Wool, the commander of the fort; on whose arrival it was decided to consult at once with Admiral Goldsborough, the commander of the fleet, whose flag-ship, the 'Minnesota,' a superb model of naval architecture, lay a short distance off the shore. The result of this conference was a plan to get up an engagement the next day between the 'Merrimac' and the 'Monitor,' so that during the fight the 'Vanderbilt,' which had been immensely strengthened for the purpose, might put on all steam and run her down. Accordingly, the next morning, the President and party went over to the Rip Raps to see the naval combat. The 'Merrimac' moved out of the mouth of the Elizabeth river, quietly and steadily, just as she had come out only a few weeks before when she had sunk the 'Congress' and the 'Cumberland.' She wore an air of defiance and determination even at that distance. The 'Monitor' moved up and waited for her. All the other vessels got out of the way to give the 'Vanderbilt' and the 'Minnesota' room to bear down upon the rebel terror as soon as she should clear the coast line. It was a calm Sabbath morning, and the air was still and tranquil. Suddenly the stillness was broken by the cannon from the vessels and the great guns from the Rip Raps, that filled the air with sulphurous smoke and a terrific noise that reverberated from the fortress and the opposite shore like thunder. The firing was maintained for several hours, but all to no purpose; the 'Merrimac' moved sullenly back to her position. It was determined that night that on the following day vigorous offensive operations should be undertaken. The whole available naval force was to bombard Sewall's Point, and under cover of the bombardment the available troops from Fortress Monroe were to be landed at that point and move on Norfolk. Accordingly, the next morning a tremendous cannonading of Sewall's Point took place. The wooden sheds at that place were set on fire and the battery was silenced. The 'Merrimac,' coated with mail and lying low in the water, looked on but took no part. Night came on, and the cannonading ceased. It was so evident that the 'Merrimac' intended to act only on the defensive, and that as long as she remained where she was no troops could be landed in that vicinity, that they were ordered to disembark. That night the President, with the Secretary of War and the Secretary of the Treasury, went over on the 'Miami' to the Virginia shore, and by the light of the moon landed on the beach and walked up and down a considerable distance to assure himself that there could be no mistake in the matter. How little the Confederacy dreamed what a visitor it had that night to the 'sacred soil.'"

The following morning an advance was made upon Norfolk by the route proposed by General Viele. The attempt was successful, and before night our forces were in control of the captured city. Some time after midnight, as General Viele records, "with a shock that shook the city, and with an ominous sound that could not be mistaken, the magazine of the 'Merrimac' was exploded, the vessel having been cut off from supplies and deserted by the crew; and thus this most formidable engine of destruction, that had so long been a terror, not only to Hampton Roads, but to the Atlantic coast, went to her doom, a tragic and glorious *finale* to the trip of the 'Miami.'"

Secretary Chase had accompanied the expedition against Norfolk, returning to Fortress Monroe with General Wool immediately after the surrender of the city. The scene which ensued on the announcement of the good tidings they brought back to the anxious parties awaiting news of them was thus described by the President himself: "Chase and Stanton had accompanied me to Fortress Monroe. While we were there, an expedition was fitted out for an attack on Norfolk. Chase and General Wool disappeared about the time we began to look for tidings of the result, and after vainly waiting their return till late in the evening, Stanton and I concluded to retire. My room was on the second floor of the Commandant's house, and Stanton's was below. The night was very warm,—the moon shining brightly,—and, too restless to sleep, I sat for some time by the table, reading. Suddenly hearing footsteps, I looked out of the window, and saw two persons approaching, whom I knew by their relative size to be the missing men. They came into the passage, and I heard them rap at Stanton's door and tell him to get up and come upstairs. A moment afterward they entered my room. 'No time for ceremony, Mr. President,' said General Wool; 'Norfolk is ours!' Stanton here burst in, just out of bed, clad in a long night-gown which nearly swept the floor, his ear catching, as he crossed the threshold, Wool's last words. Perfectly overjoyed, he rushed at the General, whom he hugged most affectionately, fairly lifting him from the floor in his delight. The scene altogether must have been a comical one, though at the time we were all too greatly excited to take much note of mere appearances."

Lincoln's general grasp of military strategy, and his keen understanding of the specific problems confronting the Army of the Potomac in the critical autumn of 1862, are well indicated in the following communication to General McClellan:

EXECUTIVE MANSION, WASHINGTON,
October 13, 1862

MY DEAR SIR:—You remember my speaking to you of what I called your over-cautiousness. Are you not over-cautious when you assume that you cannot do what the enemy is constantly doing? Should you not claim to be at least his equal in prowess, and act upon the claim?

As I understand, you telegraphed General Halleck that you cannot subsist your army at Winchester unless the railroad from Harper's Ferry to that point be put in working order. But the enemy does now subsist his army at Winchester, at a distance nearly twice as great from railroad transportation as you would have to do, without the railroad last named. He now wagons from Culpepper Court-House, which is just about twice as far as you would have to do from Harper's Ferry. He is certainly not more than half as well provided with wagons as you are. I certainly should be pleased for you to have the advantage of the railroad from Harper's Ferry to Winchester; but it wastes all the remainder of autumn to give it to you, and, in fact, ignores the question of *time*, which cannot and must not be ignored.

Again, one of the standard maxims of war, as you know, is, "to operate upon the enemy's communications as much as possible, without exposing your own." You seem to act as if this applies *against* you, but cannot apply in your *favor*. Change positions with the enemy, and think you not he would break your communication with Richmond within the next twenty-four hours? You dread his going into Pennsylvania. But if he does so in full force, he gives up his communications to you absolutely, and you have nothing to do but to follow and ruin him; if he does so with less than full force, fall upon and beat what is left behind all the easier. Exclusive of the water line, you are now nearer Richmond than the enemy is, by the route that you *can* and he *must* take. Why can you not reach there before him, unless you admit that he is more than your equal on the march? His route is the *arc* of a circle, while yours is the *chord*. The roads are as good on yours as on his.

You know I desired, but did not order, you to cross the Potomac below instead of above the Shenandoah and Blue Ridge. My idea was, that this would at once menace the enemy's communications, which I would seize if he would permit. If he should move northward, I would follow him closely, holding his communications. If he should prevent our seizing his communications, and move toward Richmond, I would press closely to him, fight him if a favorable opportunity should present, and at least try to beat him to Richmond on the inside track. I say "try," for if we never try, we shall never succeed. If he make a stand at Winchester, moving neither north nor south, I would fight him there, on the idea that if we cannot beat him when he bears the wastage of coming to us, we never can when we bear the wastage of going to him. This proposition is a simple truth, and is too important to be lost sight of for a moment. In coming to us, he tenders us an advantage which we should not waive. We should not so operate as to merely drive him away. As we must beat him somewhere, or fail finally, we can do it, if at all, easier near to us than far away. If we cannot beat the enemy where he now is, we never can, he again being within the intrenchments of Richmond. Recurring to the idea of going to Richmond on the inside track, the facility of supplying from the side away from the enemy is remarkable, as it were, by the different spokes of a wheel, extending from the hub toward the rim, and this whether you move directly by the chord, or on the inside arc, hugging the Blue Ridge more closely. The chord-line, as you see, carries you by Aldie, Haymarket, and Fredericksburg, and you see how turnpikes, railroads, and finally the Potomac by Aquia Creek, meet you at all points from Washington. The same, only the lines lengthened a little, if you press closer to the Blue Ridge part of the way. The gaps through the Blue Ridge I understand to be about the following distances from Harper's Ferry, to wit: Vestal's, five miles; Gregory's, thirteen; Snicker's, eighteen; Ashby's, twenty-eight; Manassas, thirty-eight; Chester, forty-five; and Thornton's, fifty-three. I should think it preferable to take the route nearest the enemy, disabling him to make an important move without your knowledge, and compelling him to keep his forces together for dread of you. The gaps would enable you to attack if you should wish. For a great part of the way you would be practically between the enemy and both Washington and Richmond, enabling us to spare you the greatest number of troops from here. When, at length, running to Richmond ahead of him enables him to move this way, if he does so, turn and attack him in the rear. But I think he should be engaged long before such point is reached. It is all easy if our troops march as well as the enemy, and it is unmanly to say they cannot do it. This letter is in no sense an order.

Yours truly, A. LINCOLN.
MAJOR-GENERAL MCCLELLAN.

Throughout the entire war President Lincoln was always keenly solicitous for the welfare of the Union soldiers. He knew that upon them everything depended; and he felt bound to them not only by official relations, but by the tenderer ties of human interest and love. In all his proclamations and public utterances he gave the fullest credit to the brave men in the field, and claimed for them the country's thanks and gratitude. His sympathy for the soldiers was as tender as that of a woman, and his tears were ever ready to start at the mention of their hardships, their bravery, their sufferings and losses. Nothing that he could do was left undone to minister to their comfort in field or camp or hospital. His most exacting cares were never permitted to divert his thoughts from them, and his anxious and tender sympathy included all whom they held dear. Said Mr. Riddle, in a speech in Congress in 1863: "Let not the distant mother, who has given up a loved one to fearful death, think that the President does not sympathize with her sorrow, and would not have been glad—oh, how glad—to so shape events as to spare the sacrifices. And let not fathers and mothers and wives anywhere think that as he sees the long blue regiments of brave ones marching away, stepping to the drum-beat, he does not contemplate them and feel his responsibility as he thinks how many of them shall go to nameless graves, unmarked save by the down-looking eyes of God's pitying angels." The feeling of the soldiers toward Lincoln was one of filial respect and love. He was not only the President, the commander-in-chief of all the armies and navies of the United States, but their good "Father Abraham," who loved every man, even the humblest, that wore the Union blue.

Of Lincoln's personal relations with the soldiers, enough interesting anecdotes could be collected to fill a volume. He saw much of them in Washington, as they marched through that city on their way to the front, or returned on furlough or discharge, or filled the overcrowded hospitals of the capital. Often they called upon him, singly or with companions; and he always had for them a word, however brief, of sympathy and cheer. He was always glad to see them at the White House. They were the one class of visitors who seldom came to ask for favors, and never to pester him with advice. It was a real treat for the harried President to escape from the politicians and have a quiet talk with a private soldier. Among the innumerable petitioners for executive clemency or favor, none were so graciously received as those who appeared in behalf of soldiers. It was half a victory to say that the person for whom the favor was desired was a member of the Union army.

As he wrote the pardon of a young soldier, sentenced to be shot for sleeping while on sentinel duty, the President remarked to a friend standing by: "I could not think of going into eternity with the blood of that poor young man on my hands. It is not to be wondered at that a boy raised on a farm, probably in the habit of going to bed at dark, should, when required to watch, fall asleep; and I cannot consent that he be shot for such an act." The youth thus reprieved was afterwards found among the slain on the field of Fredericksburg, with a photograph of Lincoln, on which he had written, "God bless President Lincoln," worn next his heart.

Rev. Newman Hall, of London, has repeated in a sermon an anecdote told him by a Union general. "The first week of my command," said the officer, "there were twenty-four deserters sentenced by court martial to be shot, and the warrants for their execution were sent to the President to be signed. He refused. I went to Washington and had an interview. I said: 'Mr. President, unless these men are made an example of, the army itself is in danger. Mercy to the few is cruelty to the many.' He replied: 'Mr. General, there are already too many weeping widows in the United States. For God's sake, don't ask me to add to the number, for *I won't do it.*'"

It came to the knowledge of Lincoln that a widow living in Boston—a Mrs. Bixby—had lost five sons in the service of their country. Without delay he addressed to the bereaved mother the following touching note:

> I have been shown on the file of the War Department a statement of the Adjutant-General of Massachusetts, that you are the mother of five sons who have died gloriously on the field of battle. I feel how weak and fruitless must be any word of mine which should attempt to beguile you from the grief of a loss so overwhelming; but I cannot refrain from tendering to you the consolation that may be found in the thanks of the Republic they died to save. I pray that our Heavenly Father may assuage the anguish of your bereavements, and leave only the cherished memory of the loved and lost, and the solemn pride that must be yours to have laid so costly a sacrifice upon the altar of freedom.
>
> Yours, very sincerely and respectfully,
> A. LINCOLN.

A case of unusual interest is that of Cyrus Pringle, a Vermont Quaker who was drafted into the military service in 1863, and refused to serve on the ground that his religion and his conscience would not permit him to bear arms. His story, as recorded in his diary, was given to the world after his death ("Atlantic Monthly," February, 1913). In spite of his protests, Pringle was taken South and forced to wear a uniform and carry a gun, though he refused to use it or even to clean it. His obstancy, as it was supposed to be, caused him much suffering, sometimes even physical punishment, all of which he bore patiently, believing that if he was steadfast in his faith relief would somehow come. It did come, but not until—after five months of hardship and distress of mind and body—his case, with that of other Quakers, finally reached the President. "I want you to go and tell Stanton," said Lincoln to the gentleman who had presented the case to him, "that it is my wish that all those young men be sent home at once." The gentleman went to Stanton with the message, but Stanton was unwilling to obey it. While they were arguing the matter, the President entered the room. "*It is my urgent wish,*" said he. Stanton yielded, and the unfortunate Quakers were given permission to return to their homes—none too soon to save the life of Pringle, who records in his diary: "Upon my arrival in New York I was seized with delirium, from which I only recovered after many weeks, through the mercy and favor of Him who in all this trial had been our guide and strength and comfort."

Anything that savored of the wit and humor of the soldiers was especially relished by Lincoln. Any incident that showed that "the boys" were mirthful and jolly amidst their privations seemed to commend itself to him. There was a story of a soldier in the Army of the Potomac, carried to the rear of battle with both legs shot off, who, seeing a pie-woman hovering about, asked, "Say, old lady, are them pies *sewed* or *pegged*?" And there was another one of a soldier at the battle of Chancellorsville, whose regiment, waiting to be called into the fight, was taking coffee. The hero of the story put to his lips a crockery mug which he had carried, with infinite care, through several campaigns. A stray bullet, just missing the coffee-drinker's head, dashed the mug into fragments and left only its handle on his finger. Turning his head in that direction, the soldier angrily growled, "Johnny, you can't do that again!" Lincoln, relating these two stories together, said, "It seems as if neither death nor danger could quench the grim humor of the American soldier."

A juvenile "brigadier" from New York, with a small detachment of cavalry, having imprudently gone within the rebel lines near Fairfax Court House, was captured by "guerillas." Upon the fact being reported to Lincoln, he said that he was very sorry to lose the horses. "What do you mean?" inquired his informant. "Why," rejoined the President, "I can make a 'brigadier' any day; but those horses cost the government a hundred and twenty-five dollars a head!"

Lincoln was especially fond of a joke at the expense of some high military or civil dignitary. He was intensely amused by a story told by Secretary Stanton, of a trip made by him and General Foster up the Broad river in North Carolina, in a tug-boat, when, reaching our outposts on the river bank, a Federal picket yelled out, "Who have you got on board that tug?" The severe and dignified answer was, "The Secretary of War and Major-General Foster." Instantly the picket roared back: "We've got Major-Generals enough up here—*why don't you bring us up some hardtack?*"

On one occasion, when the enemy were threatening the defenses of Washington, the President made a personal visit to the men in the trenches, for the purpose, as he stated, of "encouraging the boys." He walked about among them, telling them to hold their ground and he would soon give them reinforcements. His presence had a most inspiring effect, and the trenches were held by a few hundred soldiers of the Invalid Corps until the promised help came and the enemy withdrew.

On a visit to City Point, Lincoln called upon the head surgeon at that place and said he wished to visit all the hospitals under his charge. The surgeon asked if he knew what he was undertaking; there were five or six thousand soldiers at that place, and it would be quite a tax upon his strength to visit all the wards. Lincoln answered, with a smile, that he guessed he was equal to the task; at any rate he would try, and go as far as he could; he should never, probably, see the boys again, and he wanted them to know that he appreciated what they had done for their country. Finding it useless to try to dissuade him, the surgeon began his rounds with the President, who walked from bed to bed, extending his hand and saying a few words of sympathy to some, making kind inquiries of others, and welcomed by all with the heartiest cordiality. After some hours the tour of the various hospitals was made, and Lincoln returned with the surgeon to his office. They had scarcely entered, however, when a messenger came saying that one ward had been overlooked, and "the boys" wanted to see the President. The surgeon, who was thoroughly tired, and knew Lincoln must be, tried to dissuade him from going; but the good man said he must go back; "the boys" would be so disappointed. So he went with the messenger, accompanied by the surgeon, shook hands with the gratified soldiers, and then returned to the office. The surgeon expressed the fear that the President's arm would be lamed with so much hand-shaking, saying that it certainly must ache. Lincoln smiled, and saying something about his "strong muscles," stepped out at the open door, took up a very large heavy axe which lay there by a log of wood, and chopped vigorously for a few moments, sending the chips flying in all directions; and then, pausing, he extended his right arm to its full length, holding the axe out horizontally, without its even quivering as he held it. Strong men who looked on—men accustomed to manual labor—could not hold the axe in that position for a moment.

In summer Lincoln's favorite home was at "The Soldiers' Rest," a place a few miles out of Washington, on the Maryland side, where old and disabled soldiers of the regular army found a refuge. It was a lovely spot, situated on a beautifully wooded hill, reached by a winding road, shaded by thick-set branches. On his way there he often passed long lines of ambulances, laden with the suffering victims of a recent battle. A friend who met him on such an occasion, says: "When I met the President, his attitude and expression spoke the deepest sadness. He paused, and, pointing his hand towards the wounded men, he said: 'Look yonder at those poor fellows. I cannot bear it! This suffering, this loss of life, is dreadful!' Recalling a letter he had written years before to a suffering friend whose grief he had sought to console, I reminded him of the incident, and asked him: 'Do you remember writing to your sorrowing friend these words: "And this too shall pass away. Never fear. Victory will come."' 'Yes,' replied he, '*victory will come, but it comes slowly.*'"

CHAPTER XX

President Lincoln's relations with no other person have been so much discussed as those with General McClellan. Volumes have been written on this subject; many heated and intemperate words have been uttered and wrong conclusions reached. Whatever defects may have marked McClellan's qualities as a soldier, he must remain historically one of the most conspicuous figures of the war. He organized the largest and most important of the Union armies, and was its first commander in the field. He was one of the two out of the five commanders of the Army of the Potomac, before Grant, who led that army to victory; the other three having led it only to disastrous defeat. Great things were expected of him; and when he failed to realize the extravagant expectations of those who thought the war should be ended within a year, he received equally extravagant condemnation. It is noticeable that this condemnation came chiefly from civilians—from politicians, from Congress, from the press: not the best judges of military affairs. His own army—the men who were with him on the battlefield and risked their lives and their cause under his leadership—never lost faith in him. Of all the commanders of the Army of the Potomac, he was the one most believed in by his troops. Even after his removal, at a grand review of the army by the President, after the battle of Fredericksburg, it was not for the new commander, Burnside, but the old commander, McClellan, that the troops gave their heartiest cheers. It is worth remembering also that the war was not ended until two and a half years after McClellan's retirement, and until trial after trial had been made and failure after failure had been met in the effort to find a successful leader for our armies. The initial task of organization, of creating a great army in the field, fell upon him—a task so well performed that General Meade, his first efficient successor, said, "Had there been no McClellan there could have been no Grant, for the army [organization] made no essential improvements under any of his successors." And Grant, the last and finally victorious of these successors— who was at one time criticized as being "as great a discouragement as McClellan"—recorded in his Memoirs the conviction (already quoted in these pages) that the conditions under which McClellan worked were fatal to success, and that he himself could not have succeeded in his place under those conditions.

It is not in the province of the present narrative to enter into a consideration of the merits or demerits of McClellan as a soldier, but to treat of his personal relations with President Lincoln. Between the two men, notwithstanding many sharp differences of opinion and of policy, there seems to have been a feeling of warm personal friendship and sincere respect. Now that both have passed beyond the reach of earthly praise or blame, we may well honor their memory and credit each with having done the best he could to serve his country.

McClellan was appointed to the command of the Union armies upon the retirement of the veteran General Scott, in November of 1861. He had been but a captain in the regular army, but his high reputation and brilliant soldierly qualities had led to his being sent abroad to study the organization and movements of European armies; and this brought him into prominence as a military man. It was soon after McClellan took command that President Lincoln began giving close personal attention to the direction of military affairs. He formed a plan of operations against the Confederate army defending Richmond, which differed entirely from the plan proposed by McClellan. The President's plan was, in effect, to repeat the Bull Run expedition by moving against the enemy in Virginia at or hear Manassas. McClellan preferred a transference of the army to the region of the lower Chesapeake, thence moving up the Peninsula by the shortest land route to Richmond. (This was a movement, it may be remarked, which was finally carried out before Richmond fell in 1865.) The President discussed the relative merits of the two plans in the following frank and explicit letter to McClellan:

EXECUTIVE MANSION, WASHINGTON, D.C.,
February 3, 1862.

MAJOR-GENERAL MCCLELLAN.

MY DEAR SIR: You and I have distinct and different plans for a movement of the Army of the Potomac; yours to be done by the Chesapeake, up the Rappahannock to Urbana, and across to the terminus of the railroad on the York river; mine to move directly to a point on the railroad southwest of Manassas. If you will give me satisfactory answers to the following questions, I shall gladly yield my plan to yours:

1st. Does your plan involve a greatly larger expenditure of *time* and *money* than mine?

2d. Wherein is a victory more certain by your plan than mine?

3d. Wherein is a victory *more valuable* by your plan than mine?

4th. In fact, would it not be *less* valuable in this, that it would break no great line of the enemy 's communication, while mine would?

5th. In case of a disaster, would not a retreat be more difficult by your plan than mine?

Yours truly, ABRAHAM LINCOLN.

To this communication McClellan made an elaborate reply, discussing the situation very fully, and answering the inquiries apparently to the satisfaction of the President, who consented to the plan submitted by McClellan and concurred in by a council of his division commanders, by which the base of the Army of the Potomac should be transferred from Washington to the lower Chesapeake. Yet Lincoln must have had misgivings in the matter, for some weeks later he wrote to McClellan: "You will do me the justice to remember I always insisted that going down the bay in search of a field, instead of fighting at or near Manassas, was only shifting, and not surmounting, a difficulty; that we would find the same enemy, and the same or equal intrenchments, at either place."

After the transfer of the Army of the Potomac to the Peninsula there was great impatience at the delays in the expected advance on Richmond. The President shared this impatience, and his despatches to McClellan took an urgent and imperative though always friendly tone. April 9 he wrote: "Your despatches, complaining that you are not properly sustained, while they do not offend me, do pain me very much. I suppose the whole force which has gone forward for you is with you by this time. And, if so, I think it is the precise time for you to *strike a blow.* By delay, the enemy will relatively gain upon you—that is, he will gain faster by fortifications and reinforcements than you can by reinforcements alone. And once more let me tell you, it is indispensable to you that you *strike a blow....* I beg to assure you that I have never written to you or spoken to you in greater kindness of feeling than now, nor with a fuller purpose to sustain you, so far as, in my most anxious judgment, I consistently can. But you *must act.*"

While Lincoln was thus imperative toward McClellan, he would not permit him to be unjustly criticized. Considerable ill-feeling having been developed between McClellan and Secretary Stanton, which was made worse by certain meddlesome persons in Washington, the President took occasion, at a public meeting, to express his views in these frank and manly words: "There has been a very wide-spread attempt to have a quarrel between General McClellan and the Secretary of War. Now, I occupy a position that enables me to observe that these two gentlemen are not nearly so deep in the quarrel as some pretending to be their friends. General McClellan's attitude is such that, in the very selfishness of his nature, he cannot but wish to be successful, as I hope he will be; and the Secretary of War is in precisely the same situation. If the military commanders in the field cannot be successful, not only the Secretary of War but myself, for the time being the master of them both, cannot but be failures. I know General McClellan wishes to be successful, and I know he does not wish it any more than the Secretary of War wishes it for him, and both of them together no more than I wish it. Sometimes we have a dispute about how many men General McClellan has had, and those who would disparage him say he has had a very large number, and those who would disparage the Secretary of War insist that General McClellan has had a very small number. The basis for this is, there is always a wide difference, and on this occasion perhaps a wider one than usual, between the grand total on McClellan's rolls and the men actually fit for duty; and those who would disparage him talk of the grand total on paper, and those who would disparage the Secretary of War talk of those at present fit for duty. General McClellan has sometimes asked for things that the Secretary of War did not give him. General McClellan is not to blame for asking what he wanted and needed, and the Secretary of War is not to blame for not giving when he had none to give."

The summer of 1862 was a sad one for the country, and peculiarly sad for Lincoln. The Army of the Potomac fought battle after battle, often with temporary successes, but without apparent substantial results; while many thousands of our brave soldiers perished on the field, or filled the hospitals from the fever-swamps of the Chickahominy. The terrible realities of that dreadful summer, and their strain on Lincoln, are well shown in the following incident: Colonel Scott, of a New Hampshire regiment, had been ill, and his wife nursed him in the hospital. After his convalescence, he received leave of absence, and started for home; but by a steamboat collision in Hampton Roads, his noble wife was drowned. Colonel Scott reached Washington, and learning, a few days later, of the recovery of his wife's body, he requested permission of the Secretary of War to return for it. A great battle was imminent, and the request was denied. Colonel Scott thereupon sought the President. It was Saturday evening; and Lincoln, worn with the cares and anxieties of the week, sat alone in his room, coat thrown off, and seemingly lost in thought, perhaps pondering the issue of the coming battle. Silently he listened to Colonel Scott's sad story; then, with an unusual irritation, which was probably a part of his excessive weariness, he exclaimed: "Am I to have no rest? Is there no hour or spot when or where

I may escape these constant calls? Why do you follow me here with such business as this? Why do you not go to the War-office, where they have charge of all this matter of papers and transportation?" Colonel Scott told of Mr. Stanton's refusal; and the President continued: "Then probably you ought not to go down the river. Mr. Stanton knows all about the necessities of the hour; he knows what rules are necessary, and rules are made to be enforced. It would be wrong for me to override his rules and decisions in cases of this kind; it might work disaster to important movements. And then, you ought to remember that I have other duties to attend to—heaven knows, enough for one man!—and I can give no thought to questions of this kind. Why do you come here to appeal to my humanity? Don't you know that we are in the midst of war? That suffering and death press upon all of us? That works of humanity and affection, which we would cheerfully perform in days of peace, are all trampled upon and outlawed by war? That there is no room left for them? There is but one duty now—*to fight*. The only call of humanity now is to conquer peace through unrelenting warfare. War, and war alone, is the duty of all of us. Your wife might have trusted you to the care which the Government has provided for its sick soldiers. At any rate, you must not vex me with your family troubles. Why, every family in the land is crushed with sorrow; but they must not each come to me for help. I have all the burden I can carry. Go to the War Department. Your business belongs there. If they cannot help you, then bear your burden, as we all must, until this war is over. Everything must yield to the paramount duty of finishing the war." Colonel Scott withdrew, crushed and overwhelmed. The next morning, as he sat in his hotel pondering upon his troubles, he heard a rap at his door, and opening it found to his surprise the President standing before him. Grasping his hands impulsively and sympathetically, Lincoln broke out: "My dear Colonel, I was a brute last night. I have no excuse for my conduct. Indeed, I was weary to the last extent; but I had no right to treat a man with rudeness who had offered his life for his country, much more a man who came to me in great affliction. I have had a regretful night, and come now to beg your forgiveness." He added that he had just seen Secretary Stanton, and all the details were arranged for sending the Colonel down the Potomac and recovering the body; then, taking him in his carriage, he drove to the steamer's wharf, where, again pressing his hand, he wished him God-speed on his sad errand.

Such were Lincoln's harrowing experiences; and thus did his noble and sympathetic nature assert itself over his momentary weakness and depression.

In August of 1862 General McClellan was ordered to withdraw his army from the Peninsula. "With a heavy heart," says McClellan, "I relinquished the position gained at the cost of so much time and blood." Without being removed from his command, his troops were taken away from him and sent to join General Pope, who had been placed in command of a considerable force in Virginia, for the purpose of trying the President's favorite plan of an advance on Richmond by way of Manassas. Either from a confusion of orders or a lack of zeal in executing them, the Union forces failed to co-operate; and Pope's expected victory (Manassas, August 30) proved a disastrous and humiliating defeat. His army was beaten and driven back on Washington in a rout little less disgraceful than that of Bull Run a year before. This battle came to be known as the "Second Bull Run."

Thus the autumn of 1862 set in amidst gloom, disorder, and dismay. Our armies in and around the national capital were on the defensive; while the victorious Lee, following up his successes at Manassas, was invading Maryland and threatening Washington and the North. The President was anxious; the Cabinet and Congress were alarmed. The troops had lost confidence in General Pope, and there was practically no one in chief command. The situation was most critical; but Lincoln faced it, as he always did, unflinchingly. He took what he felt to be the wisest and at the same time the most unpopular step possible under the circumstances: he placed McClellan in command of all the troops in and around Washington. It was a bold act, and required no ordinary amount of moral courage and self-reliance. Outside the army, it was about the most unpopular thing that could have been done. McClellan was disliked by all the members of the Cabinet and prominent officials, and with especial bitterness by Secretary Stanton. Secretary Welles speaks, in his Diary, of "Stanton's implacable hostility to McClellan," and records his belief that "Stanton is determined to destroy McClellan." Welles relates that on the very day of Pope's defeat at Manassas, Secretary Stanton, accompanied by Secretary Chase, called on him and asked him to join in signing a communication to the President demanding McClellan's immediate dismissal from command of the Army of the Potomac, saying all the members of the Cabinet would sign it. The document was in Stanton's handwriting. Welles, though far from friendly toward McClellan, refused to sign the paper, and the matter was dropped. Welles adds the comment, "There was a fixed determination to remove, and, if possible, to disgrace, McClellan."

When it was rumored in Washington that McClellan was to be reinstated, everyone was thunderstruck. A Cabinet meeting was held on the second day of September, at which the President, without asking anyone's opinion, announced that he had reinstated McClellan. Regret and surprise were openly expressed. Mr. Stanton, with some excitement, remarked that no such order had issued from the War Department. The President then said, with great calmness, "No, Mr. Secretary, *the order was mine, and I will be responsible for it to the country.*" He added, by way of explanation, that, with a retreating and demoralized army tumbling in upon the capital, and alarm and panic in the community, something had to be done, and as there did not appear to be anyone else to do it he took the responsibility on himself. He remarked that McClellan had the confidence of the troops beyond any other officer, and could, under the circumstances, more speedily and effectually reorganize them and put them in fighting trim than any other general. "This is what is now wanted most," said he, "and these were my reasons for placing McClellan in command."

Perhaps at no other crisis of the war did Lincoln's strength of character and power of making quick and important decisions in the face of general opposition, come out more clearly than on this occasion. Secretary Welles, who was present at the dramatic and stormy Cabinet meeting referred to, says: "In stating what he had done, the President was deliberate, but firm and decisive. His language and manner were kind and affectionate, especially toward two of the members, who were greatly disturbed; but every person present felt that he was truly the chief, and every one knew his decision was as fixed and unalterable as if given out with the imperious command and determined will of Andrew Jackson. A long discussion followed, closing with acquiescence in the decision of the President. In this instance the President, unaided by others, put forth with firmness and determination the executive will—the *one-man* power—against the temporary general sense of the community, as well as of his Cabinet, two of whom, it has been generally supposed, had with him an influence almost as great as the Secretary of State. They had been ready to make issue and resign their places unless McClellan was dismissed; but knowing their opposition, and in spite of it and of the general dissatisfaction in the community, the President had in that perilous moment exalted him to new and important trusts."

It appears from the statement of General McClellan, made shortly before his death, that on the morning of his reinstatement (before the Cabinet meeting just described) the President visited him at his headquarters, near Washington, to ask if he would again assume command. "While at breakfast, at an early hour," says McClellan, "I received a call from the President, accompanied by General Halleck. The President informed me that Colonel Kelton had returned and represented the condition of affairs as much worse than I had stated to Halleck on the previous day; that there were 30,000 stragglers on the roads; that the army was entirely defeated and falling back to Washington in confusion. He then said that he regarded Washington as lost, and asked me if I would, under the circumstances, consent to accept command of all the forces. Without a moment's hesitation, and without making any conditions whatever, I at once said that I would accept the command, and would stake my life that I would save the city. Both the President and Halleck again asserted their belief that it was impossible to save the city, and I repeated my firm conviction that I could and would save it. They then left, the President verbally placing me in entire command of the city and of the troops falling back upon it from the front."

The result of the reappointment of McClellan soon vindicated the wisdom of the step. He possessed the confidence of the army beyond any other general at that time, and was able to inspire it with renewed hope and courage. Leaving Washington on the 7th of September, in command of Pope's beaten and disintegrated forces which he had to reorganize on the march, he within two weeks met the flushed and lately victorious troops of Lee and Jackson and fought the bloody but successful battle of Antietam (September 17, 1862), which compelled Lee to retreat to the southern side of the Potomac, and relieved Washington of any immediate danger.

After the Antietam campaign, the Army of the Potomac rested awhile from its exhausting and disorganizing labors. Supplies and reinforcements were necessary before resuming active operations. This delay gave rise to no little dissatisfaction in Washington, where a clamor arose that McClellan should have followed up his successes at Antietam by immediately pursuing Lee into Virginia. In this dissatisfaction the President shared to some extent. He made a personal visit to the army for the purpose of satisfying himself of its condition. Of this occasion McClellan says: "On the first day of October, his Excellency the President honored the Army of the Potomac with a visit, and remained several days, during which he went through the different encampments, reviewed the troops, and went over the battle-field of South Mountain and Antietam. I had the opportunity, during this visit, to describe to him the operations of the army since it left Washington, and gave him my reasons for not following the enemy after he recrossed the Potomac."

Before the grand review that was to be made by the President, some of McClellan's staff, knowing that the General was a man of great endurance and expertness in the saddle, laughed at the idea of Lincoln's attempting to keep up with him in the severe ordeal of "riding down the lines." "They rather hinted," says a narrator, "that the General would move somewhat rapidly, to test Mr. Lincoln's capacity as a rider. There were those on the field, however, who had seen Mr. Lincoln in the saddle in Illinois; and they were confident of his staying powers. A splendid black horse, very spirited, was selected for the President to ride. When the time came, Mr. Lincoln walked up to the animal, and the instant he seized the bridle to mount, it was evident to horsemen that he 'knew his business.' He had the animal in hand at once. No sooner was he in the saddle than the coal-black steed began to prance and whirl and dance as if he was proud of his burden. But the President sat as unconcerned and fixed to the saddle as if he and the horse were one. The test of endurance soon came. McClellan, with his magnificent staff, approached the President, who joined them, and away they dashed to a distant part of the field. The artillery began to thunder, the drums beat, and the bands struck up 'Hail to the Chief,' while the troops cheered. Mr. Lincoln, holding the bridle-rein in one hand, lifted his tall hat from his head, and much of the time held it in the other hand. Grandly did Lincoln receive the salute, appearing as little disturbed by the dashing movements of the proud-spirited animal as if he had passed through such an ordeal with the same creature many times before. Next came a further test of endurance—a long dash over very rough untraveled ground, with here and there a ditch or a hole to be jumped or a siding to be passed. But Mr. Lincoln kept well up to McClellan, who made good time. Finally, the 'riding down the lines' was performed, amidst the flaunting of standards, the beating of drums, the loud cheering of the men and rapid discharges of artillery, startling even the best-trained horses. Lincoln sat easily to the end, when he wheeled his horse into position to witness the vast columns march in review. McClellan was surprised at so remarkable a display of horsemanship. Mr. Lincoln was a great lover of the horse, and a skilled rider. His awkwardness of form did not show in the saddle. He always looked well when mounted."

After the President's return to Washington he began urging McClellan to resume active operations; desiring him to "cross the Potomac, and give battle to the enemy or drive him south." On the 13th of October he addressed to him the long letter quoted at the end of the preceding chapter. Subsequent communications from the President to McClellan showed more and more impatience. On the 25th he telegraphed: "I have just read your despatch about sore-tongue and fatigued horses. Will you pardon me for asking what the horses of your army have done since the battle of Antietam that fatigues anything?" And the next day, after receiving McClellan's answer to his inquiry, he responded: "Most certainly I intend no injustice to anyone, and if I have done any I deeply regret it. To be told, after more than five weeks' total inaction of the army, and during which period we had sent to that army every fresh horse we possibly could, amounting in the whole to 7,918, that the cavalry horses were too much fatigued to move, presented a very cheerless, almost hopeless, prospect for the future, and it may have forced something of impatience into my despatches. If not recruited and rested then, when could they ever be? *I suppose the river is rising, and I am glad to believe you, are crossing.*" But McClellan did not cross; his preparations for a new campaign were not yet complete; and the President, at last losing patience, removed him from command, and put Burnside in his place, November 5, 1862. And a disastrous step this proved to be. Burnside was under peremptory orders from Washington to move immediately against the Confederate forces. The result was the ill-advised attack upon Fredericksburg (December 12, 1862) and Burnside's bloody repulse. The movement was made against the judgment of the army officers then, and has been generally condemned by military critics since. Secretary Welles thus guardedly commented upon it in his Diary: "It appears to me a mistake to fight the enemy in so strong a position. They have selected their own ground, and we meet them there." But it was McClellan's unwillingness to do the very thing that Burnside is censured for having done, and that proved so overwhelming a disaster, that was the occasion for McClellan's removal.

A good illustration of Lincoln's disappointed, perhaps unreasonable, state of mind before McClellan's removal is furnished by Hon. O.M. Hatch, a former Secretary of State of Illinois and an old friend of Lincoln's. Mr. Hatch relates that a short time before McClellan's removal from command he went with President Lincoln to visit the army, still near Antietam. They reached Antietam late in the afternoon of a very hot day, and were assigned a special tent for their occupancy during the night. "Early next morning," says Mr. Hatch, "I was awakened by Mr. Lincoln. It was very early—daylight was just lighting the east—the soldiers were all asleep in their tents. Scarce a sound could be heard except the notes of early birds, and the farm-yard voices from distant farms. Lincoln said to me, 'Come, Hatch, I want you to take a walk with me.' His tone was serious and impressive. I arose without a word, and as soon as we were dressed we left the tent together. He led me about the camp, and then we walked upon the surrounding hills overlooking the great city of white tents and sleeping soldiers. Very little was spoken between us, beyond a few words as to the pleasantness of the morning or similar casual observations. Lincoln seemed to be peculiarly serious, and his quiet, abstract way affected me also. It did not seem a time to speak. We walked slowly and quietly, meeting here and there a guard, our thoughts leading us to reflect on that wonderful situation. A nation in peril—the whole world looking at America—a million men in arms—the whole machinery of war engaged throughout the country, while

I stood by that kind-hearted, simple-minded man who might be regarded as the Director-General, looking at the beautiful sunrise and the magnificent scene before us. Nothing was to be said, nothing needed to be said. Finally, reaching a commanding point where almost that entire camp could be seen—the men were just beginning their morning duties, and evidences of life and activity were becoming apparent—we involuntarily stopped. The President, waving his hand towards the scene before us, and leaning towards me, said in an almost whispering voice: 'Hatch—Hatch, what is all this?' 'Why, Mr. Lincoln,' said I, 'this is the Army of the Potomac' He hesitated a moment, and then, straightening up, said in a louder tone: 'No, Hatch, no. This is *General McClellan's body-guard.*' Nothing more was said. We walked to our tent, and the subject was not alluded to again."

CHAPTER XXI

The emancipation of slaves in America—the crowning act of Lincoln's eventful career and the one with which his fame is most indissolubly linked—is a subject of supreme interest in a study of his life and character. For this great act all his previous life and training had been but a preparation. From the first awakening of his convictions of the moral wrong of human slavery, through all his public and private utterances, may be traced one logical and consistent development of the principles which at last found sublime expression in the Proclamation of Emancipation. In this, as always, he was true to his own inner promptings. He would not be hurried or worried or badgered into premature and impracticable measures. He bided his time; and when that time came the deed was done, unalterably and irrevocably: approved by the logic of events, and by the enlightened conscience of the world.

The final Emancipation Proclamation was issued on the first day of January, 1863. The various official measures that preceded it may be briefly sketched, together with closely related incidents. As early as the autumn of 1861 the problem of the relation of the war to slavery was brought forcibly to the President's attention by the action of General J.C. Frémont, the Union commander in Missouri, who issued an order declaring the slaves of rebels in his department free. The order was premature and unauthorized, and the President promptly annulled it. General Frémont was thus, in a sense, the pioneer in military emancipation; and he lived to see the policy proposed by him carried into practical operation by all our armies. Lincoln afterwards said: "I have great respect for General Frémont and his abilities, but the fact is that the pioneer in any movement is not generally the best man to carry that movement to a successful issue. It was so in old times; Moses began the emancipation of the Jews, but didn't take Israel to the Promised Land after all. He had to make way for Joshua to complete the work. It looks as if the first reformer of a thing has to meet such a hard opposition and gets so battered and bespattered that afterward when people find they have to accept his reform they will accept it more easily from another man."

Lincoln at first favored a policy of gradual emancipation. In a special message to Congress, on the 6th of March, 1862, he proposed such a plan for the abolition of slavery. "In my judgment," he remarked, "gradual, and not sudden, emancipation is better for all." He suggested to Congress the adoption of a joint resolution declaring "that the United States ought to co-operate with any State which may adopt a gradual abolition of slavery, giving to such State pecuniary aid to compensate for the inconvenience, public and private, produced by such change of system." In conclusion he urged: "In full view of my great responsibility to my God and to my country, I earnestly beg the attention of Congress and the people to this subject."

On the 16th of April of this year, Congress passed a bill abolishing slavery in the District of Columbia—a measure for which Lincoln had himself introduced a bill while a member of Congress. In confirming the act as President, he remarked privately: "Little did I dream in 1849, when as a member of Congress I proposed to abolish slavery at this capital, and could scarcely get a hearing for the proposition, that it would be so soon accomplished."

Emancipation measures moved rapidly in 1862. On June 19 Congress enacted a measure prohibiting slavery forever in all present and future territories of the United States. July 17 a law was passed authorizing the employment of negroes as soldiers, and conferring freedom on all who should render military service, and on the families of all such as belonged to disloyal owners. Two days later, in a conference appointed by him at the Executive Mansion, the President submitted to the members of Congress from the Border States a written appeal, in which he said:

> Believing that you, in the border States, hold more power for good than any other equal number of members, I feel it a duty which I cannot justifiably waive, to make this appeal to you.... I intend no reproach or complaint when I assure you that, in my opinion, if you all had voted for the resolution in the gradual emancipation message of last March, the war would now be substantially ended. And the plan therein proposed is yet one of the most potent and swift means of ending it. Let the States which are in rebellion see definitely and certainly that in no event will the States you represent ever join their proposed confederacy, and they cannot much longer maintain the contest.... If the war continues long, as it must if the object be not sooner attained, the institution in your States will be extinguished by mere friction and abrasion, by the mere incidents of the war. It will be gone, and you will have nothing valuable in lieu of it. Much of its value is gone already. How much better for you and for your people to take the step which at once shortens the war

and secures substantial compensation for that which is sure to be wholly lost in any other event! How much better to thus save the money which else we sink forever in the war! How much better to do it while we can, lest the war ere long render us pecuniarily unable to do it! How much better for you as seller, and the nation as buyer, to sell out and buy out that without which the war could never have been, than to sink both the thing to be sold and the price of it in cutting one another's throats!... I do not speak of emancipation *at once*, but of a *decision* to emancipate *gradually*.... Upon these considerations I have again begged your attention to the message of March last. Before leaving the capital, consider and discuss it among yourselves. You are patriots and statesmen, and as such I pray you consider this proposition, and at the least commend it to the consideration of your States and people. As you would perpetuate popular government for the best people in the world, I beseech you that you do in nowise omit this. Our common country is in great peril, demanding the loftiest views and boldest action to bring a speedy relief. Once relieved, its form of government is saved to the world, its beloved history and cherished memories are vindicated, and its happy future fully assured and rendered inconceivably grand. To you, more than any others, the privilege is given to assure that happiness and swell that grandeur, and to link your own names therewith forever.

In an interview with Mr. Lovejoy and Mr. Arnold, of Illinois, the day following this conference, Lincoln exclaimed: "Oh, how I wish the border States would accept my proposition! Then you, Lovejoy, and you, Arnold, and all of us, would not have lived in vain! The labor of your life, Lovejoy, would be crowned with success. You would live to see the end of slavery."

The first occasion on which the President definitely discussed emancipation plans with members of his Cabinet, according to Secretary Welles, was on the 13th of July, 1862. On that day, says Mr. Welles, "President Lincoln invited me to accompany him in his carriage to the funeral of an infant child of Mr. Stanton. Secretary Seward and Mrs. Frederick Seward were also in the carriage. Mr. Stanton occupied at that time for a summer residence the house of a naval officer, some two or three miles west or northwest of Georgetown. It was on this occasion and on this ride that he first mentioned to Mr. Seward and myself the subject of emancipating the slaves by proclamation in case the Rebels did not cease to persist in their war on the Government and the Union, of which he saw no evidence. He dwelt earnestly on the gravity, importance, and delicacy of the movement; said he had given it much thought, and had about come to the conclusion that it was a military necessity absolutely essential for the salvation of the Union; that we must free the slaves or be ourselves subdued, etc.... This was, the President said, the first occasion when he had mentioned the subject to anyone, and wished us to frankly state how the proposition struck us. Mr. Seward said the subject involved consequences so vast and momentous that he should wish to bestow on it mature reflection before giving a decisive answer; but his present opinion inclined to the measure as justifiable, and perhaps he might say expedient and necessary. These were also my views. Two or three times on that ride the subject, which was of course an absorbing one for each and all, was adverted to; and before separating, the President desired us to give the question special and deliberate attention, for he was earnest in the conviction that something must be done. It was a new departure for the President, for until this time, in all our previous interviews, whenever the question of emancipation or the mitigation of slavery had been in any way alluded to, he had been prompt and emphatic in denouncing any interference by the General Government with the subject. This was, I think, the sentiment of every member of the Cabinet, all of whom, including the President, considered it a local, domestic question, appertaining to the States respectively, who had never parted with their authority over it. But the reverses before Richmond, and the formidable power and dimensions of the insurrection, which extended through all the Slave States, and had combined most of them in a confederacy to destroy the Union, impelled the Administration to adopt extraordinary measures to preserve the national existence. The slaves, if not armed and disciplined, were in the service of those who were, not only as field laborers and producers, but thousands of them were in attendance upon the armies in the field, employed as waiters and teamsters, and the fortifications and intrenchments were constructed by them."

It has been shown again and again, by the words of Lincoln and by the testimony of his friends, that he heartily detested the practice of slavery, and would joyfully have set every bondman free. Before his nomination for the Presidency—indeed, from the very beginning of his public life—he had repeatedly put himself on record as opposed to slavery, but perhaps nowhere more tersely and unequivocally than in these words: "There is no reason in the world why the negro is not entitled to all the natural rights enumerated in the Declaration of Independence—the right to life, liberty, and the pursuit of happiness. *I hold that he is as much entitled to them as the white man.*" But his respect for the laws of the land deterred him from measures that might seem of doubtful constitutionality, and he waited patiently until the right hour had struck before he issued the edict of emancipation so eagerly demanded by a large class of earnest and loyal people at the North. Many of these people, misunderstanding his views and intentions, were very impatient; and their criticisms and expostulations were a constant burden to the sorely tried Executive.

In June of this year (1862) the President was waited on by a deputation of Quakers, or Friends, fifteen or twenty in number, who had been charged by the Yearly Meeting of their association to present a "minute" to the President on the subject of slavery and the duty of immediate emancipation. The visit of these excellent people was not altogether timely. Bad news had been received from McClellan's army on the Peninsula, and Lincoln was harassed with cares and anxieties. But he gave the deputation a cordial though brief greeting, as he announced that he was ready to hear from the Friends. In the reading of the minute, it appeared that the document took occasion to remind the President that, years before, he had said, "I believe that this Government cannot permanently endure half slave and half free," and from this was implied a suggestion of his failure to perform his duty as he had then seen it. Lincoln was decidedly displeased with this criticism; and after the document had been read to the close, he received it from the speaker, then drawing himself up, he said, with unusual severity of manner: "It is true that on the 17th of June, 1858, I said, 'I believe that this Government cannot permanently endure half slave and half free,' but I said it in connection with other things from which it should not have been separated in an address discussing moral obligations; for this is a case in which the repetition of half a truth, in connection with the remarks just read, produces the effect of a whole falsehood. What I did say was, 'If we could first know where we are, and whither we are tending, we could better judge what to do and how to do it. We are now far into the fifth year since a policy was initiated with the avowed object and confident promise of putting an end to the slavery agitation. Under the operation of that policy this agitation has not only not ceased but has constantly augmented. In my opinion it will not cease until a crisis shall have been reached and passed. "A house divided against itself cannot stand." I believe that this Government cannot permanently endure half slave and half free. I do not expect the Union to be dissolved—I do not expect the house to fall—but I do expect that it will cease to be divided. It will become all one thing or all the other. Either the opponents of slavery will arrest the further spread of it, and place it where the public mind shall rest in the belief that it is in the course of ultimate extinction, or its advocates will push it forward till it shall become alike lawful in all the States, old as well as new, North as well as South.' Take this statement as a whole, and it does not furnish a text for the homily to which this audience has listened."

As Lincoln concluded, he was turning away, when another member of the delegation, a woman, requested permission to detain him with a few words. Somewhat impatiently he said, "I will hear the Friend." Her remarks were a plea for the emancipation of the slaves, urging that he was the appointed minister of the Lord to do the work, and enforcing her argument by many Scriptural citations. At the close he asked, "Has the Friend finished?" and receiving an affirmative answer, he said: "I have neither time nor disposition to enter into discussion with the Friend, and end this occasion by suggesting for her consideration the question whether, if it be true that the Lord has appointed me to do the work she has indicated, it is not probable that He would have communicated knowledge of the fact to me as well as to her?"

Something like the same views were expressed by Lincoln, on another occasion, when, in response to a memorial presented by a delegation representing most of the religious organizations of Chicago, he said, respectfully but pointedly: "I am approached with the most opposite opinions and advice, and by religious men who are certain they represent the Divine Will.... I hope it will not be irreverent in me to say that if it be probable that God would reveal His will to others, on a point so closely connected with my duty, it might be supposed he would reveal it directly to me.... If I can learn His will, I will do it. These, however, are not the days of miracles, and I suppose I am not to expect a direct revelation. I must study the plain physical facts of the case, and learn what appears to be wise and right.... Do not misunderstand me because I have mentioned these objections. They indicate the difficulties which have thus far prevented my action in some such way as you desire. I have not decided against a proclamation of emancipation, but hold the matter in advisement. The subject is in my mind by day and by night. Whatever shall appear to be God's will, I will do."

About this period the President had a very interesting conversation with Rev. William Henry Channing, in which the question of emancipation was frankly discussed. Mr. M.D. Conway, who was present at the interview, says: "Mr. Channing having begun by expressing his belief that the opportunity of the nation to rid itself of slavery had arrived, Mr. Lincoln asked how he thought they might avail themselves of it. Channing suggested emancipation, with compensation for the slaves. The President said he had for years been in favor of that plan. When the President turned to me, I asked whether we might not look to him as the coming deliverer of the nation from its one great evil? What would not that man achieve for mankind who should free America from slavery? He said, 'Perhaps we may be better able to do something in that direction after a while than we are now.' I said: 'Mr. President, do you believe the masses of the American people would hail you as their deliverer if, at the end of this war, the Union should be surviving and slavery still in it?' 'Yes, if they were to see that slavery was on the down hill.' I ventured to say: 'Our fathers compromised with slavery because they thought it on the down hill; hence war to-day.' The President said: 'I think the country grows in this direction daily, and I am not without hope that something of the desire of you and your friends may be accomplished. When the hour comes for dealing with slavery, *I trust I shall be willing to do my duty, though it costs my life.* And, gentlemen, lives will be lost.' These last words were said with a smile, yet with a sad and weary tone. During the conversation Mr. Lincoln recurred several times to Channing's suggestion of pecuniary compensation for emancipated slaves, and professed profound sympathy with the Southerners who, by no fault of their own, had become socially and commercially bound up with their peculiar institution. Being a Virginian myself, with many dear relatives and beloved companions of my youth in the Confederate ranks, I responded warmly to his kindly sentiments toward the South, albeit feeling more angry than he seemed to be against the institution preying upon the land like a ghoul. I forget whether it was on this occasion or on a subsequent one when I was present that he said, in parting: 'We shall need all the anti-slavery feeling in the country, and more; you can go home and try to bring the people to your views; and you may say anything you like about me, if that will help. Don't spare me!' This was said with some laughter, but still in earnest."

One of the severest opponents of President Lincoln's policy regarding slavery was Horace Greeley. He criticized Lincoln freely in the New York "Tribune," of which he was editor, and said many harsh and bitter things of the administration. Lincoln took the abuse good-naturedly, saying on one occasion: "It reminds me of the big fellow whose little wife was wont to beat him over the head without resistance. When remonstrated with, the man said, 'Let her alone. It don't hurt me, and it does her a power of good.'"

In August, 1862, Mr. Greeley published a letter in the New York "Tribune," headed "The prayer of twenty millions of people," in which he urged the President, with extreme emphasis, to delay the act of emancipation no longer. Lincoln answered the vehement entreaty in the following calm, firm, and explicit words:

EXECUTIVE MANSION, WASHINGTON,
Friday, Aug. 22, 1862.

HON. HORACE GREELEY.

DEAR SIR: I have just read yours of the 19th instant, addressed to myself, through the New York Tribune.

If there be in it any statements or assumptions of fact, which I may know to be erroneous, I do not now and here controvert them. If there be any inferences which I believe to be falsely drawn, I do not now and here argue against them. If there be perceptible in it an impatient and dictatorial tone, I waive it, in deference to an old friend whose heart I have always supposed to be right.

As to the policy I "seem to be pursuing," as you say, I have not meant to leave anyone in doubt. I would save the Union. I would save it in the shortest way under the Constitution. The sooner the national authority can be restored, the nearer the Union will be—the Union as it was. If there be those who would not save the Union unless they could at the same time save slavery, I do not agree with them. If there be those who would not save the Union unless they could at the same time destroy slavery, I do not agree with them. *My paramount object is to save the Union, and not either to save or destroy slavery.* If I could save the Union without freeing any slave, I would do it. And if I could save it by freeing all the slaves, I would do it. And if I could save it by freeing some, and leaving others alone, I would do that.

What I do about slavery and the colored race, I do because I believe it helps to save the Union; and what I forbear, I forbear because I do not believe it would help to save the Union. I shall do less whenever I believe what I am doing hurts the cause; and shall do more whenever I believe doing more will help the cause. I shall try to correct errors, when shown to be errors; and I shall adopt new views, so fast as they shall appear to be true views.

I have here stated my purpose, according to my view of official duty, and I intend no modification of my oft-expressed personal wish that all men everywhere could be free.

Yours,
A. Lincoln.

Mr. Greeley being dissatisfied with Lincoln's explanation, and the "Tribune" still teeming with complaints and criticisms of the administration, Lincoln requested Mr. Greeley to come to Washington and make known in person his complaints, to the end that they might be obviated if possible.

The editor of the "Tribune" came. Lincoln said: "You complain of me. What have I done, or omitted to do, which has provoked the hostility of the 'Tribune'?" The reply was, "You should issue a proclamation abolishing slavery." Lincoln answered: "Suppose I do that. There are now twenty thousand of our muskets on the shoulders of Kentuckians, who are bravely fighting our battles. Every one of them will be thrown down or carried over to the rebels." The reply was: "Let them do it. The cause of the Union will be stronger if Kentucky should secede with the rest than it is now." Lincoln answered, "Oh, I can't think that."

It is evident that these solicitations and counsellings from outside persons were unnecessary and idle. Lincoln's far-seeing and practical mind had already grasped, more surely than had his would-be advisers, the ultimate wisdom and justice of the emancipation of the slaves. But he was resolved to do nothing rashly. He would wait till the time was ripe, and then abolish slavery on grounds that would be approved throughout the world: he would destroy slavery as a necessary step to the preservation of the Union. In the first year of the war he had said to a Southern Unionist, who warned him against meddling with slavery, *"You must not expect me to give up this Government without playing my last card."* This "last card" was undoubtedly the freeing of the slaves; and when the time came, Lincoln played it unhesitatingly and triumphantly. How strong a card it was may be judged by a statement made in Congress by Mr. Ashmore, a Representative from South Carolina, who said shortly before the war: "The South can sustain more men in the field than the North can. *Her four millions of slaves alone will enable her to support an army of half a million."* This view makes the issue plain. If the South could maintain armies in the field supported, or partly supported, by slave labor, it was as much the right and the duty of the Government to destroy that support as to destroy an establishment for the manufacture of arms or munitions of war for the Southern armies. The logic of events had demonstrated the necessity and justice of the measure, and Lincoln now had with him a Cabinet practically united in its favor. The case was well stated by Secretary Welles—perhaps the most cool-headed and conservative member of Lincoln's Cabinet—at a Cabinet meeting held six or eight weeks after the Emancipation measure had been brought forward by the President. Mr. Welles, as he relates in his Diary, pointed out "the strong exercise of power" involved in the proposal, and denied the power of the Executive to take such a step under ordinary conditions. "But," said Mr. Welles, "the Rebels themselves had invoked war on the subject of slavery, had appealed to arms, and must abide the consequences." Mr. Welles admitted that it was "an extreme exercise of war powers" which he believed justifiable "under the circumstances, and in view of the condition of the country and the magnitude of the contest. The slaves were now an element of strength to the Rebels—were laborers, producers, and army attendants; they were considered as *property* by the Rebels, and *if property* they were subject to confiscation; if not property, but *persons* residing in the insurrectionary region, we should invite them as well as the whites to unite with us in putting down the Rebellion." This view was in the main concurred in by the Cabinet members present, and greatly heartened the President in his course. On the 22d of September, 1862, he issued what is known as the "Preliminary Proclamation." The text of this momentous document is as follows:

> I, Abraham Lincoln, President of the United States of America, and Commander-in-Chief of the Army and Navy thereof, do hereby proclaim and declare that hereafter, as heretofore, the war will be prosecuted for the object of practically restoring the constitutional relations between the United States and each of the States and the people thereof, in which States that relation is or may be suspended or disturbed.

> That it is my purpose, upon the next meeting of Congress, to again recommend the adoption of a practical measure tendering pecuniary aid to the free acceptance or rejection of all slave States, so called, the people whereof may not then be in rebellion against the United States, and which States may then have voluntarily adopted, or thereafter may voluntarily adopt, immediate or gradual abolishment of slavery within their respective limits; and that the effort to colonize persons of African descent, with their consent, upon this continent or elsewhere, with the previously obtained consent of the governments existing there, will be continued.

> That on the first day of January, in the year of our Lord one thousand eight hundred and sixty-three, all persons held as slaves within any State or designated part of a State, the people whereof shall then be in rebellion against the United States, shall be then, thenceforward, and forever FREE; and the Executive government of the United States, including the military and naval authority thereof, will recognize and maintain the freedom of such persons, and will do no act or acts to repress such persons, or any of them, in any efforts they may make for their actual freedom.

That the Executive will, on the first day of January aforesaid, by proclamation, designate the States and parts of States, if any, in which the people thereof respectively shall then be in rebellion against the United States; and the fact that any State, or the people thereof, shall on that day be, in good faith, represented in the Congress of the United States by members chosen thereto at elections wherein a majority of the qualified voters of such State shall have participated, shall, in the absence of strong countervailing testimony, be deemed conclusive evidence that such State, and the people thereof, are not in rebellion against the United States.

That attention is hereby called to an act of Congress entitled "An act to make an additional article of war," approved March 13, 1862, and which act is in the words and figures following:

Be it enacted by the Senate and House of Representatives of the United States of America in Congress assembled, That hereafter the following shall be promulgated as an additional article of war, for the government of the army of the United States, and shall be obeyed and observed as such.

ARTICLE. — All officers or persons in the military or naval service of the United States are prohibited from employing any of the forces under their respective commands for the purpose of returning fugitives from service or labor who may have escaped from any persons to whom such service or labor is claimed to be due, and any officer who shall be found guilty by a court-martial of violating this article shall be dismissed from the service.

SEC. 2. *And be it further enacted,* That this act shall take effect from and after its passage.

Also to the ninth and tenth sections of an act entitled "An act to suppress insurrection, to punish treason and rebellion, to seize and confiscate property of rebels, and for other purposes," approved July 17, 1862, and which sections are in the words and figures following:

SEC. 9. *And be it further enacted,* That all slaves of persons who shall hereafter be engaged in rebellion against the government of the United States or who shall in any way give aid or comfort thereto, escaping from such persons and taking refuge within the lines of the army; and all slaves captured from such persons or deserted by them, and coming under the control of the government of the United States; and all slaves of such persons found *on* [or] being within any place occupied by rebel forces, and afterwards occupied by the forces of the United States, shall be deemed captives of war, and shall be forever free of their servitude, and not again held as slaves.

SEC. 10. *And be it further enacted,* That no slave, escaping into any State, Territory, or the District of Columbia, from any other State, shall be delivered up, or in any way impeded or hindered of his liberty, except for crime, or some offense against the laws, unless the person claiming said fugitive shall first make oath that the person to whom the labor or service of such fugitive is alleged to be due is his lawful owner, and has not borne arms against the United States in the present rebellion, nor in any way given aid and comfort thereto; and no person engaged in the military or naval service of the United States shall, under any pretense whatever, assume to decide on the validity of the claim of any person to the service or labor of any other person, or surrender up any such person to the claimant, on pain of being dismissed from the service.

And I do hereby enjoin upon and order all persons engaged in the military and naval service of the United States to observe, obey, and enforce, within their respective spheres of service, the act and sections above recited.

And the Executive will in due time recommend that all the citizens of the United States who shall have remained loyal thereto throughout the rebellion, shall (upon the restoration of the constitutional relation between the United States and their respective States and people, if that relation shall have been suspended or disturbed) be compensated for all losses by acts of the United States, including the loss of slaves.

In witness whereof, I have hereunto set my hand, and caused the seal of the United States to be affixed.

Done at the city of Washington, this twenty-second day of September, in the year of our Lord, one thousand eight hundred and sixty-two, and of the Independence of the United States the eighty-seventh.

By the President: ABRAHAM LINCOLN.

WILLIAM H. SEWARD, *Secretary of State.*

Lincoln's own account of this proclamation, and of the steps that led to it, is given as reported by Mr. F.B. Carpenter. "It had," said Lincoln, "got to be midsummer, 1862. Things had gone on from bad to worse, until I felt that we had reached the end of our rope on the plan of operations we had been pursuing; that we must change our tactics and play our last card, or lose the game. I now determined upon the adoption of the emancipation policy; and, without consultation with, or the knowledge of, the Cabinet, I prepared the original draft of the proclamation, and, after much anxious thought, called a Cabinet meeting upon the subject. This was the last of July, or the first part of the month of August, 1862. This Cabinet meeting took place, I think, upon a Saturday. All were present excepting Mr. Blair, the Postmaster general, who was absent at the opening of the discussion, but came in subsequently. I said to the Cabinet that I had resolved upon this step, and had called them together, not to ask their advice, but to lay the subject-matter of a proclamation before them; suggestions as to which would be in order, after they had heard it read. Mr. Lovejoy was in error when he informed you that it excited no comment, excepting on the part of Secretary Seward. Various suggestions were offered. Secretary Chase wished the language stronger in reference to the arming of the blacks. Mr. Blair, after he came in, deprecated the policy, on the ground that it would cost the administration the fall elections. Nothing, however, was offered that I had not already fully anticipated and settled in my own mind, until Secretary Seward spoke. He said in substance: 'Mr. President, I approve of the proclamation, but I question the expediency of its issue at this juncture. The depression of the public mind, consequent upon our repeated reverses, is so great that I fear the effect of so important a step. It may be viewed as the last measure of an exhausted government, a cry for help; the government stretching forth its hands to Ethiopia, instead of Ethiopia stretching forth her hands to the government.' 'His idea,' said the President, 'was that it would be considered our last *shriek* on the retreat. ' (This was his precise expression.) 'Now, ' continued Mr. Seward, 'while I approve the measure, I suggest, sir, that you postpone its issue until you can give it to the country supported by military success, instead of issuing it, as would be the case now, upon the greatest disasters of the war!'" Lincoln continued: "The wisdom of the view of the Secretary of State struck me with very great force. It was an aspect of the case that, in all my thought upon the subject, I had entirely overlooked. The result was that I put the draft of the proclamation aside, waiting for a victory. From time to time I added or changed a line, touching it up here and there, anxiously waiting the progress of events. Well, the next news we had was of Pope's disaster at Bull Run. Things looked darker than ever. Finally, came the week of the battle of Antietam. I determined to wait no longer.[F] The news came, I think, on Wednesday, that the advantage was on our side. I was then staying at the Soldiers' Home (three miles out of Washington). Here I finished writing the second draft of the preliminary proclamation; came up on Saturday; called the Cabinet together to hear it; and it was published the following Monday."

Another interesting incident occurred at this Cabinet meeting in connection with Secretary Seward. The President had written the important part of the proclamation in these words: "That on the first day of January, in the year of our Lord one thousand eight hundred and sixty-three, all persons held as slaves within any State or designated part of a State, the people whereof shall then be in rebellion against the United States, shall be then, thenceforward, and forever FREE; and the Executive Government of the United States, including the military and naval authority thereof, will *recognize* the freedom of such persons, and will do no act or acts to repress such persons, or any of them, in any efforts they may make for their actual freedom." "When I finished reading this paragraph," remarked Lincoln, "Mr. Seward stopped me, and said, 'I think, Mr. President, that you should insert after the word "*recognize*" "*and maintain.*"' I replied that I had already fully considered the import of that expression in this connection, but I had not introduced it, because it was not my way to promise what I was not entirely *sure* that I could perform, and I was not prepared to say that I thought we were exactly able to maintain this. But Seward insisted that we ought to take this ground, and the words finally went in."

The special Cabinet meeting to which Lincoln here refers was one of uncommon interest even in that day of heroic things. An account of it is given by Secretary Welles, who was present. "At the Cabinet meeting of September 22," says Mr. Welles in his Diary, "the special subject was the Proclamation for emancipating the slaves after a certain date, in States that shall then be in rebellion. For several weeks the subject has been suspended, but the President says never lost sight of. In taking up the Proclamation, the President stated that the question was finally decided, the act and the consequences were his, but that he felt it due to us to make us acquainted with the fact and to invite criticism on the paper which he had prepared. There were, he had found, not unexpectedly, some differences in the Cabinet, but he had, after ascertaining in his own way the views of each and all, individually and collectively, formed his own conclusions and made his own decisions. In the course of the discussion on this paper, which was long, earnest, and, on the general principle involved, harmonious, he remarked that he had made a vow, a covenant, that if God gave us the victory in the approaching battle, he would consider it an indication of Divine will, and that it was his duty to move forward in the cause of emancipation. It might be thought strange, he said, that he had in this way submitted the disposal of important matters when the way was not clear to his mind what he should do. God had decided his questions in favor of the slaves. He was satisfied it was right; and he was confirmed and strengthened in his action by the vow and the results. His mind was fixed, his decision made, but he wished his paper announcing his course to be as correct in terms as it could be made without any change in his determination. He read the document. One or two unimportant amendments suggested by Seward were approved. It was then handed to the Secretary of State to publish to-morrow."

The discussion of Emancipation brought up at once the problem of what should be done with the freed negroes. The very next day after the preliminary proclamation was issued (September 23, 1862), the President presented the matter to the assembled Cabinet. Deportation was considered, and some of those present urged that this should be compulsory. The President, however, would not consider this; the emigration of the negroes, he said, must be voluntary, and without expense to themselves. It was proposed to deport the freedmen to Costa Rica, where a large tract of land (known as the Chiriqui Grant) had been obtained from the government of Central America. Lincoln favored this in a general way. He "thought it essential to provide an asylum for a race which we had emancipated but which could never be recognized or admitted to be our equals," says Mr. Welles. But there was some doubt as to the validity of the title to the Costa Rica lands, and the matter was dropped.

In his second annual message to Congress, transmitted to that body in December, 1862, Lincoln touched, in conclusion, upon the great subject of Emancipation, in these words of deep import:

> I do not forget the gravity which should characterize a paper addressed to the Congress of the nation by the Chief Magistrate of the nation. Nor do I forget that some of you are my seniors, nor that many of you have more experience than I in the conduct of public affairs. Yet I trust that in view of the great responsibility resting upon me, you will perceive no want of respect to yourselves in any undue earnestness I may seem to display.... The dogmas of the quiet past are inadequate to the stormy present. The occasion is piled high with difficulty, and we must rise with the occasion. As our case is new, so we must think anew and act anew.

Fellow citizens, we cannot escape history. We of this Congress and this administration will be remembered in spite of ourselves. No personal significance, or insignificance, can spare one or another of us. The fiery trial through which we pass will light us down, in honor or dishonor, to the latest generation. We say we are for the Union. The world will not forget that we say this. We know how to save the Union. The world knows we do know how to save it. We—even we here—hold the power and bear the responsibility. In giving freedom to the slave we assure freedom to the free—honorable alike in what we give and what we preserve. We shall nobly save, or meanly lose, the last best hope of earth. Other means may succeed, this could not fail. The way is plain, peaceful, generous, just—a way which, if followed, the world will forever applaud, and God must forever bless.

An immense concourse attended the reception at the White House on the first day of 1863, and the President stood for several hours shaking hands with the endless train of men and women who pressed forward to greet him. The exhausting ceremonial being ended, the proclamation which finally and forever abrogated the institution of slavery in the United States was handed to him for his signature. "Mr. Seward," remarked the President, "I have been shaking hands all day, and my right hand is almost paralyzed. If my name ever gets into history, it will be for this act, and my whole soul is in it. If my hand trembles when I sign the proclamation, those who examine the document hereafter will say I hesitated." Then, resting his arm a moment, he turned to the table, took up the pen, and slowly and firmly wrote, ABRAHAM LINCOLN. He smiled as, handing the paper to Mr. Seward, he said, "That will do." A few hours after, he remarked: "The signature looks a little tremulous, for my hand was tired; but my resolution was firm. I told them in September that if they did not return to their allegiance I would strike at this pillar of their strength. And now the promise shall be kept, and not one word of it will I ever recall."

The text of the great Emancipation Proclamation is as follows:

Whereas, on the 22d day of September, in the year of our Lord one thousand eight hundred and sixty-two, a proclamation was issued by the President of the United States, containing, among other things, the following, to-wit:

That on the first day of January, in the year of our Lord one thousand eight hundred and sixty-three, all persons held as slaves within any States or designated part of a State, the people whereof shall then be in rebellion against the United States, shall be then, thenceforward and forever free; and the Executive Government of the United States, including the military and naval authority thereof, will recognize and maintain the freedom of such persons, and will do no act or acts to repress such persons, or any of them, in any efforts they may make for their actual freedom.

That the Executive will, on the first day of January aforesaid, by proclamation, designate the States and parts of States, if any, in which the people thereof respectively shall then be in rebellion against the United States; and the fact that any State, or the people thereof, shall on that day be in good faith represented in the Congress of the United States, by members chosen thereto at elections wherein a majority of the qualified voters of such State shall have participated, shall, in the absence of strong countervailing testimony, be deemed conclusive evidence that such State, and the people thereof, are not then in rebellion against the United States.

Now, therefore, I, Abraham Lincoln, President of the United States, by virtue of the power in me vested as Commander-in-Chief of the Army and Navy of the United States in time of actual armed rebellion against the authority and Government of the United States, and as a fit and necessary war measure for suppressing said rebellion, do, on this first day of January, in the year of our Lord one thousand eight hundred and sixty-three, and in accordance with my purpose so to do, publicly proclaimed for the full period of one hundred days, from the day first above mentioned, order and designate as the States and parts of States wherein the people thereof respectively are this day in rebellion against the United States, the following, to-wit: Arkansas, Texas, Louisiana (except the parishes of St. Bernard, Plaquemines, Jefferson, St. John, St. Charles, St. James, Ascension, Assumption, Terre Bonne, Lafourche, Ste. Marie, St. Martin, and Orleans, including the city of New Orleans), Mississippi, Alabama, Florida, Georgia, South Carolina, North Carolina, and Virginia (except the forty-eight counties designated as West Virginia, and also the counties of Berkeley, Accomac, Northampton, Elizabeth City, York, Princess Anne, and Norfolk, including the cities of Norfolk and Portsmouth), and which excepted parts are for the present left precisely as if this proclamation were not issued.

And by virtue of the power and for the purpose aforesaid, I do order and declare that all persons held as slaves within said designated States and parts of States are and henceforward shall be FREE; and that the Executive Government of the United States, including the military and naval authorities thereof, will recognize and maintain the freedom of said persons.

And I hereby enjoin upon the people so declared to be free to abstain from all violence, unless in necessary self-defense; and I recommend to them that, in all cases when allowed, they labor faithfully for reasonable wages.

And I further declare and make known that such persons, of suitable condition, will be received into the armed service of the United States to garrison forts, positions, stations, and other places, and to man vessels of all sorts in said service.

And upon this act, sincerely believed to be an act of justice, warranted by the Constitution, upon military necessity, I invoke the considerate judgment of mankind and the gracious favor of Almighty God.

In testimony whereof, I have hereunto set my name, and caused the seal of the United States to be affixed.

Done at the City of Washington, this first day of January, in the year of our Lord one thousand eight hundred and sixty-three, and of the independence of the United States the eighty-seventh.

By the President: ABRAHAM LINCOLN.

WILLIAM H. SEWARD, Secretary of State.

It is stated that Lincoln gave the most earnest study to the composition of the Emancipation Proclamation. He realized, as he afterwards said, that the proclamation was the central act of his administration and the great event of the nineteenth century. When the document was completed a printed copy of it was placed in the hands of each member of the Cabinet, and criticisms and suggestions were invited. Mr. Chase remarked: "This paper is of the utmost importance, greater than any state paper ever made by this Government. A paper of so much importance, and involving the liberties of so many people, ought, I think, to make some reference to Deity. I do not observe anything of the kind in it." Lincoln said: "No, I overlooked it. Some reference to Deity must be inserted. Mr. Chase, won't you make a draft of what you think ought to be inserted?" Mr. Chase promised to do so, and at the next meeting presented the following: "And upon this act, sincerely believed to be an act of justice, warranted by the Constitution, upon military necessity, I invoke the considerate judgment of mankind and the gracious favor of Almighty God." When Lincoln read the paragraph, Mr. Chase said: "You may not approve it, but I thought this, or something like it, would be appropriate." Lincoln replied: "I do approve it; it cannot be bettered, and I will adopt it in the very words you have written."

To a large concourse of people who, two days after the proclamation was issued, assembled before the White House, with music, the President said: "What I did, I did after a very full deliberation, and under a heavy and solemn sense of responsibility. I can only trust in God I have made no mistake." That he realized to the full the gravity of the step before taking it is shown again in an incident related by Hon. John Covode, who, calling on the President a few days before the issue of the final proclamation, found him walking his room in considerable agitation. Reference being made to the forthcoming proclamation, Lincoln said with great earnestness: "I have studied that matter well; my mind is made up—it *must be done*. I am driven to it. There is to me no other way out of our troubles. But although my duty is plain, it is in some respects painful, and I trust the people will understand that I act not in anger but in expectation of a greater good."

Mr. Ben. Perley Poore makes the interesting statement that "Mr. Lincoln carefully put away the pen which he had used in signing the document, for Mr. Sumner, who had promised it to his friend, George Livermore, of Cambridge, the author of an interesting work on slavery. It was a steel pen with a wooden handle, the end of which had been gnawed by Mr. Lincoln—a habit that he had when composing anything that required thought."

In response to a request of the ladies in charge of the Northwestern Fair for the Sanitary Commission, which was held in Chicago in the autumn of 1863, Lincoln conveyed to them the original draft of the proclamation; saying, in his note of presentation, "I had some desire to retain the paper; but if it shall contribute to the relief or comfort of the soldiers, that will be better." The document was purchased at the Fair by Mr. Thomas B. Bryan, and given by him to the Chicago Historical Society. It perished in the great fire of October, 1871.

More than a year after the issue of the Emancipation Proclamation, Lincoln, in writing to a prominent Kentucky Unionist, gave a synopsis of his views and course regarding slavery, which is so clear in statement, and so forceful and convincing in logic, that a place must be given it in this chapter.

I am naturally anti-slavery. If slavery is not wrong, nothing is wrong. I cannot remember when I did not so think and feel; and yet I have never understood that the Presidency conferred upon me an unrestricted, right to act officially upon this judgment and feeling. It was in the oath I took that I would, to the best of my ability, preserve, protect, and defend the Constitution of the United States. I could not take the office without taking the oath. Nor was it my view that I might take an oath to get power, and break the oath in using the power. I understood, too, that in ordinary civil administration this oath even forbade me to practically indulge my primary abstract judgment on the moral question of slavery. I had publicly declared this many times and in many ways. And I aver that, to this day, I have done no official act in mere deference to my abstract judgment and feeling on slavery. I did understand, however, that my oath to preserve the Constitution to the best of my ability imposed upon me the duty of preserving, by every indispensable means, that Government—that Nation of which that Constitution was the organic law. Was it possible to lose the nation and yet preserve the Constitution? By general law, life *and* limb must be protected; yet often a limb must be amputated to save a life; but a life is never wisely given to save a limb. I felt that measures, otherwise unconstitutional, might become lawful, by becoming indispensable to the preservation of the Constitution, through the preservation of the nation. Right or wrong, I assumed this ground, and now avow it. I could not feel that, to the best of my ability, I had even tried to preserve the Constitution, if, to save slavery, or any minor matter, I should permit the wreck of government, country, and constitution, altogether. When, early in the war, General Frémont attempted military emancipation, I forbade it, because I did not then think it an indispensable necessity. When a little later, General Cameron, then Secretary of War, suggested the arming of the blacks, I objected, because I did not yet think it an indispensable necessity. When, still later,

General Hunter attempted military emancipation, I again forbade it, because I did not yet think the indispensable necessity had come. When, in March and May and July, 1862, I made earnest and successive appeals to the border States to favor compensated emancipation, I believed the indispensable necessity for military emancipation and arming the blacks would come, unless averted by that measure. They declined the proposition; and I was, in my best judgment, driven to the alternative of either surrendering the Union, and with it the Constitution, or of laying strong hand upon the colored element. I chose the latter. In choosing it, I hoped for greater gain than loss; but of this I was not entirely confident. More than a year of trial now shows no loss by it in our foreign relations, none in our home popular sentiment, none in our white military force, no loss by it anyhow or anywhere. On the contrary, it shows a gain of quite a hundred and thirty thousand soldiers, seamen, and laborers. These are palpable facts, about which, as facts, there can be no cavilling. We have the men; and as we could not have had them without the measure.

And now let any Union man who complains of the measure, test himself by writing down in one line that he is for subduing the rebellion by force of arms; and in the next, that he is for taking three hundred and thirty thousand men from the Union side, and placing them where they would be but for the measure he condemns. If he cannot face his case so stated, it is only because he cannot face the truth.

I attempt no compliment to my own sagacity. I claim not to have controlled events, but confess plainly that events have controlled me. Now, at the end of three years' struggle, the nation's condition is not what either party or any man devised or expected. God alone can claim it. Whither it is tending seems plain. If God now wills the removal of a great wrong, and wills also that we of the North, as well as you of the South, shall pay fairly for our complicity in that wrong, impartial history will find therein new causes to attest and revere the justice and goodness of God.

Yours truly,
A. LINCOLN

CHAPTER XXII

In a work which is not intended to cover fully the events of a great historic period, but rather to trace out the life of a single individual connected with that period, much must be included which, although not possessing special historical significance, cannot be overlooked in a personal study of the subject of the biography. Lincoln's life as President was by no means made up of Cabinet meetings, official messages and proclamations, or reviews of armies; interspersed with these conspicuous acts was a multitude of less heroic but scarcely less interesting details, with incidents and experiences humorous or sad, but all, even the most trivial, being expressions of the life and character of the man whom we are seeking to portray.

"Society," as now understood at the national capital, had but little existence during the war. At the White House there were the usual President's receptions, which were quite public in character and were largely attended. Aside from these democratic gatherings there was little enough of gaiety. The feeling that prevailed is shown by an incident that occurred during the winter of 1862-3, when a good deal of clamor was raised over a party given by Mrs. Lincoln, at which, it was asserted, dancing was indulged in; and Mrs. Lincoln was severely censured for what was regarded as inexcusable frivolity. Hon. A.G. Riddle, who was present on the occasion referred to, states positively that there was no dancing; the party was a quiet one, intended only to relieve the rather dull and formal receptions. But the President was pained by the rumors that "fashionable balls" were permitted at the White House in war-time; and the party was not repeated.

It was the custom of President Lincoln to open, twice a week, the doors of his office in the Executive Mansion for the admission of all visitors who might wish to speak with him. These brief interviews, quite devoid of ceremony, seemed to reveal the man in his true character, and to set forth the salient traits that fitted him for his great position, and endeared him so greatly to the popular heart. They showed how easily accessible he was to all classes of citizens, how readily he could adapt himself to people of any station or degree, how deep and true were his human sympathies, how quickly and keenly he could discriminate character, and how heartily he detested meanness and all unworthy acts and appliances to compass a selfish or sordid end. On these occasions, as may well be imagined, many curious incidents occurred. Lincoln was usually clad "in a black broadcloth suit, nothing in his dress betokening disregard of conventionality, save perhaps his neat cloth slippers, which were doubtless worn for comfort. He was seated beside a plain cloth-covered table, in a commodious arm-chair." As each visitor approached the President he was greeted with an encouraging nod and smile, and a few moments were cordially given him in which to state the object of the visit; the President listening with the most respectful and patient attention, and deciding each case with tact, sympathy, and good humor. "His *Yes*," says Mr. Riddle, "was most gracious and satisfactory; his *No*, when reached, was often spoken by the petitioner, and left only a soothed disappointment. He saw the point of a case unerringly. He had a confidence in the homely views and speech of the common people, with whom his heart and sympathies ever were."

At these informal meetings with people who usually wanted some favor from him, no case was too trivial to receive his attention. Taking advantage of the opportunity, there came one day, says Mr. C. Van Santvoord, "a sturdy, honest-looking German soldier, minus a leg, who hobbled up to the President on crutches. In consideration of his disabled condition, he wanted some situation about Washington, the duties of which he might be able to discharge; and he had come to the President, hoping that he would provide the desired situation for him. On being interrogated as to how he had lost his leg, he answered that it was the effect of a wound received in battle, mentioning the time and the place. 'Let me look at your papers,' said Mr. Lincoln. The man replied that he had none, and that he supposed his word would be sufficient. 'What!' exclaimed the President, 'no papers, no credentials, nothing to show how you lost your leg! How am I to know that you did not lose it by a trap after getting into somebody's orchard?' This was spoken with a droll expression which amused the bystanders, all except the applicant, who with a very solemn visage earnestly protested the truth of his statement, muttering something about the reasons for not being able to produce his papers. 'Well, well,' said the President, 'it is a little risky for an army man to be wandering around without papers to show where he belongs and what he is, but I will see what can be done for you.' And taking a blank card from a little pile of similar blanks on the table, he wrote some lines upon it, addressed it, and handing it to the man bade him deliver it to a certain quartermaster, who would attend to his case."

The President could, however, be emphatic and even severe when necessary on such occasions. One day, we are told, "he was approached by a man apparently sixty years of age, with dress and manner which showed that he was acquainted with the usages of good society, whose whole exterior, indeed, would have favorably impressed people who form opinions from appearances. The object of his visit was to solicit aid in some commission project, for the success of which Mr. Lincoln's favor was regarded as essential. The President heard him patiently, but demurred against being connected with or countenancing the affair, suggesting mildly that the applicant would better set up an office of the kind described, and run it in his own way and at his own risk. The man pleaded his advanced years and obscurity as a reason for not attempting this, but said if the President would only let him use his name to advertise and recommend the enterprise, he would then, he thought, need nothing more. At this the eyes of the President flashed with sudden indignation, and his whole aspect and manner underwent a portentous change. 'No!' he broke forth, with startling vehemence, springing from his seat under the impulse of his emotion. 'No! I'll have nothing to do with this business, nor with any man who comes to me with such degrading propositions. What! Do you take the President of the United States to be a commission broker? You have come to the wrong place; and for you and every one who comes for such purposes, there is the door!' The man's face blanched as he cowered and slunk away confounded, without uttering a word. The President's wrath subsided as speedily as it had risen."

Another example of Lincoln's power to dispose summarily of people who tried his patience too far is given by Secretary Welles, who records that a Mrs. White—a sister or half-sister of Mrs. Lincoln—made herself so obnoxious as a Southern sympathizer in Washington in 1864, that the President sent her word that "if she did not leave forthwith she might expect to find herself within twenty-four hours in the Old Capitol Prison."

With all his kindness and desire to do what was asked of him, Lincoln could not be persuaded to consent to anything which he felt to be distinctly wrong, regardless of any unfavorable consequences which his refusal might bring upon himself. When the members of Congress from Minnesota, late in 1862, called on him in a body to urge him to order the execution of three hundred Indian prisoners, captured in their State and charged with great atrocities, he positively refused, although realizing that it might cost him the support of those members of the House, which he greatly needed at that time.

"The President is always disposed to mitigate punishments and grant favors," says a member of his Cabinet. "As a matter of duty and friendship, I one day mentioned to him the case of Laura Jones, a young lady residing in Richmond and there engaged to be married, who came up three years ago to attend her sick mother and had been unable to pass through the lines and return. A touching appeal was made by the poor girl, who truly says her youth is passing. The President at once said he would give her a pass. I told him her sympathies were with the secessionists. But he said he would let her go; the war had depopulated the country and prevented marriages enough, and if he could do a kindness of this sort he would do it."

Another applicant for a pass through the lines was less fortunate than the one just noted. One day, in the spring of 1862, a gentleman from some Northern city entered Lincoln's private office, and earnestly requested a pass to Richmond. "A pass to Richmond!" exclaimed the President. "Why, my dear sir, if I should give you one it would do you no good. You may think it very strange, but there's a lot of fellows between here and Richmond who either can't read or are prejudiced against every man who totes a pass from me. I have given McClellan and more than two hundred thousand others passes to Richmond, *and not a single one of 'em has got there yet!*"

Lincoln sometimes had a very effective way of dealing with men who asked troublesome or improper questions. A visitor once asked him how many men the rebels had in the field. The President replied, very seriously, "*Twelve hundred thousand,* according to the best authority." The interrogator blanched in the face, and ejaculated, "Good heavens!" "Yes, sir, twelve hundred thousand—no doubt of it. You see, all of our generals, when they get whipped, say the enemy outnumbered them from three or five to one, and I must believe them. We have four hundred thousand men in the field, and three times four makes twelve. Don't you see it?"

Among the many illustrations of the sturdy sense and firmness of Lincoln's character, the following should be recorded: During the early part of 1863 the Union men in Missouri were divided into two factions, which waged a bitter controversy with each other. General Curtis, commander of the military district comprising Missouri, Kansas, and Arkansas, was at the head of one faction, while Governor Gamble led the other. Their differences were a source of great embarrassment to the Government at Washington, and of harm to the Union cause. The President was in constant receipt of remonstrances and protests from the contesting parties, to one of which he made the following curt reply:

> Your despatch of to-day is just received. It is very painful to me that you, in Missouri cannot, or will not, settle your factional quarrel among yourselves. I have been tormented with it beyond endurance, for months, by both sides. Neither side pays the least respect to my appeals to reason. I am now compelled to take hold of the case.

A. LINCOLN.

The President promptly followed up this warning by removing General Curtis, and appointing in his place General Schofield, to whom he soon after addressed the following letter:

EXECUTIVE MANSION, WASHINGTON,
May 27, 1863.

GENERAL J.M. SCHOFIELD.

DEAR SIR: Having removed General Curtis and assigned you to the command of the Department of the Missouri, I think it may be of some advantage to me to state to you why I did it. I did not remove General Curtis because of my full conviction that he had done wrong by commission or omission. I did it because of a conviction in my mind that the Union men of Missouri, constituting, when united, a vast majority of the people, have entered into a pestilent, factious quarrel among themselves; General Curtis, perhaps not of choice, being the head of one faction, and Governor Gamble that of the other. After months of labor to reconcile the difficulty, it seemed to grow worse and worse, until I felt it my duty to break it up somehow, and as I could not remove Governor Gamble, I had to remove General Curtis. Now that you are in the position, I wish you to undo nothing merely because General Curtis or Governor Gamble did it, but to exercise your own judgment, and do right for the public interest. Let your military measures be strong enough to repel the invaders and keep the peace, and not so strong as to unnecessarily harass and persecute the people. It is a difficult *rôle*, and so much greater will be the honor if you perform it well. If both factions, or neither, shall abuse you, you will probably be about right. Beware of being assailed by one and praised by the other.

Yours truly, A. LINCOLN.

Firm and unyielding as he was when necessity compelled him to be, Lincoln was by nature a peace-maker, and was ever anxious that personal differences be adjusted happily. In his efforts to this end he never failed to show tact and shrewdness, and would if necessary sacrifice his own preferences in the interests of peace and harmony. A characteristic instance of the exercise of these traits occurred in connection with the Missouri troubles just referred to. General Schofield's course in command of his department proved satisfactory, and he had been nominated for a

Major-General's commission. He was, however, a somewhat conservative man, and in spite of his efforts to carry out the President's injunctions of impartiality, he had given offense to certain Missouri radicals, who now opposed his promotion, and were able to exert sufficient influence in the Senate to prevent the confirmation of his appointment as a Major-General. The Missouri delegation appealed to the more radical Senators, and the nomination was "hung up" for about six weeks. Lincoln was very desirous that it should be confirmed, and the Missouri Congressmen were equally bent on its defeat. In this dilemma, Lincoln sent for Senator Zack Chandler of Michigan, and proposed a compromise. "General Rosecrans," said he, "has a great many friends; he fought the battle of Stone River and won a brilliant victory, and his advocates begin to grumble about his treatment. Now, I will tell you what I have been thinking about. If you will confirm Schofield in the Senate, I will remove him from the command in Missouri and send him down to Sherman. That will satisfy the radicals. Then I will send Rosecrans to Missouri, and that will please the latter's friends. In this way the whole thing can be harmonized." As soon as the Senate grasped the plan of the President there was no longer any opposition to the confirmation of Schofield. He was sent to join Sherman in the South, Rosecrans was appointed to the command in Missouri, and everything worked harmoniously and pleasantly as the President had predicted and desired.

Secretary Welles remarks that "the President was a much more shrewd and accurate observer of the characteristics of men—better and more correctly formed an estimate of their power and capabilities—than the Secretary of State or most others. Those in the public service he closely scanned, but was deliberate in forming a conclusion adverse to any one he had appointed. In giving or withdrawing confidence he was discriminating and just in his final decision, careful never to wound unnecessarily the sensibilities of any of their infirmities, always ready to praise, but nevertheless firm and resolute in discharging the to him always painful duty of censure, reproof, or dismissal." As an instance of this sure judgment of the abilities and characters of men, Mr. Welles gives an anecdote relating to the naval movement under Admiral Du Pont, against Charleston, S.C. "One day," says Mr. Welles, "the President said to me that he had but slight expectation that we should have any great success from Du Pont. 'He, as well as McClellan,' said Mr. Lincoln, 'hesitates—has *the slows*. McClellan always wanted more regiments; Du Pont is everlastingly asking for more gun-boats—more iron-clads. He will do nothing with any. He has intelligence and system and will maintain a good blockade. You did well in selecting him for that command, but he will never take Sumter or get to Charleston. He is no Farragut, though unquestionably a good routine officer, who obeys orders and in a general way carries out his instructions.'" The outcome of events proved the soundness of Lincoln's judgment.

Loyalty to his friends was always a strong trait of Lincoln's character. It was put to the proof daily during his life in Washington. Mr. Gurdon S. Hubbard, in a brief but interesting memorial, relates one or two interviews held with the President, in which the simplicity of his character and his fidelity to old friendships appear very conspicuously. Mr. Hubbard's acquaintance with Lincoln was of long standing. "I called on him in Washington the year of his inauguration," says Mr. Hubbard, "and was alone with him for an hour or more. I found him greatly changed, his countenance bearing an expression of great mental anxiety. The whole topic of our conversation was the war, which affected him deeply.... Two years after, I again visited Washington, and went to the White House to pay my respects, in company with my friend Thomas L. Forrest. It was Saturday; and, as usual, about six o'clock the band from the navy-yard appeared and began to play. The President, with Adjutant-General Thomas, was seated on the balcony. The crowd was great, marching compactly past the President, the men raising their hats in salutation. As my friend and myself passed he said to me, 'The President seems to notice you—turn toward him.' 'No,' I said, 'I don't care to be recognized.' At that instant Mr. Lincoln started from his seat, advancing quickly to the iron railing, and leaning over, beckoning with his long arm, called: 'Hubbard! Hubbard! come here!' I left the ranks and ascended the stone steps to the gate of the balcony, which was locked, General Thomas saying, 'Wait a moment, I will get the key.' 'Never mind, General,' said Mr. Lincoln, 'Hubbard is used to jumping—he can scale that fence.' I climbed over, and for about an hour we conversed and watched the large crowd, the rebel flag being in sight on Arlington Heights. This was the last time I ever saw his face in life."

It was noted by those about Lincoln during his residence at the White House that he usually avoided speaking of himself as President or making any reference to the office which he held. He used some such roundabout phrase as "since I came into this place," instead of saying "since I became President." The war he usually spoke of as "this great trouble," and he almost never alluded to the enemy as "Confederates" or "the Confederate Government." He had an unconquerable reluctance to appear to lead public opinion, and often spoke of himself as the "attorney for the people." Once, however, when a Senator was urging on him a certain course which the President was not disposed to pursue, the Senator said, "You say you are the people's attorney. Now, you will admit that this course would be most popular." "But I am not going to let my client manage the case against my judgment," Lincoln replied quickly. "As long as I am attorney for the people I shall manage the case to the best of my ability. They will have a chance to put me out by and by if my management is not satisfactory."

The President was so tormented by visitors seeking interviews for every sort of frivolous and impertinent matter, that he resorted sometimes, in desperation, to curious and effective inventions to rid himself of the intolerable nuisance. At one time, when he was importuned by some influential people to interfere to prevent the punishment of certain persons convicted of fraudulent dealings with the government—a class of cases too common at that time—the President wrote Secretary Welles that he desired to see the records of the case before it was disposed of. Upon Mr. Welles calling upon him with the desired information, the President said, as if by way of apology, "There was no way to get rid of the crowd that was upon me but by sending you a note." On another occasion, when he had been quite ill, and therefore less inclined than usual to listen to these bores, one of them had just seated himself for a long visit, when the President's physician happened to enter the room, and Lincoln said, holding out his hands, "Doctor, what are these blotches?" "That's varioloid, or mild small-pox," said the doctor. "They're all over me. It is contagious, I believe," said Lincoln. "Very contagious, indeed!" replied the doctor. "Well, I can't stop, Mr. Lincoln; I just called to see how you were," said the visitor. "Oh, don't be in a hurry, sir!" placidly remarked the Executive. "Thank you, sir; I'll call again," replied the visitor, executing a masterly retreat from the White House. "Some people," said the President, looking after him, "said they could not take very well to my proclamation; but now, I am happy to say, I have *something that everybody can take.*"

Among the innumerable nuisances and "cranks" who called on Lincoln at the White House, were the many who sought to win his favor by claiming to have been the first to suggest his nomination as President. One of these claimants, who was the editor of a weekly paper published in a little village in Missouri, called one day, and was admitted to Lincoln's presence. He at once began explaining that he was the man who first suggested Lincoln's name for the Presidency, and pulling from his pocket an old, worn, defaced copy of his paper, exhibited to the President an item on the subject. "Do you really think," said Lincoln, "that announcement was the occasion of my nomination?" "Certainly," said the editor, "the suggestion was so opportune that it was at once taken up by other papers, and the result was your nomination and election." "Ah, well," said Lincoln, with a sigh, and assuming a rather gloomy countenance, "I am glad to see you and to know this; but you will have to excuse me, I am just going to the War Department to see Mr. Stanton." "Well," said the editor, "I will walk over with you." The

President, with that apt good nature so characteristic of him, took up his hat and said, "Come along." When they reached the door of the Secretary's office, Mr. Lincoln turned to his companion and said, "I shall have to see Mr. Stanton alone, and you must excuse me," and taking him by the hand he continued, "Good-bye. I hope you will feel perfectly easy about having nominated me; don't be troubled about it; *I forgive you.*"

A gentleman who, after the dreadful disaster at Fredericksburg, called at the White House with news direct from the front, says that Lincoln appeared so overwhelmed with grief that he was led to remark, "I heartily wish I might be a welcome messenger of good news instead,—that I could tell you how to conquer or get rid of these rebellious States." Looking up quickly, with a marked change of expression, Lincoln said: "That reminds me of two boys in Illinois who took a short cut across an orchard, and did not become aware of the presence of a vicious dog until it was too late to reach either fence. One was spry enough to escape the attack by climbing a tree; but the other started around the tree, with the dog in hot pursuit, until by making smaller circles than it was possible for his pursuer to make, he gained sufficiently to grasp the dog's tail, and held with desperate grip until nearly exhausted, when he hailed his companion and called to him to come down. 'What for?' said the boy. 'I want you to help me let this dog go.' If I could only let them go!" said the President, in conclusion; "but that is the trouble. I am compelled to hold on to them and make them stay."

In speaking of Lincoln's fortitude under his trials and sufferings, Mrs. Harriet Beecher Stowe wrote: "Although we believe he has never made any religious profession, we see evidence that in passing through this dreadful national crisis he has been forced by the very anguish of the struggle to look upward, where any rational creature must look for support. No man has suffered more and deeper, albeit with a dry, weary, patient pain, that seemed to some like insensibility. 'Whichever way it ends,' he said to the writer, 'I have the impression that I sha'n't last long after it's over.' After the dreadful repulse of Fredericksburg, his heavy eyes and worn and weary air told how our reverses wore upon him; and yet there was a never-failing fund of patience at bottom that sometimes rose to the surface in some droll, quaint saying or story, that forced a laugh even from himself."

The care and sorrow which Lincoln was called upon to endure in the responsibilities of his high position graved their melancholy marks on each feature of his face. He was a changed man. A pathetic picture of his appearance at this time is given by his old friend, Noah Brooks, whose description of him as he appeared in 1856, on the stump in Ogle County, has already been given a place in these pages. "I did not see Lincoln again," says Mr. Brooks, "until 1862, when I went to Washington as a newspaper correspondent from California. When Lincoln was on the stump in 1856, his face, though naturally sallow, had a rosy flush. His eyes were full and bright, and he was in the fulness of health and vigor. I shall never forget the shock which the sight of him gave me six years later in 1862, I took it for granted that he had forgotten the young man whom he had met five or six times during the Frémont and Dayton Campaign. He was now President, and was, like Brutus, 'vexed with many cares.' The change which a few years had made was simply appalling. His whiskers had grown and had given additional cadaverousness to his face as it appeared to me. The light seemed to have gone out of his eyes, which were sunken far under his enormous brows. But there was over his whole face an expression of sadness, and a far-away look in the eyes, which were utterly unlike the Lincoln of other days. I was intensely disappointed. I confess that I was so pained that I could almost have shed tears."

CHAPTER XXIII

Of the two sons left to Lincoln after the death of Willie in 1862, Robert, the older, was a student in Harvard College until appointed to service on the staff of General Grant; and "Little Tad," or Thomas, the youngest, was the only one remaining in the White House during the last hard years. He was ten years old in 1863, a bright and lovable child, with whom his father was associated in constant and affectionate companionship. The boy was much with him in his walks and journeys about Washington, and even in his visits to the army in the field. The father would often gain a brief respite from his heavy cares by sharing in the sports and frolics of the light-hearted boy, who was a general favorite at the White House, where he was free to go and come at will. No matter who was with the President, or how intently he might be absorbed, little Tad was always welcome. "It was an impressive and affecting sight," says Mr. Carpenter, an inmate of the White House for several months, "to see the burdened President lost for the time being in the affectionate parent, as he would take the little fellow in his arms upon the withdrawal of visitors, and caress him with all the fondness of a mother for the babe upon her bosom." Hon. W.D. Kelley, a member of Congress at that time, says: "I think no father ever loved his children more fondly than he. The President never seemed grander in my sight than when, stealing upon him in the evening, I would find him with a book open before him, with little Tad beside him. There were, of course, a great many curious books sent to him, and it seemed to be one of the special delights of his life to open those books at a time when his boy could stand beside him, and they could talk as he turned over the pages, the father thus giving to the son a portion of that care and attention of which he was ordinarily deprived by the heavy duties pressing upon him." Tad lived to be eighteen years old, dying in Chicago in 1871. It was well said of him that he "gave to the sad and solemn White House the only comic relief it knew."

When President Lincoln visited General Hooker's headquarters with the Army of the Potomac, just before the battle of Chancellorsville, little Tad went with him, and rode with his father and General Hooker through the grand reviews that were held. "Over hill and dale," says a member of the Presidential party, "dashed the brilliant cavalcade of the General-in-Chief, surrounded by a company of officers in gay attire and sparkling with gold lace, the party being escorted by the Philadelphia Lancers, a showy troop of soldiers. In the midst, or at the head, rose and fell, as the horses galloped afar, the form of Lincoln, conspicuous by his height and his tall black hat. And ever on the flanks of the hurrying column flew, like a flag or banneret, Tad's little gray riding-cloak. The soldiers soon learned of Tad's presence in the army, and wherever he went on horseback he easily divided the honors with his father. The men cheered and shouted and waved their hats when they saw the dear face and tall figure of the good President, then the best-beloved man in the world; but to these men of war, far away from home and children, the sight of that fresh-faced and laughing boy seemed an inspiration. They cheered like mad."

There were various phases of Lincoln's character, as manifested during his life in the White House, that afford material for an interesting study. It has been said of him that he lacked imagination. This was certainly not one of the faculties of his mind which had been largely cultivated. He relied more upon the exercise of reason and logic, in all his intellectual processes, than upon fancy or imagination. Still, there are often striking figures of speech to be met with in his writings, and he had a great fondness for poetry and music. He had studied Shakespeare diligently in his youth, and portions of the plays he repeated with singular accuracy. He had a special liking for the minor poems of Thomas Hood and of Oliver Wendell Holmes. Dr. Holmes, writing in July, 1885, says that of all the tributes received by him, the one of which he was most proud was from "good Abraham Lincoln," who had a great liking for the poem of "The Last Leaf," and "repeated it from memory to Governor Andrew, as the Governor himself told me." Mr. Arnold says: "He had a great love for poetry and eloquence, and his taste and judgment were excellent. Next to Shakespeare among the poets, his favorite was Burns. There was a lecture of his upon Burns full of favorite quotations and sound criticisms." His musical tastes, says Mr. Brooks, who knew him well, "were simple and uncultivated, his choice being old airs, songs, and ballads, among which the plaintive Scotch songs were best liked. 'Annie Laurie,' 'Mary of Argyle,' and especially 'Auld Robin Gray,' never lost their charm for him; and all songs which had for their theme the rapid flight of time, decay, the recollections of early days, were sure to make a deep impression. The song which he liked best, above all others, was one called 'Twenty Years Ago'—a simple air, the words to which are supposed to be uttered by a man who revisits the playground of his youth. I remember that one night at the White House, when a few ladies were with the family, singing at the piano-forte, he asked for a little song in which the writer describes his sensations when revisiting the scenes of his boyhood, dwelling mournfully on the vanished joys and the delightful associations of forty years ago. It is not likely that there was much in Lincoln's lost youth that he would wish to recall; but there was a certain melancholy and half-morbid strain in that song which struck a responsive chord in his heart. The lines sank into his memory, and I remember that he quoted them, as if to himself, long afterward."

Lincoln's memory was extraordinarily retentive, and he seemed, without conscious effort, to have stored in his mind almost every whimsical or ludicrous narrative which he had read or heard. "On several occasions," says Mr. Brooks, "I have held in my hand a printed slip while he was repeating its contents to somebody else, and the precision with which he delivered every word was marvellous." He was fond of the writings of "Orpheus C. Kerr" and "Petroleum V. Nasby," who were famous humorists at the time of the Civil War; and he amused himself and others in the darkest hours by quoting passages from these now forgotten authors. Nasby's letter from "Wingert's Corners, Ohio," on the threatening prospects of a migration of the negroes from the South, and the President's "evident intenshun of colonizin' on 'em in the North," he especially relished. After rehearsing a portion of this letter to his guests at the Soldiers' Home one evening, a sedate New England gentleman expressed surprise that he could find time for memorizing such things. "Oh," said Lincoln, "I don't. If I like a thing, it *just sticks* after once reading it or hearing it." He once recited a long and doleful ballad, something like "Vilikins and his Dinah," the production of a rural Kentucky bard, and when he had finished he added with a laugh, "I don't believe I have thought of that before for forty years." Mr. Arnold testifies that "although his reading was not extensive, yet his memory was so retentive and so ready that in history, poetry, and in general literature, few if any marked any deficiency. As an illustration of the powers of his memory, may be related the following: A gentleman called at the White House one day, and introduced to him two officers serving in the army, one a Swede and the other a Norwegian. Immediately he repeated, to their delight, a poem of some eight or ten verses descriptive of Scandinavian scenery, and an old Norse legend. He said he had read the poem in a newspaper some years before, and liked it, but it had passed out of his memory until their visit had recalled it. The two books which he read most were the Bible and Shakespeare. With these he was perfectly familiar. From the Bible, as has before been stated, he quoted frequently, and he read it daily, while Shakespeare was his constant companion. He took a copy with him almost always when travelling, and read it at leisure moments."

Lincoln was never ashamed to confess the deficiencies in his early education. A distinguished party, comprising George Thompson, the English anti-slavery orator, Rev. John Pierpont, Oliver Johnson, and Hon.

Lewis Clephane, once called upon him, and during the conversation Mr. Pierpont turned to Mr. Thompson and repeated a Latin quotation from the classics. Mr. Lincoln, leaning forward in his chair, looked from one to the other inquiringly, and then remarked, with a smile, "*Which*, I suppose you are both aware, *I* do not understand."

While Edwin Forrest was playing an engagement at Ford's Theatre, Mr. Carpenter spoke to the President one day of the actor's fine interpretation of the character of Richelieu, and advised him to witness the performance. "Who wrote the play?" asked the President of Mr. Carpenter. "Bulwer," was the reply. "Ah!" he rejoined; "well, I knew Bulwer wrote novels, but I did not know he was a play-writer also. It may seem somewhat strange to say," he continued, "but *I never read an entire novel in my life*. I once commenced 'Ivanhoe,' but never finished it."

Among the few diversions which Lincoln allowed himself in Washington was an occasional visit to the theater to witness a representation of some good play by a favorite actor. He felt the necessity of some relaxation from the terrible strain of anxiety and care; and while seated behind the screen in a box at the theatre he was secure from the everlasting importunities of politicians and office-seekers. He could forget himself and his problems while watching the scenes on the mimic stage before him. He enjoyed the renditions of Booth with great zest; yet after witnessing "The Merchant of Venice" he remarked on the way home: "It was a good performance, but I had a thousand times rather read it at home, if it were not for Booth's playing. A farce or a comedy is best *played*; a tragedy is best *read* at home." He was much pleased one night with Mr. McCullough 's delineation of the character of "Edgar," which the actor played in support of Edwin Forrest's "Lear." He wished to convey his approval to the young actor, and asked Mr. Brooks, his companion at the moment, with characteristic simplicity, "Do you suppose he would come to the box if we sent word?" Mr. McCullough was summoned, and, standing at the door of the box in his stage attire, received the thanks of the President, accompanied with words of discriminating praise for the excellence of his delineation.

With his keen sense of humor, Lincoln appreciated to the utmost the inimitable presentation of "Falstaff" by a well-known actor of the time. His desire to accord praise wherever it was merited led him to express his admiration in a note to the actor. An interchange of slight civilities followed, ending at last in a singular situation. Entering the President's office late one evening, Mr. Brooks noticed the actor sitting in the waiting-room. Lincoln inquired anxiously if there were anyone outside. On being told, he said, half sadly, almost desperately, "Oh, I can't see him; I can't see him! I was in hopes he had gone away." Then he added, "Now, this illustrates the difficulty of having pleasant friends in this place. You know I liked him as an actor, and that I wrote to tell him so. He sent me a book, and there I thought the matter would end. He is a master of his place in the profession, I suppose, and well fixed in it. But just because we had a little friendly correspondence, such as any two men might have, he wants something. What do you suppose he wants?" I could not guess, and Lincoln added, "Well, he wants to be consul at London. Oh, dear!"

Lincoln was not a ready writer, and when preparing documents or speeches of special importance he altered and elaborated his sentences with patient care. His public utterances were so widely reported and so mercilessly discussed that he acquired caution in expressing himself without due preparation. It is stated, on what seems sufficient authority, that his Gettysburg speech, brief and simple as it is, was rewritten many times before it finally met his approval. He began also to be guarded in responding to demands for impromptu speeches, which were constantly being called for. Mr. Brooks relates that "once, being notified that he was to be serenaded, just after some notable military or political event, he asked me to come to dinner, 'so as to be on hand and see the fun afterward,' as he said. He excused himself as soon as we had dined, and while the bands were playing, the crowds cheering and the rockets bursting outside the house, he made his reappearance in the parlor with a roll of manuscript in his hand. Perhaps noticing a look of surprise on my face, he said, 'I know what you are thinking about. You think it mighty queer that an old stump-speaker like myself should not be able to address a crowd like this outside without a written speech. But you must remember that in a certain way I am talking to the country, and I have to be mighty careful. Now, the last time I made an off-hand speech, in answer to a serenade, I used the phrase, as applied to the rebels, "turned tail and ran." Some very nice Boston folks, I am grieved to hear, were very much outraged by that phrase, which they thought improper. So I resolved to make no more impromptu speeches if I could help it.'"

In all Lincoln's writings, even his most important state papers, his chief desire was to make himself clearly understood by the common reader. He had a great aversion to what he called "machine writing," and used the fewest words possible to express his meaning. He never hesitated to employ a homely expression when it suited his purpose. In his first message the phrase "sugar-coated" occurred; and when it was printed, Mr. Defrees, the Public Printer, being on familiar terms with the President, ventured an objection to the phrase—suggesting that Lincoln was not now preparing a campaign document or delivering a stump speech in Illinois, but constructing an important state paper that would go down historically to all coming time; and that therefore he did not consider the phrase "sugar-coated" as entirely a becoming and dignified one. "Well, Defrees," replied Lincoln, good-naturedly, "if you think the time will ever come when the people will not understand what 'sugar-coated' means, I'll alter it; otherwise, I think I'll let it go."

On the same subject, Mrs. Harriet Beecher Stowe says: "Our own politicians were somewhat shocked with his state papers at first. 'Why not let *us* make them a little more conventional, and file them to a classical pattern? ' 'No, ' was his reply, 'I shall write them myself. *The people will understand them.*' 'But this or that form of expression is not elegant, not classical.' '*The people will understand it,*' has been his invariable reply. And whatever may be said of his state papers as compared with the classic standards, it has been a fact that they have always been wonderfully well understood by the people, and that since the time of Washington the state papers of no President have more controlled the popular mind. One reason for this is that they have been informal and undiplomatic. They have more resembled a father's talk to his children than a state paper. They have had that relish and smack of the soil that appeal to the simple human heart and head, which is a greater power in writing than the most artful devices of rhetoric. Lincoln might well say with the apostle, 'But though I be rude in speech, yet not in knowledge, but we have been thoroughly *made manifest among you* in all things. ' His rejection of what is called 'fine writing ' was as deliberate as St. Paul 's, and for the same reason— because he felt that he was speaking on a subject which must be made clear to the lowest intellect, though it should fail to captivate the highest. But we say of Lincoln's writing, that for all true manly purposes there are passages in his state papers that could not be better put; they are absolutely perfect. They are brief, condensed, intense, and with a power of insight and expression which make them worthy to be inscribed in letters of gold."

Hon. William J. Bryan, certainly a competent judge of oratory, says of Lincoln as an orator: "Brevity is the soul of wit, and a part of Lincoln's reputation for wit lies in his ability to condense a great deal into a few words. He was epigrammatic. His Gettysburg speech is the world's model in eloquence, elegance, and condensation. He was apt in illustration—no one more so. A simple story or simile drawn from every-day life flashed before his hearers the argument that he wanted to present. He made frequent use of Bible language, and of illustrations drawn from Holy Writ. It is said that when he was preparing his Springfield speech of 1858 he spent hours in trying to find language that would express the central idea—that a republic could not permanently endure part free and part slave. Finally a Bible passage flashed through his mind, and he exclaimed, 'I have found it—*a house divided against itself cannot stand.*' Probably no other Bible passage ever exerted as much influence as this one in the settlement of a great controversy."

Lincoln was a tireless worker, and delegated no duties to others which he could perform himself. His health seemed to bear the strain of his terrible burdens wonderfully well. There are but few references anywhere to his being incapacitated by illness. One such reference occurs in Welles's Diary, dated March 14, 1865: "The President was somewhat indisposed, but not seriously ill. The members [of the Cabinet] met in his bedroom." His correspondence was extensive and burdensome, and as a rule he wrote his most important letters with his own hand, frequently going to the trouble of taking copies, which were filed with careful order in a cabinet, the interior of which was divided into pigeon-holes. These pigeon-holes, as Mr. Brooks tells us, "were lettered in alphabetical order, but a few were devoted to individuals. Horace Greeley had a pigeon-hole by himself; so did each of several generals who wrote often to him. One compartment, labelled 'W. & W.,' excited much curiosity, but I never asked what it meant, and one night, being sent to the cabinet for a letter which the President wanted, he said, 'I see you looking at my "W. & W." Can you guess what that stands for?' Of course it was useless to guess. 'Well,' said he, with a roguish twinkle of the eye, 'that's Weed and Wood—Thurlow and Fernandy.' Then he added, with an indescribable chuckle, 'That's a pair of 'em.' When asked why he did not have a letter-book and copying-press, he said, 'A letter-book might be easily stolen and carried off, but that stock of filed letters would be a *back-load.*'"

A lady who once rode with Lincoln, in the Presidential carriage, to the Soldiers' Home, gives some interesting details concerning his knowledge of woodcraft. "Around the 'Home,'" says this lady, "grows every variety of tree, particularly of the evergreen class. Their branches brushed into the carriage as we passed along, and left with us that pleasant woodsy smell belonging to fresh leaves. One of the ladies, catching a bit of green from one of these intruding branches, said it was cedar, and another thought it spruce. 'Let me discourse on a theme I understand,' said the President. 'I know all about trees, by right of being a backwoodsman. I'll show you the difference between spruce, pine, and cedar, and this shred of green, which is neither one nor the other, but a kind of illegitimate cypress.' He then proceeded to gather specimens of each, and explain the distinctive formation of foliage belonging to every species. 'Trees,' he said, 'are as deceptive in their likeness to one another as are certain classes of men, amongst whom none but a physiognomist's eye can detect dissimilar moral features until events have developed them. Do you know it would be a good thing if in all the schools proposed and carried out by the improvement of modern thinkers, we could have *a school of events?*' 'A school of events?' repeated the lady addressed. 'Yes,' he continued, 'since it is only by that active development that character and ability can be tested. Understand me, I now mean men, not trees; *they* can be tried, and an analysis of their strength obtained less expensive to life and human interests than man's. What I say now is a mere whim, you know; but when I speak of a school of events, I mean one in which, before entering real life, students might pass through the mimic vicissitudes and situations that are necessary to bring out their powers and mark the calibre to which they are assigned. Thus, one could select from the graduates an invincible soldier, equal to any position, with no such word as fail; a martyr to right, ready to give up life in the cause; a politician too cunning to be outwitted; and so on. These things have all to be tried, and their sometime failure creates confusion as well as disappointment. There is no more dangerous or expensive analysis than that which consists of *trying a man.*'"

Among Lincoln's callers one Sunday evening, was the distinguished scientist Louis Agassiz. The two men were somewhat alike in their simple, shy, and unpretending nature, and at first felt their way with each other like two bashful schoolboys. Lincoln began conversation by saying to Agassiz, "I never knew how to pronounce your name properly; won't you give me a little lesson at that, please?" Then he asked if the name were of French or Swiss derivation, to which the Professor replied that it was partly of each. That led to a discussion of different languages, the President speaking several words in different languages which had the same root as similar words in our own tongue; then he illustrated that by one or two anecdotes. But he soon returned to his gentle cross-examination of Agassiz, and found out how the Professor studied, how he composed, and how he delivered his lectures; how he found different tastes in his audiences in different portions of the country. When afterwards asked why he put such questions to his learned visitor, he said, "Why, what we got from him isn't printed in the books; the other things are." But Lincoln did not do all the questioning. In his turn, Agassiz asked Lincoln if he had ever engaged in lecturing. Lincoln gave the outline of a lecture, which he had partly written years before, to show the origin of inventions and prove that there is nothing new under the sun. "I think I can show," said he, "at least, in a fanciful way, that all the modern inventions were known centuries ago." Agassiz begged that Lincoln would finish the lecture sometime. Lincoln replied that he had the manuscript somewhere in his papers, "and," said he, "when I get out of this place, I'll finish it up, perhaps."

So great was Lincoln's magnanimity, and so keen his sense of justice, that he never allowed personal considerations to influence his official acts. It is probably true that it was easy for him to forgive an injury; but he was incapable of using his position as President to gratify his private resentments. It was once represented to him that a recent appointee to an important office had been bitterly opposed to him politically. "I suppose," said he, "the Judge did behave pretty ugly; but that wouldn't make him any less fit for this place, and I have a Scriptural authority for appointing him. You recollect that while the Lord on Mount Sinai was getting out a commission for Aaron, that same Aaron was at the foot of the mountain making a false god, a golden calf, for the people to worship; yet Aaron got his commission, you know." At another time, when remonstrated with upon the appointment to place of one of his former opponents, he said: "Nobody will deny that he is a first-rate man for the place, and I am bound to see that his opposition to me personally shall not interfere with my giving the people a good officer." And on another similar occasion, when remonstrated with by members of his Cabinet, he said: "Oh, I can't afford to punish every person who has seen fit to oppose my election. We want a competent man in this office, and I know of no one who could perform the duties better than the one proposed."

With all his self-abnegation, Lincoln could be stern when the occasion warranted it. As an illustration the following incident is related: An officer who had been cashiered from the service, forced himself several times into Lincoln's presence, to plead for a reversal of his sentence. Each time he read a long argument attempting to prove that he had received unjust treatment. The President listened to him patiently; but the facts, on their most favorable showing, did not seem to him to sanction his interference. In the last interview, the man became angry, and turning abruptly said: "Well, Mr. President, I see you are determined not to do me justice!" This was too much, even for the long-suffering Lincoln. Manifesting, however, no more feeling than that indicated by a slight compression of the lips, he quietly arose, laid down a package of papers he held in his hands, and then, suddenly seizing the disgraced officer by the coat collar, he marched him forcibly to the door, saying, as he ejected him into the passage, "Sir, I give you fair warning never to show yourself in this room again. I can bear censure, but not insult!" In a whining tone the man begged for his papers, which he had dropped. "Begone, sir," said the President, "your papers will be sent to you. I wish never to see your face again!"

Much has been said about Lincoln's views on religion. Like many other great men, he was not what might technically be called a Christian. He was a religious man in spirit and by nature; yet he never joined a church. Mrs.

Lincoln says that he had no religious faith, in the usual acceptation of the word, but that religion was a sort of poetry in his nature. "Twice during his life," she said, "he seemed especially to think about it. Once was when our boy Willie died. Once—and this time he thought of it more deeply—was when he went to Gettysburg." But whatever his inner thoughts may have been, no man on earth had a firmer faith in Providence than Abraham Lincoln. Perhaps he did not himself know just where he stood. He believed in God—in immortality. He did not believe in eternal punishment, but was confident of rest and peace after this life was over. He may not have felt certain of the divine origin of all parts of the Bible, but he valued its precepts, and his whole life gave evidence of faith in a higher power than that of man. Mr. Nicolay, his secretary, testifies that "his nature was deeply religious, but he belonged to no denomination; he had faith in the eternal justice and boundless mercy of Providence, and made the Golden Rule of Christ his practical creed." And Dr. Phillips Brooks, in an eloquent and expressive passage, calls him "Shepherd of the people—that old name that the best rulers ever craved. What ruler ever won it like this President of ours? He fed us faithfully and truly. He fed us with counsel when we were in doubt, with inspiration when we sometimes faltered, with caution when we would be rash, with calm, clear, trustful cheerfulness through many an hour when our hearts were dark. He fed hungry souls all over the country with sympathy and consolation. He spread before the whole land feasts of great duty and devotion and patriotism on which the land grew strong. He fed us with solemn, solid truths. He taught us the sacredness of government, the wickedness of treason. He made our souls glad and vigorous with the love of Liberty that was in his. He showed us how to love truth, and yet be charitable; how to hate wrong and all oppression, and yet not treasure one personal injury or insult. He fed all his people, from the highest to the lowest, from the most privileged down to the most enslaved. 'He fed them with a faithful and true heart.'"

CHAPTER XXIV

It is impossible, without a close study of the inner history of the war and of the acts of the administration, to conceive of the harassing and baffling difficulties which beset President Lincoln's course in every direction, and of the jealous, narrow, and bitter opposition which his more important measures provoked. As the struggle advanced he found in his front a solid and defiant South, behind him a divided and distrustful North. What might be called the party of action and of extreme measures developed a sharp hostility to the President. He would not go fast enough to suit them; they thought him disposed to compromise. They began by criticizing his policy, and his methods of prosecuting the war; from this they passed rapidly to a criticism of the President himself. In the affectionate admiration felt for him now, people have forgotten how weak and poor and craven they found him then. So far had this disapproval and hostility gone, that early in 1863 we find Mr. Greeley searching everywhere for a fitting successor to Lincoln for the Presidency at the next term. There were but few men in high official station in Washington who at that time unqualifiedly sustained him. In the House of Representatives there were but two members who could make themselves heard, who stood actively by him. This matter, long since forgotten, must be recalled to show clearly the President's straits, and his action and bearing amidst his difficulties. It should be remembered that party lines, which disappeared at the beginning of the war, were again clearly drawn; and the Democratic wing of Congress, under the leadership of Vallandigham of Ohio, actively opposed many of the necessary measures for the prosecution of the war. The cry had already been raised in Congress, "The South cannot be subjugated"; and every fresh disaster to the national arms was hailed as proof of the assertion.

The effect of this abuse and opposition was exceedingly painful to Lincoln. He said: "I have been caused more anxiety, I have *passed more sleepless nights,* on account of the temper and attitude of the Democratic party in the North regarding the suppression of the rebellion than by the rebels in the South. I have always had faith that our armies would ultimately and completely triumph; but these enemies in the North cause me a great deal of anxiety and apprehension. Can it be that there are opposing opinions in the North as to the necessity of putting down this rebellion? How can men hesitate a moment as to the duty of the Government to restore its authority in every part of the country? It is incomprehensible to me that men living in their quiet homes under the protection of laws, in possession of their property, can sympathize with and give aid and comfort to those who are doing their utmost to overthrow that Government which makes life and everything they possess valuable."

In January, 1863, a party of distinguished gentlemen from Boston visited the national capital, in order to confer with the President on the workings of the emancipation policy. They made the visit chiefly at the suggestion of Ralph Waldo Emerson, who during all the trying years of the war never lost faith in Lincoln's honesty and sense of justice. Secretary Stanton made no secret of his opposition to these gentlemen, who were spoken of rather slightingly as "that Boston set." The "Boston set" were uncompromising abolitionists, and nothing would satisfy them but immediate and aggressive measures for enforcing the policy of emancipation. As it was the President's instinct to feel his way slowly in pushing on the great measures necessary to the safe guidance of the nation in its perilous crisis, they were naturally dissatisfied with his conservative methods and tendencies. The visitors— including Senator Wilson, Wendell Phillips, Francis W. Bird, Elizur Wright, J.H. Stephenson, George L. Stearns, Oakes Ames, and Moncure D. Conway—called on the President one Sunday evening, at the White House. "The President met us," says Mr. Conway, "laughing like a boy, saying that in the morning one of his children had come to inform him that the cat had kittens, and now another had just announced that the dog had puppies, and the White House was in a decidedly sensational state. Some of our party looked a little glum at this hilarity; but it was pathetic to see the change in the President's face when he presently resumed his burden of care. We were introduced by Senator Wilson, who began to speak of us severally, when Mr. Lincoln said he knew perfectly who we were, and requested us to be seated. Nothing could be more gracious than his manner, or more simple. The conversation was introduced by Wendell Phillips, who, with all his courtesy, expressed our gratitude and joy at the Proclamation of Emancipation, and asked how it seemed to be working. The President said that he had not expected much from it at first, and consequently had not been disappointed; he had hoped, and still hoped, that something would come of it after awhile. Phillips then alluded to the deadly hostility which the proclamation had naturally excited in pro-slavery quarters, and gently hinted that the Northern people, now generally anti-slavery, were not satisfied that it was being honestly carried out by all of the nation's agents and Generals in the South. 'My own impression, Mr. Phillips,' said the President, 'is that the masses of the country generally are dissatisfied chiefly at our lack of military successes. Defeat and failure in the field make everything seem wrong.' His face was now clouded, and his next words were somewhat bitter. 'Most of us here present,' he said, 'have been nearly all our lives working in minorities, and many have got into a habit of being dissatisfied.' Several of those present having deprecated this, the President said, 'At any rate, it has been very rare that an opportunity of "running" this administration has been lost.' To this Mr. Phillips answered, in his sweetest voice: 'If we see this administration earnestly working to free the country from slavery and its rebellion, we will show you how we can "run" it into another four years of power.' The President's good humor was restored by this, and he said: 'Oh, Mr. Phillips, I have ceased to have any personal feeling or expectation in that matter—I do not say I never had any—so abused and borne upon as I have been.' ... On taking our leave we expressed to the President our thanks for his kindly reception, and for his attention to statements of which some were naturally not welcome. The President bowed graciously at this, and, after saying he was happy to have met gentlemen known to him by distinguished services, if not personally, and glad to listen to their views, added, 'I must bear this load which the country has intrusted to me as well as I can, and do the best I can with it.'"

To another self-constituted delegation—this time from the West—who called at the White House one day, excited and troubled about some of the commissions or omissions of the administration, the President, after hearing them patiently, replied: "Gentlemen, suppose all the property you were worth was in gold, and you had put it in the hands of Blondin to carry across the Niagara river on a rope; would you shake the cable, or keep shouting out to him, 'Blondin, stand up a little straighter!—Blondin, stoop a little more—go a little faster—lean a little more to the north—lean a little more to the south'? No! you would hold your breath as well as your tongue, and keep your hands off until he was safe over. The Government is carrying an immense weight. Untold treasures are in their hands. They are doing the very best they can. Don't badger them. Keep silence, and we'll get you safe across."

In 1863 the Government, following logically the policy of the Emancipation act, began the experiment of introducing colored soldiers into our armies. This caused not only intense anger at the South, but much doubt and dissatisfaction at the North. To discuss some of the practical and difficult questions growing out of this measure, Frederick Douglass, the most distinguished representative of the race which America had so long held in chains, was presented to the President. The account of the conference, given by Douglass, is singularly interesting. He says: "I was never more quickly or more completely put at ease in the presence of a great man than in that of Abraham Lincoln. He was seated, when I entered, in a low arm-chair, with his feet extended on the floor, surrounded by a large number of documents and several busy secretaries. The room bore the marks of business, and the persons in it, the President included, appeared to be much overworked and tired. Long lines of care were already deeply written on Mr. Lincoln's brow, and his strong face, full of earnestness, lighted up as soon as my name was mentioned. As I approached and was introduced to him, he arose and extended his hand, and bade me welcome. I at once felt myself in the presence of an honest man—one whom I could love, honor, and trust, without reserve or doubt. Proceeding to tell him who I was and what I was doing, he promptly but kindly stopped me, saying: 'I know who you are, Mr. Douglass; Mr. Seward has told me all about you. Sit down; I am glad to see you.' I urged, among other things, the necessity of granting the colored soldiers equal pay and promotion with white soldiers, and retaliation for colored prisoners killed by the enemy. Mr. Lincoln admitted the justice of my demand for equal pay and promotion of colored soldiers, but on the matter of retaliation he differed from me entirely. I shall never forget the benignant expression of his face, the tearful look of his eye, and the quiver in his voice, when he deprecated a resort to retaliatory measures. 'Once begun,' said he, 'I do not know where such a measure would stop.' He said he could not take men out and kill them in cold blood for what was done by others. If he could get hold of the persons who were guilty of killing the colored prisoners in cold blood, the case would be different; but he could not kill the innocent for the guilty. Afterwards we discussed the means most desirable to be employed outside the army to induce the slaves in the rebel States to come within the Federal lines. The increasing opposition to the war in the North, and the mad cry against it because it was being made an abolition war, alarmed Mr. Lincoln, and made him apprehensive that a peace might be forced upon him which would leave still in slavery all who had not come within our lines. What he wanted was to make his proclamation as effective as possible in the event of such a peace. He said, in a regretful tone, 'The slaves are not coming into our lines as rapidly and numerously as I had hoped.' I replied that the slaveholders knew how to keep such things from their slaves, and probably very few knew of his proclamation. 'Well,' he said, 'I want you to set about devising some means of making them acquainted with it, and for bringing them into our lines.' What he said showed a deeper moral conviction against slavery than I had ever seen before in anything spoken or written by him. I listened with the deepest interest and profoundest satisfaction, and, at his suggestion, agreed to undertake the organizing of a band of scouts, composed of colored men, whose business should be, somewhat after the original plan of John Brown, to go into the rebel States beyond the lines of our armies, carry the news of emancipation, and urge the slaves to come within our boundaries."

Frederick Douglass once remarked that Lincoln was one of the few white men he ever passed an hour with who failed to remind him in some way, before the interview terminated, that he was a negro. "He always impressed me as a strong, earnest man, having no time or disposition to trifle; grappling with all his might the work he had in hand. The expression of his face was a blending of suffering with patience and fortitude. Men called him homely, and homely he was; but it was manifestly a human homeliness. His eyes had in them the tenderness of motherhood, and his mouth and other features the highest perfection of a genuine manhood."

As though the political difficulties that beset President Lincoln in the first half of 1863 were not discouragement enough, they were attended by disheartening reverses to our arms. It will be remembered that on the removal of General McClellan from command of the Army of the Potomac, in November, 1862, General Burnside succeeded him. The change proved an unfortunate one. General Burnside was an earnest and gallant soldier, but was not equal to the vast responsibilities of his new position. It is said, to his credit, that he was three times offered the command of the Army of the Potomac, and three times he declined. Finally it was pressed upon him by positive orders, and he could no longer, without insubordination, refuse it. In addressing General Halleck, after his appointment, he said: "Had I been asked to take it, I should have declined; but being ordered, I cheerfully obey." After his fearful defeat at Fredericksburg (December 13, 1862), he said: "*The fault was mine.* The entire responsibility of failure must rest on my shoulders." By his manly and courageous bearing, and the strong sincerity of his character, he retained the respect and sympathy of the President and of the country. He immediately retired from command of the Army of the Potomac, which, under his brief leadership, had fought the most bloody and disastrous battle in its history.

General Joseph Hooker, the fourth commander of the heroic but unfortunate Army of the Potomac, was appointed to that position by President Lincoln in January, 1863. The two men had met briefly early in the war, when Hooker, then living in California, hastened to Washington to offer his services to the Government; but for some reason General Scott disliked him, and his offer was not accepted. After some months, Hooker, giving up the idea of getting a command, decided to return to California; but before leaving he called to pay his respects to the President. He was introduced as "Captain Hooker." The President, being pressed for time, was about to dismiss him with a few civil phrases; when, to his surprise, Hooker began the following speech: "Mr. President, my friend makes a mistake. I am not 'Captain Hooker,' but was once 'Lieutenant-Colonel Hooker' of the regular army. I was lately a farmer in California. Since the rebellion broke out I have been trying to get into the service; but I find I am not wanted. I am about to return home; but before going, I was anxious to pay my respects to you, and to express my wishes for your personal welfare and success in quelling this rebellion. And I want to say one word more. I was at Bull Run the other day, Mr. President, and it is no vanity in me to say *am a d——d sight better general than you had on that field.*" This was said, not in the tone of a braggart, but of a man who knew what he was talking about; and, as the President afterward said, he appeared at that moment as if perfectly able to make good his words. Lincoln seized his hand, making him sit down, and began an extended chat. The result was that Hooker did not return to California, but in a few weeks *Captain* Hooker was *Brigadier-General* Hooker. He served with distinction under McClellan in the Peninsular campaign and at Antietam, and commanded the right wing of the army at Fredericksburg. He had come to be known as "Fighting Joe Hooker," and was generally regarded as one of the most vigorous and efficient Generals of the Union army.

Such was the man who, in one of the darkest hours of the Union cause, was selected to lead once more the Army of the Potomac against the enemy. This army, since its defeat at Fredericksburg, had remained disorganized and ineffective. Its new commander, unlike his predecessor Burnside, was full of confidence. The President, made cautious by experience, deemed it his duty to accompany the appointment by some timely words of warning; and accordingly he addressed to General Hooker the following frank, manly, and judicious letter.

EXECUTIVE MANSION WASHINGTON, D.C.
January 26, 1863.

MAJOR-GENERAL HOOKER.

GENERAL:—I have placed you at the head of the Army of the Potomac. Of course, I have done this upon what appear to me to be sufficient reasons; and yet I think it best for you to know that there are some things in regard to which I am not satisfied with you. I believe you to be a brave and skilful soldier, which of course I like. I also believe that you do not mix politics with your profession, in which you are right. You have confidence in yourself, which is a valuable if not indispensable quality. You are ambitious, which, within reasonable bounds, does good rather than harm; but I think that during General Burnside's command of the army you have taken counsel with your ambition, and thwarted him as much as you could, in which you did a great wrong to the country and to a most meritorious and honorable brother officer. I have heard, in such a way as to believe it, of your recently saying that both the army and the Government needed a dictator. Of course, it was not for this, but in spite of it, that I have given you the command. Only those generals who gain success can be dictators. What I now ask from you is military success, and I will risk the dictatorship. The Government will support you to the utmost of its ability, which is neither more nor less than it has done and will do for all commanders. I much fear that the spirit which you have aided to infuse into the army, of criticizing their commander and withholding confidence from him, will now turn upon you. I shall assist you, as far as I can, to pull it down. Neither you nor Napoleon, if he were alive again, could get any good out of an army while such a spirit prevails in it. And now, beware of rashness. *Beware of rashness;* but with energy and sleepless vigilance, go forward and give us victories.

Yours very truly,
A. LINCOLN.

In all Lincoln's writings there are few things finer than this letter. In its candor and friendliness, its simplicity and deep wisdom, and its clearness of expression, it is almost perfect; and the President's deep solicitude for the safety of the army and anxiety for its success give a pathetic touch to the closing sentences. This solicitude found partial relief in a personal inspection of the Army of the Potomac, which was made in April, just before the battle of Chancellorsville, and occupied five or six days. The President was accompanied by Attorney-General Bates, Mrs. Lincoln, his son Tad, and Mr. Noah P. Brooks. The first night out was spent on the little steamer which conveyed the party to their destination. After all had retired to rest except the anxious President and one or two others, Lincoln gave utterance to his deep-seated apprehensions in the whispered query to his friend, "How many of our monitors will you wager are at the bottom of Charleston Harbor?" "I essayed," writes Mr. Brooks, "to give a cheerful view of the Charleston situation. But he would not be encouraged. He then went on to say that he did not believe that an attack by water on Charleston could ever possibly succeed. He talked a long time about his 'notions,' as he called them; and at General Halleck's headquarters next day, the first inquiries were for 'rebel papers,' which were usually brought in from the picket lines. These he examined with great anxiety, hoping that he might find an item of news from Charleston. One day, having looked all over a Richmond paper several times without finding a paragraph which he had been told was in it, he was mightily pleased to have it pointed out to him, and said, 'It is plain that newspapers are made for newspaper men; being only a layman, it was impossible for me to find that.'"

The out-door life, the constant riding, and the respite from the monstrous burdens at the capital, appeared to afford mental and physical benefit to the worn President. But in answer to a remark expressing this conviction, he replied sadly, "I don't know about 'the rest' as you call it. I suppose it is good for the body. But the tired part of me is *inside* and out of reach." "He rode a great deal," says Mr. Brooks, "while with the army, always preferring the saddle to the elegant ambulance which had been provided for him. He sat his horse well, but he rode hard, and during his stay I think he regularly used up at least one horse each day. Little Tad invariably followed in his father's train; and, mounted on a smaller horse, accompanied by an orderly, the youngster was a conspicuous figure, as his gray cloak flew in the wind while we hung on the flanks of Hooker and his generals."

General Hooker was now planning his great movement against Richmond, and talked freely of the matter with the President, In the course of a conversation, Lincoln casually remarked, "If you get to Richmond, General." But Hooker interrupted him with—"Excuse me, Mr. President, but there is no 'if' in the case. *I am going straight to Richmond, if I live!*" Later in the day, Lincoln, privately referring to this self-confidence of the General, said to Mr. Brooks, rather mournfully, "It is about the worst thing I have seen since I have been down here." In further illustration of Hooker's confidence in himself, Mr. Brooks says: "One night, Hooker and I being alone in his hut, the General standing with his back to the fireplace, alert, handsome, full of courage and confidence, said laughingly, 'The President says you know about that letter he wrote me on taking command.' I acknowledged that the President had read it to me. The General seemed to think that the advice was well-meant, but unnecessary. Then he added, with that charming assurance which became him so well, 'After I have been to Richmond, I am going to have that letter printed.'" But all that came of Hooker's confidence, after three months of elaborate preparation, was a grand forward movement into Virginia and another bloody and humiliating defeat for the heroic but unfortunate army under his command.

The first of May, 1863, the Army of the Potomac under Hooker met the Army of Northern Virginia under Lee and Jackson, near Chancellorsville, Virginia. It was here that Jackson executed his brilliant and successful flank movement around the Union right, ensuring a victory for his side but losing his own life. After a contest of several days, involving the fruitless sacrifice of thousands of gallant soldiers, Hooker's army fell back and recrossed the Rappahannock. [G]

The news of this fresh disaster was an almost stunning shock to President Lincoln. During the progress of the battle he was under a cruel strain of anxiety and suspense. Secretary Welles, who was with him a part of the time, says: "He had a feverish eagerness for facts; was constantly up and down, for nothing reliable came from the front." Mr. Noah Brooks relates that in company with an old friend of Lincoln's he was waiting in one of the family rooms of the White House. "A door opened and Lincoln appeared, holding an open telegram in his hand. The sight of his face and figure was frightful. He seemed stricken with death. Almost tottering to a chair, he sat down; and then I mechanically noticed that his face was of the same color as the wall behind him—not pale, not even sallow, but gray, like ashes. Extending the despatch to me, he said, with a hollow, far-off voice, 'Read it—news from the army.' The telegram was from General Butterfield, I think, then chief of staff to Hooker. It was very brief, simply saying that the Army of the Potomac had 'safely recrossed the Rappahannock,' and was now at its old position on the north bank of that stream. The President's friend, Dr. Henry, an old man and somewhat impressionable, burst into tears,—not so much, probably, at the news as on account of its effect upon Lincoln. The President regarded the old man for an instant with dry eyes, and said, '*What will the country say? Oh, what will the country say?*' He seemed hungry for consolation and cheer, and sat a little while talking about the failure. Yet it did not seem that he was disappointed so much for himself, but that he thought the country would be."

Lincoln's anxiety regarding the effect at the North of these repeated reverses was not without sufficient cause. Aside from those who were positively opposed to the war, the loyal people were wearying of the useless slaughter, the unavailing struggles, of the gallant soldiers. The growing distrust of the capacity of their military leaders was also keenly felt. The feeling of that time is so well expressed in a stirring poem entitled "Wanted, a Man," written by Mr. E.C. Stedman, that it is given place here. It has an additional personal interest connected with President Lincoln in the fact that he was so impressed with the piece that he read it aloud to his assembled Cabinet.

> Back from the trebly crimsoned field
> Terrible words are thunder-tost;
> Full of the wrath that will not yield,

Full of revenge for battles lost!
Hark to their echo, as it crost
The Capital, making faces wan:
End this murderous holocaust;
Abraham Lincoln, give us a MAN!

Give us a man of God's own mould,
Born to marshal his fellow-men;
One whose fame is not bought and sold
At the stroke of a politician's pen;
Give us the man of thousands ten,
Fit to do as well as to plan;
Give us a rallying-cry, and then,
Abraham Lincoln, give us a MAN!

No leader to shirk the boasting foe,
And to march and countermarch our brave
Till they fall like ghosts in the marshes low,
And swamp-grass covers each nameless grave;
Nor another, whose fatal banners wave
Aye in Disaster's shameful van;
Nor another, to bluster, and lie, and rave, —
Abraham Lincoln, give us a MAN!

Hearts are mourning in the North,
While the sister rivers seek the main,
Red with our life-blood flowing forth —
Who shall gather it up again?
Though we march to the battle-plain
Firmly as when the strife began,
Shall all our offerings be in vain? —
Abraham Lincoln, give us a MAN!

Is there never one in all the land,
One on whose might the Cause may lean?
Are all the common ones so grand,
And all the titled ones so mean?
What if your failure may have been
In trying to make good bread from bran,

From worthless metal a weapon keen?—
Abraham Lincoln, find us a MAN!

O, we will follow him to the death,
Where the foeman's fiercest columns are!
O, we will use our latest breath,
Cheering for every sacred star!
His to marshal us high and far;
Ours to battle, as patriots can
When a Hero leads the Holy War!—
Abraham Lincoln, give us a MAN!

CHAPTER XXV

Midsummer of 1863 brought a turn in the tide of military affairs. It came none too soon for the safety of the nation. The repeated reverses to the Union arms ending with the shocking disasters at Fredericksburg and Chancellorsville—although slightly relieved by the costly success of Stone River—had seemed to throw the chances of war in favor of the South; and the Union cause was at the crisis of its fate. But now fortune smiled upon the North, and its lost hope and lost ground were regained at Gettysburg and Vicksburg. These great battles are justly regarded as marking the turning-point of the war. It was yet far from finished; there remained nearly two years of desperate fighting, with heroic struggles and terrible sacrifice of life, before the end should come. But from this time the character of the struggle seemed to change. The armies of the South fought, not less desperately, but more on the defensive; and their final overthrow was in all human probability chiefly a question of time.

Emboldened by his success at Chancellorsville in May, General Lee again assumed the offensive, and recrossed the Potomac river into Maryland. Late in June he invaded Pennsylvania, and occupied a position threatening Philadelphia, Baltimore, and Washington. The situation was most critical. If Lee could once more beat the Army of the Potomac, as he had done so many times, these three great cities, and even New York, might be at his mercy. The feeling in Washington is reflected in entries made at the time in Mr. Welles's Diary. "Something of a panic pervades the city," says Mr. Welles. "Singular rumors reach us of Rebel advances into Maryland. It is said they have reached Hagerstown, and some of them have penetrated as far as Chambersburg in Pennsylvania.... The city is full of strange, wild rumors of Rebel raids in the vicinity and of trains seized in sight of the Capital. The War Department is wholly unprepared for an irruption here, and J.E.B. Stuart might have dashed into the city to-day [June 28] with impunity.... I have a panic telegraph from Governor Curtin of Pennsylvania, who is excitable and easily alarmed, entreating that guns and gunners may be sent from the Navy Yard at Philadelphia to Harrisburg without delay.... I went again, at a late hour, to the War Department, but could get no facts or intelligence from the Secretary. All was vague, opaque, thick darkness. I really think Stanton is no better posted than myself, and from what Stanton says am afraid

Hooker does not comprehend Lee's intentions nor know how to counteract them. It looks to me as if Lee was putting forth his whole energy and force in one great and desperate struggle which shall be decisive."

Following Lee, the Army of the Potomac, under General Hooker, also recrossed the Potomac, and pursued the enemy by a somewhat parallel route, but keeping carefully between him and Washington. The occasion was one calling for the best resources of a great military commander; and General Hooker, realizing his unfitness for the responsibility, asked to be relieved of the command. Thus was thrown upon the President the hazardous necessity of changing commanders upon the very eve of a great battle. It was a terrible emergency. Even the stout-hearted Stanton was appalled. He afterward stated that when he received the despatch from Hooker, asking to be relieved, his heart sank within him, and he was more depressed than at any other moment of the war. "I could not say," said Mr. Stanton, "that any other officer knew General Hooker's plans, or the position even of the various divisions of the army. I sent for the President to come at once to the War Office. It was in the evening, but the President soon appeared. I handed him the despatch. As he read it his face became like lead, and I said, 'What shall be done?' He replied instantly, '*Accept his resignation.*'"

Immediately an order was sent to Major-General George G. Meade, one of the most efficient of the corps commanders of the Army of the Potomac, appointing him to the chief command. Meade was a quiet, unassuming man, very unlike Hooker. Three days after assuming command, he led his army against the Southern host at Gettysburg, where, after a most bloody and memorable battle of three days' duration (July 1, 2, and 3, 1863), was won the first decisive victory in the history of the gallant Army of the Potomac. Lee retired, with disastrous losses, across the Potomac to Virginia; and Washington and the North breathed free again.

Senator Chandler of Michigan, speaking of the terrible strain on Lincoln during the progress of the battle of Gettysburg, said: "I shall never forget the painful anxiety of those few days when the fate of the nation seemed to hang in the balance; nor the restless solicitude of Mr. Lincoln, as he paced up and down the room, reading despatches, soliloquizing, and often stopping to trace the position of the contending armies on the map which hung on the wall; nor the relief we all felt when the fact was established that victory, though gained at such fearful cost, was indeed on the side of the Union."

Amidst the murk and gloom of those dark days in Washington, when the suspense was breathless and the heart of the nation responded in muffled beats to the dull booming of the cannon of Meade and Lee at Gettysburg, an episode occurred, with Lincoln as the central figure, which reveals perhaps more poignantly than any other in his whole career the depths of feeling in that tender and reverential soul. On Sunday evening, July 4,— the fourth day of that terrible battle, with nothing definite yet known of the result,—the President drove out in a carriage, in company with two daughters of Secretary Stanton, to the line of defenses near Arlington. It was toward sundown; and a brigade of troops were forming in position for an evening parade or review. The commander of the brigade, General Tannatt, recognizing the President and his party, rode up to the carriage and invited them to witness the parade. The President assented. His face was drawn and haggard in its expression of anxiety and sorrow. As it was Sunday evening, some of the regimental bands played familiar religious pieces. The President, hearing them, inquired of General Tannatt if any of his bands could play "Lead Kindly Light." Then in a low voice and with touching accents he repeated, as if to himself, the familiar lines—never more expressive or appropriate than now,—

Lead, kindly light, amid the encircling gloom,

Lead thou me on.

Keep thou my feet; I do not ask to see

The distant scene,—one step enough for me.

As the sweet strains of the familiar hymn floated on the evening air, Lincoln's sad face became sadder still, and tears were seen coursing down his cheeks. What emotions were his, who can tell, as he thought of that great battle-field not far away, its issues yet unknown, its ground still covered with dead and wounded soldiers whose heroic deeds—to use his noble words spoken a few months later on that historic field—"have consecrated it far above our power to add or detract."

General Tannatt, who knew Lincoln well and had spoken with him many times, never saw him again; and his view of that tragic, tear-wet face remains to him a vivid and precious memory. [H]

While the eyes of the nation were fastened upon the great drama being enacted near the capital, events scarcely less momentous were occurring in the Southwest. The campaign against Vicksburg, the great Confederate stronghold on the Mississippi river, had been in active progress, under the personal command of General Grant, for several months. The importance of this strategic point was fully understood by the enemy, and it was defended most stubbornly. At first Grant's plans proved unsuccessful; the cutting of canals and opening of bayous failed—as President Lincoln had expected and predicted. But these failures only served to develop the unsuspected energy of Grant's character and the extent of his military resources. He boldly changed his entire plan of operations, abandoned his line of communication, removed his army to a point *below* Vicksburg and attacked the city in the rear. With dogged persistence he pressed forward, gaining point by point, beating off General Johnston's forces on one side and driving Pemberton before him into Vicksburg; until finally, by the aid of Admiral Porter's gunboats on the Mississippi, he had entirely invested the city. Gradually and persistently his lines closed in, pushed forward by assault and siege; until Vicksburg accepted its doom, and on the 4th of July, 1863,—the day of Lee's retreat from Gettysburg,—the city and garrison surrendered to the victorious Grant.

Lincoln's exuberant joy over the capture of Vicksburg is revealed in an entry made at the time in Mr. Welles's Diary. "I was handed a despatch from Admiral Porter, communicating the fall of Vicksburg on the Fourth of July," says Mr. Welles. "I immediately returned to the Executive Mansion. The President was detailing certain points relative to Grant's movements on the map to Chase and two or three others, when I gave him the tidings. Putting down the map he rose at once, said he would drop these topics, and added, 'I myself will telegraph this news to General Meade.' He seized his hat, but suddenly stopped, his countenance beaming with joy; he caught my hand, and throwing his arm around me, exclaimed, 'What can we do for the Secretary of the Navy for this glorious intelligence? He is always giving us good news. I cannot, in words, tell you my joy over this result. It is great, Mr. Welles, it is great!' ... We walked the lawn together. 'This,' said he, 'will relieve Banks. It will inspire me.'"

The Union victories at Vicksburg and Gettysburg caused great rejoicing at the North, and gave added zest to the celebration of the national patriotic holiday. President Lincoln, mindful of the "almost inestimable services," as he termed them, of General Grant, and as it was his wont to do in such circumstances, made haste to acknowledge his own and the country's indebtedness to the man who had accomplished a great deed. He addressed to the conqueror of Vicksburg the following letter:

EXECUTIVE MANSION, WASHINGTON, D.C.
July 13, 1863.

MAJOR-GENERAL GRANT.

MY DEAR GENERAL:—I do not remember that you and I ever met personally. I write this now as a grateful acknowledgment for the almost inestimable services you have done the country. I write to say a word further. When you first reached the vicinity of Vicksburg, I thought you should do what you finally did—march the troops across the neck, run the batteries with the transports, and thus go below; and I never had any faith, except a general hope that you knew better than I, that the Yazoo Pass expedition, and the like, could succeed. When you got below, and took Port Gibson, Grand Gulf, and vicinity, I thought you should go down the river, and join General Banks, and when you turned northward, east of the Big Black, I feared it was a mistake. I now wish to make the personal acknowledgment that you were right and I was wrong.

Yours truly, A. LINCOLN.

An officer who was the first from Grant's army to reach Washington after the surrender of Vicksburg, has recorded the circumstances of his interview with the President. "Mr. Lincoln received me very cordially," says this officer, "and drawing a chair near to himself and motioning me to be seated said, 'Now I want to hear all about Vicksburg.' I gave him all the information I could, though he appeared to be remarkably well posted himself. He put to me a great many questions in detail touching the siege, the losses, the morale of the army, its sanitary condition, the hospital service, and General Grant. Said he: 'I guess I was right in standing by Grant, although there was great pressure made after Pittsburg Landing to have him removed. I thought I saw enough in Grant to convince me that he was one on whom the country could depend. That 'unconditional surrender' message to Buckner at Donelson suited me. It indicated the spirit of the man."

It is interesting to note that before the capture of Vicksburg the protracted campaign had occasioned no little dissatisfaction with General Grant; the President had been importuned to remove him, and had much formidable opposition to encounter in his determination to stand by him. Only a few days before the capitulation of the beleaguered city, Senator Wade of Ohio—"Bluff Ben Wade," as he was termed—called upon the President and urged Grant's dismissal; to which Lincoln good-naturedly replied, "Senator, that reminds me of a story." "Yes, yes," rejoined Wade petulantly, "that is the way it is with you, sir, all *story—story*! You are the father of every military blunder that has been made during the war. You are on your road to h—l, sir, with this Government, and you are not a mile off this minute." Lincoln calmly retorted, "Senator, that is just about the distance from here to the Capitol, is it not?" The exasperated Wade grabbed his hat and rushed angrily from the White House.

It is not pleasant to record that the cordial and generous congratulations to Grant for his achievements at Vicksburg were in marked contrast to the rather grudging recognition of Meade's much more important and hard-won victory at Gettysburg. In the latter case the despatches from Washington took the form not so much of acknowledgments of what had been done as of complaints at what had not been done. It is hard to believe that the President dictated, or even authorized, the ill-timed and peevish despatch sent to General Meade [I] by the inopportune Halleck, a few days after the battle of Gettysburg, in which the victor on that desperate field is officially informed that "the escape of Lee 's army has created great dissatisfaction in the mind of the President, and it will require an active and energetic pursuit to remove the impression that it has not been sufficiently active before." To this extraordinary message Meade at once made a simple and manly rejoinder in which he said: "Having performed my duty conscientiously and to the best of my ability, the censure of the President, as conveyed in your despatch, is in my judgment so undeserved that I feel compelled most respectfully to ask to be immediately relieved from the command of this army." Halleck replied, rather ineptly, that his despatch had not been intended as a censure, but as a "stimulus," and was not regarded as a sufficient cause for Meade's request to be relieved. When one thinks of the ill-fortunes of the Army of the Potomac under previous commanders, and of the unlikelihood of finding a successor to Meade as capable as he had shown himself to be, one shudders at the chances of what might have happened had another change of leaders been forced upon that long-suffering and now victorious army. General Meade did not press his resignation after Halleck's conciliatory telegrams, and remained in immediate command of the Army of the Potomac until the close of the war—Grant's accession to the chief command of all the armies having marked the end of the well-meant but often ill-advised and troublesome interference with military affairs from Washington.

Mr. Isaac R. Pennypacker, in his Life of General Meade, speaks of Halleck and other prominent officials in Washington in these terms: "Possessing much of the skill of the lawyer and disputant, Halleck was without military ability. The Secretary of War, like many other men who exercise vast power, was not great enough to refrain from the use of his authority in matters where his knowledge and experience did not qualify him to form the soundest views. Acting with these military authorities were men like Wade and Chandler, whose patriotism was of the exuberant kind, whose judgment in military affairs was without value, but whose personal energy impelled them to have a controlling hand, if possible, in the conduct of the war."

Lincoln's dissatisfaction with General Meade after the battle of Gettysburg was due, as we now see, to his elation over the splendid victory for the Union, his intense desire for further and overwhelming successes, and his failure (a quite natural one) to realize that what might seem desirable and feasible viewed from Washington might look very different to the practical and experienced men actually on the ground and familiar as he could not be with all the factors in the situation.[J] "He thought," wrote General Halleck in an explanatory letter sent to Meade two weeks after his despatch of censure, "that Lee 's defeat was so certain that he felt no little impatience at his unexpected escape." Among military authorities, such a retreat as that of Lee after Gettysburg is hardly regarded as an "escape." If it were, then great must be the fault of Lee as a general in allowing the defeated armies of Burnside and Hooker to "escape" after the battles of Fredericksburg and Chancellorsville, where their repulse was much worse than was Lee's at Gettysburg. That Lincoln's first feelings of disappointment and dissatisfaction with General Meade were greatly modified with fuller knowledge of the actual situation after the battle of Gettysburg is shown by a remark made by him to Senator Cameron, referring to Meade: "Why should we censure a man who has done so much for his country because he did not do a little more?" And if any debt of recognition or of gratitude yet remained due from him, it was more than paid a few months later in the unsurpassed tribute at Gettysburg to "the brave men, living and dead," who gained the victory on that hallowed field.

The improved condition of public affairs, and the increasing cheerfulness of the President, after the victories at Gettysburg and Vicksburg, are exhibited in a letter written by him a few weeks later to friends at Springfield, Illinois, who had urgently invited him to attend "a mass-meeting of Unconditional Union men" at his old home. In this letter he took occasion to declare his sentiments on various questions paramount at the time. Among these was the subject of a compromise with the South, against which he argued with great force and feeling. Again, he defended the Emancipation Proclamation, a measure to which many Union men were still unreconciled. He referred also to the arming of the negroes as a just and wise expedient; finally concluding with these expressive and felicitous words:

> The signs look better. The Father of Waters again goes
> unvexed to the sea. Thanks to the great Northwest for it;
> nor yet wholly to them. Three hundred miles up they met
> New England, Empire, Keystone, and Jersey, hewing their
> way right and left. The sunny South, too, in more colors
> than one, also lent a helping hand. On the spot, their part
> of the history was jotted down in black and white. The job

was a great national one, and let none be slighted who bore an honorable part in it. And while those who have cleared the great river may well be proud, even that is not all. It is hard to say that anything has been more bravely and well done than at Antietam, Murfreesboro, Gettysburg, and on many fields of less note. Nor must Uncle Sam's web-feet be forgotten. At all the watery margins they have been present, not only on the deep sea, the broad bay, and the rapid river, but also up the narrow, muddy bayou, and wherever the ground was a little damp they have been and made their tracks. Thanks to all. For the great Republic— for the principle it lives by and keeps alive—for man's vast future—thanks to all. Peace does not appear so distant as it did. I hope it will come soon and come to stay; and so come as to be worth the keeping in all future time. It will then have been proved that among freemen there can be no successful appeal from the ballot to the bullet, and that they who take such appeal are sure to lose their case and pay the cost. And there will be some black men who can remember that, with silent tongue, and clinched teeth, and steady eye, and well-poised bayonet, they have helped mankind on to this great consummation; while I fear there will be some white ones unable to forget that with malignant heart and deceitful speech they have striven to hinder it. Still, let us not be over-sanguine of a speedy final triumph. Let us be quite sober. Let us diligently apply the means, never doubting that a just God, in His own good time, will give us the rightful result.

In a public proclamation, issued October 3, the President gives more formal expression to his satisfaction and gratitude, and calls upon the loyal people of the Union to unite in a day of thanksgiving for the improved prospects of the country.

The year that is drawing toward its close has been filled with the blessings of fruitful fields and healthful skies. To these bounties, which are so constantly enjoyed that we are prone to forget the source from which they come, others have been added which are of so extraordinary a nature that they cannot fail to penetrate and soften even the heart which is habitually insensible to the ever-watchful providence of Almighty God. In the midst of a civil war of unequalled magnitude and severity, which has sometimes seemed to invite and provoke the aggressions of foreign states, peace has been preserved with all nations, order has been maintained, the laws have been respected and obeyed, and harmony has prevailed everywhere except in the theatre of military conflict, while that theatre has been greatly contracted by the advancing armies and navies of the Union. The needful diversion of wealth and strength from the fields of peaceful industry to the national defense has not arrested the plough, the shuttle, or the ship. The axe has enlarged the borders of our settlements, and the mines, as well of iron and coal as of the precious metals, have yielded even more abundantly than heretofore. Population has steadily increased, notwithstanding the waste that has been made in the camp, the siege, and the battle-field; and the country, rejoicing in the consciousness of augmented strength and vigor, is permitted to expect a continuance of years with large increase of freedom. No human counsel hath devised nor hath any mortal hand worked out these great things. They are the gracious gifts of the Most High God, who, while dealing with us in anger for our sins, hath nevertheless remembered mercy. It has seemed to me fit and proper that they should be solemnly, reverently, and gratefully acknowledged, as with one heart and voice, by the whole American people. I do, therefore, invite my fellow-citizens in every part of the United States, and also those who are at sea, and those who are sojourning in foreign lands, to set apart and observe the last Thursday of November next as a day of thanksgiving and prayer to our beneficent Father, who dwelleth in the heavens. And I recommend to them that, while offering up the ascriptions justly due to Him for such singular deliverances and blessings, they do also, with humble penitence for our national perverseness and disobedience, commend to His tender care all those who have become widows, orphans, mourners, or sufferers in the lamentable civil strife in which we are unavoidably engaged, and fervently implore the interposition of the Almighty Hand to heal the wounds of the nation, and to restore it, as soon as may be consistent with the divine purposes, to the full enjoyment of peace, harmony, tranquility, and union.

The brightening prospects of the Union cause quickly produced a better state of feeling at the North. In the fall elections of 1863, every State except New Jersey gave solid majorities on the Republican side, thus strengthening the administration and giving the President welcome assurances of popular approval. He had awaited with special anxiety the returns from Ohio, where the contest was fraught with peculiar significance. The Democrats had chosen for their candidate the notorious peace-at-any-price Vallandigham, against whom the Republicans had placed John Brough of Cleveland. On the night of the election, about ten o'clock, a message clicked on the wires in the telegraph office of the latter city, saying, "Where is John Brough? A. Lincoln." Brough was at hand, and directly the electric voice inquired, "Brough, about what is your majority now?" Brough replied, "Over 30,000." Lincoln requested Brough to remain at the office during the night. A little past midnight the question came again from Lincoln, "Brough, what is your majority by this time?" Brough replied, "Over 50,000." And the question was thus repeated and answered several times, with rapidly increasing majorities, till five o'clock in the morning, when the question came again, "Brough, what is your majority now?" The latter was able to respond, "Over 100,000." As soon as the words could be flashed back over the wire, there came: "*Glory to God in the highest. Ohio has saved the Nation. A. Lincoln.*"

The day after the election in Ohio (October 14, 1863) Lincoln said to Secretary Welles that he had felt more anxiety in regard to the results than he had in 1860 when he was chosen President. He could not have believed four years ago, he said, that one genuine American would or could be induced to vote for such a man as Vallandigham. Yet he had been made the candidate of a large party, and received a vote that is a discredit to the country. Mr. Welles adds: "The President showed a good deal of emotion as he dwelt on this subject."

After the battle of Gettysburg, a portion of the ground on which the engagement was fought was purchased by the State of Pennsylvania for a burial-place for the Union soldiers who were slain in that bloody encounter. The tract included seventeen and a half acres adjoining the town cemetery. It was planned to consecrate the ground with imposing ceremonies, in which the President, accompanied by his Cabinet and a large body of the military, was invited to assist. The day appointed was the 19th of November; and the chief orator selected was Massachusetts' eloquent son, Hon. Edward Everett. Following him it was expected that the President would add some testimonials in honor of the dead.

Lincoln and Everett were representatives of two contrasting phases of American civilization: the one, an outgrowth of the rough pioneer life of the West; the other, the product of the highest culture of the East. They had met for the first time on this memorable day. Everett's oration was a finished literary production. Smooth, euphonious, and elegant, it was delivered with the silvery tones and the graceful gestures of a trained and consummate speaker. When he had finished, and the applause that greeted him had died away, the multitude called vociferously for an address from Lincoln. With an unconscious air, the President came forward at the call, put his spectacles on his nose, and read, in a quiet voice which gradually warmed with feeling, while his careworn face became radiant with the light of genuine emotion, the following brief address:

> Fourscore and seven years ago our fathers brought forth on this continent a new nation, conceived in liberty, and dedicated to the proposition that all men are created equal. Now we are engaged in a great civil war, testing whether that nation, or any nation so conceived and so dedicated, can long endure. We are met on a great battle-field of that war. We have come to dedicate a portion of that field as a final resting-place of those who here gave their lives that that nation might live. It is altogether fitting and proper that we should do this. But in a larger sense we cannot dedicate, we cannot consecrate, we cannot hallow this ground. The brave men, living and dead, who struggled here, have consecrated it, far above our poor power to add or detract. The world will little note nor long remember what we *say* here, but it can never forget what they *did* here. It is for us, the living, rather, to be dedicated here to the unfinished work which they who fought here have thus far so nobly carried on. It is rather for us to be here dedicated to the great task remaining before us, that from these honored dead we take increased devotion to that cause for which they gave the last full measure of devotion; that we here highly resolve that these dead shall not have died in vain; that this nation, under God, shall have a new birth of freedom; and that government of the people, by the people, for the people, shall not perish from the earth.

The simple and sublime words of this short address shook the hearts of the listeners, and before the first sentence was ended they were under the spell of a mighty magician. They stood hushed, awed, and melted, as the speaker enforced the solemn lesson of the hour, and brought home to them, in plain unvarnished terms, the duty which remained for them to do—to finish the work which the dead around them had given their lives to carry on. It was one of the briefest of the many speeches with which Lincoln had swayed the impulses and opinions of crowds of his fellow-men, but it is the one which will be remembered above all others as hallowed by the truest and loftiest inspiration. As the final sentence ended, amid the tears and sobs and cheers of the excited throng, the President turned to Mr. Everett, and, grasping his hand, exclaimed with sincerity, "I congratulate you on your success." Mr. Everett responded in the fervor of his emotion, "Ah, Mr. President, how gladly would I exchange all my hundred pages to have been the author of your twenty lines!"

Of all Lincoln's public utterances, this is unquestionably the most remarkable. The oration, brief and unpretending as it is, will remain a classic of the English language. "The Westminster Review," one of the foremost of the great English quarterlies, said of it: "It has but one equal, in that pronounced upon those who fell in the first year of the Peloponnesian War; and in one respect it is superior to that great speech. It is not only more natural, fuller of feeling, more touching and pathetic, but we know with absolute certainty that *it was really delivered*. Nature here takes precedence of art—even though it be the art of Thucydides."

"An illustration of the difference between oratory and inspiration" is Mr. John Bigelow's happy characterization of the Gettysburg address. "It was," he adds, "one of the most momentous incidents in the history of the Civil War. It may be doubted whether anything had then, or has since, been said of that national strife conceived upon a higher and wiser spiritual plane.... It is perhaps, on the whole, the most enduring bit of eloquence that has ever been uttered on this continent; and yet one finds in it none of the tricks of the forum or the stage, nor any trace of the learning of the scholar, nor the need of it."

Major Harry T. Lee, who was himself a participant in the battle of Gettysburg and occupied a seat on the platform at the dedication, says that the people listened with marked attention through the two hours of Everett's noble and scholarly oration; but that when Lincoln came forward, and in a voice burdened with emotion uttered his simple and touching eulogy on "the brave men, living and dead, who struggled here," there was scarcely a dry eye in the whole vast audience.

Mr. John Russell Young, afterwards U.S. Minister to China, was present at the Gettysburg dedication, and says: "I sat behind Mr. Lincoln while Mr. Everett delivered his oration. I remember the great orator had a way of raising and dropping his handkerchief as he spoke. He spoke for two hours, and was very impressive, with his white hair and venerable figure. He was a great orator, but it was like a bit of Greek sculpture—beautiful, but cold as ice. It was perfect art, but without feeling. The art and beauty of it captured your imagination and judgment. Mr. Everett went over the campaign with resonant, clear, splendid rhetoric. There was not a word or a sentence or a thought that could be corrected. You felt that every gesture had been carefully studied out beforehand. It was like a great actor playing a great part.... Mr. Lincoln rose, walked to the edge of the platform, took out his glasses, and put them on. He was awkward. He bowed to the assemblage in his homely manner, and took out of his coat pocket a page of foolscap. In front of Mr. Lincoln was a photographer with his camera, endeavoring to take a picture of the scene. We all supposed that Mr. Lincoln would make rather a long speech—a half-hour at least. He took the single sheet of foolscap, held it almost to his nose, and in his high tenor voice, without the least attempt at effect, delivered that most extraordinary address which belongs to the classics of literature. The photographer was bustling about, preparing to take the President's picture while he was speaking, but Mr. Lincoln finished before the photographer was ready."

It is stated that when President Lincoln reached the town of Gettysburg, on his way to attend the exercises at the cemetery, he inquired for "Old John Burns," the hero of the battle of Gettysburg, who left his farm and fought with the Union soldiers upon that bloody field. The veteran was sent for; and on his arrival the President showed him marked attention, taking him by the arm and walking with him in the procession through the streets to the cemetery.

Edward Everett, who was associated with Lincoln during these two or three days, says of the impression the President made on him: "I recognized in the President a full measure of the qualities which entitle him to the personal respect of the people. On the only social occasion on which I ever had the honor to be in his company, viz., the Commemoration at Gettysburg, he sat at the table of my friend David Willis, by the side of several distinguished persons, foreigners and Americans; and in gentlemanly appearance, manners, and conversation, he was the peer of any man at the table."

CHAPTER XXVI

From the hour of Grant's triumph at Vicksburg to the close of the war, Lincoln never withdrew his confidence from the quiet, persistent, unpretending man who led our armies slowly but surely along the path of victory. As soon as the campaign at Vicksburg was over, Grant's sphere of operations was enlarged by his appointment to the command of the military division of the Mississippi. In November following he fought the famous battles of Chattanooga, including Lookout Mountain and Missionary Ridge; and, aided by his efficient corps commanders, Sherman, Thomas, and Hooker, gained a succession of brilliant victories for the Union cause. The wisdom of Grant's policy of concentration and "fighting it out" had now become apparent.

President Lincoln had watched closely the progress of these events, and had come to recognize in Grant the master spirit of the war, on the Northern side. Accordingly he determined to give him general command of all the Union armies. In December, 1863, a bill was introduced in the Senate by Hon. E.B. Washburne, of Illinois, and passed both houses of Congress, creating the rank of Lieutenant-General in the army. President Lincoln approved the act, and immediately nominated Grant for the position. The nomination was confirmed; and on the 17th of March, 1864, Grant issued his first order as Lieutenant-General, assuming command of the armies of the United States, and announcing that his headquarters would be in the field and until further orders with the Army of the Potomac. Of this army he shrewdly remarked that it seemed to him it "had never fought its battles *through*." He proposed, first of all, to teach that army "not to be afraid of Lee." "I had known him personally," said Grant, "and *knew that he was mortal*." With characteristic energy he formed a simple but comprehensive plan of operations both East and West; sending Sherman on his great march to Atlanta and the sea, while he, with the Army of the Potomac, pushed straight for Richmond. These operations were vigorously urged, and when they were ended the war was ended. It was but little more than a year from the date of Grant's commission as Lieutenant-General till he received Lee's surrender at Appomattox.

Immediately upon Grant's appointment as Lieutenant-General, he was summoned to Washington. It was his first visit to the capital since the war began, and he was a stranger to nearly everyone from the President down. He arrived in the city on the 8th of March (1864), taking quarters at Willard's Hotel, where, when he went in to dinner, none knew "the quiet, rather stumpy-looking man, who came in leading a little boy — the boy who had ridden by his father's side through all the campaign of Vicksburg." But soon it was whispered about who was in the room, and there was a loud call for three cheers for Ulysses S. Grant, which were given with a will. In the evening General Grant attended a reception at the White House, passing in with the throng alone and unannounced. The quick eye of the President discovered the identity of the modest soldier, and he was most heartily welcomed. "As soon as it was known that he was present, the pressure of the crowd to see the hero of Vicksburg was so great that he was forced to shelter himself behind a sofa. So irrepressible was the desire to see him that Secretary Seward finally induced him to mount a sofa, that this curiosity might be gratified. When parting from the President, he said, 'This has been rather the warmest campaign I have witnessed during the war.'" A graphic account of this interesting event is given by Secretary Welles, who records in his Diary (March 9, 1864): "Went last evening to the Presidential reception. Quite a gathering; very many that are not usually seen at receptions were attracted thither, I presume, from the fact that General Grant was expected to be there. He came about half-past nine. I was near the centre of the reception-room, when a stir and buzz attracted attention, and it was whispered that General Grant had arrived. The room was not full, the crowd having passed through to the East Room. I saw some men in uniform standing at the entrance, and one of them, a short, brown, dark-haired man, was talking with the President. There was hesitation, a degree of awkwardness, in the General. Soon word was passed around — 'Mr. Seward, General Grant is here,' and Seward, who was just behind me, hurried and took the General by the hand and led him to Mrs. Lincoln, near whom I was standing. The crowd gathered around the circle rapidly, and it being intimated that it would be necessary the throng should pass on, Seward took the General's arm and went with him to the East Room. There was clapping of hands in the next room as he passed through, and all in the East Room joined in it as he entered."

The next day at noon the General waited on the President to receive his commission. The interview took place in the Cabinet room. There were present, besides the members of the Cabinet, General Halleck, a member of Congress, two of General Grant's staff-officers, his eldest son, Frederick D. Grant, and the President's private secretary. The ceremony was simple, the President saying, as he proffered the papers: "The nation's appreciation of what you have done, and its reliance upon you for what remains to be done in the existing great struggle, are now presented with this commission, constituting you Lieutenant-General in the Army of the United States. With this high honor devolves upon you also a corresponding responsibility. As the country herein trusts you, so, under God, it will sustain you. I scarcely need to add that with what I here speak for the nation goes my own hearty personal concurrence." The General responded briefly, promising to "accept the commission with gratitude for the high honor conferred. With the aid of the noble armies that have fought on so many fields for our common country, it will be my earnest endeavor not to disappoint your expectations. I feel the full weight of the responsibilities now devolving on me, and I know that if they are met it will be due to those armies, and above all to the favor of that Providence which leads both nations and men."

Before assuming personal command of the Army of the Potomac, as he had determined to do, General Grant found it necessary to return once more to the West. In his parting interview with Lincoln, he was urged to remain to dinner the next day and meet a brilliant party whom the lady of the White House had invited to do him special honor. The General answered, apologetically: "Mrs. Lincoln must excuse me. I must be in Tennessee at a given time." "But we can't excuse you," said the President. "Mrs. Lincoln's dinner without you would be Hamlet with Hamlet left out." "I appreciate the honor Mrs. Lincoln would do me," said the General, "but time is very important now. I ought to be at the front, and a dinner to me means a million dollars a day lost to the country." Lincoln was pleased with this answer, and said cheerfully, "Well, we'll have the dinner without you."

After Lincoln's first meeting with General Grant he was asked regarding his personal impressions of the new commander. He replied, "Well, I hardly know what to think of him. He's the quietest little fellow you ever saw. He makes the least fuss of any man I ever knew. I believe on several occasions he has been in this room a minute or so before I knew he was here. It's about so all around. The only evidence you have that he's in any particular place is that he makes things move." To a subsequent inquiry as to his estimate of Grant's military capacities, Lincoln responded, with emphasis: "Grant is the first General I've had. *He's a General.*" "How do you mean, Mr. Lincoln?" his visitor asked. "Well, I'll tell you what I mean," replied Lincoln. "You know how it's been with all the rest. As soon as I put a man in command of the army, he'd come to me with the plan of a campaign, and about as much as to say: 'Now I don't believe I can do it, but if you say so I'll try it on,' and so put the responsibility of success or failure on me. They all wanted *me* to be the General. Now, it isn 't so with Grant. He hasn't told me what his plans are. I don't know and I don't want to know. I am glad to find a man who can go ahead without me. When any of the rest set out on a campaign they'd look over matters and pick out some one thing they were short of and they knew I couldn't give them, and tell me they couldn't hope to win unless they had it—and it was most generally cavalry. Now when Grant took hold I was waiting to see what his pet impossibility would be, and I reckoned it would be cavalry, of course, for we hadn't horses enough to mount what men we had. There were fifteen thousand men, or thereabouts, up near Harper's Ferry, and no horses to put them on. Well, the other day Grant sent to me about these very men, just as I expected; but what he wanted to know was whether he could make infantry of 'em or disband 'em. He doesn't ask impossibilities of me, and he's the first General I've had that didn't." On another occasion Lincoln said of Grant: "The great thing about him is his cool persistency of purpose. He is not easily excited, and he has the grip of a bulldog. *When he once gets his teeth in, nothing can shake him off.*"

The President's satisfaction with the new commander was speedily communicated to him in a characteristically frank manner, in a letter dated April 30, 1864.

> LIEUTENANT-GENERAL GRANT:—
>
> Not expecting to see you before the Spring campaign opens, I wish to express in this way my entire satisfaction with what you have done up to this time, so far as I understand it. The particulars of your plan I neither know nor seek to know. You are vigilant and self-reliant; and, pleased with this, I wish not to obtrude any restraints or constraints upon you. While I am very anxious that any great disaster or capture of our men in great numbers shall be avoided, I know that these points are less likely to escape your attention than they would be mine. If there be anything wanting which is in my power to give, do not fail to let me know it. And now, with a brave army and a just cause, may God sustain you.
>
> Yours very truly, A. LINCOLN.

General Grant himself wrote, on this point: "In my first interview with Mr. Lincoln alone, he stated to me that he had never professed to be a military man, or to know how campaigns should be conducted, and never wanted to interfere in them; but that procrastination on the part of commanders, and the pressure of the people at the North and Congress, *which was always with him,* forced him into issuing his series of 'Military Orders'—one, two, three, etc. He did not know but they were all wrong, and did know that some of them were. All he wanted or had ever wanted was someone who would take the responsibility and act, and call on him for all the assistance needed, pledging himself to use all the power of the government in rendering such assistance.... The President told me he did not want to know what I proposed to do. But he submitted a plan of campaign of his own which he wanted me to hear and then do as I pleased about. He brought out a map of Virginia on which he had evidently marked every position occupied by the Federal and Confederate armies up to that time. He pointed out on the map two streams which empty into the Potomac, and suggested that the army might be moved on boats and landed between the mouths of these streams. We would then have the Potomac to bring our supplies, and the tributaries would protect our flanks while we moved out. I listened respectfully, but did not suggest that the same streams would protect Lee's flanks while he was shutting us up."

General Horace Porter, for some time Grant's chief of staff, says: "The nearest Mr. Lincoln ever came to giving General Grant an order for the movement of troops was during Early's raid upon Washington. On July 10, 1864, he telegraphed a long despatch from Washington, which contained the following language: 'What I think is that you should provide to retain your hold where you are, certainly, and bring the rest with you personally, and make a vigorous effort to defeat the enemy's force in this vicinity. I think there is really a fair chance to do this, if the movement is prompt. This is what I think—given upon your suggestion,—and is not an order.' Grant replied that on reflection he thought it would have a bad effect for him to leave City Point, then his headquarters, in front of Richmond and Petersburg; and the President was satisfied with the dispositions which Grant made for the repulse of Early without taking command against him in person."

A curious incident revealing the intense interest with which Lincoln watched the career of Grant is related by Mr. J. Russell Jones, an old and trusted friend of the President, who joined the army at Vicksburg in time to witness its final triumph. Soon after Mr. Jones's return to Chicago, the President summoned him to Washington. With eager haste, after the first salutations were over, Lincoln declared the object for which he had secured the interview: "'I have sent for you, Mr. Jones, to know if that man Grant wants to be President.' Mr. Jones, although somewhat astonished at the question and the circumstances under which it was asked, replied at once, 'No, Mr. President.' 'Are you sure?' queried the latter. 'Yes,' said Mr. Jones, 'perfectly sure. I have just come from Vicksburg. I have seen General Grant frequently, and talked fully and freely with him about that and every other question; and I know he has no political aspirations whatever, and certainly none for the Presidency. His only desire is to see you re-elected and to do what he can under your orders to put down the rebellion and restore peace to the country.' 'Ah, Mr. Jones,' said Lincoln, 'you have lifted a great weight off my mind, and done me an immense amount of good; for I tell you, my friend, no man knows how deeply that Presidential grub gnaws till he has had it himself.'" We cannot believe that Lincoln cherished any feeling of jealousy of the rising commander, or desired to interfere with whatever political ambition he might nourish. It was rather his desire to be assured of the single-hearted purpose of a military leader whom he had trusted and to whom he wished to confide still more important services in the conduct of the war.

It may be remembered that early in the war an anecdote went the rounds of the press to the effect that, in reply to a complaint that Grant had been guilty of drunkenness in the campaigns in the West, Lincoln remarked that he would "like to find out what kind of liquor Grant drank," so that he might "send some of it to the other Generals." The true version of that characteristic anecdote is this, as given by the late Judge T. Lyle Dickey, who was a Judge of the Illinois Supreme Court at the time of his death, and at the time of Grant's famous Vicksburg campaign was on the General's staff as chief of cavalry. Judge (then Colonel) Dickey had been sent to Washington with private despatches for the President and the Secretary of War. Lincoln and Dickey had been intimate friends for years, and during the latter's visit to the former on that occasion, Dickey remarked, "I hear that some one has been trying to poison you against Grant by reporting that he gets drunk. I wish to assure you, Mr. President, that there is not a scintilla of truth in the report." "Oh, Colonel," replied the President, "we get all sorts of reports here, but I'll say this to you: that if those accusing General Grant of getting drunk will tell me *where he gets his whiskey*, I will get a lot of it and send it around to some of the other Generals, who are badly in need of something of the kind."

After Lincoln and General Grant had become personally intimate, they had many enjoyable conversations and exchanges of anecdotes. Lincoln especially enjoyed telling the General of the various persons who had come to him with complaints and criticisms about the Vicksburg campaign. "After the place had actually surrendered," said the President, "I thought it was about time to shut down on this sort of thing. So one day, when a delegation came to see me, and had spent half an hour trying to show me the fatal mistake you had made in paroling Pemberton's army, and insisting that the rebels would violate their paroles and in less than a month confront you again in the ranks and have to be whipped all over again, I thought I could get rid of them best by telling them a story about Sykes's dog. 'Have you ever heard about Sykes's yellow dog?' said I to the spokesman of the delegation. He said he hadn't. 'Well, I must tell you about him,' said I. 'Sykes had a yellow dog he set great store by, but there were a lot of small boys around the village, and that's always a bad thing for dogs, you know. These boys didn't share Sykes's views, and they were not disposed to let the dog have a fair show. Even Sykes had to admit that the dog was getting unpopular; in fact, it was soon seen that a prejudice was growing up against that dog that threatened to wreck all his future prospects in life. The boys, after meditating how they could get the best of him, finally fixed up a cartridge with a long fuse, put the cartridge in a piece of meat, dropped the meat in the road in front of Sykes's door, and then perched themselves on a fence a good distance off with the end of the fuse in their hands. Then they whistled for the dog. When he came out he scented the bait, and bolted the meat, cartridge and all. The boys touched off the fuse with a cigar, and in about a second a report came from that dog that sounded like a small clap of thunder. Sykes came bouncing out of the house, and yelled: "What's up! Anything busted?" There was no reply, except a snicker from the small boys roosting on the fence; but as Sykes looked up he saw the whole air filled with pieces of yellow dog. He picked up the biggest piece he could find—a portion of the back, with a part of the tail still hanging to it, and, after turning it around and looking it all over, he said, "Well, I guess he'll never be much account again—*as a dog*." And I guess Pemberton's forces will never be much account again—*as an army*.' The delegation began looking around for their hats before I had quite got to the end of the story, and I was never bothered any more about superseding the commander of the Army of the Tennessee."

When General Grant was ready to begin active operations with the Army of the Potomac, he sent forward all available men from Washington. Secretary Stanton, anxious about the safety of the city, said to Grant one day: "General, I suppose you have left us enough men to strongly garrison the forts?" "No, I can't do that," was Grant's quiet answer. "Why not? Why not?" repeated the Secretary nervously. "Because I have already sent the men to the front." Said the Secretary, still more nervously: "That won't do. It's contrary to my plans. I cannot allow it. I will order the men back." To this Grant returned with quiet determination: "I shall need the men there, and you cannot order them back." "Why not? Why not?" cried the Secretary. "I believe that I rank the Secretary in this matter," remarked Grant. "Very well, we will see the President about that," responded the Secretary sharply. "I will have to take you to the President." "That is right. The President ranks us both." So they went to the President; and the Secretary, turning to General Grant, said, "Now, General, state your case." But the General calmly replied, "I have no case to state. I am satisfied as it is." This threw the burden of statement on Secretary Stanton, and was excellent strategy. Meanwhile, General Grant had the men. When the Secretary had concluded, Lincoln crossed his legs, rested his elbow on his knee, and said in his quaint way and with a twinkle in his eye: "Now, Mr. Secretary, you know we have been trying to manage this army for nearly three years, and you know we haven't done much with it. We sent over the mountains and brought Mr. Grant, as Mrs. Grant calls him, to manage it for us; and now I guess we'd better let Mr. Grant *have his own way.*" And Mr. Grant had it.

The favorable opinion which Lincoln held of Grant was strongly reciprocated. A short time before the former's death, Grant said: "I regard Lincoln as one of the greatest of men. He is unquestionably the greatest man I have ever encountered. The more I see of him and exchange views with him, the more he impresses me. I admire his courage, and respect the firmness he always displays. Many think from the gentleness of his character that he has a yielding nature; but while he has the courage to change his mind when convinced that he is wrong, he has all the tenacity of purpose which could be desired in a great statesman. His quickness of perception often astonishes me. Long before the statement of a complicated question is finished, his mind will grasp the main points, and he will seem to comprehend the whole subject better than the person who is stating it. He will take rank in history alongside of Washington."

CHAPTER XXVII

The year 1864 witnessed another Presidential election, and one which was attended by the most novel and extraordinary circumstances. It was held while a considerable portion of the people were engaged in armed rebellion against the authority of the National Government; and it was not participated in by the voters of several entire States. Aside from these unique features, it marked a most critical epoch in the history of the country, and in that of Abraham Lincoln as well. The policy and acts of the administration, even the question of the further prosecution of the war, were to be submitted to the sovereign tribunal of the people; and with their verdict would be recorded also the popular measure of approval or disapproval of President Lincoln. Those who knew him best during his first official term pronounce him singularly free from plans and calculations regarding his own political future. He was too absorbed in public cares and duties, too nearly crushed by the great burdens resting upon him, to give thought or attention to questions of personal ambition. It had never been his aim, during his Presidential life, to look far ahead. He was content to deal wisely and soberly with important questions as they arose from day to day and hour to hour; to adapt himself and his actions to the exigencies of the present, and in that way to earn security for the future. He himself said, using a forcible and apt illustration borrowed from his early life: "The pilots on our Western rivers steer from *point to point*, as they call it—setting the course of the boat no farther than they can see; and that is all I propose to do in the great problems that are set before me."

Such a policy as that outlined by Lincoln, embraced in his homely and characteristic phrase of "pegging away," caused him to be greatly misunderstood and even distrusted in some quarters. As the time for the new election drew near, there was very pronounced dissatisfaction with him, particularly in New England. It was said of him, among other things, that he "lacked the essential qualities of a leader." Mr. Henry Greenleaf Pearson, the biographer of Governor Andrew of Massachusetts, illuminates this point in a few instructive sentences. "To comprehend this objection, which to us seems so astonishingly wide of the mark," says Mr. Pearson, "we must realize that whenever a New Englander of that generation uttered the word 'leader' his mind's eye was filled with the image of Daniel

Webster. Even those who called the fallen statesman 'Ichabod' could not forget his commanding presence, his lofty tone about affairs of state, his sonorous professions of an ideal, his whole *ex cathedra* attitude. All these characteristics supplied the aristocratic connotation of the word 'leader.' Of the broad democratic meaning of the term, the world had as yet received no demonstration. That Lincoln was in very truth the 'new birth of a new soil,' Lowell, with the advantage of literary detachment, was one of the first to discover and proclaim, both in his political essays and in the splendid stanzas of the 'Commemoration Ode.'"

While Lincoln seemingly gave little heed to the question of a second Presidential term, it must not be inferred that he was indifferent regarding it. His nature was one of those strong ones which, though desiring approbation, are yet able to live without it. His whole life had been a schooling in self-reliance and independence, and the last three years especially had rendered him an adept in that stern philosophy. But he was thoroughly human, and deep down in his nature was a craving for human sympathy and support. Knowing that he had done his best and was entitled to the full approval of his countrymen, he no doubt felt that it would be a pleasant thing to receive that approval by being called to serve them for another term. To one friend he remarked, using his old figure of "the people's attorney," "If the people think I have managed their case for them well enough to trust me to *carry it up to the next term*, I am sure I shall be glad to take it." He evidently dreaded the rebuke that would be implied in a failure to be renominated; yet it seemed unbecoming to him, in the critical condition of the country, to make any personal effort to that end. To these considerations were added his extreme weariness and longing for release from his oppressive burdens. He was also, as Mr. Welles records in his Diary, "greatly importuned and pressed by cunning intrigues."

From these various complications, Lincoln's embarrassment and perplexity as the time for holding the Republican Convention drew near were extreme. A journalistic friend (Mr. J.M. Winchell), who had a lengthy conversation with him on the subject, gives what is no doubt a correct idea of his state of mind at that period. "Mr. Lincoln received me," says Mr. Winchell, "kindly and courteously; but his manner was quite changed. It was not now the country about which his anxiety prevailed, but himself. There was an embarrassment about him which he could not quite conceal. I thought it proper to state in the outset that I wished simply to know whatever he was free to tell me in regard to his own willingness or unwillingness to accept a renomination. The reply was a monologue of an hour's duration, and one that wholly absorbed me, as it seemed to absorb himself. He remained seated nearly all the time. He was restless, often changing position, and occasionally, in some intense moment, wheeling his body around in his chair and throwing a leg over the arm. This was the only grotesque thing I recollect about him; his voice and manner were very earnest, and he uttered no jokes and told no anecdotes. He began by saying that as yet he was not a candidate for renomination. He distinctly denied that he was a party to any effort to that end, notwithstanding I knew that there were movements in his favor in all parts of the Northern States. These movements were, of course, without his prompting, as he positively assured me that with one or two exceptions he had scarcely conversed on the subject with his most intimate friends. He was not quite sure whether he desired a renomination. Such had been the responsibility of the office—so oppressive had he found its cares, so terrible its perplexities—that he felt as though the moment when he could relinquish the burden and retire to private life would be the sweetest he could possibly experience. But, he said, he would not deny that a re-election would also have its gratification to his feelings. He did not seek it, nor would he do so; he did not desire it for any ambitious or selfish purpose; but after the crisis the country was passing through under his Presidency, and the efforts he had made conscientiously to discharge the duties imposed upon him, it would be a very sweet satisfaction to him to know that he had secured the approval of his fellow citizens and earned the highest testimonial of confidence they could bestow. This was the gist of the hour's monologue; and I believe he spoke sincerely. His voice, his manner, gave his modest and sensible words a power of conviction. He seldom looked me in the face while he was talking; he seemed almost to be gazing into the future. I am sure it was not a pleasant thing for him to seem to be speaking in his own behalf. For himself, he affirmed that he should make no promises of office to anyone as an inducement for support. If nominated and elected, he should be grateful to his friends; but the interests of the country must always be first considered."

The principal candidates talked of as successors to Lincoln were Secretary Chase, General Frémont, and General Grant. Of the latter, Lincoln said, with characteristic frankness and generosity: "If he could be more useful as President in putting down the rebellion, I would be content. He is pledged to our policy of emancipation and the employment of negro soldiers; and if this policy is carried out, it will not make much difference who is President." But General Grant's good sense prevailed over his injudicious advisers, and he promptly refused to allow his name to be presented to the convention.

The most formidable candidate for the Republican nomination was Secretary Chase. The relations between him and the President had not latterly been very harmonious; and the breach was greatly widened by a bitter personal assault on Mr. Chase by General F.P. Blair, a newly elected

Congressman from Missouri, made on the floor of the House, about the middle of April, under circumstances which led Mr. Chase to believe that the President inspired, or at least approved, the attack. Mr. Chase was very angry, and an open rupture between his friends and those of the President was narrowly averted. Mr. Riddle, Congressman from Mr. Chase's State (Ohio), relates that on the evening after General Blair's offensive speech he was to accompany Mr. Chase on a visit to Baltimore. "I was shown," says Mr. Riddle, "to the Secretary's private car, where I found him alone and in a frenzy of rage. A copy of Blair's speech had been shown him at the station, and I was the sole witness of his Achillean wrath. He threatened to leave the train at once and send the President his resignation; but was persuaded to go on to Baltimore. He wished to forward his resignation from there, but concluded to withhold it till his return to Washington the next day. At Baltimore," continues Mr. Riddle, "I excused myself, and took the return train for Washington. I did not overestimate the danger to the Union cause. It would be a fatal error to defeat Mr. Lincoln at the Baltimore Convention; yet how could he succeed, with the angry resignation of Mr. Chase, and the defection of his friends—the powerful and aggressive radicals? Reaching Washington, I went to the White House direct. I knew the President could not have been a party to Blair's assault, and I wanted his personal assurances to communicate to Mr. Chase at the earliest moment. I was accompanied by Judge Spaulding, an eminent member of the House, fully sharing Mr. Chase's confidence, and somewhat cool toward the President. We found Mr. Lincoln drawn up behind his table, with papers before him, quite grim, evidently prepared for the battle which he supposed awaited him. Without taking a seat, hat in hand, I stated frankly, not without emotion, the condition of affairs,—the public danger, my entire confidence in him, my sole purpose there, the reason of Judge Spaulding's presence, and that we were there in no way as representatives of Mr. Chase. Mr. Lincoln was visibly affected. The tones of confidence, sympathy, personal regard, were strangers to him at that time. Softening, almost melting, he came round to us, shook our hands again and again, returned to his place, and standing there, took up and opened out, from their remote origin, the whole web of matters connected with the present complication. He spoke an hour— calm, clear, direct, simple. He reprehended Blair severely, and stated that he had no knowledge of his speech until after Blair left Washington. We were permitted to communicate this to Mr. Chase. He was satisfied with the President's explanation, and at the Baltimore Convention my large acquaintance enabled me to open the way for Governor Dennison of Ohio to become its presiding officer. All recognized the good effect of the organization of that body by the friends of Mr. Chase."

The National Republican Convention which met at Baltimore on the 8th of June adopted resolutions heartily approving the course of the administration and especially the policy of emancipation, and completed its good work by nominating Abraham Lincoln as its candidate for President for another term. Andrew Johnson, of Tennessee, was nominated for Vice-President. That Lincoln was gratified at this proof of confidence and esteem there can be no doubt. In his acceptance of the nomination, he said, with the most delicate modesty: "I view this call to a second term as in no wise more flattering to myself than as an expression of the public judgment that I may better finish a difficult work than could one less severely schooled to the task." And with characteristic humor, he thanked a visiting delegation for their good opinion of him, saying, "I have not permitted myself to conclude that I am the best man in the country; but I am reminded of the old Dutch farmer who remarked to a companion that *it was not best to swap horses while crossing a stream.*"

In July, 1864, great excitement and alarm were occasioned in Washington by a body of Confederate cavalry under General Early, who actually attacked the fortifications of the city, cut off its railroad communication with the North, and ravaged the country about with fire and sword. For several days skirmishing was going on between the raiders and the troops in our fortifications. The fact that the President himself was under fire from the enemy on this occasion gave the episode a decided thrill of realism. He, with other government officials—largely, no doubt, from motives of curiosity—visited the scene of the disturbance and witnessed the miniature but sometimes spirited engagements. Among these visitors was Secretary Welles, who thus records his experiences (Diary, July 12, 1864): "Rode out today to Fort Stevens. Looking out over the valley below, where the continual popping of pickets was going on, I saw a line of our men lying close near the bottom of the valley. Senator Wade came up beside me. We went into the Fort, where we found the President, who was sitting in the shade, his back against the parapet toward the enemy.... As the firing from the Fort ceased, our men ran to the charge and the Rebels fled. We could see them running across the fields, seeking the woods on the brow of the opposite hills. Below, we could see here and there some of our own men bearing away their wounded comrades. Occasionally a bullet from some long-range rifle passed over our heads. It was an interesting and exciting spectacle." Another account says: "President Lincoln visited the lines in person, and refused to retire, although urged to do so. He exposed himself freely at Fort Stevens, and a surgeon standing alongside of him was wounded by a ball which struck a gun and glanced." A gentleman named Neill, who lived in the country, about twelve miles from the city, gives a vivid conception of the imminence of the danger. "After breakfast, on Tuesday, July 12," says Mr. Neill, "I went as usual in a railway car to the city, and before noon my house was surrounded by General Bradley Johnson's insurgent cavalry, who had made an attempt to capture the New York express train, and had robbed the country store near by of its contents. The presence of the cavalry stopped all travel by railroad; and Senator Ramsey of Minnesota, who happened to be in Washington, could find no way to the North except by descending the Potomac to its mouth and then ascending Chesapeake Bay to Baltimore. While the cavalry was in the fields around my home, the enemy's infantry was marching toward the capital by what was called the Seventh Street road, and they set fire to the residence of Hon. Montgomery Blair, who had been Postmaster-General. As I sat in my room at the President's, the smoke of the burning mansion was visible; but business was transacted with as much quietness as if the foe were hundreds of miles distant. Mr. Fox, the assistant Secretary of the Navy, had in a private note informed the President that if there should be a necessity for him to leave the city he would find a steamer in readiness at the wharf at the foot of Sixth Street. About one o'clock in the afternoon of each day of the skirmishing, the President would enter his carriage, and drive to the forts, in the suburbs, and watch the soldiers repulse the invaders." For several days Washington was in great danger of capture. Nearly all the forces had been sent forward to reinforce Grant, and the city was comparatively defenseless. But its slender garrison, mostly raw recruits, held out gallantly under the encouragement of the President, until Grant sent a column to attack Early, who promptly withdrew, and the crisis was over. This was the last time the enemy threatened the national capital. From that time he had enough to do to defend Richmond.

Lincoln labored under deep depression during the summer of 1864. The Army of the Potomac achieved apparently very little in return for its enormous expenditure of blood and treasure. Until the victories of Farragut in Mobile Bay, late in August, and Sherman at Atlanta a few days later, the gloom was unrelieved. The people were restless and impatient, and vented their displeasure upon the administration, holding it responsible for all reverses and disappointments, and giving grudging praise for success at any point. The popular displeasure was increased by the President's call for 500,000 additional troops, made July 18,—a measure which some of his strongest friends deprecated, as likely to jeopardize his re-election in November. "It is not a personal question at all," said Lincoln. "It matters not what becomes of *me. We must have the men.* If I go down, I intend to go like the Cumberland, with my colors flying." To the question, When is the war to end? he said, "Surely I feel as deep an interest in this question as any other can; but I do not wish to name a day, a month, or a year, when it is to end. We accepted this war *for an object*—a worthy object; and the war will end *when that object is attained.* Under God, I hope it *never will end until that time.*"

The President's mind seemed constantly weighted with anxiety as to the movements and fortunes of our armies in the field. He could not sleep at night under this crushing load. Secretary Welles's Diary gives frequent instances of this. Once, after an engagement between the Western armies, the President, says Mr. Welles, "came to me with the latest news. He was feeling badly. Tells me a despatch was sent to him at the Soldiers' Home last night shortly after he got asleep, and so disturbed him that he had no more rest, but arose and came to the city and passed the remainder of the night awake and watchful." At another time, after a desperate battle between Grant and Lee, Mr. Welles says: "The President came into my room about one P.M. and told me he *had slept none last night.* He lay down for a short time on the sofa in my room, and detailed all the news he had gathered."

Ex-Governor Bross of Illinois furnishes an account of an interview with Lincoln during this dark period: "The last time I saw Mr. Lincoln, till, as a pallbearer, I accompanied his remains to their last resting-place, was in the early part of August, 1864. It was directly after the frightful disaster at Petersburg, and I was on my way to the front, to recover, if possible, the body of my brother, Colonel John A. Bross, who fell there at the head of his regiment. I found the President with a large pile of documents before him. He laid down his pen and gave me a cordial but rather melancholy welcome, asking anxiously for news from the West. Neither of us could shut our eyes to the gloom which hung over the entire country. The terrible losses of the Wilderness, and the awful disaster at Petersburg, weighed heavily upon our spirits. To a question, I answered that the people expected a still more vigorous prosecution of the war; more troops and needful appliances would, if called for, be forthcoming. 'I will tell you what the people want,' said the President, 'they want, and must have, *success.* But whether that come or not, I shall stay *right here* and do my duty. Here I shall be; and they may come and hang me on that tree' (pointing out of the window to one), 'but, God helping me, I shall never desert my post.' This was said in a way that assured me that these were the sentiments of his inmost soul."

The President, about this time, was greatly worried by Horace Greeley and others, who importuned him to receive negotiations for peace from the Confederate authorities. He at length said to Mr. Greeley, "I not only intend a sincere effort for peace, but you shall be a personal witness that it is made." On the same day that the call for additional troops was made, the President issued, through Mr. Greeley, the famous letter, "To Whom It May Concern," promising safe conduct to any person or persons authorized to present "any proposition which embraces the restoration of peace, the *integrity of the whole Union,* and the *abandonment of slavery.*" Nothing came of the proposed negotiations, except to stop for a time the mischievous fault-finding; which was, of course, the result aimed at by Lincoln. The act was severely condemned by many Republicans; but Lincoln only said, "It is hardly fair for them to say the letter amounts to *nothing*. It will shut up Greeley, and satisfy the people who are clamoring for peace. That's *something*, anyhow!"

So much blame was heaped upon the Government, and so great was the dissatisfaction at the North, that Lincoln looked upon the election of his competitor, General McClellan, and his own retirement, as not improbable. An incident in evidence of his discouragement is related by Secretary Welles. Entering the Executive office one day, Mr. Welles was asked to write his name across the back of a sealed paper which the President handed him. The names of several other members of the Cabinet were already on the paper, with the dates of signature. After the election, Lincoln opened the document in the presence of his Cabinet and read to them its contents, as follows:

EXECUTIVE MANSION, WASHINGTON,
August 23, 1864.

This morning, as for some days past, it seems exceedingly probable that this administration will not be re-elected. Then it will be my duty to co-operate with the President-elect so as to save the Union between the election and the inauguration.

A. LINCOLN.

By this careful prevision had Lincoln pledged himself to give to his successor that unselfish and patriotic assistance of which he himself had stood so sorely in need.

As the desperation of the South and the opposition to Lincoln at the North increased, fears were entertained by his friends that an attempt might be made upon his life. Lincoln himself paid but little heed to these forebodings of evil. He said, philosophically: "I long ago made up my mind that if anybody wants to kill me, he will do it. If I wore a shirt of mail and kept myself surrounded by a bodyguard, it would be all the same. There are a thousand ways of getting at a man if it is desired that he should be killed. Besides, in this case, it seems to me, the man who would succeed me would be just as objectionable to my enemies—if I have any." One dark night, as he was going out with a friend, he took along a heavy cane, remarking good-humoredly that "mother" (Mrs. Lincoln) had "got a notion into her head that I shall be assassinated, and to please her I take a cane when I go over to the War Department at nights—when I don't forget it."

It is probable that the attempts upon the life of President Lincoln were more numerous than is generally known. An incident of a very thrilling character, which might easily have involved a shocking tragedy, is related by Mr. John W. Nichols, who from the summer of 1862 until 1865 was one of the President's body-guard. "One night, about the middle of August, 1864," says Mr. Nichols, "I was doing sentinel duty at the large gate through which entrance was had to the grounds of the Soldiers' Home, near Washington, where Mr. Lincoln spent much time in summer. About eleven o'clock I heard a rifle-shot in the direction of the city, and shortly afterwards I heard approaching hoof-beats. In two or three minutes a horse came dashing up, and I recognized the belated President. The horse he rode was a very spirited one, and was Mr. Lincoln's favorite saddle-horse. As horse and rider approached the gate, I noticed that the President was bareheaded. As soon as I had assisted him in checking his steed, the President said to me: 'He came pretty near getting away with me, didn't he? He got the bit in his teeth before I could draw the rein.' I then asked him where his hat was; and he replied that somebody had fired a gun off down at the foot of the hill, and that his horse had become scared and had jerked his hat off. I led the animal to the Executive Cottage, and the President dismounted and entered. Thinking the affair rather strange, a corporal and myself started off to investigate. When we reached the place whence the sound of the shot had come—a point where the driveway intersects, with the main road—we found the President's hat. It was a plain silk hat, and upon examination we discovered a *bullet-hole* through the crown. We searched the locality thoroughly, but without avail. Next day I gave Mr. Lincoln his hat, and called his attention to the bullet-hole. He made some humorous remark, to the effect that it was made by some foolish marksman and was not intended for him; but added that he wished nothing said about the matter. We all felt confident it was an attempt to kill the President, and after that he never rode alone."

Amidst his terrible trials, Lincoln often exhibited a forced and sorrowful serenity, which many mistook for apathy. Even his oldest and best friends were sometimes deceived in this way. Hon. Leonard Swett relates a touching instance: "In the summer of 1864, when Grant was pounding his way toward Richmond in those terrible battles of the Wilderness, myself and wife were in Washington trying to do what little two persons could do toward alleviating the sufferings of the maimed and dying in the vast hospitals of that city. We tried to be thorough and systematic. We took the first man we came to, brought him delicacies, wrote letters to his friends, or did for him whatever else he most needed; then the next man, and so on. Day after day cars and ambulances were coming in, laden with untold sorrows for thousands of homes. After weeks of this kind of experience my feelings became so wrought up that I said to myself: The country cannot long endure this sacrifice. In mercy, both to North and South, every man capable of bearing arms must be hurried forward to Grant to end this, fearful slaughter at the earliest possible moment. I went to President Lincoln at the White House, and poured myself out to him. He was sitting by an open window; and as I paused, a bird lit upon a branch just outside and was twittering and singing most joyously. Mr. Lincoln, imitating the bird, said: '*Tweet, tweet, tweet*; isn't he singing sweetly?' I felt as if my legs had been cut from under me. I rose, took my hat, and said, 'I see the country is safer than I thought.' As I moved toward the door, Mr. Lincoln called out, in his hearty, familiar way, 'Here, Swett, come back and sit down.' Then he went on: 'It is impossible for a man in my position not to have thought of all those things. Weeks ago every man capable of bearing arms was ordered to the front, and everything you have suggested has been done.'"

The burdens borne by Lincoln seemed never to tell so seriously on his strength and vitality as in this terrible battle-summer of 1864. For him there had been no respite, no holiday. Others left the heat and dust of Washington for rest and recuperation; but he remained at his post. The demands upon him were incessant; one anxiety and excitement followed another, and under the relentless strain even his sturdy strength began to give way. "I sometimes fancy," said he, with pathetic good-humor, "that every one of the numerous grist ground through here daily, from a Senator seeking a war with France down to a poor woman after a place in the Treasury Department, darted at me with thumb and finger, picked out *their especial piece of my vitality*, and carried it off. When I get through with such a day's work there is only one word which can express my condition, and that is *flabbiness*." Once Mr. Brooks "found him sitting in his chair so collapsed and weary that he did not look up or speak when I addressed him. He put out his hand, mechanically, as if to shake hands, when I told him I had come at his bidding. Presently he roused a little, and remarked that he had had '*a mighty hard day*.'" Mr. Riddle, who saw him at this period, after some months' absence, says he was shocked, on gaining admission to the President, "by his appearance—that of a *baited, cornered man*, always on the defense against attacks that he could not openly meet and defy or punish." Mr. Carpenter, an inmate of the White House, says: "Absorbed in his papers, he would become unconscious of my presence, while I intently studied every line and shade of expression in that furrowed face. There were days when I could scarcely look into it without crying. During the first week of the battles of the Wilderness he scarcely slept at all. Passing through the main hall of the domestic apartment on one of these days, I met him, clad in a long morning wrapper, pacing back and forth a narrow passage leading to one of the windows, his hands behind him, great black rings under his eyes, his head bent forward upon his breast,—altogether such a picture of the effects of sorrow, care, and anxiety as would have melted the hearts of the worst of his adversaries, who so mistakenly applied to him the epithets of tyrant and usurper."

Mr. Edward Dicey, the English historian, says: "Never in my knowledge have I seen a sadder face than that of the late President during the time his features were familiar to me. It is so easy to be wise after the event; but it seems to me now that one ought somehow to have foreseen that the stamp of a sad end was impressed by nature on that rugged, haggard face. The exceeding sadness of the eyes and their strange sweetness were the one redeeming feature in a face of unusual plainness, and there was about them that odd, weird look, which some eyes possess, of seeming to see more than the outer objects of the world around."

Lincoln's family and friends strove to beguile him of his melancholy. They took him to places of amusement; they walked and drove with him in the pleasantest scenes about the capital; and above all, they talked with him of times past, seeking to divert his mind from its present distress by reviving memories of more joyous days. His old friends were, as Mr. Arnold states, "shocked with the change in his appearance. They had known him at his home, and at the courts in Illinois, with a frame of iron and nerves of steel; as a man who hardly knew what illness was, ever genial and sparkling with frolic and fun, nearly always cheery and bright. Now they saw the wrinkles on his face and forehead deepen into furrows; the laugh of old days was less frequent, and it did not seem to come from the heart. Anxiety, responsibility, care, thought, disasters, defeats, the injustice of friends, wore upon his giant frame, and his nerves of steel became at times irritable. He said one day, with a pathos which language cannot describe, 'I feel as though I shall *never be glad again*.'"

Hon. Schuyler Colfax repeats a similarly pathetic expression which fell from the lips of the afflicted President. "One morning," says Mr. Colfax, "calling upon him on business, I found him looking more than usually pale and careworn, and inquired the reason. He replied with the bad news he had received at a late hour the previous night, which had not yet been communicated to the press, adding that he had not closed his eyes or breakfasted; and, with an expression I shall never forget, he exclaimed, 'How willingly would I exchange places today with the soldier who sleeps on the ground in the Army of the Potomac!'"

A lady who saw Lincoln in the summer of 1864 for the first time, and who had expected to see "a very homely man," says: "I was totally unprepared for the impression instantly made upon me. So bowed and sorrow-laden was his whole person, expressing such weariness of mind and body, as he dropped himself heavily from step to step down to the ground. But his face!—oh, the pathos of it!—haggard, drawn into fixed lines of unutterable sadness, with a look of loneliness, as of a soul whose depth of sorrow and bitterness no human sympathy could ever reach. I was so penetrated with the anguish and settled grief in every feature, that I gazed at him through tears, and felt I had stepped upon the threshold of a sanctuary too sacred for human feet. The impression I carried away was that I had seen, not so much the President of the United States, as *the saddest man in the world.*"

The changes in Lincoln's appearance were noted in the subdued, refined, purified expression of his face, as of one struggling almost against hope, but still patiently enduring. Mr. Brooks says, "I have known impressionable women, touched by his sad face and his gentle bearing, to go away in tears." Another observer, Rev. C.B. Crane, wrote at the time: "The President looks thin and careworn. His form is bowed as by a crushing load; his flesh is wasted as by incessant solicitude; and his face is thin and furrowed and pale, as though it had become spiritualized by the vicarious pain which he endured in bearing on himself all the calamities of his country." Truly it might be said of him, in the words of Matthew Arnold:

> With aching hands and bleeding feet
>
> We dig and heap, lay stone on stone;
>
> We bear the burden and the heat
>
> Of the long day, and wish 't were done.
>
> Not till the hours of light return
>
> All we have built do we discern.

In the tragic experiences of Lincoln in these dark days, the outlook was less gloomy than it had seemed to his tortured soul. He was even then, as Mr. John Bigelow puts it, "making for himself a larger place in history than he had any idea of." He "builded better than he knew"; and the "hours of light" were soon to come when he would know what he had built and see the signs that promised better things. The Presidential election of 1864 demonstrated the abiding confidence of the people in him and his administration. Every loyal State but three—New Jersey, Delaware, and Kentucky—gave him its electoral vote; and his popular majority over McClellan, the Democratic candidate, was upwards of 400,000. Lincoln was cheered but not exultant at the news. Late in the evening of election day (November 8, 1864) he said, in response to public congratulations: "I am thankful to God for this approval of the people. But while deeply grateful for this mark of their confidence in me, if I know my own heart my gratitude is free from any taint of personal triumph. It is not in my nature to triumph over anyone; but I give thanks to Almighty God for this evidence of the people's resolution to stand by free government and the rights of humanity."

While the election returns were coming in, early in the evening, Lincoln was at the War Department with a little group assembled to hear them read. How different the scene from that in the quiet country town where he had waited for the returns on a similar occasion four years before! Then all was peace—the lull before the storm. Now the storm had broken, and its greatest fury was raging about that patient and devoted man who waited to hear the decision of the nation's supreme tribunal—the voice of the people whose decree would settle the fate of himself and of the country. Mr. Charles A. Dana, Assistant Secretary of War, who was in the group, gives this description of the scene: "General Eckert was coming in continually with telegrams containing election returns. Mr. Stanton would read them, and the President would look at them and comment upon them. Presently there came a lull in the returns, and Mr. Lincoln called me up to a place by his side. 'Dana,' said he, 'have you ever read any of the writings of Petroleum V. Nasby?' 'No, sir,' I said, 'I have only looked at some of them, and they seemed to me funny.' 'Well,' said he, 'let me read you a specimen,' and pulling out a thin yellow-covered pamphlet from his breast pocket he began to read aloud. Mr. Stanton viewed this proceeding with great impatience, as I could see; but Mr. Lincoln paid no attention to that. He would read a page or a story, pause to con a new election telegram, and then open the book again and go ahead with a new passage. Finally Mr. Chase came in; and presently Mr. Whitelaw Reid, and then the reading was interrupted. Mr. Stanton went to the door and beckoned me into the next room. I shall never forget his indignation at what seemed to him disgusting nonsense."

The morning following the election one of his private secretaries, Mr. Neill, coming to the Executive office earlier than usual, found Lincoln at his table engaged in his regular routine of official work. "Entering the room," says Mr. Neill, "I took a seat by his side, extended my hand, and congratulated him upon the vote, for the country's sake and for his own sake. Turning away from the papers which had been occupying his attention, he spoke kindly of his competitor, the calm, prudent General, and great organizer."

The importance of Lincoln's re-election, to the country and to himself, is forcibly stated by General Grant and Secretary Seward. The former telegraphed from City Point, the day following: "The victory is worth more to the country than a battle won." And the same evening, at a public gathering held to celebrate the event, Mr. Seward said: "The election has placed our President beyond the pale of human envy or human harm, as he is above the pale of human ambition. Henceforth all men will come to see him as we have seen him—a true, loyal, patient, patriotic, and benevolent man. Having no longer any motive to malign or injure him, detraction will cease, and Abraham Lincoln will take his place with Washington and Franklin and Jefferson and Adams and Jackson—among the benefactors of the country and of the human race."

Lincoln evidently felt greatly reassured by the result of what had seemed to him a very doubtful contest; but with the return of cheerfulness came also the dread of continuing his official labors. He began to long and plan for that happy period at the end of the second term when he should be free from public burdens. "Mrs. Lincoln desired to go to Europe for a long tour of pleasure," says Mr. Brooks. "The President was disposed to gratify her wish; but he fixed his eyes on California as a place of permanent residence. He had heard so much of the delightful climate and the abundant natural productions of California that he had become possessed of a strong desire to visit the State and remain there if he were satisfied with the results of his observations. 'When we leave this place,' he said, one day, 'we shall have enough, I think, to take care of us old people. The boys must look out for themselves. I guess mother will be satisfied with six months or so in Europe. After that I should really like to go to California and take a look at the Pacific coast.'"

After the Baltimore Convention, Mr. Chase proposed to resign his position as Secretary of the Treasury, but he was persuaded by influential friends of himself and Lincoln to reconsider his determination. Chief among these friends was Hon. John Brough, the sturdy "War Governor" of Ohio. Later in the summer of 1864 the relations between the President and Secretary Chase again became inharmonious; the latter determined a second time to resign, and communicated that fact in a confidential letter to Governor Brough. Hon. Wm. Henry Smith, at that time Ohio's Secretary of State, and intimately acquainted with the circumstances as they occurred, says: "Mr. Brough went directly to Washington to bring about another reconciliation. After talking the matter over with Mr. Chase and Mr. Stanton, he called on the President and urged a settlement that would retain the services of Mr. Chase in the Treasury Department. Mr. Lincoln was very kind, and admitted the force of all that was urged; but finally said, with a quiet but impressive firmness, 'Brough, I think you had better *give up the job* this time.' And thereupon he gave reasons why it was unwise for Mr. Chase to continue longer in the Cabinet."

In the autumn, the Chief-Justiceship became vacant by the death of Judge R.B. Taney (October 11, 1864), and the friends of Mr. Chase, who was then in retirement, desired his elevation to that honorable seat. Congressman Riddle, who was designated to present the matter to the President, says: "After hearing what I had to say, Mr. Lincoln asked, 'Will this content Mr. Chase?' 'It is said that those bitten of the Presidency die of it,' I replied. His smile showed he would not take that answer. I added: 'Mr. Chase is conscious of ability to serve the country as President. We should expect the greatest from him.' 'He would not disappoint you, were it in his reach. But I should be sorry to see a Chief-Justice anxious to *swap* for it. ' I said then what I had already said to Mr. Chase: that I would rather be the Chief Justice than the President. I urged that the purity and elevation of Mr. Chase 's character guaranteed the dignity of the station from all compromise; that momentous questions must arise, involving recent exercises of power, without precedents to guide the court; that the honor of the Government would be safe in the hands of Mr. Chase. 'Would you *pack* the Supreme Court?' he asked, a little sharply. 'Would you have a Judge with no preconceived notions of law?' was my response. 'True, true,' was his laughing reply; 'how could I find anyone, fit for the place, who has not some definite notions on all questions likely to arise?'"

The proposed appointment of Mr. Chase as Chief-Justice was severely criticized by certain friends of Lincoln, who believed Mr. Chase was personally hostile to the President, and could not understand the latter's magnanimity in thus ignoring personal considerations. When told of these criticisms, Lincoln said: "My friends all over the country are trying to put up the bars between me and Governor Chase. I have a vast number of messages and letters from men who think they are my friends, imploring and warning me not to appoint him. Now I know more about Governor Chase's hostility to me than any of these men can tell me; but *I am going to nominate him.*" Which he did, and Chase became Chief-Justice in December, 1864.

The withdrawal of Secretary Chase from the Cabinet was soon followed by that of Postmaster-General Blair, who was succeeded by ex-Governor Dennison of Ohio. Blair received, says Mr. Welles in his Diary, a letter from the President, which, though friendly in tone, informed him that the time had arrived when it seemed best that he should retire, and requesting his resignation, which was promptly given. Mr. Welles says that the President subsequently informed him that "Mr. Chase had many friends who felt wounded that he should have left the Cabinet, and left alone. The friends of

Blair had been his assailants, and the President thought that if he also left the Cabinet Chase and his friends would be satisfied and the administration would be relieved of irritating bickerings. The relations of Blair with Stanton also were such that it was difficult for the two to remain." A little later came the resignation of Attorney-General Bates, which, says Mr. Welles, "has initiated more intrigues. A host of candidates are thrust forward—Evarts, Holt, Gushing, Whiting, and the Lord knows who, are all candidates." This gives but a faint idea of the embarrassments and dissensions among Lincoln's friends and official advisers, and of the ceaseless efforts and infinite tact that were needed to maintain a decent degree of harmony among them.

Early in December the President submitted to Congress his fourth annual message—a brief and businesslike statement of the prospects and purposes of the Government. Its first sentence is: "The most remarkable feature in the military operations of the year is General Sherman's attempted march of three hundred miles directly through the insurgent region." Then follows a reference to the important movements that had occurred during the year, "to the effect of moulding society for durability in the Union." The document closes with the following explicit statement: "In presenting the abandonment of armed resistance to the national authority, on the part of the insurgents, as the only indispensable condition to ending the war on the part of the Government, I *retract nothing* heretofore said as to slavery. If the people should, by whatever mode or means, make it an executive duty to re-enslave such persons, *another, and not I*, must be their instrument to perform it. In stating a single condition of peace, I mean simply to say that the war will cease on the part of the Government whenever it shall have ceased on the part of those who began it."

New Year's day, 1865, was marked by a memorable incident. Among the crowds gathered in the White House grounds stood groups of colored people, watching with eager eyes the tide of people flowing in at the open door to exchange salutations with the President. It was a privilege heretofore reserved for the white race; but now, as the line of visitors thinned, showing that the reception was nearly over, the boldest of the colored men drew near the door with faltering step. Some were in conventional attire, others in fantastic dress, and others again in laborers' garb. The novel procession moved into the vestibule and on into the room where the President was holding the republican court. Timid and doubting, though determined, they ventured where their oppressed and down-trodden race had never appeared before, and with the keen, anxious, inquiring look on their dark faces, seemed like a herd of wild creatures from the woods, in a strange and dangerous place. The reception had been unusually well attended, and the President was nearly overcome with weariness; but when he saw the dusky faces of his unwonted visitors, he rallied from his fatigue and gave them a hearty welcome. They were wild with joy. Thronging about him, they pressed and kissed his hand, laughing and weeping at once, and exclaiming, "God bless Massa Linkum!" It was a scene not easy to forget: the thanks and adoration of a race paid to their deliverer.

Ever since issuing the Emancipation Proclamation Lincoln had earnestly desired that that measure should be perfected by a Constitutional amendment forever prohibiting slavery in the territory of the United States. He had discussed the matter fully with his friends in Congress, and repeatedly urged them to press it to an issue. Just before the Baltimore Convention, he urged Senator Morgan of New York, chairman of the National Republican Committee, to have the proposed amendment made the "key-note of the speeches and the key-note of the platform." Congressman Rollins of Missouri relates that the President said to him, "The passage of the amendment will *clinch the whole matter*." The subject was already definitely before Congress. In December, 1863, joint resolutions for this great end had been introduced in the House by Hon. James M. Ashley of Ohio, and in the Senate by Hon. Charles Sumner of Massachusetts and Hon. J.B. Henderson of Missouri. Senator Trumbull of the Judiciary Committee, to whom the Senate resolutions were referred, reported a substitute for the amendment, which, in April, 1864, passed the Senate by a vote of thirty-eight to six; but reaching the House, June 15, it failed to get the necessary two-thirds vote and was defeated. At the next session of Congress the resolutions were again presented to the House, and after a protracted debate were passed (January 13, 1865) by a vote of one hundred and nineteen to fifty-six. Illinois was the first State to ratify the amendment; and others promptly followed. Lincoln was grateful and delighted. He remarked, "This ends the job"; adding, "I feel proud that Illinois is a little ahead."

Overtures having been made, through General Grant, for a meeting between the President and certain "peace commissioners" representing the belligerents, Lincoln, anxious that nothing should be left undone that might evidence his desire to bring the war to a close, consented to the interview. On the morning of February 2, 1865, he left Washington, quite privately, in order to accomplish his mission without awakening the gossip and criticism which publicity would excite. At Fortress Monroe he was joined by Secretary Seward, who seems to have been the only member of the Cabinet who knew of the President's intention to meet the Southern Commissioners. Lincoln took the full responsibility, as he often did when dealing with risky or unpopular measures. "None of the Cabinet were advised of this move, and without exception I think it struck them unfavorably that the Chief Magistrate should have gone on such a mission," is the comment of Secretary Welles,—although he adds, "The discussion will be likely to tend to peace."

The next morning (February 3) the President and Mr. Seward received the Southern Commissioners—Stephens, Hunter, and Campbell—on board the U.S. steam transport "River Queen" in Hampton Roads. The conference, says Mr. Seward, "was altogether informal. There was no attendance of secretaries, clerks, or other witnesses. Nothing was written or read. The conversation, although earnest and free, was calm and courteous and kind on both sides. The Richmond party approached the subject rather indirectly, and at no time did they either make categorical demands or tender formal stipulations or absolute refusals. Nevertheless, during the conference, which lasted four hours, the several points at issue between the Government and the insurgents were distinctly raised and discussed, fully, intelligently, and in an amicable spirit."

The meeting was fruitless. The commissioners asked, as a preliminary step, the recognition of Jefferson Davis as President of the Southern Confederacy. Lincoln declined, stating that "the only ground on which he could rest the justice of the war—either with his own people or with foreign powers—was that it was not a war of conquest, for the States had never been separated from the Union. Consequently he could not recognize another government inside of the one of which he alone was President, nor admit the separate independence of States that were yet a part of the Union. 'That,' said he, 'would be doing what you have so long asked Europe to do in vain, and be resigning the only thing the armies of the Union have been fighting for.' Mr. Hunter, one of the commissioners, made a long reply to this, insisting that the recognition of Davis's power to make a treaty was the first and indispensable step to peace, and referred to the correspondence between King Charles I. and his Parliament as a trustworthy precedent of a constitutional ruler treating with rebels. Lincoln's face then wore that indescribable expression which generally preceded his hardest hits, as he remarked: 'Upon questions of history I must refer you to Mr. Seward, for he is posted in such things, and I don't pretend to be. My only distinct recollection of the matter is that *Charles lost his head.*'"

Alexander H. Stephens, one of the commissioners at the meeting on board the "River Queen," and the Vice-President of the waning Confederacy, was a very small man physically, with a complexion so yellow as to suggest an ear of ripe corn. Lincoln gave the following humorous account of the meeting with him: "Mr. Stephens had on an overcoat about three sizes too big for him, with an old-fashioned high collar. The cabin soon began to get pretty warm, and after a while he stood up and pulled off his big coat. He slipped it off just about as you would husk an ear of corn. I couldn't help thinking, as I looked first at the overcoat and then at the man, 'Well, that's the *biggest shuck* and the *smallest nubbin* I ever laid eyes on. '"

So strongly were Lincoln's hopes fixed on finding some possible basis for a peaceful restoration of the Union that a few days after his return from his meeting with the Southern Peace Commissioners he presented to the Cabinet (February 5, 1865) a scheme for paying to the Southern States a partial compensation for the loss of their slaves, provided they would at once discontinue armed resistance to the Federal Government. It was, says Mr. Welles, who was present at the meeting referred to, as "a proposition for paying the expenses of the war for two hundred days, or four hundred millions of dollars, to the rebellious States, to be for the extinguishment of slavery. The scheme did not meet with favor, and was dropped." But it showed, adds Mr. Welles, "the earnest desire of the President to conciliate and effect peace."

The evening of March 3, 1865, the President had remained with his Cabinet at the Capitol until a late hour, finishing the business pertaining to the last acts of the old Congress. His face had the ineffaceable care-worn look, yet his manner was cheerful, and he appeared to be occupied with the work of the moment, to the exclusion of all thoughts of the future or of the great event of the morrow.

Rain prevailed during the morning of inauguration day, but before noon it had ceased falling. The new Senate, convened for a special session, was organized, and Andrew Johnson was sworn in its presence into the office of Vice-President. Shortly after twelve o'clock, Lincoln entered the chamber and joined the august procession, which then moved to the eastern portico. As Lincoln stepped forward to take the oath of office, a flood of sunlight suddenly burst from the clouds, illuminating his face and form as he bowed to the acclamations of the people. Speaking of this incident next day, he said, "Did you notice that sunburst? It made my heart jump." Cheers and shouts rent the air as the President prepared to speak his inaugural. He raised his arm, and the crowd hushed to catch his opening words. He paused, as though thronging memories impeded utterance; then, in a voice clear and strong, but touched with pathos, he read that eloquent and imperishable composition, the Second Inaugural Address.

> *Fellow-Countrymen:* At this second appearing to take the oath of the Presidential office, there is less occasion for an extended address than there was at the first. Then a statement, somewhat in detail, of a course to be pursued, seemed fitting and proper. Now, at the expiration of four years, during which public declarations have been constantly called forth on every point and phase of the great contest which still absorbs the attention and engrosses the energies of the Nation, little that is new could be presented.

The progress of our arms, upon which all else chiefly depends, is as well known to the public as to myself; and it is, I trust, reasonably satisfactory and encouraging to all. With high hope for the future, no prediction in regard to it is ventured.

On the occasion corresponding to this, four years ago, all thoughts were anxiously directed to an impending civil war. All dreaded it, all sought to avoid it. While the inaugural address was being delivered from this place, devoted altogether to saving the Union without war, insurgent agents were in the city, seeking to destroy it with war,—seeking to dissolve the Union, and divide the effects by negotiation. Both parties deprecated war, but one of them would make war rather than let the Nation survive, and the other would accept war rather than let it perish; and the war came. One-eighth of the whole population were colored slaves, not distributed generally over the Union, but localized in the southern part of it. These slaves constituted a peculiar and powerful interest. All knew that this interest was somehow the cause of the war. To strengthen, perpetuate, and extend this interest was the object for which the insurgents would rend the Union by war, while the Government claimed no right to do more than to restrict the territorial enlargement of it.

Neither party expected for the war the magnitude or the duration which it has already attained. Neither anticipated that the cause of the conflict might cease when, or even before the conflict itself should cease. Each looked for an easier triumph, and a result less fundamental and astounding. Both read the same Bible, and pray to the same God, and each invokes His aid against the other. It may seem strange that any men should dare to ask a just God's assistance in wringing their bread from the sweat of other men's faces; but let us judge not, that we be not judged. The prayer of both could not be answered. That of neither has been answered fully. The Almighty has his own purposes. "Woe unto the world because of offenses, for it must needs be that offenses come, but woe to that man by whom the offense cometh." If we shall suppose that American slavery is one of those offenses, which, in the Providence of God, must needs come, but which, having continued through

His appointed time, He now wills to remove, and that He gives to North and South this terrible war, as the woe due to those by whom the offense came, shall we discern therein any departure from those Divine attributes which the believers in a living God always ascribe to Him? Fondly do we hope, fervently do we pray, that this mighty scourge of war may speedily pass away. Yet if God wills that it continue until all the wealth piled by the bondman's two hundred and fifty years of unrequited toil shall be sunk, and until every drop of blood drawn by the lash shall be paid by another drawn with the sword, as was said three thousand years ago, so still it must be said: "The judgments of the Lord are true and righteous altogether."

With malice toward none, with charity for all, with firmness in the right, as God gives us to see the right, let us strive on to finish the work we are in; to bind up the nation's wounds; to care for him who shall have borne the battle, and for his widow and for his orphan; to do all which may achieve and cherish a just and lasting peace among ourselves and with all nations.

This address was probably, next to the Gettysburg oration, Lincoln's most eloquent and touching public appeal. Gladstone of England said of it: "I am taken captive by so striking an utterance as this. I see in it the effect of sharp trial, when rightly borne, to raise men to a higher level of thought and action. It is by cruel suffering that nations are sometimes born to a better life. So it is with individual men. Lincoln's words show that upon him anxiety and sorrow have wrought their true effect."

As the procession moved from the Capitol to the White House, at the close of the inaugural ceremonies, a bright star was visible in the heavens. The crowds gazing upon the unwonted phenomenon noted it as an auspicious omen, like the baptism of sunshine which had seemed to consecrate the President anew to his exalted office.

CHAPTER XXVIII

Great events crowded upon each other in the last few weeks of the Civil War; and we must pass rapidly over them, giving special prominence only to those with which President Lincoln was personally connected. The Army of the Potomac under Grant, which for nearly a year had been incessantly engaged with the army of General Lee, had forced the latter, fighting desperately at every step, back through the Wilderness, into the defenses about Richmond; and Lee's early surrender or retreat southward seemed the only remaining alternatives. But the latter course, disastrous as it would have been for the Confederacy, was rendered impracticable by the comprehensive plan of operations that had been adopted a year before. Interposed between Richmond and the South was now the powerful army of General Sherman. This daring and self-reliant officer, after his brilliant triumph at Atlanta the previous fall, had pushed on to Savannah and captured that city also; then turning his veteran columns northward, he had swept like a dread meteor through South Carolina, destroying the proud city of Charleston, and then Columbia, the State capital. General Johnston, with a strong force, vainly tried to stay his progress through North Carolina; but after a desperate though unsuccessful battle at Bentonville (March 20, 1865), the opposition gave way, and the Union troops occupied Goldsboro, an important point a hundred miles south of Richmond, commanding the Southern railway communications of the Confederate capital. The situation was singularly dramatic and impressive. In this narrow theatre of war were now being rendered, with all the leading actors on the stage, the closing scenes of that great and bloody tragedy. Grant on the north and Sherman on the south were grinding Lee and Johnston between them like upper and nether millstones.

The last days of March brought unmistakable signs of the speedy breaking-up of the rebellion. Lincoln, filled with anticipation not unmixed with anxiety, wished to be at the front. "When we came to the end of the War and the breaking-up of things," says General Grant, "one of Lincoln's friends said to me, 'I think Lincoln would like to come down and spend a few days at City Point, but he is afraid if he does come it might look like interfering with the movements of the army, and after all that has been said about other Generals he hesitates.' I was told that if Lincoln had a hint from me that he would be welcome he would come by the first boat. Of course I sent word that the President could do me no greater honor than to come down and be my guest. He came down, and we spent several days riding around the lines. He was a fine horseman. He talked, and talked, and talked; he seemed to enjoy it, and said, 'How grateful I feel to be with the boys and see what is being done at Richmond!' He never asked a question about the movements. He would say, 'Tell me what has been done; not what is to be done.' He would sit for hours tilted back in his chair, with his hand shading his eyes, watching the movements of the men with the greatest interest." Another account says: "Lincoln made many visits with Grant to the lines around Richmond and Petersburg. On such occasions he usually rode one of the General's fine bay horses, called 'Cincinnati.' He was a good horseman, and made his way through swamps and over corduroy roads as well as the best trooper in the command. The soldiers invariably recognized him, and greeted him, wherever he appeared amongst them, with cheers that were no lip service, but came from the depth of their hearts. He always had a pleasant salute or a friendly word for the men in the ranks."

Aside from the President's desire to be at the front at this critical time, he had an almost feverish anxiety to escape from the petty concerns and details of official life in Washington. In Welles's Diary is this entry (March 23, 1865): "The President has gone to the front, partly to get rid of the throng [office-seekers, politicians, etc.] that is pressing on him. The more he yields, the greater the pressure. It has now become such that he is compelled to flee. There is no doubt he is much worn down. Besides, he wishes the war terminated, and, to this end, that severe terms shall not be exacted of the Rebels."

Much of the time during the President's visit to the army he had his quarters on the steamer "River Queen," lying in the James river at City Point. It was the same vessel on which he had received the Southern peace commissioners a month before, and the one on which he had made the journey from Washington. On the 27th of March a memorable interview occurred in the cabin of this vessel, between President Lincoln, Generals Grant and Sherman, and Admiral Porter. General Sherman thus describes the interview: "I left Goldsboro on the 25th of March and reached City Point on the afternoon of the 27th. I found General Grant and staff occupying a neat set of log huts, on a bluff overlooking the James river. The General's family was with him. We had quite a long and friendly talk, when Grant remarked that the President was near by in a steamer lying at the dock, and he proposed that we should call at once. We did so, and found Mr. Lincoln on board the 'River Queen.' We had met in the early part of the war; he recognized me, and received me with a warmth of manner and expression that was most grateful. We sat some time in the after-cabin, and Mr. Lincoln made many inquiries about the events which attended the march from Savannah to Goldsboro, and seemed to enjoy the humorous stories about 'our bummers,' of which he had heard much. When in lively conversation his face brightened wonderfully, but if the conversation flagged it assumed a sad and sorrowful expression. General Grant and I explained to him that my next move from Goldsboro would bring my army, increased to 80,000 men by Schofield's and Terry's reinforcements, in close communication with Grant's army then investing Lee and Richmond; and that unless Lee could effect his escape and make junction with Johnston in North Carolina, he would soon be shut up in Richmond with no possibility of supplies, and would have to surrender. Mr. Lincoln was extremely interested in this view of the case, and we explained that Lee's only chance was to escape, join Johnston, and, being then between me in North Carolina and Grant in Virginia, he could choose which to fight. Mr. Lincoln seemed impressed with this; but General Grant explained that at the very moment of our conversation General Sheridan was pressing his cavalry across James River from the north to the south, that with this cavalry he would so extend his left below Petersburg as to meet the South Shore Road, and that if Lee should 'let go' his fortified lines he (Grant) would follow him so close that he could not possibly fall on me alone in North Carolina. I in like manner expressed the fullest confidence that my army in North Carolina was willing to cope with Lee and Johnston combined, till Grant could come up. But we both agreed that one more bloody battle was likely to occur before the close of the war. Mr. Lincoln repeatedly inquired as to General Schofield's ability to maintain his position in my absence, and seemed anxious that I should return to North Carolina. More than once he exclaimed, 'Must more blood be shed? Cannot this last bloody battle be avoided?' We explained that we had to presume that General Lee was a real general; that he must see that Johnston alone was no barrier to my progress, and that if my army of 80,000 veterans should reach Burksville he was lost in Richmond; and that we were forced to believe he would not await that inevitable conclusion, but would make one more desperate effort."

General Sherman adds this personal tribute to Lincoln to the account of the interview on board the "River Queen": "When I left Mr. Lincoln I was more than ever impressed by his kindly nature, his deep and earnest sympathy with the afflictions of the whole people, resulting from the war, and by the march of hostile armies through the South. I felt that his earnest desire was to end the war speedily, without more bloodshed or devastation, and to restore all the men of both sections to their homes. In the language of his second inaugural address, he seemed to have 'charity for all, malice toward none,' and above all an absolute faith in the courage, manliness, and integrity of the armies in the field. When at rest or listening, his legs and arms seemed to hang almost lifeless, and his face was careworn and haggard; but the moment he began to talk his face lightened up, his tall form, as it were, unfolded, and he was the very impersonation of good humor and fellowship. The last words I recall as addressed to me were that he would feel better when I was back at Goldsboro. We parted at the gangway of the 'River Queen,' about noon of March 28, and I never saw him again. Of all the men I ever met, he seemed to possess more of the elements of greatness, combined with goodness, than any other."

A few days after the interview described by General Sherman, the President changed his quarters to the cabin of the "Malvern," Admiral Porter's flagship. The Admiral says: "The 'Malvern' was a small vessel with poor accommodations, and not at all fitted to receive high personages. She was a captured blockade-runner, and had been given to me as a flag-ship. I offered the President my bed, but he positively declined it, and elected to sleep in a small state-room outside of the cabin occupied by my secretary. It was the smallest kind of a room, six feet long by four and a half feet wide—a small kind of a room for the President of the United States to be domiciled in; but Mr. Lincoln seemed pleased with it. When he came to breakfast the next morning, I inquired how he had slept: 'I slept well,' he answered, 'but you can't put a long sword into a short scabbard. I was *too long* for that berth. ' Then I remembered he was over six feet four inches, while the berth was only six feet. That day, while we were out of the ship, all the carpenters were put to work; the state-room was taken down and increased in size to eight feet by six and a half feet. The mattress was widened to suit a berth of four feet width, and the entire state-room remodelled. Nothing was said to the President about the change in his quarters when he went to bed; but next morning he came out smiling, and said: 'A miracle happened last night; I shrank six inches in length and about a foot sideways. I got somebody else's big pillow, and slept in a better bed than I did on the "River Queen."' He enjoyed it greatly; but I do think if I had given him two fence-rails to sleep on he would not have found fault. That was Abraham Lincoln in all things relating to his own comfort. He would never permit people to put themselves out for him under any circumstances."

On the 2d of April the stronghold of Petersburg fell into the hands of the Union troops. Lincoln, accompanied by Admiral Porter, visited the city. They joined General Grant, and sat with him for nearly two hours upon the porch of a comfortable little house with a small yard in front. Crowds of citizens soon gathered at the fence to gaze upon these remarkable men of whom they had heard so much. The President's heart was filled with joy, for he felt that this was "the beginning of the end." Admiral Porter says: "Several regiments passed us *en route*, and they all seemed to recognize the President at once. 'Three cheers for Uncle Abe!' passed along among them, and the cheers were given with a vim which showed the estimation in which he was held by the soldiers. That evening," continues Admiral Porter, "the sailors and marines were sent out to guard and escort in some prisoners, who were placed on board a large transport lying in the stream. There were about a thousand prisoners, more or less. The President expressed a desire to go on shore. I ordered the barge and went with him. We had to pass the transport with the prisoners. They all rushed to the side with eager curiosity. All wanted to see the Northern President. They were perfectly content. Every man had a chunk of meat and a piece of bread in his hand, and was doing his best to dispose of it. 'That's Old Abe,' said one, in a low voice. 'Give the old fellow three cheers,' said another; while a third called out, Hello, Abe, your bread and meat's better than pop-corn!' It was all good-natured, and not meant in unkindness. I could see no difference between them and our own men, except that they were ragged and attenuated for want of wholesome food. They were as happy a set of men as ever I saw. They could see their homes looming up before them in the distance, and knew that the war was over. 'They will never shoulder a musket again in anger,' said the President, 'and if Grant is wise he will leave them their guns to shoot crows with. It would do no harm.'"

The next day (April 3) the Union advance, under General Weitzel, reached and occupied Richmond. Lee was in retreat, with Grant in close pursuit. When the news of the downfall of the Confederate capital reached Lincoln on board the "Malvern," he exclaimed fervently: "Thank God that I have lived to see this! It seems to me I have been dreaming a horrid dream for four years, and now the nightmare is gone. *I want to see Richmond.*"

The vessel started up the river, but found it extremely difficult to proceed, as the channel was filled with torpedoes and obstructions, and they were obliged to wait until a passage could be cleared. Admiral Porter thus describes what followed: "When the channel was reported clear of torpedoes (a large number of which were taken up), I proceeded up to Richmond in the 'Malvern,' with President Lincoln. Every vessel that got through the obstructions wished to be the first one up, and pushed ahead with all steam; but they grounded, one after another, the 'Malvern' passing them all, until she also took the ground. Not to be delayed, I took the President in my barge, and with a tug ahead with a file of marines on board we continued on up to the city. There was a large bridge across the James about a mile below the landing, and under this a party in a small steamer were caught and held by the current, with no prospect of release without assistance. I ordered the tug to cast off and help them, leaving us in the barge to go on alone. Here we were in a solitary boat, after having set out with a number of vessels flying flags at every masthead, hoping to enter the conquered capital in a manner befitting the rank of the President of the United States, with a further intention of firing a national salute in honor of the happy result. Mr. Lincoln was cheerful, and had his 'little story' ready for the occasion. 'Admiral, this brings to my mind a fellow who once came to me to ask for an appointment as minister abroad. Finding he could not get that, he came down to some more modest position. Finally he asked to be made a tide-waiter. When he saw he could not get that, he asked me for *an old pair of trousers*. It is sometimes well to be *humble*.'

"I had never been to Richmond before by that route," continues Admiral Porter, "and did not know where the landing was; neither did the cockswain nor any of the barge's crew. We pulled on, hoping to see someone of whom we could inquire, but no one was in sight. The street along the river-front was as deserted as if this had been a city of the dead. The troops had been in possession some hours, but not a soldier was to be seen. The current was now rushing past us over and among rocks, on one of which we finally stuck; but I backed out and pointed for the nearest landing. There was a small house on this landing, and behind it were some twelve negroes digging with spades. The leader of them was an old man sixty years of age. He raised himself to an upright position as we landed, and put his hands up to his eyes. Then he dropped his spade and sprang forward. 'Bress de Lord,' he said, 'dere is *de great Messiah*! I knowed him as soon as I seed him. He's bin in my heart fo' long yeahs, an' he's cum at las' to free his chillun from deir bondage! Glory, Hallelujah!' And he fell upon his knees before the President and kissed his feet. The others followed his example, and in a minute Mr. Lincoln was surrounded by these people, who had treasured up the recollection of him caught from a photograph, and had looked up to him for four years as the one who was to lead them out of captivity. It was a touching sight—that aged negro kneeling at the feet of the tall, gaunt-looking man who seemed in himself to be bearing all the grief of the nation, and whose sad face seemed to say, 'I suffer for you all, but will do all I can to help you.' Mr. Lincoln looked down on the poor creatures at his feet. He was much embarrassed at his position. 'Don't kneel to me,' he said, 'that is not right. You must kneel to God only, and thank Him for the liberty you will hereafter enjoy. I am but God's humble instrument; but you may rest assured that as long as I live no one shall put a shackle on your limbs, and you shall have all the rights which God has given to every other free citizen of this Republic.' It was a minute or two before I could get the negroes to rise and leave the President. The scene was so touching that I hated to disturb it, yet we could not stay there all day; we had to move on; so I requested the patriarch to withdraw from about the President with his companions, and let us pass on. 'Yes, Mars,' said the old man, 'but after bein' so many yeahs in de desert widout water, it's mighty pleasant to be lookin' at las' on our spring of life. 'Scuse us, sir; we means no disrepec' to Mars Lincoln; we means all love and gratitude.' And then, joining hands together in a ring, the negroes sang a hymn, with the melodious and touching voices possessed only by the negroes of the South. The President and all of us listened respectfully while the hymn was being sung. Four minutes at most had passed away since we first landed at a point where, as far as the eye could reach, the streets were entirely deserted; but now what a different scene appeared as that hymn went forth from the negroes' lips! The streets seemed to be suddenly alive with the colored race. They seemed to spring from the earth. They came tumbling and shouting, from over the hills and from the water-side, where no one was seen as we had passed. The crowd immediately became very oppressive. We needed our marines to keep them off. I ordered twelve of the boat's crew to fix bayonets to their rifles and surround the President, all of which was quickly done; but the crowd poured in so fearfully that I thought we all stood a chance of being crushed to death. At length the President spoke. He could not move for the mass of people—he had to do something. 'My poor friends,' he said, 'you are free—free as air. You can cast off the name of slave and trample upon it; it will come to you no more. Liberty is your birthright. God gave it to you as He gave it to others, and it is a sin that you have been deprived of it for so many years. But you must try to deserve this priceless boon. Let the world see that you merit it, and are able to maintain it by your good works. Don't let your joy carry you into excesses. Learn the laws and obey them; obey God's commandments and thank Him for giving you liberty, for to Him you owe all things. There, now, let me pass on; I have but little time to spare. I want to see the capital, and must return at once to Washington to secure to you that liberty which you seem to prize so highly.' The crowd shouted and screeched as if they would split the firmament, though while the President was speaking you might have heard a pin drop."

Presently the little party was able to move on. "It never struck me," says Admiral Porter, "there was anyone in that multitude who would injure Mr. Lincoln; it seemed to me that he had an army of supporters there who could and would defend him against all the world. Our progress was very slow; we did not move a mile an hour, and the crowd was still increasing. It was a warm day, and the streets were dusty, owing to the immense gathering which covered every part of them, kicking up the dirt. The atmosphere was suffocating; but Mr. Lincoln could be seen plainly by every man, woman, and child, towering head and shoulders above that crowd; he overtopped every man there. He carried his hat in his hand, fanning his face, from which the perspiration was pouring. He looked as if he would have given his Presidency for a glass of water—I would have given my commission for half that.

"Now came another phase in the procession. As we entered the city every window flew up, from ground to roof, and every one was filled with eager, peering faces, which turned one to another, and seemed to ask, 'Is this large man, with soft eyes, and kind, benevolent face, the one who has been held up to us as the incarnation of wickedness, the destroyer of the South?' There was nothing like taunt or defiance in the faces of those who were gazing from the windows or craning their necks from the sidewalks to catch a view of the President. The look of every one was that of eager curiosity—nothing more. In a short time we reached the mansion of Mr. Davis, President of the Confederacy, occupied after the evacuation as the headquarters of General Weitzel and Shepley. There was great cheering going on. Hundreds of civilians—I don't know who they were—assembled at the front of the house to welcome Mr. Lincoln. General Shepley made a speech and gave us a lunch, after which we entered a carriage and visited the State House—the late seat of the Confederate Congress. It was in dreadful disorder, betokening a sudden and unexpected flight; members' tables were upset, bales of Confederate scrip were lying about the floor, and many official documents of some value were scattered about.

"After this inspection I urged the President to go on board the 'Malvern.' I began to feel more heavily the responsibility resting upon me through the care of his person. The evening was approaching, and we were in a carriage open on all sides. He was glad to go; he was tired out, and wanted the quiet of the flag-ship. I was oppressed with uneasiness until we got on board and stood on the deck with the President safe; then there was not a happier man anywhere than myself."

On Sunday, April 9, the President returned to Washington; and there he heard the thrilling news that Lee, with his whole army, had that day surrendered to Grant at Appomattox. Lincoln's first visit, after reaching the capital, was to the house of Secretary Seward, who had met with a severe accident during his absence, and was a prisoner in a sick room. Lincoln's heart was full of joy, and he entered immediately upon an account of his visit to Richmond and the glorious successes of the Union army; "throwing himself," as Mr. Carpenter says, "in his almost boyish exultation, at full length across the bed, supporting his head upon one hand, and in this manner reciting the story of the collapse of the Rebellion. Concluding, he lifted himself up and said, 'And now for a day of Thanksgiving!'"

In Washington, as in every city and town in the loyal States, there was the wildest enthusiasm over the good news from the army. Flags were flying everywhere, cannon were sounding, business was suspended, and the people gave themselves up to the impulses of joy and thanksgiving. Monday afternoon the workmen of the navy-yard marched to the White House, joining the thousands already there, and with bands playing and a tumult of rejoicing, called persistently for the President. After some delay Lincoln appeared at the window above the main entrance, and was greeted with loud and prolonged cheers and demonstrations of love and respect. He declined to make a formal speech, saying to the excited throng beneath:

> I am very greatly rejoiced that an occasion has occurred so pleasurable that the people can't restrain themselves. I suppose that arrangements are being made for some sort of formal demonstration, perhaps this evening or to-morrow night. If there should be such a demonstration, I, of course, shall have to respond to it, and I shall have nothing to say if I dribble it out before. I see you have a band. I propose now closing up by requesting you to play a certain air or tune. I have always thought "Dixie" one of the best tunes I ever heard. I have heard that our adversaries over the way have attempted to appropriate it as a national air. I insisted yesterday that we had fairly captured it. I presented the question to the Attorney-General, and he gave his opinion that it is our lawful prize. I ask the band to give us a good turn upon it.

The band did give "a good turn" not only to "Dixie," but to the whimsical tune of "Yankee Doodle," after which Lincoln proposed three cheers for General Grant and all under his command; and then "three more cheers for our gallant navy," at the close of which he bowed and retired amid the inspiring strains of "Hail Columbia" discoursed with vigor by the patriotic musicians.

As additional despatches were received from the army, the joyful excitement in Washington increased. Tuesday evening, April 11, the President's mansion, the Executive Departments, and many of the business places and private residences, were illuminated, bonfires were kindled, and fireworks sent off, in celebration of the great event which stirred the hearts of the people. A vast mass of citizens crowded about the White House, as Lincoln appeared at the historic East window and made his last speech to the American public. It was a somewhat lengthy address, and had been prepared and written out for the occasion. "We meet this evening, not in sorrow but in gladness of heart," began the President. "No part of the honor or praise is mine. To General Grant, his skilful officers and brave men, all belongs." Mr. Brooks, who was in the White House during the delivery of this address, gives the following glimpses behind the scenes: "As Lincoln spoke, the multitude was as silent as if the court-yard had been deserted. Then, as his speech was written on loose sheets, and the candles placed for him were too low, he took a light in his hand and went on with his reading. Soon coming to the end of a page, he found some difficulty in handling the manuscript and holding the candlestick. A friend who stood behind the drapery of the window reached out and took the candle, and held it until the end of the speech, and the President let the loose pages fall on the floor, one by one, as fast as he was through with them. Presently Tad, having refreshed himself at the dinner-table, came back in search of amusement. He gathered up the scattered sheets of the President's speech, and then amused himself by chasing the leaves as they fluttered from the speaker's hand. Growing impatient at his father's delay to drop another page, Tad whispered, 'Come, give me another!' The President made a queer motion with his foot toward the boy, but otherwise showed no sign that he had other thoughts than those which he was dropping to the listeners beneath. Without was a vast sea of upturned faces, each eye fixed on the form of the President. Around the tall white pillars of the portico flowed an undulating surface of human beings, stirred by emotion and lighted with the fantastic colors of fireworks. At the window, his face irradiated with patriotic joy, was the much-beloved Lincoln, reading the speech that was to be his last to the people. Behind him crept back and forth, on his hands and knees, the boy of the White House, gathering up his father's carefully written pages, and occasionally lifting up his eager face waiting for more. It was before and behind the scenes. Sometimes I wonder, when I recall that night, how much of a father's love and thought of his boy might have been mingled in Lincoln's last speech to the eager multitude."

The President's speech on this occasion was largely devoted to the impending problem of Reconstruction in the South. The problem was complex and difficult, with no recognized principles or precedent for guidance. Said Lincoln: "Unlike the case of a war between independent nations, there is no authorized organization for us to treat with. No one man has authority to give up the rebellion for any other man. We simply must begin with and mould from disorganized and discordant elements. Nor is it a small additional embarrassment, that we, the loyal people, differ amongst ourselves as to the mode, manner, and measure of reconstruction. Let us all join in doing the acts necessary to restoring the proper practical relations between these States and the Union." The problem thus touched upon was one that had long occupied the thoughts of Lincoln, especially since the downfall of the Confederacy had been imminent. His practical and far-seeing mind was already addressing itself to the new issues, duties, and responsibilities, which he saw opening before him, and which he well knew would demand all of his wisdom, firmness, and political sagacity. As was to be expected, a great diversity of views prevailed. A powerful faction in Congress, sympathized with by some members of the Cabinet, was for "making treason odious" and dealing with the insurgent States as conquered provinces that had forfeited all rights once held under the Constitution and were entitled only to such treatment as the Government chose to give them. Lincoln's ideas were very different. His mind was occupied with formulating a policy having for its object the welfare of the Southern people and the restoration of the rebellious States to the Union. His broad and statesmanlike views were outlined, the day after the public address just referred to, in discussing Secretary Welles's plans for convening the legislature of Virginia. Says Mr. Welles in his Diary: "His idea was that the members of the legislature, comprising the prominent and influential men of their respective counties, had better come together and undo their own work. Civil government must be reestablished, he said, as soon as possible; there must be courts, and law and order, or society would be broken up, the disbanded armies would turn into robber bands and guerillas, which we must strive to prevent. These were the reasons why he wished prominent Virginians who had the confidence of the people to come together and turn themselves and their neighbors into good Union men." Lincoln had no thought of leaving any of these questions to the military authorities. In March he had directed a despatch from Stanton to Grant, saying: "The President wishes you to have no conference with General Lee, unless it be for the capitulation of his army, or on some other minor and purely military matter. He instructs me to say that you are not to decide, discuss, or confer upon any political question. Such questions the President *holds in his own hands*, and will submit them to no military conferences or conventions." During his meeting with Grant at Petersburg the President revealed to the General many of his plans for the rehabilitation of the South, and it could easily be seen that a spirit of magnanimity was uppermost in his heart. And at the conference with Grant, Sherman, and Porter, on board the "River Queen," the same subject was broached. "Though I cannot attempt to recall the words spoken by any one of the persons present on that occasion," says General Sherman, "I know we talked generally about what was to be done when Lee's and Johnston's armies were beaten and dispersed. On this point Mr. Lincoln was very full. He said that he had long thought of it, that he hoped this end could be reached without more bloodshed, but in any event he wanted us to get the men of the Southern armies disarmed and back to their homes; that he contemplated no revenge, no harsh measures, but quite the contrary, and that their suffering and hardships during the war would make them the more submissive to law." Says Hon. George Bancroft: "It was the nature of Mr. Lincoln to forgive. When hostilities ceased he who had always sent forth the flag with every one of its stars in the field was eager to receive back his returning countrymen."

One of the last stories of personal interviews with President Lincoln relates to his feeling of clemency for the men lately in rebellion. It is told by Senator Henderson of Missouri. "About the middle of March, 1865," says Senator Henderson, "I went to the White House to ask the President to pardon a number of men who had been languishing in Missouri prisons for various offenses, all political. Some of them had been my schoolmates, and their mothers and sisters and sweethearts had persisted in appeals that I should use my influence for their release. Since it was evident to me that the Confederacy was in its last throes, I felt that the pardon of most of these prisoners would do more good than harm. I had separated them, according to the gravity of their offenses, into three classes; and handing the first list to him, I said, 'Mr. President, the session of the Senate is closed, and I am about to start for home. The war is virtually over. Grant is pretty certain to get Lee and his army, and Sherman is plainly able to take care of Johnston. In my opinion the best way to prevent guerilla warfare at the end of organized resistance will be to show clemency to these Southern sympathizers.' Lincoln shook his head and said, 'Henderson, I am deeply indebted to you, and I want to show it; but don't ask me at this time to pardon rebels. I can't do it. People are continually blaming me for being too lenient. Don't encourage such fellows by inducing me to turn loose a lot of men who perhaps ought to be hanged.' I answered, 'Mr. President, these prisoners and their friends tell me that for them the war is over; and it will surely have a good influence now to let them go.' He replied, 'Henderson, my conscience tells me that I must not do it.' But I persisted. 'Mr. President, you *should* do it. It is necessary for good feeling in Missouri that these people be released. ' 'If I sign this list as a whole, will you be responsible for the future good behavior of these men? ' he asked. 'Yes,' I replied, 'I will.' 'Then I'll take the risk.' He wrote the word *Pardoned*, signed the order of release, and returned the paper to me. 'Thank you, Mr. President,' I said, 'but that is not all. I have another list.' 'You're not going to make me let loose another lot!' he exclaimed. 'Yes,' I answered, 'and my argument is the same as before. The guilt of these men is doubtful. Mercy must be the policy of peace.' With the only words approaching profanity that I ever heard him utter, he exclaimed, '*I'll be durned if I don't sign it!* Now, Henderson, ' he said, as he handed me the list, 'remember that you are responsible to me for these men, and if they don't behave '*I'll put you in prison for their sins.*'"

Lincoln's whole feeling toward the vanquished Southern people was one of peace and magnanimity. While many were clamoring for the execution of the Southern leaders, and especially Jefferson Davis, Lincoln said, only a day or two before his death: "This talk about Mr. Davis wearies me. I hope he will mount a fleet horse, reach the shores of the Gulf of Mexico, and ride *so far into its waters* that we shall never see him again." And then he told a pat story—perhaps his last—of a boy in Springfield, "who saved up his money and bought a 'coon,' which, after the novelty wore off, became a great nuisance. He was one day leading him through the streets, and had his hands full to keep clear of the little vixen, who had torn his clothes half off him. At length he sat down on the curb-stone, completely fagged out. A man passing was stopped by the lad's disconsolate appearance, and asked the matter. 'Oh,' was the only reply, 'this coon is such a *trouble* to me!' 'Why don't you get rid of him, then?' said the gentleman. '*Hush!*' said the boy, 'don't you see he is gnawing his rope off? I am going to let him do it, and then I will go home and tell the folks *that he got away from me.*'"

At the last Cabinet meeting ever attended by Lincoln, held in the morning of the day on which he was shot, the subject of Reconstruction was again uppermost, and various plans were presented and discussed. Secretary Stanton brought forward a plan or ordinance which he said he had prepared with much care and after a great deal of reflection. It was arranged that a copy of this should be furnished to each member of the Cabinet, for criticism and suggestion. "In the meantime," says Secretary Welles, "we were requested by the President to deliberate and carefully consider the proposition. He remarked that this was *the great question* now before us, and *we must soon begin to act.*" What that action would have been had Lincoln lived—what wrong and misery would have been spared to the South and shame and dishonor to the North—no one can doubt who comprehends the fibre of that kindly, just, and indomitable soul.

CHAPTER XXIX

It is something to be ever gratefully remembered, that the last day of Lincoln's life was filled with sunshine. His cares and burdens slipped from him like a garment, and his spirit was filled with a blessed and benignant peace.

On the morning of that fatal Friday, the 14th day of April, the President had a long conversation at breakfast with his son Robert, then a member of Grant's staff, who had just arrived from the front with additional particulars of Lee's surrender, of which event he had been a witness. The President listened with close attention to the interesting recital; then, taking up a portrait of General Lee, which his son had brought him, he placed it on the table before him, where he scanned it long and thoughtfully. Presently he said: "It is a good face. It is the face of a noble, brave man. I am glad that the war is over at last." Looking upon Robert, he continued: "Well, my son, you have returned safely from the front. The war is now closed, and we will soon live in peace with the brave men who have been fighting against us. I trust that the era of good feeling has returned, and that henceforth we shall live in harmony together."

After breakfast the President received Speaker Colfax, spending an hour or more in discussing his plans regarding the adjustment of matters in the South. This was followed by an interview with Hon. John P. Hale, the newly appointed Minister to Spain, and by calls of congratulation from members of Congress and old friends from Illinois. Afterwards he took a short drive with General Grant, who had just come to the city to consult regarding the disbandment of the army and the parole of prisoners. The people were wild with enthusiasm, and wherever the President and General Grant appeared they were greeted with cheers, the clapping of hands, waving of handkerchiefs, and every possible demonstration of delight.

At the Cabinet meeting held at noon the President was accompanied by General Grant. The meeting is thus described by one who was present, Secretary Welles: "Congratulations were interchanged, and earnest inquiry was made whether any information had been received from General Sherman. General Grant, who was invited to remain, said he was expecting hourly to hear from Sherman, and had a good deal of anxiety on the subject. The President remarked that the news would come soon and come favorably, he had no doubt, for he had last night his usual dream which had preceded nearly every important event of the war. I inquired the particulars of this remarkable dream. He said it was in my department—it related to the water; that he seemed to be in a singular and indescribable vessel, but always the same, and that he was moving with great rapidity toward a dark and indefinite shore; that he had had this singular dream preceding the firing on Sumter, the battles of Bull Run, Antietam, Gettysburg, Stone River, Vicksburg, Wilmington, etc. General Grant remarked, with some emphasis and asperity, that Stone River was no victory—that a few such victories would have ruined the country, and he knew of no important results from it. The President said that perhaps he should not altogether agree with him, but whatever might be the facts his singular dream preceded that fight. Victory did not always follow his dream, but the event and results were important. He had no doubt that a battle had taken place or was about being fought, 'and Johnston will be beaten, for I had this strange dream again last night. It must relate to Sherman; my thoughts are in that direction, and *I know of no other very important event which is likely just now to occur.*'" "Great events," adds Mr. Welles in his Diary, "did indeed follow; for within a few hours the good and gentle as well as truly great man who narrated his dream closed forever his earthly career."

After the Cabinet meeting the President took a drive with Mrs. Lincoln, expressing a wish that no one should accompany them. His heart was filled with a solemn joy, which awoke memories of the past to mingle with hopes for the future; and in this subdued moment he desired to be alone with the one who stood nearest to him in human relationship. In the course of their talk together, he said: "Mary, we have had a hard time of it since we came to Washington; but the war is over, and with God's blessing we may hope for four years of peace and happiness, and then we will go back to Illinois and pass the rest of our lives in quiet." He spoke, says Mr. Arnold, "of his old Springfield home; and recollections of his early days, his little brown cottage, the law office, the court room, the green bag for his briefs and law papers, his adventures when riding the circuit, came thronging back to him. The tension under which he had for so long been kept was removed, and he was like a boy out of school. 'We have laid by,' said he to his wife, 'some money, and during this term we will try and save up more, but shall not have enough to support us. We will go back to Illinois, and I will open a law office at Springfield or Chicago, and practise law, and at least do enough to help give us a livelihood.' Such were the dreams, the day-dreams of Lincoln, on the last day of his earthly life."

Mr. Neill, the President's private secretary, states that between three and four o'clock of this day he had occasion to seek the President to procure his signature to a paper. "I found," says Mr. Neill, "that he had retired to the private parlor of the house for lunch. While I was looking over the papers on his table, to see if I could find the desired commission, he came back, eating an apple. I told him what I was looking for, and as I talked he placed his hand upon the bell-pull. I said: 'For whom are you going to ring?' Placing his hand upon my coat, he spoke but two words: 'Andrew Johnson.' 'Then,' I said, 'I will come in again.' As I was leaving the room, the Vice-President had been ushered in, and the President advanced and took him by the hand."

Charles A. Dana, the Assistant Secretary of War, says that his last recollections of President Lincoln are indelibly associated with the seditious Jacob Thompson. "Late in the afternoon," says Mr. Dana, "a despatch was received at the War Department from the provost marshal of Portland, Maine, saying that he had received information that Jacob Thompson would arrive in Portland during that night, in order to take there the Canadian steamer which was to sail for Liverpool. On reading this despatch to Mr. Stanton, the latter said, 'Order him to be arrested—but no; you had better take it over to the President.' I found Mr. Lincoln in the inner room of his business office at the White House, with his coat off, washing his hands preparatory to a drive. 'Hello,' said he, 'what is it?' Listening to the despatch, he asked, 'What does Stanton say?' 'He thinks he ought to be arrested,' I replied. 'Well,' he continued, drawling his words, 'I rather guess not. When you have an elephant on your hands, and he wants to run away, better let him run.'"

During the afternoon the President signed a pardon for a soldier sentenced to be shot for desertion; remarking, as he did so, "Well, I think the boy can do us more good above ground than under ground." He also approved an application for the discharge, on taking the oath of allegiance, of a Southern prisoner, on whose petition he wrote, "*Let it be done.*" This act of mercy was his last official order.

It had been decided early in the day that the President and Mrs. Lincoln would attend Ford's Theatre in the evening, to witness the play of "The American Cousin." Lincoln had invited General Grant to accompany his party to the theatre, saying that the people would expect to see him and should not be disappointed. But the General had declined, as Mrs. Grant was anxious to start that afternoon to visit their children, who were at school in Burlington, New Jersey.

As the hour approached for leaving for the theatre, the President was engaged in a conversation with two friends—Speaker Colfax and Hon. George Ashmun of Massachusetts. The business on which they had met not being concluded, the President gave Mr. Ashmun a card on which he had written these words: "Allow Mr. Ashmun and friend to come in at 9 A.M. tomorrow—A. Lincoln." He then turned to Mr. Colfax, saying, "You are going with Mrs. Lincoln and me to the theatre, I hope." Mr. Colfax pleaded other engagements, when Lincoln remarked: "Mr. Sumner has the gavel of the Confederate Congress, which he got at Richmond to hand to the Secretary of War. But I insisted then that he must give it to you; and you tell him for me to hand it over." He then rose, but seemed reluctant to go, expressing a half-determination to delay a while longer. It was undoubtedly to avoid disappointing the audience, to whom his presence had been promised, that he went to the play-house that night. At the door he stopped and said to Speaker Colfax, who was about to leave for the Pacific coast, "Colfax, do not forget to tell the people in the mining regions, as you pass through, what I told you this morning about the development when peace comes. I will telegraph you at San Francisco."

It was nine o'clock when the Presidential party reached the theatre. The place was crowded; "many ladies in rich and gay costumes, officers in their uniforms, many well-known citizens, young folks, the usual clusters of gaslights, the usual magnetism of so many people, cheerful, with perfumes, music of violins and flutes—and over all, and saturating all, that vast, vague wonder, Victory, the Nation's victory, the triumph of the Union, filling the air, the thought, the sense, with exhilaration more than all perfumes." As the President entered he was greeted with tremendous cheers, to which he responded with genial courtesy. The box reserved for him, at the right of the stage, a little above the floor, was draped and festooned with flags. As the party were seated, the daughter of Senator Harris of New York occupied the corner nearest the stage; next her was Mrs. Lincoln; and behind them sat the President and Major Rathbone, the former being nearest the door.

> In his quiet chair he sate,
>
> Pure of malice or guile,
>
> Stainless of fear or hate;
>
> And there played a pleasant smile
>
> On the rough and careworn face,—
>
> For his heart was all the while
>
> On means of mercy and grace.

The brave old flag drooped o'er him,—

A fold in the hard hand lay;

He looked perchance on the play,—

But the scene was a shadow before him,

For his thoughts were far away.

It was half-past ten o'clock, and the audience was absorbed in the progress of the play, when suddenly a pistol shot, loud and sharp, rang through the theatre. All eyes were instantly directed toward the President's box, whence the report proceeded. A moment later, the figure of a man, holding a smoking pistol in one hand and a dagger in the other, appeared at the front of the President's box, and sprang to the stage, some eight or ten feet below, shouting as he did so, "*Sic semper tyrannis!*" He fell as he struck the stage; but quickly recovering himself, sprang through the side-wings and escaped from the theatre by a rear door.

At the moment of the assassination a single actor, Mr. Hawk, was on the stage. In his account of the tragical event he says: "When I heard the shot fired, I turned, looked up at the President's box, heard the man exclaim, '*Sic semper tyrannis!*' saw him jump from the box, seize the flag on the staff, and drop to the stage. He slipped when he struck the stage, but got upon his feet in a moment, brandished a large knife, crying, 'The South shall be free,' turned his face in the direction where I stood, and I recognized him as John Wilkes Booth. He ran towards me, and I, seeing the knife, thought I was the one he was after, and ran off the stage and up a flight of stairs. He made his escape out of a door directly in the rear of the theatre, mounted a horse, and rode off. The above all occurred in the space of a quarter of a minute, and at the time I did not know the President was shot."

Scarcely had the horror-stricken audience witnessed the leap and flight of the asassin when a woman's shriek pierced through the theatre, recalling all eyes to the President's box. The scene that ensued is described with singular vividness by the poet Walt Whitman, who was present: "A moment's hush—a scream—the cry of murder—Mrs. Lincoln leaning out of the box, with ashy cheeks and lips, with involuntary cry, pointing to the retreating figure, '*He has killed the President!*' And still a moment's strange, incredulous suspense—and then the deluge!—then that mixture of horror, noises, uncertainty—(the sound, somewhere back, of a horse's hoofs clattering with speed)—the people burst through chairs and railing, and break them up—that noise adds to the queerness of the scene—there is inextricable confusion and terror—women faint—feeble persons fall and are trampled on—many cries of agony are heard—the broad stage suddenly fills to suffocation with a dense and motley crowd, like some horrible carnival—the audience rush generally upon it—at least the strong men do—the actors and actresses are there in their play costumes and painted faces, with mortal fright showing through the rouge—some trembling, some in tears—the screams and calls, confused talk—redoubled, trebled—two or three manage to pass up water from the stage to the President's box—others try to clamber up. Amidst all this, a party of soldiers, two hundred or more, hearing what is done, suddenly appear; they storm the house, inflamed with fury, literally charging the audience with fixed bayonets, muskets, and pistols, shouting, 'Clear out! clear out!'.... And in the midst of that pandemonium of senseless haste—the infuriated soldiers, the audience, the stage, its actors and actresses, its paints and spangles and gaslights,—the life blood from those veins, the best and sweetest of the land, drips slowly down, and death's ooze already begins its little bubbles on the lips."

It appears that Booth, the assassin, had long been plotting the murder of the President, and was awaiting a favorable moment for its execution. He had visited the theatre at half-past eleven on the morning of the 14th, and learned that a box had been taken for the President that evening. He engaged a fleet horse for a saddle-ride in the afternoon, and left it at a convenient place. In the evening he rode to the theatre, and, leaving the animal in charge of an accomplice, entered the house. Making his way to the door of the President's box, and taking a small Derringer pistol in one hand and a double-edged dagger in the other, he thrust his arm into the entrance, where the President, sitting in an arm-chair, presented to his view the back and side of his head. A flash, a sharp report, a puff of smoke, and the fatal bullet had entered the President's brain.

Major Rathbone, who occupied a seat in the President's box, testifies that he was sitting with his back toward the door, when he heard the discharge of a pistol behind him, and looking around saw through the smoke a man between the door and the President. Major Rathbone instantly sprang toward him and seized him; the man wrested himself from his grasp, and made a violent thrust at the Major's breast with a large knife. The Major parried the blow by striking it up, and received a wound in his left arm. The man rushed to the front of the box, and the Major endeavored to seize him again, but only caught his clothes as he was leaping over the railing of the box. Major Rathbone then turned to the President. His position was not changed; his head was slightly bent forward, and his eyes were closed.

As soon as the surgeons who had been summoned completed their hasty examination, the unconscious form of the President was borne from the theatre to a house across the street, and laid upon his death-bed. Around him were gathered Surgeon-General Barnes, Vice-President

Johnson, Senator Sumner, Secretaries Stanton and Welles, Generals Halleck and Meigs, Attorney-General Speed, Postmaster-General Dennison, Mr. McCulloch, Speaker Colfax, and other intimate friends who had been hastily summoned. Mrs. Lincoln sat in an adjoining room, prostrate and overwhelmed, with her son Robert. The examination of the surgeons had left no room for hope. The watchers remained through the night by the bedside of the stricken man, who showed no signs of consciousness; and a little after seven o'clock in the morning—Saturday the 15th of April—he breathed his last.

A vivid account of the death-bed scene, together with particulars of the attacks upon Secretary Seward and his son Frederick a half-hour later than the attack upon the President, is furnished in the contemporaneous record of Secretary Welles, a singularly cool observer and clear narrator. "I had retired to bed about half-past ten on the evening of the 14th of April," writes Mr. Welles, "and was just getting asleep when Mrs. Welles, my wife, said some one was at our door.... I arose at once and raised a window, when my messenger, James Smith, called to me that Mr. Lincoln, the President, had been shot; and said Secretary Seward and his son, Assistant Secretary Frederick Seward, were assassinated.... I immediately dressed myself, and, against the earnest remonstrance and appeals of my wife, went directly to Mr. Seward's, whose residence was on the east side of the square, mine being on the north.... Entering the house, I found the lower hall and office full of persons, and among them most of the foreign legations, all anxiously inquiring what truth there was in the horrible rumors afloat.... At the head of the first stairs I met the elder Mrs. Seward, who was scarcely able to speak, but desired me to proceed up to Mr. Seward's room.... As I entered, I met Miss Fanny Seward, with whom I exchanged a single word, and proceeded to the foot of the bed. Dr. Verdi, and, I think, two others, were there. The bed was saturated with blood. The Secretary was lying on his back, the upper part of his head covered by a cloth, which extended down over his eyes. His mouth was open, the lower jaw dropping down. I exchanged a few whispered words with Dr. Verdi. Secretary Stanton, who came after but almost simultaneously with me, made inquiries in a louder tone till admonished by a word from one of the physicians. We almost immediately withdrew and went into the adjoining front room, where lay Frederick Seward. His eyes were open, but he did not move them, nor a limb, nor did he speak. Doctor White, who was in attendance, told me he was unconscious and more dangerously injured than his father.... As we descended the stairs, I asked Stanton what he had heard in regard to the President that was reliable. He said the President was shot at Ford's Theatre, that he had seen a man who was present and witnessed the occurrence. I said

I would go immediately to the White House. Stanton told me the President was not there but was at the theatre. 'Then,' said I, 'let us go immediately there.' ... The President had been carried across the street from the theatre, to the house of a Mr. Peterson. We entered by ascending a flight of steps above the basement and passing through a long hall to the rear, where the President lay extended on a bed, breathing heavily. Several surgeons were present, at least six, I should think more. Among them I was glad to observe Dr. Hall, who, however, soon left. I inquired of Dr. H., as I entered, the true condition of the President. He replied the President was dead to all intents, although he might live three hours or perhaps longer.... The giant sufferer lay extended diagonally across the bed, which was not long enough for him. He had been stripped of his clothes. His large arms, which were occasionally exposed, were of a size which one would scarce have expected from his spare appearance. His slow, full respiration lifted the clothes with each breath that he took. His features were calm and striking. I had never seen them appear to better advantage than for the first hour, perhaps, that I was there. After that, his right eye began to swell and that part of his face became discolored ... Senator Sumner was there, I think, when I entered. If not, he came in soon after, as did Speaker Colfax, Mr. Secretary McCulloch, and the other members of the Cabinet, with the exception of Mr. Seward. A double guard was stationed at the door and on the sidewalk, to repress the crowd, which was of course highly excited and anxious. The room was small and overcrowded. The surgeons and members of the Cabinet were as many as should have been in the room, but there were many more, and the hall and other rooms in the front or main house were full. One of these rooms was occupied by Mrs. Lincoln and her attendants, with Miss Harris. Mrs. Dixon and Mrs. Kinney came to her about twelve o'clock. About once an hour Mrs. Lincoln would repair to the bedside of her dying husband and with lamentations and tears remain until overcome by emotion.... A door which opened upon a porch or gallery, and also the windows, were kept open for fresh air. The night was dark, cloudy, and damp, and about six it began to rain. I remained in the room until then without sitting or leaving it, when, there being a vacant chair which some one left at the foot of the bed, I occupied it for nearly two hours, listening to the heavy groans, and witnessing the wasting life of the good and great man who was expiring before me.... A little before seven in the morning I re-entered the room where the dying President was rapidly drawing near the closing moments. His wife soon after made her last visit to him. The death-struggle had begun. Robert, his son, stood with several others at the head of the bed. The respiration of the President became suspended at intervals, and at last entirely ceased at twenty-two minutes past seven o'clock."

The news of the President's assassination flashed rapidly over the country, everywhere causing the greatest consternation and grief. The revulsion from the joy which had filled all loyal hearts at the prospects of peace was sudden and profound. All business ceased, and gave way to mourning and lamentation. The flags, so lately unfurled in exultation, were now dropped at half-mast, and emblems of sorrow were hung from every door and window. Men walked with a dejected air. They gathered together in groups in the street, and spoke of the murder of the President as of a personal calamity. The nation's heart was smitten sorely, and signs of woe were in every face and movement.

A scene which transpired in Philadelphia, the morning after the murder, reflects the picture presented in every city and town in the United States. "We had taken our seats," says the delineator, "in the early car to ride down town, men and boys going to work. The morning papers had come up from town as usual, and the men unrolled them to read as the car started. The eye fell on the black border and ominous column-lines. Before we could speak, a good Quaker at the head of the car broke out in horror: 'My God! What's this? *Lincoln is assassinated.*' The driver stopped the car, and came in to hear the awful tidings. There stood the car, mid-street, as the heavy news was read in the gray dawn of that ill-fated day. Men bowed their faces in their hands, and on the straw-covered floor hot tears fell fast. Silently the driver took the bells from his horses, and we started like a hearse cityward. What a changed city since the day before! Then all was joy over the end of the war; now we were plunged in a deeper gulf of woe. The sun rose on a city smitten and weeping. All traffic stood still; the icy hand of death lay flat on the heart of commerce, and it gave not a throb. Men stood by their open stores saying, with hands on each other's shoulders, 'Our President is dead.' Over and over, in a dazed way, they said the fateful syllables, as if the bullet that tore through the weary brain at Washington had palsied the nation. The mute news-boy on the corner said never a word as he handed to the speechless buyers the damp sheets from the press; only he brushed, with unwashed hand, the tears from his dirty cheeks. Groups stood listening on the pavement with faces to the earth, while one, in choking voice, read the telegrams; then with a look they departed in unworded woe, each cursing bitterly in his breast the 'deep damnation of his taking off.' Mill operatives, clerks, workers, school children, all came home, the faltering voice of the teacher telling the wondering children to 'go home, there will be no school to-day.' The housewife looked up amazed to see husband and children coming home so soon. The father's face frightened her and she cried, 'What is wrong, husband?' He could not speak the news, but the wee girl with the school-books said, 'Mamma, they've killed the President.' Ere noon every house wore crape; it was as if there lay a dead son in every home. For hours a sad group hung around the bulletins, hoping against hope; then, when the last hope died, turned sullenly homeward, saying, 'When all was won, and all was done, then to strike him down!' The flags in the harbor fell to half-mast; the streets were rivers of inky streamers; from door-knobs floated crape; and even the unbelled car-horses seemed to draw the black-robed cars more quietly than before."

On Saturday the remains were borne to the White House, where they were embalmed and placed on a grand catafalque in the East Room. Little "Tad" was overcome with grief. All day Saturday he was inconsolable, but on Sunday morning the sun rose bright and beautiful and into his childish heart came the thought that all was well with his father. He said to a gentleman who called upon Mrs. Lincoln, "Do you think, sir, that my father has gone to heaven?" "I have not a doubt of it," was the reply. "Then," said the little fellow in broken voice, "I am glad he has gone there, for he was never happy after he came here. This was not a good place for him!" Tuesday the White House was thrown open to admit friends who desired to look upon the still form as it lay in death. Wednesday, the 19th, the funeral services took place. Mrs. Lincoln was too ill to be present; but her two sons sat near the coffin in the East Room. Next in order were ranged Andrew Johnson (now President) and the members of the Cabinet, and after them the foreign representatives, the chief men of the nation, and a large body of mourning citizens. The services were conducted jointly by the Rev. Dr. Hall, Bishop Simpson, Dr. Gray, and the Rev. Dr. Gurley, the latter delivering the discourse. At two o'clock the funeral cortege started for the Capitol, where the remains were to lie in state until the following morning. The procession was long and imposing. "There were no truer mourners," says Secretary Welles, "than the poor colored people who crowded the streets, joined the procession, and exhibited their woe, bewailing the loss of him whom they regarded as a benefactor and father. Women as well as men, with their little children, thronged the streets, sorrow and trouble and distress depicted on their countenances and in their bearing. The vacant holiday expression had given way to real grief." The body was borne into the rotunda, amidst funeral dirges and military salutes; and the religious exercises of the occasion were concluded. A guard was stationed near the coffin, and the public were again admitted to take their farewell of the dead. While these obsequies were being performed at Washington, similar ceremonies were observed in every part of the country. It had been decided to convey the remains of Lincoln to the home which he left four years before with such solemn and affectionate words of parting. The funeral train left Washington on the 21st. Its passage through the principal Eastern States and cities of the

Union was a most mournful and impressive spectacle. The heavily craped train, its sombre engine swathed in black, moved through the land like an eclipse. At every point vast crowds assembled to gain a tearful glimpse as it sped past.

Over the breast of the spring, the land, amid cities,
Amid lanes and through old woods, where lately the
violets peep'd from the ground, spotting thegray debris,
Amid the grass in the fields each side of the lanes,
passing the endless grass,
Passing the yellow-spear'd wheat, every grain from
its shroud in the dark-brown fields uprisen,
Passing the apple-tree blows of white and pink in the
orchards,
Carrying a corpse to where it shall rest in the grave,
Night and day journeys a coffin.
Coffin that passes through lanes and streets,
Through day and night with the great cloud darkening
the land,
With the pomp of the inloop'd flags, with the cities
draped in black,
With the show of the States themselves as of crape-veil'd
women standing,
With processions long and winding and the flambeaus
of the night,
With the countless torches lit, with the silent sea of
faces and the unbared heads,
With the waiting depot, the arriving coffin, and the
sombre faces,
With dirges through the night, with the thousand
voices rising strong and solemn,
With all the mournful voices of the dirges pour'd
around the coffin,
The dim-lit churches and the shuddering organs—
With the tolling, tolling bells' perpetual clang.

At the principal cities delays were made to enable the people to pay their tribute of respect to the remains of their beloved President. Through Baltimore, Harrisburg, Philadelphia, the train passed to New York City, where a magnificent funeral was held; thence along the shore of the Hudson river to Albany, thence westward through the principal cities of New York, Ohio, and Northern Indiana, the cortege wended its solemn way, reaching, on the 1st of May, the city of Chicago. Here very extensive preparations for funeral obsequies had been made by the thousands who had known him in his life, and other thousands who had learned to love him and now mourned his death.

On the 3d of May the funeral train reached Springfield, where old friends and neighbors tenderly received the dust of their beloved dead. Funeral services were held, and for twenty-four hours the catafalque remained in the hall of the House, where thousands of tear-dimmed eyes gazed for the last time upon the familiar face. Then, on the morning of the 4th of May, a sorrowing procession escorted the remains to the beautiful grounds of Oak Ridge Cemetery, to rest at last from the care and tumult of a troubled life. To this hallowed spot have come the gray-haired soldiers of that stormy war, reverently to salute their great commander's tomb. Here shall long be paid the loving homage of the dusky race that he redeemed. And pilgrims from every land, who value human worth and human liberty, bring here their tributes of respect. And here, while the Government that he saved endures, shall throng his patriot countrymen, not idly to lament his loss, but to resolve *that from this honored dead they take increased devotion to that cause for which he gave the last full measure of devotion; that the dead shall not have died in vain; that the nation, under God, shall have a new birth of freedom; and that government of the people, by the people, for the people, shall not perish from the earth.*

INDEX

[*The abbreviation "L.," as used in this index, refers in every case to the subject of this biography.*]

Abolitionists

Bloomington convention

crusade against slavery

"Boston set" visits L.

Adams, Charles Francis

Adams, John Quincy

Agassiz, Louis, visits L.

Alabama, secedes

Allen, Robert, L's letter to

Ames, Dr.

Ames, Oakes

Anderson, Robert

meetings with L.

holds Fort Sumter

Andrew, John A.

mentioned

impression of L.

Anecdotes of L.

Aaron's commission from the Lord

Abolitionist call for a convention

About his wealth

Actor who wanted consulship

Anderson and L's good memory

Anxiety during summer of 1864

Artemus Ward, reading of

Attorney for the people

Authenticity of

Baker rescued from opponents

"Biggest shuck and smallest nubbin,"

Birds restored to nest

Black Hawk War

Bob Lewis and the Mormon lands

Booth's acting

Bores, getting rid of

Breach of promise suit

Bread and butter dinner

Bullet-hole through L's hat

Burnside's brigadiers, promoted

Butterfield's son, appointment

"Cabinet a-sittin',"

Call for additional troops "not a personal question,"

Cashiered officer, censured

Challenge to work in field for votes

"Charles I. lost his head,"

Chase's appointment as chief-justice

Client's fee divided with defendant

Cogdal note returned by L.

Confederate soldiers greeting at Petersburg

Congress, first speech in

Credits of troops, Stanton overmatched

Coward, "If any man calls me coward let him test it,"

Darkey arithmetic

Dennis Hanks' recollections

Douglas reproved

Dreams significant

DuPont's slowness

Earning the first dollar

Editor who nominated L.

Election clerk, first official act

Five Points Sunday School visit

Forced serenity deceptive

Free-soil party, prediction

Gavel of Confederate congress

Gettysburg battle, L's anxiety during

"Give and take" rule for office-seekers

Government on a tight rope

Grant accused of drunkenness

Grant invited to dinner

Grant's ability to manage the army

Grant's political aspirations

Greeley's criticism

Gunboat advice to New Yorkers

Herndon's convictions on slavery

Hooker's appointment

Hooker's self-confidence

Horsemanship tested by McClellan

Horses captured by guerillas

Horse-trading

Ignorance of Latin admitted

Impromptu speeches written

Inaugural message, loss of

Indian protected by L.

Jack-knife given him because of ugliness

Jacob Thompson, proposed arrest

Jefferson Davis and the troublesome coon story

Johnnie Kongapod

Joseph Jefferson and his players

Kerr's papers enjoyed

Kindness to birds

Kindness to old colored woman

Kindness to old John Burns

Last drive with wife

Law cases refused on moral grounds

Lawsuits, gaining advantage in

Lee, attitude of L. toward

Lightning rod and Forquer

Logan and his shirt

"Long sword in a short scabbard,"

Loyalty to old friends, Hubbard

McClellan's body-guard

McClellan's fatigued horses

McClellan's pass to Richmond

McCormick reaper case

McCullough thanked by L.

Major-generals and hard tack

Manners, first lesson

Measuring backs with Sumner

Measuring height with Ab McElrath

Measuring height with a Southerner

Measuring height with a young "Sucker,"

Meeting with Smoot

Mrs. White, southern sympathizer

"Monarch of all you survey,"

Name refused for commercial use

Negroes at White House reception

Negroes welcome their "Great Messiah,"

Noisy and boastful fighter

Office-seeker from Wisconsin repulsed

Office-seeker, unfit

Old sign, "Lincoln and Herndon,"

Old woman and the bread and milk

One-legged soldier, lack of credentials

Oratorical success discussed with Gulliver

Pardon for deserters

Pardon for young soldier

Pardoning prisoners of war

Pass given Laura Jones, Southerner

Paymaster, appointment

Philadelphia receives news of L's death

Pig rescued from a pit

Pigeon holes versus letter files

Powder sample, testing

Quaker demand for emancipation

Quakers sent home

Rail making

Reading Nasby during election returns

Rebel mail examined

Rebels number twelve hundred thousand

Revolutionary War defended

Sandwich Islands, commissioner, applicants

School of events, suggestion

Scott's request concerning wife's body

Scott "unable as a politician,"

Sherman and the officer

Sherman after Bull Run

Sherman's visit from Louisiana

Sitting for life-mask

Skunks, shooting

Slave girl sold

Slavery speech criticised by Long

Soldiers' humor

"Something everybody can take,"

South Carolina lady's visit

Stanton calls L. a d——d fool

"Stoning Stephen,"

Storekeeper in New Salem

Strength, physical

Stump speech, first appearance

Sun doesn't set

Swapping horses mid stream

Sykes's yellow dog

Tad and the scattered pages of L's speech

Tad's grief over death of father

"Taking the wind out of his sails,"

Talking against time

Taylor's fine clothes

Thrashing a bully

"To whom it may concern,"

Trousers requested by office-seeker,;

Trust in God

Use of old-fashioned words

Used on adversaries

Verses written from memory

Vicksburg, joy of L.

Wade's effort to remove Grant

Weem's life of Washington

Whigs all dead

Wood-craft knowledge

Wrestling match with Jack Armstrong

Antietam, battle of

L's dream

Appomattox, Lee's surrender at

Armstrong, Hannah

Armstrong, Hugh

Armstrong, Jack, trial of strength

early friend

Armstrong, John, quoted

Armstrong, William D., defended by L.

Arnold, Isaac N., quoted

interview with L.

mentioned

Arnold, Matthew, quoted

Ashley, Hon. James M., constitutional
amendment introduced by

Ashmore, Congressman, of South Carolina

quoted

Ashmun, George, mentioned

Austin, G.L., quoted

Baker, Edward D., mentioned

refuses to defend slaves

Whig debater

personal and political friend of L.

elected congressman

killed at Balls' Bluff

magnanimity of L. towards

introduced L. at inauguration

Balch, George B., quoted

Baltimore, republican convention at, 1864

Bancroft, George, contrasted with L.

quoted

Banks, Nathaniel P.

Barnes, Surgeon-General

Barrett, J.H., quoted

Bateman, Newton, quoted

Bates, Edward, candidate for president

made attorney general

characterized

visits army with L.

resignation

Beckwith, H.W.

Beecher, Henry Ward, abolition sermons read by L.

invites L. to speak in his church

eloquent abolitionist

Bell, John, nominated for president

Bennett, John, impressions of L.

Bible, L's knowledge of

L. quotes from

L's opinion of

Bigelow, John, quoted

Bird, Francis, W.

Birney, Zachariah, L's school-master

Bissell, William H., mentioned

Bixby, Mrs.

Black Hawk War, L's military experience in

Blaine, James G., compares Lincoln and Douglas

Blair, F.P., attacks Chase

reprehended by L.

Blair, Montgomery, made postmaster general

arming of negroes deprecated by

residence fired

resignation

Bloomington Convention

Bonham, Jeriah, quoted

Boone, Daniel

Booneville, Ind., L. attends court

Booth, Edwin, L's enjoyment of his acting

Booth, John Wilkes, assassination of L.

Boston delegation, conference with L.

Boutwell, George S., quoted

Bowles, Samuel, quoted

Brainard and Knott, quoted

Breckenridge, John A., early influence on L.

Breckenridge, John C, nominated for president

Breese, Sidney, dignity

quoted

Brewster, Father

Bright, John

Brooklyn, L's lecture trip

Brooks, Senator, knocks down Sumner

quoted

Brooks, Noah P.

quoted

describes L's last speech

Brooks, Phillips, quoted

Bross, John A.

Bross, William, first meeting with L.

interview with L.

Brough, John, victorious governor of Ohio

effort to reconcile L. and Chase

Brown, John

Browne, Francis Fisher, biographical sketch

Browning, O.H., mentioned

Whig debater

inaugural party, member of

Browning Robert, L's fondness for his poetry

Bryan, Thomas B., purchases MS. of emancipation proclamation

Bryan, William J., on L. as an orator

Bryant, William Cullen

presided over Cooper Institute meeting

abolitionist

favored L. for presidency

Buchanan, James

mentioned

treachery during his administration

escorts L. to Capitol

characterized

escorts L. to White House

Bull Run, battle of

depression after

L's dream

second battle

Bulwer-Lytton, mentioned

Burns, John

Burns, Robert, L's fondness for his poetry

Burnside, Ambrose E.

Fredericksburg repulse,,;

victories in N.C.

unpopularity

replaces McClellan

L's opinion of

Bushnell, C.S., agent for Ericsson

Butler, William, L. boards with, in Springfield

Butterfield, Daniel

Butterfield, Justin

mentioned

appointed commissioner of land office

son of, desires appointment

Byron, Lord

L's fondness for his poetry

quoted

Cabinet

L's political rivals chosen

L's non-partisan ideas

makeup discussed with Weed

with Riddle

Banks considered

final appointments and how decided

changes during administration

meetings enlivened by stories

L's relations with

misconceptions of rights and duties

unfriendly feeling between members

earliest meetings informal

attitude toward the war

personal dissensions

Seward's removal demanded

Chase and Seward resignations

Stanton the master-mind

Cameron's relations with L.

Stanton succeeds Cameron

Senators advise reconstruction of

Stanton's relations with L.

opposes L's reinstatement of McClellan

attitude toward emancipation

preliminary proclamation discussed, L's own account

second draft discussed

disposal of freedmen discussed

Chase finally disposed of

Blair succeeded by Dennison

Bates resigns

ignored by L.

last meeting attended by L.

Calhoun, John C

mentioned

appoints L. deputy surveyor

democratic debater

congressman

California, L.'s desire to live in

Cameron, Simon

mentioned

congressman

presidential candidate

cabinet possibility

secretary of war

retirement from the cabinet

advocates arming the blacks

Campbell, Major, rescues fugitive slaves

Campbell, John A., Southern peace commissioner

Canada, rebel agents in

Capital and labor.

See

Labor and capital

Carpenter, Francis B.

mentioned

quoted

Cartwright, Peter
Cass, Lewis, mentioned
ridiculed by L.
Caton, John Dean
first meeting with L.
opinion of L. as lawyer
fugitive slave decision
advice on war policy
Chancellorsville, battle of
Chandler, Zack
aids L. in Schofield matter
quoted
lack of military judgment
Channing, William Henry
abolitionist
conversation with L. on slavery
Chapman, Colonel, quoted
Chapman, Mrs.
quoted
Charleston, L.'s opinion of situation
Chase, Salmon P.
mentioned
opposes Nebraska bill
presidential candidate
logic of
cabinet possibility
secretary of the treasury
rivalry with Seward
upholds Stanton
resignation and withdrawal
consulted about Stanton

opposes negro enlistment

visits Fortress Monroe with L.

opinion of emancipation proclamation

contribution to emancipation proclamation

rupture with Lincoln

second resignation offered

accepted

appointed Chief Justice

quoted

Chattanooga, Grant's success

Chicago

L. visits N.B. Judd

national republican convention

memorial on emancipation

Northwestern fair

funeral services for L.

Chicago Historical Society, owned emancipation proclamation MS.

Cincinnati

L's first visit

L's second visit

visits on inaugural journey

City Point, visited by L.

Civil War

L's peace pleas before war, extract

L. foresees coming struggle

L. promises to promote peace

workingmen offer support for freedom

L's reluctance to express opinion

L's peace plea in inaugural speech

Washington swarms with rebels

desperate condition of treasury

secession a political issue

Stanton's loyalty to Union

faithless officials in departments

L's conquest of a South Carolinian

Louisiana's war preparations

Sumter attack

call for volunteers

Massachusetts first in field

Baltimore attack

Douglas stands by government

Washington thrills over Sumter

blockade of Southern ports, proclamation

Key West, Tortugas, and Santa Rosa proclamation

Virginia asks expression of federal policy

L's reply

L's hope for Union

L's desire to retain Kentucky

Kentucky saved to Union

special session of Congress

L's appeal for funds and men

preparations

review of N.Y. troops

Bull Run

L. visits army in Virginia

L's anxiety after Bull Run

Harper's Ferry

fleet urged to draw rebels from Washington

L. refuses gun-boat to New Yorkers

Trent affair, Mason and Slidell

English neutrality established

English controversies

Ericsson's "Monitor,"

Ross's mission to Canada;

L's reply on number of losses

friction concerning direction

negro enlistment, recommended

Sabin's appointment

inertia of proceedings

L. develops military sagacity

brightening prospects, proclamation

L. visits Fortress Monroe

Merrimac and Monitor

Norfolk captured

L's letter to McClellan on over-cautiousness

L's sympathy for soldiers

visits hospitals

L's letter to McClellan concerning route to Richmond

impatience over approach to Richmond

strain of summer of 1862

refusal of leave for Scott

McClellan's army ordered withdrawn

Pope's defeat at Manassas

McClellan's reinstatement

Washington peril

Antietam victory

L. visits Army of Potomac

Fredericksburg attacked

L's dissatisfaction with McClellan

Missouri factional quarrels

L's dissatisfaction with DuPont

Fredericksburg, L's grief over

L's visit to army before Chancellorsville

L's method criticised

negro enlistment

retaliation opposed by L.

Fredericksburg defeat

Hooker succeeds Burnside

naval operations

Chancellorsville defeat

defeat, dissatisfaction of North

turning-point of war

Pennsylvania invaded

Northern fear of Lee

Hooker succeeded by Meade

Gettysburg

Vicksburg campaign

L's joy over victory

Wade urges Grant's dismissal

Gettysburg victory

Washington criticisms

Meade's leadership

Chancellorsville defeat

Fredericksburg defeat

L. against compromise

brightening prospects after elections

L's confidence in Grant

Grant's victories after Vicksburg

his plans

Grant's commission received

L's plan of campaign for Grant

Early's raid, L's plan against

Grant's reply

Vicksburg, criticisms of campaign, anecdote

Grant and Stanton clash

Early's attack on Washington

call for additional troops, July 18, 1864

gloomy prospects

Wilderness and Petersburg losses

peace negotiations, "To whom it may concern,"

effect of L's re-election

Sherman's march to the sea

L's conditions for peace

peace negotiations with Southern commissioners

Lee's last efforts

closing events

L. visits army

fall of Petersburg

fall of Richmond

Lee's surrender

end of war

pardoning prisoners, .

See also Emancipation; Secession

Clary Grove boys

attack on L.

volunteers in Black Hawk War

smash store in New Salem

Clay, Cassius M.

Clay, Henry

influence of speeches on L.

L's admiration and disillusion

gradual emancipation speech

L's eulogy of

Clephane, Lewis

Cleveland, Grover

Cleveland, Ohio, visit on inaugural journey

Clinton, DeWitt

Cobb, Howell, distinguished in civil war

Cogdal's note

Colfax, Schuyler

interview with L.

L.'s death-bed

Collamer, Jacob

Collyer, Robert, quoted

Columbus, Ohio, welcome on inaugural journey

Confederate States

considered a fact by Wigfall

knowledge of Union moves

Trent affair

favored capital

Canadian machinations

Congress

special session, July 4, 1861

emancipation measures

Conkling, James C.

quoted

Constitution, slavery amendment

Constitutional Union Party

Conway, Moncure D.

impression of L.

interview with L.

quoted

Cook, Mr., of Illinois

Cooper Institute speech

Costa Rica, asylum for freedom

Covode, John

Crane, C.B., quoted

Crawford, Andrew, L's schoolmaster

Crawford, Josiah, incident of the ruined book

Crawford, Mrs. Josiah, quoted

Crittenden, John J.

Curdy, Dr.

Curtin, Andrew G.

Curtis-Gamble controversy

Cushing, Caleb

candidate for attorney general

quoted

Dahlgren, John A., quoted

Dana, Charles A., quoted

Davis, David

mentioned

quoted

advised L. on cabinet;

member of inaugural party

Davis, Jefferson

in Black Hawk War

in senate

recognition asked by Southern commissioners

mansion occupied by Weitzel

L's clemency toward

Davis, O.L.

Dayton, William L., vice-presidential nominee

Defrees, public printer, objects to L's colloquialisms

Deming, Henry Champion, quoted

Democratic Party

dominates Illinois

pro-slavery tendencies

rebel sympathisers

opposes congressional war measures

Dennison, William

postmaster general

presides over Baltimore convention

replaces Blair

at L's death-bed

Dicey, Edward, quoted

Dickey, T. Lyle, quoted

Dickson, W.M., quoted

District of Columbia, slavery abolished

Dixon, Father, quoted

Dominican question, Seward's embarrassment

Dorsey, Azel, L's schoolmaster

Douglas, Stephen A.

mentioned

groggery taunt about L.

L's first impression of

debates with L.

courts Mary Todd

Mexican War, blames L. for opposition

opens campaign, 1852

defends Missouri compromise

claims Whigs are dead

senatorial nomination

oratory compared with L.

debater and orator

appearance and characteristics

quoted

senator in 1846

magnetism

re-elected senator in 1858

speeches in Ohio in 1859

L's attitude toward

democratic nominee for president

magnanimity

sustains the government

death

Douglass, Frederick

conference with L.

impression of L.

Dresser, Rev. Nathan, residence of, in Springfield, purchased by L.

Drummond, Thomas, quoted

Dummer, H.C., quoted

Duncan, Major, teaches L. use of broadsword

DuPont, Admiral, characterized by L.

Early, Dr., L's reply to

Early, Jubal A., raid on Washington

Eaton, Page, quoted

Eckert, General

Edwards, Matilda, admired by L.

Edwards, Ninian W.

mentioned

candidate for legislature

Edwards, Mrs. Ninian W., sister of Mary Todd

Egan, Dr., of Chicago

Eggleston, Edward, quoted

Elkin, Elder, funeral services for Nancy Hanks

Ellis, A.Y., quoted

Ellsworth, E.E., member of inaugural party

Emancipation

discussion of measures

Frémont's proclamation
gradual, advocated
first discussed by L. with cabinet members
military, authorized
Quaker delegation demands
Chicago clergymen demand
Lincoln and Channing interview
Lincoln and Greeley
Greeley's "Prayer of twenty millions," and L's reply
compensation suggested
deportation suggested
L's message to congress, 1862
"Boston set" discussed with L.
defended by L.
Emancipation proclamation
issued
official measures preceding
preliminary text
L's own account of
Seward's view of
Welles's account
text
signed
pen used
Emerson, Ralph Waldo
quoted
belief in L.
England
neutrality established
controversies with
Ericsson, John, inventor of "Monitor,"

Evarts, Mr., of N.Y., grieved over Seward's defeat

Everett, Edward

nominated for vice-president

appreciation of L's Gettysburg address

impression of L.

Ewing, Lee D., opposed to change in Illinois State capital

Farragut, David G.

compared with DuPont

Fell, Jesse W.

Fessenden, William P.

secretary of the treasury

Ficklin, O.B.

Fithian, Dr.

Flatboat, constructed by L.

Florida, secedes

Ford's Theatre, scene of assassination

Forquer, George, lightning rod anecdote

Forrest, Edwin

Forrest, Thomas L.

Fort Sumter

held by Anderson

attack

L's dream

Fortress Monroe, L. visits

Foster, Major-General

Fox, G.V., assistant secretary of the navy

Franklin, Benjamin, L. ranked with

Fredericksburg

repulse at

attacked

L's grief over

defeat

Free-Soil Party

Free-state cause, L. sympathises with

Freedmen.

See

Negroes

Frémont, John C.

nominated for president

defeated

pioneer emancipator

presidential possibility in, 1864

Fry, J.B., quoted

Fugitive Slave Law

detested by L.

text

Fusion Party, L. candidate of, for senator

Gamble, Governor, Curtis-Gamble faction

Gentry, Allen

Gentry, Mrs. Allen, quoted

Georgia, seceded

Germans in Cincinnati, welcome L.

Gettysburg

mentioned

victory

L's feeling during battle

victory cheers L.

battle-field purchase and dedication

L's dream

Gettysburg Address

rewritten many times

world's model

text

Gillespie, Joseph

quoted

conversation with L. on slavery

Grant, Frederick D.

Grant, Ulysses S.

mentioned

opinion of McClellan's difficulties

victories in Tenn.

Vicksburg campaign

L's letter on Vicksburg

L's dissatisfaction before Vicksburg

commands military division of Miss.

rank of Lieut.-General created for

assumes command of army

summoned to Washington

at White House reception

receives commission from L.

refusal to dine at White House

L's impressions of personality and military capacities

L.'s letter of commendation

interview with L. on military matters, Grant's own account

L's suggestion about Early's repulse

Grant's reply

L. seeks to know his political aspirations

true version of whiskey anecdote

L. tells story of Sykes's dog

dispute with Stanton

upheld by president

presidential possibility

attacks Early

telegram to L. on re-election

peace overture made through

forces Lee to Richmond

visited by L. at City Point

interview with L. at City Point

L's visit at Petersburg

Lee's surrender

praised by L.

instructions for conference with Lee

denies Stone River victory

drives with L. and attends last cabinet meeting

declines invitation to theater

Grant, Mrs. Ulysses S.

Gray, Dr., officiated at L's funeral

Great Britain.

See

England

Gladstone, William Ewart, opinion of second inaugural address

Globe Tavern, Springfield, Ill., L's first home after marriage

Godbey, Squire, quoted

Goldsborough, Lewis M.

Goodrich, Judge, L. declines partnership

Greeley, Horace

opposes L's policy in N.Y. "Tribune,"

publishes "The prayer of twenty millions,"

L's reply

conference with L.

L.'s "pigeonhole" for

seeks successor to L.

peace importunities and L's famous reply

Green, L.M., quoted

Greene, Bowlin, friend of L.

Greene, W.G.

Gridley, G.A.

Grigsby, Aaron

Grigsby, Nat, quoted

Griswold, John A., builder of "Monitor,"

Grimes, James W.

Grover, A.J., quoted

Gulliver, John P., estimate of L's speeches

Gurley, Rev. Dr., officiated at L's funeral

Haines, Elijah M., quoted

Hale, John P.

mentioned

calls on L.

Hall, Doctor, attends L.

Hall, John

Hall, Newman

quoted

officiated at L's funeral

Halleck, Henry W.

mentioned

telegrams to Meade

military ability

at L's death-bed

Halpine, Colonel

Hamlin, Hannibal, nominated for vice-president

Hampton Roads, meeting of peace commissioners

Hanks, Dennis

recollections of L's boyhood

story-telling ability

L. visits

Hanks, John

L's fellow-laborer

bears campaign banner

Hanks, Nancy.

See

Lincoln; Nancy Hanks

Hannegan, Edward A.

Hapgood, Norman, quoted

Hardin, Colonel

Hardin, John J.

mentioned

congressional candidate

killed in Mexican War

Harding, George, attorney in McCormick Reaper case

Harper's Ferry, Union forces driven out

Harris, G.W., quoted

Harris, Ira

daughter

Harris, Thomas L.

Harrisburg, L's visit on inaugural journey

Hatch, O.M.

mentioned

quoted

Hawk, Mr., actor, describes assassination

Hay, John M.

private secretary

quoted

Hayes, General

Hazel, Caleb, L's schoolmaster

Henderson, J.B.

constitutional amendment introduced by

interviews L. about pardons

Henry, Dr.

Herndon, William H.

law partnership with L.

letter of advice from L.

quoted

sympathy for L.

abolitionist efforts

"Lincoln and Herndon" law sign

Hitt, Robert R.

Holland, Josiah G., quoted

Holmes, Oliver Wendell, L's fondness for his poetry

Holt, Joseph

appeals for Union

possibility as secretary of war

candidate for attorney general

Homestead law, opinion of L. on

Hood, Thomas, L's fondness for his poetry

Hooker, Joseph

visited by L. before Chancellorsville

interview with L. and promotion

"Fighting Joe Hooker,"

L's letter to

Hooker's comment

accused of drunkenness

Sumner's opinion of

self-confidence

unequal to responsibility

asked to be relieved

aids Grant in victories

Hossack, John

"House-Divided-Against-Itself" speech, quoted

Howard, Senator

Hoyne, Thomas

Hoyt, Governor

Hubbard, Gurdon S.

quoted

works for Illinois and Michigan Canal

interview with L.

Hunter, David, attempts military emancipation

Hunter, Robert M.T., Southern peace commissioner

Iles, Elijah, service in Black Hawk War

Illinois

Lincoln family settles in

slavery sentiment

first to ratify 13th amendment

Illinois and Michigan Canal, favored by Lincoln

Indiana, early home of Lincoln

Indianapolis, speech, on inaugural journey

Indians

hostile in Kentucky

execution refused by L.

Invention

L's interest in history of

navigation device

Jackson, Andrew, L. compared with

Jackson, Thomas Jonathan (Stonewall)

death

Jayne, William, quoted

Jefferson, Joseph, quoted

Jefferson, Thomas

L. ranked with

Johnson, Andrew

mentioned

nominated for vice-president

sworn in

at L's death-bed

at funeral

Johnson, Bradley, Confederate general

raid of country around Washington

Johnson, Oliver, visit to L.

Johnson, Reverdy, attorney in McCormick case

Johnston, Albert Sidney, at Vicksburg

Johnston, Joseph E.

mentioned

Sherman defeats

plan to force surrender

L's dream

Johnston, John

step-brother of L.

indolent and shiftless nature

L's letters to

Jones, J. Russell, L. consults about Grant

Jones, Laura, L's leniency to

Joy, James F.

Judd, Norman B.

L. visits

member of inaugural party

mentioned

Judd, Mrs. Norman B., quoted

Julian, George W., quoted

Kansas, L's visit to

Kansas-Nebraska Bill, controversy

Kelly, William D., quoted

Kelton, Colonel

Kentucky

Lincoln family in

plea for neutrality

importance of neutrality

concessions made to

"Kerr, Orpheus C," (Robert Henry Newell)

footnote

L's great fondness for his writings

Keyes, General, quoted

King, Preston

Kirkpatrick, William

Know-Nothing-Party

Knox, Joe

Labor and capital discussed by Lincoln

Laboring-men, L's speech to Cincinnati Germans

Lamborn, Josiah

Lamon, Ward H.

mentioned

member of inaugural party

quoted

Lane, General

Lectures.

See

Speeches and Lectures

Lee, Harry T., impression of Gettysburg address

Lee, Robert E.

mentioned

Pennsylvania invasion

Manassas successes

Antietam defeat

Chancellorsville victory

Gettysburg defeat

Appomattox surrender

Richmond, retreat to

Union plans for capture

Richmond, retreat from

Grant ordered not to confer with

L's comment on portrait

Letters and telegrams

acceptance of presidential nomination

correspondence burdensome

written by hand

to Bryant concerning party pledges

to Mrs. Bixby on loss of sons

to Curtis on factional quarrels

to Douglas, invitation to debate

telegram to Grant during Early's raid

to Grant after Vicksburg

to Grant, expressing satisfaction

to Greeley on emancipation

to Herndon, giving advice

to Hooker, on latter's appointment

to Judd about campaign contribution

to Judd regarding the presidency

to Kentucky unionist on slavery

to McClellan on over-cautiousness

to McClellan concerning route to Richmond

to McNeill relating to fees for speeches

to Schofield, advice on factional quarrels

to Speed on slavery

to Speed's sister on slavery
to Springfield friends after Gettysburg and Vicksburg
to step-brother on death of father
to Washburne, about forts
to Washburne, against compromises
to Weed on secession
"To whom it may concern," safe conduct for peace envoys
Lewis, Robert
Lincoln, Abraham, grandfather of L.
settles in Kentucky
death
LINCOLN, ABRAHAM
CHARACTERISTICS
inherited
in boyhood and youth
handwriting
elements of greatness
claims to be a fatalist
absent-mindedness
debt abhorred
as a lawyer
as a public speaker
master of himself
compared with Jackson
attitude toward public visitors
lack of sovereignty
simplicity of manner
qualities of a leader
morbid dislike of guard
forbearance
precision and minuteness of information

living power of integrity and elasticity

greatness in moral strength

summed up by Nicolay

peace-maker

wisdom and moderation

guileless and single-hearted

power to make quick and important decisions

will compared to Andrew Jackson

easily accessible to visitors

no case too trivial

ability to say no,;

diplomacy in Schofield-Rosecrans episode

loyalty to friends

fortitude

imagination versus reason

tireless worker

magnanimity toward opponents

stern when necessary

candor and friendliness in criticism

willingness to admit errors

quickness of perception

tenacity

Sherman's tribute

unselfishness

magnanimity toward southern leaders

clemency in granting pardons,

Ambitions

presentiment of future greatness

desire to be the "DeWitt Clinton of Illinois,"

encouraged by friends

generous quality of

senatorial

presidential

not concerned over political future

Appearance

at fifteen

at nineteen

in 1832

in 1847

in 1849

"man of sorrows,"

singular walk

on the circuit

face transformed in speaking

in repose and on the stump

in 1858

in 1860

height

as President-elect

arrival at Washington

inauguration

in his reception room

changed by anxiety

Nicolay's description

face a surprise to Winchell

unconventional dress

changed by grief

Frederick Douglass' impressions

saddest man in the world

Courage

fighting qualities

encounter with a bully

in Black Hawk War

rescues Baker from a fight

duel with Shields

under discouragements

did not fear attempt upon his life

Honesty

at nineteen

as a salesman

"Honest Abe,"

trust funds never used

in voting

as a lawyer

refused to defend the guilty

intellectual and moral

Horsemanship

Justice

anecdote of Black Hawk War

refusal to countenance injustice

sense of

injustice to Gen. Meade

Literary methods and *style*

early example

example from Douglas debates

methods

style

Kindness and *sympathy*

to animals

everybody's friend

in his home

regard for old friends and relatives

to old colored woman

to young attorneys

for Col. Scott

for soldiers

embarrassing results of friendliness

Melancholy and *sadness*

caused by love of Anne Rutledge

temporary attack

causes

struggles with

depression in 1854

evidence of

over defeat for senate

on inaugural journey

after Bull Run

over war victims

engraved on features

summer of 1864

Matthew Arnold's poem

Memory

for faces and names

for events

retentive

Military sagacity

Modesty

unassuming manner in politics

about printing speeches

in regard to presidential nomination

as president

natural

about second nomination

on news of second election

Popularity

as a young man

in New Salem

in Black Hawk War

universal favorite

in Kansas

at Republican convention in 1860

among old friends and relatives

Confederate soldiers' greeting at Petersburg

Physical strength

in boyhood

incidents showing

Religious nature

knowledge of the Bible

shown in letter to step-brother

reliance on Divine help

influence of son's death

spirituality highly organized

religious spirit

shown in fortitude

quotes the Bible

his views on

not a church member

shown in second inaugural address

Tact

in official relations

anecdotes illustrating

Temperance

reply to Douglas's taunt

Voice

magnetism of

not pleasing

clear and vigorous

high but clear

Wit and *humor*

power of satire

examples of

love of practical joke

no end to his fund of

used against adversaries

chief attraction at dinners

cultivated

stories not always dignified

repartee

advantage of L. over Douglas

indelicacy charge refuted

safety-valve of L.

enjoyment of "Orpheus C. Kerr,"

at cabinet meetings

soldiers' humor appreciated by L.

humorists liked by L.

PRIVATE LIFE:

ancestry

L's own account

birth,;

illegitimate parentage legend

Lincoln family in Kentucky

removal to Indiana

in Indiana

reminiscences by Dennis Hanks

death of his mother

love for his mother

tribute to her influence

his father remarries

affection for step-mother

moves to Macon Co., Ill.

his father's possessions

death of father

L. helps build log cabin

splitting rails

flatboat voyages down the Mississippi

settles in New Salem

patent for navigation device

athletic skill

first meeting with Smoot

meets Governor Yates

love of story-telling

home life

autobiography

struggle with poverty

love for Anne Rutledge

close of his boyhood and youth

New Salem a desolate waste

moves to Springfield

struggles of a young lawyer

meeting with Speed

shares his home

in state politics

Mary Todd's satirical article

love affairs with Matilda Edwards and Mary Todd

derangement

goes to Kentucky with Speed

marriage to Mary Todd

lives at Globe Tavern

purchases Dressar home

enters national politics

back in Springfield

simplicity of home life in Springfield

income from law practice

property owned

his children

L. as husband and father

marriage unhappy

did his own marketing

visits Chicago

regard for relatives

purchases home for father

letters to step-brother

idol of his step-mother

wealth, not desired by L.

L. as a lawyer

careless about money

keeping partnership accounts

anecdote about his wealth

summer home during presidency

home life in White House

desire to live in California

plans for retirement, .

Education

early education

early schools attended

his copy book inscription

first efforts in composition

mental training from reading

scrap-book kept in youth

handwriting at seventeen

book of arithmetic examples

knowledge of astronomy and geology

study of grammar

L.'s own account

knowledge of drama

L. as a student

musical taste

unashamed of early deficiencies

Books and *reading*

influence of first books

his own testimony

the ruined volume

method of reading

wrote verses

books in White House office

love for Shakespeare, Browning, and Byron

memory for poetry

poets best loved

humorists liked

best-loved books

novel reading

Employments

first work

first dollar earned

flatboat constructed for commercial enterprise

his first employer

first flatboat journey to New Orleans

second flatboat journey to New Orleans

clerk at New Salem

Offutt's store closed

brief career as country merchant

blacksmith trade considered

surveys and plans Petersburg

notion to become a carpenter

Law career

early interest in law

study and practice

begins study of

begins practice

period covered

reverence for law

in Springfield

without plans or money

asking credit

partnership with Stuart and Logan

with Herndon

riding the circuit

borrows, then owns a horse

welcome by other lawyers

humility

court scene

freedom in social intercourse

leading lawyers of the day

adventures and hardships

popularity and appearance

not afraid of unpopular cases

wins case of widow of revolutionary pensioner

wins case for Jefferson

ridiculing the eloquence of opponent

breach of promise suit

ready wit

dissolved partnership with Logan

partnership with Herndon

declined partnership with Goodrich

resumes practice in 1849

legal fee ridiculously small

appearance in court

defending a colored woman

dividing fee with defendant

refused to take unjust cases

keeping accounts

fees moderate

defends son of Jack Armstrong

would not press for pay

refused to defend guilty

would never advise unwise suits

returns fee

anecdotes of L. at the bar

his rank as a lawyer

special characteristics

Recreations

games

dancing

theatre

fondness for walking

PUBLIC LIFE

Nicknames

"Railsplitter,"

"Uncle Abe,"

"Old Abe,"

"Honest Abe,"

Oratory

first efforts

reputation

spoke without manuscript

manner of speaking described

used old-fashioned words

jury speeches

eloquence of Bloomington speech

compared with Douglas

Cooper Institute speech

New England tour

W.J. Bryan's opinion

Gettysburg address

eloquence of second inaugural

Public questions, L's views on:

Mexican war

Missouri compromise

Kansas-Nebraska bill

secession views

labor and capital

emancipation

reconstruction policy

Slavery

L. opposes pro-slavery enactment in Illinois

attitude shown in Douglas debates,

sale of slave girl

early views

opposed slavery in Congress and in speeches

views in letters to Speed

argues eternal right at Bloomington Convention

resolution adopted

"House divided against itself,"

Cincinnati speech

L.'s policy

Channing interview

Chicago clergymen's delegation

Greeley and L.

L's own account

4th annual message

Early political career

change in views

made election clerk

appointed postmaster at Salem

made deputy surveyor

natural taste for politics

candidate for presidential elector

Whig leader

canvassed Illinois in Clay-Polk campaign

leader of Whigs in Congress

Whig delegate to National Convention

seeks appointment as land commissioner

little interested in politics until 1854

building up the Free Soil party

admits being a Whig

generosity toward rivals

considered for vice president

activity in Frémont campaign

no political enemies

bored with talk on politics

Illinois legislature

defeat and election

first candidacy unsuccessful

campaign of 1834, and election

aids canal bill

reputation in

renominated, 1836

campaign methods

lightning rod anecdote

not an aristocrat

reply to Early

letter to Allen

election

journey to capital

meets Judge Caton

first meeting with Douglas

removal of Illinois Capitol

an early speech

opposes pro-slavery enactment

contest with Ewing

campaign of 1838 and election

end of legislative service

election and resignation, 1864

senatorial contest

Black Hawk War

candidate for captain

memories of L.

first experience drilling troops

rescues an Indian

meeting with Stuart

L. re-enlists

recollects Major Anderson after 29 years

courage as a soldier

his own account of his service

popularity with comrades

Congress

aspirations

elected to lower house, 1846

Whig leader

reputation in

first speech

Mexican War attitude

notable speech and ridicule of Gen. Cass

bill for abolition of slavery

campaign methods

senatorial contest, 1855

defeated

senatorial contest with Douglas, 1858

defeated

depression of L. over

Presidency

presentiment of L. concerning

modest over proposed nomination

almost in his grasp

Cooper Institute speech aids toward

suggested as a candidate

nomination

sittings for life mask

cast of hands

notified of nomination

opposition of Springfield clergymen

election, 1860

non-partisan appointments

unembarrassed by promises

preparation for inauguration

journey to Washington

stories of disguises

week preceding inauguration

ceremonies described

oath administered

first night at the White House

cabinet appointments

cabinet changes

difficulties selecting loyal and capable men

impression on people

modest as president

fears for attempted assassination

L's dislike for guard

Civil War begun

first call for troops

creates excitement

Boston riots

loyalty of Douglas

proclamation of blockade of Southern ports

blockade extended

Virginia convention waits on L.

L's war policy outlined

L's conciliatory course

tries to save Kentucky

special session of Congress

L's first message

difficulties of a new administration

Bull Run disaster

visits the army in Virginia

depression following Bull Run

unfaltering courage

relief in story-telling

depression relieved by humor

measuring up with Sumner

diplomacy in Mason and Slidell affair

in French invasion of Mexico

building the "Monitor,"

first annual message

reception at White House

illness and death at the White House

secret service incidents

annoyed by office-seekers

Mr. Ross at the White House

William Kelley at the White House

Goldwin Smith's impressions

tributes from Hapgood, Bigelow, and Nicolay

cabinet relations

with Stanton

with Seward

Cameron and Stanton

L. considers McClellan over-cautious

L. visits hospitals

differences of opinion with McClellan

letter to him about campaign

urges action

L's defence of him

L. recalls him

reinstates him

McClellan's own account

correspondence

L's summing up of McClellan

signs emancipation proclamation

his life as president

society at the White House

public receptions

tact with favor seekers and bores

sense of justice

answering improper questions

settles the Curtis-Gamble dispute

appoints Schofield

views of his own position

dealing with cranks

Fredericksburg disaster

responsibility of his position

home life in the White House

visits Army of the Potomac

tireless worker

health

his letter file

Agassiz and L.

his official acts not influenced by personal consideration

criticism of the administration

war policy opposed by Greeley

by high official

Democrats of the North

Boston abolitionists

effect of abuse

Western delegation

personal responsibility for policy

interview with Douglas on enlisting colored soldiers

McClellan's removal

relations with Burnside

with Hooker

candor and friendliness with officers

visits army of the Potomac

his view of Charleston attack

effect of Chancellorsville on L.

reads Stedman's poem to cabinet

the tide turns

Lee invades Pennsylvania

Hooker proves unfit

Meade appointed

L's feelings during Gettysburg battle

joy over Vicksburg

praise of Grant

criticism of Meade for Lee's escape

Meade asks to be relieved

criticism answered

resignation not insisted upon

L's opinion modified

improved conditions

defence of emancipation proclamation

Thanksgiving proclamation

fall election, 1863

L. upheld

his own comment

Gettysburg dedication

relations with Grant

appoints Grant Lieut-General

summons him to Washington

Grant receives commission

first meeting with Grant

L's letter of satisfaction

military orders issued by L.

interested in Grant's career

interest in Grant's political aspirations

Grant-Stanton episode

Grant's opinion of Lincoln

campaign of 1864

L's attitude toward a second term

New England's attitude toward the administration

relations with Chase

candidates of 1864

L's nomination, 1864

acceptance speech

Early's raid

call for more troops

war policy criticized

depression of L.

campaign of 1864

McClellan a candidate

L's secret pledge to support successor

attempt on life

effect of burdens and anxiety during war

election of 1864, victory

Grant's telegram

Seward's tribute

Chase's resignation

other cabinet changes

fourth annual message

colored people at White House reception

negotiates with Southern peace commissioners

assumes responsibility for unpopular measures

scheme for compensation emancipation

second inauguration

close of the war

escapes office-seekers

with Grant, Sherman, and Porter at City Point

on the River Queen

concern about Schofield

on the Malvern

at Petersburg

at Richmond

news of Richmond's fall

visit to Richmond

welcomed by the negroes

Southerners' reception

joy over Lee's surrender

scene at Capitol

L.'s speech to the multitude

reconstruction views

instructions to Grant on final conference with Lee

feeling toward the South

pardoning confederates

the last day: talk with Robert

receives visitors

last cabinet meeting

significant dreams

drive with Mrs. Lincoln

last official acts

reaches theatre

the shot fired

Booth's escape

Walt Whitman's description

Booth's plan

Rathbone's account

death-bed

Welles's account

a nation's grief

funeral ceremonies at the White House

lying in state at Capitol

funeral train to Springfield

interment

Lincoln, Edward Baker, L's son, birth

Lincoln, John, L's great-grandfather

Lincoln, John, L's half-brother

Lincoln, Josiah, L's uncle

Lincoln, Mary Todd, L's wife

published satirical articles about James Shields

ambitions

characteristics

engagement to L. broken

marriage

hospitality

pro-slavery views

meeting with Volk

on inaugural journey

opinion of Riddle on

censured for frivolity

defines L's religion

visits Army of Potomac

receives Grant

fears of L's assassination

desired to visit Europe

last drive with L.

plans to visit theatre

at theatre

shock at assassination

prostrated by L's death

at L's death-bed

unable to attend obsequies

Lincoln, Matilda, L's half-sister

Lincoln, Mordecai, son of Samuel Lincoln

Lincoln, Mordecai, L's uncle

adventure with Indians

character

L's characterization of

opinion of L. about

Lincoln, Nancy Hanks, L's mother

marriage

slurs upon her name

character and appearance

Dennis Hanks's opinion of

death and funeral

epitaph

love of L. for

influence on L.

tribute of L. to

Lincoln, Robert Todd, L's son

birth

student at Harvard

gripsack anecdote

student and soldier

interview with L. about war

with his mother after assassination

at L's death-bed

Lincoln, Samuel, L's English forbear

Lincoln, Sarah, L's half-sister

death

Lincoln, Sarah, L's sister, birth

Lincoln, Sarah Johnston, L's step-mother

marries Thomas Lincoln

mutual fondness of L. and

quoted

death

visit of L. before inauguration

Lincoln, Thomas, L's father

birth

rescue from Indians

marriage to Nancy Hanks

moves to Rock Spring farm

moves to Indiana

second marriage

moves to Illinois

nicknames

character-sketch death

epitaph

story-telling ability

death

solicitude for

L. visits grave

Lincoln, Thomas, L's son

birth

"Little Tad,"

companion of father

death

loved by soldiers

anecdote of L's last speech

grief over death of father

Lincoln, William Wallace, L's son

birth

death

influence of death on L.

Lincoln-Douglas Debates

comparative powers of speakers, .

Extracts, Springfield

Peoria

Quincy and Alton,

Linder, General

quoted

talks against time

Livermore, George, given proclamation pen

Logan, John A., quoted

Logan, Mrs. John A., quoted

Logan, Stephen T.

mentioned

law partner of L.

Whig debater

partnership dissolved

anecdote of shirt

favors L. for legislature

elected to legislature

L's champion in legislature

Longfellow, Henry Wadsworth, abolitionist

Long, Dr., quoted

"Long Nine," delegates to senate convention, 1836

Lookout Mountain, Grant's success

Loring, George B., quoted

Lossing, Benson J., quoted

Louisiana, seceded

Louisville "Journal," L's liking for

Lovejoy, Elijah

Lovejoy, Owen

abolitionist

mentioned

Lowell, James Russell

abolitionist

quoted

Lucas, Major, quoted

Lyons, Lord

McClellan, George B.

mentioned

Stanton's hostility

difficulties with Army of Potomac

letter from L. on over-cautiousness

as a soldier

Meade and Grant quoted

L's personal regard for

appointed general of Union armies

L.'s letter about plan of campaign

urging action

L. defends

recalled from Peninsula; succeeded by Pope

reinstated

own account

Antietam victory

inaction after Antietam criticized

quoted on L's visit to army

correspondence with L.

replaced by Burnside

L's opinion

bad news from the Peninsula

fails to reach Richmond

removal from Army of the Potomac

L's presidential competitor

defeated for presidency

McCormick, R.C., quoted

McCormick reaper case, in 1857

McCulloch, Hugh

quoted

secretary of the treasury

at L's death-bed

McCullough, John Edward, summoned to meet L.

McDonald, Senator

McHenry, Henry, quoted

McNeill, James, (McNamar), Anne Rutledge's suitor

Macon County, Ill., Lincoln family settle in

Manassas defeat

Markland, Mr., quoted

Mason, Senator

Mason and Slidell affair

Massachusetts, first to put regiment in the field in Civil War

Meade, George G.

mentioned

opinion of McClellan

succeeds Hooker

criticized for Lee's escape

asks to be relieved

answers criticism

does not press resignation

L.'s opinion modified

Meigs, Montgomery C.

at L's death-bed
"Merrimac,"
frightens New Yorkers
Hampton Roads defeat
engagement with "Monitor,"
Messages and proclamations
inaugural message, loss feared
colloquialisms in
Messages and proclamations, quotations
inaugural address
volunteers called for
blockade of southern ports
Key West, Tortugas, and Santa Rosa, concerning authority
Virginia convention, response to
to congress, July 4, 1861
first annual message
President's general order, No. 1, Feb. 22, 1862
thanksgiving proclamation, April 10, 1862
emancipation, appeal to border states
final proclamation
second annual message
Thanksgiving, 1863
fourth annual message
inaugural address, second
Gladstone's tribute, .
See also Speeches and Lectures
Metzgar murder case
Mexican War, attitude of L. toward
Mexico, French invasion
"Miami," Federal steamboat
Milroy, R.H.

Milwaukee, speech of L. at State Fair

Minnesota, asks execution of Indians

Minter, Graham, L's schoolmaster, quoted

"Mirror," The Manchester (N.H.), quoted

Missionary Ridge, Grant's success

Mississippi, seceded

Missouri Compromise, views of L. and Douglas

Missouri, factional quarrels

Mitchell, General, telegram from

"Monitor,"

engagement with "Merrimac,"

origin of

Moore, Ex-governor

Moore, Mrs., step-sister

Morgan, Edwin D.

Morse, John T., quoted

"Nasby, Petroleum V." (David Ross Locke), read by L.

Nebraska Bill.

See

Kansas-Nebraska Bill

Negroes

enlistment in army

justified by L.

New Year's reception

grief over death of L., .

See also Emancipation; Slavery

Neill, Secretary to L., quoted

New Brunswick affair

New England

dissatisfaction with L.

speeches and visit of L.

New Salem, Ill.

L. settles at

L. appointed postmaster

speech of L. before literary society

now a desolate waste

New Year's presidential reception

in 1862

in 1863

in 1865

New York City

visit of L. in 1860

on inaugural journey

funeral ceremonies

New York "Tribune."

See

Greeley, Horace

New York troops, reviewed July 4, 1861

Newpapers

L's favorite newspaper

surveillance

Nichols, John W., quoted

Nicolay, John G.

L's private secretary

quoted

Norfolk captured

Norris, James H.

Nott and Brainard, quoted

Noyes, George C., quoted

Oberkleine, Frederick

address to L. at Cincinnati

L's reply

Office-seekers

patience of L. toward

demands of

annoy L.

actor who wanted consulship

Offutt, Denton

relations with L.,

quoted

store closed in 1832

Oglesby, Richard J., quoted

Oregon, federal office offered L.

Pain, John

Parke, John G.

Parker, Theodore, abolitionist

Parks, C.S., quoted

Pearson, John, quoted

Pearson, Henry Greenleaf, quoted

Peck, Ebenezer

mentioned

quoted

Pemberton, J.C.

Pennsylvania, invaded by Lee

Pennypacker, Isaac R., quoted

Petersburg, Ill., surveyed and planned by L.

Petersburg, Va., victory, and visit by L.

Philadelphia

visited on inaugural journey

receives news of L's death

Phillips, Wendell

abolitionist

interview with L.

Piatt, Don, quoted

Pierce, Franklin

Pierpont, John, visits L.

Pinkerton, Allan

Polk, James K., campaign

Pomeroy, Senator

Poore, Benjamin Perley, quoted

Pope, John

defeat at Manassas

succeeded by McClellan

Bull Run disaster

Porter, D.D.

aids Grant

interview with L. at City Point

L's visit to the Malvern

visits Petersburg with L.

described visit to Richmond with L.

interview with L. at City Point

quoted

Prime, Irenæus, quoted

Pringle, Cyrus, the case of

Proclamations.

See

Messages and Proclamations

Quakers

L's ancestry

war scruples

demand emancipation

Rail-splitting episode

Ramsey, Senator

Rathbone, Major

at Ford's Theatre

struggles with Booth

Raymond, Henry J., quoted

Rebellion, War of.

See

Civil War

Reconstruction

L.'s speech on, quoted

policy of L.

Reid, Whitelaw

Reno, Jesse L.

Republican party

birth of

organized in Illinois

national convention in 1856

asked L. to speak in Ohio

advice of L. to

Illinois convention of 1860

national convention, 1860

growth and tendencies

fears for L's loyalty

partisan and unreasonable

office-seekers

elections of 1863

national convention of 1864

Reynolds, John, call for volunteers

Rhett, Robert B.

Richardson, William A., resolution supported by L.

Richmond

plans to capture

fall of

visited by L.

Riddle, A.G.

part in Lincoln-Chase affair

urges Chase's appointment as chief justice

quoted

Rock Valley

Rollins, James S., quoted

Rosecrans, W.S., sent to Missouri

Ross, A.M., quoted

Rothschild, Alonzo, quoted

Rousseau, Kentucky legislator

Russell, Lord John, protest of, in Trent affair

Rutledge, Anne, L's love-affair with

Schenck, Robert C.

Schofield, J.M.

mentioned

replaces Curtis, L's letter of appointment

joins Sherman

L's concern about ability

Scott, Colonel, refused leave on death of wife

Scott, Winfield

L's order to hold or retake forts

warns L. of danger

pays respects to L.

lacking as politician

dislike of Hooker

Schurz, Carl

seconded L's nomination

quoted

Secession

states that withdrew

attitude of L. toward

not considered rebellion

Sedgwick, John, view of Meade's failure to attack Lee

Selby, Paul, quoted

Seward, Fanny

Seward, Frederick W.

warns L. of danger

attacked and wounded

Seward, Mrs. Frederick W.

Seward, William H.

mentioned

opposes Nebraska bill

doubt of his nomination

statesmanship

candidate for president

eloquence of

cabinet possibility

sends warning to L.

appointment as secretary of state

press refused information

diplomacy, credited to

"Premier," self-styled

arrogance

rivalry with Chase

resignation

senate, opposition of

L's objection to his resignation

opposes negro enlistment

emancipation views

preliminary proclamation views

with Grant at White House reception

tribute to L. on his re-election

with L. meets peace commission

L's visit, after Richmond

attacked and wounded

Seward, Mrs. William H.

Shakespeare, L's fondness for his works

Shepley, General, receives L. at Richmond

Sherman, John, introduces brother to L.

Sherman, William T.

mentioned

quoted

march to the sea

L's opinion

at Atlanta

victories after Atlanta

interview with L. at City Point

tribute to L.

anxiety of L. and Grant

Shields, James

ridiculed by Mary Todd

duel with L.

L. wishes to succeed in congress

Shuman, Andrew

reports Lincoln-Douglas debates

quoted

Sibley, Judge, quoted

Simpson, Bishop, officiates at L's funeral

Slavery

protest against pro-slavery act in Illinois

L's defense of fugitive slaves

Independence Hall flag-raising

L. introduces bill against

L's growing opposition to

L's attitude in letter to Speed

Peoria speech, extract

L's growing opposition to

knowledge of L. regarding

Cincinnati speech

Cooper Institute speech

L's hatred for, growing

fugitive slave law

political issue

attitude of L. toward

L. opposes compromises

legislation against, 1862

L's own account of his views

L's attitude in fourth annual message

constitutional amendment, .

See also Emancipation

Slocum, Henry W.

Smith, Caleb B.

secretary of the interior

non-committal on Ericsson's invention

Smith, Goldwin

visits L.

quoted

Smith, James

Smith, William Henry, quoted

Smoot, Coleman, friendship with L.

"Soldiers' Rest," Lincoln's summer home during presidency

South Carolina, seceded

Southern Confederacy.

See

Confederate states

Sparrow, Thomas and Betsy

Spaulding, Judge

Speeches and lectures

in congress in 1848

candidate for member of legislature

to New Salem literary society

stump-speaking

on "Spot Resolutions,"

on the presidency and general politics

age of different inventions

to Scott club of Springfield

eulogy on death of Clay

Bloomington convention

"House-divided-against-itself,"

lectures in winter of 1859

political speeches in Ohio

political speeches in Kansas

invitation to lecture in Beecher's church

Cooper Institute speech

in New England

accusation of fees received for speeches

Five Points Sunday School, N.Y., talk

inaugural journey

Wisconsin state fair

Speeches and lectures, quotations

influence of Weem's life of Washington

Perpetuation of our political institutions

Peace plea

Bloomington ratification meeting

"House-divided-against-itself,"

Appeal for a hearing in southern Illinois

Cincinnati, 1859

Cooper Institute speech

Presidential nomination, response

Springfield farewell

Cincinnati in 1861

Cincinnati, reply to Oberkleine

Philadelphia, on inaugural journey

after Bull Run

Slavery

Emancipation proclamation, speech following

Gettysburg address

text

comments

Grant's commission, presentation of

Richmond, to negroes

Close of war

Reconstruction, last speech, .

See also

Lincoln-Douglas debates;

Messages and proclamations

Speed, Joshua F.

mentioned

first interview with L.

L's home with

intimate friend of L.

opinion of L's ability as a lawyer

L's letter to sister of Speed, quoted

L's letter to, on slavery

compares L. and Douglas

appointed attorney general

at L's death-bed

"Spot Resolutions," speech

Springfield, Ill.

L. moves to

agitation over removal of capital

removal accomplished

L. returns to

L's departure, Feb. 11, 1861

recollections of L. about

funeral ceremonies for L.

Stanton, Edwin M.

mentioned

professional meeting with L.

contempt for L.

appointed secretary of war

member of Buchanan's cabinet

applicant for office

press refused information

Mason and Slidell capture approved

impulsiveness and violence

antagonism to Welles

relations with L.

resignation threatened

resignation withdrawn

master-mind of cabinet

replaces Cameron in cabinet

Cameron's own account

Fortress Monroe, visit to

hostility to McClellan

refuses Col. Scott leave of absence

death of his child

opposes the "Boston set,"

discouraged at Hooker's resignation

dispute with Grant

irritated by L's humor

relations with Blair

dispatch to Grant

reconstruction plan proposed

at L's death-bed

at Seward's bedside

Steamboat Invention, L's

Stearns, George L.

Stedman, E.C., quoted

Stephens, Alexander H.

mentioned

opinion of L. as a speaker

Southern peace commissioner

L's description of

Stephenson, J.H.

Stewart, Harry W., quoted

Stewart, James G., recollection of L's visit to Kansas

Stone, Charles P., quoted

Stone River

costly success

L's dream

Grant denies victory

Stories told by L.

Bob Lewis and the Mormon lands

Big fellow beaten by little wife

Boy and the troublesome coon

Darkey arithmetic

Horse sold at cross-roads

Johnnie Kongapod

Jones and his bridge to the infernal regions

Letting the dog go

Plaster of psalm-tunes

Sausages and cats

Shooting skunks

Sick man of Illinois and his grudge

Swapping horses in mid-stream

Sykes's yellow dog

Taking to the woods

Story-telling

used on troublesome visitors

fondness of L. for

L. entertains Van Buren

indelicacy charge refuted

application of stories

safety-valve of L.

chagrins friends

relieves bad news by

Stowe, Harriet Beecher

"Uncle Tom's Cabin,"

quoted

Stuart, J.E.B.

Stuart, John T.

mentioned

L's first acquaintance with

law partner of L.

on L's method of accounting

Sumner, Charles

mentioned

opposes Nebraska Bill

eloquence of

assault upon

member of inaugural party

declined to measure backs with L.

lacks confidence in Hooker

introduces constitutional amendment

at L's death-bed

Sumter.

See

Fort Sumter

Swett, Leonard

associate of L. in law case

quoted

Sykes, George

Taney, R.B.

administered oath of office to L.

death

Tannatt, T.R.

Taylor Club, "the young Indians,"

Taylor, Richard (Dick), L's discomfiture of

Taylor, Zachary

Black Hawk War

presidency supported by L. and Stephens

Terry, Alfred H.

Texas, seceded

Thirteenth Amendment passed

Thomas, Jesse

Thomas, George H.

Thompson George

Thompson, Jacob

Thompson, Richard

Todd, Captain, guards L. at White House

Todd, Mary.

See

Lincoln, Mary Todd

Todd, Robert S.

Toombs, Robert

Treat, Judge

Trent Affair

friendly attitude of France and Spain

L's diplomacy in

Trumbull, Lyman

mentioned, ;

elected senator

substitute amendment introduced by

Usher, John D.

appointed secretary of the interior

Vallandigham, Clement L.

opposes war policy

candidate for governor of Ohio

L's opinion of

Van Buren, Martin

mentioned

entertained by L's stories

Vandalia, Ill., proposed change of state capital

Van Santvoord, C., quoted

Verdi, Dr.

Vicksburg

mentioned

turning-point in war

campaign

L's joy over victory

L. meets criticism with anecdote

L's dream

Viele, General, describes visit to Fortress Monroe

Virginia Convention, asks expression of Federal policy

Volk, Leonard W.

impressions of L.

makes cast of L.

Voorhees, Daniel W.

Wade, Benjamin

mentioned

urges Grant's dismissal

lack of military judgment

Wadsworth, James S.

Walker, Isaac, recollections of L.

Washburne, E.B.

mentioned

L's letters to, against compromise

giving orders for Scott

quoted

bill creating rank of lieutenant-general

Washington, D.C.

L. reluctant to leave in 1849

L's arrival, Feb. 23, 1861

inaugural week

rebels and rebel sympathizers in

defenses visited by L.

regarded as lost

relieved

society in 1862-1863

Early's attack

enthusiasm over Lee's surrender

Washington, George

mentioned

influence of Weem's life of W. on L.

life read by L. as case preparation

L. ranked with

Watson, assistant secretary of state

Watterson, Henry, quoted

Webster, Daniel

mentioned

considered a leader

Weed, Thurlow

mentioned

quoted

discusses cabinet appointments

L's letter to, Dec. 17, 1860, extract

objects to Welles

Weitzel, Godfrey

occupies Richmond

headquarters in Richmond

Weldon, Lawrence, quoted

Welles, Gideon

mentioned

cabinet possibility

appointed secretary of the navy

approves Mason and Slidell capture

calmness of

antagonism to Stanton

at L's death-bed

quoted

Welles, Mrs. Gideon, mentioned

"Westminster Review," on Gettysburg address

Wheeler, William A., quoted

Whig Party

L. a delegate to presidential convention

L. believes he is a Whig

symptoms of disintegration

L. a leader

dissolution

White, Dr.

White, Mrs.

White House

L.'s first night at

L's family life

office of L. described

official precedence

New Year's receptions

society in 1862-63

L's informal receptions

freedom of access

Grant's ovation at reception

reception, 1865, negroes attend

Whiting

solicitor of war department

candidate for attorney general

Whitman, Walt, quoted

Whittier, John Greenleaf, abolitionist

"Wide-awake" clubs

Wigfall, Senator

Wilcox, Major, quoted

Willard's Hotel, Washington, headquarters of L.

Willis, David

Wilmington, L's dream

Wilmot Proviso, L. votes for

Wilkes, Charles

Wilson, Robert L., quoted

Wilson, Henry

Winchell, J.M.

quoted

interview with L.

Winslow, John F., builder of "Monitor,"

Winthrop, Robert C., quoted

Wisconsin State Fair, addressed by L. in 1859

Wood, Fernando

Wool, John E.

Workingmen, L's speech to

Wright, Elizur

Wright, Horatio

Writings.

See Letters and telegrams;

Messages and proclamations;

Speeches and lectures

Yates, Richard

mentioned

beginning of friendship with L.

opposes Missouri Compromise

election to Congress

"Young Indians," Taylor club

Young, John Russell, quoted

Young Men's Lyceum, address of L. quoted

NOTES

[A] The popular vote was as follows: Lincoln, 1,857,610; Douglas, 1,291,574; Breckenridge, 850,082; Bell, 646,124. Of the electoral votes, Lincoln had 180; Breckenridge, 72; Bell, 39; and Douglas, 12.

[B] On the very day of Lincoln's arrival in Washington, he said to some prominent men who had called upon him at his hotel, "As the country has placed me at the helm of the ship, I'll try to steer her through."

[C] This first call for troops was supplemented a month later (May 16) by a call for 42,034 volunteers for three years, for 22,114 officers and men for the regular army, and 18,000 seamen for the navy.

[D] Orpheus C. Kerr (*Office Seeker*) was the pseudonymn of Robert H. Newell, a popular humorist of the war period, who dealt particularly with the comic aspects of Washington and army life.

[E] Lincoln never lost his interest in exhibitions of physical strength, and involuntarily he always compared its possessor with himself. On one occasion—it was in 1859—he was asked to make an address at the State Fair of Wisconsin, which was held at Milwaukee. Among the attractions was a "strong man" who went through the usual performance of tossing iron balls and letting them roll back down his arms, lifting heavy weights, etc. Apparently Lincoln had never seen such a combination of strength and agility before. He was greatly interested. Every now and then he gave vent to the ejaculation, "By George! By George!" After the speech was over, Governor Hoyt introduced him to the athlete; and as Lincoln stood looking down at him from his great height, evidently pondering that one so small could be so strong, he suddenly gave utterance to one of his quaint speeches. "Why," he said, "I could lick salt off the top of your hat!"

[F] Hon. George S. Boutwell of Massachusetts stated Lincoln said to him personally: "When Lee came over the river, I made a resolution that if McClellan drove him back I would send the proclamation after him. The battle of Antietam was fought Wednesday, and until Saturday I could not find out whether we had gained a victory or lost a battle. It was then too late to issue the proclamation that day; and the fact is, I fixed it up a little on Sunday, and Monday I let them have it."

[G] The cause of General Hooker's seeming stupefaction at the critical point of the Chancellorsville battle has been much discussed but never satisfactorily explained. It has been thought that he was disabled by the shock of a cannon-ball striking a post or pillar of the house where he had his headquarters. An interesting entry in Welles's Diary, made soon after the battle, reflects somewhat the feeling at the time. "Sumner expresses an absolute want of confidence in Hooker; says he knows him to be a blasphemous wretch; that after crossing the Rappahannock and reaching Centreville, Hooker exultingly exclaimed, 'The enemy are in my power, and God Almighty cannot deprive me of them.' I have heard before of this, but not so direct and positive. The sudden paralysis that followed, when the army in the midst of a successful career was suddenly checked and commenced its retreat, has never been explained. Whiskey is said by Sumner to have done the work. The President said that if Hooker had been killed by the shot which knocked over the pillar that stunned him, we should have been successful."

[H] General T.R. Tannatt, a graduate of West Point in 1858, is now (1913) an active and honored citizen of Spokane, Washington.

[I] The criticism of Meade for not attacking Lee before he recrossed the Potomac is based on the assumption that the attack must be successful. On this point Meade's words to Halleck, written in reply to the latter's conciliatory letter of July 28, can hardly be ignored. "Had I attacked Lee the day I proposed to do so, and in the ignorance that then existed of his position, I have every reason to believe the attack would have been unsuccessful, and would have resulted disastrously. This opinion is founded on the judgment of a number of distinguished officers after inspecting Lee's vacated works and position. Among these officers I could name Generals Sedgwick, Wright, Slocum, Hays, Sykes, and others." In other words the attack which Meade has been so severely blamed for not making might have ended in reversing the results at Gettysburg, losing all we had gained at such terrible cost, placed Washington and other Northern cities in far more deadly peril, and changing the whole subsequent issues of the war.

[J] A curious revelation of the estimate of General Halleck held by at least one member of the Cabinet, and of the relations between Halleck and the President, is found in Welles's Diary in the record of a rather free conversation with the President during the anxious period about the time of the battle of Gettysburg. Says Mr. Welles: "I stated I had observed the inertness if not the incapacity of the General-in-Chief, and had hoped that he [the President], who had better and more correct views, would issue peremptory orders. The President immediately softened his tone, and said, 'Halleck knows better than I what to do. He is a military man, has had a military education. I brought him here to give me military advice. His views and mine are widely different. It is better that I, who am not a military man, should defer to him, rather than he to me.' This," continues Mr. Welles, "is the President's error. His own convictions and conclusions are infinitely superior to Halleck's; even in military operations, more sensible and more correct always.... Halleck has no activity; never exhibits sagacity or foresight." And in another place in the same Diary we are given this singular picture by a Cabinet minister of the man who was at that moment the General-in-Chief of the Union armies and the military adviser of the President: "Halleck sits and smokes, and swears, and scratches his arm, but exhibits little military capacity or intelligence; is obfuscated, muddy, uncertain, stupid as to what is doing or to be done."